Universal Generalization (UG)

$A(a/x)$
$(\forall x)A$

Provided:
  (i) *a* does not occur in the hypotheses.
  (ii) *a* is not introduced in any line justified by the rule of existential instantiation.
(iii) *a* does not occur in $(\forall x)A$.

Two-Way Rules

Association (Assoc)

$(A \lor (B \lor C)) :: ((A \lor B) \lor C)$
$(A \& (B \& C)) :: ((A \& B) \& C)$

Contraposition (Contra)

$(A \rightarrow B) :: (\sim B \rightarrow \sim A)$

Commutation (Com)

$(A \lor B) :: (B \lor A)$
$(A \& B) :: (B \& A)$

De Morgan's Law (DeM)

$\sim(A \& B) :: (\sim A \lor \sim B)$
$\sim(A \lor B) :: (\sim A \& \sim B)$

Conditional Exchange (Con Exch)

$(A \rightarrow B) :: (\sim A \lor B)$
$(A \rightarrow B) :: \sim(A \& \sim B)$

Tautology (Taut)

$A :: (A \lor A)$
$A :: (A \& A)$

Exportation (Exp)

$((A \& B) \rightarrow C) :: (A \rightarrow (B \rightarrow C))$

Double Negation (DN)

$\sim\sim A :: A$

Distribution (Dist)

$(A \& (B \lor C)) :: ((A \& B) \lor (A \& C))$
$(A \lor (B \& C)) :: ((A \lor B) \& (A \lor C))$

Quantifier Negation (QN)

$(\forall x)A :: \sim(\exists x)\sim A$
$\sim(\forall x)A :: (\exists x)\sim A$
$(\forall x)\sim A :: \sim(\exists x)A$
$\sim(\forall x)\sim A :: (\exists x)A$

ABOUT THE AUTHOR

Kathleen Johnson Wu became interested in logic while an undergraduate at Bryn Mawr College, an interest she pursued at Yale University, where she received her Ph.D. She has published a number of articles on modal and free logics that have appeared in the *Journal of Philosphical Logic, Notre Dame Journal of Formal Logic,* and *Logique et Analyse,* as well as in a collection of essays published by Yale University Press in honor of Frederic B. Fitch. For many years, she has taught courses in logic at the University of Alabama, where she is an associate professor of philosophy.

DISCOVERING FORMAL LOGIC

KATHLEEN JOHNSON WU

University of Alabama

DPG

THE DUSHKIN PUBLISHING GROUP, INC.
Guilford, Connecticut

Copyright © 1994 by The Dushkin Publishing Group, Inc.
All rights reserved. No part of this publication may
be reproduced, stored, or transmitted in any form or by
any means, mechanical, electronic, photocopying,
recording, or otherwise, without prior written permission
of the copyright holder except in the case of brief
quotations embodied in critical articles and reviews.

Printed in the United States of America

Library of Congress Catalog Card Number: 93-73091

International Standard Book Number (ISBN) 1-56134-233-5

First Printing

The Dushkin Publishing Group, Inc.,
Sluice Dock, Guilford, Connecticut 06437

PREFACE

This book is concerned primarily with the logic of connectives and the logic of quantifiers. Much of it was written for two sequenced undergraduate courses that I have taught for some years at the University of Alabama. The introductory course covers material from chapters 1 through 8, while the more advanced course combines a review of chapters 1 through 7 with careful study of chapters 9 through 12. As the title "Discovering Formal Logic" suggests, the approach is gradual and intuitive, and is intended to lead to a clear, secure grasp of the subject matter.

The text is divided into three parts. Part I consists of the first three chapters. These chapters, while making minimal use of symbols, nevertheless introduce many of the fundamental concepts of logical analysis, such as validity, truth conditions, logical form, the domain of discourse, and universal and existential quantifiers. In the first chapter, fairy tales and counterarguments are employed to detect invalid arguments; in the third, Venn diagrams are applied to argument forms.

Two formal languages are introduced in Part II, one for the logic of connectives and the other for the logic of quantifiers. Students easily understand the need for these languages from their experience with the problem-solving limitations of ordinary language in Part I. For each formal language, there is a separate chapter devoted to its applications to English. In the last chapter of Part II, Copi-style inference rules are presented as an introduction to the derivation method for beginning students.

In Part III, formal systems consisting of natural deduction rules similar to those of Frederic B. Fitch are developed. A system for the logic of connective is constructed first, then one for standard quantifier logic with identity, and finally two for alternative free logics.

Besides covering the usual topics, this book also addresses questions of underlying motivation and of the significance and justification of formal techniques and procedures. Even if time does not permit discussion of every one of these topics, reading about them in the text will give students a more appreciative attitude toward logic and a better conception of how to exploit its resources.

Exercises that range from the straightforward to the complex are included throughout the text. Solutions to those exercises designated with an asterisk can be found at the end of the text. Solutions to the rest of the exercises are given in the separate student solutions manual. An instructor's resource guide is also available.

I am greatly indebted to my teachers, especially Frederic B. Fitch and Hugues Leblanc, for inspiring my interest in logic and philosophy and for their guidance and counsel. I am indebted to others through their writings, particularly Bas C. van Fraassen and John T. Kearns. For corrections and useful suggestions related to earlier drafts of this book, I wish to thank Ellery Eells, University of Wisconsin; William G. Lycan, University of North Carolina; Robert G. Meyers, State University of New York–Albany; Clifton McIntosh, University of Utah; Walter H. O'Briant, University of Georgia; Melville Y. Stewart, Bethel College; Michael Scanlan, Oregon State University; Douglas N. Walton, University of Winnipeg; and Frank Wilson, Bucknell University.

In addition, I should like to thank my colleagues, James W. Clark and J. B. McMinn, who provided many helpful comments and unflagging encouragement. Thanks are due also to William Harper for his keen observations. I am also indebted to my students with whom I often felt that I was conversing when writing this text. Two of them, Robert Jackson and Julia Tumasova, helped me with the exercises and solutions. Ms. Tumasova, especially, made a number of constructive suggestions. I would also like to thank Irving Rockwood, John Holland, Jacqueline T. Cannon, and Joshua Safran of The Dushkin Publishing Group. Finally, I wish to thank my husband Hsiu-Kwang Wu for his invaluable encouragement and support.

CONTENTS

2

LOGICAL CONTENT AND LOGICAL FORM 29

3

PRELIMINARY LOGICAL ANALYSIS 55

PART II   FORMAL METHODS

4

THE LANGUAGE OF THE LOGIC OF CONNECTIVES 87

5

LOGIC OF CONNECTIVES: APPLICATIONS TO ENGLISH 123

8

COPI-STYLE INFERENCE RULES 219

PART III   FORMAL LOGICAL SYSTEMS

9

AN INTRODUCTION TO FORMAL SYSTEMS 259

10

ADDITIONAL CONNECTIVE RULES 293

11

12

PART I

WHAT IS LOGIC?

1

WHAT IS LOGIC?

This chapter introduces the reader to the subject matter of logic and provides a framework for analysis. Some fundamental concepts may be difficult to grasp initially but can be mastered gradually as they reoccur throughout the text. In the last section, two informal methods for detecting incorrect reasoning are presented.

1.1 WHAT IS REASONING?

When you reason, you move from one proposition or a series of propositions to another. Your initial propositions are premises; the terminal proposition you reach and affirm on the basis of the premises is your conclusion. You may know that your premises are true, but you may also simply believe them, or even just assume them to be true for the sake of argument. For example, you could assume, together with certain other premises, that the level of water in the Atlantic Ocean is rising by 1 foot per week and conclude from those propositions that Miami Beach will be submerged in 2 months.

Note: Definitions for the words underlined may be found in the Glossary beginning on page 411.

Propositions and Sentences

Propositions are the sort of things that you can believe, know, and reason from and to. True propositions are called <u>facts</u> or <u>truths</u>, while false propositions are called <u>errors of fact</u> or <u>untruths</u>. Most <u>declarative sentences</u> express propositions. For example, the declarative sentence 'Hydrogen is heavier than water' expresses a false proposition; on the other hand, 'Water freezes at 0°C' expresses a true one. Sentences that are not declarative, such as exclamations, imperatives, and interrogatives, may also express propositions. For example, the rhetorical question 'What is the use?' conveys the same proposition as 'There is no use'. The proposition that 'Today is Thursday' expresses depends on the context in which the sentence is used. The proposition a sentence expresses in a given context is the meaning of the sentence in that context. Our primary concern in this text is with sentences that express true or false propositions. Thus, unless otherwise stated, hereafter we simply use 'sentence' as short for 'sentence that expresses a true or false proposition'.

A proposition may have various linguistic expressions or <u>verbalizations</u>. Indeed, just as a place may have several names in different languages and even in the same language, a proposition may have more than one verbalization. For example, 'Boston' and 'The Hub' both name the same place; and 'Scotland', the place the French call '*Écosse*'. Analogously, the sentences 'The glass is exactly half empty' and 'The glass is exactly half full' verbalize the same proposition. And 'All philosophers are wise' has the same meaning in English as '*Tous les philosophes sont sages*' has in French.

Many propositions are not verbalized because they are known to be false or are simply not thought of. Others are not verbalized because to mention them would be either inappropriate, impolite, or just boring. For example, I rarely tell anyone what I had for breakfast or make a written estimate of how many paper clips are in my desk drawer. That would be boring. Verbalized or not, a proposition is not a sentence or any other part of language.

The notion of a proposition is helpful in understanding how sentences in one languages are translatable in another. Translation is possible because the propositions verbalized are the same. As for how the same sentence can be true in one context and false in another, an explanation is also readily at hand. 'I am an American citizen', for example, is true if spoken by President Clinton in 1994, but is false if spoken by President Yeltsin in 1994. Although the same sentence is involved, two different propositions are expressed. In addition to explaining various puzzles of language, the notion of a proposition provides a needed and convenient framework for an introduction to formal logic. In this text, our talk of propositions is justified by its heuristic value and does not imply that the philosophical debate over whether propositions do or do not exist is settled.

Use and Mention

When we placed single quotation marks around words and phrases above, we were *mentioning* them rather than *using* them. This is a common convention. To better understand it, consider the following sentences.

'Love' is spelled with four letters.

Love is a state of mind.

The first sentence says something about the word 'love', namely, that it is spelled with four letters, which is true; the word is mentioned and not used. The second sentence says something about love, namely, that it is a state of mind. You cannot decide whether the second sentence is true without knowing what love is. In the second sentence, the word 'love' is not mentioned but used. [In the sentence preceding this, is 'love' being used or mentioned?]

The distinction between use and mention may help you in appreciating the difference between a sentence and a proposition. A sentence is used to express or verbalize a proposition. When a sentence is mentioned, it is placed within single quotation marks. Notice how sentences are used and mentioned in our previous discussion of propositions and sentences.

Arguments and Language

As walking is a physical activity that takes you from one place to another, reasoning is a mental activity that takes you from premises to a conclusion. The premises and conclusion together we call a <u>premise-conclusion argument</u> or, for short, an <u>argument</u>. Our use of the term 'argument' in this text should not be confused with the more ordinary use of the term, such as that in the sentence 'They broke their engagement because of an argument over the prenuptial agreement'.

When verbalizing an argument, you use sentences to state the premises and conclusion. In addition, you usually distinguish the premises from the conclusion by using a word, such as 'therefore', 'so', 'it follows that', or 'hence', to identify the conclusion, or by using another kind of a word, such as 'given', 'suppose', 'because', or 'provided that', to identify the premises. Here is an example of a verbalization of an argument:

(1) All pumas are animals of the cat family.

(2) This is a puma.

Therefore,

(3) This is an animal of the cat family.

Of course, outside of textbooks, premises and conclusion are rarely numbered and the conclusion is often stated first. Moreover, in the verbalization of some arguments, premises are left unstated and, occasionally, the conclusion is left for you yourself to draw.

The following is an example of a verbalization of an argument that omits the statement of a premise.

> Hector reads only mystery novels. Therefore, Hector will never read Thomas Hardy's novel *The Mayor of Casterbridge*.

The unstated premise is

> Thomas Hardy's novel *The Mayor of Casterbridge* is not a mystery novel.

An example of a verbalization that leaves the conclusion unstated is below.

> Suppose you are approached by an individual with a gun who says, "I will shoot you unless you give me $100. I see you do not have $100. Well, that is too bad." Hearing this, you run for your life.

The conclusion that he will shoot you is left for you to draw. It is not stated.

Inductive and Deductive Reasoning

Inductive reasoning is often incorrectly defined as reasoning from specific propositions (for example, this apple is red) to a general one (for example, all apples are red). In contrast, deductive reasoning is often defined, equally incorrectly, as reasoning from general propositions (all apples are red) to a specific one (this apple is red). Such definitions as these are incorrect because specific and general propositions can serve as premises and conclusions in both sorts of reasoning.

Reasoning is <u>inductive</u> when the reasoner considers the truth of the premises to make the conclusion probable, though not certain. For instance, finding over half a crate of oranges rotten and then concluding with confidence, but not certainty, that the remainder are also rotten is an example of inductive reasoning. Other examples are forecasting the weather, predicting the outcome of a sports event, speculating on an individual's motives, estimating how long it will take to complete a task, and surmising that two individuals who look alike are twins.

Inductive reasoning is stronger or weaker depending on the degree of probability to which the conclusion is supported by the premises. Since the conclusion can be probable without being true, inductive reasoning from true premises may be strong even though the conclusion is false. For example, if one of the remaining oranges in the crate is not rotten, the previously mentioned conclusion that the remainder are rotten is false. Yet, your inductive reasoning is strong if you reached that conclusion after randomly checking over half and finding all of those rotten. Moreover, since a conclusion may be improbable and, nevertheless, be true, inductive reasoning may be weak even though the premises and conclusion are true. For example, even if all of the oranges are rotten, if you reached that conclusion after having inspected only one orange and finding it rotten, your inductive reasoning is weak. Phrases prefixed to conclusions, such as 'it is likely that', 'it is probable that', and 'I believe that', usually indicate inductive reasoning.

In contrast, reasoning is <u>deductive</u> when the reasoner considers the truth of the premises to require the truth of the conclusion. This deductive attitude is often expressed by a phrase prefixed to the conclusion, such as 'it follows that', 'it must be that', or 'I know that'. Balancing a checkbook, calculating the circumference of a circle given its radius, and determining the shortest day of the year from the principles of astronomy are all examples of deductive reasoning. Deductive reasoning is *correct* if and only if the truth of the conclusion is necessitated by the truth of the premises or, in other words, the truth of the premises requires the truth of the conclusion. If reasoning from the premises to the conclusion of an argument is deductively correct, we say that the argument is <u>valid</u>.

Examples of valid arguments are the following:

Argument A

(1) Timothy is a poet.

(2) All poets are poor.

Therefore,

(3) Timothy is poor.

Argument B

(1) There is someone that everyone loves.

Therefore,

(2) Everyone loves someone.

Reasoning deductively from the premises to the conclusion of either of these arguments would represent correct deductive reasoning.

Examples of arguments that are not valid are the two below:

Argument C

(1) Timothy is a poet.

(2) Some poets are poor.

Therefore,

(3) Timothy is poor.

Argument D

(1) Everyone loves someone.

Therefore,

(2) There is someone that everyone loves.

Reasoning deductively from the premises to the conclusion of either of these arguments would be incorrect. [Can you explain why Argument A is valid and Argument C is invalid? What about Arguments B and D?]

Errors of fact are found in the premises or conclusions of both valid and invalid arguments. For example, if in fact Timothy is not a poet, an error of fact occurs in both Argument A (which is valid) and Argument C (which is invalid). In contrast, an error of deductive reasoning is committed in reasoning from the premises to the conclusion of an invalid argument. No such error is committed in reasoning from the premises to the conclusion of a valid argument. Thus, although an error of fact may occur in both valid and invalid arguments, an error of deductive reasoning is always associated with an invalid argument. So, you may start from or end with an error of fact without committing an error of deductive reasoning and may commit an error of deductive reasoning without starting from or ending with an error of fact. So, deductive reasoning may be incorrect even though the premises and conclusion are true. But, unlike inductive reasoning, deductive reasoning from true premises is never correct if the conclusion is false.

A sound argument is one kind of valid argument. It is a valid argument having all true premises and a true conclusion. Put another way, a sound argument is an argument that contains no error of fact and no error of deductive reasoning. For example, if there is a person whom everyone loves, then Argument B is a sound argument. In reasoning deductively from the premises to the conclusion of a sound argument, you commit no error of fact and no error of deductive reasoning. Because a valid argument with all true premises must have a true conclusion, a sound argument can also be defined simply as a valid argument with all true premises. An argument that either is not valid or has a false premise is unsound, that is, not sound.

Argument A is unsound because its second premise 'All poets are poor', is false. Both Arguments C and D are invalid and, thus, unsound. [Is Argument B sound or unsound?]

In this text, our interest in inductive reasoning is limited to explaining how it differs from deductive reasoning. Our primary concern is with deductive reasoning. Thus, with the exception of the exercises at the end of this section, for the sake of brevity, we shall simply omit the qualifying words 'deductive' and 'deductively,' as this is the only type of reasoning or logic with which we shall be dealing.

Implication and Inference

Whether an argument is valid depends upon how the premises and conclusion are related. In logic, implication or implying is understood as a relationship between the premises and conclusion of valid arguments. As the relation of *being less than* holds or does not hold between two numbers (3 is less than 7, but 7 is not less than 3), so the relation of implication or implying holds or does not hold between the premises and conclusion of arguments. If the relationship holds (in other words, if the premises imply the conclusion), the argument is valid; but not otherwise.

Unlike implication, inference involves a doer. If an individual infers a conclusion from premises and the premises imply the conclusion, then the inference is correct. If the premises do not imply the conclusion, then the inference is incorrect. Reasoning logically, you make correct inferences; reasoning illogically, you make incorrect ones. In the absence of reasoning, you make neither. While inferences are correct or incorrect, those attributes do not apply to implications.

Conventions

Because of the close relationship between a sentence and the proposition its verbalizes, when no misunderstanding is likely and the presentation is simplified, we may speak of them as if they are interchangeable. For example, we speak of sentences being true or false, even though, strictly speaking, only the propositions they express are true or false. Similarly, when the premises of an argument imply (or do not imply) the conclusion, we may say that the sentences verbalizing the premises imply (or do not imply) the sentence verbalizing the conclusion. For example, in the next section, we refer to the sentence 'The earth cannot be circumnavigated' as the conclusion of an argument, not as a verbalization of the conclusion, even though, strictly speaking, only propositions are conclusions of arguments.

An inference is a mental act in which a transition is made from premises to the conclusion of an argument. The inference is correct or incorrect depending upon whether the argument is valid or invalid. Because of this close relationship between arguments and inferences, inferences are sometimes simply said to be valid or invalid. Moreover, for purposes of brevity, we may refer to an inference as an argument and an argument as an inference. For example, in explaining what counts as a sound argument above, we wrote that "a sound argument is an argument that contains no error of fact and no error of reasoning," although, strictly speaking, it is inferences and not arguments that contain or fail to contain errors of reasoning. Similarly, an individual may be referred to as committing both an error of fact and an error of reasoning in making an inference, although, strictly speaking, errors of fact (that is, false propositions) are the sort of things that are believed, not the sort of things that are committed. Where this kind of interchange might lead to misunderstanding, the distinction between an argument and an inference is maintained.

EXERCISES FOR SECTION 1.1

[*Note:* Solutions to exercises marked with asterisks are given at the end of the text.]

1. In walking, you move from one place to another. In reasoning, you move from what to what?

*2. Is a verbalized proposition a sentence?

3. Give examples of propositions that you have not verbalized previously because to do so would have been either impolite, inappropriate, or boring.

*4. Is an argument no more than a collection of propositions? Explain your answer.

*5. Using the concept of a proposition, explain how two individuals could solve the same problem the same way, although one speaks only French and the other speaks only English.

6. Construct an argument with a premise you know is false.

*7. Give five examples of words other than those offered in the text that you could use to indicate either the premises or the conclusion of an argument. Be sure to specify which function each performs.

8. Determine how long it would take an individual running at 7 miles per hour to traverse 65 miles nonstop. Did you reason deductively or inductively? Explain your answer.

9. Describe a situation in which you reason inductively. Do the same for one in which you reason deductively.

*10. Can you always tell without a doubt whether a person is reasoning deductively or inductively, if you are told only the premises and conclusion? Explain your answer. What if the reasoner tells you that the conclusion follows necessarily from the premises or that the conclusion is only probable given the truth of the premises?

11. Assume that you arrive at a conclusion having reasoned inductively and your conclusion turns out to be false, even though your premises are true. Must you admit that your reasoning is not acceptable, or could you still maintain that it is acceptable? Would it make any difference if you had reasoned deductively?

*12. Assume that a person arrives at a conclusion from true premises and you ask, "Will you eat your hat if your conclusion is wrong?" Would the answer more likely be "Yes" if the person's reasoning is deductive rather than inductive? Explain your answer.

13. Will the study of logic be more likely to improve your ability to distinguish between true and false propositions than between valid and invalid arguments?

*14. Consider the following definition: Logic is the study of rational deductive processes by which the truth of a statement is determined. What are the weak and strong points of this definition?

15. Can propositions be communicated without being verbalized? Give examples if you think they can be.

*16. In idiomatic English, persons are said to imply this or that. Strictly speaking, persons do not imply; it is what a person says that has implications. Discuss.

17. Give your own example of a valid argument that is unsound. Be sure to provide facts if the truth or falsehood of your premises is not generally known.

*18. Can an individual who is reasoning commit an error of fact without committing an error of reasoning? Why or why not? Can an individual commit an error of reasoning without committing an error of fact? Why or why not?

*19. Can you explain why Arguments A and B on page 7 are valid? Why Arguments C and D on page 8 are invalid?

1.2 SEMANTIC PROPERTIES

Reasoning is very difficult—if not impossible—to deal with directly. Hence, logicians study reasoning only indirectly, as a completed process, after the premises and conclusion have been articulated in a language, in other words, after the argument is verbalized. Once an argument is verbalized, the correctness of reasoning from its premises to its conclusion can be decided on the basis of whether the argument is valid or not. The reasoning is correct if the argument is valid, incorrect if it is not.

Because verbalizations of arguments are linguistic entities, logic is, in large part, a study of the syntax and semantics of languages. In studying the syntax of a language, one looks at the language's structure or grammar considered independently of what specific meaning its expressions may have. In studying the semantics, one deals with the meanings of its words and phrases and the conditions under which sentences are true or false, as well as various semantic properties of sentences and arguments that are of special interest to logicians. The semantic property of greatest interest to logicians is the validity of arguments. We begin our discussion below with a topic that is closely related to the validity of arguments but easier to grasp, namely, the validity of sentences.

Semantic Possibility

As previously mentioned, we are using the term 'sentence' as short for 'a sentence that expresses either a true or false proposition'. Understood in this way, every sentence has one and only one of two truth values: truth or falsehood. To recognize which truth value a sentence has, you must understand it. In some cases, understanding is enough; but in others, additional information is needed.

For example, consider the following sentences:

(1) February 19, 1999, is on a Monday.

(2) February 19, 1999, is not on a Monday.

(3) February 19, 1999, is on a Monday and is the day that George Washington's Birthday is observed.

(4) February 19, 1999, is either on a Monday or on some other day of the week.

(5) February 19, 1999, is both on a Monday and on a Tuesday.

Simply understanding (1), you cannot detect its truth value; additional information is needed. The same is true of (2) and (3), because neither of these is constrained in and of itself to either truth value. But (4) and (5) are. Simply understanding them, you can see that (4) must be true and (5) must be false.

We call <u>valid</u> any sentence that does not have the <u>semantic possibility</u> of being false. In this text, we use the term 'semantic possibility' to describe the kind of possibility that exists with respect to the truth values of sentences relative only to the constraints of the language. For example, sentence (4) is valid because truth is the only value that is possible for (4) given the constraints of the language on that sentence. Another example of a valid sentence is 'Maroon is a shade of red'. We call <u>self-contradictory</u> or, simply, <u>contradictory</u> any sentence that does not have the semantic possibility of being true. For example, sentence (5) is self-contradictory. Another example of a contradiction is '2 + 2 = 5'.

When either truth value is semantically possible for a sentence, the sentence is neither valid nor contradictory. Examples of such sentences are (1), (2), and (3). This does not mean, of course, that a sentence for which either truth value is possible is without a truth value. Every sentence has a truth value and only one truth value. However, if a sentence is neither valid nor contradictory, then its truth value cannot be determined simply from knowing what proposition it expresses.

Understanding the difference between sentences that are valid and those that are not valid is not difficult. But deciding which sentences in a natural language, such as English or Japanese, are valid and which are not is not always a simple matter. For example, is the sentence 'All humans are mortal' valid or not? Your answer will depend upon what you take 'human' and 'mortal' to signify. If you regard mortality as essential to being a human, then you will say that the sentence is valid. But if you do not, then you will say that the sentence is not valid. The situation is analogous for the other semantic properties discussed in this section.

You may wonder why we use 'valid' to describe a property of sentences when we have used the same term previously for arguments. We could have called valid sentences 'analytically true' or 'semantically true'. However, our use of 'valid' for sentences is standard and based on the relationship between valid propositions and valid arguments. An argument, with or without premises, is valid if it has a valid conclusion. An argument without premises is just one proposition, the conclusion. Consequently, a valid proposition is just a valid argument without premises.

Logical Possibility

We use the term 'logical possibility' to describe the kind of possibility that exists with respect to the truth values of sentences relative only to the constraints of the <u>logical content</u> of the language. Notice how this definition differs from that of 'semantic possibility' only in containing the qualifying phrase 'logical content'. The logical content of a sentence is only part of its meaning. What is meant by 'logical content' we shall indicate through examples below.

Because the logical content of a sentence is only part of its meaning, two sentences may have the same logical content even though they express different propositions. For example, the following sentences have the same logical content:

(6) Today is Halloween and today is not Halloween.

(7) The missile exploded and the missile did not explode.

Each says that a given proposition is both true and false; that is their entire logical content. Now, if you based your judgement solely on the logical content of these sentences, you would conclude that both are self-contradictory.

Now replace the word 'and' with 'or' in (6) and (7). You will get the following:

(8) Today is Halloween or today is not Halloween.

(9) The missile exploded or the missile did not explode.

Both of these sentences have the same logical content. Each says that a given proposition is either true or false. In virtue of their logical content, both are valid sentences.

A sentence that is self-contradictory simply because of its logical content is self-contradictory. But not every self-contradictory sentence is self-contradictory simply because of its logical content. For example, consider the following sentence:

(10) All monkeys are squirrels.

From the point of view of its logical content, all that (10) says is that all these things are those things. It is irrelevant to the logical content of the sentence that these things are monkeys and those things are squirrels. But without knowing that, you cannot even decide whether the sentence is true or false. Consequently, although (10) is self-contradictory, it is not self-contradictory simply because of its logical content.

The situation is analogous with validity. A sentence that is valid simply because of its logical content is valid, but not all valid sentences are valid in this way. For example, consider the sentence

(11) All bachelors are men.

If your judgment is based solely on what this sentence says, you will conclude that there is no way that the sentence can be false. However, if your judgment is based solely on its logical content (which is the same as that of (10)), you will not conclude that (11) is valid. Thus (11) is not valid simply because of its logical content.

The distinction between the meaning of a sentence and its logical content is related to the distinction between <u>logical expressions</u> (that is, logical words and phrases) and <u>nonlogical expressions</u>. Logical expressions may occur in any book on any subject. Examples of these are 'and', 'or', 'if . . . then', 'not', 'if and only if', 'some' and 'all'. In contrast, nonlogical expressions are descriptive and used to refer to things or to say something about them. Examples of these expressions are 'George Washington', 'my friend', 'taller than', and 'after'. The logical content of a sentence is the meaning it has apart from the specific meaning of the nonlogical expressions.

Incompatibility and Equivalence

Generally speaking, a sentence has two possibilities with respect to truth value: (i) truth or (ii) falsehood. For two sentences, there are four such possibilities: (i) both are true, (ii) the first is true while the second is false, (iii) the first is false while the second is true, or (iv) both are false. For each increase in the number of sentences, the number of such possibilities doubles. Thus, for three sentences, there are eight such possibilities; and there are 2^n for n sentences. When you consider specific sentences, the number of possibilities usually declines. For example, in the listing of sentences (1)–(5) on page 12, (1) and (2) cannot be true together; (2) and (3) is another combination for which being true together is not possible. [Stop now to explain why.]

Combinations like (1) and (2), or (2) and (3), or (1), (2), and (3) are said to be <u>incompatible</u> because their being true together is not semantically possible. Other sentences that are incompatible are 'John is 6 feet tall' and 'John is not taller than 5 feet', where 'John' in both sentences designates the same individual. Combinations, such as (1) and (3) or (1) and (4) are compatible because there is a semantic possibility for them to be true together. Other sentences that are compatible are 'John is under 6 feet tall' and 'John is not over 5 feet tall', where 'John' again in both sentences designates the same individual. Some logic texts prefer the terminology 'consistent' and 'inconsistent' instead of 'compatible' and 'incompatible', but the properties are the same.

Another important semantic property is that of equivalence. Sentences are said to be <u>equivalent</u> if and only if it is not semantically possible that they have different truth values. An example of a sentence that is equivalent to (1) is 'February 19, 1999, is on the second day of the week', when Sunday is understood to be the first day of the week. A sentence equivalent to (2) is 'February 19, 1999, is on some day of the week other than Monday'. 'Kansas was a dry state' and 'The sale of alcoholic liquors was prohibited in Kansas' are equivalent sentences. When a sentence is free to have a truth value different from that of another sentence, the sentences are not equivalent—in other words, they are nonequivalent. Among the sentences (1) through (5), no two are equivalent.

Validity

In our initial definition of a valid argument, we said that an argument is valid when and only when the truth of the premises requires the truth of the conclusion. Using the notion of semantic possibility, we can now offer the following definition: An argument is valid if and only if there is no semantic possibility that the premises are true while the conclusion is false. An argument is invalid if and only if there is such a possibility.

Below is an example of an invalid argument. (For the sake of brevity, the symbol '∴' is used to stand for 'therefore'.)

> (1) If Shanghai has a larger population than London, then Shanghai has a larger population than Paris.
>
> (2) Shanghai has a larger population than Paris.
>
> ∴ (3) Shanghai has a larger population than London.

To convince yourself that this argument is not valid, you need only recognize that the premises could be true while the conclusion is false. If London has, in fact, a larger population than Paris and Shanghai ranks in between, the conclusion is false and the premises are true.

The following is an example of a valid argument.

> (1) If Shanghai has a larger population than London, then Shanghai has a larger population than Paris.
>
> (2) Shanghai has a larger population than London.
>
> ∴ (3) Shanghai has a larger population than Paris.

To convince yourself that this argument is valid, ask yourself whether Shanghai could fail to have a larger population than Paris if both premises were true. Answering this question for yourself should help you see that the premises of this argument cannot be true without the conclusion's also being true.

The premises, as well as the conclusion, of both of the arguments displayed above are true, but one is valid and the other is invalid. The following argument also has true premises and a true conclusion.

> (1) Albrecht Dürer was born on May 21, 1471.
>
> (2) Martin Johnson Heade was born on August 11, 1819.
>
> ∴ (3) Pablo Picasso was born on October 25, 1881.

The truth of the premises does not require that the conclusion also be true; therefore, the argument is invalid. So, despite the fact that the conclusion is true, as are the premises, anyone reasoning from the premises to the conclusion would be reasoning incorrectly. This example should help you remember that an argument with true premises and a true conclusion may be invalid. What is essential to validity is the semantic impossibility of the premises being true and the conclusion false.

In Columbus's time, a person concluding that the earth cannot be circumnavigated because the earth is flat might well have reasoned correctly. And today, someone attempting to follow that same reasoning could construct a valid argument with 'The earth is flat' among its premises and 'The earth cannot be circumnavigated' as its conclusion. The argument would be valid, even though one of its premises is false and known to be false. [Although valid, is such an argument sound?]

A somewhat simpler example of a valid argument with a false premise is

      (1) All human beings are mammals.

      (2) All mammals are vegetarians.

∴ (3) All human beings are vegetarians.

The second premise of this argument is clearly false. But, because there is no semantic possibility for the premises to be true while the conclusion is false, the argument is valid. Thus, if you think that no valid argument has a false premise, you are mistaken. A false premise alone never prevented an argument from being valid.

The following is an example of a valid argument with a false premise and a true conclusion:

      (1) All undergraduates at UCLA (the University of California at Los Angeles) are women.

      (2) Some undergraduates at UCLA are tennis players.

∴ (3) Some tennis players are women.

Even though one of the premises of this argument is false, it is perfectly logical to reason from the given premises to the conclusion. If the first or second premise is interchanged with the conclusion, however, reasoning from the premises to conclusion of the resulting argument is illogical. [Can you explain why?]

As our examples above illustrate, some arguments with true premises and a true conclusion are valid, but others are invalid. And some arguments with one or more false premises are invalid, but others are valid. There is only one case in which knowledge of truth values is useful in determining that an argument is invalid; that is, when the premises are all true yet the conclusion is false. An example is the following:

(1) Some cars are Fords.

(2) Some cars are Pontiacs.

∴ (3) Some Fords are Pontiacs.

The fact that the premises are true and the conclusion false tells you in the most forceful way that the semantic possibility of true premises and a false conclusion exists. When such a possibility exists, the argument is not valid. Consequently, valid arguments can have true premises and a true conclusion, a false premise and a false conclusion, or a false premise and a true conclusion, but they can never have true premises and a false conclusion.

EXERCISES FOR SECTION 1.2

*1. Is it possible for 'February 19, 1999, falls on a Monday' and 'February 19, 1999, falls on a Monday and is the day George Washington's Birthday is observed' to be true together? The first true and the second false? The first false and the second true? Both false?

*2. Which of the following sentences are valid?

   a. Every bachelor is an unmarried man.
   b. No apples are apples.
   c. Some tomatoes are red.
   d. One's siblings are one's brothers and sisters.
   e. You will see me or you won't.
   f. Today is my birthday or today is my birthday.

3. Which of the following sentences are self-contradictory?

   a. Some bachelor is married.
   b. Some apples are oranges.
   c. No snakes are poisonous.
   d. To be a whale is to be a vegetable.
   e. Today is my birthday and today is not my birthday.

4. Are valid sentences compatible with self-contradictory ones? Explain your answer, giving examples if appropriate.

*5. Are valid sentences compatible with ones that are not contradictory? Explain your answer, giving examples if appropriate.

6. Can two neither contradictory nor valid sentences be incompatible? Explain your answer, giving examples if appropriate.

*7. Is any sentence compatible with a self-contradictory sentence? Explain your answer, giving examples if appropriate.

*8. Are there sentences that are equivalent yet incompatible? Explain your answer, giving examples if appropriate.

9. Give your own example of an invalid argument that has all true premises and a true conclusion. Be sure to provide facts if the truth values of your premises and conclusion are not generally known.

*10. Specify whether the following sentences are true or false.

   a. No valid argument has a false premise.
   b. Some valid arguments have a false conclusion.
   c. Every valid argument has at least one false premise.
   d. Some invalid arguments have a true conclusion.
   e. Every sound argument has true premises.
   f. Some valid arguments have a false premise and a true conclusion.
   g. There is a valid argument with all premises true and a false conclusion.
   h. Every unsound argument contains an error of fact.
   i. An argument with a self-contradictory premise is valid.
   j. An argument with a valid conclusion is valid.

11. Which of the arguments displayed on pages 16–18 are unsound? Explain why each (if any) is unsound.

12. Compare the argument about human beings, mammals, and vegetarians on page 17 with the one below by noting specific similarities and differences with respect to vocabulary and patterns of placement of expressions.

   (1) All humans are tennis players.

   (2) All humans are lacrosse players.

   ∴ (3) All lacrosse players are tennis players.

   Now compare it with the argument about undergraduates at UCLA, women, and tennis players.

*13. Compare the first argument about London, Paris, and Shanghai on page 16 with the one below by noting specific similarities and differences with respect to vocabulary and patterns of placement of expressions.

   (1) If Bugs Bunny is an elephant, then Bugs Bunny has floppy ears.

   (2) Bugs Bunny has floppy ears.

   ∴ (3) Bugs Bunny is an elephant.

14. Describe a situation in which the premises of the following argument are true while the conclusion is false. The situation you describe may be hypothetical.

  (1) The Eiffel Tower is taller than the Tower of London.

  (2) The Empire State Building is taller than the Tower of London.

∴ (3) The Empire State Building is taller than the Eiffel Tower.

*15. Follow the same directions as in exercise 14 for this argument:

  (1) All chimpanzees eat bananas.

  (2) Some banana eaters are orange eaters.

∴ (3) Some chimpanzees are orange eaters.

1.3 DETECTING INVALIDITY

Detecting that an argument is not valid is easy when you know that the argument has true premises and a false conclusion. No valid argument has true premises and a false conclusion. In contrast, when a premise is false, the conclusion is true, or the truth values of the premises and conclusion are not known, detecting that an argument is not valid may be more of a problem. Described below are two methods for detecting invalidity.

The Fairy-Tale Method

One way to detect that an argument is not valid is to imagine a possible situation in which the premises *are true* and the conclusion *is false*. You may not know it, but you are probably already using this method.

Since fairy tales are descriptions of imagined situations, we call this method for detecting invalidity the fairy-tale method. The following is an example of a fairy tale: Tuscaloosa is the capital of Alabama (as it once was) and Montgomery is not (although it really is). Using this fairy tale, you can see that the following argument is not valid.

  (1) Either Tuscaloosa or Montgomery is the capital of Alabama.

∴ (2) Montgomery is the capital of Alabama.

In the fairy tale, the premises are true and the conclusion false.

  Now consider the next argument:

(1) All flautists are pianists.

(2) All violinists are pianists.

∴   (3) All flautists are violinists.

Just imagine a world that is like ours except that in that world all flautists and violinists are pianists but some flute players do not play the violin. In that world, the premises of the argument are true and the conclusion false. Therefore, the argument is not valid.

The following are arguments that appeared earlier in the chapter.

Argument C

(1) Timothy is a poet.

(2) Some poets are poor.

Therefore,

(3) Timothy is poor.

Argument D

(1) Everyone loves someone.

Therefore,

(2) There is someone that everyone loves.

Imagine that some poets are poor but Timothy is a poet who is not poor. In this imagined situation, the premises of Argument C are true and the conclusion false. So, the argument is not valid. To see that Argument D is not valid, construct a fairy tale in which there are exactly two persons called 'Jon' and 'Jan' and state that Jon loves Jan but not himself and that Jan loves Jon but not herself. In this fairy tale, every person loves at least someone but no one is loved by everyone. So, the premise of Argument D is true but the conclusion is false in the fairy tale and the argument is, therefore, not valid.

The Counterargument Method

The fairy-tale method works well when you can imagine a situation in which the premises are true and the conclusion false. However, such imagining is not always easy when arguments are complicated or you need to convince someone else who cannot follow your imaginings. If you are not successful with the fairy-tale method, you can try the counterargument method, also known as the counterexample method. This method is commonly used in debate for didactic purposes and represents a more explicit type of demonstration than the fairy-tale method.

Using this second method, instead of coming up with a fairy tale, you come up with a new argument that resembles the original argument in important respects but has premises that are true and a conclusion that is false. The new argument is the counterargument. It is constructed by replacing nonlogical expressions throughout the original argument with other expressions of the same grammatical type.

In constructing a counterargument, there are certain principles that must be observed. They are the following:

> I. You cannot replace logical expressions.

> II. You can replace nonlogical expressions only with expressions of the same grammatical type. For example, you can replace a proper name with another proper name and you can replace a sentence with another sentence.

> III. The same replacement must be made for the same nonlogical expression throughout.

You will understand these principles and their significance from the examples of counterarguments given below.

To see how the counterargument method works, ask yourself whether the following argument is valid:

> (1) No pets are dogs.

> (2) No dogs are birds.

> ∴   (3) No pets are birds.

Now instead of imagining that the world is just the same as it is except that no pets are dogs, just replace the word 'pets' throughout with the word 'quails'. You will get the counterargument that follows:

> (1) No quails are dogs.

> (2) No dogs are birds.

> ∴   (3) No quails are birds.

Notice that the premises of this counterargument are true while its conclusion is false.

Any invalid argument has numerous counterarguments. For example, you can construct another counterargument to the same argument above by simultaneously replacing 'pets' with 'men' and 'birds' with 'humans'. [Take the time now to do that. Then come up with a counterargument of your own.]

Note how in the construction of the counterargument above no logical words or phrases are replaced and the same <u>plural substantive general term</u>

replaces the same plural substantive general term throughout. As you may know, an expression is *plural* if it takes a plural verb; *substantive* if it can serve as a subject; and *general* if it is true of any one of a class of things. For example, 'men' is plural, but 'man' is not; 'exotic things' is substantive, but 'exotic' is not; and 'chimpanzee' is general, but 'King Kong' is not. You can determine whether an English expression qualifies as a plural substantive general term by using it to complete the phrase 'class of _____'. When the result is grammatical, the expression is a plural substantive general term. So 'red' is not a plural substantive general term because 'class of red' is not grammatically correct; but 'red things' is because 'class of red things' is correct. Some other plural substantive general terms are 'apples', 'mortals', 'people', 'things with seeds', 'drinkers of wine or beer'. For brevity, we will use 'general term' as short for 'plural substantive general term' unless otherwise stated.

As the fairy-tale method shows, the following argument is not valid.

(1) Either Tuscaloosa or Montgomery is the capital of Alabama.

∴ (2) Montgomery is the capital of Alabama.

You can get a counterargument to it by interchanging 'Tuscaloosa' with 'Montgomery' throughout. 'Tuscaloosa' and 'Montgomery' are both proper names so your replacements are within the same grammatical type. [Before continuing, construct the counterargument.]

The following is a counterargument to the argument on page 21 about flautists and violinists.

(1) All flautists are bipeds.

(2) All violinists are bipeds.

∴ (3) All flautists are violinists.

[Stop now to explain how the counterargument was constructed and why it qualifies as a counterargument.]

Next is a counterargument to Argument D above.

(1) Every integer is less than some integer.

∴ (2) There is some integer that every integer is less than.

[As an exercise, explain how the counterargument was constructed. Then construct a counterargument for Argument C.]

Now consider the following argument:

(1) If Pinky is a rabbit, then Pinky has floppy ears.

(2) Pinky has floppy ears.

∴ (3) Pinky is a rabbit.

You can construct a counterargument to this argument by replacing 'Pinky' throughout with 'Dumbo' (the elephant). You can also construct a counterargument to the same argument by replacing a sentence with another sentence. For example, you can replace the entire sentence 'Pinky is a rabbit' with the sentence 'All chinchillas are armadillos' and the entire sentence 'Pinky has floppy ears' with the sentence 'All chinchillas have noses'. Making these sentence replacements, you will obtain the following counterargument:

(1) If all chinchillas are armadillos, then all chinchillas have noses.

(2) All chinchillas have noses.

∴ (3) All chinchillas are armadillos.

You may think that there is something wrong with this counterargument. Both replacement sentences ('All chinchillas are armadillos' and 'All chinchillas have noses') contain the logical word 'all', while the sentences they replace ('Pinky is a rabbit' and 'Pinky has floppy ears') contain no logical expression. But there is nothing wrong. Even though the expression replaced in the original argument cannot contain a logical word, so long as the grammatical type is the same, the replacement can. In choosing a replacement, you are only restricted as to grammatical type and you have satisfied that restriction in replacing a sentence with a sentence.

Justification and Limits of the Counterargument Method

An argument Y is a counterargument to an argument X if and only if (i) Y has true premises and a false conclusion, (ii) Y is obtained from X by replacing nonlogical expressions in X with other expressions of the same grammatical type, and (iii) the same replacement for the same nonlogical expression is made throughout. Because of these conditions on the construction of a counterargument, an argument X has a counterargument Y only if it is logically possible for X to have true premises and a false conclusion. Consequently, constructing a counterargument Y to an argument X demonstrates that X is not valid because of its logical content.

To understand why the counterargument method works, you need to keep in mind not only how the counterargument differs from the original argument but also how it is similar. A counterargument preserves the logical expressions of the original argument, as well as the grammatical type and pattern of repetition of each nonlogical expression replaced. For example, in constructing a counterargument to the argument about pets, you replaced 'pets' with 'quails' throughout. In the counterargument, the pattern of repetition of 'quails' is the same as that of 'pets' in the original argument. Similarly, the pattern of repetition of 'All chinchillas are armadillos' and that of 'All chinchillas have noses' in the counterargument to the argument about

Pinky's being a rabbit and having floppy ears are, respectively, the same as the pattern of repetition of 'Pinky is a rabbit' and that of 'Pinky has floppy ears' in the original.

Keeping all of this in mind, you can see that, by having true premises and a false conclusion, a counterargument shows that there is nothing in the logical content of the original argument that prevents it from also having true premises and a false conclusion. Debaters often employ the counterargument method to show that an opponent's argument is not valid because of its logical content. An effective counterargument in debate is one (i) that has premises that are obviously true, (ii) that has a conclusion that is obviously false, and (iii) that is an obvious result of the kind of expression replacement described above.

No argument that is valid because of its logical content has a counterargument. Therefore, no counterargument can be constructed to such an argument. *However, for someone to try to construct a counterargument and fail does not mean that a counterargument cannot be constructed.* Thus, although constructing a counterargument is a reliable basis on which to conclude that an argument is not valid because of its logical content, trying and failing is not a reliable basis on which to conclude that it is valid. The counterargument method simply is not a procedure for establishing validity.

EXERCISES FOR SECTION 1.3

1. Consider the following arguments, and answer the questions at the top of page 26.

   i. (1) All pieces of furniture are wooden objects.
      (2) Some supports are wooden objects.
      ∴ (3) Some supports are pieces of furniture.

   ii. (1) All pieces of furniture are wooden objects.
       (2) All supports are pieces of furniture.
       ∴ (3) All supports are wooden objects.

   iii. (1) All mothers are parents.
        (2) Some males are parents.
        ∴ (3) Some males are mothers.

   iv. (1) All Bill's friends are swingers.
       (2) All my friends are Bill's friends.
       ∴ (3) All my friends are swingers.

a. Which arguments have nonlogical expressions in common?

b. Which arguments share a pattern of repetition of nonlogical expressions of the same grammatical type? Remember a pattern of repetition may be the same without the repeated expression being the same.

c. Which arguments have logical expressions and their placement in common?

*d. Is ii a counterargument to i? Why or why not?

e. Is iii a counterargument to i? Why or why not?

*f. Is ii a counterargument to iv? Why or why not?

2. Use the fairy-tale method to show that each of the arguments below is invalid.

*a. (1) All physics majors are collard greens eaters.
    (2) All physics majors are okra eaters.
∴ (3) All collard greens eaters are okra eaters.

b. (1) The chalkboard is green or broken.
∴ (2) The chalkboard is green.

*c. (1) If I am human, then I am mortal.
    (2) I am mortal.
∴ (3) I am human.

d. (1) All chemists are scientists.
    (2) Some scientists are women.
∴ (3) Some women are chemists.

*e. (1) No football players are philosophy majors.
    (2) No friends of Sarah are philosophy majors.
∴ (3) No football players are friends of Sarah.

*3. Construct a counterargument to each of the arguments in exercise 2. Be sure to provide facts if the truth of the premises of your counterargument or the falsehood of its conclusion is not generally known. For instance, if the conclusion of your counterargument to argument 2c above is 'I will buy a model airplane', then state that you will not buy one, thus making it clear that the conclusion is false.

4. For each of the following arguments, decide for yourself whether it is valid or invalid.

a. (1) Mary is a Catholic and Jeff is a Catholic.
∴ (2) Mary is a Catholic.

*b. (1) All turtles are underwater swimmers.
    (2) Some underwater swimmers are green.
∴ (3) Some turtles are green.

c. (1) All my pets are carnivorous.
  (2) All poodles are carnivorous.
∴ (3) All my pets are poodles.

*d. (1) I was happy on St. Valentine's Day.
  (2) I was happy on Halloween.
∴ (3) I will be happy on Christmas.

e. (1) One or three is even.
  (2) One is not even.
∴ (3) Three is even.

*f. (1) If Henry Ford is president of the United States, then he is of Italian descent.
  (2) Henry Ford is not president of the United States.
∴ (3) Henry Ford is not of Italian descent.

g. (1) Some athletes are smokers.
  (2) Some smokers have cancer.
∴ (3) Some athletes have cancer.

*h. (1) All Jack's children are Bill's nephews.
  (2) All Bill's nephews have red hair.
∴ (3) All Jack's children have red hair.

i. (1) All antelopes are animals.
  (2) Some things are not animals.
∴ (3) Some things are not antelopes.

*j. (1) All dogs are mammals.
  (2) Some dogs are pets.
∴ (3) Some animals are pets.

5. For each of the arguments in exercise 4 that you judged invalid, construct a counterargument.

LOGICAL CONTENT AND LOGICAL FORM

The concepts of logical content and logical form are essential to an appreciation of the methods of logic, but they are not easily grasped. To make the notions more understandable, this chapter provides a gradual introduction through the study of forms of English sentences and arguments.

2.1 SENTENCES AND SENTENCE FORMS

The construction of an English sentence is often directly related to its meaning, though not always. For example, the following sentences are both similar in construction and similar in meaning.

> Today is Sunday and I will go to church.

> Dumbo washes with Ivory soap and so does my brother.

Each results from connecting two sentences with 'and'. And each is true if and only if the connected sentences are true.

Now consider the following sentences:

> My car is a brown Ford.

> Heade, who is an American, painted orange blossoms.

Neither has the structure of the first two; yet, both can be paraphrased with sentences that do.

My car is brown and my car is a Ford.

Heade is an American and Heade painted orange blossoms.

Therefore, as far as logicians are concerned, the third and fourth sentence have the same logical content as the first two.

In this section, you will begin to learn how to recognize the logical content of English sentences and to display that content in English sentence forms, such as '*A* and *B*', where '*A*' and '*B*' are placeholders for sentences. In later chapters, you will be doing the same thing using artificial languages instead of English forms. Dealing first with English forms should make your work with artificial languages much easier.

Logical Connectives

Logical connectives are quite important when one considers logical content. Examples of such connectives are 'not', 'and', 'or', and 'if . . . then'. Sentences containing these connectives are negations, conjunctions, disjunctions, and conditionals, respectively. We discuss each of these sentence types below.

Negations

Negations are constructed in English from simpler sentences in several ways: (i) by placing 'not' within a simpler sentence (e.g., 'Mars is not a planet'); (ii) by prefixing an adjective or verb with 'non-', 'un-', or 'il-' (e.g., 'Coke is nonalcoholic'); (iii) by prefixing a simpler sentence with a phrase such as 'It is not the case that', 'It is not true that', or 'It is false that' (e.g., 'It is not the case that the Moon is made of green cheese); and (iv) by replacing an adjective or verb with its opposite (e.g., by replacing 'passed' with 'failed').

But not all sentences formed in these ways are negations. For example, 'Some of my friends are not married' is not a negation of 'Some of my friends are married'. A sentence is incompatible with its negation, but both of the sentences above can be true. Other examples are given in section 5.2 (see pp. 130–131).

Conjunctions

Like negations, conjunctions appear in various forms. The following sentences are examples of conjunctions:

(1)   Brasilia and Buenos Aires are cities.

(2)   Paris is known for its architecture and its high fashion salons.

(3)   Paris is known for its architecture, and Paris is known for its high fashion salons.

Notice how (1) is formed by using a connective to join two subjects with a common predicate, and how (2) is formed by using a connective to join two predicates with a common subject. Such sentences are said to be <u>telescoped</u> versions of longer sentences in which the connective joins two sentences.

For example, (2) is a telescoped version of (3). [From what sentence is (1) telescoped?] Telescoped or not, for the purposes of logical analysis, a conjunction is thought of as composed of two sentences called its <u>conjuncts</u>. Thus the conjuncts of (3) (which are 'Paris is known for its architecture' and 'Paris is known for its high fashion salons') are also the conjuncts of (2). [What are the conjuncts of (1)?]

Other expressions commonly used to form conjunctions are 'but', 'although', 'even though', and 'whereas'. English conjunctions are also formed without connectives. For example, 'Bertrand Russell is a British logician' is a conjunction even though it contains no connective. Its conjuncts are 'Bertrand Russell is British' and 'Bertrand Russell is a logician'. Similarly, 'My pet is a poisonous snake' is a conjunction of 'My pet is poisonous' and 'My pet is a snake'. However, 'My pet is a sea horse' cannot and should not be understood in this way. Conjunctions may also be formed by using relative pronouns, such as 'that', 'who', and 'which'. For example, 'Ross Perot, who is a Texan, ran for president in 1992' has as its conjuncts 'Ross Perot is a Texan' and 'Ross Perot ran for president in 1992'. Sometimes, even a comma suffices to form a conjunction, as in 'It is known who did it, when he did it, and how he did it'.

Disjunctions

<u>Disjunctions</u> are constructed in much the same way as conjunctions, except that 'or' and 'either . . . or' are the usual connectives. The following are disjunctions:

(4)   The ship will take on supplies in Hong Kong or Canton.

(5)   Either Cairo or Atlanta will host the Olympics.

(6)   Cairo will host the Olympics or Atlanta will host the Olympics.

Like the conjunctions (1) and (2), the disjunctions (4) and (5) are telescoped. The two sentences used to form a disjunction are called its <u>disjuncts</u>. Because (5) is a telescoped version of (6), the disjuncts of (6), namely, 'Cairo will host the Olympics' and 'Atlanta will host the Olympics', are also the disjuncts of (5).

Conditionals

Telescoping is also used in the construction of <u>conditionals</u>, although less frequently than with conjunctions and disjunctions. An example of a telescoped conditional is 'The overpass is dangerous if icy'. [What is the longer, untelescoped version?] The following are some conditionals that are not telescoped:

(7) Ukraine will sign the treaty only if Russia signs the treaty.

(8) There will be peace in the world if the United States and China cooperate.

(9) If the president of the United States is 55 years old, then he is middle-aged.

[Telescope (9) before continuing.]

Of any two sentences connected to form a conditional, one is the <u>antecedent</u> and the other is the <u>consequent</u> of the conditional. To help determine which is the antecedent and which is the consequent, the following rule is a reliable guide:

> *When a conditional is formed from two sentences using just 'if', the antecedent of the conditional follows 'if'.*

> *When a conditional is formed from two sentences using 'only if', the consequent of the conditional follows 'only if'.*

According to this rule, the consequent of (7) is 'Russia will sign the treaty', and the antecedent is 'Ukraine will sign the treaty'. On the other hand, the antecedent of (8) is 'the United States and China will cooperate', and the consequent is 'there will be peace in the world'. The antecedent of (9) is 'the president of the United States is 55 years old', and the consequent is 'the president of the United States is middle-aged'.

You will have trouble appreciating the difference between uses of 'if . . . then', 'if', and 'only if', especially as they are often used in contexts where more is understood than stated. Keeping in mind the pair of sentences below may be helpful.

> You will graduate if you fulfill the foreign language requirement.

> You will graduate only if you fulfill the foreign language requirement.

According to the first sentence, all you need to graduate is to fulfill the foreign language requirement (nothing else need be done). In other words, if the first sentence is true and you fulfill the foreign language requirement, you will graduate. In contrast, according to the second sentence, your fulfilling the foreign language requirement is necessary for you to graduate but may not be sufficient. In other words, if the second sentence is true and you fulfill the foreign language requirement, you still may not graduate.

Another pair of sentences that should help you see the distinction is the following:

> I shall open the door only if you tell me who you are.

> If you tell me who you are, then I shall open the door.

In reading these sentences, imagine that you are home alone, you have just heard that a person on the FBI's Most Wanted List has been seen in your neighborhood, and the doorbell rings. Imagine you give one of the two sentences as your response. If the person tells you who he or she is and you had responded with the first sentence, you are not committed to opening the door. But if the person tells you who he or she is and you had responded with the second sentence, you are committed to opening the door regardless of whether the person is the criminal.

Truth Conditions

English syntax, like that of other natural languages, is not a reliable guide to whether a sentence is a negation, conjunction, disjunction, or conditional. The same word that functions as a logical connective in one context may not in another. For example, 'not' inserted in a sentence does not always result in a negation of that sentence. After all, 'Some people do not like to dance' is not the negation of 'Some people do like to dance'. Furthermore, 'Jane is unhappy' is not a negation of 'Jane is happy'. Jane may not be happy without being unhappy.

The situation is similar for 'and'. 'The United States and China will cooperate' is not a conjunction of 'The United States will cooperate' and 'China will cooperate'. 'The United States will cooperate' makes no sense unless with whom the United States will cooperate is understood. If it is with China, then 'The United States will cooperate' is equivalent to 'The United States and China will cooperate'.

Certain problems with 'if . . . then' are discussed in chapter 5 (see pp. 131–133). In the meantime, the type of conditional we shall be concerned with is the material conditional.

Whether a sentence is a negation, conjunction, disjunction, or material conditional ultimately depends upon its truth conditions. The conditions under which a sentence is true are the truth conditions of that sentence. These conditions are stated below for negations, conjunctions, disjunctions, and material conditionals. The same information is also contained in a table. If the truth conditions of a sentence fit the truth conditions of one of these types of sentences, then the sentence is of that type.

I. A negation is true if and only if the simpler, or negated, sentence from which the negation is constructed is false.

Simpler Sentence	Negation of Simpler Sentence
True	False
False	True

This table and those below should be read horizontally line by line. The first line indicates that when the simpler sentence is true, its negation is false; the second, that when the simpler sentence is false, its negation is true.

II. A conjunction is true if and only if both its conjuncts (the right as well as the left conjunct) are true.

Left Conjunct	Right Conjunct	Conjunction
True	True	True
True	False	False
False	True	False
False	False	False

The first line indicates that when the right and left conjuncts are both true, the conjunction is true; and so on.

III. A disjunction is true if and only if at least one of its disjuncts is true.

Left Disjunct	Right Disjunct	Disjunction
True	True	True
True	False	True
False	True	True
False	False	False

IV. A material conditional is true if and only if either its antecedent is false or its consequent is true.

Antecedent	Consequent	Material Conditional
True	True	True
True	False	False
False	True	True
False	False	True

From studying the truth conditions of a conjunction, you can see that the order of the conjuncts has no effect on the truth value of a conjunction. Interchange the right and left conjunct and you still have a conjunction with the same truth value. The situation is analogous with disjunctions and their disjuncts. However, if you interchange the antecedent and consequent of a conditional, you may get a conditional with a different truth value. For example, 'If one is even, then so is two' is true because it has a false antecedent. But 'If two is even, then so is one' is false because its antecedent is true and its consequent is false.

Logical Quantifiers

Besides logical connectives, there are logical quantifiers, such as 'all' and 'some'. The Greek philosopher Aristotle (384–322 B.C.) identified four types of sentences using those quantifers. Medieval logicians later named them 'A', 'I', 'E', and 'O', using the first two vowels in the Latin words '*affirmo*' and '*nego*'. Each type is analyzed below. Although the English forms are the same as those found in Aristotelian logic, the truth conditions for both A- and E-types differ as explained below.

A-Type Sentences

An A-type sentence is a sentence of the form 'All *F* are *G*', where '*F*' and '*G*' are placeholders for general terms. A classic example is 'All humans are mortals'. An A-type sentence is true if and only if whatever belongs to the class of *F* belongs to the class of *G*. For example, 'All roses are flowers' is true because whatever is a rose is a flower. And 'All movie-goers are play-goers' is false because there are individuals who are movie-goers that are not play-goers.

E-Type Sentences

An E-type sentence is a sentence of the form 'No F are G'. 'No monks are married men' is E-type. A sentence of this type is true if and only if whatever belongs to the class of F does not belongs to the class of G. Put another way, such a sentence is true if and only if the class of F and the class of G have no member in common. For example, 'No figs are vegetables' is true because the class of figs and the class of vegetables have no member in common. And 'No figs are fruits' is false because it is not true that whatever is a fig is not a fruit (or, in other words, it is not true that the class of figs and the class of fruits have no member in common).

I-Type Sentences

An I-type sentence is a sentence of the form 'Some F are G'. So, 'Some pandas are performers' is I-type. An I-type sentence is true if and only if at least one thing belonging to the class of F belongs also to the class of G or, in other words, the two classes have at least one member in common. For example, 'Some pandas are performers' is true because at least one thing that is a panda is also a performer. And 'Some pandas are lawyers' is false because the class of pandas and the class of lawyers have no member in common.

O-Type Sentences

An O-type sentence is a sentence of the form 'Some F are not G'. An example is 'Some women are not mothers'. An O-type sentence is true if and only if there is at least one thing that belongs to the class of F that does not belong to the class of G. For example, 'Some women are not mothers' is true because at least one woman is not a mother (or, in other words, at least one thing belongs to the class of women that does not belong to the class of mothers). And 'Some mothers are not women' is false because it is not the case that there is a mother that is not a woman.

In Aristotelian logic, a sentence of the form 'All F are G' is true if and only if whatever belongs to the class of F belongs to the class of G and at least one thing belongs to the class of F. The truth conditions for E-type sentences also include the requirement that at least one thing belong to the class of F. Consequently, in Aristotelian logic, 'All unicorns are beings with one horn' implies that 'There are unicorns with one horn'. Likewise, 'No unicorns are beings with one horn' implies 'There are unicorns without one horn'. But there are no unicorns; therefore, in Aristotelian logic, 'All unicorns are beings with one horn' is just as false as 'No unicorns are beings with one horn'. In contrast, according to the truth conditions we stated above for the A- and E-sentences, those same two sentences are true.

Sentence Forms and Idiomatic Variants

For purposes of logical analysis, logicians construct artificial languages that display their logical content in their structure or form. Without such a language, for purposes of discussion below, the best that we can do is to identify some typical English sentence forms and give them the status of logical forms. A logical form is a structural representation of logical content.

Sentence Forms with Logical Connectives

Negations, conjunctions, disjunctions, and conditionals all have typical sentence forms. Some of these are listed below in Table 2.1.

TABLE 2.1

Negation
It is not the case that A (abbreviated 'Not A')

Conjunction
A and B
A but B

Disjunction
Either A or B

Conditional
if A then B
B if A
A only if B

Note that 'Not A' is used as short for 'It is not the case that A'. The letters 'A', 'B', 'C', 'D', and 'E' are sentence placeholders and are replaceable only with sentences unless otherwise specified.

In algebra, you can get '(2 + 3) = (3 + 2)' from '(a + b) = (b + a)' by replacing 'a' with '2' and 'b' with '3'. From a sentence form, you can get a sentence by replacing the form's placeholders with sentences. For example, in the form '*A* and *B*', replace '*A*' with 'Mary is 12 years old' and replace '*B*' with 'Ralph is 10 years old' and you get 'Mary is 12 years old and Ralph is 10 years old'.

Sentence Forms with Quantifiers

Sentence forms of A-, E-, I-, and O-type sentences are listed in Table 2.2. Unlike the forms in Table 2.1, those in Table 2.2 use placeholders for general terms instead of for sentences.

TABLE 2.2

A-type
All *F* are *G*

E-type
No *F* are *G*

I-type
Some *F* are *G*

O-type
Some *F* are not *G*

The letters '*F*', '*G*', '*H*', '*I*', and '*J*' are the <u>general term placeholders</u>.

You can get a sentence from any of these four forms by replacing the placeholders with general terms. For example, the following results from replacing '*F*' with 'towers' and '*G*' with 'minarets' in the table above.

A-type
All towers are minarets.

E-type
No towers are minarets.

I-type
Some towers are minarets.

O-type
Some towers are not minarets.

Idiomatic Variants

A linguistic expression is said to be an <u>idiomatic variant</u> of another when the two expressions are interchangeable without a change in meaning. The conjunctions (2) and (3) above are idiomatic variants, as are the disjunctions (5) and (6). Other examples of idiomatic variants are the three negations that follow.

It is not the case that this issue is negotiable.

This issue is not negotiable.

This issue is nonnegotiable.

Of the three sentences listed below, only the first is, strictly speaking, an I-type sentence. The second and third are idiomatic variants of the first.

Some bibliophiles are females.

Some bibliophiles are female.

There are bibliophiles who are female.

Generally speaking, we say that a sentence X exemplifies (or has) a sentence form Y if X or an *idiomatic variant* of X can be obtained from Y by replacing its placeholders, making the same replacement for the same placeholder throughout. For example, the first of the three negations above has the form 'Not A' because you can obtain 'It is not the case that this issue is negotiable' from 'Not A' (which is short for 'It is not the case that A') through replacing 'A' with 'This issue is negotiable'. Because the second and third negations are idiomatic variants of the first, we also say that they have the form 'Not A'. Similarly, you can obtain an idiomatic variant of (5) and (6) from 'A or B' by replacing 'A' with 'Cairo will host the Olympics' and 'B' with 'Atlanta will host the Olympics'. So, both (5) and (6) exemplify 'A or B'. [Which forms do the conditionals (7)–(9) exemplify?]

The sentences considered so far exemplify forms in Table 2.1, but the situation is the same for sentences exemplifying forms in Table 2.2. For example, the I-type sentence in the list above exemplifies 'Some F are G', since 'Some bibliophiles are females' results from replacing 'F' with 'bibliophiles' and 'G' with 'females'. Moreover, because the second and third sentences are idiomatic variants of the I-type sentence, they also are said to exemplify the form 'Some F are G'. The situation is analogous for A-type, E-type, and O-type forms and sentences with those forms.

Principal Logical Form

As previously stated, a sentence X exemplifies a form Y if X, or an idiomatic variant of X, can be gotten from Y by making the same replacement for the same placeholder throughout. The form is said to be the principal logical form of the sentence if (i) the replacements for different placeholders are different and (ii) none of the replacements contains a logical expression explicitly or implicitly.

For example,

Jack studies hard only if he's not tired

exemplifies each of the forms displayed at the top of page 40.

> *A* only if *B*
>
> *A* only if not *B*

The first form is not the principal logical form, inasmuch as you can get the sentence from the form only by replacing '*B*' with a sentence that contains the logical word 'not'. [What is that sentence?] However, the second form is the principal logical form because you can obtain the sentence from that form by replacing '*A*' with 'Jack studies hard' and '*B*' with 'Jack is tired'. Both replacements contain no logical expression and each is different from the other.

Now consider the sentence

> If Jack climbed the bean stalk, then Jack climbed the bean stalk.

This sentence exemplifies both of the following sentence forms:

> If *A* then *B*
>
> If *A* then *A*

However, only the second is the principal logical form. [Can you explain why?]

Complex Sentence Forms

We call the sentence forms listed in Tables 2.1 and 2.2 <u>basic forms</u>. The following are examples of <u>complex forms</u>.

> Not *A* if *B*
>
> *A* and (*B* or *C*)
>
> (Some *F* are *G*) but (no *H* are *G*)

Complex forms are constructed from basic forms by replacing the sentence placeholders with forms. For example, the first form results from replacing '*A*' in '*A* if *B*' with 'Not *A*'. In like manner, the second form results from replacing '*B*' in '*A* and *B*' with '(*B* or *C*)'. In turn, the third results from replacing the placeholders in '*A* but *B*' with 'Some *F* are *G*' and 'No *H* are *G*', respectively.

Sentences that exemplify complex forms also exemplify basic ones (in other words, forms from Table 2.1 or Table 2.2). For instance,

> The patient will not get worse if the patient is dressed warmly

has the complex form 'Not *A* if *B*', which is its principal logical form. But the same sentence also has the basic form '*A* if *B*'. Notice how the sentence can be gotten from '*A* if *B*' by replacing '*A*' with 'The patient will not get worse' and '*B*' with 'The patient is dressed warmly'. The sentence

> The game is Saturday and our team will either win or lose

has the form '*A* and *B*', as well as the complex form '*A* and (*B* or *C*)'. [Can you explain why?]

Now consider the sentence

Some grapes are seeded, but no plums are seeded.

It has the basic form '*A* but *B*' and is, therefore, a conjunction. But it also has the complex form '(Some *F* are *G*) but (no *H* are *G*)'. To see this, take the complex form and replace '*F*' with 'grapes', '*G*' with 'seeded things', and '*H*' with 'plums'. What results is an idiomatic variant of the original sentence.

The difference between ((1 – 2) – 3) and (1 – (2 – 3)) is the difference between –4 and 2. Parentheses are just as important in expressing complex sentence forms. For example, compare the forms 'Not (*A* and *B*)' and 'Not *A* and *B*'. The first form is exemplified by the first sentence below, while the second form is exemplified by the second sentence.

It is not the case that Bill Clinton and Hillary Rodham Clinton were both elected president in 1992.

Bill Clinton was not elected president in 1992 and Hillary Rodham Clinton was elected president in 1992.

Notice that the first sentence is true but the second is false.

EXERCISES FOR SECTION 2.1

1. Explain how the following sentences differ in meaning.

    (1) You will win the lottery if you are present at the draw.

    (2) You will win the lottery only if you are present at the draw.

2. In each of the exercises below, a sentence is listed together with one or more of its forms. For each form, specify a replacement scheme enabling you to show that the sentence has that form. The first two exercises are completed as examples.

    a. Popeye can concentrate, but he is tired.
        A but *B*

        A: Popeye can concentrate.
        B: Popeye is tired.

    b. Some gourmets eat caviar.
        Some *F* are *G*

        F: gourmets
        G: eaters of caviar

c. The United States will prosper if it is not at war.
   (i) *A* if *B*
   (ii) *A* if not *B*

*d. All grapefruit are edible, and some do not have seeds.
   (i) *A* and *B*
   (ii) (All *F* are *G*) and (some *F* are not *H*)

e. If Caesar and Brutus win, Cleopatra won't.
   (i) If *A* then *B*
   (ii) If (*A* and *B*) then *C*

*f. If Caesar and Brutus win and Cleopatra comes in second, then Marcus Antonius will have a banana split if there are bananas in the Forum.
   (i)   If *A* then *B*
   (ii) If (*A* and *B*) then *C*
   (iii) If ((*A* and *B*) and *C*) then (*D* if *E*)
   (iv) If ((*A* and *B*) and *C*) then (*D* if some *F* are *G*)

3. For each sentence in exercise 2 above, indicate which form is the principal logical form. If none is, then provide one together with an appropriate replacement scheme.

4. Specify the principal logical form of each of the following sentences, and provide an appropriate replacement scheme. In working out these exercises, consult Tables 2.1 and 2.2 on pages 37–38.

   a. You must promise to drive carefully or you may not borrow my car.
   *b. Johann Strauss is an Austrian composer.
   *c. Either Marcus Antonius or Julius Caesar will speak to Cleopatra.
   d. I did not bury Paul.
   *e. Some men are not tennis players.
   f. All philosophers drink wine.
   *g. No camels have humps.
   h. Some apples are red, and some are yellow.
   *i. Jack will pass if Jack does not fail.
   *j. This apple is red, but some are not.

*5. Identify the antecedent and the consequent of each conditional sentence in exercises 2 and 4 above.

6. Identify the conjuncts of each conjunction in exercises 2 and 4 above.

7. Identify the disjuncts of each disjunction in exercises 2 and 4 above.

*8. Identify the sentences that exemplify A-, I-, E-, and O-type forms in exercises 2 and 4 above. [Remember the exemplification of a type only requires idiomatic variance with a sentence of that type.]

9. Describe what kind of sentence has each of the following forms. For example, a sentence having the form 'A and A' is a conjunction, where the right conjunct is the same as the left.

  *a. If A then A
   b. Not A
  *c. Not (A or B)
  *d. Not A or B
   e. Not (A and B)
   f. Not (all F are G)
   g. (Some F are G) and (some F are not G)
  *h. If (some F are not G), then (some F are G)
  *i. (All F are G) but (no G are H)

*10. Give examples of English sentences that exemplify each of the forms in exercise 9.

 11. Is every sentence with the form 'Either A or not A' valid? Are sentences that exemplify the form 'A and not A' contradictory?

*12. There are sentences of the form 'A and B' that are valid; some that are contradictory; and some that are neither valid nor contradictory. Give your own examples of all three.

2.2 ARGUMENTS AND ARGUMENT FORMS

Sentences have logical content and so do arguments. When an argument is valid simply because of its logical content, we say that the argument is <u>logically valid</u>. The following are two examples of arguments that have the same logical content.

> (1) Jon is late or Lys is late.
>
> (2) Lys is not late.
>
> ∴ (3) Jon is late.

> (1) Lys is Jon's sister or Joy is.
>
> (2) Joy is not Jon's sister.
>
> ∴ (3) Lys is Jon's sister.

The premises of both arguments state that at least one of two propositions is true and, furthermore, that the second of the two is false. In turn, the conclusion states that the first of the two propositions is true. This is the logical content of both arguments. If at least one of two propositions is true but the second is false, it follows that the first is true. Consequently, both arguments are logically valid, that is, each is valid simply because of its logical content.

In these examples, the similarity in content is reflected in the way the arguments are expressed. In both, the first premise is constructed by placing 'or' between two simpler sentences: one of the simpler sentences is to the left and the other is to the right of 'or'. The second premise is the negation of the sentence to the right of 'or', and the conclusion is the affirmation of the sentence to the left of 'or'. In short, in these arguments logical content and logical form coincide.

Argument Forms

Argument forms are analogous to sentence forms in every respect. The following is an example of an argument form:

(1) *A* or *B*

(2) Not *B*

∴   (3) *A*

From studying this form, you can see that any argument having this form must have exactly two premises and, of course, a conclusion. The first premise must be a disjunction; the second, the negation of the right disjunct of that disjunction; and the conclusion of the argument, the left disjunct. Arguments of this form are known as <u>disjunctive syllogisms</u>. The two arguments above about Jon and Lys are disjunctive syllogisms.

The following are other argument forms:

(1) If *A* then *B*

(2) *A*

∴   (3) *B*

(1) All *F* are *G*

(2) All *G* are *H*

∴   (3) All *F* are *H*

Arguments of the form at top are known as *modus ponens* arguments; those that have the form at bottom, as <u>chain arguments</u>. The argument that follows is an example of *modus ponens*:

(1) If oxygen is lighter than hydrogen, then the Pope is the Aga Khan.

(2) Oxygen is lighter than hydrogen.

∴ (3) The Pope is the Aga Khan.

The next is a chain argument:

(1) All tennis players are campers.

(2) All campers are hunters.

∴ (3) All tennis players are hunters.

To see that the first exemplifies *modus ponens*, replace '*A*' throughout the *modus ponens* form with 'Oxygen is lighter than hydrogen' and replace '*B*' throughout with 'The Pope is the Aga Khan'. [As an exercise, explain what replacements in the chain argument form can be made to show that the second argument is a chain argument.]

An argument form is *valid* if it is not possible for an argument with that form to have true premises and a false conclusion, but *invalid* if it is possible for an argument with that form to have true premises and a false conclusion. The three argument forms above are valid. The following is a form that is not valid. It is known as the fallacy of affirming the consequent.

(1) If *A* then *B*

(2) *B*

∴ (3) *A*

If you have any doubt that this form is invalid, the following argument with true premises and a false conclusion should convince you.

(1) If turtles are fish, then turtles can swim.

(2) Turtles can swim.

∴ (3) Turtles are fish.

An argument, like a sentence, usually exemplifies more than one form. The more complex the argument, the more complex and varied are the forms it exemplifies. As with sentence forms, a form exemplified by an argument is the *principal logical form* if (i) the replacements for different placeholders are different and (ii) none of the replacements contains a logical word. Like a sentence, an argument, no matter how complex, has only one principal logical form (if some notational and idiomatic differences are disregarded).

To better understand the relationship between an argument and its forms, consider the following relatively complex argument:

(1) If Geoffrey is sleepy, then he is uncooperative.

(2) If Geoffrey is funny and uncooperative, then he is a nuisance.

∴   (3) If Geoffrey is sleepy and funny, then he is a nuisance.

Like any argument with just two premises, this argument has the form

(1) *A*

(2) *B*

∴   (3) *C*

But it also has the form

(1) If *A* then *B*

(2) If *C* then *D*

∴   (3) If *E* then *D*

as well as the still more complex form

(1) If *A* then *B*

(2) If (*C* and *B*) then *D*

∴   (3) If (*A* and *C*) then *D*

To convince yourself that the argument about Geoffrey above exemplifies the last form, use the replacement scheme that follows:

A: Geoffrey is sleepy.

B: Geoffrey is uncooperative.

C: Geoffrey is funny.

D: Geoffrey is a nuisance.

In this scheme, the replacement sentence for '*B*' ('Geoffrey is uncooperative') is an idiomatic variant of 'Geoffrey is not cooperative'. Therefore, the replacement sentence contains a logical word.

None of the forms displayed, as yet, is the principal logical form of the argument. However, the following form is.

(1) If *A* then not *B*

(2) If (*C* and not *B*) then *D*

∴   (3) If (*A* and *C*) then *D*

To convince yourself that this form is the principal logical form, use the scheme that results from substituting 'Geoffrey is cooperative' for 'Geoffrey is uncooperative' in the replacement scheme above. No replacement sentence contains a logical word and each is different from the others.

Valid and Invalid Forms

If an argument form is valid, any argument exemplifying that form is valid. Put another way, only valid arguments exemplify valid forms. In contrast, both valid and invalid arguments exemplify invalid forms. Of the forms exemplified by the valid argument about Geoffrey above, only the last two forms displayed are valid. The other forms are invalid; yet, the same valid argument exemplifies them all. [Stop now to review those forms. For each invalid form, construct both a valid and an invalid argument that has that form.]

A form is not valid if an invalid argument has that form. So, finding that an invalid argument has an argument form is enough to establish that the form is invalid. For example, replace 'A' with 'Two is even' and 'B' with 'Three is even' in the form

(1) A or B

∴   (2) B

What results is the following argument:

(1) Two is even or three is even.

∴   (2) Three is even.

With a true premise and a false conclusion, this argument is obviously invalid. Therefore, the form it exemplifies is also invalid. Finding that an invalid argument exemplifies a certain form, you can conclude that the form is invalid. But trying and failing to find such an argument does not warrant your concluding that the form is valid. As with counterarguments, failing to find one does not mean that none exists.

So far we have only discussed arguments that are valid because of their logical content. There are some arguments that are valid because of their nonlogical content. For example, consider the following valid argument:

(1) John McEnroe is a professional tennis player.

∴   (2) John McEnroe is a professional athlete.

The principal logical form of this valid argument is the invalid form

>(1) A
>
>∴   (2) B

But the argument is valid, nevertheless, because of its nonlogical content.

Forms of Forms

Logicians talk not only of the forms of sentences and arguments but also of the forms of forms. In general, a form X has a form Y if X results from replacing the same sentence placeholders in Y with the same sentence forms throughout. Remember that sentence placeholders are themselves forms (the simplest type). For instance, each of the three sentence forms

>(A or B) and C
>
>A and not B
>
>(A if B) and (A only if B)

has the form 'A and B'. To see this, note that the first sentence form results from 'A and B' by replacing 'A' with '(A or B)' and replacing 'B' with 'C'. [Now stop to explain how the second and third result from making replacements in 'A and B'.]

The situation is analogous with argument forms. The *modus ponens* form

>(1) If A then B
>
>(2) A
>
>∴   (3) B

is exemplified by both of the forms below.

>(1) If (A and B) then C
>
>(2) A and B
>
>∴   (3) C

>(1) If not A then not B
>
>(2) Not A
>
>∴   (3) Not B

To see that the form at top exemplifies *modus ponens*, replace '*A*' in the *modus ponens* form with '*A* and *B*' and replace '*B*' with '*C*'. [What replacements in *modus ponens* are needed to get the second form?]

Valid argument forms are never exemplified by invalid argument forms. Thus, knowing that a form is valid, you can conclude that any form exemplifying it is also valid. However, knowing that an argument form exemplifies an invalid form is not enough to conclude that the form is invalid. The only exception is the case in which the forms can be gotten from one another by simply interchanging replacement letters, the same replacement letter for the same replacement letter throughout. For example, the following are two such forms:

(1) If *A* then *B*

(2) *B*

∴ (3) *A*

(1) If *B* then *A*

(2) *A*

∴ (3) *B*

Logicians regard forms that are related in this way as the same form. In this case, both forms are the form of the fallacy of affirming the consequent.

EXERCISES FOR SECTION 2.2

1. Each English argument a–d below is listed with two of its forms. For each form, specify a replacement scheme enabling you to show that the argument has that form.

a. (1) Either Gaby or Hans is coming.
∴ (2) Gaby is coming.

   | (1) *A* | (1) *A* or *B* |
   | ∴ (2) *B* | ∴ (2) *A* |

*b. (1) Harvey is annoyed if Jack is.
   (2) Jack is not annoyed.
∴ (3) Harvey is not annoyed.

(1) *A* if *B*	(1) *A* if *B*
(2) *C*	(2) Not *B*
∴ (3) Not *A*	∴ (3) Not *A*

  c. (1) No turtles are alligators.
     (2) Some alligators are in captivity, and some are not.
  ∴ (3) No turtles are in captivity.

    (1) *A*   (1) No *F* are *G*
    (2) *B* and *C*   (2) Some *G* are *H* and some *G* are not *H*
  ∴ (3) *D*   ∴ (3) No *F* are *H*

*d. (1) If all piano players are European, then no piano players are
      Chinese.
    (2) All piano players are European.
  ∴ (3) No piano players are Chinese.

    (1) If *A* then *B*   (1) If all *F* are *G* then no *F* are *H*
    (2) *A*   (2) All *F* are *G*
  ∴ (3) *B*   ∴ (3) No *F* are *H*

*2. For each argument in exercise 1, indicate which of the forms is the principal logical form. If neither is, then provide one, together with an appropriate replacement scheme.

3. Some of the arguments in exercise 1 are invalid and some valid. As best you can, indicate which are valid and which are invalid.

4. Specify the principal logical form of each of the following arguments, and provide a replacement scheme to show that the argument has that form.

*a. (1) All my sisters-in-law are New Englanders.
    (2) All my sisters-in-law are descendants of Paul Revere.
  ∴ (3) All New Englanders are descendants of Paul Revere.

 b. (1) The window is green or broken.
  ∴ (2) The window is broken.

*c. (1) If I am a dolphin, then I am a cetacean.
    (2) I am a dolphin.
  ∴ (3) I am a cetacean.

 d. (1) All bridge players are backgammon players.
    (2) Some bridge players are lion tamers.
  ∴ (3) Some lion tamers are backgammon players.

*e. (1) Harry will come only if John does.
    (2) Harry or Peter will come.
    (3) John will not come.
  ∴ (4) Peter will come.

 f. (1) If Harvey is not old enough to vote, then he is under 21.
    (2) He can drink legally if he is not under 21.
  ∴ (3) He can drink legally only if he is old enough to vote.

*g. (1) If Harvey is not old enough to vote, then he is under 21.
    (2) He can drink legally if and only if he is not under 21.
∴ (3) He can drink legally only if he is old enough to vote.

 h. (1) All drug takers are freaks.
    (2) Some risk takers are not freaks.
∴ (3) Some risk takers are not drug takers.

*i. (1) Some apples are not yellow.
∴ (2) Some yellow things are not apples.

 j. (1) No violinists in Saudi Arabia are microbiologists.
∴ (2) No microbiologists are violinists in Saudi Arabia.

*k. (1) All canines are pets.
∴ (2) All pets are canines.

 l. (1) Some artichokes are purple things.
∴ (2) Some purple things are artichokes.

*m. (1) Some apples are not red.
∴ (2) Not all apples are red.

 n. (1) All apples are red.
∴ (2) It is false that some apples are not red.

*o. (1) Some apples are red.
∴ (2) It is false that no apples are red.

 p. (1) No apples are red.
∴ (2) It is false that some apples are red.

*5. Indicate which arguments in exercise 4 are valid and which are invalid. If you think that an argument is invalid, try to establish that it is by using either the fairy-tale method or the counterargument method.

 6. For each invalid argument form in the text, construct an argument of your own with true premises and a false conclusion that exemplifies the form.

*7. Which of the argument forms b–f below have the form a?

 a. (1) If A then B
    (2) Not B
∴ (3) Not A

 b. (1) If (A or B) then C
    (2) Not C
∴ (3) Not (A or B)

    c. (1) If A then A
       (2) Not A
    ∴ (3) Not A

    d. (1) If not A then B
       (2) Not B
    ∴ (3) Not A

    e. (1) If A then B
       (2) Not A
    ∴ (3) Not B

    f. (1) If A then (B and C)
       (2) Not (B and C)
    ∴ (3) Not A

8. Are all forms that exemplify valid forms valid? Are all forms that exemplify invalid forms invalid?

*9. Indicate whether you believe that the following argument forms are valid or invalid. For each argument form that you believe to be invalid, construct an English argument that exemplifies that form but has true premises and a false conclusion.

    a. (1) If A then B
       (2) B
    ∴ (3) A

    b. (1) If (A and B) then C
       (2) A and B
    ∴ (3) C

    c. (1) All F are G
       (2) All G are H
    ∴ (3) All F are H

    d. (1) No F are G
       (2) No G are H
    ∴ (3) No F are H

    e. (1) If A then B
       (2) Not B
    ∴ (3) Not A

    f. (1) A or B
       (2) Not B
    ∴ (3) A

g. (1) *A* or *B*
∴ (2) *A*

h. (1) *A* and *B*
∴ (2) *B*

i. (1) *A* only if *B*
　(2) *B*
∴ (3) *A*

j. (1) If *A* then *B*
　(2) If *B* then *C*
∴ (3) If *A* then *C*

k. (1) *A* if *B*
　(2) *B*
∴ (3) *A*

l. (1) All *F* are *G*
　(2) No *G* are *H*
∴ (3) No *F* are *H*

m. (1) All *F* are *G*
　(2) Some *F* are not *H*
∴ (3) Some *G* are not *H*

n. (1) If *A* then *B*
　(2) *A*
∴ (3) *B*

o. (1) All *F* are *G*
∴ (2) All *G* are *F*

p. (1) No *F* are *G*
∴ (2) No *G* are *F*

q. (1) All *F* are *G*
　(2) All *F* are *H*
∴ (3) All *G* are *H*

r. (1) All *F* are *G*
　(2) Some *F* are *H*
∴ (3) Some *G* are *H*

s. (1) Some *F* are *G*
∴ (2) Some *G* are *F*

t. (1) Some *F* are *G*
∴ (2) Some *F* are not *G*

u. (1) *A* only if *B*
   (2) *A*
∴ (3) *B*

v. (1) If *A* then *B*
∴ (2) *B*

w. (1) Some *F* are not *G*
∴ (2) Some *G* are not *F*

x. (1) *A* if *B*
   (2) *A*
∴ (3) *B*

y. (1) All *F* are *G*
   (2) Some *G* are *H*
∴ (3) Some *F* are *H*

z. (1) All *F* are *G*
   (2) Some *H* are not *G*
∴ (3) Some *H* are not *F*

CHAPTER

3

PRELIMINARY LOGICAL ANALYSIS

To represent logical content, we have so far relied upon typical sentence forms. Proceeding in this way, we follow in the footsteps of earlier logicians. By the nineteenth century, however, logicians, seeking a deeper understanding, began to look beyond the structure of ordinary expressions. As a consequence, they introduced novel syntactical structures derived from a conceptual analysis of quantification. In this chapter, following the conceptual approach, we develop some of the essential analytical tools of contemporary logic.

3.1 INDIVIDUALS AND ATTRIBUTES

Analysis of sentences in terms of what they say about <u>individuals</u> is fundamental to the conceptual approach. Understood in this way, there are three basic types of sentences. Each of the sentences at the top of the next page is an example of one of these three types.

The Golden Gate Bridge is being painted.

Some are paleontologists.

All are happy.

The first type of sentence we call <u>designatory</u>. A sentence belongs to this type if the sentence designates an individual and says that a certain <u>attribute</u> is true of it. 'The Golden Gate Bridge is being painted' designates the Golden Gate Bridge and says that the attribute of *being painted* is true of it. So, it is a sentence of the first type.

The second type of sentence we call <u>existential</u>. A sentence belongs to this type if the sentence is about a group of individuals and the sentence says that a certain attribute is true of at least one of those individuals. 'Some are paleontologists' is an example of this type of sentence. It is about a group and it says that at least one of that group is a paleontologist. In this second type of sentence, what individuals belong to the group depends upon what is being talked about when the sentence is uttered. The group could be wide open or just include the family members of the person who utters the sentence.

The third type of sentence we call <u>universal</u>. A sentence is of this type if the sentence is about a group of individuals and the sentence says that a certain attribute is true of every one of those individuals. 'All are happy' is an example of this type. It is about a group and says that everyone in that group is happy. To understand a sentence of the second or third type fully, one needs to know what individuals make up the group. This is usually indicated by context and understood by those who are party to the discourse.

Sentences may belong to more than one of the three types of sentences just discussed. For example, 'Everyone loves rock-and-roll music' belongs to both the first and third types. This is a designatory sentence in that it designates an individual and says that a certain attribute is true of it. The specific individual in question is a type of music, namely, rock-and-roll music. The attribute the sentence says is true of rock-and-roll music is that of *being loved by everyone*. The same sentence is also universal in that it says that a certain attribute is true of every individual. The attribute that the sentence says is true of every individual is the attribute of *loving rock-and-roll music if one is a person*. [Stop now and think of your own examples of each of the three basic types of sentences. Can you think of one that belongs to both the first and second types?]

In this section, we discuss the notion of an individual and that of an attribute, used in the three classifications of sentences above. Also discussed are types of linguistic expressions used to designate individuals and attributes. Study of these types of expressions will help you understand and appreciate the syntactical structures that have superseded the natural language A-, E-, I-, and O-type forms of chapter 2.

Individuals and Singular Terms

The most familiar individuals are physical objects. Human beings, books, kiwis, and electrons are individuals. Events (World War I) and actions (the bombing of Hiroshima) also qualify, as do mental pictures and fictional entities. An individual has, or exemplifies, attributes and is linked to other individuals by relations.

Linguistic expressions used to designate individuals we call <u>singular terms</u>. In natural languages, such as English, singular terms belong to various grammatical categories which include, but are not limited to, proper names (for example, 'George Washington' and 'Princeton University'), definite descriptions (for example, 'the capital of California' and 'the trial of Joan of Arc'), and singular pronouns (for example, 'it', 'he', 'she' and 'you'). 'Pegasus' and 'it' are singular terms in the following sentence:

Pegasus stopped Mount Helicon's ascent by giving it a kick.

And so are the phrases 'Mount Helicon's ascent' and 'giving it [Mount Helicon] a kick', which designate an event and an action, respectively. Generally speaking, any linguistic expression used to designate an individual, we count as a singular term.

Individuals, such as physical objects and historical events, that have spatial and temporal locations are called <u>concrete</u> individuals. Besides these, there are others that have no spatial or temporal location. They are called <u>abstract</u> individuals. Geometric figures, numbers, classes, attributes, relations, and propositions are abstract individuals. An example is the number *two*. Although there is an Arabic numeral '2', a Roman numeral 'II', as well as a Chinese numeral '<u>二</u>' for the number two, the number itself has no location in either space or time. Other examples of abstract individuals are the attribute of *being both round and square* and the attribute of *being a kidney specialist*. The relation of *being taller than* and the relation of *implication* are still other examples of abstract individuals.

Because abstract individuals have no spatial or temporal location, there is uncertainty and philosophical debate with respect to which, if any, are real. For example, some philosophers do not accept mathematical objects as real, not even the natural numbers (1, 2, 3, . . .). These philosophers regard the natural numbers as no more than convenient fictions that allow for greater simplicity in speech. Questions concerning which individuals are real and which are not belong to ontology, a branch of metaphysics, rather than to logic.

To avoid paradoxical constructions, some restrictions on what counts as an individual are needed in some logics. An example of such a paradoxical construction is the class of all classes that are not members of themselves. What is paradoxical about this "class" is that it is a member of itself if it is not a member of itself and it is not a member of itself if it is a member of itself. There is no need to qualify what counts as an individual in first-order quantification, the logic developed in this text. Consequently, we do not restrict the use of the term 'individual' here.

Attributive Expressions

Attributes, or properties, are the sort of things that an individual has or exemplifies. For example, *athletic ability* is an attribute that some individuals have. The sentence 'Monica Seles has athletic ability' says that the attribute is true of Monica Seles. This is an attribute that she has.

We say that an attribute <u>applies</u> to an individual when the attribute is true of that individual. And we say that a sentence <u>assigns</u> an attribute to an individual when the sentence says that the attribute applies to the individual. Whether a sentence that assigns an attribute to an individual is true or false depends upon whether the attribute it assigns applies to the individual. If the attribute assigned applies, then the sentence is true; otherwise, it is false. The attribute *athletic ability* applies to Monica Seles. So, 'Monica Seles has athletic ability' is true. But the attribute of *being a professional football player* does not apply to her; therefore, the sentence 'Monica Seles is a professional football player' is false.

Any designatory sentence, as discussed above, is a sentence that designates an individual. From this type of sentence, an <u>attributive expression</u> is formed by selecting one or more singular terms, all designating one and the same individual, and replacing each with 'x'. Such expressions are also know as *open sentences* or *propositional functions*. For example, take

John Wayne lassoed the beast.

Replace 'John Wayne' with 'x' and what results is the attributive expression

x lassoed the beast.

The following are other attributive expressions:

x hates Hitler

Hitler hates x

x hates x

Each results from replacing one or more occurrences of 'Hitler' with 'x' in

Hitler hates Hitler.

[As an exercise, form as many attributive expressions as you can from the following sentences:

Pegasus stopped Mount Helicon's ascent by giving it a kick.

John Wayne lassoed the beast.

'Bore' does not have the same meaning as 'boar'.

Remember that you have formed an attributive expression from a sentence only when the expression results from your putting '*x*' in place of one or more singular terms designating the *same* individual.]

Attributes and Abstracts

The <u>extension</u> of an attribute is the class of individuals that have the attribute. For example, the extension of the attribute of *being a mountain climber* is the class of individuals that are mountain climbers. And the extension of the attribute of *being both round and square* is the class of individuals that are both round and square (of which there are none). A class with no members is the <u>null</u> or <u>empty class</u>. For present purposes, we make no distinction between an attribute and its extension. The only exception is that, when speaking of classes, we say that an individual *is a member of a class* rather than *has an attribute* and that a class *contains* rather than *applies to* or *is true of* an individual.

To designate an attribute (or its extension), we use what logicians call an <u>abstract</u>. This is an expression having the form

$$\hat{x}(Fx)$$

where '*Fx*' is a placeholder for an attributive expression, regardless of how often '*x*' occurs in that expression. For example, 'John Wayne lassoed *x*', '*x* hates Hitler', and '*x* hates *x*' are all replacements for '*Fx*'.

The expression '$\hat{x}(Fx)$' is read 'the attribute *F*', but its usefulness is primarily as a written expression. For example, you can write

$$\hat{x}(\text{John Wayne lassoed } x)$$

to designate the attribute of *being lassoed by John Wayne*. This is the attribute that the sentence 'John Wayne lassoed the beast' assigns the beast. And you can write

$$\hat{x}(x \text{ lassoed the beast})$$

to designate the attribute of *having lassoed the beast*. This is the attribute that the same sentence assigns to John Wayne.

As for attributes that the sentence 'Hitler hates Hitler' assigns Hitler, there are the following:

$$\hat{x}(x \text{ hates Hitler})$$

$$\hat{x}(\text{Hitler hates } x)$$

$$\hat{x}(x \text{ hates } x)$$

These are, respectively, the attribute of *hating Hitler*, the attribute of *being hated by Hitler*, and the attribute of *self-hate*.

Complements, Intersections, and Unions

As illustrated above, abstracts are convenient when one wants to talk about attributes that sentences assign to individuals. As illustrated below, abstracts are also useful when one wants to talk about attributes that are formed from other attributes.

Complements of Attributes

Corresponding to every attribute, there is an attribute called its <u>complement</u>. Given a relevant group, the complement of an attribute applies to just those individuals (if any) that the attribute does not apply to. For example, given a group of mushrooms, the attribute of *not being poisonous* applies to just those mushrooms to which the attribute of *being poisonous* does not apply. In talking about which individuals have an attribute and which do not, a relevant group is essential. For example, the class of elementary particles is not a relevant group for the attribute of *being poisonous*. Talk about which elementary particles are poisonous and which are not is nonsense.

An attribute and its complement are designated by expressions of the following form:

$\hat{x}(Fx)$

$\hat{x}$(it is not the case that *Fx*)

For example, replace '*Fx*' with '*x* is alive' and the following abstracts result:

$\hat{x}(x$ is alive)

$\hat{x}$(it is not the case that *x* is alive)

Notice how the second abstract results from the first through the insertion of 'it is not the case that'. English has coined special words for a few complements. For example, *being dead* is the complement of *being alive*. [Take the time now to express the complement of the attribute of *hating one's enemies* in terms of the standard form above. In the class of people now living, is *loving one's enemies* the complement of *hating spinach*? If not, explain why not.]

Unions of Attributes

Corresponding to any two attributes, there is an attribute called their <u>union</u>. The union of two attributes applies to just those individuals (if any) that have *either* attribute. For example, the attribute of *being a parent* is the union of the attribute of *being a mother* with the attribute of *being a father*.

But what is the union of the attribute of *being a University of North Carolina (UNC) graduate* with that of *being an Oregon State University (OSU) graduate*? English has no special word for this union. To designate two attributes and their union, logicians use abstracts having the following forms:

$$\hat{x}(Fx), \quad \hat{x}(Gx), \quad \hat{x}(Fx \text{ or } Gx)$$

Using the form for the union, one can express the union of the attribute $\hat{x}(x$ is a UNC graduate) with the attribute $\hat{x}(x$ is a OSU graduate) as follows:

$$\hat{x}(x \text{ is a UNC graduate or } x \text{ is a OSU graduate})$$

Notice how 'x is a UNC graduate' replaces 'Fx' and 'x is an OSU graduate' replaces 'Gx' in the form for the union. Expressed in English, the attribute is that of *being either a UNC graduate or an OSU graduate*.

[As an exercise, express the union of the attribute of *being a mother* and the attribute of *being a father* in terms of an abstract of the form $\hat{x}(Fx$ or $Gx)$. Of what two attributes is the attribute of *being a sibling* the union? Express the union of those two attributes through an abstract of the form $\hat{x}(Fx$ or $Gx)$.]

Intersections of Attributes

Corresponding to any two attributes, there is also an attribute called their <u>intersection</u>. The intersection of two attributes applies to just those individuals (if any) that have *both* attributes. For example, the attribute of *being a rotten egg* is the intersection of the attribute of *being rotten* with that of *being an egg*. This attribute belongs to just those individuals that are both rotten and eggs.

For logicians, three abstracts having the forms

$$\hat{x}(Fx), \quad \hat{x}(Gx), \quad \hat{x}(Fx \text{ and } Gx)$$

designate, respectively, the attribute F, the attribute G, and their intersection. Accordingly, the intersection of the attribute $\hat{x}(x$ is rotten) with the attribute $x(x$ is an egg) is

$$\hat{x}(x \text{ is rotten and } x \text{ is an egg})$$

Notice that the form used to designate an intersection differs from that used to designate a union only in having 'and' where the other has 'or'. [As an exercise, express the intersection of the attribute of *being a child* with that of *having lost one's parents* through an abstract of the standard form given above.]

English often juxtaposes two words to express an intersection of attributes, as in 'rotten egg'. But, in English, juxtaposed words do not always indicate an intersection. For example, the attribute of *being a sea horse* is not the intersection of the attribute of *being a sea* with that of *being a horse*. As with complements and unions, English has some special words for intersections. For example, the attribute of *being an orphan* is the intersection of the attribute of *being a child* with the attribute of *having lost one's parents*.

EXERCISES FOR SECTION 3.1

1. In the sentences below, identify words or phrases that are singular terms. Then describe the kind of individual each singular term designates (physical object, fictional object, time, attribute, relation, set, event, action, and so forth).

   a. 'Role' does not have the same meaning as 'roll'.
   *b. The assassination of President Lincoln occurred in 1865.
   c. Paul Revere announced the Redcoats' arrival.
   *d. Seven minus three equals four.
   *e. Maternity is a joy.
   *f. To err is human, to forgive divine.
   g. The set of natural numbers is the same size (in other words, has the same number of members) as the set of even numbers.

2. Form a sentence from each of the attributive expressions below.

   *a. *x* is shorter than the World Trade Center
   b. *x* is easier than division
   *c. I forgot *x* on the exam
   d. *x* is quite a responsibility
   *e. *x* has been scheduled for tomorrow
   f. *x* is a virtue
   *g. *x* is in the eyes of the beholder
   *h. John is sitting next to *x* and *x* is sitting next to Harry

3. For each of the attributes listed below, indicate two or more attributes of which it is the union. Express those attributes in English. For example, the attribute of *being married* is the union of the attribute of *being a wife* with the attribute of *being a husband*.

   *a. the attribute of *being a real number*
   b. the attribute of *being a parent*
   *c. the attribute of *being a sibling*
   d. the attribute of *being one of the British Isles*
   *e. the attribute of *being an animal, vegetable, or mineral*
   f. the attribute of *being a science major*

*4. Each of the attributes listed in exercise 3 is the union of two or more attributes. Show this by expressing the union in terms of an abstract of the form $\hat{x}(Fx$ or $Gx)$. For example, the attribute of *being married* is the union of $\hat{x}(x$ is a wife) with $\hat{x}(x$ is a husband). Therefore, the union expressed in terms of an abstract is $\hat{x}(x$ is a wife or x is a husband).

5. For each of the attributes listed below, indicate two attributes of which it is the intersection. Express these attributes in idiomatic English. For example, the attribute of *being a teenage bride* is the intersection of the attribute of *being a teenager* with the attribute of *being a bride*.

  *a. the attribute of *being a bachelor*
  b. the attribute of *being a green apple*
  *c. the attribute of *being a seventeenth-century philosopher*
  d. the attribute of *being a square*
  *e. the attribute of *being an isosceles triangle*
  f. the attribute of *being an American student*

6. Each of the attributes listed in exercise 5 is the intersection of two attributes. Show this by expressing the intersection in terms of an abstract of the form $\hat{x}(Fx$ and $Gx)$. For example, the attribute of *being a teenage bride* is the intersection of $\hat{x}(x$ is a bride) and $\hat{x}(x$ is a teenager). Therefore, the intersection expressed in terms of an abstract is $\hat{x}(x$ is a bride and x is a teenager).

7. Each of the abstracts listed below designates an attribute. Designate the same attribute using idiomatic English. Then write an idiomatic sentence that assigns that attribute to either Bertrand Russell (a British philosopher and logician), Beethoven (a German composer), or Nietzsche (a German philosopher).

  *a. $\hat{x}(x$ is a philosopher)
  b. $\hat{x}($it is not the case that x is a philosopher)
  *c. $\hat{x}(x$ is a human)
  d. $\hat{x}($it is not the case that x is a human)
  *e. $\hat{x}(x$ is a philosopher or x is a composer)
  f. $\hat{x}(x$ is British and x is a logician)
  *g. $\hat{x}(x$ is a philosopher and it is not the case that x is a logician)
  h. $\hat{x}($if x is a philosopher then x is a logician)
  *i. $\hat{x}($if x is a philosopher then it is not the case that x is a logician)

3.2 UNIVERSALITY AND EXISTENCE

As mentioned previously, to fully understand what is meant by 'all' and 'some', one needs to know what individuals constitute the subject of discussion. We discuss this topic further in this section. The next topic is also related to quantification and deals with three uses of the pronoun 'it'. The section ends with a presentation of alternative structures for existential and universal sentences, in general, and for A-, E-, I-, and O-type sentences, in particular.

Domain of Discourse

On one occasion, you can say "All are rotten" and be talking about just the oranges in a crate. On another occasion, you can say "All are rotten" and be talking about just the members of the Mafia. On still another occasion, you can make the very same utterance and be talking about just the halyards of a sailboat. On each occasion, the same words are uttered. What differs is what logicians call the <u>domain of discourse</u> or, for short, the <u>domain</u>. The domain is a group or class of individuals, specifically, the class of individuals talked about.

The phrase 'the domain of ___', as in 'the domain of Mafia members', specifies the class that contains just those individuals that belong to the Mafia. Thus, for example, the domain of Mafia members has as members all and only the members of the Mafia, just as the domain of the oranges in the crate has as members all and only the oranges in the crate. The domain that includes everything in the universe (whatever that might be) is said to be *universal* or *unlimited*. In contrast, the domain that contains nothing is said to be *empty*.

Limiting the domain allows for simpler argument descriptions. Because the simpler the argument description, the easier the argument is to analyze, logicians often limit the domain. For example, consider the following argument description with an unlimited domain:

> (1) All violinists are either Latvian or Korean.
>
> (2) Not all violinists are Latvian.
>
> ∴ (3) Some violinists are Korean.

Now limit the domain to violinists. With this limitation on the domain, the following argument description is equivalent to the original.

> (1) All are either Latvian or Korean.
>
> (2) Not all are Latvian.
>
> ∴ (3) Some are Korean.

Three Uses of 'It'

The pronoun 'it' may be used in sentences in three ways; each way corresponds to one of the three types of sentences discussed in the previous section. In the first use, 'it' occurs in a sentence that assigns a certain attribute to an individual and 'it' is used in place of a singular term to designate that individual. For example, assume that you take a spoonful of ice cream and then remark, "It is peppermint," meaning the ice cream. Your remark assigns the attribute of *being peppermint flavored* to the individual you designate using 'it'. A sentence using 'it' in this way is a designatory sentence. So, we call this use of 'it' the <u>designatory use of 'it'</u>. The following passage also illustrates the designatory use of 'it':

> Only the King James Bible counts. It acts as a major initiator
> of personal action, behavior, and decision-making in their
> lives. It defines them (*Science83*, May 1983, p. 50).

In this passage, each occurrence of 'it' designates the King James Bible.

For an example of the second of the three uses of 'it', consider the following situation. A fortune-teller gazes into a crystal ball and says to you, "It will arrive next week, and it will bring good news." You ask, "What is it?" But the fortune-teller responds, "My crystal ball is cloudy now; I cannot tell." The fortune-teller used 'it' simply to say that the attribute $\hat{x}(x$ will arrive next week and x will bring good news) is true of at least one individual in the domain. A sentence that says that a certain attribute is true of at least one individual in the domain while not designating which one or ones is an existential sentence. So, we call the second use of 'it' its <u>existential use</u>.

An example of the third use of 'it' is the following. Not using 'it' to designate an individual, a person says, "If it is a dog, then it has fleas." What that person says, in effect, is that everything in the domain has the attribute $\hat{x}(if x is a dog, then x has fleas), or, in other words, that everything has the attribute of *having fleas if it is a dog*. When 'it' is used to say that a certain attribute is true of everything in the domain, as in this example, that use is said to be an example of the <u>universal use of 'it'</u>.

If you only consider a sentence in which 'it' occurs and not the context in which the sentence is uttered or written, you will have no way of knowing which of the three uses of 'it' is being employed. For example, the same sentence "It will arrive next week, and it will bring good news" uttered by the fortune-teller could be spoken under different circumstances, using 'it' to designate a specific letter just posted. In this case, the use of 'it' would be designatory. Similarly, a man saying "If it is a dog, then it has fleas" could conceivably be referring specifically to a shaggy animal in the distance.

The question of which way 'it' is being used can be made independent of context through the addition of quantifier phrases. For example, there would be no doubt that 'it' is being used existentially with the addition of the quantifier phrase

> there is at least one individual such that

as in 'There is at least one individual such that it will arrive next week and it will bring good news'. Similarly, no universal use of 'it' could be mistaken for a designatory use once it is prefixed with the quantifier phrase

> every individual is such that

as in 'Every individual is such that if it is a dog, then it has fleas'.

Existential and Universal Quantifiers

Logicians use two quantifier phrases that are very similar to those just suggested for existential and universal uses of 'it'. One is the existential quantifier; the other, the universal quantifier.

Existential Quantifier

The existential quantifier is

> there is at least one individual x such that.

For the sake of brevity, the word 'individual' is often dropped and the quantifier given as

> there is at least one x such that.

For still greater brevity, the existential quantifier is written in the form

> $(\exists x)$

This symbolic expression may be read in the same way as one of its longer versions. In addition, it can also be read using quantifier phrases, such as 'for some x' or 'some x is such that', that are interchangeable with the existential expressions above.

Existential sentences result from prefixing an existential quantifier to an attributive expression. The following is an example:

> There is at least one individual x such that x will arrive next week and x will bring good news.

A shorter version is

> $(\exists x)(x$ will arrive next week and x will bring good news$)$

Notice the similarity that the longer version of this sentence bears to 'There is at least one individual such that it will arrive next week and it will bring good news'. The only difference is the insertion of 'x' in the quantifier phrase and the use of 'x' in place of 'it'. Both sentences say that the attribute of *arriving next week with good news* is true of at least one individual in the domain.

Universal Quantifier

The <u>universal quantifier</u> is

every individual x is such that.

A shorter version is

every x is such that.

For still greater brevity, you can write

$(\forall x)$

but continue to read it as if it were one of the longer versions. Other equivalent readings are 'for all x', 'all x are such that', and 'take any x you will'.

Universal sentences result from prefixing the universal quantifier to an attributive expression. The following is an example:

$(\forall x)$(if x is a dog then x has fleas)

Notice the similarity that this sentence bears to 'Every individual is such that if it is a dog, then it has fleas'. Both sentences say that the attribute of *having fleas if a dog* is true of every member of the domain. If you limit the domain to dogs, '$(\forall x)$(if x is a dog then x has fleas)' and '$(\forall x)(x$ has fleas)' are equivalent.

Universal and Nonempty Attributes

Using quantifiers, logicians have developed standard ways for saying that attributes are universal, nonuniversal, empty, and nonempty. These ways are discussed below.

Universal Attributes

An attribute is universal in a domain if and only if every individual in the domain has that attribute. For example, an attribute that is universal in the domain of pianos is the attribute of *being a musical instrument*. Take any individual you will from the class of pianos and you will have a musical instrument. An attribute that is universal in the universal domain, that is, universal without qualification, is the attribute of *being self-identical*. Take any individual you will from all that there is and you will have something that is identical to itself.

Logicians use sentences of the following form to say that an attribute is universal:

$(\forall x)Fx$

'*Fx*' serves as a placeholder for attributive expressions. The result of replacing '*Fx*' with '*x* is male' is the following sentence:

$(\forall x)(x$ is male$)$

An equivalent English sentence is 'All are male'.

To state that the attribute of *being male if one is a father* is universal, follow the same procedure. Replace '*Fx*' in the form above with 'if *x* is a father then *x* is male' to get

$(\forall x)($if x is a father then x is male$)$

This sentence is true in the universal domain. Compare it with '$(\forall x)(x$ is male$)$', which is false when the domain is universal.

The Venn diagram below provides a graphic way of representing the content of the form 'Every *x* is such that *Fx*' or, for short, '$(\forall x)Fx$'.

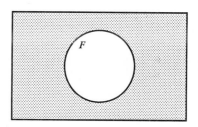

In this diagram, a circle labeled '*F*' is drawn within a rectangle. The rectangle represents the domain of discourse and the circle represents the attribute $\hat{x}(Fx)$ or, for short, the attribute *F*. The part of the rectangle outside the circle is the complement of the *F* circle. Not surprisingly, the complement of the *F* circle represents $\hat{x}$(it is not the case that *Fx*), that is, the complement of the attribute *F*. For simplicity in presentation, we shall refer both to the areas and to the attributes they represent as *F* or the *F*-complement and let the context make clear which is meant.

An area is shaded on a Venn diagram to indicate that the attribute that area represents is not true of anything. In the diagram above the *F*-complement is shaded. This indicates that the *F*-complement applies to nothing.

As the complement of an attribute applies to just those things that the attribute does not, the complement applies to nothing if and only if the attribute is universal. Thus the diagram tells us that *F* is universal.

Nonuniversal Attributes

An attribute is nonuniversal in a domain if and only if at least one individual in the domain does not have the attribute. For example, the attribute of *being female* is not universal if the domain is the class of human beings. There are both males and females in the class of human beings and males are not females.

To say that an attribute is nonuniversal, you can prefix the phrase 'It is not the case that' or simply 'Not' to a sentence of the form '$(\forall x)Fx$', which says that the attribute is universal. For example, to say that wisdom is nonuniversal, just write the following:

Not$(\forall x)(x$ is wise$)$

An English sentence corresponding to this is 'Not all are wise'. [As an exercise, use the form above to express the proposition that womanhood is nonuniversal.]

Just as there is a Venn diagram that graphs the content of '$(\forall x)Fx$', there is also a Venn diagram that graphs the content of 'Not$(\forall x)Fx$'. It is the following:

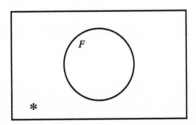

An asterisk drawn within any area of a Venn diagram indicates that the attribute that the area represents is true of at least one individual. Thus the diagram above indicates that the *F*-complement applies to at least one individual. But the *F*-complement applies to at least one individual if and only if *F* is nonuniversal. Therefore, the diagram tells us that *F* is nonuniversal.

If an area of a Venn diagram does not contain an asterisk and is also not shaded, then the diagram provides no information about the attribute that area represents. For example, the diagram above does not tell us whether *F* is true of anything or not.

Nonempty Attributes

An attribute is nonempty in a domain if and only if at least one individual in the domain has the attribute. For example, the attribute of *being an orchid* is nonempty in the universal domain, although the same attribute is empty in the domain of buzzards and coyotes.

To say that an attribute is nonempty, you can use an existential sentence having the form

$(\exists x)Fx$

An example of a sentence having this form is the following:

$(\exists x)(x$ hates $x)$

An equivalent sentence in English is 'Some are self-haters'. Both sentences are true only in cases in which the attribute of *hating oneself* applies to at least one individual.

The form '$(\exists x)Fx$' is graphed in the following Venn diagram.

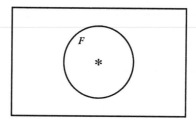

In this diagram, an asterisk is drawn within the circle to indicate that F applies to at least one individual and, therefore, that F is nonempty. For example, if F is triangularity, the diagram tells us that something is triangular (in other words, that the attribute of triangularity is nonempty). This diagram also indicates that the complement of triangularity (the attribute of *not being triangular*) is nonuniversal. [If F is superficiality, what does the diagram tell us about the F-complement?]

Empty Attributes

An attribute is empty in a domain if and only if no individual in the domain has that attribute. For example, since no toadstool is an apricot, the attribute of *being a toadstool* is empty in the domain of apricots. But the same attribute is nonempty in the domain of fungi, since toadstools belong to the class of fungi.

To say that an attribute is empty, you can simply add the phrase 'It is not the case that' or 'Not' to an existential sentence that says that the attribute is nonempty. For example, to say that the attribute of self-hate is empty, write

Not($\exists x$)(x hates x)

Equivalent English sentences are 'It is not the case that some are self-haters' and 'None are self-haters'. [Note that 'Some are not self-haters' does not express the same proposition.]

The Venn diagram below is a graph of 'Not($\exists x$)Fx'.

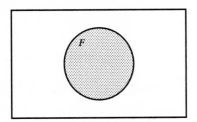

In this diagram, the circle is shaded. This indicates that F is empty, or, in other words, that nothing has that attribute. [Does it also indicate that the F-complement is universal? If so, explain why.]

Relations among Attributes

In chapter 2, we used English A-, E-, I-, and O-type forms. In Table 3.1, equivalent forms using quantifiers appear below the earlier type of forms.

TABLE 3.1

A-type	**E-type**
All F are G	No F are G
($\forall x$)(if Fx then Gx)	($\forall x$)(if Fx then not Gx)

I-type	**O-type**
Some F are G	Some F are not G
($\exists x$)(Fx and Gx)	($\exists x$)(Fx and not Gx)

References to A-, E-, I-, and O-type forms are henceforth to the new quantifier forms rather than to the English forms unless otherwise stated.

Below, the new forms are used to make statements about relations among attributes. Their contents are also represented graphically in Venn diagrams. Seeing how the new forms can be used and how they are graphed will help you understand them.

Overlapping Attributes

Two attributes <u>overlap</u> in a domain if and only if at least one individual in the domain has both attributes. Put another way, F overlaps with G just in cases in which their intersection $\hat{x}(Fx$ and $Gx)$ is nonempty. For example, the attribute of *being yellow* and that of *being a balloon* overlap in the universal domain because there is at least one thing that is both yellow and a balloon.

Sentences of the form 'Some F are G' are commonly used in English to say that two attributes overlap. In logic, sentences of the following I-type form serve the same purpose:

$$(\exists x)(Fx \text{ and } Gx)$$

The following sentence, which says there are yellow balloons, has that form.

$$(\exists x)(x \text{ is yellow and } x \text{ is a balloon})$$

The Venn diagram below graphs the information contained in the I-type form.

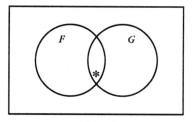

The diagram consists of a rectangle and two intersecting circles within the rectangle. The rectangle represents the domain of discourse. The F circle represents F and the G circle represents G. The intersection of the two circles represents the intersection of the two attributes. The asterisk within the intersection of the two circles indicates that the intersection of the two attributes is nonempty or, in other words, that the attributes overlap.

Disjoint Attributes

Two attributes are said to be <u>disjoint</u> in a domain if and only if they do not overlap in the domain. In other words, F is said to be disjoint from G if and only if their intersection $\hat{x}(Fx$ and $Gx)$ is empty. For example, the attribute of *being round* and the attribute of *being a square* are disjoint because nothing has both attributes.

To say that two attributes are disjoint, you can use a negation of an I-type sentence, that is, a sentence having the following form:

Not($\exists x$)(Fx and Gx)

You can also express disjointness by using an E-type sentence having the form

($\forall x$)(if Fx then not Gx)

The following sentences have those forms:

Not($\exists x$)(x is round and x is a square)

($\forall x$)(if x is round then x is not a square)

English sentences equivalent to these are 'It is not the case that there are round squares' and 'No round things are squares'.

The information contained in the E-type form is represented in the Venn diagram below.

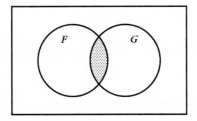

Notice that in this diagram the intersection of the two circles is shaded. Because shading indicates emptiness, this diagram tells us that the intersection of F and G is empty or, in other words, that the attributes are disjoint. Notice how this diagram differs from that of the I-type form. Where an asterisk appears in the I-type diagram (namely, at the intersection of the two circles), the E-type diagram is shaded.

Extension of an Attribute Outside Another

F is said to <u>extend outside</u> G in a domain if and only if there is at least one individual in the domain to which F applies but G does not. For example, the attribute of *being a mammal* extends outside the attribute of *being a human being* in the universal domain because there is at least one individual that is a mammal and is not a human being.

To state that *F* extends outside *G*, you can use the following O-type form:

$(\exists x)(Fx$ and not $Gx)$

The form says that the intersection of *F* with the *G*-complement is nonempty. An equivalent form is

$\text{Not}(\forall x)(\text{if } Fx \text{ then } Gx)$

The following sentences have those forms:

$(\exists x)(x$ is a mammal and x is not a human being)

$\text{Not}(\forall x)(\text{if } x$ is a mammal then x is a human being)

Equivalent English sentences are 'Some mammals are not human beings' and 'Not all mammals are human beings'.

The Venn diagram for both forms is below.

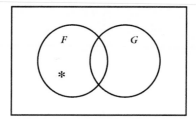

The part of *F* that extends outside *G* represents the attribute $\hat{x}(Fx$ and not $Gx)$. An asterisk occurring within this area indicates that $\hat{x}(Fx$ and not $Gx)$ is nonempty or, in other words, that at least one individual has that attribute.

To say that some fur hats are not on sale, you can limit the domain to hats and write

$(\exists x)(x$ is made of fur and x is not on sale)

To say that some fur hats are not on sale without limiting the domain, write

$(\exists x)(x$ is a hat and $(x$ is made of fur and x is not on sale$))$

The phrase 'x is a hat and' adds the needed qualification.

Inclusion of an Attribute in Another

An attribute *F* is said to be <u>included</u> in an attribute *G* in a domain if and only if every individual in the domain that has the attribute *F* also has the attribute *G*. For example, take anything you will that is an opossum and you will have a tree-dweller. Therefore, the attribute of *being an opossum* is included in the attribute of *being a tree-dweller*.

To say that an attribute is included in another, a sentence having the A-type form

$$(\forall x)(\text{if } Fx \text{ then } Gx)$$

is appropriate. For the same purpose, you can use also a sentence of the form

$$\text{Not}(\exists x)(Fx \text{ and not } Gx)$$

For example, to say that the attribute of *being an opossum* is included in the attribute of *being a tree-dweller*, either of the following will do:

$$(\forall x)(\text{if x is an opossum then x is a tree-dweller})$$

$$\text{Not}(\exists x)(\text{x is an opossum and x is not a tree-dweller})$$

Sentences in idiomatic English comparable to these two are 'All opossums are tree-dwellers' and 'It is not the case that some opossums are not tree-dwellers.'

The Venn diagram below graphs both forms.

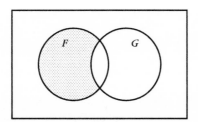

Compare this diagram with that for the O-type previously given. In the O-type diagram, there is an asterisk within the part of *F* that is outside *G*. In the diagram above, that area is shaded. The shading indicates that *F* is included in *G*. Notice that the unshaded part of *F* is entirely within *G*, in other words, it is *included in G*.

To say that the attribute of *being made of fur* is included in the attribute of *being on sale* in the domain of hats using the A-type form above, you write

$$(\forall x)(\text{if } x \text{ is made of fur then } x \text{ is on sale})$$

This sentence is equivalent to the more idiomatic sentence 'All those made of fur are on sale'. To say that all fur hats are on sale when the domain is universal, write

$(\forall x)$(if x is a hat and x is made of fur, then x is on sale)

This sentence is equivalent to 'All hats made of fur are on sale'.

EXERCISES FOR SECTION 3.2

*1. Determine whether each of the following attributes is universal or nonuniversal, and empty or nonempty, in the domain that contains just Bertrand Russell (a British philosopher and logician), Beethoven (a German composer), and Nietzsche (a German philosopher).

   a. $\hat{x}(x$ is a philosopher)
   b. $\hat{x}(x$ it is not the case that x is a philosopher)
   c. $\hat{x}(x$ is a human)
   d. $\hat{x}(x$ it is not the case that x is a human)
   e. $\hat{x}(x$ is a philosopher or x is a composer)
   f. $\hat{x}(x$ is British and x is a logician)
   g. $\hat{x}(x$ is a philosopher and it is not the case that x is a logician)
   h. $\hat{x}(x$ if x is a philosopher then x is a logician)
   i. $\hat{x}(x$ if x is a philosopher then it is not the case that x is a logician)

2. Determine whether each of the following attributes is universal or nonuniversal, and empty or nonempty, in the domain of green apples and yellow bananas.

   a. the intersection of $\hat{x}(x$ is yellow) with $\hat{x}(x$ is a banana)
   b. the intersection of $\hat{x}(x$ is red) with $\hat{x}(x$ is an apple)
   c. the intersection of $\hat{x}(x$ is yellow) with $\hat{x}(x$ is not an apple)
   d. the intersection of $\hat{x}(x$ is not red) with $\hat{x}(x$ is not yellow)
   e. the union of $\hat{x}(x$ is an apple) with $\hat{x}(x$ is a banana)
   f. the union of $\hat{x}(x$ is not an apple) with $\hat{x}(x$ is not a banana)

*3. Is the intersection of an attribute and its complement always empty? Explain your answer. Given that the domain is nonempty, is the union of an attribute and its complement always nonempty? Explain your answer. What if the domain itself is empty?

4. If the domain is universal, which attributes listed below overlap with the attribute of *being a poodle*? Which attributes are included in the attribute of *being a poodle*? Answer the same questions for each of the other attributes listed below.

   *a. the attribute of *being a poodle*
   b. the attribute of *being a dog*
   *c. the attribute of *being a cat*
   d. the attribute of *being a grasshopper*
   *e. the attribute of *being a mammal*
   f. the attribute of *being an animal*
   *g. the attribute of *not being a poodle*
   h. the attribute of *not being a dog*
   *i. the attribute of *not being a cat*
   j. the attribute of *not being a grasshopper*
   *k. the attribute of *not being a mammal*
   l. the attribute of *not being an animal*

5. If the domain is universal, which of the attributes listed in exercise 4 are disjoint from the attribute of *being a poodle*? Which attributes extend outside but are not disjoint from the attribute of *being a poodle*? Answer the same questions with respect to the next three attributes on the list.

6. Simplify the following arguments by limiting the domain as suggested.

   *a. (1) All animals are either vegetarians or carnivores.
       (2) Some animals are vegetarians.
   ∴ (3) Some animals are carnivores.
           Limit domain to animals.

   b. (1) All new hats are red.
      (2) No red hats are for children.
   ∴ (3) No hats for children are new.
           Limit domain to hats.

   *c. (1) All dogs that are gentle are desirable as pets.
       (2) No pit bull terriers are gentle.
   ∴ (3) No pit bull terriers are desirable as pets.
           Limit domain to dogs.

   d. (1) Only students who are prepared for class will pass.
      (2) Some students will not pass.
   ∴ (3) Some students are not prepared for class.
           Limit domain to students.

7. Using the A-, E-, I-, and O-type forms introduced in this section, paraphrase the arguments in exercise 6 (assuming an unlimited domain).

8. Using the A-, E-, I-, and O-type forms introduced in this section, para-phrase the simplifications of the arguments in exercise 6 that result from limiting the domain as suggested.

9. Replace the argument forms in exercise 9 of section 2.2 (pp. 52–54), which are composed of English A-, E-, I-, and O-type forms, with argument forms composed of the corresponding A-, E-, I-, and O-type forms intro-duced in this chapter.

*10. Assume that the domain includes everything in the world with the exception of apples that are not red. Explain why, in this domain, sentence (1) below is true but sentence (2) is false.

(1) $(\forall x)$(if x is an apple then x is red)

(2) $(\forall x)$(x is an apple and x is red)

Would both sentences be true if the domain contained red apples and only red apples?

3.3 VALIDITY AND VENN DIAGRAMS

One can detect whether an argument form composed of A-, E-, I-, O-type forms is valid by constructing a Venn diagram. The procedure is simple. Graph the information contained in the premises and then see if the result-ing diagram contains the information in the conclusion. If the diagram con-tains that information, then the argument form is valid; otherwise, it is not valid. Because an argument is valid if it has a valid form, once you detect validity in the form of an argument, you can also conclude that the argument is valid.

For example, consider the following argument form:

(1) $(\forall x)$(if Fx then Gx)

(2) $(\forall x)$(if Gx then Hx)

∴   (3) $(\forall x)$(if Fx then Hx)

To graph the content of the premises, you need a Venn diagram with three overlapping circles labeled with the letters 'F', 'G', and 'H'. The following is such a diagram.

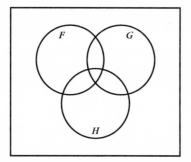

The first premise says that F is included in G. So to graph that premise, shade the part of F that is outside of G.

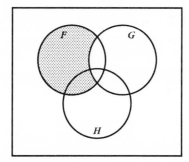

Now all of the unshaded part of F is included in G. This indicates that whatever has F also has G. The second premise says that G is included in H. So to graph that premise on the same diagram, shade the part of G that is outside of H.

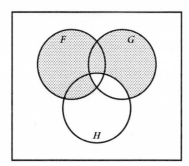

This graph represents the information contained in both premises. Notice that the part of *F* that is outside *H* is shaded. This tells you that *F* is included in *H*, which is exactly what the conclusion tells you. So the argument form is valid.

Now consider the following argument form:

(1) ($\forall x$)(if *Fx* then *Gx*)

(2) ($\exists x$)(*Fx* and *Hx*)

∴   (3) ($\exists x$)(*Gx* and *Hx*)

Graph the first premise as before by shading the part of *F* that is outside *G*. The second premise says that *F* and *H* overlap, so place an asterisk in the unshaded part of the intersection of *F* and *H*. An asterisk can never be placed in an area that is shaded. For this reason, always graph premises that are universal before you graph those that are existential regardless of the order of the premises in the argument form.

After graphing both premises, you will have the following diagram:

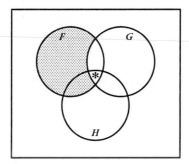

Notice that the asterisk appears not only in the intersection of *F* with *H* but also in the intersection of *G* with *H*. Therefore, the diagram tells you that *G* and *H* overlap. But that is also what the conclusion of the argument form tells you. Therefore, the argument form is valid.

The following is another valid form:

(1) ($\forall x$)(if *Fx* then not *Gx*)

(2) ($\exists x$)(*Fx* and *Hx*)

∴   (3) ($\exists x$)(*Hx* and not *Gx*)

The first premise says that *F* and *G* are disjoint. To graph this premise, you shade the area where *F* and *G* intersect. The second premise tells you that *F* and *H* overlap, so you place an asterisk in the unshaded part of the intersection of *F* and *H*. The following diagram results:

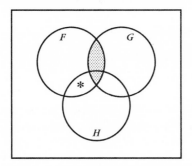

Notice that the asterisk appears in the part of *H* that is outside of *G*. This tells you that *H* extends outside *G*. Of course, that is just what the conclusion tells you. Therefore, the argument form is valid.

The three argument forms above are all valid. The one below is invalid.

(1) (∀*x*)(if *Fx* then *Gx*)

(2) (∃*x*)(*Gx* and *Hx*)

∴   (3) (∃*x*)(*Fx* and *Hx*)

The first premise is graphed as before by shading the part of *F* that is outside of *G*. The second premise says that *G* overlaps with *H*. To graph this, you place an asterisk in the intersection of *G* with *H*. But the intersection of those two circles has two parts: one part is outside *F* and the other is inside *F*. As the second premise says nothing about *F*, place the asterisk on the circumference of the *F* circle so that the asterisk is neither in nor outside of *F*. The diagram is below.

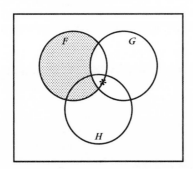

The conclusion of the argument form tells you that *F* and *H* overlap. However, the diagram does not provide that information. Notice that no asterisk appears in the intersection of *F* with *H*. When the information in the conclusion does not appear on the diagram, the argument form is not valid.

Now diagram the next argument form.

(1) (∀*x*)(if *Fx* then not *Gx*)

(2) (∀*x*)(if *Gx* then not *Hx*)

∴   (3) (∀*x*)(if *Fx* then not *Hx*)

Both premises are *E*-type. To diagram the first, shade the intersection of *F* with *G*. To diagram the second, shade the intersection of *G* with *H*. The result is the following:

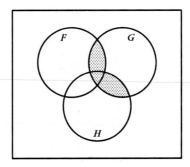

Notice that the conclusion of the argument tells you that *F* and *H* are disjoint. However, only part of the intersection of *F* with *H* is shaded. Therefore, the diagram does not tell you that *F* and *H* are disjoint. So, the argument form is not valid.

EXERCISES FOR SECTION 3.3

Use Venn diagrams to identify which argument forms are valid and which are invalid.

*1. (1) (∀*x*)(if *Fx* then *Gx*)
  ∴ (2) (∀*x*)(if *Gx* then *Fx*)

2. (1) (∀*x*)(if *Fx* then not *Gx*)
  ∴ (2) (∀*x*)(if *Gx* then not *Fx*)

3. (1) (∃x)(*Fx* and *Gx*)
∴ (2) (∃x)(*Gx* and *Fx*)

*4. (1) (∃x)(*Fx* and not *Gx*)
∴ (2) (∃x)(*Gx* and not *Fx*)

*5. (1) (∃x)(*Fx* and *Gx*)
(2) (∃x)(*Gx* and *Hx*)
∴ (3) (∃x)(*Fx* and *Hx*)

6. (1) (∀x)(if *Fx* then *Gx*)
(2) (∃x)(*Fx* and not *Hx*)
∴ (3) (∃x)(*Gx* and not *Hx*)

*7. (1) (∀x)(*Fx* and *Gx*)
∴ (2) (∀x)*Fx* and (∀x)*Gx*

*8. (1) (∀x)*Fx* and (∀x)*Gx*
∴ (2) (∀x)(*Fx* and *Gx*)

9. (1) (∃x)(*Fx* and *Gx*)
∴ (2) (∃x)*Fx* and (∃x)*Gx*

*10. (1) (∃x)*Fx* and (∃x)*Gx*
∴ (2) (∃x)(*Fx* and *Gx*)

*11. (1) (∀x)(if *Fx* then *Gx*)
(2) (∃x)(not *Gx*)
∴ (3) (∀x)(not *Fx*)

*12. (1) (∀x)(if *Fx* then *Gx*)
(2) (∃x)(*Hx* and not *Gx*)
∴ (3) (∃x)(*Fx* and not *Hx*)

PART II

FORMAL METHODS

CHAPTER 4

THE LANGUAGE OF THE LOGIC OF CONNECTIVES

Natural languages are primarily spoken languages, such as English and ancient Greek. They develop over a long period of time to enable speakers to express a wide variety of feelings and thoughts, and to point out and describe things in the outer world. Natural languages are well known to be vague, ambiguous, and changeable. In contrast, artificial languages are primarily written or printed languages. Constructed for specific purposes of analysis and problem solving, they have precise, unambiguous, and fixed vocabularies and grammars. Computer languages are examples of artificial languages. Mathematicians, linguists, and logicians have developed still others. One that you already know is the language of arithmetic.

In the next four chapters, you will be studying two artificial languages and learning how to use them to analyze English sentences and arguments. This chapter introduces the first language, a language for the logic of connectives. The logic of connectives is also known as *sentential, propositional*, and *truth-functional logic*. Study of the syntax of the language comes first, including the symbols and various syntactic categories, such as that of a sentence. The semantic issues covered include truth conditions for sentences and tests for semantic properties.

4.1 THE LANGUAGE

This section begins by distinguishing logical from nonlogical symbols of the language of the logic of connectives, here called <u>language C</u> or simply <u>C</u>. Next defined are various syntactical categories of the language, such as that of a <u>C-sentence</u>. C-sentences display the type of sentence they represent in their structure, so that, for example, what looks like a conjunction *is* always a conjunction. Because of the syntactical uniformity of C and the direct dependence of its semantics on its syntax, simple procedures for detecting semantic properties are possible.

Symbols

The symbols of C are of three kinds: nonlogical symbols, logical symbols, and auxiliary signs. Their identity and function are discussed below. The <u>sentence letters</u> that follow are the only nonlogical symbols.

$$P, Q, R, P_1, Q_1, R_1, \ldots$$

They are infinite in number and understood to express propositions.

The proposition a sentence letter expresses is specified, however, only in a <u>translation scheme</u> that consists of one or more assignments of English sentences to sentence letters. In such a scheme, the assigned sentence is the translation of the sentence letter; and the sentence letter is the translation of the assigned sentence. For example, when the English sentence 'The Dow Jones average lost 508 points on October 19, 1987' is assigned to the sentence letter 'P', the English sentence is the English translation of 'P' and 'P' is the C-translation of the English sentence. Translation schemes are analogous to the replacement schemes you used in chapter 2. Just as placeholders have different replacement sentences under different replacement schemes, sentence letters have different translations (or translate different sentences) under different translation schemes.

The logical symbols are just the four <u>sentence connectives</u> exhibited below.

$$\sim, \&, v, \rightarrow$$

You can use these sentence connectives to form negations, conjunctions, disjunctions, and conditionals in much the same way as you use 'It is not the case that', 'and', 'or', and 'if . . . then' in English. For example, if you apply 'it is not the case that' to 'There is life on Mars', you form the new sentence 'It is not the case that there is life on Mars'. Similarly, if you apply '$\sim$' to 'P', you form the new sentence '$\sim P$'. The negation sign '$\sim$' is called the <u>tilde</u>; the conjunction sign '$\&$', the <u>ampersand</u>; the disjunction sign 'v', the *vel*; and the material conditional sign '$\rightarrow$', the <u>arrow</u>.

Because '~' takes one sentence to form a new sentence, it is a one-place or unary sentence connective. The other sentence connectives, which take two sentences to form a new sentence, are two-place or binary sentence connectives. Each of these four sentence connectives has a fixed meaning fully specified by a rule given in the next section of this chapter. Other binary connectives ($|$, $\downarrow$, $\equiv$, $\underline{\vee}$) are defined in terms of the official ones listed above. Logicians often use the triple bar '$\equiv$' to form biconditionals.

Besides sentence letters and sentence connectives, the language also contains the parentheses symbols, '( )'. The parentheses function as auxiliary signs for punctuation, in the same way as parentheses do in arithmetic. For example, because of a different placement of parentheses, $(4 - 2) \times 6$ is equal to 12 but $4 - (2 \times 6)$ is equal to -8. In like manner, because of a different placement of parentheses, '$\sim(P \& Q)$' is a negation but '$(\sim P \& Q)$' is a conjunction. Furthermore, under the translation scheme

P: Canada is a member of the British Commonwealth

Q: Cuba is a member of the British Commonwealth

'$\sim(P \& Q)$' translates as 'Canada and Cuba are not both members of the British Commonwealth', which is true; while '$(\sim P \& Q)$' translates as 'Canada is not a member of the British Commonwealth but Cuba is', which is false.

We have been following the convention of placing quotation marks around linguistic expressions that are being talked about unless they are displayed on separate lines. While continuing to use quotation marks around English expressions, we shall omit them around symbolic expressions where there is no danger of ambiguity or misunderstanding and they are not otherwise helpful.

Sentences

Some combinations of English words are English sentences, and some combinations are not. For example, 'singing in the rain' is not a sentence, but 'Singing in the rain is fun' is. Similarly, some combinations of symbols are C-sentences, and some combinations are not. Because of the complexity and linguistic richness of English, no one has yet been able to specify unequivocally what counts as an English sentence. But, due to the simplicity of C, what counts as a sentence in C can be specified with little difficulty. The following rules describe how sentences in C are formed.

I. A sentence letter is a sentence. Examples are P, Q, and R.

II. The result of placing a tilde before a sentence is a sentence. An example is $\sim P$.

III. The result of placing an ampersand, a *vel*, or an arrow between two sentences and enclosing the result in parentheses is a sentence. Examples are $(P \& Q)$, $(P \vee R)$, and $(R \rightarrow Q)$.

IV. Nothing is a sentence unless it qualifies under the above rules.

From these rules, you can easily decide which expressions count as sentences and which do not.

For example, each sentence letter $(P, Q, R, P_1, Q_1, R_1, \ldots)$ is a sentence by rule I. So,

$(P \vee R)$

is a sentence by rule III.

$\sim(P \vee R)$

results from placing a tilde before the preceding sentence and is, therefore, a sentence in virtue of rule II. By rule III,

$(\sim(P \vee R) \rightarrow Q)$

is a sentence. It is the outcome of placing an arrow between two sentences and enclosing the result in parentheses. [What are the two sentences between which the arrow is placed?]

To see how the C-sentences above relate to English, assign to 'P' and 'Q' the same English sentences you assigned to them in the translation scheme above and assign 'India is a member of the British Commonwealth' to 'R'. Under this scheme, each English sentence below is preceded by its C-translation.

$(P \vee R)$

Either Canada or India is a member of the British Commonwealth.

$\sim(P \vee R)$

It is not the case that either Canada is a member of the British Commonwealth or India is.

Neither Canada nor India is a member of the British Commonwealth.

$(\sim(P \vee R) \rightarrow Q)$

If neither Canada nor India is a member of the British Commonwealth, then Cuba is.

The following are examples of combinations of symbols that are not C-sentences:

$(PQ), \rightarrow R, (P_1 \sim Q_1), (P), (\sim P)$

You may wonder why (P) and $(\sim P)$ are not sentences. The rules for sentence formation were designed to exclude them because parenthetical marks are not needed around either a sentence letter or a negation to distinguish it as a sentence when it is taken by a sentence connective to form a new sentence.

Letting 'A', 'B', and 'C' function as placeholders for sentences, we can also define what counts as a sentence as follows:

> The sentences consist of the following and only the following:
>
> (i) any sentence letter, standing alone; and
>
> (ii) any combinations of C-symbols having one of the following forms: $\sim A$, $(A \& B)$, $(A \vee B)$, $(A \rightarrow B)$.

You can justify that an expression is a sentence by breaking it down as illustrated below.

$(\sim(P \vee R) \rightarrow Q)$

$\sim(P \vee R) \qquad Q$

$(P \vee R)$

$P \qquad R$

A form is said to be <u>the form of a sentence</u> if and only if the form differs from the sentence only in having placeholders for sentences where the sentence has sentence letters. Thus, $(\sim(A \vee B) \rightarrow C)$ is *the* form of $(\sim(P \vee R) \rightarrow Q)$ because they differ only in one having A, B, and C where the other has P, Q, and R, respectively. In contrast, $(A \rightarrow B)$ is only *a* form of $(\sim(P \vee R) \rightarrow Q)$ and not *the* form because there is no way of replacing the placeholders in $(A \rightarrow B)$ with individual sentence letters to end up with $(\sim(P \vee R) \rightarrow Q)$. [Is $(A \rightarrow B)$ *the* form of $(P \rightarrow P)$ or just *a* form?]

Dominant Connectives and Sentence Components

To say what we want to about the language C, we need to make a few additional syntactical distinctions. There is no need to try to memorize the definitions; you will learn them as you apply them in solving various exercises and problems. Nevertheless, understanding the definitions will give you a better command of C.

Dominant Connectives

One or more sentence connectives may occur in a sentence. An occurrence of a sentence connective is the <u>dominant connective</u> of a sentence if and only if within that sentence, there is no shorter sentence in which the occurrence appears. The connective is then said to *dominate* the sentence. For example, in each of:

$$\sim P, \ \sim(P \text{ v } R), \ \sim\sim P$$

the leftmost occurrence of the tilde is the dominant connective of that sentence. The occurrence of the *vel* in $\sim(P \text{ v } R)$ does not dominate the entire sentence. That occurrence dominates just the sentence to the right of the tilde because that sentence is the shortest sentence in which it occurs. The connective that dominates $((P \text{ v } Q) \& \sim(P \& Q))$ is the ampersand that appears between $(P \text{ v } Q)$ and $\sim(P \& Q)$. The arrow in $(\sim(P \text{ v } Q) \to R)$ dominates that sentence. [Of what part of that sentence is the occurrence of the tilde the dominant connective?]

As you may have already recognized, a sentence with a tilde as its dominant connective is a <u>negation</u>. A sentence with an ampersand as its dominant connective is a <u>conjunction</u>. A sentence with a *vel* as its dominant connective is a <u>disjunction</u>. And, finally, a sentence with an arrow as its dominant connective is a <u>conditional</u>.

Components

The <u>components</u> of a sentence are defined as follows:

I. The sentence is a component of itself.

II. If a sentence with a tilde as its dominant connective is a component of the sentence, then the sentence that the tilde precedes is also one of its components.

III. If a sentence with an ampersand, *vel*, or arrow as its dominant connective is a component of the sentence, then the sentence to the left and to the right of the sentence connective are also among its components.

Note that *only* sentences count as components of sentences. The following list of sentences includes all and only the components of the first sentence in the list.

$$((P \text{ v } Q) \& \sim(P \& Q))$$

$$(P \text{ v } Q)$$

$$\sim(P \& Q)$$

(P & Q)

P

Q

[By appealing to specific clauses in the definition, explain why each sentence above, including the first, qualifies as a component of the first.]

To illustrate further how the language C and English translate one another, the list of sentences in C above is translated into English below. The assignments to the sentence letters are those given previously.

((P v Q) & ~(P & Q))

Canada or Cuba is a member of the British Commonwealth but not both.

(P v Q)

Canada or Cuba is a member of the British Commonwealth.

~(P & Q)

Canada and Cuba are not both members of the British Commonwealth.

(P & Q)

Canada and Cuba are members of the British Commonwealth.

P

Canada is a member of the British Commonwealth.

Q

Cuba is a member of the British Commonwealth.

[As an exercise, choose your own translation scheme, and provide your own translations.]

Immediate Components

The <u>immediate components</u> of a sentence are those that the dominant connective of the sentence takes to form the sentence. The immediate component of a negation is the sentence it negates. For example, ~(P v Q) is a negation of (P v Q), so (P v Q) is the immediate component of ~(P v Q). Similarly, ~P is the immediate component of ~~P. The immediate component of a conjunction are its left and right <u>conjuncts</u>. Thus,

((P v Q) & ~(P & Q))

has as its immediate components its left conjunct $(P \vee Q)$ and its right conjunct $\sim(P \& Q)$. The immediate components of a disjunction are its left and right disjuncts. So, the immediate components of

$$((P \& Q) \vee (\sim P \& \sim Q))$$

are its left disjunct $(P \& Q)$ and its right disjunct $(\sim P \& \sim Q)$. The immediate component of a conditional are its <u>antecedent</u> and <u>consequent</u>. The antecedent is the left immediate component and the consequent is the right immediate component. For example, the immediate components of $(\sim(P \vee R) \to Q)$ are its antecedent $\sim(P \vee R)$ and its consequent Q.

Atomic Components

An <u>atomic component</u> of a sentence is a component that is a sentence letter. In short, the atomic components are the individual sentence letters in the sentence. Thus P and Q are the atomic components of

$$((P \& Q) \vee (\sim P \& \sim Q))$$

[What are its immediate components? What are its components? Compare the list of these components with the list of components of $((P \vee Q) \& \sim(P \& Q))$ given above. Now translate the list into English using the earlier assignments to the sentence letters or assignments of your own.]

Scope

The <u>scope</u> of a connective in a sentence is the sentence that connective dominates. For example, the dominant connective of $(\sim(P \vee R) \to Q)$ is the arrow; therefore, the scope of the arrow is the entire conditional. Every sentence connective in the sentence–including the arrow itself–is within the scope of the arrow. The dominant connective of the antecedent of this conditional is the tilde; therefore, the scope of the tilde is the entire antecedent and the tilde has both itself and the *vel* within its scope. [Within the antecedent, what is the scope of the *vel*?]

Some ambiguities in English can be resolved through distinctions of scope. For instance, depending upon what is meant,

(1) Both John and Mary are not coming

could be equivalent to

(2) It is not the case that both John and Mary are coming.

But (1) could also be equivalent to

(3) John is not coming, and Mary is not coming.

If you take 'John is coming' to be the meaning of 'P' and 'Mary is coming' to be the meaning of 'Q', (2) and (3) translate, respectively, as follows:

(2′) $\sim(P \& Q)$

(3′) $(\sim P \& \sim Q)$.

In (2′) the tilde has a wider scope than the ampersand. In (3′), both occurrences of the tilde are within the scope of the ampersand. Analogously, we can explain the ambiguity in (1) as an ambiguity with respect to the relative scopes of 'and' and 'not'. In (2), 'and' is within the scope of 'not'; on the other hand, 'not' is within the scope of 'and' in (3).

EXERCISES FOR SECTION 4.1

1. Answer the following questions:

   *a. What are some differences between an artificial language and a natural language?

   b. On the basis of what you have learned about artificial languages, would you say that the language of arithmetic that you learned in school qualifies as one? If so, how?

   *c. Give an example of a combination of English words which is not a sentence.

   d. By appealing to the definition of a component, explain why each sentence in the list below is a component of the first.

$$((P \& Q) \text{ v } (\sim P \& \sim Q))$$
$$(P \& Q)$$
$$(\sim P \& \sim Q)$$
$$\sim P$$
$$\sim Q$$
$$P$$
$$Q$$

2. Circle the dominant connective of each of the following sentences:

   a. $(\sim P \text{ v } Q)$

   *b. $(P \rightarrow Q)$

   c. $\sim(P \& \sim Q)$

   *d. $(\sim Q \rightarrow \sim P)$

   e. $(P \text{ v } Q)$

   *f. $(\sim P \rightarrow Q)$

   *g. $(\sim Q \rightarrow P)$

   h. $(\sim P \text{ v } \sim Q)$

   *i. $(P \rightarrow \sim Q)$

   j. $(Q \rightarrow \sim P)$

   *k. $\sim(P \& Q)$

   l. $\sim(P \text{ v } Q)$

*m. $(\sim P \& \sim Q)$ *q. $((P \& \sim Q) \vee (Q \& \sim P))$

n. $((P \& Q) \vee (\sim P \& \sim Q))$ r. $((P \vee Q) \rightarrow R)$

*o. $((P \rightarrow Q) \& (Q \rightarrow P))$ *s. $((P \rightarrow R) \& (Q \rightarrow R))$

p. $((P \vee Q) \& \sim(P \& Q))$ t. $(((P \rightarrow Q) \& (Q \rightarrow R)) \rightarrow (P \rightarrow R))$

3. List the immediate components of the sentences in exercise 2.

*4. Identify which sentences in exercise 2 are conditionals. Then list the antecedent and the consequent of each.

5. Which sentences in exercise 2 have the same atomic components? Which have the same immediate components?

*6. List the components of 2p and 2q. Which components do they have in common?

7. For each of the forms below, list the sentences in exercise 2 which have that form.

a. $\sim A$ *f. $\sim(A \& B)$

*b. $(A \& B)$ g. $((A \& B) \vee (\sim A \& \sim B))$

c. $(A \vee B)$ *h. $((A \& \sim B) \vee (\sim A \& B))$

*d. $(A \rightarrow B)$ i. $((A \rightarrow B) \& (B \rightarrow A))$

e. $(\sim A \& \sim B)$ *j. $((A \& B) \rightarrow C)$

*8. For each of the forms a–j in exercise 7, list the sentence (if any) in exercise 2 for which it is *the* form.

9. Which sentences in exercise 2 have $(Q \vee R)$ as a component?

*10. Identify the scope of each ampersand in 2c, 2k, 2n, 2p, 2q, and 2t.

11. Identify the scope of each arrow in 2o, 2s, and 2t.

12. Give a C-translation of the following English sentences. In each translation, reveal as much content as possible. State the translation scheme you use.

a. Popeye can concentrate, but he is tired.
*b. Some gourmets eat caviar.
c. The United States will prosper if it is not at war.
*d. All grapefruit are edible, and some do not have seeds.
e. If Caesar and Brutus win, Cleopatra won't.
*f. If Caesar and Brutus win and Cleopatra comes in second, then Marcus Antonius will have a banana split if there are bananas in the Forum.
g. You must promise to drive carefully or you may not borrow my car.
*h. Johann Strauss is an Austrian composer.
i. Either Marcus Antonius or Julius Caesar will speak to Cleopatra.

*j. I did not bury Paul.

k. Some men are not tennis players.

*l. All philosophers drink wine.

13. Give a C-translation of the following English arguments. Provide a translation scheme for each argument you translate. In your translation, reveal as much content as possible.

a. (1) Either Gaby or Hans is coming.
∴ (2) Gaby is coming.

*b. (1) Harvey is annoyed if Jack is.
(2) Jack is not annoyed.
∴ (3) Harvey is not annoyed.

c. (1) No turtles are alligators.
(2) Some turtles are in captivity, and some are not.
∴ (3) No turtles are in captivity.

*d. (1) If all piano players are European, then no piano players are Chinese.
(2) All piano players are European.
∴ (3) No piano players are Chinese.

e. (1) The window is green or broken.
∴ (2) The window is broken.

*f. (1) If I am a dolphin, then I am a cetacean.
(2) I am a dolphin.
∴ (3) I am a cetacean.

g. (1) Harry will come only if John does.
(2) Harry or Peter will come.
(3) John will not come.
∴ (4) Peter will come.

*h. (1) If Harvey is not old enough to vote, then he is under 21.
(2) Harvey can drink legally if he is not under 21.
∴ (3) Harvey can drink legally if he is not old enough to vote.

i. (1) If Harvey is not old enough to vote, then he is under 21.
(2) Harvey can drink legally if and only if he is not under 21.
∴ (3) Harvey can drink legally only if he is old enough to vote.

*14. Explain why $(P \rightarrow Q)$ does not have the form $(A \rightarrow A)$. Then explain why $(A \rightarrow B)$ is *a* form of $(P \rightarrow P)$ but not *the* form. Finally, explain why $(A \rightarrow A)$ is *the* form of $(P \rightarrow P)$.

4.2 TRUTH CONDITIONS

In the previous section, we listed the symbols of the language and defined various syntactical notions. Our concern here is with semantic notions, chiefly, the truth conditions of the sentences.

Truth- and Non-Truth-Functional Connectives

A dominant connective is truth-functional in a sentence if and only if the truth value of the sentence is determined solely by (i) the meaning of the connective and (ii) the truth values of the immediate components of the sentence, whatever those truth values might be. For example, consider the following sentence:

(1) It is not the case that Monica Seles was born in Serbia.

The unary connective 'it is not the case that' dominates the sentence, and 'Monica Seles was born in Serbia' is the immediate component. From the meaning of 'it is not the case that', one can determine the truth value of (1) given the truth value of its immediate component, regardless of what that value might be. The matter is simple: (1) is false if its immediate component is true, but true if its immediate component is false. Therefore, the occurrence of 'it is not the case that' in (1) is truth-functional.

Another example of a truth-functional connective is 'and' as it appears in the following sentence:

(2) Monica Seles was born in Serbia and is a tennis player.

The connective 'and' dominates, and the immediate components are 'Monica Seles was born in Serbia' and 'Monica Seles is a tennis player'. Because of the meaning of 'and', (2) is true if both its immediate components are true, but false if either one or both are false. Therefore, 'and' in this sentence is truth-functional.

Now consider the next sentence:

(3) All fans of Monica Seles know that Monica was born in Serbia.

The phrase 'All fans of Monica Seles know that' is a unary connective grammatically similar to 'it is not the case that'. Notice how applying 'All fans of Monica Seles know that' to 'Monica Seles was born in Serbia' results in (3). But is 'All fans of Monica Seles know that' a truth-functional connective? Given the meaning of 'All fans of Monica Seles know that' and the fact that 'Monica Seles was born in Serbia' is true, you cannot determine the truth value of (3). After all, Seles could have been born in Serbia with or without all of her fans knowing that she had been. To determine the truth value of (3), you need to know what all of Monica Seles's fans know. Knowing the truth value of the immediate component and understanding what the sentence connective means are simply not enough. So, 'all Monica Seles fans know that' is non-truth-functional.

On at least some occasions, 'because' functions as a sentence connective. It does in the following sentence:

(4) Monica Seles was stabbed in the back because she was born in Serbia.

But knowing the meaning of 'because' and knowing that Monica Seles was stabbed in the back and that she was born in Serbia is not a sufficient basis on which to conclude that (4) is either true or false. One must also know whether there is a causal relationship between the stabbing and the fact that she was born in Serbia.

As the examples above illustrate, English has both truth-functional and non-truth-functional connectives. In contrast, all of the C-connectives (~, &, v, →) are truth-functional. As a consequence, no C-connective or combination of those connectives can fully translate non-truth-functional connectives of English, such as 'all fans of Monica Seles know that' and 'because'.

Valuation Rules and Truth Tables

The following <u>valuation rules</u> state the truth conditions for the four basic sentence types.

I. A negation ~A is true if and only if its immediate component A is false.

II. A conjunction (A & B) is true if and only if both its left conjunct A and its right conjunct B are true.

III. A disjunction (A v B) is true if and only if either its left disjunct A or its right disjunct B is true.

IV. A conditional ($A \rightarrow B$) is true if and only if either its antecedent A is false or its consequent B is true.

A standard way of codifying these rules is with <u>truth tables</u>. Using these tables, you can determine in a mechanical fashion the truth value of any sentence given the truth values of its immediate components. Moreover, since the immediate components of a sentence are either sentence letters, negations, conjunctions, disjunctions, or conditionals, you can use the tables to determine the truth value of any sentence given the truth values of its atomic components, that is, its sentence letters. In short, to determine in a mechanical fashion the truth value of a sentence, all that one needs are the truth values of the sentence letters it contains and the tables that follow.

Truth Table for Negations

The following table presents the truth conditions of sentences of the form ~*A*.

A	~*A*
T	F
F	T

In the column below *A* are the two values that the immediate component of a negation might have: T (the value of *being true*) and F (the value of *being false*). Below the tilde are the corresponding values for the negation, that is, the value when the immediate component is true and the value when the immediate component is false. Corresponding values are always written on the same row. For example, in the first row, T is the value of the immediate component and F is the value of the negation.

If you know the value of the immediate component, you can fix the value of the negation by consulting the row in which the value of the immediate component is listed below *A*. On that row, the truth value of the negation is listed below the tilde. For example, to ascertain the truth value of ~(*P* & *Q*) given that (*P* & *Q*) is false, consult the second row. On that row, ~(*P* & *Q*) is true.

Truth Table for Conjunctions

The table below records the truth conditions for sentences of the form (*A* & *B*).

A	*B*	(*A* & *B*)
T	T	T
T	F	F
F	T	F
F	F	F

In the first two columns, you will find row by row the four combinations of truth values that the right and left conjuncts of a conjunction might have: TT (both are true), TF (left is true and right is false), FT (left is false and right is true), FF (both are false). Below the ampersand are the values of the conjunction that correspond to each of those four possible combinations.

Thus, to ascertain the truth value of a conjunction when its left and right conjuncts are both true, consult the first row (the TT row). If its left conjunct is true and the right conjunct is false, consult the second row (the TF row). Consult the third row (the FT row) if the left conjunct is false and the right conjunct is true. And if the left and the right conjuncts are both false, consult the fourth row (the FF row). On the row consulted, the truth value listed below the ampersand is the truth value of the conjunction. For example, to find the truth value of $((P \vee Q) \& \sim(P \& Q))$, given that $(P \& Q)$ is true and $\sim(P \& Q)$ is false, consult the second row. On that row, $((P \vee Q) \& \sim(P \& Q))$ is false.

Truth Table for Disjunctions

The truth table for sentences of the form $(A \vee B)$ is next.

A	B	$(A \vee B)$
T	T	T
T	F	T
F	T	T
F	F	F

The four truth-value combinations that the right and left disjuncts of a disjunction might have are the same as those for the right and left conjuncts of a conjunction. Below the *vel* are the corresponding values for the disjunction.

So, to determine the truth value of a disjunction given the truth values of its left and right disjuncts, consult the row on which those values of the disjuncts are listed. On the row consulted, the truth value in the column below the *vel* is the truth value of the disjunction. For example, to determine the truth value of $(\sim P \vee \sim Q)$ given that $\sim P$ and $\sim Q$ are both false, consult the fourth row where the right disjunct and left disjunct are both listed as false. On that row, $(\sim P \vee \sim Q)$ is false.

Truth Table for Conditionals

The table for sentences of the form $(A \rightarrow B)$ comes next.

A	B	$(A \rightarrow B)$
T	T	T
T	F	F
F	T	T
F	F	T

Notice that the four truth-value combinations that the antecedent and consequent of a conditional might have are the same as those appearing in the tables for the other binary connectives. Below the arrow and written on the same row as the values of the antecedent and consequent is the value of the conditional.

In the same row-by-row fashion as the other tables, this table will tell you the truth value of a conditional (no matter how complex) given the truth values of its antecedent and consequent. For example, to determine the truth value of $((P \lor Q) \to \sim R)$ given that the antecedent $(P \lor Q)$ is false and the consequent $\sim R$ is true, consult the third row, where the antecedent is false and the consequent is true. On this row, $((P \lor Q) \to \sim R)$ is true.

EXERCISES FOR SECTION 4.2

*1. The phrase 'it is required by law' as it occurs in 'It is required by law that no one drives over 35 miles an hour in Tanzania' is a unary sentence connective. Is it a truth-functional connective? Explain your answer.

2. Is the connective 'after' in 'John phoned me after he had breakfast' truth-functional? Explain your answer.

*3. Is 'neither . . . nor' in 'Neither John will come nor Mary will come' a truth-functional connective? Justify your answer.

4. Construct a truth table for 'neither A nor B'.

*5. Determine the truth value of each of the following given that $(P \to Q)$ is true and $(Q \to P)$ is false.

    a. $((P \to Q) \& (Q \to P)$
    b. $((Q \to P) \& (P \to Q))$
    c. $((P \to Q) \lor (Q \to P)$
    d. $((Q \to P) \lor (P \to Q))$
    e. $((P \to Q) \to (Q \to P)$
    f. $((Q \to P) \to (P \to Q))$
    g. $\sim(P \to Q)$
    h. $\sim(Q \to P)$

*6. Determine the truth value of sentences a–h in exercise 5 given that $(P \to Q)$ and $(Q \to P)$ are both true.

4.3 COMPLEX TRUTH TABLES

From the four basic tables given in the previous section, one can construct truth tables for forms with more than one connective. We call such forms <u>complex forms</u> to contrast them with the four <u>basic forms</u>, namely, $\sim A$, $(A \ \& \ B)$, $(A \ v \ B)$, and $(A \rightarrow B)$.

Truth Table Construction

The general procedure for constructing a truth table for a complex form is the following:

I. Write the form in question.

II. Draw a horizontal line below the form and extending to the left.

III. On the same horizontal line as the form but to the left of it, list in alphabetical order the distinct placeholders in the form. Ordering the placeholders alphabetically will help insure that all are listed.

IV. Post values below each placeholder in the alphabetical listing. When there is one and only one placeholder, the values are as in the table for negations: T and then F. When there are two placeholders, the listing is as in the table for conjunctions: T and F alternating twice below the second placeholder, and two Ts and then two Fs appearing below the first placeholder. In general, to complete the columns below the alphabetic listing of placeholders, follow this procedure: Below the last placeholder, that is, the nth placeholder in alphabetical order (where $n \geq 1$), alternate T and F until the column contains 2^n entries; below the next to the last placeholder, alternate two Ts and two Fs until the column contains 2^n entries; and so on, each time doubling the number of Ts and Fs alternated until there are no more placeholders. For example, if there are three placeholders (A, B, and C) so that $n = 3$, you would construct the table like this: Below the third placeholder, alternate T and F until the column contains 2^3 (that is, 8) entries; below the second, alternate two Ts and two Fs until the column contains 8 entries; and below the first, alternate four Ts and four Fs until the column contains 8 entries. The proper construction is illustrated at the top of page 104.

A	B	C
T	T	T
T	T	F
T	F	T
T	F	F
F	T	T
F	T	F
F	F	T
F	F	F

V. In the complex form for which you are constructing the table, identify the basic forms (that is, those with only one connective and sentence letters as immediate components). Complete a column for each of these forms. Having calculated these, you can then post columns for the forms that have basic forms as their immediate components, and so on. Do not stop until you complete the column below the connective that dominates the complex form for which the table is being constructed.

Now study the incomplete table for $((A \rightarrow B) \& (B \rightarrow A))$ below.

A	B	$((A \rightarrow B) \& (B \rightarrow A))$
T	T	
T	F	
F	T	
F	F	

Review the directions above in I–IV to see how each part was constructed.

To complete the table, follow the directions in V. Begin by completing the column for $(A \rightarrow B)$ and then complete the one for $(B \rightarrow A)$. Both can be done by consulting the table for the arrow to determine the value of the conditional given the values of its antecedent and consequent on each row. Once you have the values of its immediate components, you can complete the column for $((A \rightarrow B) \& (B \rightarrow A))$ by consulting the table for the ampersand. On the first row, the value below $(A \rightarrow B)$ is T and the value below $(B \rightarrow A)$ is also T; therefore, the value below their conjunction is T. On the second row, the value below $(A \rightarrow B)$ is F and the value below $(B \rightarrow A)$ is T; therefore, the value below their conjunction is F. On the third row, the value below $(A \rightarrow B)$ is T and the value below $(B \rightarrow A)$ is F; therefore, the value below their conjunction is F. On the fourth row, the value below $(A \rightarrow B)$ is T and the value below $(B \rightarrow A)$ is also T; therefore, the value below their conjunction is T.

The table is completed below. This extended format can be adapted for any complex form.

A B	$(A \rightarrow B)$	$(B \rightarrow A)$	$((A \rightarrow B)\ \&\ (B \rightarrow A))$
T T	T	T	T
T F	F	T	F
F T	T	F	F
F F	T	T	T

Notice that the column of values for each form is written directly below the connective that dominates that form.

A more compact table is the following:

A B	$((A$	$\rightarrow B)$	$\&$	$(B$	$\rightarrow A))$
T T		T	T		T
T F		F	F		T
F T		T	F		F
F F		T	T		T

Note that on the second row F is listed below $(A \rightarrow B)$, but T is listed below $(B \rightarrow A)$; and on the third row the reverse is true. [Can you explain this?]

The instructions contained above in clauses I-V on pages 103-104 convert easily into instructions for the construction of a table for a sentence. Just replace 'form' with 'sentence', 'placeholder' with 'sentence letter', '*A*' with '*P*', and '*B*' with '*Q*'. The table for a sentence is the same as that for the form of the sentence. If the sentence letters of a sentence have the values posted for them in a row of the table, then the sentence has the value posted for it in that same row.

The truth table for $(P \rightarrow \sim Q)$ is below.

P Q	$(P \rightarrow \sim Q)$
T T	F
T F	T
F T	T
F F	T

The listing of values on the first row indicates that if its atomic components are both true, then $(P \to \sim Q)$ is false. The other listings should be read analogously.

Alternative Denials and Joint Denials

Besides negations, conjunctions, disjunctions, and conditionals, English contains other types of sentences of a truth-functional nature that are used often enough to have given names. Among these are alternative denials and joint denials.

Alternative Denials

An <u>alternative denial</u> is typically expressed in English through a negation of a conjunction or a disjunction of two negations. The following are examples:

(1) Pierce and Frege are not both logicians.

(2) Either Pierce or Frege is not a logician.

The two sentences that (1) and (2) alternatively deny are 'Pierce is a logician' and 'Frege is a logician'. With 'Pierce is a logician' assigned to 'P' and 'Frege is a logician' assigned to 'Q', (1) and (2) translate in C, respectively, as follows:

(1') $\sim(P \& Q)$

(2') $(\sim P \vee \sim Q)$

(1') is the negation of a conjunction and (2') the disjunction of two negations. A joint truth table for those sentences is below.

P	Q	$\sim(P \& Q)$	$(\sim P \vee \sim Q)$
T	T	F	F
T	F	T	T
F	T	T	T
F	F	T	T

According to this table, both (1') and (2') are true if at least one of the sentences they alternatively deny is false (see rows 2, 3, and 4). They are false if both are true (see row 1).

Joint Denials

A joint denial is often expressed in English using the phrase 'neither . . . nor . . .'. A joint denial can also be expressed through a conjunction of two negations. The following are examples of joint denials.

(3) Neither Pierce nor Frege is a logician.

(4) Pierce is not a logician and Frege is not a logician.

The two sentences that (3) and (4) jointly deny are 'Pierce is a logician' and 'Frege is a logician'. With the scheme above, (3) and (4) translate in C, respectively, as

(3′) ~(P v Q)

and

(4′) (~P & ~Q)

Note that (3′) is the negation of a disjunction and that (4′) is the conjunction of two negations.

Joint denials are typically translated with sentences having the form of either (3′) or (4′). A joint truth table for these sentence is as follows.

P	Q	~(P v Q)	(~P & ~Q)
T	T	F	F
T	F	F	F
F	T	F	F
F	F	T	T

According to this table, (3′) and (4′) are true if the two sentences jointly denied are false (see row 4), but are false if either one or both of the sentences jointly denied are true (see rows 1, 2, and 3).

Biconditionals and Exclusive Disjunctions

Biconditionals and exclusive disjunctions are related in the same way as conjunctions and alternative denials, and disjunctions and joint denials. In other words, a biconditional and an exclusive disjunction of the same two sentences invariably have opposite truth values.

Biconditionals

Biconditionals are expressed in English in a variety of ways. The following are some examples of ways one could express the biconditional of 'Pierce is a logician' and 'Frege is a logician'.

(5) If Frege is a logician, then Pierce is; and if Pierce is a logician, then Frege is.

(6) Pierce is a logician if Frege is; and Pierce is a logician only if Frege is.

(7) Pierce is a logician if and only if Frege is.

(8) Either Pierce and Frege are both logicians or Pierce and Frege are both not logicians.

With 'if and only if' as the sentence connective, (7) is an obvious contraction or abbreviation of (6). Other phrases usually interchangeable with 'if and only if' in forming English biconditionals are 'just in case', 'just if', and 'is a necessary and sufficient condition that'. The English biconditionals above translate in C, respectively, as follows:

(5') $((P \to Q) \& (Q \to P))$

(6') $((P \to Q) \& (Q \to P))$

(7') $((P \to Q) \& (Q \to P))$

(8') $((P \& Q) \lor (\sim P \& \sim Q))$

In translating biconditionals, sentences of the form of (5')–(7') and (8') are commonly used. A joint truth table for those sentences is below.

P Q	$((P \to Q) \& (Q \to P))$	$((P \& Q) \lor (\sim P \& \sim Q))$
T T	T	T
T F	F	F
F T	F	F
F F	T	T

This table shows clearly the truth conditions of a biconditional of two sentences. The <u>biconditional</u> is true if both sentences have the same truth value (see the first and fourth rows) but false if they have different ones (see the second and third rows). Thus (5) through (8) above are true if 'Pierce is a logician' and 'Frege is a logician' have the same truth values but false if their truth values differ. Details in the construction of the table are left to the reader as an exercise.

Exclusive Disjunctions

In Latin, 'aut' is the sentence connective for exclusive disjunction, and 'vel' is the sentence connective for disjunction. But, unlike Latin, English and most other natural languages have no sentence connective for exclusive disjunction. The following are examples of English sentences that express the exclusive disjunction of 'Pierce is a logician' and 'Frege is a logician'.

(9) Either Frege or Pierce is a logician but not both.

(10) Either Pierce is a logician but not Frege, or Frege is logician but not Pierce.

You can translate (9) and (10) as follows using the same translation scheme as before.

(9′) $((P \lor Q) \mathbin{\&} {\sim}(P \mathbin{\&} Q))$

(10′) $((P \mathbin{\&} {\sim}Q) \lor (Q \mathbin{\&} {\sim}P))$

Sentences exemplifying the form of (9′) or (10′) typically translate exclusive disjunctions. A joint truth table for those sentences is below.

P Q	$((P \lor Q) \mathbin{\&} {\sim}(P \mathbin{\&} Q))$	$((P \mathbin{\&} {\sim}Q) \lor (Q \mathbin{\&} {\sim}P))$
T T	F	F
T F	T	T
F T	T	T
F F	F	F

This table indicates that the <u>exclusive disjunction</u> of two sentences is true if they have different truth values (see the second and third rows), but false if they have the same ones (see the first and fourth rows). Thus (9) and (10) are true if 'Pierce is a logician' and 'Frege is a logician' have different truth values, but false if their truth values are the same.

Defined Connectives

Logicians often abbreviate complex C-sentences by employing <u>defined connectives</u>. These are sentence connectives that do not belong to the language proper but are introduced as convenient devices to abbreviate C-sentences without adding to the <u>official connectives</u> of the language. <u>Sheffer's stroke</u> (|) is the sentence connective used for alternative denials; <u>dagger</u> (↓), for joint denials; <u>triple bar</u> (≡), for biconditionals; and *aut* (⊻), for exclusive disjunction.

The following are definitions of Sheffer's stroke, dagger, triple bar, and *aut*.

$(A \mid B) =$df $(\sim\!A$ v $\sim\!B)$

$(A \downarrow B) =$df $(\sim\!A$ & $\sim\!B)$

$(A \equiv B) =$df $((A \rightarrow B)$ & $(B \rightarrow A))$

$(A \veebar B) =$df $((A$ v $B)$ & $\sim\!(A$ & $B))$

In these expressions, the placeholders stand for any sentences, no matter how complex; so the result of replacing placeholders with sentences throughout (the same placeholder with the same sentence) also qualifies as a definition. For example, in virtue of the definition of Sheffer's stroke above,

$\sim\!Q$ v $\sim\!(P$ & $R)$

can be abbreviated with

$Q \mid (P$ & $R)$

Notice that in these sentences the outermost parentheses are omitted. There is no harm in this as no ambiguity results.

In the definitions of Sheffer's stroke, dagger, triple bar, and *aut*, one combination of symbols is introduced simply as an abbreviation for another. These are syntactical definitions as they make no reference to truth values or truth conditions. Because Sheffer's stroke, dagger, triple bar, and *aut* are defined sentence connectives and do not belong to the official set of symbols, their meaning is derived from the meaning of the combination of symbols that they abbreviate.

The joint truth table below is based on the truth tables for tilde, ampersand, *vel*, and arrow and the syntactical definitions of Sheffer's stroke, dagger, triple bar, and *aut*.

A B	$(A \mid B)$	$(A \downarrow B)$	$(A \equiv B)$	$(A \veebar B)$
T T	F	F	T	F
T F	T	F	F	T
F T	T	F	F	T
F F	T	T	T	F

To understand how the table was constructed, one need only recognize that the column in the table for $(A \mid B)$ is the same as that for $(\sim\!A$ v $\sim\!B)$; that for $(A \downarrow B)$, the same as that for $(\sim\!A$ & $\sim\!B)$; that for $(A \equiv B)$, the same as that for $((A \rightarrow B)$ & $(B \rightarrow A))$; and that for $(A \veebar B)$, the same as that for $((A$ v $B)$ & $\sim\!(A$ & $B))$.

EXERCISES FOR SECTION 4.3

*1. Determine the truth value of the sentences below given that *P* is true, *Q* is false, and *R* is false. Exercise a is completed as an example.

a. (~*P* v *Q*)

P *Q*	(~*P* v *Q*)
T F	F

b. (*P* → *Q*)
c. ~(*P* & ~*Q*)
d. (~*Q* → ~*P*)
e. (*P* v *Q*)
f. (~*P* → *Q*)
g. (~*Q* → *P*)
h. (~*P* v ~*Q*)
i. (*P* → ~*Q*)
j. (*Q* → ~*P*)
k. ~(*P* & *Q*)

l. ~(*P* v *Q*)
m. (~*P* & ~*Q*)
n. ((*P* & *Q*) v (~*P* & ~*Q*))
o. ((*P* → *Q*) & (*Q* → *P*))
p. ((*P* v *Q*) & ~(*P* & *Q*))
q. ((*P* & ~*Q*) v (*Q* & ~*P*))
r. ((*P* v *Q*) → *R*)
s. ((*P* → *R*) & (*Q* → *R*))
t. (((*P* → *Q*) & (*Q* → *R*)) → (*P* → *R*))

2. Determine the truth values of sentences a–t in exercise 1 given that *P*, *Q*, and *R* are all false.

*3. Determine the truth value of sentences a–t in exercise 1 given that *P* is false, *Q* is true, and *R* is true.

4. Determine the truth value of sentences a–t in exercise 1 given that *P*, *Q*, and *R* are all true.

5. Complete a truth table for each form a–j at the top of page 112. Follow the example given for ((*A* v *B*) & ~(*A* & *B*)). In other words, before completing a truth table for the form in question, complete truth tables for its immediate components, the immediate components of its immediate components, and so on.

A *B*	(*A* & *B*)	~(*A* & *B*)	(*A* v *B*)	((*A* v *B*) & ~(*A* & *B*))
T T	T	F	T	F
T F	F	T	T	T
F T	F	T	T	T
F F	F	T	F	F

*a. $(\sim A \lor B)$ f. $(A \,\&\, (B \,\&\, \sim C))$

b. $((A \,\&\, B) \lor (\sim A \,\&\, \sim B))$ *g. $(A \to (B \to A))$

*c. $((A \,\&\, \sim B) \lor (B \,\&\, \sim A))$ h. $(\sim B \to \sim A)$

d. $(A \to \sim B)$ *i. $((A \lor B) \to C)$

*e. $(\sim B \to A)$ j. $(A \to (B \to C))$

6. Match each sentence a–h with a form (i)–(viii) that it exemplifies. If there is none, answer "none."

(i) $(\sim A \lor \sim B)$ (v) $((A \to B) \,\&\, (B \to A))$

(ii) $\sim(A \,\&\, B)$ (vi) $((A \,\&\, B) \lor (\sim A \,\&\, \sim B))$

(iii) $(\sim A \,\&\, \sim B)$ (vii) $((A \lor B) \,\&\, \sim(A \,\&\, B))$

(iv) $\sim(A \lor B)$ (viii) $((A \lor \sim B) \lor (B \,\&\, \sim A))$

*a. $(\sim(P \,\&\, Q) \,\&\, \sim R)$

b. $((P \,\&\, \sim(Q \,\&\, S)) \lor ((Q \,\&\, S) \,\&\, \sim P))$

*c. $(\sim Q \lor \sim R)$

d. $\sim(Q \lor \sim R)$

*e. $((\sim P \to \sim Q) \,\&\, (\sim Q \to \sim P))$

f. $(((P \,\&\, R) \,\&\, (Q \,\&\, R)) \lor (\sim(P \,\&\, R) \,\&\, \sim(Q \,\&\, R)))$

*g. $\sim(\sim Q \,\&\, \sim P)$

h. $((Q \lor P) \,\&\, \sim(Q \,\&\, P))$

7. Give examples in English of alternative denials, joint denials, biconditionals, and exclusive disjunctions. Use the sentences 'Sue gets an A' and 'Sue goes to the party' or others of your choice. Be sure to identify the type of sentence each of your examples illustrates.

*8. Translate into English sentences a–h in exercise 6 using a translation scheme of your choice.

9. Rewrite the following with only official connectives. To eliminate defined connective, apply the syntactical definitions of the stroke, dagger, triple bar, and *aut*.

a. $(Q \mid P)$ c. $(Q \equiv P)$

*b. $(Q \downarrow \sim R)$ *d. $\sim(Q \veebar P)$

4.4 TRUTH TABLES AND SEMANTIC PROPERTIES

C-sentences differ from those of natural languages in certain important respects. A sentence letter has meaning only relative to a translation scheme or an assignment of a truth value. The role of sentence connectives in the construction of sentences is defined; moreover, the meaning of each connective is specified and constant. As a consequence, the syntax of a C-sentence is an unfailing guide to its content so that, for example, what looks like a C-conditional syntactically is a C-conditional semantically. Because of this match between syntax and semantics, we can define semantic properties for the language C in terms of the truth tables that you have just learned to construct.

Valid and Contradictory Sentences

Generally speaking, a sentence is valid in virtue of the content displayed in its form if and only if there is no possibility for a sentence of that form to be false. When a C-sentence is valid in virtue of the content displayed in its form, we call the sentence C-valid. A truth table for a sentence represents the content that is displayed in the form of the sentence. Thus, when Ts and only Ts appear under the dominant connective in the truth table of a sentence, no sentence of that form has the possibility of being false. So, we can define C-validity for a sentence in term of its truth table as follows.

> A sentence is C-valid if and only if the sentence is true upon every row of its truth table.

Given this definition, one can decide whether a sentence is C-valid simply by constructing a truth table and then looking at the column below its dominant connective. The sentence is C-valid just in case the column contains Ts and only Ts.

A sentence is contradictory in virtue of the content displayed in its form if and only if no sentence of that form can be true. When a C-sentence is contradictory in virtue of its form, we say that it is C-contradictory. Because a truth table for a sentence records all possible truth values for sentences of that form, we can define C-contradiction as we did C-validity, that is, in terms of a characteristic truth table.

> A sentence is C-contradictory if and only if the sentence is false upon every row of its truth table.

With this definition, one can decide whether a sentence is C-contradictory by constructing a truth table for it. The sentence is C-contradictory just in case the column below the dominant connective of the sentence contains Fs and only Fs.

A form is C-valid if and only if it is the form of a C-valid sentence and C-contradictory if and only if it is the form of a C-contradictory sentence. So, you can decide whether a form is either C-valid, C-contradictory, or neither in the same way as you make that decision for a sentence. The following is a truth table for two sentence forms.

A	B	$A \rightarrow (B \rightarrow A)$	$(A \& B) \& (\sim A \lor \sim B)$
T	T	T	F
T	F	T	F
F	T	T	F
F	F	T	F

The truth value column below the dominant connective of $(A \rightarrow (B \rightarrow A))$ contains all Ts. This tells you that any sentence of the form $(A \rightarrow (B \rightarrow A))$ is true regardless of the truth values of the sentences taking the place of A and B or, for short, that $(A \rightarrow (B \rightarrow A))$ is C-valid. The truth value column below the second form, namely, $((A \& B) \& (\sim A \lor \sim B))$ contains all Fs. This tells you that any sentence of that form is false regardless of the truth values of the sentences taking the place of A and B or, in other words, that $((A \& B) \& (\sim A \lor \sim B))$ is a C-contradictory form.

Only valid sentences exemplify C-valid forms. So once you become familiar with a number of C-valid forms, you will be able to detect a C-valid sentence simply by recognizing that it has a C-valid form. For example, knowing that the form $(A \lor \sim A)$ is C-valid, one can easily see that $(\sim Q \lor \sim \sim Q)$ is C-valid as well. If this puzzles you, just replace A with $\sim Q$ in $(A \lor \sim A)$ to obtain $(\sim Q \lor \sim \sim Q)$. Examples of various C-valid forms are given below.

$$A \rightarrow A$$
$$A \rightarrow (B \rightarrow A)$$
$$A \lor \sim A$$
$$(A \& B) \rightarrow A$$
$$\sim (A \& \sim A)$$
$$A \rightarrow (A \lor B)$$

[As an exercise, construct truth tables for some or all of these forms. If the column for the form contains an F, then your table is wrong.]

Just as only valid sentences exemplify C-valid forms, only contradictory sentences exemplify C-contradictory ones. Therefore, you can conclude that a sentence is C-contradictory once you recognize that it has a C-contradictory form. Two examples of C-contradictory forms are (A & ~A) and ~(A v ~A). [As an exercise, stop to construct truth tables for these forms. The column below each form should contain all and only Fs. If it does not, try again to construct the table correctly.]

There are forms which are neither C-valid nor C-contradictory. For example, consider the truth table below.

A	B	(A v B) → B
T	T	T
T	F	F
F	T	T
F	F	T

This table shows that ((A v B) → B) is neither C-valid nor C-contradictory. Notice that there are both Ts and Fs in the table. But, from the fact that a form is neither C-valid nor C-contradictory, it does not follow that every sentence exemplifying this form is neither C-valid nor C-contradictory. For example, the C-valid sentence ((P v P) → P) has the form ((A v B) → B) and so does the C-contradictory sentence (((Q v ~Q) v (P & ~P)) → (P & ~P)). [Take the time now to show that those sentences do both have that form.] Remember a sentence's having a form and a form's being the form of a sentence are different matters. Both of the sentences have the form ((A v B) → B), but ((A v B) → B) is not *the* form of either one.

Equivalent Sentences

A sentence is equivalent to another in virtue of the content displayed in their joint form if and only if no possibility exists that a pair of sentences of that form have different truth values. When a C-sentence is equivalent to another C-sentence in virtue of the content displayed in their joint form, we call the sentences C-equivalent. The following is a definition of C-equivalence in terms of a characteristic truth table.

> Sentences are C-equivalent if and only if, in a joint truth table for those sentences, there is no row upon which the sentences differ from one another in truth value.

Given this definition, whether sentences are C-equivalent can be decided by constructing a joint truth table for them and then making a row-by-row comparison of the truth values below the dominant connective of each. The pair is equivalent when the columns of truth values below the dominant connectives are the same; otherwise, the pair is not C-equivalent.

The procedure for determining whether forms are C-equivalent is the same as for sentences. The first truth table below shows that $(\sim A \vee B)$ and $\sim(A \ \& \sim B)$ are C-equivalent. Notice how the columns below these forms are identical.

A B	$\sim A \vee B$	$\sim(A \ \& \sim B)$
T T	T	T
T F	F	F
F T	T	T
F F	T	T

The next truth table shows that $(A \rightarrow B)$ and $(B \rightarrow A)$ are not C-equivalent.

A B	$A \rightarrow B$	$B \rightarrow A$
T T	T	T
T F	F	T
F T	T	F
F F	T	T

Note that the values below the dominant connectives of $(A \rightarrow B)$ and $(B \rightarrow A)$ differ in the second and third rows. By merging the two tables above, one can see that $(\sim A \vee B)$ and $\sim(A \ \& \sim B)$ are C-equivalent to $(A \rightarrow B)$ but not to $(B \rightarrow A)$.

Because only pairs of C-equivalent sentences exemplify pairs of C-equivalent forms, one can conclude that sentences are C-equivalent once one recognizes that they have C-equivalent forms. The following are lists of C-equivalent forms that will be helpful to you in detecting C-equivalent sentences.

$A, \ \sim\sim A, \ (A \ \& \ A), \ \text{and} \ (A \vee A)$

$(A \ \& \ B), \ (B \ \& \ A), \ \text{and} \ \sim(\sim A \vee \sim B)$

$(A \vee B), \ (B \vee A), \ (\sim A \rightarrow B), \ \text{and} \ \sim(\sim A \ \& \sim B)$

$(A \rightarrow B), \ (\sim A \vee B), \ (\sim B \rightarrow \sim A), \ \text{and} \ \sim(A \ \& \sim B)$

$((A \ \& \ B) \ \& \ C) \ \text{and} \ (A \ \& \ (B \ \& \ C))$

$((A \vee B) \vee C) \ \text{and} \ (A \vee (B \vee C))$

$\sim(A \ \& \ B) \ \text{and} \ (\sim A \vee \sim B)$

$\sim(A \vee B) \ \text{and} \ (\sim A \ \& \sim B)$

$((A \rightarrow B) \ \& \ (B \rightarrow A)) \ \text{and} \ ((A \ \& \ B) \vee (\sim A \ \& \sim B))$

For example, if you know that (*A* & *B*) is C-equivalent to (*B* & *A*), you should be able to recognize immediately that ((*P* v *R*) & ~*Q*) is C-equivalent to (~*Q* & (*P* v *R*)).

Validity of Arguments

An argument is valid in virtue of the content displayed in its form if and only if there is no possibility for an argument of that form to have true premises and a false conclusion. A C-argument that is valid in virtue of the content displayed in its form is called a <u>C-valid argument</u>. A joint truth table for the premises and conclusion of a C-argument contains all (and only) the truth value combinations that are possible for the premises and conclusion of arguments of that form. So, we can define C-validity as follows.

> An argument is C-valid if and only if, in a joint truth table for its premises and conclusion, every row upon which all the premises are true is one upon which the conclusion is true.

Given this definition, you can decide whether an argument is C-valid or not C-valid by constructing a joint truth table for the premises and conclusion and then checking each row to see whether there is one in which Ts appear below all premises and an F below the conclusion. If there is no such row, the argument is C-valid. If there is such a row, the argument is not C-valid. However, if a C-argument is not C-valid, it means only that it is not valid in virtue of its form. The argument could still be valid in virtue of what is hidden in its translation scheme.

To determine whether an argument form is C-valid, you follow the same procedure as for an argument. Construct a joint truth table for the premises and conclusion of the argument form, then scan each row of the table. For the form of an argument, if there is no row in which F is listed below the conclusion and T is listed below each and every one of the premises, the argument form is C-valid; if there is at least one such row, then the argument form is not C-valid.

The table at the top of page 118 shows that (*A* → *B*), ~*B* /∴ ~*A* is C-valid. Note that in this form, commas separate the premises from one another and '/' separates the last premise from '∴', which precedes the conclusion.

A B	$A \rightarrow B$	~B	~A
T T	T	F	F
T F	F	T	F
F T	T	F	T
F F	T	T	T

The truth values appearing below the premises and conclusion in the first row are TFF; in the second, FTF; in the third, TFT; and in the fourth TTT. On no row are they TTF. Therefore, the argument form is C-valid.

The next table shows that $(A \rightarrow B)$, B /∴ A is not C-valid.

A B	$A \rightarrow B$	B	A
T T	T	T	T
T F	F	F	T
F T	T	T	F
F F			

In the third row, the truth values of the premises and conclusion are TTF. This shows that it is possible for an argument of that form to have true premises and a false conclusion. Because the third row demonstrates that the argument form is not C-valid, there is no need to complete the fourth row. In fact, for the same reason, there was no need to do the first and second rows either.

Only C-valid arguments exemplify C-valid argument forms. Thus, recognizing that an argument exemplifies a C-valid form (as *the* form or just as *a* form), one can conclude that the argument is C-valid. Examples of C-valid forms are the following:

A, $(A \rightarrow B)$ /∴ B

A /∴ $(A \lor B)$

$(A \rightarrow B)$, ~B /∴ ~A

$(A \rightarrow B)$, $(C \rightarrow B)$ /∴ $((A \lor C) \rightarrow B)$

$(A \lor B)$, ~B /∴ A

$(A \rightarrow B)$, $(A \rightarrow C)$ /∴ $(A \rightarrow (B \& C))$

$(A \& B)$ /∴ A

$((A \& B) \rightarrow C)$ /∴ $(A \rightarrow (B \rightarrow C))$

A /∴ $(B \rightarrow A)$

$(A \rightarrow C)$, $(B \rightarrow C)$, $(A \lor B)$ /∴ C

$A, B /\therefore (A \& B)$

$(A \to B), (B \to C) /\therefore (A \to C)$

Any argument having one of these forms is a C-valid argument.

Examples of argument forms that are not C-valid are below.

$(A \to B), B /\therefore A$

$(A \lor B) \therefore A$

$(A \to B) /\therefore B$

$(A \to B), \sim A /\therefore \sim B$

$(A \to B) /\therefore A$

$(A \to B), (C \to B) /\therefore (A \to C)$

Because an argument has one of these forms just as *a* form, it does not follow that the argument is not C-valid. However, if the form is *the* form of the argument, then the argument is not C-valid.

Incompatibility of Sentences

Sentences are incompatible in virtue of the content displayed in their joint form if and only if no possibility exists that sentences of that form are all true. C-sentences that are incompatible in virtue of the content they display in their joint form are called C-incompatible sentences. A joint truth table for C-sentences lists all (and only) the truth value combinations that are possible for sentences of that joint form. So we can define C-incompatibility as follows:

> Sentences are C-incompatible if and only if, in a joint truth table for those sentences, there is no row upon which all the sentences are true.

To decide whether sentences are C-incompatible, construct a joint truth table for them and then scan each row of the table to see if in any row all the sentences have Ts. If there is no such row, the sentences are C-incompatible; if there is at least one such row, then the sentence are not C-incompatible or, in other words, are C-compatible.

To decide whether forms are C-incompatible, you follow the same procedure as for sentences. The table at the top of page 120 shows that the forms $\sim(A \lor B)$, B, and $\sim A$ are C-incompatible.

A B	~(A v B)	B	~A
T T	F	T	F
T F	F	F	F
F T	F	T	T
F F	T	F	T

Note that there is *no* row in which all three forms have T. However, since both ~(A v B) and ~A have T on the fourth row, the table tells us that ~(A v B) and ~A are not C-incompatible. For the same reason, the third row shows that B and ~A are not C-incompatible.

EXERCISES FOR SECTION 4.4

1. Determine which of the forms below are C-valid, which are C-contradictory, and which are neither. Use truth tables.

a. A → A

*b. (A → B) → A

c. (A → B) & (A & ~B)

*d. ~(A v ~A)

e. (A & B) & (~A v ~B)

*f. (A & B) ≡ (B & A)

g. (A → B) → (B → A)

*h. (A v B) → B

i. (A v B) & (~A & ~B)

*j. (A | B) ↓ A

2. Use truth tables to determine which forms below are C-equivalent. Is there a form among them to which none of the other forms is equivalent?

a. A & B

b. ~(A & ~B)

c. ~(A & B)

d. ~(~A & ~B)

e. ~A & ~B

f. A v B

g. ~(A v ~B)

h. ~(A v B)

i. ~(~A v ~B)

j. ~A v ~B

*3. Use the C-equivalent forms listed on page 116 to determine which of the sentences that follow are C-equivalent to one another. Equivalent sentences may appear in the same column. Is there any sentence among them to which none of the others is C-equivalent?

a. ~Q & ~Q

b. Q & (R v P)

c. ~P v (Q v S)

d. ~Q v ~Q

e. (R v P) & Q

f. P → (Q v S)

g. $(Q \& R) \& P$

h. $\sim Q$

i. $(\sim P \lor Q) \lor S$

j. $\sim (P \& \sim (Q \lor S))$

4. Which of the following arguments are C-valid? Use truth tables to justify your answer.

   a. $((P \& Q) \to R) / \therefore (P \to (Q \to R))$

   *b. $((P \& R) \to Q), Q / \therefore (P \& R)$

   c. $(P \lor Q) / \therefore Q$

   *d. $\sim (P \& Q), Q / \therefore P$

   e. $(\sim P \to Q) / \therefore \sim P$

   *f. $(P \lor Q), \sim P / \therefore Q$

5. Use the C-valid argument forms i–xii to determine that the arguments a–t below are C-valid. Specify which form you use for which argument.

   (i) $A, (A \to B) / \therefore B$

   (ii) $A / \therefore (A \lor B)$

   (iii) $(A \to B), \sim B / \therefore \sim A$

   (iv) $(A \to B), (C \to B) / \therefore ((A \lor C) \to B)$

   (v) $(A \lor B), \sim B / \therefore A$

   (vi) $(A \to B), (A \to C) / \therefore (A \to (B \& C))$

   (vii) $(A \& B) / \therefore A$

   (viii) $((A \& B) \to C) / \therefore (A \to (B \to C))$

   (ix) $A / \therefore (B \to A)$

   (x) $(A \to C), (B \to C), (A \lor B) / \therefore C$

   (xi) $A, B / \therefore (A \& B)$

   (xii) $(A \to B), (B \to C) / \therefore (A \to C)$

   *a. $Q, (Q \to \sim R) / \therefore \sim R$

   b. $Q / \therefore (Q \lor \sim R)$

   *c. $(Q \to \sim R), \sim\sim R / \therefore \sim Q$

   d. $(Q \to \sim R), (P \to \sim R) / \therefore ((Q \lor P) \to \sim R)$

   *e. $(Q \lor \sim R), \sim\sim R / \therefore Q$

   f. $(Q \to \sim R), (Q \to P) / \therefore (Q \to (\sim R \& P))$

   *g. $(Q \& \sim R) / \therefore Q$

   h. $((Q \& \sim R) \to P) / \therefore (Q \to (\sim R \to P))$

   *i. $Q / \therefore (\sim R \to Q)$

   j. $(Q \to P), (\sim R \to P), (Q \lor \sim R) / \therefore P$

   *k. $Q, \sim R / \therefore (Q \& \sim R)$

*1. $(Q \rightarrow \sim R), (\sim R \rightarrow P) / \therefore (Q \rightarrow P)$

m. $(P \rightarrow Q) / \therefore (R \rightarrow (P \rightarrow Q))$

*n. $(Q \& Q) / \therefore Q$

o. $((Q \& R) \vee P), \sim P / \therefore (Q \& R)$

*p. $(\sim Q \rightarrow R), (\sim P \rightarrow R), (\sim P \vee \sim Q) / \therefore R$

q. $(R \rightarrow (P \& Q)), ((P \& Q) \rightarrow \sim R) / \therefore (R \rightarrow \sim R)$

*r. $((P \vee Q) \rightarrow R), (R \rightarrow R) / \therefore (((P \vee Q) \vee R) \rightarrow R)$

s. $(P \rightarrow Q), (P \rightarrow \sim Q) / \therefore (P \rightarrow (Q \& \sim Q))$

*t. $(Q \rightarrow R), (\sim (P \vee R) \rightarrow R) / \therefore ((Q \vee \sim (P \vee R)) \rightarrow R)$

6. Use truth tables to decide which of the sets of sentence forms below are C-incompatible.

*a. $A, (B \rightarrow \sim A)$

b. $(\sim A \rightarrow \sim B), (\sim A \& B)$

*c. $\sim (A \vee \sim B), (A \rightarrow (\sim B \& C))$

d. $(A \vee B), \sim A, \sim B$

*e. $(A \equiv \sim B), \sim A, \sim B$

f. $(A \rightarrow B), (A \rightarrow \sim B)$

7. Give a yes or no answer to each of the following questions about the language C. As an optional exercise, explain your answer.

*a. If two sentences are C-equivalent, is the sentence that results from placing a triple bar between the two and enclosing the result in parentheses C-valid? Remember that the triple bar ($\equiv$) is the biconditional sign.

b. If two sentences are C-equivalent, is an argument with one as the premise and the other as conclusion C-valid?

*c. Could the premises and conclusion of a C-valid argument be C-incompatible?

d. If the premises and conclusion of an argument are C-incompatible, does it follow that the argument is not C-valid?

*e. Does it follow that a conditional is C-valid if its consequent is C-valid? What if its antecedent is?

f. Does it follow that a conditional is C-valid if its antecedent is C-contradictory? What if its consequent is?

*g. Two C-contradictory sentences are C-equivalent, but are they C-compatible?

h. Is an argument that has a C-valid sentence as its conclusion also C-valid?

*i. Is an argument that has a C-contradictory sentence as a premise C-valid?

5

LOGIC OF CONNECTIVES: APPLICATIONS TO ENGLISH

Because of the idiomatic character and hidden logical structure of natural languages, no efficient general procedure exists for detecting semantic properties, such as validity and the like. However, when natural language expressions are translated into an artificial language, standardized procedures can then be applied to the translation and thus, indirectly, to the natural language.

This chapter begins with general considerations about translating a natural language into an artificial language, then provides guidelines for translating from English. The final section deals with the detection of semantic properties through C-translations. The student need not master totally all of the details and refinements so long as the general issues illustrated are understood.

5.1 TRANSLATING WITH AN ARTIFICIAL LANGUAGE

In chapter 2, you displayed the content of English sentences and argument descriptions by employing English sentence forms, argument forms, and replacement schemes. In chapter 4, you began displaying logical content through C-translations. This practice is continued in this chapter. Because many of the issues you met in chapter 2 are important for translating English, be sure to review that chapter again before reading this one.

Translation Schemes

As explained previously, translation schemes are analogous to the replacement schemes of chapter 2. While replacement schemes provide temporary replacements for placeholders, translation schemes provide temporary meanings for sentence letters.

Under the same translation scheme, a sentence letter can never translate more than one English sentence. Thus, no scheme can ever list 'P' once followed by one sentence—for instance, 'July is rainy'—and then list 'P' again followed by a different sentence such as 'August is rainy'. Nevertheless, under the same translation scheme, two different sentence letters can have the same English translation. For example, you can translate 'If July is rainy, then both July and August will be rainy' with '$(P \rightarrow (R \& Q))$' if you assign 'July is rainy' to 'P' and 'August is rainy' to 'Q', and assign 'R' the same sentence you assign 'P', namely, 'July is rainy'. But you can also translate the same English sentence with '$(P \rightarrow (P \& Q))$' and drop 'R' from the scheme. Notice that the second translation reveals more of the content of the original English sentence by exposing not only the fact that it is a conditional with a conjunction as its consequent but also the fact that the left conjunct of its consequent is the same sentence as its antecedent. As a rule, assignment of different English sentences to different sentence letters delivers more content.

Equivalent Translations

In translating English with an artificial language, the usual objectives are (i) to achieve an equivalent translation and (ii) to reveal as much content as possible. A C-translation is equivalent to an English sentence when the C-translation implies the English sentence and the English sentence, in turn, implies the C-translation.

For some English sentences, a sentence letter is the most appropriate equivalent translation. For example, to translate equivalently 'July is rainy', your best choice is a sentence letter. Other English sentences for which a sentence letter is the most suitable equivalent translation are the following:

Some whales are quails.

Hitler lost World War II because he invaded Russia.

All of the citizens are in debt.

Notice that none of these sentences contains a truth-functional connective.

Now consider the following English sentences, which do contain truth-functional connectives:

(1) Marx or Hegel is a philosopher.

(2) Neither Marx nor Hegel is a philosopher.

(3) Either Marx or Hegel is a philosopher but not both.

To show that (1) is a disjunction, you can begin by rewriting it using the *vel* as follows:

Marx is a philosopher v Hegel is a philosopher.

Notice how the rewrite exposes the fact that (1) is a disjunction. You can complete the translation by (i) assigning 'Marx is a philosopher' to '*P*' and 'Hegel is a philosopher' to '*Q*' and then (ii) replacing in the rewrite each English sentence with the sentence letter it translates to get

(1′) $P \lor Q$

You can translate (2) in an analogous way by noticing that it is a negation and rewriting it with the tilde:

~(Either Marx or Hegel is a philosopher)

You can then rewrite the sentence negated as a disjunction:

~(Marx is a philosopher v Hegel is a philosopher)

Now replace the English sentences with the C-sentence letters each translates to get

(2′) $\sim(P \lor Q)$

As for (3), first rewrite it as a conjunction:

(Either Marx is a philosopher or Hegel is a philosopher) &
(not both)

To reveal further that (3) is not only a conjunction but also a conjunction the left conjunct of which is a disjunction, rephrase again as follows:

(Marx is a philosopher v Hegel is a philosopher) & (not both)

Using the prior translation scheme, you can now shorten what you have to

$(P \lor Q)$ & (Marx and Hegel are not both philosophers)

The following rewrite exhibits the fact that the right conjunct is a negation:

$(P \vee Q)$ & ~(Marx and Hegel are philosophers)

The next shows that the right conjunct is a negation of a conjunction.

$(P \vee Q)$ & ~(Marx is a philosopher & Hegel is a philosopher)

Replacing the remaining English sentences with the appropriate sentence letters, you can complete the translation of (3) as

(3') $(P \vee Q)$ & ~$(P$ & $Q)$

Once you are accustomed to translating, you will be able to go directly from an English sentence to its C-translation without having to mix the two languages in intermediate rewrites as was done for (1)–(3) above. But whenever the translation is difficult, go step by step until you gain the mastery that you need.

In the scheme used to translate (1)–(3), there are no logical words. This indicates that their C-translations display all of the logical content of the sentences they translate. Now consider the sentence

(4) Though the federal government is in debt, not all of the citizens are.

You can translate it as

(4') P & ~Q

with the translation scheme

P: The federal government is in debt.

Q: All of the citizens of the federal government are in debt.

In this scheme, the English sentences are different from one another and neither contains a truth-functional connective. Nevertheless, the translation is of an English sentence that has logical content. Therefore, although '$(P$ & ~$Q)$' displays some of the logical content of (4), it does not display all of its logical content.

Nonequivalent Translations

The usual rule of thumb for translating is to make equivalent translations and to display as much content as the artificial language allows. However, the suitability of a translation ultimately depends upon how you intend to use it. For example, if your objective is to establish that an English argument is valid and you can do that through a C-translation that displays less content than allowed, your translation is still suitable. Moreover, although equivalent translations are usually desirable, nonequivalent ones can occasionally do a better job. The nonequivalent translations considered below are ones that are either weaker or stronger than the English sentences they translate. The value of such translations will be explained further on.

Weaker Translations

Of any two sentences, the first is <u>weaker</u> than the second if and only if the first is implied by the second but does not imply it. Put another way, a sentence is weaker than another when the latter says as much and more than the former. An example of two English sentences the first of which is weaker than the second is: 'My socks are a shade of red' and 'My socks are maroon'. Note that 'My socks are maroon' implies 'My socks are a shade of red', but not vice versa. To see this clearly, ask yourself the following question: Can my socks be maroon and not be a shade of red? The correct answer is negative. Therefore, 'My socks are maroon' implies 'My socks are a shade of red'. Now ask yourself the next question: Can my socks be a shade of red and not be maroon? The correct answer is positive. Therefore, 'My socks are a shade of red' does not imply 'My socks are maroon'. Because 'My socks are a shade of red' is implied by but does not imply 'My socks are maroon', 'My socks are a shade of red' is weaker than 'My socks are maroon'.

An example of a C-translation that is weaker than the sentence it translates is the translation of 'Nia and Meta climbed Kilimanjaro together' as '(P & Q)', where 'P' translates 'Nia climbed Kilimanjaro' and 'Q' translates 'Meta climbed Kilimanjaro'. The translation is weaker than the English sentence for the following reasons: (i) the translation can be true and the English sentence false (for instance, if Nia and Meta climbed Kilimanjaro separately) but (ii) the English sentence cannot be true and its translation false.

Now consider the following sentence:

(5) Monica Seles was stabbed in the back because a fan of Steffi Graf wanted Steffi to win.

This sentence implies, but is not implied by,

(6) Monica Seles was stabbed in the back and a fan of Steffi Graf wanted Steffi to win.

Thus (6), a conjunction, is weaker than (5). By assigning 'Monica Seles was stabbed in the back' to 'P' and 'a fan of Steffi Graf wanted Steffi to win' to 'Q', you can translate both (5) and (6) with '(P & Q)', achieving a translation that is equivalent to (6), but weaker than (5).

Stronger Translations

Given any two sentences, the first is <u>stronger</u> than the second if and only if the second is weaker than the first. That is, a sentence is *stronger* than another if and only if the sentence implies the other but is not implied by it. So 'My socks are maroon' is stronger than 'My socks are a shade of red', and 'Monica Seles was stabbed in the back because a fan of Steffi Graf wanted Steffi to win' is stronger than 'Monica Seles was stabbed in the back and a fan of Steffi Graf wanted Steffi to win'. Notice that the stronger sentence says as much as and more than the weaker of the two.

Although (5) is stronger than (6),

> **(7)** It is not true that (Monica Seles was stabbed in the back and a fan of Steffi Graf wanted Steffi to win)

is stronger than

> **(8)** It is not true that (Monica Seles was stabbed in the back because a fan of Steffi Graf wanted Steffi to win).

If you are having trouble seeing why (7) is stronger than (8), note that the truth of (7) requires the truth of (8) but that the truth of (8) does not require the truth of (7). For example, (8) can be true and (7) false even if (i) Monica Seles was stabbed in the back and (ii) a fan of Steffi Graf wanted Steffi to win, as long as (iii) it was not *because* a fan of Steffi Graf wanted Steffi to win that Monica Seles was stabbed.

Notice that (7) is the negation of (6), while (8) is the negation of (5). Though (6) is weaker than (5), the negation of (6) is stronger than the negation of (5). This fact illustrates the following general rule: if one sentence is weaker than another, the negation of the former is stronger than the negation of the latter. This rule also applies to translations. So translating (7) and (8) under the same scheme as you translated (6), you get '~(P & Q)' for each. This translation is equivalent to (7), but stronger than (8).

EXERCISES FOR SECTION 5.1

1. Indicate whether the first sentence in each of the following pairs is stronger than, equivalent to, or weaker than the second, or whether none of these conditions hold.

   *a. Butterfield has a beaver coat.
       Butterfield has a pet beaver.
    b. The stove is hot.
       The stove is extremely hot.

*c. Harold is almost finished with the exam.
   Harold is not finished with the exam.

 d. Pico is famous because he wrote poetry.
   Pico is famous and Pico wrote poetry.

*e. I shall attend if you invite my best friend.
   I shall attend if and only if you invite my best friend.

 f. This is a square.
   This is a rectangle.

*g. Mr. Trump has a sea horse.
   Mr. Trump has a horse.

 h. Raoul will win and Mario will come in second.
   Mario and Raoul will each place.

 i. Not both came.
   Neither came.

*j. This is a square.
   This is a rectangle with four equal sides.

 k. John or Mary is coming.
   John is coming.

*l. John and Mary are coming.
   John is coming.

 m. John and Mary are coming together.
   John and Mary are coming.

*n. His hiccups stopped after he counted to ten.
   He counted to ten and then his hiccups stopped.

 o. It will rain on Monday or Tuesday.
   It will rain on either Monday or Tuesday but not on both Monday and Tuesday.

*p. John will not come without Mary.
   John will come only if Mary comes.

 q. John will come only if Mary does.
   John will not come unless Mary does.

*r. John will come if Mary does.
   John will come only if Mary does.

2. Use the translation scheme below to translate the English sentences that follow. Aim for translations that reveal as much content as possible.

   P: John will win.
   Q: Harry will win.
   R: Peter will win.
   S: John can concentrate.
   T: John is tired.

   *a. Either John, Harry, or Peter will win.
   b. John and Harry will win.
   *c. John will win but not Peter.

    d. John will win because he is not tired.

  *e. John will not win because he cannot concentrate.

    f. John or Peter will win but not both.

  *g. Neither Peter nor Harry will win.

    h. Not both Peter and Harry will win.

  *i. Either John will win and Peter will not or Peter will win and John will not.

    j. Either John and Peter both will win or both John and Peter will not win.

  *3. Explain why translating sentence 2d above as '$(P \,\&\, {\sim}T)$' reveals more content than translating it as '$(P \to {\sim}T)$'.

5.2 TRANSLATING ENGLISH

Translating from one language into another is difficult. You need a good understanding of both languages and you need to be able to fathom the speaker's or writer's intentions. In this section, our concern is primarily with specific problems related to the English idiom. Some were discussed previously in chapter 2.

Translating 'Not' and 'And'

As a rule you are safe in translating a sentence with an internal 'not' as a negation if the sentence is about a specific individual. For example, there is no question that 'Jan is not joining the Navy' is equivalent to '${\sim}P$', where 'P' translates 'Jan is joining the Navy'. However, you cannot translate every sentence with an internal 'not' in this way. For example, consider the two sentences below.

  (1) Some apples are not yellow.

  (2) It is not true that some apples are yellow.

Although (2) is equivalent to '${\sim}P$', when 'P' has the same meaning as 'Some apples are yellow', (1) is not. To see this, note that (1) is true while '${\sim}P$' is false.

    Examples of other sentences that contain 'not' or 'un-' but are not negations are the following:

  (3) Three of my friends do not have jobs on Wall Street.

  (4) All drinkers of alcohol are unhealthy.

(5) Several students will not receive a passing grade.

Extract 'not' from the first and third sentence and 'un' from the second and you get

(3′) Three of my friends do have jobs on Wall Street.

(4′) All drinkers of alcohol are healthy.

(5′) Several students will receive a passing grade.

Now ask yourself the following questions: Could (3) and (3′) both be true? Could (4) and (4′) both be false? Could (5) and (5′) both be true? When the answer to any of these questions is "yes," the first sentence is not a negation of the second. Remember one sentence is the negation of another *only if* it is not possible for them to have the same truth value, that is, to be either both true or both false.

In translating with the ampersand, watch for uses of 'and' in which 'and' means 'and then'. If 'and then' is meant, a translation with a C-sentence of the form (*A* & *B*) will be weaker than the English sentence it translates. Unlike 'and then', the ampersand does not indicate temporal order. Other English connectives used to form conjunctions as well as to express temporal order (or simultaneity) are 'while', 'since', and 'as'. If temporal order is expressed or implied and the original sentence is translated with the ampersand, the translation will be weaker than the original.

When functioning as connectives, a number of English words and phrases contrast the phrases they connect. Examples of these include: 'but', 'yet', 'although', 'besides', 'nevertheless', 'even though', 'whereas', 'despite the fact that', 'but even so', 'not only . . . but also'. You can translate sentences with these connectives as conjunctions. Your translations will usually be equivalent to the original English sentences, although some emphasis may be lost.

Translating 'If . . . Then' and 'Only If'

In our initial discussion of conditionals in chapter 2, we gave no indication of the variety of English conditionals or of how they differ from C-conditionals. The truth conditions for material conditionals were simply given. These truth conditions are the same as those for C-conditionals. Now, it is time to discuss English conditionals at greater length and provide some warnings for the translator.

Any student who carefully compares the truth conditions of a C-conditional with those of an indicative 'if . . . then' sentence notices some disparities. Unlike C-conditionals, the truth of English conditionals often depends not on just the truth values of their immediate components but on whether some causal relationship holds or on the motivations of individuals. For example, consider the sentence

(6) If you turn the key, then the door will open.

All would agree that (6) is false if you turn the key and the door does not open. But what if (i) the door opens either before, after, or at the same time you turn the key, or (ii) you do not turn the key and the door remains shut, or (iii) you do not turn the key and the door opens?

In each of the last three cases, the truth value of the sentence is indeterminate if a causal connection is claimed. Yet, if you translate (6) with a C-conditional and ask the same three questions, the answer in each case is that the C-conditional is true. So, in general, translating an indicative 'if . . . then' conditional with a C-sentence of the form $(A \rightarrow B)$ does not result in an equivalent translation. Instead of an equivalent translation, what results is a weaker one. To see this, note that whenever (6) is true, its translation as a C-conditional is also true, but the C-translation may be true without (6) being true.

The following table shows how the truth conditions of an indicative 'if . . . then' may differ from those of a C-conditional.

A	B	If A then B	$A \rightarrow B$
T	T	?	T
T	F	F	F
F	T	?	T
F	F	?	T

Notice that, on each row on which an indicative conditional is indeterminate, the corresponding C-conditional is true, and vice versa. So, a C-translation of an indicative conditional could be true even though the indicative conditional is false. But an indicative conditional cannot be true without its translation as a C-conditional also being true. Therefore, the C-translation will be weaker than the indicative conditional, if it is not equivalent. Only the meaning of 'if . . . then' as used in mathematics, and related subjects, and occasional uses in English correspond exactly to the meaning of '$\rightarrow$'.

In chapter 2, 'only if' sentences are classified as conditionals. And the sentence following 'only if' is labeled the *consequent*. To see how such sentences are translated, consider

(7) You will become president only if you graduate from Yale.

Like a C-conditional, this sentence is false if its antecedent is true and its consequent is false, that is, if you become president and do not graduate from Yale. But what if (i) you become president and graduate from Yale, (ii) you do not become president but do graduate from Yale, or (iii) you do not become president and do not graduate from Yale? The fact that you cannot determine the truth value of (7) in any of these three cases indicates that this use of 'only if' is non-truth-functional.

You can achieve an equivalent translation of (7) simply by using a sentence letter. But translating an 'only if' sentence with a C-conditional will expose more content than translating it with just a sentence letter. And, as stated previously, some determinations with respect to semantic properties can be made with translations that are weaker than the original sentences. So, you can continue to translate 'only if' sentences as C-conditionals even though the translation will be weaker, as a rule, than the original English sentence.

In most, if not all, contexts, 'unless' is interchangeable in English with 'if . . . not'. For example, the sentences below are equivalent:

> **(8)** The patient will die unless we operate.

> **(9)** The patient will die if we do not operate.

Consequently, letting 'P' translate 'the patient will die' and 'Q' translate 'we operate', you can translate both (8) and (9) with '$(\sim Q \rightarrow P)$', which is equivalent to '$(P \lor Q)$'. Translating (8) with '$(P \lor Q)$' is convenient, as the order of the sentence letters corresponds to the order of the English sentence. In either case, your C-translation will be weaker than the original.

Translating 'If and Only If'

An English sentence of the form 'A if and only if B' may be thought of as a contraction of a sentence of the form 'A if B and A only if B'. For example, viewed in this way,

> You will go if and only if I say so

is short for

> You will go if I say so, and you will go only if I say so.

Other phrases often used to express English biconditionals are 'is equivalent to', 'is a necessary and sufficient condition for', 'just in case', and 'just if'. Sometimes people utter sentences of the form 'A only if B' and leave as understood but unstated a second conditional of the form 'A if B'; in other words, they may, in effect, use a sentence of the form 'A only if B' as short for one of the form 'A if and only if B'. In translating, you should attempt to capture the intent of the speaker. But you should not assume more than is said unless you are confident that more is understood but unstated. For example, if you are told that you can purchase a permit to drive an automobile *only if* you pass an eye examination, do not understand 'only if' as 'if and only if'. Although it may be necessary for purchasing a permit, passing an eye examination is not likely to be sufficient. In working the exercises in this text, *never* read 'only if' as 'if and only if' unless it is obvious that 'if and only if' is meant. In that case, make it clear that you are translating what you consider to be understood but unstated.

In chapter 4, the triple bar ($\equiv$) was introduced as a defined connective as follows:

$$(A \equiv B) =\text{df} ((A \to B) \,\&\, (B \to A))$$

Just as translating 'if' sentences and 'only if' sentences with C-sentences of the form $(A \to B)$ results in translations that are often weaker than the originals, translating 'if and only if' sentences with C-sentences of the form $((A \to B) \,\&\, (B \to A))$ or the form $(A \equiv B)$ also results in translations that are often weaker than the originals.

Subjunctive Conditionals

Thus far we have discussed only indicative conditionals. Indicative conditionals make claims about what was, is, or will be the case if something else (or even the same thing) was, is, or will be the case. In contrast, <u>subjunctive conditionals</u> make claims about what would be the case if something else were the case.

The following are examples of subjunctive conditionals that belong to a special category called <u>counterfactuals</u>.

> If Robert Campeau had not bought Bloomingdale's, then Bloomingdale's would have continued to ride high.

> If Robert Campeau had not bought Bloomingdale's, then Bloomingdale's would not have continued to ride high.

One obvious difficulty in translating these sentences with C-conditionals is the fact that their immediate components cannot stand alone as independent sentences. Thus, for purposes of translation, you have to rewrite the immediate components with the verbs in the indicative, rather than subjunctive, mood.

You might attempt this for the first two sentences by rewriting them as follows:

> If Robert Campeau did not buy Bloomingdale's, then Bloomingdale's will continue to ride high.

> If Robert Campeau did not buy Bloomingdale's, then Bloomingdale's will not continue to ride high.

Under an appropriate translation scheme, you can then translate these sentences in C, respectively, as follows:

$$\sim P \rightarrow Q$$

$$\sim P \rightarrow \sim Q$$

Because Robert Campeau did buy Bloomingdale's, the antecedent of each of these conditionals is false. Thus both conditionals are true. Yet, the sentences they translate appear to have opposite truth values even though one may not know which has which.

    If translating leads from sentences with different truth values to sentences with the same truth value, then the translation is inappropriate. When translation as a C-conditional is not appropriate, assign a sentence letter to the sentence you wish to translate and leave it at that. Although the topic of translating English conditionals has by no means been exhausted, we shall stop here and let what has been presented serve as an introduction to a fascinating, though complex, topic.

EXERCISES FOR SECTION 5.2

1. Stating your translation scheme, give a C-translation for each of the following. Your translation scheme should show as much content as possible. Explain why each of your translations must be weaker than the original sentence.

  *a. Hans hit the ball and then ran for first base.
  b. I shall attend the picnic if you invite Jill.
  *c. Jack is jovial and charming unless his stepmother is present.
  d. After Mr. Baker met with the Israelis, he met with the Egyptians.
  *e. As Mr. Stevens paused from his task of repairing a scythe, a small bird alighted beside him.
  *f. Charles will become the king of England only if he remains married to Di.

2. Explain why the following pairs of sentences are not equivalent.

  a. (i) Three of my friends are not football fans.
    (ii) It is false that three of my friends are football fans.
  *b. (i) All teenagers are unemployed.
    (ii) Not all teenagers are employed.
  c. (i) Several students will not graduate.
    (ii) It is not the case that several students will graduate.

3. Using the translation scheme below, give a C-translation for each of the English sentences that follow. Your translation should display as much content as possible. Indicate which, if any, translations are weaker and which stronger than the originals.

   P: Tom and Barbara will marry.
   Q: Tom has a job.
   R: Barbara has a job.
   S: Mary has a job.

*a. Tom and Barbara will marry if Barbara has a job.
 b. Neither Tom nor Barbara has a job.
*c. Barbara does not have a job.
*d. Tom has a job only if Barbara does not.
 e. Both Tom and Mary have jobs.
 f. Barbara has a job although Tom does not.
*g. Barbara and Tom will marry only if Barbara and Tom are working.
 h. Either Barbara or Tom is out of work.
*i. Not both Barbara and Tom have jobs.
 j. They (Tom and Barbara) will marry unless Tom is out of work.
*k. Not only Tom is working but also Barbara.
 l. Barbara is working because Tom is not.
*m. Tom has a job unless Barbara does.
*n. It is not true that if Tom has a job, then Tom and Barbara will marry.
 o. Both Barbara and Tom have a job or neither do.
 p. One (Barbara or Tom) has a job.
*q. One (Barbara or Mary) has a job but not both.
*r. Tom has a job if and only if Barbara does not.

4. Use the translation scheme below to translate the English sentences that follow.

   P: John will win.
   Q: Harry will win.
   R: Peter will win.
   S: John can concentrate.
   T: John is tired.

*a. John will win unless he is tired.
 b. John will win only if Harry does not.
*c. Harry will win just in case Peter does.
 d. If either Peter or Harry wins, then John will not.
*e. Not more than one (John, Peter, or Harry) will win.
*f. Exactly one (John, Peter, or Harry) will win.
 g. John will win if and only if Peter and Harry do not.

*5. Construct a joint truth table for '*A* only if *B*' and '*A* unless *B*'. Use a question mark where a truth value cannot always be determined.

6. Below is a list of C-sentences and a list of English sentences. For each English sentence, select a C-sentence as its translation and provide an appropriate translation scheme. Aim for translations that are equivalent and show as much content as possible. Identify those translations that are stronger or weaker than the original English sentences.

(i) P

(ii) $P \rightarrow Q$

(iii) $\sim Q$

(iv) $P \& Q$

(v) $P \vee Q$

(vi) $\sim (P \& Q)$

(vii) $P \vee \sim Q$

(viii) $\sim (P \vee Q)$

(ix) $P \vee \sim P$

(x) $(P \rightarrow Q) \& (Q \rightarrow P)$

(xi) $\sim P \& Q$

(xii) $(P \vee Q) \& \sim (P \& Q)$

  a. You will not be elected unless you campaign.

*b. Either everyone is invited or no one is.

  c. Some things are right and some things are wrong.

*d. If you invite her, she will be pleased.

  e. We will attend if and only if we are invited.

*f. Neither the Alpha nor the Beta team will score.

  g. They will have dinner this evening at either the Union Oyster House or Durgin Park.

*h. It is not true that the boat sank because it was attacked by whales.

  i. Your party can visit the island fortress only if Ek agrees.

*j. Photography is not permitted during the procession or in the church.

  k. If you do not invite her, she will not be pleased.

*l. Either someone is invited or no one is.

  m. The Alpha team will win unless John fumbles.

*n. If life is too short, then no day is too long.

7. Write English sentences equivalent to the following sentences, using 'if . . . not' as the dominant connective instead of 'unless'.

*a. Jack is jovial and charming unless his stepmother is present.

  b. Tom and Barbara will marry unless Tom is out of work.

  c. Tom has a job unless Barbara does.

*d. You will not be elected unless you campaign.

  e. The Alpha team will win unless John fumbles.

8. Using 'unless' as your dominant connective, write English sentences equivalent to those that follow.

*a. Tom and Barbara will marry if Barbara has a job.

  b. Tom has a job only if Barbara does not.

*c. Barbara and Tom will marry only if Barbara and Tom are working.

  d. It is true that if Tom has a job, then Tom and Barbara will marry.

*e. John will win only if Harry does not.

  f. If either Peter or Harry wins, then John will not.

*g. If you invite her, she will be pleased.

   *h. If you do not invite her, she will not be pleased.
   i. If life is too short, then no day is too long.

 *9. Which of the following sentences are equivalent to one another? Are any stronger than the others?

   a. You will go only if I say so.
   b. You will go if I say so.
   c. You will not go unless I say so.
   d. If I do not say so, you will not go.
   e. If I say so, you will go.

5.3 DETECTING SEMANTIC PROPERTIES IN NATURAL LANGUAGES

There are no standardized procedures, such as truth tables, for detecting semantic properties in natural languages. Nevertheless, through C-translations, the methods available to C can be applied to natural languages. For example, if through C-methods you can establish that a C-argument is C-valid and the C-argument is a suitable translation of an English argument, you can conclude that the original argument is valid.

Detecting Valid and Contradictory Sentences

Without a translation scheme, you can understand from reading a C-sentence only what is displayed in its form. For example, '$(P \ \& \ Q)$' informs you (correctly or not) that P and Q are true. And '$(P \ v \ {\sim}P)$' tells you that P is true or false. The situation is different when a translation scheme is available. For example, with 'Puccini is an Italian operatic composer' translating 'P' and 'Kafka is an Austrian novelist' translating 'Q', the meaning of '$(P \ \& \ Q)$' is the same as that of the English sentence 'Puccini is an Italian operatic composer and Kafka is an Austrian novelist'; '$(P \ v \ {\sim}P)$' is equivalent to 'Puccini is or is not an Italian operatic composer'.

  An equivalent C-translation may display enough of the content of a sentence for you to establish by methods available to C that the sentence is valid. The translation of 'Puccini is or is not an Italian operatic composer' as '$(P \ v \ {\sim}P)$' is a case in point. The situation is analogous for contradictions. If you can detect by some method available to C that a C-translation is a contradiction and the translation is equivalent to the original sentence, you can conclude that the original sentence is also contradictory. For example, if '$(P \ \& \ {\sim}P)$' is an equivalent translation of a sentence, you can conclude that the sentence is contradictory as well.

However, if an equivalent C-translation is neither C-valid nor C-contradictory, it does not follow that the original sentence or the C-translation itself, for that matter, is neither valid nor contradictory. The reason is simple. Whether a C-translation is C-valid, C-contradictory, or neither depends upon and only upon the partial content displayed in its form and not on that contained in the translation scheme. There may be other logical as well as nonlogical content in the translation scheme in virtue of which the original sentence and its equivalent C-translation are, in fact, valid or contradictory. Therefore, when a C-translation is neither C-valid nor C-contradictory, do not conclude that the original sentence is neither valid nor contradictory unless you are convinced that there is nothing in the translation scheme in virtue of which the sentence is valid or contradictory.

For example, consider the valid sentence

> Either no anti-nuke protesters are environmentalists or some anti-nuke protesters are environmentalists.

You can translate its immediate components as

> *P*: No anti-nuke protesters are environmentalists

> *Q*: Some anti-nuke protesters are environmentalists

and then translate the original sentence as

> *P* v *Q*

The translation is obviously not C-valid. From that fact, however, you should not conclude that the original English sentence is not valid. To reflect the validity of the sentence in an artificial language, you need a richer language than C.

The situation is analogous for the contradictory sentence

> No anti-nuke protesters are environmentalists and some anti-nuke protesters are environmentalists.

An equivalent C-translation is '(*P* & *Q*)', but this translation does not reveal enough of the content of the sentence to expose its contradictoriness. Let these two examples be good warning: Validity and contradictoriness can exist as properties of C-translations even though those properties are not detectable through their structure.

Detecting Equivalent Sentences

Some C-translations exhibit enough content for their equivalence to be detected and, thus, the equivalence of the English sentences they translate. For example, consider the following sentences:

(1) July and August are idle months for wine growers.

(2) It is not true that either July or August is an active month for wine growers.

The first is a conjunction and the second is a negation of a disjunction. To show this, rewrite them, using C-connectives, as

> July is an idle month for wine growers & August is an idle month for wine growers

and

> ~(either July is an active month for wine growers or August is an active month for wine growers)

Given that 'July is an idle month for wine growers' is an idiomatic variant of 'July is not an active month for wine growers', the rewrite of (1) just given is equivalent to

> ~ (July is an active month for wine growers) & ~(August is an active month for wine growers)

Now, using the translation scheme

> *P*: July is an active month for wine growers

> *Q*: August is an active month for wine growers

you can translate (1) and (2), respectively, as follows:

(1′) ~*P* & ~*Q*

(2′) ~(*P* v *Q*)

You can then establish the equivalence of (1′) and (2′) through constructing a joint truth table. The table shows that regardless of how '*P*' and '*Q*' are translated, (1′) and (2′) will always have the same truth value; thus, they are equivalent. Because (1) and (1′), and (2) and (2′), as well as (1′) and (2′), are equivalent, it follows that (1) and (2) are also equivalent.

The general procedure for detecting equivalence is first to make a suitable C-translation of the pair. To be suitable the translation must be equivalent to the original English. The next step is to construct a truth table for the C-translation. If the table indicates equivalence, you can then conclude that the original English sentences are equivalent. If the table does not indicate equivalence, however, it does not mean that the original English sentences are not equivalent. Remember that methods available to C apply only to what appears in the syntactical structure of C-translations and the sentences may, nevertheless, be equivalent because of what is contained in the translation scheme. Only after convincing yourself that there is nothing in the translation scheme in virtue of which there is equivalence, should you then conclude that there is none.

Detecting Valid Arguments

Like the equivalence of English sentences, the validity of English arguments can be detected through C-translations. However, in translating, two conditions must be met. The first condition is that the translation of each premise be equivalent to or weaker than the original. The second is that the translation of the conclusion be equivalent to or stronger than the original conclusion. As stated previously, a sentence is stronger than another just in those cases in which it implies but is not implied by the other and weaker than another just in those cases in which the other is stronger than it.

These two conditions ensure that the original premises imply their C-translations and that the C-translation of the conclusion implies the original conclusion. In other words, they ensure that

> *Original Premises* imply *C-Premises*

and

> *C-Conclusion* implies *Original Conclusion.*

All that is then needed is to show that

> *C-Premises* imply *C-Conclusion*

or, in other words, that the C-translation is itself valid, in order to conclude that

> *Original Premises* imply *Original Conclusion.*

Thus, in short, to ascertain that an English argument is valid, give equivalent or weaker C-translations of the premises and an equivalent or stronger C-translation of the conclusion. Then establish that the C-translation is C-valid, that is, valid by some method available to C. This done, you can conclude that the original English argument is valid.

For example, consider the argument below:

> Jiang Qing married Mao Tse-tung because the marriage was arranged by their parents. Jiang Qing wanted to marry someone else. Therefore, Jiang Qing married Mao even though she wanted to marry someone else.

With the following scheme, you achieve a suitable translation.

> *P*: Jiang Qing married Mao.

> *Q*: The parents of Jiang Qing and the parents of Mao arranged the marriage of Jiang Qing to Mao.

> *R*: Jiang Qing wanted to marry someone other than Mao.

The translation is

$$(P \ \& \ Q), \ R \ /\therefore \ (P \ \& \ R)$$

The premises and the conclusion of the translation are equivalent to those of the English except that the translation of the first premise is weaker than the original. But weaker translations of the premises are admissible. That the translation above is C-valid can be easily shown by constructing a truth table.

If a translation is not C-valid, that does not mean that the original argument is not valid. For example, consider the simple English argument below:

> All apples are red. I have an apple in my hand. Therefore, I have a red apple in my hand.

This argument has the C-translation

$$P, \ Q \ /\therefore \ R$$

under the following scheme:

> P: All apples are red.
>
> Q: I have an apple in my hand.
>
> R: I have a red apple in my hand.

The English argument is obviously valid, but its validity cannot be detected through this translation. And no C-translation through which its validity could be detected is possible given the limitations of C. C is simply incapable of exposing all the elements important to the validity of that argument.

As previously stated, to detect validity through a C-translation, you must have a suitable C-translation. To be suitable, the C-translation of the conclusion must be equivalent to or stronger than the original. Without this requirement, our procedure for detecting valid arguments would count as valid some arguments that are, in fact, invalid. For example, the following argument is obviously invalid:

> If Harris is promoted, Johnson will resign. If Johnson is fired, Harris will be promoted. Therefore, if Johnson is fired, Johnson will resign.

Yet, if there were no requirement that the C-conclusion be equivalent or stronger than the original conclusion, the following C-valid argument would qualify as a suitable C-translation:

$$(P \rightarrow Q), \ (R \rightarrow P) \ /\therefore \ (R \rightarrow Q)$$

However, because the C-conclusion is weaker than the original conclusion, the translation is not suitable. So you cannot conclude from it that the original argument is valid.

Another example of an obviously invalid argument is the following:

The weather is hot. Therefore, the weather is hot if it is snowing.

A C-translation is

$$P / \therefore (Q \rightarrow P)$$

The translation is C-valid. However, the translation is not a suitable translation because the C-conclusion is weaker than the original conclusion. Therefore, it does not follow from the validity of the translation that the original argument is valid, which in fact it is not.

The requirement that the C-conclusion be equivalent to or stronger than the English conclusion blocks your concluding that the argument about Harris and Johnson and the one about the weather are valid. But this requirement presents difficulties for detecting the validity of arguments that have 'if', 'only if', 'if and only if', or 'unless' as the dominant connective of their conclusions. Some logicians make an exception for weaker translations of conclusions so long as the conclusion is compatible with the premises, the unstated premises, and sentences that are valid. Others make no exceptions. You must decide for yourself what to do. But caution is advised.

Detecting Incompatible Sentences

The procedure for detecting incompatibility among English sentences is to give them equivalent or weaker C-translations. If the translations are shown incompatible, then the original English sentences are also incompatible. But if the translations are not shown incompatible, it does not follow that the English sentence are compatible. The content of English sentences may be only partially revealed in their C-translations. The translation scheme contains the rest, and English sentences may be incompatible in virtue of what the scheme contains.

You may wonder why weaker translations, as well as equivalent ones, are suitable for testing for incompatibility. The reason is that only sentences that are incompatible with one another imply incompatible sentences. So, if the translations are incompatible and they are implied by the sentences they translate, those sentences are incompatible as well. And weaker translations, as well as equivalent ones, are implied by the sentences they translate.

Extended Applications

You can conclude that an English argument is valid if you can establish that a suitable C-translation is C-valid. For example, you can establish by a truth table that 'P, $(P \rightarrow Q)$ /∴ Q' is C-valid; therefore, we can conclude that any argument that it suitably translates is also valid. In contrast, given that a C-translation is not C-valid, it does not follow that any argument it suitably translates is not valid. For example, you can establish with a truth table that 'Q, $(P \rightarrow Q)$ /∴ P' is not C-valid. Nevertheless, there are some arguments that it suitably translates that are valid. An argument may be valid in virtue of content in its translation scheme. And content in its translation scheme is not displayed in the structure of the C-translation.

In detecting semantic properties through translation in an artificial language, the usefulness of the translation is directly related to the content displayed. Thus, to extend the application of an artificial language, you must incorporate as much relevant content as possible into your translation; in other words, you must minimize the relevant content hidden in the translation scheme and maximize that revealed in the structure of the translation. We did that in recognizing that 'idle' and 'not active' are idiomatic variants while translating the passages about the wine growers. Another way to increase content is to add relevant premises that are valid, such as 'All bachelors are unmarried males'. Still another is to include unstated premises essential to the validity of the argument. These are discussed below.

Incorporating Valid Premises

The following is an example of a valid argument that appeared previously in chapter 2.

John McEnroe is a professional tennis player.

Therefore, John McEnroe is a professional athlete.

A suitable C-translation that exposes as much content as possible is 'P /∴ Q'. The translation is not C-valid. To reveal validity through a C-translation, you need to supplement your C-translation by adding

$$P \rightarrow Q$$

as a valid premise. As you can see, this C-sentence translates the valid English sentence 'If John McEnroe is a professional tennis player, then he is a professional athlete'. With this addition, the C-translation is the C-valid argument 'P, $(P \rightarrow Q)$ /∴ Q'.

Another example is the following:

The object in my hand is a red apple.

Therefore, the object in my hand is a piece of fruit.

Translate this argument under the translation scheme

P: The object in my hand is red.

Q: The object in my hand is an apple.

R: The object in my hand is a piece of fruit.

You will get

$(P \ \& \ Q) \ / \therefore \ R$

This translation is not adequate to show that the English argument is valid. Add to the premises of the original argument the valid sentence

> If the object in my hand is an apple, then the object in my hand is a piece of fruit.

Translating again, you get the C-valid argument

$(P \ \& \ Q), \ (Q \rightarrow R) \ / \therefore \ R$

which a truth table will show to be C-valid.

Through incorporating a valid premise in the translation, the translation reveals more of the content of the English argument. This enables you to show that the English argument is valid. In a similar way, valid sentences may also be added to lists of sentences when testing for incompatibility.

Incorporating Unstated Premises

Often arguments that you encounter have unstated premises. Such arguments, called <u>enthymemes</u>, cannot properly be evaluated by means of C-translations unless those unstated premises are included. Therefore, another way of making C more useful is to allow translations to include unstated premises. Of course, in taking the liberty of supplying what you think are unstated premises, you must be careful about including only those sentences that the individual expressing the argument would consider understood but unstated. Through the addition of premises, you can eventually get a valid argument no matter what you start from.

For example, consider the following argument:

> Bill won't win the election unless Ross runs. George does not have a chance if Ross runs. Ross will run but lose. Therefore, Bill will win the election.

Set up the following translation scheme:

P: Bill will win the election.

Q: Ross will run for the office.

R: George has a chance to win the election.

S: Ross will win the election.

Under this scheme, the following is a suitable translation.

$$(\sim Q \rightarrow \sim P), (Q \rightarrow \sim R), (Q \ \& \ \sim S) \ /\therefore \ P$$

But the translation is not C-valid. Does this surprise you? If it does, the reason may be that you incorporated among your premises an unstated premise as well as a valid one. The unstated premise is 'Either Bill, Ross, or George will win'. The valid premise is 'If George does not have a chance to win, then he will not win'.

Now add to your translation scheme the following:

T: George will win the election.

Then translate the valid premise and the unstated premise, respectively, as

$$(\sim R \rightarrow \sim T)$$

and

$$((P \ v \ S) \ v \ T)$$

Adding both of these at the end of the premises of your initial translation, you get the following C-valid argument:

$$(\sim Q \rightarrow \sim P), (Q \rightarrow \sim R), (Q \ \& \ \sim S), (\sim R \rightarrow \sim P),$$
$$((P \ v \ S) \ v \ T) \ /\therefore \ P$$

Now consider the next example:

> If some part of Jack's Vitorinox knife is broken and the trademark is visible on the largest blade's shank, then Vitorinox will repair it for free. The trademark is not visible on the shank of the largest blade of Jack's Vitorinox knife. Therefore, Vitorinox will not repair the knife for free.

Should you add the following as an unstated premise?

> If the trademark is not visible on the shank of the largest blade of Jack's knife, then Vitorinox will not repair the knife for free.

The argument translates with the additional premise as follows:

$$((P \ \& \ Q) \rightarrow R), \sim Q, (\sim Q \rightarrow \sim R) \ /\therefore \ \sim R$$

As you can show with a truth table, this argument is C-valid. However, you may think that adding this premise is unjustified and that the argument is, in fact, invalid. In adding "unstated" premises, you are exercising your own judgment. If the addition of some obvious premise makes an argument valid, then add the premise. But unless the premise is fairly obvious, proceed with caution. If the arguer is present and the matter is of importance, ask.

EXERCISES FOR SECTION 5.3

1. Find equivalent C-translations for the following sentences. Show the translation scheme that you use. Then identify each translation that reveals through its form either validity or contradiction in the sentence it translates. If your translation does not reveal either validity or contradiction, consult the translation scheme before deciding whether the sentence is valid, contradictory, or neither.

   *a. Either Spain is a land of castles or cathedrals, or Spain is a land neither of castles nor of cathedrals.
   b. Mars and Venus are both inhabited, or Mars is inhabited but Venus is not, or Mars is not inhabited.
   *c. It is not true that Joe is either an astronaut or not an astronaut.

2. Showing the translation scheme that you use, give equivalent C-translations of the following pairs of sentences. Then identify each translation that reveals through its form the equivalence of the sentences translated. If your translation does not reveal that the sentences are equivalent, consult the translation scheme before deciding whether they are or are not.

   *a. (i) Neither Church nor Bierstadt is a painter.
      (ii) Church and Bierstadt are not both painters.
   b. (i) Church and Bierstadt are not both painters.
      (ii) Either Church or Bierstadt is a painter.
   *c. (i) Church and Bierstadt are painters.
      (ii) It is false that Church and Bierstadt are not both painters.
   d. (i) Neither Church nor Bierstadt is a painter.
      (ii) Church is not a painter and Bierstadt isn't one either.

3. With the intention of using the translations to detect valid arguments, translate the following. Identify the arguments that your translations show to be valid. For those translations that are not C-valid, consult the translation scheme before deciding whether the argument is valid or not.

   *a. The clay will not release water if either there is no water in the clay or the particles are too fine. The particles are too fine. Therefore, the clay will not release water.

   b. The clay will release water if there is water in the clay and the particles are not too fine. The particles are not too fine. Therefore, the clay will release water.

   *c. The child is blowing bubbles through a straw into a glass of milk. She will be spanked if she does not stop. She will continue. Therefore, she will be spanked and sent to her room.

d. The child is blowing bubbles through a straw into a glass of milk. She will be spanked if she does not stop. She will continue. Therefore, she will be spanked.

*e. The child is blowing bubbles through a straw into a glass of milk. She will be spanked only if she does not stop. She will continue. Therefore, she will be spanked.

*f. If you forget your opera glasses, I shall supply you with a long thin tube. If I supply you with a long thin tube, you will be able to look at the exotic landscape in small sections. Therefore, even if you forget your opera glasses, you will be able to look at the exotic landscape in small sections.

g. If you forget your opera glasses, I shall supply you with a long thin tube. If I supply you with a long thin tube, you will be able to look at the exotic landscape in small sections. Therefore, you will be able to look at the exotic landscape in small sections only if you forget your opera glasses.

h. If Alex either dances all night or works all night, he will be exhausted in the morning. Alex will not be exhausted in the morning. Therefore, he will not dance all night but will work until daybreak.

*i. If Alex either dances all night or works all night, he will be exhausted in the morning. Alex will not be exhausted in the morning. Therefore, he will not dance all night and he will not work until daybreak.

j. If Alex either dances all night or works all night, he will be exhausted in the morning. Alex will be exhausted in the morning. Therefore, he will either dance all night or work until daybreak.

*k. The president has a cocker spaniel. The first lady has a Siamese cat. If the president has a cocker spaniel and the first lady has a Siamese cat, then they both love animals. They belong to the Animal Rights Society only if they love animals. Therefore, they both love animals and belong to the Animal Rights Society.

l. The president and the first lady both love animals only if the president has a cocker spaniel and the first lady has a Siamese cat. The first lady does not have a Siamese cat. Therefore, either the president or the first lady does not love animals.

*m. If the United States has a trade deficit with Japan, the Japanese yen will increase in value relative to the U.S. dollar. If the U.S. dollar declines in value relative to the Japanese yen, the ability of the United States to sell goods in Japan will increase unless Japan has trade barriers unfavorable to the United States. Therefore, if the ability of the United States to sell goods in Japan does not increase, then either Japan has trade barriers unfavorable to the United States or the United States does not have a trade deficit with Japan.

n. If the United States has a trade deficit with Japan, the Japanese yen will increase in value relative to the U.S. dollar. The U.S. dollar will increase in value relative to the Japanese yen only if the ability of the United States to sell goods in Japan increases. If Japan has trade barriers unfavorable to the United States, the ability of the United States to sell goods in Japan will not increase. Therefore, if either Japan has unfavorable trade barriers or the United States has a trade deficit with Japan, the Japanese yen will increase in value relative to the U.S. dollar.

*o. The U.S. dollar will increase in value relative to the Japanese yen if the United States does not have a trade deficit with Japan. The United States will not have a trade deficit with Japan if Japan does not have trade barriers unfavorable to the United States. The ability of the United States to sell goods in Japan will not increase if the U.S. dollar increases in value relative to the Japanese yen. Therefore, if Japan does not have trade barriers unfavorable to the United States, the ability of the United States to sell goods in Japan will not increase.

p. The ability of the United States to sell goods to Europe will increase if the quality of U.S. goods increases or the price declines. There will be no increase in quality or decrease in the price of U.S. goods. Therefore, the ability of the United States to sell goods to Europe will not increase.

*q. If the quality of U.S. goods increases, then the ability of the United States to sell goods to Europe will increase. If the price of U.S. goods declines, then the ability of the United States to sell goods to Europe will increase. The price of U.S. goods will decline unless the quality increases. Therefore, the ability of the United States to sell goods to Europe will increase.

r. If Tom is sober, then he is interesting. If he is polite and interesting, then Suzy likes him. Therefore, if Tom is sober, Suzy likes him.

*s. If Tom is sober, then he is interesting and polite. If he is polite and interesting, then Suzy likes him. Therefore, if Tom is sober, Suzy likes him.

t. Tom is polite only if he is sober. Suzy likes him only if he is polite. Tom is not sober. Therefore, Suzy doesn't like him.

*u. Lee is old enough to vote if she is 21 or over. If she's under 21, she can't drink legally; and if she's over 21, she'll have to join the army. So, if she is old enough to vote, Lee either can't drink legally or will have to join the army.

v. Lee is old enough to vote if she is 21 or over. If she's under 21, she'll have to join the army. So if Lee is not old enough to vote, then she either can't drink legally or will have to join the army.

*w. If Bill heard Nancy, then he was eavesdropping. He was eavesdropping if he was in the pay of the FBI. So, if he wasn't in the pay of the FBI, he didn't hear Nancy.

x. If Bill heard Nancy, then he was eavesdropping. He was eavesdropping only if he was in the pay of the FBI. So, if he wasn't in the pay of the FBI, he didn't hear Nancy.

*y. If the number of hens stays about the same but people start buying more eggs, then omelettes will cost more. If omelettes cost more, then the chicken farmers will make a fortune. The number of hens will stay about the same and people will start buying more eggs. Therefore, chicken farmers will make a fortune.

z. If the number of hens stays about the same but people start buying more eggs, then omelettes will cost more. If omelettes cost more, then the chicken farmers will make a fortune. People will start buying more eggs. Therefore, chicken farmers will make a fortune.

4. With the intention of using the translations to detect incompatible lists of sentences, provide C-translations of each of the following. Identify the sentences that your translations show to be incompatible. For the others, consult the translation scheme before deciding whether they are incompatible or not.

*a. If the mayor follows tradition, he will visit his "lucky" subway stop. The mayor will not follow tradition, but he will visit his "lucky" subway stop.

b. We will prevail or I shall lose the mayoral contest. If I lose the mayoral contest, I shall get a better job. We will prevail and I shall not get a better job.

*c. Dinkins will win unless he does not have the support of the labor unions. Giuliani will win only if Dinkins loses. Dinkins will not win even though he has the support of the labor unions.

*d. Representatives of the Sons of the Revolution and the Yale Club were at the Hale ceremony, which Giuliani did not attend. If Giuliani does not get the votes from the Yale Club, he will not win the election. He will not get the votes from the Yale Club if he did not attend the Hale ceremony. Nevertheless, Giuliani will win the election.

5. With the intention of using the translations to detect valid arguments, provide C-translations of the following. You may add valid premises where appropriate as well as any premises that you regard as unstated. Then decide whether the arguments are valid and justify your answer.

*a. I shall eat either salmon or liver. I shall not eat fish. Therefore, I shall eat liver.

b. Pauline was born in the capital of France if she was not born in the capital of Spain. She was not born in Madrid. Therefore, she was born in Paris.

*c. I shall order either a tuna or lobster salad for lunch. If I order a tuna salad, I shall spend $4. If I order a lobster salad, I shall spend $10. I shall not spend more than $6 for lunch. Therefore, I shall order a tuna salad for lunch.

d. If you want to avoid being burglarized, you should have a security system installed or bury all of your valuables. Therefore, you should have a security system installed.

*e. Mr. Cartier will have an allergic reaction if he drinks at least two glasses of wine. Mr. Cartier will drink at least three glasses of wine. Therefore, Mr. Cartier will have an allergic reaction.

f. Jim Dorsey stays indoors and studies the interior of his house. He thinks of new ways to renovate and remodel if he studies the interior of his house. Therefore, Jim Dorsey will buy an issue of *Livable House.*

*g. Buddy will live in the mountains the rest of his life unless he is not indicted for the murder of the lost children. Buddy will be convicted for the murder of the lost children. Therefore, Buddy will live in the mountains the rest of his life.

h. It was the Fourth of July. Therefore, the mail was not delivered.

*i. If the government closes legitimate private companies or ignores problems with public companies, the clock is being turned back on economic reforms. The government is paying no attention to the problems of public companies. Therefore, the economy will decline.

j. The pro-democracy movement will succeed unless the people are repressed. If the people are repressed, they will fight back until they win. Therefore, the pro-democracy movement will succeed.

*k. The president has a cocker spaniel. The first lady has a Siamese cat. If the president has a dog and the first lady has a cat, then they both love animals. Therefore, they both love animals.

l. The clay will release water if there is water in the clay and the particles are not too fine to release water. The particles are too fine to release water. Therefore, the clay will not release water.

6

LOGIC OF QUANTIFIERS: SYNTAX AND SEMANTICS

In chapter 3, you were introduced to some of the fundamental notions upon which the contemporary analysis of quantifiers depends. In this chapter, you will be learning an artificial language for the logic of quantifiers. The syntax of the language is described first, followed by English translations of some of its sentences. Truth conditions are taken up next and then, detection of semantic properties through various types of translation.

6.1 SYNTAX

The new artificial language, to be known as the <u>language Q</u> or simply Q, is a richer and more complex language than C. Consequently, you will be able to exhibit content and detect semantic properties through Q-translations that you have not been able to using C.

For example, consider the following argument, which is obviously valid.

> Some apples I buy are Fuji apples. All Fuji apples are from Japan. Therefore, some apples I buy are from Japan.

The maximum content that one can reveal through a C-translation is

$$P, Q /\therefore R$$

The scheme for this translation is

P: Some apples I buy are Fuji apples.

Q: All Fuji apples are from Japan.

R: Some apples I buy are from Japan.

Because the C-translation is not C-valid, the validity of the English argument is not detectable from the translation.

In contrast, the same English argument translates in Q as follows:

$$(\exists x)(Fx \,\&\, Gx), (\forall x)(Gx \to Hx) /\therefore (\exists x)(Fx \,\&\, Hx)$$

*F*_: _ is an apple I buy

*G*_: _ is a Fuji apple

*H*_: _ is from Japan

To see how the Q-translation relates to the English argument, compare the Q-translation with the rephrasal of the English argument below in the style of chapter 3.

$(\exists x)(x$ is an apple I buy and x is a Fuji apple)

$(\forall x)($if x is a Fuji apple then x is from Japan)

$\therefore$ $(\exists x)(x$ is an apple I buy and x is from Japan)

The Q-translation displays more content than the C-translation. Moreover, the Q-translation is Q-valid, while the C-translation is not C-valid. Because the Q-translation is Q-valid, we can conclude that the original English argument is valid.

This section deals specifically with the syntax of language Q. Some of the terminology may be difficult to remember. But after reading the definitions carefully and working out a few exercises, you should grasp the new language well enough to understand and use it successfully. Try to reread the definitions periodically to avoid errors.

Symbols

The language Q contains all the logical symbols of C and three others of its own. These are the identity sign '=' and the quantifier symbols '$\forall$' and '$\exists$'. The quantifier symbols should be familiar to you as they are the same as those introduced informally in chapter 3; the identity sign is the same as that used in mathematics. Among the nonlogical symbols, Q includes predicate letters, singular terms, and term variables, as well as the same sentence letters as C.

Although Q is more complex than C, in comparison to English and many other artificial languages, the new language is still a relatively simple language and easily learned. Clauses I–V below list all the symbols in five syntactical categories: terms, predicate letters, sentence letters, logical symbols, and auxiliary signs. There are no symbols in addition to these.

I. Terms
  a. Singular terms: a, b, c, a_1, b_1, c_1, . . .
  b. Term variables: x, y, z, x_1, y_1, z_1, . . .

II. Predicate letters
  a. One-place predicate letters: $F\_$, $G\_$, $H\_$, $F_1\_$, $G_1\_$, $H_1\_$, . . .
  b. n-place predicate letters (where $n > 1$): $F^2\_\_$, $G^2\_\_$, $H^2\_\_$, . . . , $F^n\_\cdots\_$, $G^n\_\cdots\_$, $H^n\_\cdots\_$, ... If $n = 2$, the superscript is '2' and the predicate letter is two-place; if $n = 3$, the superscript is '3' and the predicate letter is three-place; and so on.

III. Sentence letters: P, Q, R, P_1, Q_1, R_1, . . .

IV. Logical symbols
  a. Connectives: $\sim$, &, v, $\rightarrow$
  b. Quantifier symbols: $\forall$, $\exists$
  c. The identity sign: =

V. Auxiliary signs
  a. Parentheses: (,)

Note that Q has in common with C the four connectives, the sentence letters, and the auxiliary signs, which are the right and left parentheses. Terms, predicate letters, quantifier symbols, and the identity sign do not appear in C. The role of these new symbols is explained below.

Singular Terms

The singular <u>terms</u> in clause I above are the letters 'a', 'b', 'c', 'a_1', 'b_1', 'c_1', . . . A <u>singular term</u> is used to designate an individual. As explained in chapter 3, individuals are physical objects (the Golden Gate Bridge, the World Trade Center), properties (being honest, playing tennis), relations (marriage, loyalty), sets (the null set, the jet set), events (the Ascension, the wedding of Andrew and Sarah), and other kinds of things. By the way, although problems do occur for richer languages, letting singular terms designate properties presents no problem for Q.

Which individual a singular term designates depends on how it is translated. The following is an example of a translation scheme listing several singular terms.

> a: Andrew
>
> b: Sarah
>
> c: playing tennis
>
> d: the man with the goatee

Under this scheme, 'a' designates the same individual as 'Andrew'; 'b', the same individual as 'Sarah'; and so on. Notice that 'd' appears in the scheme above although 'd' is not officially classified as a singular term in clause I(a). For variety, we use other lowercase letters from the beginning of the alphabet as "unofficial" singular terms. However, we never use the letters 'x', 'y', and 'z' in this way because they are <u>term variables</u>.

Predicate Letters

The <u>predicate letters</u>, listed in clause II on the preceding page, are <u>one-place</u> or <u>n-place</u> (where $n > 1$). They are used to translate English phrases as in the following translation scheme.

> $F\_$: _ is a student
>
> $G\_ \_$: _ likes _
>
> $H\_ \_ \_$: _ arranged for _ to meet _

None of the English phrases contains a logical word and none is the same or an idiomatic variant of any other in this scheme. This just happens to be the case in this example and is not required of all schemes.

Superscripts do not appear in '$G\_ \_$' or in '$H\_ \_ \_$' because the number of blanks is sufficient to indicate how many places the predicate letters have. This is done for easier reading with no loss of precision. For variety and convenience, other uppercase letters from the alphabet can be used as "unofficial" predicate letters.

Quasi-Sentences

We have listed the various symbols and explained the function of the singular terms and predicate letters. We now need to specify what counts as a <u>quasi-sentence</u>. To do that, we begin by defining two other notions on which the concept depends.

Atoms

An <u>atom</u> is an *n*-place predicate letter with *n* singular terms in its *n* blank places (where $n \geq 1$). Under the combined translation schemes on page 156, each atom below has the same meaning as the English sentence to its right.

> *Fb*: *Sarah* is a student.
>
> *Gac*: *Andrew* likes *playing tennis*.
>
> *Hdba*: *The man with the goatee* arranged for *Sarah* to meet *Andrew*.

English translations of the singular terms are in italic.

Quantifiers

A <u>quantifier</u> is formed by placing one of the quantifier symbols, $\forall$ or $\exists$, before a term variable and enclosing the result in parentheses. Examples of quantifiers are $(\exists x)$, $(\forall y)$, and $(\exists z)$. <u>Existential quantifiers</u> are those that contain the symbol $\exists$; <u>universal quantifiers</u> are those that contain the symbol $\forall$. A singular term never appears in a quantifier. Thus $(\exists a)$ and $(\forall b)$ are *not* quantifiers. We say that a quantifier is a <u>quantifier in the variable</u> that occurs in it. For example, $(\forall y)$ is a quantifier in the variable *y* and $(\exists z)$ is a quantifier in the variable *z*.

Quantifiers translate as read in chapter 3. For example, $(\exists z)$ translates as 'there is at least one individual *z* such that' or, for short, 'there is at least one *z* such that'. And $(\forall y)$ translates as 'every individual *y* is such that' or, for short, 'Every *y* is such that'. Be sure to reread section 3.2, which explains the function of quantifiers.

You may have noticed that expressions of Q appear without single quotation marks in the two preceding paragraphs. We shall omit such quotation marks in this section when no misunderstanding is likely.

Quasi-Sentences

We can now specify what counts as a quasi-sentence as follows:

> I. A sentence letter is a quasi-sentence.
>
> II. An atom (as defined above) is a quasi-sentence.
>
> III. The result of replacing a singular term in an atom with a term variable is a quasi-sentence. Examples are *Fx* and *Gxc*. Using the translation scheme above, the first translates in

English as '*x* is a student' and the second translates as '*x* likes playing tennis'.

IV. The result of placing a tilde before a quasi-sentence is a quasi-sentence. Examples are ~*Fx* and ~*Fa*. The first translates as '*x* is not a student' and the second as 'Andrew is a student'.

V. The result of placing one of the binary connectives (that is, the ampersand, *vel,* or arrow) between two quasi-sentences and enclosing the result in parentheses is a quasi-sentence. An example is (*Fx* → *Gxc*). This translates as 'If *x* is a student then *x* likes playing tennis'.

VI. The result of placing the identity sign between two singular terms or term variables and enclosing the result in parentheses is a quasi-sentence. Examples are (*x* = *b*) and (*a* = *b*). The first translates as '*x* is the same individual as Sarah' and the second translates as 'Andrew and Sarah are the same individual'.

VII. The result of placing a quantifier (either existential or universal) before a quasi-sentence is a quasi-sentence. Examples are (∃*x*)(*Fx* & *Gxc*) and (∀*x*)(*Fx* → *Gxc*). Their translations are discussed below.

VIII. Nothing is a quasi-sentence except in virtue of the preceding clauses.

Using the same translation scheme as above, you can translate

(∃*x*)(*Fx* & *Gxc*)

as

There is at least one individual *x* such that *x* is a student and *x* likes playing tennis

or, more idiomatically, as

Some students like playing tennis.

Similarly, you can translate

(∀*x*)(*Fx* → *Gxc*)

as

Every individual *x* is such that if *x* is a student then *x* likes playing tennis

or, more idiomatically, as

Every student likes playing tennis.

Sentences

The sentences of Q or Q-sentences are a subclass of the quasi-sentences. In other words, a sentence is a special type of quasi-sentence. To describe the subclass of quasi-sentences that count as sentences, we first need to define the notions upon which our description depends.

Dominant Operator

The logical operators in Q are the sentence connectives and the quantifiers. An occurrence of an operator is the dominant operator of the quasi-sentence in which it appears if and only if within that quasi-sentence, there is no shorter quasi-sentence in which the occurrence appears. The operator is then said to *dominate* that quasi-sentence. Notice the similarity between this definition and the definition in chapter 4 of a dominant connective (see p. 92). The difference is that dominant operators include quantifiers as well as connectives, and the shortest quasi-sentence rather than the shortest sentence is decisive.

Scope

An occurrence of an operator has as its scope the quasi-sentence for which it is the dominant operator. For example, the ampersand is the dominant operator of

$$(Fa \ \& \ Gac)$$

so the entire quasi-sentence is within the scope of the ampersand. However, in

$$(\exists x)(Fx \ \& \ Gxc)$$

the existential quantifier is the dominant operator. Therefore, the existential quantifier has the entire quasi-sentence within its scope; and the scope of the ampersand is only

$$(Fx \ \& \ Gxc)$$

Similarly, in

$$(\forall x)(Fx \rightarrow Gxc)$$

the scope of the arrow is the quasi-sentence to the right of the universal quantifier, in other words

$$(Fx \rightarrow Gxc)$$

But the scope of the universal quantifier includes not only the quasi-sentence to its right but also the quantifier itself. In other words, the scope of the quantifier includes the entire quasi-sentence.

Overlapping Quantifiers

When a quantifier occurs within the scope of another quantifier, the scopes of the quantifiers overlap and the quantifiers are said to be <u>overlapping quantifiers</u>. The quantifiers overlap in

$$(\exists x)(Fx \ \& \ (\exists y)Gxy)$$

The scope of the existential quantifier in x is $(\exists x)(Fx \ \& \ (\exists y)Gxy)$, while the scope of the existential quantifier in y is only $(\exists y)Gxy$. Because the scope of the one in y occurs within the scope of the one in x, the quantifiers are overlapping quantifiers.

Another example of overlapping quantifiers is

$$(\forall x)(Fx \ \rightarrow \ (\exists x)Gxx)$$

In this case, the scope of the existential quantifier is within the scope of the universal quantifier. As both quantifers contain an occurrence of the same variable, we say that they are <u>overlapping quantifiers in the same variable</u>.

Bound and Free Variables

An occurrence of a term variable is <u>bound</u> if it is within the scope of a quantifier in that variable. An occurrence of a term variable is <u>free</u> if it is not bound. For example, consider the sentences and quasi-sentences displayed above in the discussion of scope. In $(Fx \rightarrow Gxc)$, both occurrences of the variable are free as neither is within the scope of any quantifier whatsoever. On the other hand, in both $(\exists x)(Fx \ \& \ Gxc)$ and $(\forall x)(Fx \rightarrow Gxc)$, there are three occurrences of the variable x; the first is in the quantifier, the second is in Fx, and the third is in Gxc. Since all three occurrences are within the scope of a quantifier in x, all three are bound, including the one in the quantifier itself. Note that, although the occurrence of c is within the scope of the quantifier, the occurrence is of a singular term and is, therefore, neither bound nor free. [Are the occurrences of y in $(Fa \ \& \ (\exists y)Gay)$ bound or free? Are the occurrences of y in $(Fx \ \& \ (\exists y)Gxy)$ bound or free? What about the occurrences of x in $(Fx \ \& \ (\exists y)Gxy)$?]

Vacuous Quantifers

A quantifier is a <u>vacuous quantifier</u> when the quantifier is in a variable that occurs once and only once within the scope of the quantifier. For example, $(\exists x)Fa$ has a vacuous quantifier because $(\exists x)$ is a quantifier in x and x occurs once and only once within the quantifier's scope. The singular occurrence is in the quantifier itself.

Sentences

A sentence of Q is a quasi-sentence which contains (i) no overlapping quantifiers in the same variable, (ii) no free occurrence of a term variable, and (iii) no vacuous quantifier. With this definition, you can identify which of the quasi-sentences numbered (1)–(7) below are full-fledged sentences.

(1) $(Fx \ \& \ Gxc)$

(2) $(\exists y)(Fx \ \& \ Gxc)$

(3) $(\forall x)(Fx \rightarrow Gxc)$

(4) $(Fx \rightarrow Gxc)$

(5) $(\exists x)(Fx \ \& \ (\exists y)Gxy)$

(6) $(\forall x)(Fx \rightarrow (\exists x)Gxx)$

(7) $(\exists x)Fa$

Expression (1) is not a sentence because it has a free occurrence of a term variable. Expression (2) is not a sentence because it has a vacuous quantifier; it also has free variables. Expression (3) is a sentence. Expression (4) is not a sentence because it has free variables. Expression (5) is a sentence. Expression (6) is not a sentence because it has overlapping quantifiers in the same variable. Expression (7) is not a sentence because it has a vacuous quantifier.

Quantified Sentences and Their Instances

Of particular importance to logic is the relationship between quantified sentences and their instances. What a quantified sentence is and what counts as an instance, as well as how the two are related, are discussed below.

Quantified Sentences

Quantified sentences are either existentially or universally quantified. A sentence is an <u>existentially quantified sentence</u> (or an <u>existential sentence</u>, for short) if its dominant operator is an existential quantifier. A sentence is a <u>universally quantified sentence</u> (or a <u>universal sentence</u>, for short) if its dominant operator is a universal quantifier. For example,

$$(\exists x)(Fx \ \& \ Gxc)$$

is an existential sentence. But

$$(\forall x)(Fx \rightarrow Gxc)$$

is a universal one.

Instances

An <u>instance</u> of a quantified sentence is formed from the quantified sentence by dropping the dominant operator, which is either an existential or universal quantifier, and replacing the variable which becomes free with the same singular term throughout. The singular term that replaces the variable is called the <u>instantial term</u>.

For example, drop the dominant operator from

$$(\exists x)(Fx \ \& \ Gxc)$$

and you get

$$(Fx \ \& \ Gxc)$$

Now replace the variable x throughout with the singular term a (the instantial term) and you get

$$(Fa \ \& \ Gac)$$

which is an instance of $(\exists x)(Fx \ \& \ Gxc)$ with a as the instantial term.

Analogously, the result of dropping the dominant operator from

$$(\forall x)(Fx \rightarrow Gxc)$$

is

$$(Fx \rightarrow Gxc)$$

And the instance that results from replacing the variable x throughout with the singular term b (the instantial term) is

$$(Fb \rightarrow Gbc)$$

The procedure is the same in forming instances of sentences with overlapping quantifiers. For example, to form an instance of

$$(\exists x)(\forall y)Gxy$$

drop the dominant operator to get

$(\forall y)Gxy$

and then replace x with a singular term throughout. If you choose a, the result will be

$(\forall y)Gay$

As this instance is itself a universal sentence, it has instances of its own. To form its instances, you follow the same procedure as above. The instance with a as the instantial term is *Gaa*. That with b as the instantial term is *Gab*.

Translating Quantified Sentences and Their Instances

On the translation scheme used previously, the existential sentence

$(\exists x)(Fx \ \& \ Gxc)$

translates as

> There is at least one individual x such that x is a student and x likes playing tennis.

Or, more idiomatically, it also translates as either of the following:

> Some students like playing tennis.

> There are students who like to play tennis.

The instance

$(Fa \ \& \ Gac)$

translates as

> Andrew is a student and Andrew likes to play tennis

or, more idiomatically, as

> Andrew is a student who likes to play tennis.

Note that what the existential sentence says to be true of at least one thing, its instance says to be true of Andrew. In other words, while $(\exists x)(Fx \ \& \ Gxc)$ says that at least one thing has the attribute of *being a student who likes to play tennis*, $(Fa \ \& \ Gac)$ says that Andrew has that attribute.

Now, under the same translation scheme, the universal sentence

$(\forall x)(Fx \rightarrow Gxc)$

translates as

> Every individual x is such that if x is a student, then x likes playing tennis

or, more idiomatically, as

> Every student likes playing tennis.

The instance

> $(Fb \rightarrow Gbc)$

translates as

> If Sarah is a student, then Sarah likes playing tennis

or, more idiomatically, as

> Sarah likes to play tennis if she is a student.

Note that what $(\forall x)(Fx \rightarrow Gxc)$ says to be true of everything, $(Fb \rightarrow Gbc)$ says to be true of Sarah. In other words, while the universal sentence says that everything has the attribute of *liking to play tennis if a student*, its instance (with b as the instantial term) says that Sarah has that attribute.

The following is another universal sentence:

> $(\forall x)(Fx \ \& \ Gxc)$

Note that this differs from the universal sentence above only in having an ampersand where the other has an arrow. An instance of this sentence with b as the instantial term is

> $(Fb \ \& \ Gbc)$

Under the same translation scheme as above, $(\forall x)(Fx \ \& \ Gxc)$ translates as

> Every individual x is such that x is a student and x likes playing tennis

or, more idiomatically, as

> All are students who like to play tennis.

The instance $(Fb \ \& \ Gbc)$ translates as

> Sarah is a student who likes to play tennis.

Notice how $(\forall x)(Fx \rightarrow Gxc)$ and $(\forall x)(Fx \ \& \ Gxc)$ differ in meaning. The former says that everything has the attribute of *liking to play tennis if a student*, while the latter says that everything has the attribute of *being a student who likes to play tennis*. Notice also the difference between their respective instances, $(Fb \rightarrow Gbc)$ and $(Fb \ \& \ Gbc)$. The difference is due to the fact that one has an arrow where the other has an ampersand. These connectives are not interchangeable, so be very careful in your use of them.

An instance of a quantified sentence has one fewer quantifier than the sentence of which it is an instance. For this reason, in translating a quantified sentence into idiomatic English, you may find it helpful first to translate an instance. This is especially true if the quantified sentence contains overlapping quantifiers. For example, assume that the domain is the class of human beings and the translation scheme is the same as the one you have been using. You could then translate $(\exists x)(\forall y)Gxy$ in English as

> There is an individual x such that every individual y is such that x likes y.

This English translation may, however, seem no clearer to you than the sentence it translates.

What we suggest is that you form an instance of $(\exists x)(\forall y)Gxy$ such as $(\forall y)Gay$, which has a as its instantial term. You can then translate the instance as

> Every individual y is such that Andrew likes y

or, more idiomatically, as

> Andrew likes everyone.

Remembering that what $(\forall y)Gay$ says is true of Andrew, $(\exists x)(\forall y)Gxy$ says is true of at least one individual, you can now translate $(\exists x)(\forall y)Gxy$ as

> Someone likes everyone.

[Does $(\forall y)(\exists x)Gxy$ say the same thing as $(\exists x)(\forall y)Gxy$? To answer this question, begin by forming an instance of $(\forall y)(\exists x)Gxy$ with a. The instance will claim to be true of Andrew what $(\forall y)(\exists x)Gxy$ claims to be true of everyone. What does $(\exists x)Gxa$ claim to be true of Andrew? What does $(\forall y)(\exists x)Gxy$ claim to be true of everyone? Now answer the question at the beginning of this paragraph.]

Square of Opposition and Quantified Sentences

The first square of opposition you met was in chapter 2 (see p. 38). In chapter 3, that square was amplified with the addition of forms conforming more closely to contemporary logical analysis (see p. 71). The following square includes versions of those same forms in Q.

A-type
All F are G
$(\forall x)$(if Fx then Gx)
$(\forall x)(Fx \rightarrow Gx)$

E-type
No F are G
$(\forall x)$(if Fx then not Gx)
$(\forall x)(Fx \rightarrow {\sim}Gx)$

I-type
Some F are G
$(\exists x)(Fx$ and $Gx)$
$(\exists x)(Fx$ & $Gx)$

O-type
Some F are not G
$(\exists x)(Fx$ and not $Gx)$
$(\exists x)(Fx$ & ${\sim}Gx)$

As stated previously, this square of opposition differs from that of Aristotelian logic. In this square, A-types do not imply I-types, and E-types do not imply O-types. So, the following arguments are not Q-valid:

$$(\forall x)(Fx \rightarrow Gx) \; / \therefore \; (\exists x)(Fx \; \& \; Gx)$$

$$(\forall x)(Fx \rightarrow \sim Gx) \; / \therefore \; (\exists x)(Fx \; \& \; \sim Gx)$$

The square should help you in translating from English to Q. For example, if the English sentence is of the form 'All F are G', your translation should be of the form $(\forall x)(Fx \rightarrow Gx)$. To remember Q-versions in the square is not difficult. The E-type differs from the A-type, and the O-type from the I-type, only in having '$\sim Gx$' in the place of 'Gx'. Furthermore, the I-type differs from the A-type, and the O-type from the E-type, only in having '$\exists$' in the place of '$\forall$' and '&' in the place of '$\rightarrow$'.

The following are some examples of existential sentences:

(1) $(\exists x)(Fx \; \& \; Gx)$

(2) $(\exists x)(Fx \; \& \; \sim Gx)$

(3) $(\exists x)((Fx \; \& \; Gx) \; \& \; Hx)$

(4) $(\exists x)(\exists y)((Fx \; \& \; Hx) \; \& \; (Gy \; \& \; Hy))$

With the translation scheme

$F\_$: _ is an island dweller

$G\_$: _ is a sailor

$H\_$: _ eats fish

(1)–(4) translate in English, respectively, as follows:

(1′) Some island dwellers are sailors.

(2′) Some island dwellers are not sailors.

(3′) Some island dwellers who are sailors eat fish.

(4′) Some island dwellers and (some) sailors eat fish.

Note the difference in meaning between (3′) and (4′) and the difference in construction of (3) and (4). The following are also translations of (4):

(4″) $(\exists x)(Fx \; \& \; Hx) \; \& \; (\exists y)(Gy \; \& \; Hy)$

(4‴) $(\exists x)(Fx \; \& \; Hx) \; \& \; (\exists x)(Gx \; \& \; Hx)$

Both translations are equivalent to (4), but neither of the alternatives has overlapping quantifiers. Because they do not have overlapping quantifiers, they are easier to read than (4). Be sure to note the difference between (4″) and (4‴). As neither has overlapping quantifiers, the syntactical difference makes no difference in their meaning.

The following are examples of universal sentences:

(5) $(\forall x)(Fx \rightarrow Gx)$

(6) $(\forall x)(Fx \rightarrow {\sim}Gx)$

(7) $(\forall x)((Fx \mathbin{\&} Gx) \rightarrow Hx)$

(8) $(\forall x)((Fx \mathbin{v} Gx) \rightarrow Hx)$

On the translation scheme given above, these sentences translate in English, respectively, as follows:

(5′) All island dwellers are sailors.

(6′) No island dwellers are sailors.

(7′) All island dwellers who are sailors eat fish.

(8′) All island dwellers and (all) sailors eat fish.

Note the difference in meaning between the last two English sentences and the difference in the construction of their translations. [How else could (8′) be translated? To get an idea, look at how (4″) translates (4′).]

Metalanguage

When one talks about a language, one uses a metalanguage. We tried to keep our metalanguage as simple as possible in describing the syntax of Q. However, in later sections and especially in Part III of the text, a more sophisticated metalanguage is needed. This language will be described here. The reader can return to this description when needed.

Previously, in talking about the language of connectives, we used the capital letters 'A', 'B', and 'C' as placeholders for sentences. In contrast, when talking about the language of quantifiers, we use the same letters to talk in a general way about quasi-sentences, unless otherwise noted. To talk in a general way about singular terms, we use the singular terms themselves. For example, the following are all sentences of the form $(a = a)$:

$$(b = b), \ (c = c), \ldots.$$

In a similar way, we also use term variables to talk in a general way about term variables. So, an expression of the form $(x = y)$ is any expression that results from replacing x and y with term variables (possibly the same one). Examples of such expressions are $(x = y)$, $(z = z)$, $(y = z)$, and $(y = y)$. To talk in general about terms (both singular terms and term variables), we use 't_1', 't_2', 't_3', . . . Thus, an expression of the form $(t_1 = t_2)$ is one which results from replacing t_1 with a term and t_2 with a term. Examples are $(a = b)$, $(x = y)$, $(z = c)$. The quantifiers symbols '$\forall$' and '$\exists$' and parentheses serve as names of themselves.

A sentence of the form $(\forall x)A$ is any sentence which results from replacing the quasi-sentence A with a quasi-sentence and the term variable x with a term variable. A sentence of the form $(\exists x)A$ is any sentence which results from replacing the quasi-sentence A with a quasi-sentence and the term variable x with a term variable.

We use the notation

$$A(a/x)$$

to designate the expression which results from replacing every free occurrence of the term variable x in the quasi-sentence A with the singular term a. So $A(a/x)$ is

$$(Fa \rightarrow Ga)$$

when A is

$$(Fx \rightarrow Gx)$$

x is 'x', and a is 'a'. But $A(a/x)$ is

$$(Fb \rightarrow Gb)$$

when A is

$$(Fy \rightarrow Gy)$$

x is 'y', and a is 'b'. In sum,

$$(\forall x)(Fx \rightarrow Gx), \qquad (Fx \rightarrow Gx), \qquad (Fa \rightarrow Ga)$$

as well as

$$(\forall y)(Fy \rightarrow Gy), \qquad (Fy \rightarrow Gy), \qquad (Fb \rightarrow Gb)$$

are sequences of the form

$$(\forall x)A, \qquad A, \qquad A(a/x)$$

When $(\forall x)A$ is a sentence, every occurrence of x is bound in $(\forall x)A$ because every occurrence of x is in the scope of $(\forall x)$. However, because no sentence has overlapping quantifiers in the same variable, x is free in A. For example, every occurrence of 'y' is bound in

$$(\forall y)(Fy \rightarrow Gy)$$

but free in

$$(Fy \rightarrow Gy)$$

We use the more general notation $A(t_1/t_2)$ to designate the result of replacing every occurrence of t_2 in A, where t_2 is a singular term or *freely occurring* term variable, with an occurrence of a singular term or term variable t_1 that is not bound in the resulting expression. For example, consider the following pair of quasi-sentences:

$$(\exists y)(Fx \ \& \ Gx), \qquad (\exists y)(Fz \ \& \ Gz)$$

That pair has the form

$$A, \qquad A(t_1/t_2)$$

Notice how the second quasi-sentence results from replacing 'x' with 'z' throughout the first. In contrast, the next pair does *not* have that form:

$$(\exists y)(Fx \ \& \ Gx), \qquad (\exists y)(Fy \ \& \ Gy)$$

Replacing 'x' with 'y' in the first quasi-sentence results in 'y' becoming bound in the second. In no expression of the form $A(t_1/t_2)$ is t_1 a bound variable.

A special case of an expression of the form $A(t_1/t_2)$ is one of the form $A(a/x)$. For example, let $(\forall x)A$ be

$$(\forall x)(Fx \rightarrow {\sim}Gx)$$

Then A is

$$(Fx \rightarrow {\sim}Gx)$$

And each of the following are of the form $A(a/x)$:

$$(Fa \rightarrow {\sim}Ga)$$

$$(Fb \rightarrow {\sim}Gb)$$

$$(Fc \rightarrow {\sim}Gc)$$

and so on.

As previously defined, an instance of a quantified sentence results from dropping the quantifier that is the dominant operator and replacing every occurrence of the variable which becomes free with the same singular term throughout. Thus, given any pair of sentences of the form

$$(\forall x)A, \qquad A(a/x)$$

the second is an instance of the first with a as the instantial term. In like manner, given any pair of the form

$$(\exists x)A, \qquad A(a/x)$$

the second is an instance of the first with a as the instantial term.

Some instances of quantified sentences are known as <u>generating instances</u>. An instance of a quantified sentence is a generating instance when the instantial term does not appear in the quantified sentence. For example, 'Gaa' is not a generating instance of '$(\forall y)Gay$' because the instantial term 'a' appears in '$(\forall y)Gay$.' On the other hand, 'Gab' is a generating instance of '$(\forall y)Gay$' because the instantial term 'b' does not appear in '$(\forall y)Gay$.' In terms of the metalanguage, we can say that $A(a/x)$ is a generating instance of $(\exists x)A$ as well as of $(\forall x)A$ if a does not occur in A. For example, '$(c = b)$' is a generating instance of '$(\exists x)(c = x)$' as well of '$(\forall x)(c = x)$' because '*b*' does not occur in '$(c = x)$'. Observe how you can form a quantified sentence $(\forall x)A$ or $(\exists x)A$ from one of its generating instances $A(a/x)$ by replacing a in $A(a/x)$ with x and placing the quantifier $(\forall x)$ or $(\exists x)$ before the resulting expression. This works only for generating instances. [Is '*Gac*' a generating instance of '$(\forall y)Gay$'? If so, why? What are other generating instances of '$(\forall y)Gay$'?].

EXERCISES FOR SECTION 6.1

*1. Which of the following are sentences? Which are quasi-sentences but not sentences? Which are neither sentences nor quasi-sentences?

a. $((\exists x)Fx \ \& \ Gx)$

b. (Fa)

c. $(\exists y)(Gy \ v \ (\exists y)Fy)$

d. $(\exists z)(Fz \ \& \ Ga)$

e. $(\forall x)(F^2xx)$

f. $(\forall a)\sim Ga$

g. $((\forall x)Fx \rightarrow G^3ab)$

h. $(\exists z)F^2zz$

i. $((\forall x)Fx \ \& \ (\exists y)Gy)$

j. $(\exists x)(Gx \ \& \ (\exists y)F^2xy)$

k. $(\exists y)(\forall x)F^2xy$

l. $((\exists x)Fx \rightarrow (\forall y)Gy)$

m. $(\forall x)(\exists y)(Fy \rightarrow Gx)$

n. $(\exists x)(\exists y)F^2xy$

o. $(a = b)$

p. $(\exists x)(a = b)$

2. For each sentence in exercise 1, identify the dominant operator.

*3. Identify the scope of each quantifier that occurs in a sentence in exercise 1.

4. Identify the sentences in exercise 1 that have overlapping quantifiers.

5. List two instances of each of the following sentences. Identify the instantial term of each instance.

*a. $(\forall z)(Gz \ v \ Hz)$

b. $(\exists x)(Gx \ v \ Hx)$

*c. $(\forall y)((Fy \ \& \ Gy) \rightarrow Hy)$

d. $(\exists y)(a = y)$

*e. $(\exists z)(Fz \ \& \ (\exists x)(Fx \ \& \ Gxz))$

f. $(\forall x)((\exists y)Fy \rightarrow Gxx)$

*g. $(\forall x)(\forall y)(x = y)$

6. Using the translation scheme provided and assuming that the domain is the class of human beings, translate the following sentences into English.

> *a*: Platt   *b*: Nancy
> *F*_: _ is an island dweller
> *G*_: _ is a sailor
> *H*_: _ eats fish
> *I* _ _: _ likes _

a. *Fa*

*b. *Fa & Ga*

c. *Fa & Fb*

*d. *(∃x)Fx*

e. *(∃x)(Fx & Gx)*

*f. *(∃x)Fx & (∃y)Fy*

g. *~(∃x)Fx*

h. *(∃x)~Fx*

*i. *~(∃x)(Fx & Gx)*

j. *(∃x)~(Fx & Gx)*

*k. *(∃x)(~Fx & Gx)*

l. *(∃x)(Fx & ~Gx)*

*m. *(∃x)Fx & (∃y)~Fy*

n. *~(Fa & Ha)*

*o. *~(Fa & Fb)*

p. *~(Fa v Ha)*

*q. *Fa → Ga*

r. *~Fa → Ga*

*s. *Fa → ~Ga*

t. *Fa → (Ga & Ha)*

*u. *(Fa & Ga) → Ha*

v. *(Fa v Ga) → Ha*

*w. *(∀x)(Fx → Gx)*

x. *(∀x)(Fx → ~Gx)*

*y. *(∀x)((Fx & Gx) → ~Hx)*

*z. *(∀x)((Fx v Gx) → Hx)*

7. Using the translation scheme in exercise 6, translate the following into English. Take the domain to be the class of human beings.

a. *Iab & Iba*

*b. *Iab → Iba*

c. *Iab → ~Iba*

*d. *Iab v ~Iab*

e. *(∃x)(Ixb & Ibx)*

*f. *(∀x)(Iax & Ibx)*

g. *(∀x)(Ixb & ~Ibx)*

*h. *(∀x)(Iax v Ibx)*

i. *(∃x)(Ixb & ~Ibx)*

*j. *(∀x)(Iax → Ixa)*

k. *~(∀x)(Ixb → Ibx)*

*l. *(∀x)(Iax v Ibx)*

m. *~Iaa*

*n. *(∀x)(Gx → Iax)*

o. *(∀x)(Iax → Gx)*

*p. *(∀x)Ixa → (∀x)Ixb*

q. *(∃x)Ixa → (∃x)Ixb*

*r. *(∃x)Ixa → (∀x)Ixb*

s. *~(∃x)(Fx & Ibx)*

*t. *(∃x)(Fx & ~Ibx)*

u. *(∀x)(Fx & ~Ibx)*

*v. *~(∀x)(Fx → Ibx)*

w. *(∀x) (Gx → ~(Fx v Hx))*

*x. *(∀x)((Fx v Hx) → ~Gx)*

y. *(∀x)Ixx*

*z. *(∀z)Izz → Ibb*

8. Using the scheme in exercise 6, translate the following English sentences.

  a. Platt likes Nancy.
 *b. Platt is a sailor.
  c. All island dwellers eat fish.
 *d. Every island dweller eats fish and every island dweller is a sailor.
  e. If Platt is an island dweller, then he eats fish.
 *f. Every island dweller eats fish and is a sailor.
  g. Some island dwellers are not sailors but Nancy is an island dweller who is.
 *h. Neither Nancy nor Platt eat fish.
  i. No sailor who is an island dweller eats fish.
 *j. Not one sailor eats fish.
  k. Not one sailor likes Nancy.
 *l. If any sailor eats fish, then Platt does.
  m. If every sailor eats fish, then some sailor does.
 *n. Every sailor who is an island dweller eats fish.
  o. Every sailor and island dweller eats fish.
 *p. Only sailors are island dwellers.
  q. The only sailors are island dwellers.
 *r. All and only sailors eat fish.
  s. No fish eaters are sailors or island dwellers.
 *t. Not just sailors eat fish.
  u. Some fish eaters are not sailors.
 *v. Not all fish eaters are either sailors or island dwellers.
 *w. Some sailors and island dwellers do not like to eat fish.
  x. An island dweller is not a sailor unless that island dweller eats fish.
 *y. Nancy is the one and only sailor who does not eat fish.
 *z. All island dwellers like all sailors.

6.2 SEMANTICS

We have described the syntax of Q. Our concern now is with the semantics of the language, specifically, the truth conditions of its sentences. Truth conditions will be defined for the following types of sentences:

> (i) sentences that contain no logical symbol (sentence letters and atoms);

(ii) <u>identity sentences</u> (those formed from placing the identity sign between two singular terms and enclosing the result in parentheses);

(iii) sentences dominated by a connective;

(iv) existential sentences;

(v) universal sentences.

Although spelling out the truth conditions for these sentences is not a simple matter, understanding those conditions is essential to understanding Q.

In this section, we use <u>natural translation</u> in discussing the truth conditions of the five types of sentences listed above. Natural translation uses words and phrases from a natural language, such as English, to specify the individuals that singular terms designate and the attributes or relations that predicate letters express. You are already familiar with this method of translation. Two other translation methods are also used: extensional translation and abstract translation. Studying these will give you a deeper understanding of the artificial language.

Sentence Letters, Atoms, and Identity Sentences

The truth conditions for sentence letters are easily defined. If the proposition the sentence letter expresses is true, the sentence letter is true; otherwise, it is false. Thus, if '*P*' translates 'Mars has more moons than Jupiter', '*P*' is false on that translation. If '*P*' translates 'Luna moths are attracted to light', '*P*' is true on that translation.

An atom consists of a predicate letter combined with an appropriate number of singular terms. An atom composed of a one-place predicate letter and a singular term, such as '*Fa*', says that the individual designated by the singular term has the attribute expressed by the predicate letter. Without knowing to which individual the singular term refers or what the attribute is, there is no way of deciding the truth value of the sentence. However, using a translation scheme, you can determine whether the sentence is true or false on the basis of what it says about the world. For example, if '*F_*' translates '_ is a country' and '*a*' translates 'Luxembourg', the sentence '*Fa*' (which says that Luxembourg is a country) is true. But, with the same translation for '*F_*' but '*a*' as the translation for 'Cairo', '*Fa*' (which says that Cairo is a country) is false.

The situation is analogous, though somewhat more complex, for atoms composed of a two-place predicate letter and two singular terms. An example is '*Gab*'. In this sentence, '*G_ _*' expresses a relation, such as *being taller than*, that one individual bears (or does not bear) to another and the two singular terms '*a*' and '*b*' designate individuals. The sentence is true if and only if *a* bears the relation to *b*. A more technical way of expressing the truth conditions of '*Gab*' is to say that '*Gab*' is true if and only if *a* and *b*, taken in that order, have the relation G^2. The concept of order is very important in considering relations because a relation may be borne by individuals in one order but not in another.

Placing in proper order the names of the individuals and enclosing them in angular parentheses is the convention commonly used to write about <u>ordered couples</u>. Thus

⟨the World Trade Center, the Empire State Building⟩

designates the couple with the World Trade Center first and the Empire State Building second. On the other hand,

⟨the Empire State Building, the World Trade Center⟩

designates the same couple of individuals but in reverse order. Two-term relations may be treated as classes of ordered couples. For example, the relation of *being taller than* may be viewed as the class of all ordered couples such that the first is taller than the second. Viewed in that way, ⟨the World Trade Center, the Empire State Building⟩ belongs to this relation because the World Trade Center is taller than the Empire State Building. But ⟨the Empire State Building, the World Trade Center⟩ does not belong because the relation does not hold in the reverse order. Thus, when '_ is taller than _' translates '*G_ _*', 'the World Trade Center' translates '*a*', and 'the Empire State Building' translates '*b*', '*Gab*' is true because ⟨*a*, *b*⟩ belongs to the relation G^2, but '*Gba*' is false because ⟨*b*, *a*⟩ does not belong to that relation.

Besides ordered pairs or couples, there are ordered triples, ordered quadruples, and so on. In general, any atom composed of an *n*-place predicate letter and *n* singular terms is true on a translation if and only if the <u>ordered *n*-tuple</u> of individuals (in the order designated by the singular terms) belongs to the relation on that translation. For example, if you translate '_ is the result of dividing _ by _' with '*H_ _ _*', '2' with '*a*', '3' with '*b*', and '6' with '*c*', then '*Hacb*' (which says that 2 is the result of dividing 6 by 3) is true but '*Habc*' (which says that 2 is the result of dividing 3 by 6) is false. In other words, the ordered triple ⟨2, 6, 3⟩ belongs to the relation H^3. But the ordered triple ⟨2, 3, 6⟩ does not.

As previously stated, an identity sentence results from placing a singular term on each side of an identity sign and enclosing the result in parentheses. Such sentences are true on a translation if and only if the singular terms flanking the identity sign designate the same individual on that translation. So, if you let '*b*' and '*c*' both translate '17', or '*b*' translate '17' and '*c*' translate '10 + 7', '(*b* = *c*)' is true. On the other hand, if '*b*' translates '17' and '*c*' translates '7', '(*b* = *c*)' is false.

Sentences Dominated by a Connective

As previously defined, a sentence dominated by a connective is a sentence with a tilde, ampersand, *vel,* or arrow as its dominant operator. Put another way, it is a sentence that has the form $\sim A$, $(A \mathbin{\&} B)$, $(A \vee B)$, or $(A \to B)$, where A and B are sentences. Any sentence of the form $\sim A$ is a negation, any sentence of the form $(A \mathbin{\&} B)$ is a conjunction, any sentence of the form $(A \vee B)$ is a disjunction, and any sentence of the form $(A \to B)$ is a conditional. Examples of negations are the following:

$$\sim Fa, \qquad \sim(\exists x)(Fx \mathbin{\&} Gx), \qquad \sim(\forall y)(\exists x)Gxy$$

[What are some examples of conjunctions, disjunctions, and conditionals?]

The truth conditions for these sentences are the same in Q as in C. A negation is true if and only if its immediate component is false. A conjunction is true if and only if its left conjunct and its right conjunct are both true. A disjunction is true if and only if either its left disjunct is true, its right disjunct is true, or both disjuncts are true. And a conditional is false if and only if its antecedent is true and its consequent false. For example,

$$(\exists x)Fx \to Fa$$

is a conditional. Therefore, it is false if '$(\exists x)Fx$' is true and 'Fa' is false; otherwise, it is true.

You can determine the truth value of some truth-functional sentences from their forms. For example, any sentence that has the form $(A \vee \sim A)$ is clearly true. And any exemplifying the form $(A \mathbin{\&} \sim A)$ is obviously false. An example of a sentence that has the form $(A \vee \sim A)$ is

$$(\exists x)Fx \vee \sim(\exists x)Fx$$

To determine the truth value of other truth-functional sentences, you need to know the truth value of their immediate components. For example, the immediate components of

$$\sim(\forall x)Fx \mathbin{\&} (\forall y)Gy$$

are its left conjunct

$$\sim(\forall x)Fx$$

and its right conjunct

$$(\forall y)Gy$$

To determine the truth values of these conjuncts, you need to know of what individuals the domain consists and how the predicate letters are translated.

Existential Sentences

An existential sentence is any sentence with an existential quantifier as its dominant operator. Put another way, an existential sentence is any sentence $(\exists x)A$, where x and A are a term variable and a quasi-sentence, respectively.

Every existential sentence claims that there is at least one individual that has a certain attribute. Thus an existential sentence is true if and only if there is an individual that has the attribute. For example, let '_ is a Frenchman' correspond for purposes of translation to '$F\_$', '_ is a friend of _' to '$G\_\ \_$', and 'George Washington' to 'a'. Then $\hat{x}(Fx)$ is the attribute of *being a Frenchman*, $\hat{x}(Gxa)$ is the attribute of *being a friend of George Washington*, and $\hat{x}(Fx\ \&\ Gxa)$ is the attribute of *being a Frenchman and a friend of George Washington*. This is an attribute that is true of the Marquis de Lafayette; therefore, $(\exists x)(Fx\ \&\ Gxa)$ is true. If you are not familiar with abstracts, reread section 3.1, where abstracts are first discussed.

The following is a general procedure that you may find helpful in determining whether an existential sentence is true on a translation with respect to a domain. First, pick a singular term that does not occur in the translation scheme. Form an instance with the singular term as the instantial term. Scan the domain. If the instance is true as a result of letting the instantial term designate an individual in the domain, then the existential sentence is true. If the instance is false regardless of what individual in the domain the instantial term designates, then the existential sentence is false. For example, take

$$(\exists x)(Gx\ \&\ Hx)$$

and let '$G\_$' correspond to '_ is a country', '$H\_$' to '_ has a communist government', and the domain consist of political organizations in Asia in 1993. Remove the existential quantifier, then replace 'x' throughout with 'c' (a term that does not appear in the translation scheme) to form the following instance:

$$Gc\ \&\ Hc$$

Let c be North Korea or any other individual that is in the domain and has the attribute of $\hat{x}(x$ is a country and x has a communist government). Then '$(Gc\ \&\ Hc)$' says that North Korea is a country with a communist government. Because '$(Gc\ \&\ Hc)$' is true, '$(\exists x)(Gx\ \&\ Hx)$' is also true. Now suppose that the domain is political organizations in the mainland of North America in 1993. Regardless of what individual c is in this domain, '$(Gc\ \&\ Hc)$' is false. Therefore, if the translation scheme is the same as above but the domain is political organizations in the mainland of North America in 1993 rather than Asia, '$(\exists x)(Gx\ \&\ Hx)$' is false.

Universal Sentences

A universal sentence is any sentence with a universal quantifier as its dominant operator. In other words, it is any sentence $(\forall x)A$, where x and A are, respectively, a term variable and a quasi-sentence.

Because a universal sentence claims that every individual has an attribute, the sentence is true if and only if every individual in the domain has the attribute. Thus it is false if at least one individual in the domain does not. In general, to determine whether a universal sentence is true on a translation with respect to a domain, proceed as follows: Pick a singular term that does not occur in the translation scheme. Form an instance with the singular term as the instantial term. Scan the domain. If the instance is true regardless of what individual in the domain the instantial term designates, then the universal sentence is true. If the instance is false as a result of letting the instantial term designate a specific individual in the domain, then the universal sentence is false.

For example, consider the sentence

$$(\forall x)(Fx \rightarrow Gx)$$

where 'F_' translates '_ is a president of the United States', 'G_' translates '_ graduated from Yale', and the domain is universal. Is this sentence, which says that every president of the United States graduated from Yale, true? To answer this question, pick a singular term that does not occur in the translation scheme to form an instance. As no singular term occurs in the translation scheme, any will do. So, take 'a' to form the following instance:

$$Fa \rightarrow Ga$$

Letting a be Jimmy Carter, the instance is false because the antecedent 'Fa' (which says that Jimmy Carter is a president of the United States) is true but the consequent 'Ga' (which says that Jimmy Carter graduated from Yale) is false. Therefore, '$(\forall x)(Fx \rightarrow Gx)$' is false. If you had let a be George Bush, Gerald Ford, or Mao Tse-tung, the instance '$(Fa \rightarrow Ga)$' would have been true. But the universal sentence is true if and only if the instance is true for *all* possible designations of the instantial term, not just a few, and we have shown the instance is false for at least one.

Extensional and Abstract Translations

The method of translation we have been using so far is that of natural translation. Two other methods of translation or interpretation are discussed next.

Extensional Translations

In a natural translation, singular terms and phrases from a natural language translate in a direct and obvious way the singular terms, predicate letters, and the sentence letters that belong to the artificial language. For example, to indicate that the attribute *F* is the attribute of *being a president of the United States*, '*F_*' was read '_ is a president of the United States'. You can also translate a predicate letter by assigning to it the extension of an attribute and thus giving it an <u>extensional translation</u>.

The extension of an attribute is the class of individuals that have the attribute. For example, the extension of the attribute of *being a president of the United States* is a class of all the presidents. As of 1994, it is the following class:

> {George Washington, John Adams, Thomas Jefferson, . . . ,
> George Bush, Bill Clinton}

In an analogous fashion, you can translate a two-place predicate letter by assigning it a class of ordered couples and translate an *n*-place predicate letter by assigning it a class of ordered *n*-tuples. For example, you can translate '*G_ _*' by assigning it the class of ordered pairs indicated below.

> {⟨George Washington, John Adams⟩, ⟨John Adams, Thomas
> Jefferson⟩, ⟨Thomas Jefferson, James Madison⟩, . . . , ⟨Jimmy
> Carter, Ronald Reagan⟩, ⟨Ronald Reagan, George Bush⟩,
> ⟨George Bush, Bill Clinton⟩}

[Can you articulate in English a relationship for which this class appears to be the extension?]

Under an extensional translation, a sentence composed of a one-place predicate letter and a singular term is true if and only if the individual the singular term names is a member of the class assigned to the predicate letter. Thus, under the extensional translation above, '*Fa*' is true if *a* is George Washington but false if *a* is Winston Churchill, because George Washington is a member of the class assigned to '*F_*' but Winston Churchill is not.

Similarly, a sentence composed of a two-place predicate letter and two singular terms is true if and only if the pair of individuals in the order named is a member of the class assigned to the two-place predicate letter; and so on. Thus, under the extensional translation of '*G_ _*' above, '*Gab*' is true if *a* is Jimmy Carter and *b* is Ronald Reagan but false if *b* is Jimmy Carter and *a* is Ronald Reagan, because ⟨Jimmy Carter, Ronald Reagan⟩ is a member of the class assigned '*G_ _*' but ⟨Ronald Reagan, Jimmy Carter⟩ is not. In extensional translations, sentence letters are not translated by sentences from another language. They are simply assigned one of the two truth values.

An example of an extensional translation with respect to the domain {1, 2, 3, 4} is as follows:

>   *a*: 1   *b*: 2   *c*: 3   *d*: 4   *P*: T
>
>   *F_*: {2, 4}
>
>   *G_*: {1, 3}
>
>   *H_ _*: {⟨1, 2⟩, ⟨2, 3⟩, ⟨1, 3⟩, ⟨1, 4⟩, ⟨2, 4⟩, ⟨3, 4⟩}
>
>   *I_ _ _*: {⟨1, 1, 2⟩, ⟨1, 2, 3⟩, ⟨2, 2, 4⟩}

Under this scheme, '*Fa*' is false because 1 is not a member of the class assigned to '*F_*', which is {2, 4}. But '*Fb*' is true because 2 is a member of {2, 4}. As for '*Ibcd*', it is false because ⟨2, 3, 4⟩ is not a member of class assigned to '*I_ _ _*', which is {⟨1, 1, 2⟩, ⟨1, 2, 3⟩, ⟨2, 2, 4⟩}. Given that the domain is {1, 2, 3, 4}, '(∃*x*)*Fx*' is true because the class assigned to '*F_*' is nonempty. However, '(∀*x*)*Fx*' is false because the class is also nonuniversal, that is, there are members of the domain that are not members of {2, 4}. '(*Fa* → *P*)' is true because '*P*' is true and '*Fa*' is false.

Abstract Translations

Both natural translations and extensional translations involve a second language for translation. For example, English words and phrases appear in the natural translations and Arabic numerals appear in the extensional translation above. In an <u>abstract translation</u>, the artificial language translates itself and no reference is made to recognizable individuals, attributes, or relations.

With such a translation, you simply place singular terms in braces to specify the domain. For example, you can let the domain be

>   {*a*, *b*}

To translate predicate letters, you follow the extensional method described above, but place singular terms from the language itself in braces. The following is an example of an abstract translation with respect to the domain {*a*, *b*}.

>   *F_*: {*a*}
>
>   *G_*: {*a*, *b*}
>
>   *H_ _*: {⟨*a*, *b*⟩}.

On this translation, '*Fa*' is true because *a* is in the class assigned to '*F_*', but '*Fb*' is false because *b* is not in that class. Similarly, '*Hab*' is true because ⟨*a*, *b*⟩ is a member of the class assigned to '*H_ _*', but '*Hba*' is false because ⟨*b*, *a*⟩ is not a member of that class.

To determine the truth value of a quantified sentence on an abstract translation, the only instances you need to consider are those formed with the instantial terms used in specifying the domain. For example, when the domain is $\{a, b\}$, to determine the truth value of either '$(\exists x)Fx$' or '$(\forall x)Fx$', you need only know the truth value of 'Fa' and 'Fb'. A universal sentence is true if and only if every one of the relevant instances are true, while an existential sentence is true if and only if at least one of the relevant instances is true. Therefore, on the abstract translation above, '$(\forall x)(Fx \rightarrow Gx)$' is true because both '$(Fa \rightarrow Ga)$' and '$(Fb \rightarrow Gb)$' are true. But '$(\forall x)(Gx \rightarrow Fx)$' is false because '$(Gb \rightarrow Fb)$' is false. And '$(\exists x)(Fx \ \& \ Gx)$' is true because '$(Fa \ \& \ Ga)$' is true.

Quantification Theory

Quantification is usually taught from the perspective of standard quantification theory, which is also known as standard logic. In standard logic, $(\forall x)(Fx \rightarrow Gx)$ does not imply $(\exists x)(Fx \ \& \ Gx)$. Nevertheless, standard logic does make some existential assumptions. It assumes that the domain is nonempty and that every singular term designates exactly one individual in the domain. For example, if the domain is the class of presidents of the United States, each singular term designates exactly one president. None designates any individual, such as yourself, who is not a president and, thus, not in the domain. Because the domain of presidents of the United States is finite and the number of singular terms is infinite, there will be a superfluity of singular terms to go around. In fact, at least one president will be designated by not only one or two but an infinite number of singular terms.

Standard quantification theory does not assume that every individual in the domain is designated by at least one singular term. Nevertheless, if this assumption is added to the assumption of standard theory, namely, that every singular term designates at least one individual, we can define the truth conditions of quantified sentences quite simply as follows:

> An existential sentence is true if and only if at least one of its instances is true.

> A universal sentence is true if and only if all of its instances are true.

Using these definitions, '$(\exists x)(a = x)$' is true because one of its instances, namely '$(a = a)$', is true. And '$(\forall x)(x = x)$' is true because all of its instances are true. Similarly, '$(\forall x)Fx \rightarrow (\exists x)Fx$' is true because the only way for it to be false is for '$(\forall x)Fx$' to be true and '$(\exists x)Fx$' to be false. But '$(\exists x)Fx$' is false only if none of its instances are true. But, as the instances of '$(\exists x)Fx$' are the same as the instances of '$(\forall x)Fx$', if '$(\exists x)Fx$' is false, so is '$(\forall x)Fx$'. So the conditional cannot be false; therefore, it is true.

EXERCISES FOR SECTION 6.2

*1. Explain why (∃y)Gz does not qualify as an existential sentence.

2. Determine the truth value of each of the following sentences on the translation scheme below.

 a: 1   *b*: 2   *c*: 3   *d*: 4

 *F_*: _ is even
 *G_*: _ is odd
 H_ _: _ is less than _
 I_ _: _ is greater than _
 J_ _ _: _ is the sum of _ and _

 a. *Fa* v *Gb*
 b. *Iab* v *Hba*
 c. *Icb* → *Ica*
 d. *Iab* ≡ *Hba*
 e. ~(*b* = *c*)

 f. *Jbba*
 g. *Jcbb* → *Jbaa*
 h. *Jcab* → (*c* = *b*)
 i. *Iaa* & *Ibb*
 j. *Jaab* → *Iab*

*3. Using the translation scheme provided, translate the sentences in exercise 2 into idiomatic English.

*4. Determine the truth value of each of the following sentences with respect to the domain {1, 2, 3, 4} on the translation scheme of exercise 2.

 a. (∃x)(Fx & Gx)
 b. (∃x)Fx & (∃x)Gx
 c. (∃x)Hxa
 d. (∃x)Ixd
 e. (∀y)(Iya v (y = a))
 f. ~(∃y)Jyyy
 g. (∃y)Jdyy
 h. (∀y)Gy
 i. (∀x)(Hxc → Icx)
 j. (∀x)((Hxc & Hcb) → Hxb)

 k. (∀x)(Jxbc → Fx)
 l. (∀x)(∀y)(Hxy → Ixb)
 m. (∃x)(∀y)Ixy
 n. (∀y)(∃x)Hxy
 o. (∀x)(Fx → (∃y)Jxyy)
 p. (∃x)(∀y)(x = y)
 q. (∃x)(∃y)Hxy
 r. (∀x)(∃y)(x = y)
 s. (∀x)((Ixb v Ibx) v (x = b))

5. Repeat exercise 4 with {1, 2, 3, . . .} as the domain.

6. Using the translation scheme in exercise 2, translate into idiomatic English the sentences in exercise 4. Assume that the natural numbers make up the domain.

7. Determine which of the following sentences are true on the translation scheme in exercise 2 with respect to the domain {1, 2, 3, 4}, and translate into English those that are true.

   a. $(\forall x)(Fx \rightarrow Gx)$

   *b. $(\exists x)(Fx \;\&\; \sim Gx)$

   c. $Fa \;\&\; (\exists x)Hax$

   *d. $Fb \;\&\; (\exists x)Hxb$

   e. $(\forall x)(((x = a) \;v\; (x = b)) \rightarrow (\exists y)Jxxy)$

   f. $(\forall x)(Fx \rightarrow (\exists y)Jxxy)$

   *g. $(\forall x)(\forall y)((Fx \;\&\; Gy) \rightarrow \sim(x = y))$

   h. $(\forall x)(Gx \rightarrow (\exists y)(Fy \;\&\; Ixy))$

   *i. $(\forall x)(\forall y)(\sim(x = y) \rightarrow (Hxy \;v\; \sim Hxy))$

   *j. $(\forall x)(\forall y)(\forall z)((Ixy \;\&\; Iyz) \rightarrow Ixz)$

*8. Determine which of the following sentences are true on the translation scheme below.

   a: 1 b: 2 c: 3 d: 4

   $F\_$: {2, 4} $G\_$: {1, 3}

   $H\_\_$: {⟨1, 2⟩, ⟨2, 3⟩, ⟨1, 3⟩, ⟨1, 4⟩, ⟨2, 4⟩}

   $I\_\_\_$: {⟨1, 1, 2⟩, ⟨1, 2, 3⟩, ⟨2, 2, 4⟩}

a. $Icbb$	f. $Iaab \rightarrow Ga$
b. $Ibbc$	g. $\sim(Fa \;v\; Ga)$
c. Hdd	h. $\sim(Fb \;\&\; Fc)$
d. $\sim(Fb \;\&\; Fc) \equiv (b = c)$	i. $Fc \;v\; Gc$
e. $(Fa \;\&\; \sim Fc) \rightarrow \sim(a = c)$	j. $Fa = Ga$

9. Identify the extension of the attribute or relation expressed by each of the following on the translation scheme in exercise 2 with respect to the domain {1, 2, 3, 4}. Blanks are added for easier reading.

a. $Ia\_$	g. $(\exists x)Ix\_$
*b. I_b	*h. $(\exists y)I\_y$
c. Jb_c	i. $(\forall x)Jxx\_$
*d. Ja_a	*j. $(\forall x)(Fx \rightarrow Ix\_)$
e. $J\_\_c$	*k. $(\forall y)(\sim(y = d) \rightarrow (\exists x)J\_xy)$
*f. $Jd\_\_$	

*10. Determine which of the following sentences is true on the translation scheme below with respect to the domain $\{a, b\}$.

F_: $\{a\}$

G_: $\{a, b\}$

H_ _: $\{\langle a, b \rangle\}$

a. $(\exists x)Hxb$

b. $(\forall x)Hxb$

c. $(\exists x)Hxa$

d. $(\exists x)(\exists y)Hxy$

e. $(\forall x)(Fx \rightarrow Hxb)$

f. $(\forall x)(Hxx \rightarrow Fx)$

g. $(\exists x)(Fx \,\&\, (\forall y)(\sim(x = y) \rightarrow Hxy))$

6.3 SEMANTIC EVALUATION

Some semantic properties belong to sentences and arguments because certain truth values or combinations of truth values are possible for them; others, because certain truth values or combination of such values are not possible for them. The first we call "possibility" properties; the second, "impossibility" properties.

For example, the property of *not being contradictory* is a "possibility" property. A sentence that is not contradictory has the possibility of being true. In contrast, *being contradictory* is an "impossibility" property. A sentence that is contradictory has no possibility of being true. Other "possibility" properties are those of *non-validity*, *non-equivalence*, and *compatibility*. On the other hand, the properties of *validity*, *equivalence*, and *incompatibility* are "impossibility" properties. For example, an argument is valid if and only if it is impossible for the premises to be true while the conclusion is false.

In this section, you will learn how to detect "possibility" properties in terms of Q. This is done by finding translations that demonstrate the possibility of the truth value or combinations of truth values upon which the property depends. The problem of detecting "impossibility" properties is then discussed.

Detecting Semantic Properties through Translations

Our definitions of semantic properties in chapter 1 are quite general and not designed for any specific language. For example, the definition of a valid argument states that an argument is valid if and only if it is not semantically possible for the premises to be true while the conclusion is false. We then defined analogous "logical properties" depending on logical content only. For the language C, we defined C-properties, such as C-validity. It is now time to define analogous Q-properties.

A sentence is either Q-valid, Q-contradictory, or neither.

> A sentence is Q-valid if and only if there is no translation with respect to any domain on which the sentence is false.

> A sentence is Q-contradictory if and only if there is no translation with respect to any domain on which the sentence is true.

An obvious example of a sentence that is neither Q-valid nor Q-contradictory is

(1) *Fa*

Translate '*a*' with 'Yeltsin' and '*F_*' with '_ is a Russian', and (1) says that Yeltsin is a Russian, which is true. But translate '*a*' with 'Yeltsin' and '*F_*' with '_ is a Spaniard', and (1) says that Yeltsin is a Spaniard, which is false. The fact that '*Fa*' translates both ways shows that it is neither Q-valid nor Q-contradictory.

Another sentence that is neither Q-valid nor Q-contradictory is the following:

(2) $(\forall x)(Fx \to Gx)$

If you translate '*F_*' with '_ is a rhomboid', and '*G_*' with '_ is a parallelogram', (2) says that all rhomboids are parallelograms. But, if you translate '*F_*' with '_ is a parallelogram' and '*G_*' with '_ is a rhomboid', (2) says all parallelograms are rhomboids. One translation is true, the other is false. [Which is which?]

Still another example of a sentence that is neither Q-valid nor Q-contradictory is

(3) $(\exists x)(\exists y)(x \neq y)$

Here, we follow the common convention of abbreviating '$\sim(x = y)$' with '$(x \neq y)$'. Sentence (3) tells us that there is an individual x and there is an individual y such that x is not identical with y, or, in more idiomatic English, that there are at least two distinct individuals in the domain. Let the domain have exactly one member, and (3) is false. Let the domain have more than one member, and (3) is true. Therefore, (3) is neither Q-valid nor Q-contradictory.

We define the conditions under which an argument is Q-valid as follows:

An argument is <u>Q-valid</u> if and only if there is no translation with respect to any domain on which all the premises are true and the conclusion is false.

Given this definition, to show that an argument is not Q-valid, one need only present a translation with respect to some domain on which all the premises are true and the conclusion is false.

For example, consider the argument below:

(4) $(\forall x)(Fx \rightarrow Gx)$, $(\exists x)(Gx \,\&\, Hx)$ /∴ $(\forall x)(Fx \rightarrow Hx)$

Let the domain be universal and let '_ is a whale' translate '$F\_$', '_ is an underwater swimmer' translate '$G\_$', and '_ is a human being' translate '$H\_$'. On this translation, the premises are true and the conclusion is false. If you have any trouble seeing this, translate the entire argument into English. You will get essentially the following:

(4′) All whales are underwater swimmers. Some underwater swimmers are human beings. Therefore, all whales are human beings.

The premises are true while the conclusion is false.

We define the conditions under which two sentences are Q-equivalent as follows:

Two sentences are <u>Q-equivalent</u> if and only if there is no translation with respect to any domain on which those sentences have different truth values.

Following this definition, one can detect that two sentences are not Q-equivalent by coming up with a translation with respect to a domain on which the two sentences have different values.

For example, consider the following pair:

(5) $(\forall x)(Fx \,\text{v}\, Gx)$

(6) $(\forall x)Fx \,\text{v}\, (\forall x)Gx$

Let the domain be the class of parents and translate '$F\_$' with '_ is a mother' and '$G\_$' with '_ is a father'. On this translation, (5) is true but (6) is false. Therefore, the sentences are not Q-equivalent. The full English translation of the pair is

(5′) Each is either a mother or a father.

(6′) All are mothers or all are fathers.

[What is the truth value of (5′)? Is it the same as that of (6′)?]

We define Q-incompatibility as follows:

Sentences are <u>Q-incompatible</u> if and only if there is no translation with respect to any domain on which all of them are true.

As shown above, there is a translation with respect to a domain on which (5) is true and (6) is false. There is also a translation on which they are both true. To see this, let the domain be {1, 2, 3} and let '_ is greater than 0' translate '*F*_' and '_ is less than 4' translate '*G*_'. Then (5) and (6) are respective Q-translations of the sentences below.

(5″) Each is greater than 0 or less than 4.

(6″) All are greater than 0 or all are less than 4.

Because both are true, (5) and (6) are not incompatible.

By finding a translation with respect to a domain on which a sentence is true, you can show that the form of the sentence does not prevent it from being true. But how can you show that the form of a sentence prevents the sentence from being true? If the sentence is valid, you will never find a translation with respect to a domain on which the sentence is false. But, because such translations are infinite in number, you will never be able to prove by a one-by-one process of elimination that no such translation exists. Finding translations that demonstrate that certain combinations of truth values are possible is sufficient for detection of the "possibility" properties. But not finding such a translation after checking any finite number is not sufficient for detection of the "impossibility" properties of validity, equivalence, and incompatibility. In this respect, the translation method employed above is analogous to the fairy-tale and counterargument methods described in section 1.3 (see pp. 20–25).

Model Domains

A model domain is specified in the same way as the domain for an abstract translation. As with abstract translations, the members of the domain are not identified. So, of the model domain {*a*}, one knows only that it has exactly one member, but not what member. Similarly, of the model domain {*a, b*}, one knows only that it has at least one and no more than two members but not what member or members. If both *a* and *b* are the same individual, the domain has only one member; if they are different individuals, it has two members. Both possibilities are open. Nevertheless, when only one singular term occurs in braces, the domain is said to be a one-member domain; when two occur, a two-member domain; and so on.

The expansion of a sentence relative to an *n*-member domain is a sentence that contains no quantifiers and is equivalent to the original sentence in that domain. For example, for the domain {*a*}, the expansion of '$(\forall x)Fx$' is '*Fa*.' It is not difficult to see that '$(\forall x)Fx$' is equivalent to '*Fa*' when the domain is {*a*}. Similarly, for the domain {*a*},

$$(\forall x)(Fx \rightarrow Gx)$$

expands to

> $Fa \rightarrow Ga$

For the domain $\{a, b\}$, it expands to

> $(Fa \rightarrow Ga)$ & $(Fb \rightarrow Gb)$

And, for the domain $\{a, b, c\}$, it expands to

> $(Fa \rightarrow Ga)$ & $(Fb \rightarrow Gb)$ & $(Fc \rightarrow Gc)$

[What is the expansion for the domain $\{a, b, c, d\}$?]

The expansion of existential sentences is somewhat different. For the domain $\{a\}$,

> $(\exists x)(Fx$ & $Gx)$

expands to

> Fa & Ga

For the domain $\{a, b\}$, it expands to

> $(Fa$ & $Ga)$ v $(Fb$ & $Gb)$

And, for the domain $\{a, b, c\}$, it expands to

> $(Fa$ & $Ga)$ v $(Fb$ & $Gb)$ v $(Fc$ & $Gc)$

[What is the expansion for the domain $\{a, b, c, d\}$?]

To form the expansion of

> $(\forall x)(\exists y)Fxy$

for the domain $\{a, b, c\}$, first eliminate '$(\forall x)$' by forming the following conjunction of the relevant instances:

> $(\exists y)Fay$ & $(\exists y)Fby$ & $(\exists y)Fcy$

Then form the expansion of each of the conjuncts (each of which is an existential sentence) to get

> $(Faa$ v Fab v $Fac)$ & $(Fba$ v Fbb v $Fbc)$ & $(Fca$ v Fcb v $Fcc)$

As with the example above, when there are overlapping quantifiers, always begin by eliminating the quantifier with the widest scope and work inward.

The examples above indicate how to form an expansion of any sentence for any model domain. A universal sentence expands to a *conjunction* of its relevant instances. An existential sentence expands to a *disjunction* of its relevant instances. The expansion of a sentence for a model domain is complete when every quantified sentence that is a component of the sentence or of the result of expanding it is expanded until no quantifiers remain.

One caution is needed. When it is assumed—as in standard quantification theory—that every singular term designates an individual in the domain, and a given sentence contains a singular term, be sure the singular term appears in any model domain for which it is expanded. For example, if you want to form the expansion of

$$(\forall x)Fx \rightarrow Fc$$

for a domain with two members, be sure that 'c' is one of the singular terms within braces. For example, a suitable domain for such an expansion is $\{a, c\}$. The expansion for that domain is

$$(Fa \text{ \& } Fc) \rightarrow Fc$$

Notice that the original sentence is a conditional, but its antecedent is a universal sentence. The expansion results from expanding its antecedent.

That any universal or existential sentence is equivalent in a model domain to its expansion for the model domain can be easily understood. The expansion of a universal sentence for a model domain is a conjunction; its conjuncts are those and just those instances of the universal sentence that have as their instantial terms the singular terms used to designate members of the domain. The expansion is true if and only if all of those instances are true. The universal sentence is true in the model domain if and only if all of those same instances are true. Therefore, the expansion of a universal sentence for a model domain is true if and only if the universal sentence is true in the domain.

The expansion of an existential sentence for a model domain is a disjunction; its disjuncts are those and just those instances of the existential sentence that have as their instantial terms the singular terms used to designate the members of the domain. The expansion is true if and only if at least one of those instances is true. The existential sentence is true in the model domain if and only if at least one of those same instances is true. Therefore, the expansion of an existential sentence for a model domain is true if and only if the existential sentence is true in that domain.

Decision Procedures

You can use model domains to detect that an argument is not Q-valid. Start with a domain with only one member, such as $\{a\}$ or $\{b\}$, and determine by a truth table whether the expansion for that domain is Q-valid. If the expansion is not Q-valid, you can conclude that the original argument is not Q-valid. If the expansion for that domain is Q-valid, proceed to a two-member domain, such as $\{a, b\}$, and so on. Once you have found an expansion for a domain that is not Q-valid, you can conclude that the original argument is not Q-valid.

For example, you can detect by this method that the following argument is not Q-valid:

$$(\forall x)(Fx \rightarrow Gx), (\exists x)(Gx \,\&\, Hx) \; / \therefore \; (\exists x)(Fx \,\&\, Hx)$$

The expansion of its premises and conclusion for the domain $\{a\}$ is

$$(Fa \rightarrow Ga), (Ga \,\&\, Ha) \; / \therefore \; (Fa \,\&\, Ha)$$

On the truth-table row displayed below, the premises of the expansion are true but the conclusion is false. So, the expansion is not Q-valid.

Fa	Ga	Ha	(Fa → Ga)	(Ga & Ha)	(Fa & Ha)
F	T	T	T	T	F

The row gives you a translation with respect to the domain $\{a\}$ on which the original argument has true premises and a false conclusion. The translation is the following:

$F\_$: empty class

$G\_$: $\{a\}$

$H\_$: $\{a\}$

To understand the connection between the translation and the truth-table row, note that 'Fa' is false if and only if the class assigned '$F\_$' is empty. Similarly, 'Ga' and 'Ha' are both true if and only if both '$G\_$' and '$H\_$' are assigned $\{a\}$. The original argument is not Q-valid on this translation with respect to the domain $\{a\}$. But if an argument is not Q-valid on some translation with respect to a domain, it is not Q-valid. Thus, the original argument is not Q-valid.

In cases of Q-validity, the situation is different. An expansion of an argument for a model domain can be Q-valid and the original argument not be. For example,

(1) $Fc \; / \therefore \; Fc$

is the expansion of

(2) $(\exists x)Fx \; / \therefore \; Fc$

for the domain $\{c\}$. Yet (1) is Q-valid and (2) is not.

A decision procedure is a mechanical method that will give an answer to a question in a finite number of steps. Truth tables provide a decision procedure with respect to semantic properties when there are no quantifiers. A decision procedure also exists for what is known as monadic predicate logic. The language of this logic is a fragment of Q, namely, what is left after removing the identity sign and the n-place predicate letters (where $n > 1$).

The decision procedure for monadic predicate logic is to select a model domain with 2^n members, where n is the number of different predicate letters involved, and then to form the expansion for that domain. If a truth table shows that the expansion has a semantic property, then one can conclude that the original expression has that property in every domain. For example, consider the argument

$$Fa \; /\therefore \; (\exists x)(Fx \vee Gx)$$

Because it contains two predicate letters, you form its expansion for a domain with four members. The following is its expansion for the domain $\{a, b, c, d\}$:

$$Fa \; /\therefore \; ((Fa \vee Ga) \vee (Fb \vee Gb) \vee (Fc \vee Gc) \vee (Fd \vee Gd))$$

A truth table will show that the expansion is Q-valid. Therefore, you can conclude that the original argument is Q-valid.

The procedure described above works for monadic predicate logic for two reasons. First, a semantic property that applies in a domain with 2^n members (where n is as above) also applies in any nonempty domain with fewer members. This is not difficult to understand. For example, whatever is valid in the domain $\{a, b, c\}$ will be valid if $(a = b)$ or if $(a = b)$ and $(b = c)$. Second, for monadic predicate logic a semantic property that applies in a domain with 2^n members (where n is as above) also applies in any larger domain, including infinite ones. The truth of this is not obvious. Unfortunately, the proof is beyond the scope of this text.

No decision procedure has been found for languages as rich as Q. Indeed, it has been proven that a decision procedure for such languages is impossible to devise.

EXERCISES FOR SECTION 6.3

1. For each sentence below, find an English translation with respect to a domain on which it is false. Besides giving a full English translation, specify your translation scheme and the domain if it is not universal.

    *a. $Fa \rightarrow (\forall x)Fx$

    b. $(\exists x)Gx \rightarrow Gb$

    *c. $(\forall x)((Fx \vee Gx) \rightarrow Fx)$

    d. $(\exists x)(Fx \; \& \sim Gx)$

    *e. $((\exists x)Fx \; \& \; (\exists y)Gy) \rightarrow (\exists x)(Fx \; \& \; Gx)$

    *f. $(\exists x)(\exists y)((Fx \; \& \; Gy) \; \& \; (x \neq y))$

2. For each sentence a, *b, c, *d, e, and f in exercise 1, find an abstract translation with respect to a domain on which it is false.

3. For each sentence a, *b, c, *d, e, and *f in exercise 1, find an English translation with respect to a domain on which the sentence is true. Besides giving a full English translation, specify your translation scheme and the domain if it is not universal.

4. For each sentence *a, b, *c, d, *e, and *f in exercise 1, find an abstract translation with respect to a domain on which the sentence is true.

5. For each of the arguments below, find an English translation with respect to a domain on which its premises are true while its conclusion is false. Besides giving a full English translation, specify your translation scheme and the domain if it is not universal.

  *a. $(\forall x)(Fx \to Gx)$, $(\forall x)(Fx \to Hx)$ /∴ $(\forall x)(Gx \to Hx)$

  b. $(\forall x)(Fx \to Gx)$, $(\exists x)Gx$ /∴ $(\exists x)Fx$

  *c. Fa, $\sim Gb$ /∴ $(\exists x)(Fx \,\&\, \sim Gx)$

  d. $(\forall x)(Fx \to Gx)$, $(\exists x)\sim Fx$ /∴ $(\exists x)\sim Gx$

  *e. $(\forall x)(Fx \to Gx)$, $(\exists x)(Gx \,\&\, Hx)$ /∴ $(\exists x)(Fx \,\&\, Hx)$

  f. $(\exists x)(Fx \text{ v } Gx)$ /∴ $(\exists x)Gx$

  *g. $(\forall x)(Fx \text{ v } Gx)$ /∴ $(\forall x)Gx$

  h. $(\forall x)(\exists y)Gxy$ /∴ $(\exists x)(\forall y)Gxy$

6. For each of the arguments a, *b, c, *d, e, *f, g, and *h in exercise 5 above, find an abstract translation with respect to a domain on which its premises are true and its conclusion is false.

7. For each of the pairs of sentences below, find an English translation with respect to a domain on which their truth values differ. Besides giving a full English translation, specify your translation scheme and the domain if it is not universal.

  a. $(\exists x)(Fx \text{ v } Gx)$, $(\exists x)(Fx \,\&\, Gx)$

  *b. $(\forall x)(Fx \,\&\, Gx)$, $(\forall x)(Fx \text{ v } Gx)$

  c. $(\exists x)(\forall y)Fxy$, $(\forall x)(\exists y)Fxy$

8. For each of the pairs *a, b, and *c in exercise 7, find an abstract translation with respect to a domain on which the sentences have different truth values.

9. Give the expansion of the following for the model domain $\{a, b, c\}$.

  a. $(\forall x)(Fx \,\&\, Gx)$

  *b. $(\forall x)Fx \to (\exists x)Gx$

  c. $(\exists x)(Hx \text{ v } Gx)$

*d. $Gb \ \& \ (\forall x)Fx$

e. $(\forall x)(\forall y)(x = y)$

f. $(\forall x)(\exists y)(x = y)$

*g. $(\exists x)(\forall y)(x = y)$

10. You can conclude that a sentence is neither Q-valid nor Q-contradictory if you show that the sentence has an expansion for a model domain that is neither Q-valid nor Q-contradictory. For each of the sentences a, *b, c, *d, e, and f in exercise 1, find an expansion in a model domain that is neither Q-valid nor Q-contradictory. In your search, begin with a one-member domain. If you cannot find the expansion you are looking for there, try a two-member domain. Keep going until you find an expansion of the type described.

11. You can conclude that an argument is not Q-valid if you show that the argument has an expansion for a model domain that is not Q-valid. For each of the arguments *a, b, *c, d, *e, f, *g, and h in exercise 5, find an expansion for a model domain that is not Q-valid. In your search, begin with a one-member domain. If you cannot find the expansion you are looking for there, try a two-member domain. Keep going until you find an expansion of the type described.

12. You can conclude that a pair of Q-sentences are not Q-equivalent if you show that for a model domain, the pair have expansions that are not Q-equivalent. For each of the pairs *a, b, and *c in exercise 7, find expansions for a model domain that are not Q-equivalent. In your search, begin with a one-member domain. If you cannot find the expansion you are looking for there, try a two-member domain. Keep going until you find an expansion of the type described.

13. Show by the decision procedure for monadic predicate logic that each of the following sentences is Q-valid.

*a. $(\exists x)(Fx \ v \ {\sim}Fx)$

b. $Fa \rightarrow (\exists x)Fx$

*c. $(\forall x)Fx \rightarrow (\exists x)Fx$

*d. $(\forall x)Fx \rightarrow Fa$

14. Show by the decision procedure for monadic predicate logic that the sentences in each of the following pairs are Q-equivalent.

*a. $(\exists x)(Fx \ \& \ {\sim}Gx)$, ${\sim}(\forall x)(Fx \rightarrow Gx)$

b. $(\forall x)(Gx \ v \ Fx)$, $(\forall x)(Fx \ v \ Gx)$

*c. ${\sim}(\exists x)(Fx \ \& \ {\sim}Gx)$, $(\forall x)(Fx \rightarrow Gx)$

d. $(\exists x)(Fx \ \& \ Gx), \ \sim(\forall x)(Fx \rightarrow \sim Gx)$

*e. $\sim(\exists x)(Fx \ \& \ Gx), \ (\forall x)(Fx \rightarrow \sim Gx)$

15. Show by the decision procedure for monadic predicate logic that each of the following arguments is Q-valid.

*a. $(\forall x)Fx \ / \therefore \ Fa$

b. $(\forall x)(Fx \ \& \ Gx) \ / \therefore \ (\forall x)Fx$

*c. $(\exists x)(Fx \ \& \ Gx) \ / \therefore \ (\exists x)Gx$

d. $(\forall x)(Fx \rightarrow Gx), \ (\forall x)Fx \ / \therefore \ (\forall x)Gx$

*e. $(\exists x)\sim Fx \ / \therefore \ \sim(\forall x)Fx$

f. $(\forall x)Fx \ / \therefore \ (\exists x)Fx$

*g. $(\forall x)(Fx \rightarrow Gx), \ (\forall x)(Gx \rightarrow Hx) \ / \therefore \ (\forall x)(Fx \rightarrow Hx)$

h. $(\forall x)(\sim Fx \rightarrow \sim Gx), \ (\exists x)(Gx \ \& \ Hx) \ / \therefore \ (\exists x)(Fx \ \& \ Hx)$

*i. $(\forall x)(Fx \rightarrow Gx), \ (\exists x)(Hx \ \& \ \sim Gx) \ / \therefore \ (\exists x)(Hx \ \& \ \sim Fx)$

16. Translate into English each of the arguments *a, b, *c, d, *e, f, *g, h, and *i in the previous exercise. For each translation specify the translation scheme and the domain if it is not universal.

LOGIC OF QUANTIFIERS: APPLICATIONS TO ENGLISH

Even though Q is a more complex language than C and the English idiom expressible through it is more varied, the same general principles apply with regard to translating and evaluating English. To translate well, you must know the purpose and suitability of the translation. In addition, you must have a good understanding of the language you are translating from, as well as of the language you are translating to. If you suitably translate an English argument and detect through a method available to Q that the translation is valid, you are justified in concluding that the original English argument is also valid. However, if your translation is not Q-valid, you are not justified in concluding that the original argument is not valid. The situation is analogous for the other semantic properties.

7.1 TRANSLATING WITH Q

Translating with Q provides options that are not available in translating with C. In addition to sentence letters, connectives, and parentheses, there are singular terms, term variables, predicate letters, quantifiers, and the identity sign to work with. This section illustrates the capacity of Q to display the content of English sentences and arguments. The focus is primarily on translating with quantifiers and the identity sign. The next section deals more directly with the English idiom.

Options for Translating

There are several options for translating any English sentence into Q. Which option you select depends upon what you want the syntactical structure of the translation to reveal.

For example, consider the following sentence:

Hans is keeping something from Danielle.

When 'G_' translates '_ is keeping something from Danielle' and 'a' translates 'Hans', the sentence translates as

Ga

An alternative translation that reveals something different is

$(\exists x)Fx$

Here 'F_' translates 'Hans is keeping _ from Danielle'. Now consider the next translation of the same sentence, where 'H_ _' translates '_ is keeping _ from Danielle' and 'a' designates Hans:

$(\exists x)Hax$

This translation tells us that a bears the relation H^2 to some individual.

Still another possible translation of the same English sentence is

$(\exists x)Iaxb$

where 'I_ _ _' translates '_ is keeping _ from _', 'a' translates 'Hans', and 'b' translates 'Danielle'. This last translation contains two singular terms and a three-place predicate letter, as well as a term variable and a quantifier. Its structure exhibits more of the content of the original English sentence than any of the other translations.

In practice, which way you translate depends on the purpose of the translation. Being aware of your options is essential to translating for the purpose of detecting semantic properties.

Quantifiers

In Q, there are two quantifier signs, $\forall$ and $\exists$, which appear in the universal and existential quantifiers. Below we discuss translating with these quantifiers.

Universal Claims

A sentence makes a <u>universal claim</u> if it states that every individual has a certain attribute. The following are examples of sentences making universal claims:

(1) Every student is eager to learn.

(2) No student is eager to learn.

Sentence (1) says that every individual has the attribute of *being eager to learn if a student*. And sentence (2) says that every individual has the attribute of *not being eager to learn if a student*. The most obvious way to translate such sentences is with a Q-sentence of the form $(\forall x)A$.

A helpful first step is to rephrase the sentence using a universal quantifier and an attributive expression (see chapter 3, p. 67). For example, to translate (1), first rephrase it as

$(\forall x)(x$ is eager to learn if a student)

Using this rewrite as a guide and translating '_ is eager to learn if a student' with 'F _', you can then translate (1) as

$(\forall x)Fx$

An alternative rewrite that shows more of the logical content of (1) is

$(\forall x)(x$ is a student $\rightarrow x$ is eager to learn)

Using this rewrite as a guide and translating '_ is a student' with 'F_' and '_ is eager to learn' with 'G_', you can translate (1) as

$(\forall x)(Fx \rightarrow Gx)$

To translate (2) in a way that reveals how it differs from (1), you can first rewrite it as

$(\forall x)(x$ is a student $\rightarrow \sim(x$ is eager to learn$))$

Then, using the scheme above, translate (2) as

$(\forall x)(Fx \rightarrow \sim Gx)$

One could also translate (2) as '$(\forall x)Fx$' or as '$(\forall x)(Fx \rightarrow Gx)$'. [What would be the translation scheme if '$(\forall x)Fx$' translated (2)? What if '$(\forall x)(Fx \rightarrow Gx)$' were the translation?]

Now consider translating the following sentences:

(3) Tigers, but not elephants, are carnivorous.

(4) All doctors and lawyers are professionals.

To translate (3) in a way that reveals as much content as possible, rewrite it first as the following conjunction of two universally quantified sentences:

$$(\forall x)(x \text{ is a tiger} \to x \text{ is carnivorous}) \ \& \ (\forall x)(x \text{ is an elephant} \to \sim(x \text{ is carnivorous}))$$

Then translate it as

$$(\forall x)(Fx \to Hx) \ \& \ (\forall x)(Gx \to \sim Hx)$$

with '_ is a tiger' assigned to '$F\_$', '_ is an elephant' to '$G\_$', and '_ is carnivorous' to '$H\_$'.

To exhibit as much of the content of (4) as possible, rewrite it as a conjunction of two universally quantified sentences:

$$(\forall x)(x \text{ is a doctor} \to x \text{ is a professional}) \ \& \ (\forall x)(x \text{ is a lawyer} \to x \text{ is a professional})$$

And then, with this rewrite as a guide, translate (4) as

$$(\forall x)(Fx \to Hx) \ \& \ (\forall x)(Gx \to Hx)$$

with '$F\_$' for '_ is a doctor', '$G\_$' for '_ is a lawyer', and '$H\_$' for '_ is a professional'.

One could also translate (4) as

$$(\forall x)((Fx \to Hx) \ \& \ (Gx \to Hx))$$

Notice that the dominant operator of this translation is a universal quantifier, while the dominant operator of the previous translation is the ampersand. Another possible translation is

$$(\forall x)((Fx \text{ v } Gx) \to Hx)$$

[Would there be a difference in meaning if the *vel* were replaced with an ampersand? To see the difference, give an English translation of '$(\forall x)((Fx \ \& \ Gx) \to Hx)$'.]

Existential Claims

A sentence makes an <u>existential claim</u> if it states that there is at least one individual that has a certain attribute. Examples of sentences of this sort are the following:

(5) A student is absent.

(6) There are sailors who do not eat fish.

(7) Some people who are in love are foolish.

Sentence (5) says that there is at least one individual that has the attribute of *being an absent student*. Sentence (6) says that there is at least one individual that has the attribute of *being a sailor who does not eat fish*. And sentence (7) says that there is at least one individual that has the attribute of *being a person who is in love and also foolish*. All of these sentences can be translated as sentences of the form $(\exists x)A$.

To translate (5) in a way that reveals that it makes an existential claim, rephrase it first as

$(\exists x)(x$ is an absent student)

To show more logical content, rephrase it as

$(\exists x)(x$ is absent & x is a student)

Notice how the second rewrite shows more logical content than the first. Using the second rewrite as a guide and '$F\_$' for '$\_$is absent' and '$G\_$' for '$\_$is a student', you can translate (5) as

$(\exists x)(Fx$ & $Gx)$

To show as much of the logical content of (6) as possible, rephrase it as

$(\exists x)(x$ is a sailor & ~$(x$ eats fish$))$

Then translate it as

$(\exists x)(Fx$ & ~$Gx)$

where '$F\_$' translates '$\_x$ is a sailor' and '$G\_$' translates '$\_$ eats fish'.

Once you become confident in translating, you can skip intermediate rewrites and, for example, translate (7) directly as

$(\exists x)((Fx$ & $Gx)$ & $Hx)$

where '$F\_$' translates '$\_$ is a person', '$G\_$' translates '$\_$ is in love', and '$H\_$' translates '$\_$ is foolish'. However, to avoid error, intermediate rewrites are always advisable whenever you find the task of translation particularly difficult.

Overlapping Quantifiers

According to the definition in section 6.1 (see p. 160), quantifiers overlap if one is within the scope of the other. If both quantifiers appear, one after the other, at the beginning of the sentence, and both are existential or both are universal, which quantifier occurs within the scope of the other makes no difference. Put another way, any two sentences are equivalent if together they have the joint form

$(\exists x)(\exists y)A$, $(\exists y)(\exists x)A$

or the joint form

$(\forall x)(\forall y)A$, $(\forall y)(\forall x)A$

In contrast, if the quantifiers are mixed, that is, one universal and the other existential, which one occurs within the scope of the other *does* matter. For example, consider the following sentences:

(1) Each thing has a cause.

(2) There is some thing that is a cause of all things.

Sentence (1) says that every individual has the attribute of *having a cause*. In contrast, sentence (2) says that there is at least one individual that has the attribute of *being a cause of all things*.

To translate (1), first paraphrase it as

$(\forall x)(x$ has a cause)

with the universal quantifier as the dominant operator. Then rewrite 'x has a cause' as

$(\exists y)(y$ is a cause of x)

to get

$(\forall x)(\exists y)(y$ is a cause of x)

Let '_ is a cause _' translate 'F_ _'. Then (1) translates as

(1′) $(\forall x)(\exists y)Fyx$.

As previously mentioned, when the quantifiers are both universal or both existential, the order makes no difference. When the quantifiers are mixed, as in the cases of (1) and (2) above, the order is important. When a universal claim is made, then the existential quantifier is within the scope of the universal quantifier. When an existential claim is made, then the universal quantifier is within the scope of the existential. Thus, to translate (2), which says that at least one thing is a cause of all things, rewrite it with an existential quantifier as the dominant operator:

$(\exists y)(y$ is a cause of all things)

Then translate with the universal quantifier to get

$(\exists y)(\forall x)(y$ is a cause of x)

Then eliminate the English expression to get

(2′) $(\exists y)(\forall x)Fyx$

Notice that in appearance (1′) is the same as (2′) except that the quantifiers are in reverse order.

The expansions of these Q-sentences for the domain $\{a, b\}$ (see section 6.3, pp. 186–190) illustrate how important the order of the quantifiers is to the meaning of the sentences. The first step in expanding (1′) for the domain {*a, b*} is to eliminate the quantifier that is the dominant operator. The result is

$$(\exists y)Fya \ \& \ (\exists y)Fyb$$

which says that something is a cause of *a* and that something is a cause of *b*. From this, the expansion is easily completed as follows:

$$(Faa \ v \ Fba) \ \& \ (Fab \ v \ Fbb)$$

This sentence says that either *a* or *b* is a cause of *a* and that either *a* or *b* is a cause of *b*.

In contrast, the initial step in the expansion of (2′) is

$$(\forall x)Fax \ v \ (\forall x)Fbx$$

which says that *a* is a cause of all things or *b* is a cause of all things. The completed expansion is

$$(Faa \ \& \ Fab) \ v \ (Fba \ \& \ Fbb)$$

[What does this expansion say? How does this differ in meaning from the expansion of (1′)?]

Identity

We use the identity sign '=' to translate claims that two individuals are the same individual. Such claims are made in English using proper names and what are commonly classified as definite descriptions. Generally speaking, a definite description is an expression of the form 'the so-and-so'. Examples of definite descriptions are 'the governor of New York', 'George Bush's mother', 'the king of England', 'the captain of the University of North Dakota baseball team'. A definite description is used to claim that two individuals are the same individual in the sentence

(1) The capital of Alabama is either Montgomery or Tuscaloosa

which translates as

$$(a = b) \ v \ (a = c)$$

where 'the capital of Alabama' translates '*a*', 'Montgomery' translates '*b*', and 'Tuscaloosa' translates '*c*'.

Some examples of other sentences that translate with the identity sign are the following:

(2) Edith is smarter than everyone (else) but Jon.

(3) Edith and only Edith is smarter than Jon.

(4) Edith is the smartest in the class.

Respective intermediary rewrites of (2)–(4) are

(2′) $(\forall x)((x$ is a person & $x \neq$ Edith & $x \neq$ Jon$) \rightarrow$ Edith is smarter than $x)$

(3′) Edith is smarter than Jon & $(\forall x)(x$ is smarter than Jon $\rightarrow x =$ Edith$)$

and

(4′) Edith is in the class & $(\forall x)((x$ is in the class & $x \neq$ Edith$) \rightarrow$ Edith is smarter than $x)$

Rewrite (2′) says that every individual has the attribute of *being such that Edith is smarter than it if it is a person and it is not Edith and it is not Jon.* Rewrite (3′) says that Edith is smarter than Jon and that every individual has the attribute of *being such that it is Edith if it is smarter than Jon.* And rewrite (4′) says that Edith is in the class and that every individual has the attribute of *being such that if it is in the class and it is not Edith, then Edith is smarter than it.*

Where '$F\_$' translates '$\_$ is a person', '$G\_ \_$' translates '$\_$ is smarter than $\_$', '$H\_$' translates '$\_$ is in the class', 'a' translates 'Edith', and 'b' translates 'Jon', (2)–(4) translate as follows:

(2″) $(\forall x)((Fx$ & $x \neq a$ & $x \neq b) \rightarrow Gax)$

(3″) Gab & $(\forall x)(Gxb \rightarrow x = a)$

(4″) Ha & $(\forall x)((Hx$ & $x \neq a) \rightarrow Gax)$

Note that, in these translations and hereafter, parentheses around identities are usually omitted as a simplification. We also omit parentheses among expressions separated by multiple ampersands, as in (2″), when which ampersand dominates is irrelevant to the meaning of the sentence. [Can you explain why '$F\_$' appears in (2″) but not in (3″) or (4″)? Can you simplify (2) after specifying that the domain is the class of people? If so, how? Simplify the translation of (4) by limiting the domain to the individuals in the class.]

EXERCISES FOR SECTION 7.1

1. Using predicate letters, give two different Q-translations of each of the following. Be sure to provide a translation scheme for each translation and specify the domain if it is not universal.

  *a. Pansy is sitting between Lily and Rose.
  b. Someone is sitting between Lily and Rose.
  *c. No one is sitting between Lily and Rose.

    d. Ann likes dancing more than Stephen does.

 *e. Some number plus 3 is 7 only if 7 minus 3 is equal to that number.

2. Showing as much content as possible, translate each English sentence below. Use the translation scheme provided.

> *a*: Platt
>
> *b*: Nancy
>
> *F_*: _ is an island dweller
>
> *G_*: _ eats fish
>
> *H_*: _ is a sailor
>
> *I_ _*: _ likes _

   a. All island dwellers eat fish.

 *b. If Platt is an island dweller, then he eats fish.

   c. All island dwellers eat fish but some are not sailors.

 *d. Some island dwellers are not sailors, but Nancy is.

   e. Neither Nancy nor Platt eats fish.

 *f. No sailor who is an island dweller eats fish.

 *g. Some island dwellers who are sailors do not eat fish.

   h. Any sailor who eats fish is an island dweller.

 *i. All sailors and island dwellers eat fish.

   j. Platt likes Nancy.

 *k. Nancy eats fish gladly.

   l. Platt is a good sailor.

 *m. Some sailors do not eat fish and some island dwellers do not eat fish.

   n. Nancy likes something and something likes Nancy.

 *o. Nancy likes nothing Platt likes.

   p. An island dweller likes Nancy.

 *q. Nancy likes a sailor.

   r. Every sailor likes Platt.

 *s. Every sailor who likes Nancy likes Platt.

   t. No sailor eats fish.

*3. Explain why 'All doctors and lawyers are professionals' should not be translated '$(\forall x)((Fx \,\&\, Gx) \rightarrow Hx)$' with '*F_*' as the translation for '_ is a doctor', '*G_*' as the translation for '_is a lawyer', and '*H_*' as the translation for '_ is a professional'.

4. Using the translation scheme in exercise 2 above, translate the English sentences below. Show as much content as possible.

 *a. Every sailor likes something (or other).

   b. Some sailors like everything.

 *c. Nancy likes nothing but herself.

   d. Nancy is the only sailor Platt likes.

*e. Nancy is the only sailor Platt does not like.
 f. Only Platt likes Nancy.
*g. If no sailor likes Nancy, then Nancy does not like herself.
 h. Nancy likes Platt only if Platt is Nancy.
*i. Just Platt and Nancy eat fish.
 j. If Platt likes anyone he likes Nancy. (In translating this sentence, limit the domain to people.)

7.2 TRANSLATING ENGLISH

Translating English into Q, just like translating English into any other language, is not a mechanical affair. To translate well, you must understand both languages. In this section, we discuss some of the difficulties presented by the English idiom and some of the limitations of Q.

Translating Adjectives

Some adjectives have a meaning independent of the noun they modify, but others do not. Others, when applied to a noun, can change the meaning of the noun. Before translating, you must know with which kind of adjective you are dealing, especially if you intend to display maximal content.

For example, the adjective 'cultured' (meaning obtained through cultivation, not simply through nature) in sentence (1) below has its meaning independently of the noun with which it is used. Thus the sentence

> **(1)** This object is a cultured pearl

has the same meaning as

> **(2)** This object is cultured and is a pearl.

Therefore, in translating (1), the adjective 'cultured' can be separated from the noun and (1) translated as

> *Fa & Ga*

where '*a*' translates 'this object', '*F_*' translates '_ is cultured', and '*G_*' translates '_ is a pearl'.

Now consider the following sentence:

> **(3)** This object is a large pearl.

To say that something is large is to say that it is large relative to other things of a certain kind. Thus, unlike 'cultured' in sentence (1), the adjective 'large' cannot be split away from the noun it modifies in sentence (3) and translated independently.

An example of an adjective that can change the meaning of the noun to which it is applied is the adjective 'artificial'. This is what it does in the sentence

(4) This object is an artificial pearl.

In translating, the adjective 'artificial' can be separated from the noun 'pearl' only if (4) is equivalent to

(5) This object is artificial and is a pearl.

But (5) is contradictory, as, by definition, no pearl is artificial. Therefore, although you can translate 'This object is a cultured pearl' as we did above, you cannot translate either 'This object is a large pearl' or 'This object is an artificial pearl' in that way.

Translating 'Any', 'Every', and 'All'

The following are examples of sentences in which the English quantifiers 'any', 'every', and 'all' serve essentially the same purpose.

(1) I know anything Harriet knows.

(2) I know everything Harriet knows.

(3) I know all Harriet knows.

All three rephrase as

$$(\forall x)(\text{Harriet knows } x \rightarrow \text{I know } x)$$

and translate as

$$(\forall x)(Fx \rightarrow Gx)$$

where '$F\_$' translates 'Harriet knows _' and '$G\_$' translates 'I know _'.

Now insert 'do not' between 'I' and 'know' in the sentences above. You will get the following:

(4) I do not know anything Harriet knows.

(5) I do not know everything that Harriet knows.

(6) I do not know all Harriet knows.

These three sentences do not all have the same translation. The translation of (4) is

$$(\forall x)(Fx \rightarrow \sim Gx)$$

while the translation of (5) and (6) is

$$\sim(\forall x)(Fx \rightarrow Gx)$$

Notice that in the translation of (4), the tilde is within the scope of the universal quantifier. In contrast, in the translation of (5) and (6), the reverse is true. In other words, in the translation of the *any*-sentence, the universal quantifier is the dominant operator. But the tilde dominates in the translation of the *every*- and *all*-sentences.

When 'any', 'every', and 'all' are used with conditional expressions such as 'if . . . then', the situation is analogous. For example, the sentences

(7) If any book is read, I will be surprised,

(8) If every book is read, I will be surprised,

and

(9) If all books are read, I will be surprised

are virtually identical in outward appearance except for their respectives uses of 'any', 'every', and 'all'. Yet, when '*F_*' translates '_ is a book', '*G_*' translates '_ is read', '*H_*' translates '_ will be surprised', and '*a*' translates 'I', the *any*-sentence translates as

$$(\forall x)((Fx \ \& \ Gx) \rightarrow Ha)$$

and the *every*- and *all*-sentences translate as

$$(\forall x)(Fx \rightarrow Gx) \rightarrow Ha$$

Notice how, in the translation of the *any*-sentence, the arrow is within the scope of the universal quantifier. In contrast, in the translation of the other two, the universal quantifier is within the scope of the arrow.

Because (7) says the same thing as

(10) If some book is read, I will be surprised,

(10) translates as

$$(\forall x)((Fx \ \& \ Gx) \rightarrow Ha)$$

But (10) also translates as

$$(\exists x)(Fx \ \& \ Gx) \rightarrow Ha$$

Both translations are equivalent.

Unlike (10), the sentence

(11) If some book is read, I will read it

does not translate as a conditional with an existential antecedent. Let '*F_*' translate '_ is a book', '*G _*' translate '_ is read', '*H_ _*' translate '_ will read _', and '*a*' translate 'I', and then (11) translates as

(6) All the plums in the bowl are delicious.

Some translate as Q-sentences about their members and some do not. [Which of these sentences about collections do you think translate properly as sentences about their members? And which do not? Try to explain your answers.]

Just as collections have members, types have instances. But a collection cannot exist without its members, while a type is an individual in its own right. Examples of types are: the Greek alphabet (a type of alphabet), the first letter of the Greek alphabet (a type of letter of a type of alphabet), chartreuse (a color type), and the platypus (a type of mammal). An instance of the Greek alphabet is any written or spoken record of it. The following is an instance of its first letter: α. Erase this instance and every other instance of it and the type still exists. Similarly, you yourself are an instance of a type called *the human being*.

Some sentences about types translate as sentences about their instances, and others do not. For example, (7) and (8) below do, but (9) and (10) do not.

(7) The platypus is a mammal.

(8) The universal Q-sentence contains the sign '∀'.

(9) The Greek alphabet is difficult to remember.

(10) Chartreuse is my favorite color.

Translations of sentences about types as sentences about their instances are weaker than the English sentences they translate. To understand why, note that (7) translates as

(7′) $(\forall x)(Fx \rightarrow Gx)$

with '*F_*' translating '_ is a platypus' and '*G_*' translating '_ is a mammal'. Sentence (7′) says that whatever is a platypus is also a mammal. But sentence (7) says that whatever is a platypus must be a mammal. Sentence (7′) does not capture the modal necessity in sentence (7). Thus (7′) is weaker than (7).

There are formal languages logicians have developed for the purpose of expressing modalities of necessity, possibility, and so forth. For example, in such a language, (7) translates as

(7″) $\Box(\forall x)(Fx \rightarrow Gx)$

with '□' read 'necessarily' or as 'it is necessarily the case that'. Although of great interest, modal logics are beyond the scope of this text.

Numerical Quantifiers

The identity sign is useful in translating English sentences that assert that at least, at most, or exactly n individuals have a certain attribute, where $n \geq 1$. Examples of "at least" sentences are the following:

(1) I have at least one friend.

(2) I have at least two friends.

(3) I have at least three friends.

If '$F\_$' translates '$\_$ is my friend', (1) through (3) translate as shown below, with unnecessary parentheses omitted.

(1′) $(\exists x)Fx$

(2′) $(\exists x)(\exists y)(Fx \ \& \ Fy \ \& \ x \neq y)$

(3′) $(\exists x)(\exists y)(\exists z)(Fx \ \& \ Fy \ \& \ Fz \ \& \ x \neq y \ \& \ x \neq z \ \& \ y \neq z)$

Sentence (1′) says there is at least one individual who is my friend. Sentence (2′) says that there are at least two individuals who are my friends and that those individuals are not the same. And sentence (3′) says the same thing, but of three individuals instead of two. From these translations, it is not difficult to see how to translate the phrase 'at least four', and so on.

Examples of sentences of the type asserting that there are at most n individuals are

(4) I have at most one friend

and

(5) I have at most two friends.

Note that, although both (4) and (5) set an upper limit, neither sets a lower limit on the number of friends I have. In other words, both could be true even if I had no friends whatsoever. To capture this meaning, translate (4) and (5), under the same translation scheme used above, as follows:

(4′) $(\forall x)(\forall y)((Fx \ \& \ Fy) \rightarrow x = y)$

(5′) $(\forall x)(\forall y)(\forall z)((Fx \ \& \ Fy \ \& \ Fz) \rightarrow (x = y \ \text{v} \ x = z \ \text{v} \ y = z))$

Notice that there are two ampersands and two *vels* in (5′). Parentheses may be omitted among expressions separated by multiple *vels*, just as among expressions separated by multiple ampersands, when the truth values of the sentence is not affected by which *vel* dominates.

The translation of (4) says that if two individuals (possibly the same individual) are my friends, then they are the same individual. In an analogous fashion, the translation of (5) says that if three individuals (possibly the same individual) are my friends, then at least two of them are the same individual. The translation for 'at most three' would say that if four individuals are my friends, then at least two of them are the same individual. From these examples, you can see how to translate 'at most four', and so on.

Examples of sentences asserting that there are exactly n individuals having a certain attribute are the following:

> **(6)** I have exactly one friend.

> **(7)** I have exactly two friends.

To translate (6), form a conjunction of (1') with (4'), or translate it more compactly as

> **(6′)** $(\exists x)(Fx \ \& \ (\forall y)(Fy \rightarrow x = y))$

Sentence (6′) says that there is an individual who is my friend and any other individual who is my friend is the same individual.

To translate (7), form a conjunction of (2') and (5'). An alternative and more succinct translation is

> **(7′)** $(\exists x)(\exists y)(Fx \ \& \ Fy \ \& \ x \neq y \ \& \ (\forall z)(Fz \rightarrow (z = x \ \text{v} \ z = y)))$

This says that there are two nonidentical individuals who are my friends and any individual who is my friend is identical to one of them. You can translate 'exactly three', and so on, analogously.

Definite Descriptions

There are various ways of translating definite descriptions. Translating with a singular term, a universal sentence, or an existential one are the usual options. Which way is more appropriate in any one case depends on how the definite description is used and the objective of the translation.

For example,

> **(1)** The person who can speak 50 languages is remarkable

can be translated as

> *Fa*

This translation is appropriate if (1) is being used to designate a unique individual who can speak 50 languages and to characterize him or her as a remarkable person. In this case, a singular term translates the definite description.

If (1) means that any instance of this type of person is remarkable and not that there is one, (1) translates better as

> $(\forall x)(Fx \rightarrow Gx)$

with '*F*_' having the same meaning as '_ is a person who can speak 50 languages' and '*G*_' having the same meaning as '_ is a remarkable person'. But if (1) is not used to designate an individual but simply to claim that there is exactly one individual who speaks 50 languages and that individual is a remarkable person, then the translation should be

$$(\exists x)(Fx \ \& \ (\forall y)(Fy \rightarrow x = y) \ \& \ Gx)$$

Plural Nouns and Implicit Existence Claims

Whether a universal claim is made using a singular or a plural noun usually makes no difference. For example, consider the following sentences:

(1) Every student is eager to learn.

(2) No student is interested.

(3) Tigers, but not elephants, are carnivorous.

(4) All doctors and lawyers are professionals.

If you replace 'every student is' with 'all students are' in (1), you get

(5) All students are eager to learn,

a sentence that says the same thing as (1). In a similar way, if you replace 'tigers' with 'a tiger' and 'elephants' with 'an elephant' in (3), you have

(6) A tiger, but not an elephant, is carnivorous.

Sentence (6) is equivalent to (3). Now replace 'no student is' with 'no students are' in (2); what you get is the equivalent sentence

(7) No students are interested.

With existential sentences, however, the situation is different. For example, consider the following sentences:

(8) Some student is absent.

(9) There are sailors who do not eat fish.

(10) Some people who are in love are foolish.

(11) Most immigrants are eager to become citizens.

(12) Several leaders resigned.

(13) Many sailors are island dwellers.

If 'some students are' replaces 'some student is' in (8), the result is

(14) Some students are absent.

Depending on context, this can mean that at least two students are absent. Therefore, the new sentence may be stronger than the original rather than equivalent to it. And, instead of translating 'Some students are absent' as

$$(\exists x)(Fx \ \& \ Gx)$$

you may want to translate it as

$$(\exists x)(\exists y)(x \neq y \ \& \ Fx \ \& \ Fy \ \& \ Gx \ \& \ Gy)$$

This says that there are at least two different individuals, both students and both absent.

The second translation may come closer to the meaning of 'Some students are absent' than the first. But, for the purposes of analysis, the first translation may be strong enough. Furthermore, in translating English sentences such as (9) and (10), specifying that at least two individuals have a certain attribute, rather than at least one, may be pointless unless the number of sailors or people in love is small. The sentences (11), (12), and (13) contain the phrases 'most immigrants', 'several leaders', and 'many sailors'. From what you now know, you can see that there is no way of providing equivalent Q-translations for these sentences. Although one can translate them specifying only that at least one individual is thus-and-so, such translations may be too weak to be of much use.

Standard quantification theory dictates that

$$(\forall x)(Fx \rightarrow Gx)$$

is implied by

$$\sim(\exists x)Fx$$

but not that it implies

$$(\exists x)Fx$$

However, many ordinary English sentences that make universal claims also make an implicit claim that there is an individual of the kind the sentence is about. For example,

(15) All Pamela's children are at camp

would normally be understood as true only if Pamela had children. With this understanding, to get an equivalent translation of (15), you need to rephrase it as

$(\forall x)(x$ is a child of Pamela $\rightarrow x$ is at camp) $\& \ (\exists x)(x$ is a child of Pamela)

and then translate it as

$$(\forall x)(Fx \rightarrow Gx) \ \& \ (\exists x)Fx$$

with '*F_*' translating '_ is a child of Pamela' and '*G_*' translating '_ is at camp'. But, as we already noted in discussing plural nouns, a stronger, more complex translation may not be required for the problem of analysis at hand.

Whether a sentence that makes a universal claim translates equivalently with the addition of an existential claim depends upon context and idiom. An example of a sentence that makes no existential claim and, thus, translates equivalently simply as a Q-universal is

(16) Any trespasser will be prosecuted.

Clearly, its truth does not depend upon there being a trespasser. Indeed, under ordinary circumstances, anyone making such a declaration hopes that there are none and that there never will be any.

EXERCISES FOR SECTION 7.2

1. For each of the following English sentences, give an equivalent or weaker translation. Use the translation scheme below.

    a: Mr. Parker

    *F_*: _ is a person

    *G_*: _ will attend

    *H_*: _ is a candidate

    *I_*: _ is a Democrat

    a. Everyone who is a candidate will attend.
    *b. If anyone attends, Mr. Parker will.
    *c. If everyone attends, Mr. Parker will.
    d. Not all candidates will attend.
    *e. Not any candidates will attend.
    *f. Only candidates will attend.
    g. All and only candidates will attend.
    *h. Only Democratic candidates are attending.
    i. Only Democrats who are attending are candidates.
    *j. The only Democrats attending are candidates.
    k. If someone attends, Mr. Parker will.
    *l. If someone attends, he or she is a candidate.
    m. Each person who attends is a Democratic candidate.
    *n. No one will attend unless he or she is a candidate.
    o. Some candidates will attend and some will not.
    *p. All the Democrats who are attending are candidates.
    *q. Only the Democrats who are attending are candidates.
    *r. All the Democratic candidates are attending.

2. Translate each of the following English sentences. Use the identity sign where suitable and the singular terms and predicate letters given in parentheses.

   *a. Mr. Trump is the richest man in Manhattan ($a, F\_, G\_, H\_ \_$).
   *b. There is a woman who lives in Manhattan who is richer than Mrs. Astor ($c, F\_, G\_, H\_ \_$).
   c. Everyone except Bozo laughs at Bozo ($b, F\_, G\_ \_$).
   *d. Only Bozo laughs at Bozo ($b, G\_ \_$).
   e. Not only Bozo laughs at Bozo ($b, G\_ \_$).
   *f. John loves no one but Mary ($a, b, F\_, G\_ \_$).
   g. Mrs. Astor lives in Manhattan, but she is not the richest woman in Manhattan ($c, F\_, G\_, H\_ \_$).

3. Using the translation scheme below, translate each of the following English sentences.

   $F\_$: _ is a brother of Abby

   $G\_$: _ is a sister of Abby

   *a. Abby has at least two brothers.
   b. Abby has at most one brother.
   c. Abby has at least one brother or sister.
   *d. Abby has exactly two siblings.
   *e. Abby has at most two sisters.

4. Translate each of the following English sentences. Simplify your translation scheme by assuming that the domain is restricted to human beings.

   *a. Everyone likes everyone.
   b. Everyone likes someone or other.
   *c. Everyone likes everyone else.
   d. Everyone likes oneself.
   *e. Someone likes someone.
   f. Someone is liked by no one.
   *g. Someone likes everyone.
   h. Someone does not like anyone.
   *i. Someone does not like everyone.

5. Translate again the sentences in exercise 4 without limiting the domain.

6. Using the translation scheme below, translate each of the following English sentences.

   $F\_$: _ is a friend of mine

   $G\_$: _ is fair-minded

   *a. All my friends are fair-minded.
   b. A friend of mine by definition is fair-minded.

*c. Any individual who is a friend of mine is fair-minded.
 d. A friend of mine who is not fair-minded is not my friend.
*e. Every fair-minded individual is my friend.
 f. My friends are fair-minded.
*g. Each friend of mine is fair-minded.

7. Translate each of the following sentences, and, using Q, determine whether each is valid, contradictory, or neither.

 a. Everything is self-identical.
*b. Nothing is self-identical.
 c. Not everything is self-identical.
*d. Something is self-identical.
 e. Something is identical to something.
*f. Something is not identical to something.
 g. Either everything is round and everything is a square or not everything is a round square.
*h. If something is red, then it is not true that something is red or black.
 i. If everything is a cabbage or a king, then everything is a king.
*j. If some woman attends, no man will.
 k. No golden mountain is golden.
*l. If everything is a dinosaur, then something is not.
 m. Everyone is coming but John is not.
*n. Someone is coming but John is not.
 o. If no one but John is coming, then no one is.
*p. Something caused everything but not everything is caused by something or other.
 q. Everything is caused by something or other but some one thing did not cause everything.

8. With the intention of using the translations to detect incompatible lists of sentences, translate the following. Add valid sentences when appropriate.

*a. Every even number is in the set. Twelve is not an odd number. Every number is odd or even. Twelve is not in the set.
 b. All columnists are men or all reporters are women. Some reporters are women and so are some men.
*c. All columnists are men and all reporters are women. But some female reporters are columnists.
 d. All of Hans's daughters are beautiful. Only one is married. The one who is married has a daughter. Unfortunately, Hans has no granddaughters.
*e. If Jack comes, I shall not be surprised. I shall be surprised only if somebody comes or nobody does.

9. With the intention of identifying those that are valid, translate the following arguments into Q. Add valid or unstated premises when appropriate. Do not assume all arguments are valid.

   a. The interests of the state are the same as the interests of its citizens. The interests of General Motors are the same as the interests of its citizens. Therefore, the interests of the state are the same as the interests of General Motors.

   *b. Everything is identical to itself. Therefore, everything is identical to everything.

   *c. There are exactly two Nobel Prize winners at the wedding reception. I will photograph one and so will Harold. So, every Nobel Prize winner at the wedding reception will be photographed by either Harold or myself.

   *d. Sebastian gave the *I Ching* to Rachel. Rachel has returned every book that anyone has given her. Therefore, Rachel returned the *I Ching* to Sebastian.

   *e. One person at the party was spoken to by everybody at the party. Therefore, everybody at the party was spoken to by somebody who was at the party.

COPI-STYLE INFERENCE RULES

Like truth tables, derivations can be used to detect semantic properties of sentences and arguments. But, unlike truth tables, derivations are carried out on the basis of rules of inference written in terms of syntactic rather than semantic features of the language, in other words, in terms of the structure of the language rather than the meaning of the connectives.

The rules of inference presented in this chapter are similar to, though not exactly the same as, those used by Irving M. Copi in his popular text *Introduction to Logic*. They differ in important respects from the introduction and elimination rules presented in Part III of this text. Studying this chapter before the chapters in Part III is recommended for students who have had no previous introduction to derivations. For those that have had an introduction, this chapter can be omitted.

8.1 INFERENCE RULES FOR C

For the language C, the derivation method could be set out as an algorithm consisting of mechanical procedures, telling you how to arrive at the correct answer in a finite number of steps. However, instead of having you learn another mechanical method (the truth table method is one you already know), we emphasize intelligent use of rules of inference. This approach is more engaging and usually more efficient.

Derivations

A <u>derivation</u>, sometimes referred to also as a "deduction" or "proof," is a sequence of sentences, some of which are hypotheses and the others of which are each sanctioned by an application of a rule of inference. <u>Rules of inference</u> are constructed to allow you to take steps from the hypotheses to the conclusion. The last sentence in a derivation is the <u>conclusion</u>. With a proper set of rules, the conclusion of a derivation can be either true or false if a hypothesis is false. But, with a proper set of rules, the conclusion can never be false if all the hypotheses are true.

The following is an example of a derivation.

1	$(P \vee Q) \rightarrow \sim R$	Hyp
2	P	Hyp
3	$P \vee Q$	2, Add
4	$\sim R$	1, 3, MP (Conclusion)

Note how each step is numbered to the left and justified on the right. 'Hyp', as an abbreviation for 'Hypothesis', is written as the justification for steps 1 and 2. Written to the right of step 3, '2, Add' records that step 3 is sanctioned by application of one of the rules of inference to step 2. This rule allows you to write a disjunction as a step in any derivation if one of its disjuncts is a preceding step, though not necessarily an immediately preceding step. '1, 3, MP' appears to the right of step 4 to indicate that it results from applying another rule of inference to steps 1 and 3. According to this other rule, you can write the consequent of a conditional as a step in a derivation if the conditional and its antecedent are preceding steps.

Derivations show how to move from hypotheses to conclusion in a step-by-step fashion. Each step is taken through application of a rule of inference. A correct rule of inference can never lead from truth to falsity. Therefore, the conclusion must be true if the hypotheses are. So, when you list the premises of an argument as the hypotheses of a derivation and derive the argument's conclusion, you can rest assured that the argument is valid. The derivation displayed above establishes the validity of the following argument:

$$((P \vee Q) \rightarrow \sim R), P \therefore \sim R$$

Observe how the premises of the argument are the derivation's hypotheses and the conclusion of the argument is the conclusion of the derivation.

To see how this derivation relates to an English translation, let '*P*' have the same meaning as 'Pat is employed as a financial analyst', '*Q*' have the same meaning as 'Pat is employed as a CIA agent', and '*R*' have the same meaning as 'Pat will be bored'. Then the steps in the derivation have the same meaning as the following English sentences.

1   If Pat is employed as either a financial analyst or a CIA agent, then Pat will not be bored.
2   Pat is employed as a financial analyst.
3   Pat is employed as either a financial analyst or a CIA agent.
4   Pat will not be bored.

One-Way Rules

As illustrated in the derivation above, your applying a rule of inference to a preceding step or steps allows you to write a new step in a derivation. Because of the way in which these rules are written, no rule allows you to enter a false sentence in a derivation when the sentence or sentences to which the rule is applied are true. The following are rules of inference. All are <u>one-way rules</u> in contrast to the <u>two-way rules</u> presented in the next section. The abbreviation for the name of each rule is placed in parentheses after the name.

Modus Ponens (MP).   The rule of *modus ponens* allows you to write the consequent of a conditional as a step in a derivation if the conditional and its antecedent are preceding steps.

This rule is expressed schematically as follows:

$$
\begin{array}{lll}
i & A & \\
j & A \rightarrow B & \\
k & B & \text{i, j, MP}
\end{array}
$$

with i, j, and k representing the numbering in a sequence of steps, where $i \geq 1$ and $i < j < k$. The scheme tells you that in any sequence of sentences of this form step k is justified by application to steps i and j of the rule of *modus ponens*. The abbreviated name of the rule of *modus ponens* is 'MP'. Although in this schematic expression of the rule, the conditional is preceded by its antecedent, their order is not important. For example, when the rule of *modus ponens* is applied in the sample derivation on page 220 to get step 4 from steps

1 and 3, the conditional $((P \vee Q) \rightarrow \sim R)$ is step 1 and the antecedent $(P \vee Q)$ of the conditional is step 3.

Addition (Add).   The rule of addition allows you to write a disjunction as a step in a derivation if either the right or left disjunct is a preceding step.

The schematic expression of this rule is as follows:

i	A			i	B	
j	$A \vee B$	i, Add		j	$A \vee B$	i, Add

Note that there are two schemes, one for the case in which the left disjunct is the preceding step and the other for the case in which the right disjunct is. In the sample derivation above, the rule of addition was applied to step 2 to get step 3.

Simplification (Simp).   The rule of simplification allows you to write either the left or right conjunct of a conjunction as a step in a derivation if the conjunction is a preceding step.

Schematically expressed, the rule is as follows:

i	$A \& B$			i	$A \& B$	
j	A	i, Simp		j	B	i, Simp

[Note that there are two schemes. Can you explain why?]

Conjunction (Conj).   The rule of conjunction allows you to write a conjunction as a step in a derivation if both its right and left conjuncts are preceding steps.

[As an exercise, provide your own schematic expression of this rule, using those given for the preceding rules as your guide.]

Modus Tollens (MT).   The rule of *modus tollens* allows you to write the negation of the antecedent of a conditional as a step in a derivation if the conditional and the denial of its consequent are preceding steps. We count a sentence and its negation as denials of one another.

This rule is expressed schematically as follows:

i	$A \rightarrow B$			i	$A \rightarrow \sim B$	
j	$\sim B$			j	B	
k	$\sim A$	i, j, MT		k	$\sim A$	i, j, MT

Disjunctive Syllogism (DS).   The rule of disjunctive syllogism allows you to write as a step in a derivation the left disjunct of a disjunction if the disjunction and the denial of its right disjunct are preceding steps. This rule also allows you to write as a step in a derivation the right disjunct of a disjunction if the disjunction and the denial of its left disjunct are preceding steps.

The second part of this rule is expressed schematically as follows:

i	$A \vee B$		i	$\sim A \vee B$	
j	$\sim A$		j	A	
k	B	i, j, DS	k	B	i, j, DS

[As an exercise, provide a schematic expression of the first part of the rule.]

A derivation using both the rule of *modus tollens* and the rule of disjunctive syllogism is the following:

1	$\sim P \vee (Q \,\&\, S)$	Hyp
2	$R \rightarrow (Q \,\&\, S)$	Hyp
3	$\sim(Q \,\&\, S)$	Hyp
4	$\sim P$	1, 3, DS
5	$\sim R$	2, 3, MT
6	$\sim P \,\&\, \sim R$	4, 5, Conj

Now compare the steps in this derivation and the steps in the list of English sentences below.

1. Pat will not join the Philosophy Club unless both Quincy and Sally do.
2. Rachel will join only if both Quincy and Sally do.
3. Quincy and Sally will not both join.
4. Pat will not join.
5. Rachel will not join.
6. Pat will not join and Rachel will not join.

[Do you see a relationship between the derivation and the list of English sentences? If so, explain what it is.]

In addition to those above, there are three other one-way rules. These three rules, which follow, are difficult to state using just English. So, we only express them schematically.

Hypothetical Syllogism (HS).   The rule of hypothetical syllogism is stated schematically as follows:

$$
\begin{array}{ll}
\text{i} & A \rightarrow B \\
\text{j} & B \rightarrow C \\
\text{k} & A \rightarrow C \qquad\qquad \text{i, j, HS}
\end{array}
$$

The scheme tells you that given any sequence of sentences having this form, step k is justified by application to i and j of the rule of hypothetical syllogism. Where step j precedes step i, the rule also applies. What is essential is that steps i and j precede step k in the derivation.

Constructive Dilemma (CD).   The rule of constructive dilemma is stated schematically as follows:

$$
\begin{array}{ll}
\text{i} & A \rightarrow C \\
\text{j} & B \rightarrow C \\
\text{k} & (A \vee B) \rightarrow C \qquad\qquad \text{i, j, CD}
\end{array}
$$

The scheme tells you that given any sequence of sentences having this form, step k is justified by application of the rule of constructive dilemma to i and j. Where step j precedes step i, the rule also applies.

Destructive Dilemma (DD).   The rule of destructive dilemma is expressed schematically as follows:

$$
\begin{array}{ll}
\text{i} & (A \rightarrow B) \,\&\, (C \rightarrow D) \\
\text{j} & {\sim}B \vee {\sim}D \\
\text{k} & {\sim}A \vee {\sim}C \qquad\qquad \text{i, j, DD}
\end{array}
$$

The scheme tells you that given any sequence of sentences having this form, step k is justified by citing steps i and j and the rule of destructive dilemma as indicated. As with the preceding rules, the order of the steps to which the rule is applied is irrelevant.

The following is an example of a derivation using the rule of constructive dilemma.

$$
\begin{array}{lll}
1 & Q \rightarrow {\sim}R & \text{Hyp} \\
2 & P \rightarrow {\sim}R & \text{Hyp} \\
3 & P \vee Q & \text{Hyp} \\
4 & (P \vee Q) \rightarrow {\sim}R & \text{1, 2, CD} \\
5 & {\sim}R & \text{3, 4, MP} \\
6 & (P \vee Q) \,\&\, {\sim}R & \text{3, 5, Conj}
\end{array}
$$

Steps 1, 2, and 3 are hypotheses; step 4 is justified by the rule of constructive dilemma as applied to steps 1 and 2; step 5 is justified by *modus ponens* as applied to steps 3 and 4; step 6 is justified by the rule of conjunction as applied to steps 3 and 5. [To see how this derivation relates to English, keep the initial meanings for '*P*', '*Q*', and '*R*' that were given for the first sample derivation. Then write out English sentences corresponding to each sentence in the derivation.]

Another sample derivation is

1	$(P \rightarrow Q) \& (R \rightarrow S)$	Hyp
2	$\sim Q$	Hyp
3	$\sim Q \lor \sim S$	2, Add
4	$\sim P \lor \sim R$	1, 3, DD

The derivation establishes that the following argument is valid.

$$((P \rightarrow Q) \& (R \rightarrow S)), \sim Q \; / \therefore \; (\sim P \lor \sim R)$$

The rules of inference presented above are either <u>one-premise rules</u> or <u>two-premise rules</u>. For example, the rules of addition and simplification are one-premise rules. That is, they are rules that apply to one and only one preceding step in a derivation. The other rules of inference are two-premise rules because each applies to two and only two preceding steps in a derivation.

To apply a one-premise rule to two preceding sentences is an error. For example, the justification for step 3 in the following derivation could be either '1, Add' or '2, Add'. But '1, 2, Add' is a mistake.

1	Q	Hyp
2	R	Hyp
3	$Q \lor R$	1, 2, Add (Wrong!)

It is also an error to apply a two-premise rule to only a single sentence as below.

1	$P \rightarrow (Q \rightarrow R)$	Hyp
2	$Q \rightarrow R$	1, MP (Wrong!)
3	R	2, MP (Wrong!)

Remember that *modus ponens* is a two-premise rule that can be applied to only two preceding steps; one step must be a conditional and the other must be its antecedent.

The following is another example of a way in which a rule may be misapplied.

1	$\sim(P \& \sim Q)$	Hyp
2	P	1, Simp (Wrong!)

Like all of the one-way rules, the rule of simplification applies only to entire sentences. It is never permissible for a one-way rule to apply to less than the entire sentence that is a step in a derivation. Thus, although the immediate component of step 1 is $(P \& {\sim}Q)$, the entire sentence is ${\sim}(P \& {\sim}Q)$. Therefore, the rule of simplification cannot be applied to $(P \& {\sim}Q)$ because $(P \& {\sim}Q)$ is not the entire sentence, and the rule cannot be applied to ${\sim}(P \& {\sim}Q)$ because ${\sim}(P \& {\sim}Q)$ is a negation and not a conjunction.

The following is an example of the same kind of mistake.

1	$P \rightarrow (Q \vee R)$	Hyp
2	P	Hyp
3	${\sim}Q$	Hyp
4	R	1, 3, DS (Wrong!)

No one-way rule can apply to part of a step. So the attempt to apply the rule of disjunctive syllogism to steps 1 and 3 is wrong. $(Q \vee R)$ is merely the consequent of the conditional that is step 1; $(Q \vee R)$ is *not* step 1.

You can reach the desired conclusion from the same hypotheses through correct applications of the rules as follows:

1	$P \rightarrow (Q \vee R)$	Hyp
2	P	Hyp
3	${\sim}Q$	Hyp
4	$Q \vee R$	1, 2, MP
5	R	3, 4, DS

Notice how in this derivation the rule of disjunctive syllogism is applied to $(Q \vee R)$ where it appears on a line of its own as step 4 and not to where it appears as a component of step 1.

For other examples of derivations, read ahead in the text or look at the solutions to exercises for this section. Partial solutions appear at the end of the text. Studying these solutions will help you understand how to construct derivations of your own.

Two-Way Rules

In addition to the one-way rules of inference listed above, there are also two-way rules. Application of a two-way rule always results in an equivalent step. However, the resulting step is justified not by its equivalence but by its conforming with a two-way rule. For example, the following sequence of steps is a derivation:

> 1 $\sim\sim P \vee R$ Hyp
> 2 $\sim P \to R$ 1, Con Exch

Step 2 is justified not because it is equivalent to step 1 but because step 1 and step 2 as a pair exemplify the pair of forms

$$(A \to B) \qquad (\sim A \vee B)$$

We express the two-way rules schematically by pairs of sentence forms written side by side as follows. A new symbol ': :' appears between the forms in each pair.

Association (Assoc)

$$(A \vee (B \vee C)) \; :: \; ((A \vee B) \vee C)$$

$$(A \;\&\; (B \;\&\; C)) \; :: \; ((A \;\&\; B) \;\&\; C)$$

Commutation (Com)

$$(A \vee B) \; :: \; (B \vee A)$$

$$(A \;\&\; B) \; :: \; (B \;\&\; A)$$

Conditional Exchange (Con Exch)

$$(A \to B) \; :: \; (\sim A \vee B)$$

$$(A \to B) \; :: \; \sim(A \;\&\; \sim B)$$

Contraposition (Contra)

$$(A \to B) \; :: \; (\sim B \to \sim A)$$

De Morgan's Law (DeM)

$$\sim(A \;\&\; B) \; :: \; (\sim A \vee \sim B)$$

$$\sim(A \vee B) \; :: \; (\sim A \;\&\; \sim B)$$

Double Negation (DN)

$$\sim\sim A \; :: \; A$$

Exportation (Exp)

$$((A \;\&\; B) \to C) \; :: \; (A \to (B \to C))$$

Tautology (Taut)

$$A \ :: \ (A \text{ v } A)$$

$$A \ :: \ (A \ \& \ A)$$

Distribution (Dist)

$$(A \ \& \ (B \text{ v } C)) \ :: \ ((A \ \& \ B) \text{ v } (A \ \& \ C))$$

$$(A \text{ v } (B \ \& \ C)) \ :: \ ((A \text{ v } B) \ \& \ (A \text{ v } C))$$

In a two-way rule for C, the symbol ': :' appearing between a pair of forms indicates the following: When a pair of sentences exemplifies that pair of forms and one of the pair of sentences is a preceding step or *a component of a preceding step* in a derivation, the rule allows you to repeat the step in the derivation with the other member of the pair of sentences in place of the original. The new step is justified by mentioning the number of the preceding step and the appropriate rule.

Unlike one-way rules, all two-way rules work in both directions (hence the "two-way" appellation). For example, as previously stated, the following sequence of steps is a derivation:

$$
\begin{array}{lll}
1 & \sim\sim P \text{ v } R & \text{Hyp} \\
2 & \sim P \rightarrow R & \text{1, Con Exch}
\end{array}
$$

Because step 1 and step 2 as a pair exemplify the first pair of forms in the rule of conditional exchange, step 2 is justified correctly by citing step 1 and the rule of conditional exchange. Because the rule of conditional exchange works in both directions, the justification for the following derivation is exactly the same as the previous one even though the conclusion and the hypothesis of the previous derivation have been interchanged.

$$
\begin{array}{lll}
1 & \sim P \rightarrow R & \text{Hyp} \\
2 & \sim\sim P \text{ v } R & \text{1, Con Exch}
\end{array}
$$

In applying a two-way rule, you must be careful that you follow the rule precisely. Although in the following sequence step 2 is equivalent to step 1, the sequence is not a derivation.

$$
\begin{array}{lll}
1 & P \text{ v } R & \text{Hyp} \\
2 & \sim P \rightarrow R & \text{1, Con Exch (Wrong!)}
\end{array}
$$

It is not a derivation because the pair of sentences

$$(\sim P \rightarrow R) \qquad (P \text{ v } R)$$

does not exemplify either of the pairs of forms

$$(A \rightarrow B) \qquad (\sim A \text{ v } B)$$

and

$$(A \rightarrow B) \qquad \sim(A \text{ \& } \sim B)$$

To convince yourself of this, replace '*A*' with '$\sim P$' and '*B*' with '*R*' in both pairs of forms. Making the replacements, you get

$$(\sim P \rightarrow R) \qquad (\sim \sim P \text{ v } R)$$

and

$$(\sim P \rightarrow R) \qquad \sim(\sim P \text{ \& } \sim R)$$

The left member of each pair of sentences matches step 2, but neither right member matches step 1; therefore, the transition from $(P \text{ v } R)$ to $(\sim P \rightarrow R)$ is not justified by applying the rule of conditional exchange to step 1. [As an exercise, derive $(\sim \sim P \text{ v } R)$ from $(P \text{ v } R)$ by one application of the rule of double negation. Then derive $(\sim P \rightarrow R)$ from $(P \text{ v } R)$ in three steps.]

In the following sequence, De Morgan's Law is applied incorrectly. When a rule is incorrectly applied, the sequence does not count as a derivation.

1	$P \text{ \& } \sim Q$	Hyp
2	$\sim(\sim P \text{ v } Q)$	1, DeM (Wrong!)

[As an exercise, stop to explain why the application is wrong.] The following sequence does qualify as a derivation of $\sim(\sim P \text{ v } Q)$ from $(P \text{ \& } \sim Q)$.

1	$P \text{ \& } \sim Q$	Hyp
2	$\sim \sim P \text{ \& } \sim Q$	1, DN
3	$\sim(\sim P \text{ v } Q)$	2, DeM

Unlike some one-way rules, two-way rules never apply to more than one preceding step; in other words, they are all one-premise rules. They also differ from one-way rules in being applicable to components of sentences (as defined in section 4.1), as well as to entire sentences. The following is a derivation in which a two-way rule (the rule of commutation) is applied to the immediate component of step 1 to get step 2.

1	$\sim(\sim Q \text{ \& } P)$	Hyp
2	$\sim(P \text{ \& } \sim Q)$	1, Com
3	$P \rightarrow Q$	2, Con Exch
4	$\sim Q \rightarrow \sim P$	3, Contra

Specifically, the sentence pair

$$(\sim Q \ \& \ P) \qquad (P \ \& \ \sim Q)$$

exemplifies the pair of forms

$$(A \ \& \ B) \qquad (B \ \& \ A)$$

Therefore, by the rule of commutation, step 2 can be entered with $(P \ \& \ \sim Q)$ in the place of $(\sim Q \ \& \ P)$ in step 1.

Now, in that same derivation, look at step 3. It follows by application of the rule of conditional exchange to step 2. To see how this works, note that the pair of sentences

$$(P \rightarrow Q) \qquad \sim(P \ \& \ \sim Q)$$

exemplifies the second pair of forms in the rule of conditional exchange. Since $\sim(P \ \& \ \sim Q)$ is step 2, you can write $(P \rightarrow Q)$ as step 3. Analogously, step 4 follows by applying the rule of contraposition to step 3. Note that steps 3 and 4 exemplify the pair of forms in the rule of contraposition stated above. Any pair of sentences having the form of one of these pairs is such that if one of the pair is a step or a component of a step in a derivation, the result of replacing it with the other can be written as a new step in the derivation.

To see how the derivation relates to English, assign 'P' to 'Don passed' and 'Q' to 'Sue passed', and steps 1 through 4 in the derivation immediately above translate as 1 through 4 in the following sequence of English sentences.

1   It is false that Sue did not pass while Don did.
2   It is false that Don passed and Sue did not.
3   Don passed only if Sue passed.
4   If Sue did not pass, then neither did Don.

Because all of the rules in the derivation above are two-way, the hypothesis of that derivation can be derived from its conclusion as follows:

1	$\sim Q \rightarrow \sim P$	Hyp
2	$P \rightarrow Q$	1, Contra
3	$\sim(P \ \& \ \sim Q)$	2, Con Exch
4	$\sim(\sim Q \ \& \ P)$	3, Com

Compare the two derivations and you will see that the second results from interchanging step 1 with step 4, step 2 with step 3, and 'Com' with 'Contra'. In the English translation of the first derivation, interchange 1 and 4, then 2 and 3, and you have a translation of the second derivation.

Construction Strategies for Derivations

A rule of inference is <u>truth-preserving</u> if and only if it is not possible for the step or steps to which you apply the rule to be true and the result of the application to be false. All the rules of inference you have learned are truth-preserving. Thus, in any derivation, it is not possible for the hypotheses to be true and the conclusion to be false. Understanding this, you can appreciate how derivations can be used to detect valid arguments. If there is a derivation with the conclusion of the argument as its last step and the premises of the argument as its hypotheses, the argument is valid. We recommend the following as helpful strategies to employ when constructing derivations to detect validity.

Focus on the Conclusion

On a piece of scratch paper, list the premises of the argument as hypotheses of the derivation. Then list the conclusion further down the page as the last step. Study the last step and the hypotheses and try to think of some way to reach the last step from the hypotheses. Never start off blindly from the hypotheses.

Simplify

If you have difficulty in seeing a way from the hypotheses to the conclusion, it is often helpful to apply rules that have the effect of allowing you to write sentences containing fewer connectives than, or at least the same number as, the steps to which they are applied. Rules that have this effect are the rules of simplification, *modus ponens*, *modus tollens*, disjunctive syllogism, hypothetical syllogism, constructive dilemma, destructive dilemma, and certain two-way rules.

Combine or Add

After simplifying, if you still have difficulty in seeing a way to the conclusion, think of applying the rules of addition, conjunction, and certain two-way rules, which allow you to write as steps sentences containing more connectives than the sentences to which they are applied. This strategy, of course, must be followed judiciously.

Apply Two-Way Rule to Reach Step

If you are still having difficulty in seeing how to arrive at a step, using a two-way rule to move to that step may be helpful. For example, in trying to derive $(\sim Q \rightarrow \sim P)$, you might choose to proceed to $(P \rightarrow Q)$ first, knowing, of course, that you can ultimately apply the rule of contraposition to $(P \rightarrow Q)$ to reach $(\sim Q \rightarrow \sim P)$.

Other Ways of Detecting Validity

One way that you have learned to detect that an argument is valid is to derive the conclusion from the premises. We call this method the <u>direct method</u>. We shall now present two alternative methods, the indirect method and the conditional proof method. When you use either of these alternative methods, the conclusion of the argument is not the last step of the derivation.

To detect that an argument is valid using the <u>indirect method</u>, you derive a sentence of the form $(A \,\&\, \sim A)$ from hypotheses consisting of the premises of the argument and the negation of the conclusion. The following derivation shows that

$$(P \rightarrow Q),\ (Q \rightarrow R)\ /\therefore\ (P \rightarrow R)$$

is valid.

1	$P \rightarrow Q$	Hyp (Premise of Argument)
2	$Q \rightarrow R$	Hyp (Premise of Argument)
3	$\sim(P \rightarrow R)$	Hyp (Negation of Conclusion)
4	$\sim(\sim P \,v\, R)$	3, Con Exch
5	$\sim\sim P \,\&\, \sim R$	4, DeM
6	$\sim\sim P$	5, Simp
7	P	6, DN
8	Q	1, 7, MP
9	R	2, 8, MP
10	$\sim R$	5, Simp
11	$R \,\&\, \sim R$	9, 10, Conj (has the form $(A \,\&\, \sim A)$)

Notice that the first two hypotheses are the premises of the argument and the third hypothesis is the negation of the conclusion of the argument. Derivation of a contradiction shows that there is no way for the premises to be true while the conclusion of the argument is false. So, the argument is valid.

For an argument that has a conditional as its conclusion, the <u>conditional proof method</u> provides a convenient way for detecting validity. The method is as follows: You list the premises of the argument as hypotheses of the derivation and include as an additional hypothesis the antecedent of the conditional that is the argument's conclusion. You then derive the consequent of that conditional. The derivation that follows detects validity in the same argument as the preceding derivation. But this derivation uses the conditional proof method.

1	$P \rightarrow Q$	Hyp (Premise of Argument)
2	$Q \rightarrow R$	Hyp (Premise of Argument)
3	P	Hyp (Antecedent of Conclusion)
4	Q	1, 3, MP
5	R	2, 4, MP (Consequent of Conclusion)

Notice that the first two hypotheses are the premises of the argument, the third hypothesis is the antecedent of the conditional that is the conclusion of the argument, and the last step is the consequent of that conditional.

Above we used the indirect method and the conditional proof method as alternate means of demonstrating the validity of the same argument. We could have also used the direct method. In this case the direct method is the simpler of the three to use. But there are arguments for which either the indirect or the conditional proof method would have been easier than the direct. In any case, you now have three different methods to detect a valid argument through a derivation.

Other Uses for Derivations

There are also ways to use derivations to detect a valid sentence, a contradictory sentence, equivalent sentences, and incompatible sentences. These are discussed below. Some of these are related to the indirect method and conditional proof method just discussed.

There is a simple way to see that a conditional is valid. The procedure is to construct a derivation with the antecedent of the conditional as the only hypothesis and the consequent as the conclusion. This procedure works because a derivation from a true hypothesis can only lead to a true conclusion. For example, the following derivation shows that whenever $(P \rightarrow (Q \rightarrow R))$ is true, then so is $(Q \rightarrow (P \rightarrow R))$.

1	$P \rightarrow (Q \rightarrow R)$	Hyp
2	$(P \& Q) \rightarrow R$	1, Exp
3	$(Q \& P) \rightarrow R$	2, Com
4	$Q \rightarrow (P \rightarrow R)$	3, Exp

As there is no way for the antecedent to be true and the conclusion false, there is no way for

$$(P \rightarrow (Q \rightarrow R)) \rightarrow (Q \rightarrow (P \rightarrow R))$$

to be false. Therefore, it is valid.

You can use a procedure called reductio ad absurdum to detect validity not just in conditionals but also in negations, disjunctions, and conjunctions. Following this procedure, begin with the negation of the sentence in question as your only hypothesis and then derive a sentence of the form (A & $\sim A$). Any sentence of the form (A & $\sim A$) is contradictory. On this basis, you can conclude that the hypothesis itself must be contradictory. Because the contradictory hypothesis is a negation, you can then conclude that the sentence it negates is valid.

The following derivation uses the *reductio ad absurdum* method to detect that the sentence

$$P \rightarrow (\sim P \rightarrow Q)$$

is valid.

1	$\sim(P \rightarrow (\sim P \rightarrow Q))$	Hyp
2	$\sim(\sim P \vee (\sim P \rightarrow Q))$	1, Con Exch
3	$\sim\sim P \& \sim(\sim P \rightarrow Q)$	2, DeM
4	$P \& \sim(\sim P \rightarrow Q)$	3, DN
5	$P \& \sim(\sim\sim P \vee Q)$	4, Con Exch
6	$P \& (\sim\sim\sim P \& \sim Q)$	5, DeM
7	$P \& (\sim P \& \sim Q)$	6, DN
8	$(P \& \sim P) \& \sim Q$	7, Assoc
9	$P \& \sim P$	8, Simp

To understand the *reductio ad absurdum* method better, remember that the rules of inference are truth-preserving so that if the last step cannot be true, then neither can the hypothesis. If the hypothesis (which is a negation) cannot be true, then the sentence it negates is valid, in other words, must be true.

You can also show that one or more sentences are incompatible by deriving a sentence of the form (A & $\sim A$) from them. As no sentence of the form (A & $\sim A$) can be true, it follows that the hypotheses in the derivation cannot all be true and are, therefore, incompatible. The following is a derivation demonstrating the incompatibility of the three sentences ((P & R) $\rightarrow$ Q), (R & $\sim Q$), and P.

1	$(P \,\&\, R) \to Q$	Hyp
2	$R \,\&\, {\sim}Q$	Hyp
3	P	Hyp
4	R	2, Simp
5	$P \,\&\, R$	3, 4, Conj
6	Q	1, 5, MP
7	${\sim}Q$	2, Simp
8	$Q \,\&\, {\sim}Q$	6, 7, Conj

Note how the sentences in question are listed as the hypotheses of the derivation and the last step has the form ($A \,\&\, {\sim}A$).

You can detect that two sentences are equivalent by constructing two derivations. Pick one of the sentences and construct a derivation with that sentence as the only hypothesis and the other as the conclusion. Then let the sentence that is the conclusion of the first derivation be the only hypothesis of the second and derive the hypothesis of the first derivation from it. Look back now to the derivation on page 229 of (${\sim}Q \to {\sim}P$) from ${\sim}({\sim}Q \,\&\, P)$. It is followed by a derivation of ${\sim}({\sim}Q \,\&\, P)$ from (${\sim}Q \to {\sim}P$). From these derivations you can conclude that the sentences (${\sim}Q \to {\sim}P$) and ${\sim}({\sim}Q \,\&\, P)$ are equivalent. [Try to explain in your own words how those derivations can be understood as establishing that the two sentences in question cannot have different truth values.]

EXERCISES FOR SECTION 8.1

*1. Explain why two schemes are given in the schematic expression of the rule of simplification. Would just one scheme have been sufficient?

2. Express schematically the rule of conjunction. Use the schematic expressions for other rules as a guide.

*3. Express schematically the first part of the rule of disjunctive syllogism.

4. Explain precisely the relationship between the derivation on page 223 of (${\sim}P \,\&\, {\sim}R$) from (${\sim}P$ v ($Q \,\&\, S$)) and ($R \to (Q \,\&\, S)$) and the list of English sentences 1 through 6 that follow that derivation.

*5. Using the initial meanings for the sentence letters that were given for the first sample derivation, translate into English the derivation on page 224 of ((P v Q) & ${\sim}R$) from ($Q \to {\sim}R$), ($P \to {\sim}R$), and (P v Q).

6. For each of the following arguments, construct a derivation demonstrating that the argument is valid.

 a. $(P \& Q) /\therefore P$

*b. $(P \& (Q \& {\sim}R)) /\therefore {\sim}R$

 c. $P, Q /\therefore (Q \& P)$

*d. $Q, {\sim}(P \& Q), {\sim}R /\therefore (Q \& {\sim}(P \& Q))$

 e. $(P \to R), (Q \to R) /\therefore ((P \lor Q) \to R)$

*f. $(Q \to {\sim}R), ({\sim}P \to {\sim}R) /\therefore (({\sim}P \lor Q) \to {\sim}R)$

 g. $(P \to {\sim}Q), ({\sim}Q \to R) /\therefore (P \to R)$

*h. $((Q \to R) \& ({\sim}P \to S)), ({\sim}R \lor {\sim}S) /\therefore ({\sim}Q \lor {\sim}{\sim}P)$

 i. ${\sim}P, (Q \lor P) /\therefore Q$

*j. $(R \to S), {\sim}S /\therefore {\sim}R$

7. What is a two-premise rule? Does the order of the sentences to which a two-premise rule is applied matter? Discuss.

8. Under what conditions is a rule of inference truth-preserving? Construct a truth table showing that *modus ponens* is truth-preserving. Do the same for all one-way rules of inference presented in this section.

9. Justify each step in the following derivation. Justification for the first two is given.

1	${\sim}R$	Hyp
2	$P \lor R$	Hyp
3	P	
4	${\sim}Q \lor P$	
5	$Q \to P$	
6	${\sim}P \to {\sim}Q$	

10. For each of the following arguments, construct a derivation of 2 to 3 steps showing that the argument is valid. Remember that two-way rules can be applied to components of sentences, as well as to entire sentences. However, one-way rules can be applied only to entire sentences.

*a. $((P \lor {\sim}R) \lor (Q \& R)) /\therefore (P \lor ({\sim}R \lor (Q \& R)))$

 b. $((Q \& {\sim}P) \& R) /\therefore (Q \& ({\sim}P \& R))$

*c. $(Q \& (P \lor R)) /\therefore (Q \& (R \lor P))$

 d. $(Q \& (P \lor R)) /\therefore ((P \lor R) \& Q)$

*e. $((P \& Q) \to R) /\therefore ({\sim}(P \& Q) \lor R)$

 f. $((P \& Q) \to R) /\therefore (({\sim}P \lor {\sim}Q) \lor R)$

*g. $(P \to (Q \& R)) /\therefore {\sim}(P \& {\sim}(Q \& R))$

 h. $(P \to ({\sim}R \to Q)) /\therefore ((P \& {\sim}R) \to Q)$

*i. $(P \& (Q \vee Q)) / \therefore (P \& Q)$

j. $(\sim Q \rightarrow R) / \therefore (\sim Q \rightarrow \sim\sim R)$

*k. $(P \& (\sim Q \vee R)) / \therefore ((P \& \sim Q) \vee (P \& R))$

l. $(Q \vee (P \& \sim R)) / \therefore ((Q \vee P) \& (Q \vee \sim R))$

11. For each of the following arguments, construct a derivation demonstrating that the argument is valid.

   a. $(\sim P \vee Q), P / \therefore Q$

   *b. $((P \& Q) \vee (P \& \sim Q)), (P \rightarrow Q) / \therefore (P \& Q)$

   c. $(R \rightarrow S), \sim S / \therefore \sim R$

   *d. $(P \rightarrow (Q \vee R)), \sim Q, \sim R / \therefore \sim P$

   e. $(\sim P \rightarrow \sim Q), Q / \therefore P$

   *f. $(P \rightarrow (Q \rightarrow R)), (P \& Q) / \therefore R$

12. Using the rule of double negation and the rule of conditional exchange, derive $(\sim P \rightarrow R)$ from $(P \vee R)$ in three steps.

*13. Explain why De Morgan's Law cannot be applied to step 1 to get step 2 in the following.

   | 1 | $P \& \sim Q$ | Hyp |
   | 2 | $\sim(\sim P \vee Q)$ | 1, DeM (Wrong!) |

14. For each of the following arguments, construct a derivation demonstrating that the argument is valid.

   *a. $\sim(P \& \sim Q) / \therefore (\sim P \vee \sim\sim Q)$

   b. $(\sim P \vee \sim\sim Q) / \therefore \sim(P \& \sim Q)$

   c. $\sim(P \vee \sim Q) / \therefore (\sim P \& Q)$

   *d. $(\sim P \& Q) / \therefore \sim(P \vee \sim Q)$

   e. $\sim P, (Q \vee R), (Q \rightarrow P) / \therefore R$

   f. $(\sim P \rightarrow Q), (Q \rightarrow R), (R \rightarrow P) / \therefore P$

   *g. $(P \& Q), (P \rightarrow R) / \therefore (R \vee S)$

   h. $(P \& Q), (\sim P \vee R) / \therefore (\sim R \rightarrow S)$

   i. $(P \rightarrow \sim Q), (P \vee R), \sim R / \therefore \sim(Q \vee R)$

   *j. $((P \& Q) \rightarrow R), \sim R / \therefore (P \rightarrow \sim Q)$

   k. $(P \rightarrow Q), (R \rightarrow S), (\sim Q \vee \sim S) / \therefore \sim(P \& R)$

   l. $(P \rightarrow Q), (R \rightarrow Q), (P \vee R) / \therefore \sim\sim Q$

   *m. $(P \rightarrow Q), (Q \rightarrow R), \sim R / \therefore \sim P$

*15. Is it truth-preserving to allow the consequent of a conditional to be written as a step in a derivation whenever the conditional is a preceding step? Explain your answer.

16. For each of the following sentences, construct a derivation demonstrating the sentence is valid. Use the conditional proof method.

   a. $P \rightarrow \sim\sim P$

   b. $(P \vee P) \rightarrow P$

17. Demonstrate by the truth table method that the pairs of sentence forms in the two-way rules are equivalent.

18. Other rules of inference could be added to those already stated. Can you think of one that you would like to have on hand?

*19. In the text, $(\sim Q \rightarrow \sim P)$ is derived from $\sim(\sim Q \,\&\, P)$ and vice versa (see pp. 229–230). Explain how the two derivations can be understood as establishing the equivalence of the two sentences.

20. Use derivations to show the equivalence of the premise and conclusion in each of the arguments in exercise 14.

21. For each of the following conditionals, construct a derivation demonstrating that the conditional is valid. Use the conditional proof method.

   *a. $P \rightarrow (Q \rightarrow P)$

   b. $(P \,\&\, \sim P) \rightarrow Q$

   *c. $P \rightarrow (P \vee Q)$

   d. $(P \,\&\, Q) \rightarrow Q$

   *e. $(P \rightarrow (Q \vee R)) \rightarrow ((P \rightarrow Q) \vee (P \rightarrow R))$

22. For each of the following lists of sentences, construct a derivation demonstrating that the sentences are incompatible.

   a. $P, (P \rightarrow (Q \,\&\, R)), (P \rightarrow \sim Q)$

   *b. $(P \vee Q), (\sim P \,\&\, \sim Q)$

   c. $\sim(P \vee (P \rightarrow Q))$

23. After translating into C each of the arguments in exercises 3 and 5 in section 5.3 (see pp. 147–151), construct derivations demonstrating the validity of the C-translations that are valid.

24. After translating the lists of sentences in exercise 4 in section 5.3 (p. 150), construct derivations demonstrating the incompatibility of the C-translations that are incompatible.

25. Show by the indirect proof method that the arguments in exercises 6, 10, 11, and 14 on pages 236–237 are valid.

26. Use the method of conditional proof to demonstrate the validity of each argument that has a conditional as its conclusion in exercises 6, 10, 11, and 14.

8.2 INFERENCE RULES FOR Q

The inference rules for Q include those for C that appear in the previous section. In addition to these rules, there are five inference rules strictly for quantifiers; all but one are one-way rules. With respect to detecting semantic properties, derivations in Q serve the same purposes as derivations in C.

One-Way Rules

All of the one-way rules in section 8.1 are also inference rules for Q. The only difference is that the relevant sentences are Q-sentences. The following is an example of a derivation in which two of these rules are applied.

$$
\begin{array}{lll}
1 & (\exists x)Fx \rightarrow (\exists x)Gx & \text{Hyp} \\
2 & (\exists x)Fx \text{ v } Ha & \text{Hyp} \\
3 & \sim Ha & \text{Hyp} \\
4 & (\exists x)Fx & 2, 3, \text{DS} \\
5 & (\exists x)Gx & 1, 4, \text{MP}
\end{array}
$$

Notice how step 4 results from applying the rule of disjunctive syllogism to steps 2 and 3, and step 5 results from applying the rule of *modus ponens* to steps 1 and 4.

In addition to the one-way rules for connectives, Q also has one-way rules for quantifiers. These consist of two <u>instantiation rules</u> and two <u>gen-eralization rules</u>. One of the instantiation rules is for the existential quanti-fier and the other is for the universal quantifier. Similarly, one of the generalization rules is for the existential quantifier and the other is for the universal quantifier. An instantiation rule allows you to move from a uni-versal or existential sentence to one of its instances. On the other hand, a generalization rule allows you to move to a universal or existential sentence from one of its instances.

As defined in section 6.1 (see p. 162), an instance of a universal or existential sentence is any sentence that results from dropping the dominant operator (which is either a universal or existential quantifier) and replacing every variable occurrence that becomes free with the same singular term. The singular term that replaces the free variable is the instantial term.

Of the four generalization and instantiation rules, the next is one of the easiest to understand and apply.

Universal Instantiation (UI).   The rule of universal instantiation allows you to write as a step in a derivation any instance of a universal sentence that is a preceding step.

Notice that in this rule there is no condition on the instantial term. You may write *any* instance regardless of its instantial term. You should have no trouble accepting this rule given the fact that what an instance of a universal sentence says to be true of a particular individual is what the universal sentence says to be true of every individual.

The following derivation contains two applications of the rule of universal instantiation.

1	$(\forall x)Fx$ & $(\forall y)Gy$	Hyp
2	$(\forall x)Fx$	1, Simp
3	Fa	2, UI
4	$(\forall y)Gy$	1, Simp
5	Ga	4, UI
6	Fa & Ga	3, 5, Conj

Because step 2 is a universal sentence, the rule allows you to write one of its instances as step 3. Similarly, the rule of universal instantiation as applied to step 4 allows you to write one of its instances in step 5. In both applications, the instantial terms are the same singular term, but they could have been different ones. In applying the rule of universal instantiation, you are free to choose any singular term whatsoever for the instantial term.

To see how the derivation above relates to English, let the domain be the class of first ladies, '$F\_$' have the same meaning as '$\_$ is kindhearted', '$G\_$' have the same meaning as '$\_$ is self-sacrificing', and 'a' name Martha Washington. With this understanding, the derivation translates in English as follows:

1   All first ladies are kindhearted and all first ladies are self-
     sacrificing.
2   All first ladies are kindhearted.
3   Martha Washington is kindhearted.
4   All first ladies are self-sacrificing.
5   Martha Washington is self-sacrificing.
6   Martha Washington is kindhearted and self-sacrificing.

The phrase 'first ladies' occurs in the translation because the domain is limited to first ladies. With a domain not so limited, the phrase would not appear. [As an exercise for yourself, construct a derivation from (($\forall x$)Fx & ($\forall y$)Gy) to (Fa & Gb), instead of to (Fa & Ga). Then, with 'b' naming Dolly Madison, translate each step into English. Next derive (Fa & Ga) from ($\forall x$)(Fx & Gx) and then derive (Fa & Gb) from ($\forall x$)(Fx & Gx). Translate into English each step of both derivations.]

The rule of universal instantiation, just discussed, allows you to move from a universal sentence to any one of its instances. The next rule allows you to move to an existential sentence from any one of its instances and is, thus, a generalization rule. This rule is no more difficult to understand or apply than the rule of universal instantiation just presented.

Existential Generalization (EG).   The rule of existential generalization allows you to write as a step in a derivation an existential sentence that has any one of its instances as a preceding step.

Notice that this rule also has no condition on the instantial term. You can write an existential sentence in a derivation regardless of which of its instances precedes it, in other words, regardless of which singular term is the instantial term.

The rule of existential generalization justifies the last step in the following derivation.

1	*Gb*	Hyp
2	*Fb*	Hyp
3	*Gb* & *Fb*	1, 2, Conj
4	($\exists x$)(*Gx* & *Fx*)	3, EG

The appearance of '3, EG' to the right of step 4 indicates that step 4 results from applying to step 3 the rule of existential generalization. Notice that step 3 is an instance of step 4 and has 'b' as its instantial term.

The following is an English translation of the sentences in the derivation.

1   Dolly Madison is self-sacrificing.
2   Dolly Madison is kindhearted.
3   Dolly Madison is self-sacrificing and kindhearted.
4   Some first ladies are self-sacrificing and kindhearted.

[For this translation, can you say what is the domain? What is the translation scheme? As an exercise, provide a different translation of the derivation using a different domain and a different translation scheme.]

The next derivation uses the rule of existential generalization three times.

1	Hcc	Hyp
2	$(\exists x)Hxc$	1, EG
3	$(\exists x)Hcx$	1, EG
4	$(\exists x)Hxx$	1, EG

To see how the derivation relates to English, let the domain be the class of human beings and translate '$H\_ \_$' with '$\_$ loves $\_$' and 'c' with 'Mark Twain'. Then steps 1–4 translate as follows:

1	Hcc	Mark Twain loves himself.
2	$(\exists x)Hxc$	Someone loves Mark Twain.
3	$(\exists x)Hcx$	Mark Twain loves someone.
4	$(\exists x)Hxx$	Someone loves himself or herself.

Returning to the derivation, notice that steps 2, 3, and 4 have the same justification: 1, EG. The justification is the same because the rule of existential instantiation allows you to write an existential sentence if any instance of it is a preceding step. In this case, step 1 is an instance of steps 2 and 3, as well as 4. To see that step 1 is an instance of step 2, form an instance of step 2 with 'c' as the instantial term; in other words, remove the existential quantifier from '$(\exists x)Hxc$' to get 'Hxc' and then replace 'x' with 'c'. The result is 'Hcc'. Now form an instance of step 3 and an instance of step 4 also with 'c' as the instantial term; the result in both these cases is also 'Hcc'. You could, of course, eliminate steps 2 and 3, go directly from step 1 to step 4, and have a two-step derivation. The purpose of giving all of the steps in this example is to illustrate the latitude one has in applying the rule.

So far we have presented only the rule of universal instantiation and the rule of existential generalization. We now turn to a rule that is more difficult to understand and remember because of conditions on the instantial term. These conditions are, however, necessary to ensure that no derivation reaches a false conclusion starting from all true hypotheses.

Existential Instantiation (EI).   The rule of existential instantiation allows you to write as a step in a derivation an instance of a preceding existential sentence so long as the instantial term does not appear in any preceding step of the derivation and does not appear in the last step.

In the following derivation, the rule of existential instantiation is applied to step 2 to get step 3. Notice that step 3 is an instance of step 2 and that 'a' is the instantial term.

1	$(\forall x)(Fx \rightarrow Gx)$	Hyp
2	$(\exists x)(Hx \,\&\, Fx)$	Hyp
3	$Ha \,\&\, Fa$	2, EI
4	$Fa \rightarrow Ga$	1, UI
5	Fa	3, Simp
6	Ga	4, 5, MP
7	Ha	3, Simp
8	$Ha \,\&\, Ga$	6, 7, Conj
9	$(\exists x)(Hx \,\&\, Gx)$	8, EG

The instantial term used to form step 3 from step 2 does not appear in either step 1 or step 2 and it does not appear in the last step of the derivation. Therefore, both conditions that the rule places on the instantial term are satisfied. [If the sequence of steps above had terminated with step 3, 4, 5, 6, 7, or 8, would the resulting sequence qualify as a derivation? If not, explain why not.]

In applying this new rule, the instantial term selected is a tentative name, or convenient "handle," through which to say that an individual has an attribute without making a commitment to which one. Consequently, you must pick a singular term that does not appear in a preceding step of the derivation. On occasion, you may have followed this same practice in reasoning with English. For example, suppose that you are involved in an investigation into the disappearance of a code book and you hypothesize that some spy stole the code book. You restate the hypothesis, saying "Slippery Fingers is a spy and Slippery Fingers stole the code book." You use 'Slippery Fingers' because no one involved in the investigation has that name and you are, thus, able to avoid confusing attributes of some person who actually has that name with those of your tentatively named individual.

Furthermore, because 'Slippery Fingers' is a tentative name, you do not use it in your final report because you do not want anyone reading the report to conclude that you could, in fact, identify the person you are presumably referring to by that name. Similarly, when picking a singular term to form an instance in applying the rule of existential instantiation, you avoid selecting any singular term that will appear in the last step of the derivation. In other words, you never use what is a tentative name in what amounts to your "final" report.

To help you better appreciate the parallel between the rule of existential instantiation and an example of ordinary reasoning using the name 'Slippery Fingers', each step of the derivation above is translated into English at the top of page 244, using 'Slippery Fingers' for '*b*', '_ stole the code book' for '*F_*', '_ has security clearance' for '*G_*', and '_ is a spy' for '*H_*'. The domain is limited to human beings.

1   Whoever stole the code book has security clearance.
2   Some spy stole the code book.
3   Slippery Fingers is a spy and Slippery Fingers stole the code book.
4   Slippery Fingers stole the code book only if Slippery Fingers has security clearance.
5   Slippery Fingers stole the code book.
6   Slippery Fingers has security clearance.
7   Slippery Fingers is a spy.
8   Slippery Fingers is a spy and Slippery Fingers has security clearance.
9   Some spy has security clearance.

Step 3 says that Slippery Fingers (whoever Slippery Fingers is) is a spy and stole the code book. Using 'Slippery Fingers' as a tentative name allows you to reason as if you actually had the name of the individual. However, the derivation does not end with any sentence in which the name 'Slippery Fingers' appears, because 'Slippery Fingers' is simply used in a tentative way as an aid to reasoning. The sequence ends with step 9. This says that at least one individual in the domain is a spy and has security clearance. Because 'Slippery Fingers' is a tentative name, step 9 does not really add or subtract anything from the content of step 8.

Faulty applications of the rule of existential instantiation are presented below together with English translations showing how failure to observe the conditions on the instantial term can lead from true hypotheses to a false conclusion. In the following sequence, the rule of existential instantiation is applied *incorrectly* to step 2 to get step 4.

1	$(\exists x)Gx$	Hyp
2	$(\exists x)Fx$	Hyp
3	Ga	2, EI
4	Fa	2, EI (Wrong!)
5	$Ga \& Fa$	3, 4, Conj
6	$(\exists x)(Gx \& Fx)$	5, EG

The instantial term selected for step 4 already appears in step 3. This is an error because, according to the rule of existential instantiation, the instantial term cannot appear in an earlier step.

You can appreciate the significance of this error by studying the following translation of the sequence with '_ is a kangaroo' for '$F\_$', '_ is a rhinoceros' for '$G\_$', 'a' left untranslated, and the domain unlimited.

1   There are kangaroos.
2   There are rhinoceroses.
3   *a* is a kangaroo.
4   *a* is a rhinoceros.
5   *a* is a kangaroo and *a* is a rhinoceros.
6   Some kangaroos are rhinoceroses.

Notice that the hypotheses are true but that step 6 is false.
    The following sequence of steps also involves an error.

1   (∃x)Fx   Hyp
2   Fc   1, EI (Wrong!)

The instantial term appears in the conclusion. This violates the restriction against a singular term introduced by the rule of existential instantiation occurring in the conclusion. To appreciate why you would not want this sequence to count as a derivation, let the domain be unlimited, '*F_*' have the same meaning as '_ is a desert', and '*c*' designate the Atlantic Ocean. Then the hypothesis says that there is at least one desert (which is true) and the conclusion says that the Atlantic Ocean is a desert (which is false).
    We now turn to the last of the one-way rules.

Universal Generalization (UG).   The rule of universal generalization allows you to write as a step in a derivation a universal sentence if one of its instances is a preceding step and the instantial term is not (i) in the hypotheses, (ii) introduced in any line justified by the rule of existential instantiation, or (iii) in the universal sentence itself.

The following sequence of steps is an example of a derivation in which the rule of universal generalization is correctly applied.

1   (∀x)(Fx → Gx)   Hyp
2   (∀x)(Gx → Hx)   Hyp
3   Fc → Gc   1, UI
4   Gc → Hc   2, UI
5   Fc → Hc   3, 4, HS
6   (∀x)(Fx → Hx)   5, UG

Note that the instantial term '*c*' in step 5 satisfies all of the conditions required to derive step 6: (i) '*c*' does not appear in the hypotheses, (ii) '*c*' is not introduced in any step justified by the rule of existential instantiation, and (iii) '*c*' does not appear in step 6 (the universal sentence derived by applying the rule of universal generalization to step 5). When an instantial term satisfies conditions (i) and (ii), the only way for it to be introduced in the derivation is through the rule of universal instantiation. Notice that in the derivation above, the introduction of '*c*' in step 3 is by the rule of universal instantiation. By being introduced through the rule of universal instantiation, '*c*' could be the name of any individual in the domain as far as the derivation is concerned. Thus, in applying the rule of universal generalization to step 5 to get step 6, you are deriving a sentence that could not possibly be false if step 5 is true.

The following is a translation into English of the preceding derivation. The domain is the class of human beings, '_ studies physics' translates '*F_*', '_ has heard of Einstein's theory of relativity' translates '*G_*', '_ knows the Pythagorean theorem' translates '*H_*', and '*c*' is left untranslated.

1   Anyone studying physics has heard of Einstein's theory of relativity.

2   Anyone who has heard of Einstein's theory of relativity knows the Pythagorean theorem.

3   If *c* studies physics, then *c* has heard of Einstein's theory of relativity.

4   If *c* has heard of Einstein's theory of relativity, then *c* knows the Pythagorean theorem.

5   If *c* studies physics, then *c* knows the Pythagorean theorem.

6   Anyone who studies physics knows the Pythagorean theorem.

Observe that steps 3 through 5 are true regardless of what human being '*c*' designates so long as both steps 1 and 2 are true. Thus, if steps 1 and 2 are both true, so is step 6.

Even with the explanation above, you may be puzzled by a rule that allows you to write a universal sentence as the step of a derivation when one and only one of its instances is a preceding step. After all, a universal sentence says of everything in the domain that it has a certain attribute, while an instance says of only one thing that it does. The reason the rule of universal generalization works is that it only allows generalization to a universal sentence from an instance if the instance is true regardless of which individual in the domain the instantial term designates.

We illustrate below how failure to satisfy any one of the three conditions on the instantial term in the rule of universal generalization can lead you from true hypotheses to a false conclusion. The first condition on the instantial term is that it cannot occur in a hypothesis. In the following example, the instantial term occurs in the hypothesis. Consequently, the sequence 1–2 is not a derivation.

1   *Fa*   Hyp
2    $(\forall x)Fx$ 1, UG (Wrong!)

You can easily see why no one would want this sequence to count as a derivation. Let the domain be the class of human beings, '*F_*' have the same meaning as '_ is a movie star', and '*a*' name Tom Cruise. Then the hypothesis says that Tom Cruise is a movie star (which is true) while the conclusion says that we are all movies stars (which is false).

The second condition on the instantial term is that it cannot be introduced by the rule of existential instantiation. In the following sequence, step 2 is gotten from step 1 by the rule of existential instantiation and its instantial term introduced by application of that rule. Therefore, even though step 2 is an instance of step 3, the rule of universal generalization cannot be applied to step 2.

1	$(\exists x)Gx$	Hyp
2	Gb	1, EI
3	$(\forall x)Gx$	2, UG (Wrong!)

To appreciate the importance of the second condition on the instantial term, let the domain consist of candidates for president of the United States in 1992. And let '*G_*' have the same meaning as '_ won the presidential election in 1992'. In the sequence above, the hypothesis now says that at least one candidate won the election, while the last step says that all did. The hypothesis is true but the conclusion is false. To understand in another way why step 3 is wrong, note that the singular term introduced by the rule of existential instantiation in step 2 is just a tentative name for an individual and what is true of one individual in the domain need not be true of all.

The third condition on the instantial term is that it not occur in the universal sentence derived by application of the rule. The following sequence of steps does not satisfy that condition because the instantial term in step 2 appears in step 3.

1	$(\forall x)(x = x)$	Hyp
2	$b = b$	1, UI
3	$(\forall y)(b = y)$	2, UG (Wrong!)

If such faulty "derivations" were allowed, you could easily derive a false conclusion from true hypotheses. To see this, let '*b*' designate $\sqrt{5}$ and the domain be universal. Then step 1 says that everything is self-identical (which is true), and step 2 says that $\sqrt{5}$ is self-identical (which is true), but step 3 says that everything is identical to $\sqrt{5}$ (which is false).

The rule of universal generalization is truth-preserving in monadic predicate logic (the logic of quantifiers without the multi-place predicate letters and the identity sign) and in polyadic predicate logic (the logic of quantifiers with the multi-place predicate letters and the identity sign) so long as there are no overlapping quantifiers in the derivation. As explained in section 6.1 (see p. 160), overlapping quantifiers are quantifiers one of which falls within the scope of the other. For example, $(\exists x)(\forall y)Fxy$ has overlapping quantifiers. For the rule of universal generalization to be truth-preserving in polyadic predicate logic, one more condition on the instantial term is needed. We do not add this condition here because it makes the rule too difficult for most beginning students.

Construction Strategies for Derivations

We discussed four strategies for construction of derivations in section 8.1: (i) focus on the conclusion, (ii) simplify hypotheses, (iii) combine or add, and (iv) apply a two-way rule to reach a step. These apply equally as well for Q. In addition to these strategies, there are others to recommend for dealing specifically with quantifiers.

Remove Quantifiers

The two instantiation rules, when applied to an appropriately quantified sentence, allow you to remove the quantifier that is the dominant operator and form an instance. In constructing derivations, apply these rules whenever possible to remove quantifiers.

Remove Existential Quantifiers First

When there is a choice between applying the rule of existential instantiation and applying the rule of universal instantiation, apply the rule of existential instantiation first.

The following is an example of a derivation where the rule of existential instantiation is applied first.

1	$(\forall x)(Fx \rightarrow Gx)$	Hyp
2	$(\exists x)(\sim Gx \,\&\, Hx)$	Hyp
3	$\sim Ga \,\&\, Ha$	2, EI
4	$Fa \rightarrow Ga$	1, UI
5	$\sim Ga$	3, Simp
6	$\sim Fa$	4, 5, MT
7	Ha	3, Simp
8	$\sim Fa \,\&\, Ha$	6, 7, Conj
9	$(\exists x)(\sim Fx \,\&\, Hx)$	8, EG

The next derivation is from the same hypotheses as the one above. However, the rule of universal instantiation is applied first and, as a consequence, the derivation cannot reach the same conclusion.

1	$(\forall x)(Fx \rightarrow Gx)$	Hyp
2	$(\exists x)(\sim Gx \,\&\, Hx)$	Hyp
3	$Fa \rightarrow Ga$	1, UI
4	$\sim Gb \,\&\, Hb$	2, EI
5	$\sim Gb$	4, Simp

Notice how the two derivations begin to differ at step 3. In applying the rule of existential instantiation to step 2, one is required to pick a singular term for step 4 that does not appear previously in the derivation. But without the same singular term to instantiate both hypotheses, an instance of $(\exists x)(\sim Fx \,\&\, Hx)$, such as $(\sim Fa \,\&\, Ha)$, cannot be generated. Without one of its instances as a step in the derivation, there is no way of deriving $(\exists x)(\sim Fx \,\&\, Hx)$ from the hypotheses. Therefore, only by removing the existential quantifier first, as in the first derivation, can you reach the desired conclusion.

Limit Use of New Singular Terms

When applying the rule of universal instantiation, usually the best policy is to instantiate with a singular term that appears in a preceding step. The rationale for this strategy is not difficult to see. For example, you can easily derive $(\forall x)(Fx \rightarrow Hx)$ from the hypotheses $(\forall x)(Fx \rightarrow Gx)$ and $(\forall x)(Gx \rightarrow Hx)$ by instantiating both hypotheses with the same singular term.

The following derivation also illustrates the importance of minimizing the number of instantial terms introduced to derive the conclusion.

1	$(\forall x)(Fx \rightarrow Gx)$	Hyp
2	$(\forall x)\sim Gx$	Hyp
3	$Fa \rightarrow Ga$	1, UI
4	$\sim Ga$	2, UI
5	$\sim Fa$	3, 4, MT
6	$(\forall x)\sim Fx$	5, UG

Notice that the same singular term is used to reach both step 4 and step 5.

Although usually the best policy is to stick with singular terms that have already been introduced, there are occasions when a new singular term is required. The following is an example of a derivation that requires a new singular term to reach the desired conclusion.

1	$(\forall x)(Fxa \to Gxa)$	Hyp
2	$(\forall x)Fxa$	Hyp
3	$Fba \to Gba$	1, UI
4	Fba	2, UI
5	Gba	3, 4, MP
6	$(\forall x)Gxa$	5, UG

To understand why a new singular term is needed, try to reach step 6 by instantiating steps 1 and 2 with '*a*'. Proceeding in this way, you will have a derivation with the following appearance through step 5:

1	$(\forall x)(Fxa \to Gxa)$	Hyp
2	$(\forall x)Fxa$	Hyp
3	$Faa \to Gaa$	1, UI
4	Faa	2, UI
5	Gaa	3, 4, MP

There is no way for you to reach the desired conclusion by applying the rule of universal generalization to step 5. The rule of universal generalization allows you to write a universal sentence as a step in a derivation only under the condition that one of its instances is a preceding step and the instantial term is not in the universal sentence. Step 5 is an instance of step 6 of the previous derivation, but the instantial term, which is '*a*', appears in step 6. For this reason, the rule of universal generalization cannot be applied to step 5 to reach the desired conclusion.

Two-Way Rules

The two-way rules for C also serve as two-way rules for Q. But, as rules for Q, they apply to quasi-sentences of Q.

According to the rule of contraposition, whenever one member of a pair of expressions of the form

$$(A \to B) \qquad (\sim B \to \sim A)$$

is a step or *part* of a step in a derivation, you may replace that member with the other and write the result as a new step in the derivation. Examples of such interchangeable pairs are the following:

$$(Fa \to Ga) \qquad (\sim Ga \to \sim Fa)$$

$$(Fx \to Gy) \qquad (\sim Gy \to \sim Fx)$$

$$((\forall x)Fx \to Hb) \qquad (\sim Hb \to \sim(\forall x)Fx)$$

The rule of contraposition is applied in the following derivation:

1	$(\forall x)(Fx \rightarrow Gx)$	Hyp
2	$(\forall x)(\sim Gx \rightarrow \sim Fx)$	1, Contra

Notice that step 2 results from replacing $(Fx \rightarrow Gx)$ in step 1 with $(\sim Gx \rightarrow \sim Fx)$.

Instead of restating all of the two-way rules from section 8.1, we will simply assume that they are now rules for Q. The following is a derivation that uses the two-way rule of commutation. In this derivation, no step contains a quantifier.

1	*Fa & Ga*	Hyp
2	$\sim$(*Ga & Fa*) v (*Gb & Fb*)	Hyp
3	*Ga & Fa*	1, Com
4	*Gb & Fb*	2, 3, DS
5	*Gb*	4, Simp

Notice that step 3 is the result of applying the rule of commutation to step 1. Step 4 is the result of applying the rule of disjunctive syllogism to steps 2 and 3. And, finally, step 5 is the result of applying the rule of simplification to step 4.

The next rule is the only two-way rule specifically for quantifiers.

Quantifier Negation (QN)

$(\forall x)\, A$	: :	$\sim(\exists x)\sim A$
$\sim(\forall x)\, A$	: :	$(\exists x)\sim A$
$(\forall x)\sim A$	: :	$\sim(\exists x)A$
$\sim(\forall x)\sim A$	: :	$(\exists x)A$

In a two-way rule for Q, the symbol ': :' appearing between a pair of forms indicates the following: When a pair of quasi-sentences exemplifies that pair of forms and one of the pair of quasi-sentences is a preceding step or a *component of a preceding step* in a derivation, the rule allows you to repeat the step in the derivation with the other member of the pair of quasi-sentences in place of the original.

The rule of quantifier negation is applied in the following derivation:

1	$\sim(\forall z)Fz$	Hyp
2	$(\exists z)\sim Fz$	1, QN

With '_ is a fan of country music' assigned to '$F\_$', the steps in this derivation translate into English as follows:

1   Not all are fans of country music.
2   Some are not fans of country music.

To help you remember the quantifier pairs in the rule of quantifier negation, approximate English counterparts are given below. In the listing, instead of one across from the other as above, the relevant symbolic pairs are written one below the other. Their English counterparts are written to the right.

$(\forall x)$	all are
$\sim(\exists x)\sim$	it is not the case that some are not
$\sim(\forall x)$	not all are
$(\exists x)\sim$	some are not
$(\forall x)\sim$	all are non-
$\sim(\exists x)$	it is not the case that some are
$\sim(\forall x)\sim$	it is not the case that all are non-
$(\exists x)$	some are

Just as 'all are' is interchangeable with 'it is not the case that some are not' in English, $(\forall x)$ is interchangeable with $\sim(\exists x)\sim$ in Q. The same applies to the other pairs. In the listing, 'all are non-' appears rather than 'all are not' because 'all are not' is ambiguous in English. For example, does 'All are not winners' mean 'Not all are winners' or 'All are non-winners'?

You can use inference rules for Q to detect validity the same way as you used those for C. For example, by listing the premise as the hypothesis and deriving the conclusion, you can show that

$$(\forall x)(Fx \rightarrow Gx) /\therefore \sim(\exists x)(Fx \ \& \ \sim Gx)$$

is valid. This is done in the derivation below.

1	$(\forall x)(Fx \rightarrow Gx)$	Hyp
2	$(\forall x)\sim(Fx \ \& \ \sim Gx)$	1, Con Exch
3	$\sim(\exists x)(Fx \ \& \ \sim Gx)$	2, QN

Notice that step 2 is the result of replacing $(Fx \rightarrow Gx)$ in step 1 with $\sim(Fx \ \& \ \sim Gx)$ through application of the rule of conditional exchange to step 1. Step 3 results from applying the rule of quantifier negation to step 2.

The validity of

$$\sim(\exists x)(Fx \ \& \ \sim Gx) /\therefore (\forall x)(Fx \rightarrow Gx)$$

is established by the following derivation:

$$
\begin{array}{lll}
1 & \sim(\exists x)(Fx\ \&\ \sim Gx) & \text{Hyp} \\
2 & (\forall x)\sim(Fx\ \&\ \sim Gx) & \text{1, QN} \\
3 & (\forall x)(Fx \rightarrow Gx) & \text{2, Con Exch}
\end{array}
$$

With this derivation, together with that above, one can conclude that the sentences

$$(\forall x)(Fx \rightarrow Gx)$$

and

$$\sim(\exists x)(Fx\ \&\ \sim Gx)$$

are equivalent.

The next derivation proceeds from the premise of

$$(\exists x)(Fx\ \&\ Gx)\ /\therefore\ \sim(\forall x)(Fx \rightarrow \sim Gx)$$

to its conclusion.

$$
\begin{array}{lll}
1 & (\exists x)(Fx\ \&\ Gx) & \text{Hyp} \\
2 & \sim(\forall x)\sim(Fx\ \&\ Gx) & \text{1, QN} \\
3 & \sim(\forall x)(\sim Fx\ \text{v}\ \sim Gx) & \text{2, DeM} \\
4 & \sim(\forall x)(Fx \rightarrow \sim Gx) & \text{3, Con Exch}
\end{array}
$$

As an exercise, derive step 1 from step 4. Your derivation will establish the validity of

$$\sim(\forall x)(Fx \rightarrow \sim Gx)\ /\therefore\ (\exists x)(Fx\ \&\ Gx)$$

[Does your derivation together with the one above tell you that $\sim(\forall x)(Fx \rightarrow \sim Gx)$ and $(\exists x)(Fx\ \&\ Gx)$ are equivalent?]

EXERCISES FOR SECTION 8.2

*1. Construct a derivation from $((\forall x)Fx\ \&\ (\forall y)Gy)$ to $(Fa\ \&\ Gb)$. Then, letting the domain be the first ladies, '$F\_$' have the same meaning as '$\_$ is kindhearted', '$G\_$' have the same meaning as '$\_$ is self-sacrificing', 'a' name Martha Washington, and 'b' name Dolly Madison, translate each step into English.

2. Derive (*Fa* & *Ga*) from (∀*x*)(*Fx* & *Gx*) and then derive (*Fa* & *Gb*) from (∀*x*)(*Fx* & *Gx*). Then translate into English each step of both derivations. Use the same domain and translation scheme as in exercise 1.

*3. With the same domain and translation scheme as in exercise 1, translate the following sequence of sentences into Q.

    1   Dolly Madison is self-sacrificing.
    2   Dolly Madison is kindhearted.
    3   Dolly Madison is self-sacrificing and kindhearted.
    4   Some first ladies are self-sacrificing and kindhearted.

4. Your solution to exercise 3 is a sequence of Q-sentences. Provide an English translation of that sequence. Use a translation scheme and domain different from those in exercise 1.

*5. Is (*a* = *b*) an instance of (∃*x*)(*a* = *x*)? If so, what is the instantial term? Is (*a* = *b*) an instance of (∃*x*)(*x* = *b*)? If so, what is the instantial term?

6. List three quantified sentences for which (*a* = *a*) is an instance.

7. Using one-way rules, construct a derivation of the conclusion from the premises of each of the following arguments.

  *a. (∀*x*)*Fx* /∴ (∀*x*)(*Fx* v *Gx*)

   b. (∃*y*)*Fy* /∴ (∃*y*)(*Fy* v *Gy*)

  *c. (∀*x*)*Fx*, (∀*x*)*Gx* /∴ (∀*y*)(*Fy* & *Gy*)

   d. (∀*x*)(*Fx* v *Gx*), ~*Fc* /∴ *Gc*

  *e. (∀*x*)(*Gx* → *Fx*), (∃*x*)*Gx* /∴ (∃*x*)*Fx*

   f. (∀*x*)(*Gx* → *Fx*), (∃*x*)~*Fx* /∴ (∃*x*)~*Gx*

  *g. (∀*x*)(*Gx* → *Fx*), (∀*x*)*Gx* /∴ (∀*x*)*Fx*

   h. (∀*x*)(*Gx* → *Fx*), (∀*y*)(*Hy* → *Fy*) /∴ (∀*z*)((*Gz* v *Hz*) → *Fz*)

  *i. (∀*x*)(*Fx* → *Gx*), (∃*x*)(*Fx* & *Hx*) /∴ (∃*x*)(*Gx* & *Hx*)

   j. (∀*x*)(*Fx* → *Gx*), (∃*x*)(*Hx* & ~*Gx*) /∴ (∃*x*)(*Hx* & ~*Fx*)

  *k. (∃*x*)(*Fx* & ~*Gx*), (∀*x*)(*Fx* → (*Hx* v *Gx*)) /∴ (∃*x*)*Hx*

   l. (∃*x*)(*Fx* v *Gx*), (∀*x*)~*Fx* /∴ (∃*x*)*Gx*

  *m. (∀*x*)(*Fx* → *Gx*), (∀*x*)(*Hx* → *Ix*), (∀*x*)(~*Gx* v ~*Ix*) /∴ (∀*x*)(~*Fx* v ~*Hx*)

   n. (∀*x*)(*Fx* → (*Gx* v *Hx*)), (∃*x*)(*Fx* & ~*Hx*) /∴ (∃*x*)(*Fx* & *Gx*)

8. If the sequence of steps at the top of page 255 had terminated with step 3, 4, 5, 6, 7, or 8, would the resulting sequence qualify as a derivation? If not, explain why not.

1	$(\forall x)(Fx \rightarrow Gx)$	Hyp
2	$(\exists x)(Hx \,\&\, Fx)$	Hyp
3	$Ha \,\&\, Fa$	2, EI
4	$Fa \rightarrow Ga$	1, UI
5	Fa	3, Simp
6	Ga	4, 5, MP
7	Ha	3, Simp
8	$Ha \,\&\, Ga$	6, 7, Conj
9	$(\exists x)(Hx \,\&\, Gx)$	8, EG

9. Using both one-way and two-way rules, construct a derivation of the conclusion from the premises of each of the following arguments.

*a. $\sim(\exists x)(Fx \,\&\, Gx) \,/\therefore\, (\forall x)(Fx \rightarrow \sim Gx)$

 b. $(\forall x)(Fx \rightarrow \sim Gx) \,/\therefore\, (\forall x)(Gx \rightarrow \sim Fx)$

*c. $(\exists x)(Fx \,\&\, Gx) \,/\therefore\, (\exists x)(Gx \,\&\, Fx)$

 d. $(\forall x)(Fx \rightarrow Gx) \,/\therefore\, (\forall x)(\sim Gx \rightarrow \sim Fx)$

*e. $(\forall x)(Fx \rightarrow \sim Gx), (\forall x)(Hx \rightarrow Gx) \,/\therefore\, (\forall x)(Hx \rightarrow \sim Fx)$

 f. $(\forall x)(Fx \,v\, Gx), \sim(\exists x)\sim(Fx \rightarrow Hx), (\forall x)(Gx \rightarrow Hx) \,/\therefore\, \sim(\exists x)\sim Hx$

*g. $(\forall y)(Fy \,v\, Gy), (\forall y)(\sim Gy \,v\, Hy) \,/\therefore\, (\forall z)(Fz \,v\, Hz)$

*h. $(\forall y)((Fy \,v\, Gy) \rightarrow Hy), (\forall x)((Hx \rightarrow (Ix \,\&\, Jx)) \,/\therefore\, (\forall z)(Fz \rightarrow Iz)$

 i. $(\exists x)(\exists y)(Fxy \,v\, Fxy) \,/\therefore\, (\exists x)(\exists y)Fxy$

*j. $(\forall x)(Fx \rightarrow (Gx \,v\, Hx)), \sim(\exists x)(Fx \,\&\, Hx) \,/\therefore\, (\forall x)(Fx \rightarrow Gx)$ [Difficult]

 k. $(\forall x)(Fx \rightarrow (Gx \rightarrow Hx)) \,/\therefore\, (\forall x)((Fx \,\&\, Gx) \rightarrow Hx)$

*10. Using both one-way and two-way rules, construct a derivation of the conclusion from the premises for each of the following arguments.

 a. $\sim(\forall x)(Fx \rightarrow \sim Gx) \,/\therefore\, (\exists x)(Fx \,\&\, Gx)$

 b. $(\exists x)(Fx \,\&\, Gx) \,/\therefore\, \sim(\forall x)(Fx \rightarrow \sim Gx)$

 For these two derivations, can you conclude that $\sim(\forall x)(Fx \rightarrow \sim Gx)$ and $(\exists x)(Fx \,\&\, Gx)$ are equivalent?

11. Show by derivations that the following arguments are valid.

 a. $(\forall x)(Fx \rightarrow \sim Gx) \rightarrow (\forall x)(Fx \rightarrow \sim Hx), (\exists x)(Fx \,\&\, Hx) \,/\therefore\, (\exists x)(Fx \,\&\, Gx)$

*b. $(\forall x)(Fx \rightarrow \sim Gx), ((\exists x)Fx \rightarrow (\forall x)(Gx \,v\, Hx)) \,/\therefore\, (\sim(\exists x)Hx \rightarrow (\forall x)\sim Fx)$

 [Hint: Use the indirect method.]

12. With the intention of using the translations to detect validity, translate the arguments at the top of page 256. Then derive the Q-conclusion from the Q-premises in each translation.

*a. All angels are perfect. But, no humans are perfect. Therefore, no humans are angels.

b. All who are brave take risks. All who take risks do not give up easily. Therefore, all who give up easily are not brave.

*c. Everyone who loves me will cheer for me. Everybody loves me. Therefore, the governor of California will cheer for me.

d. Every desperate or confused person will become happy after a while and enlightened after a while. Therefore, anyone who is confused will become happy after a while.

*e. Everybody is foolish sometimes. And everybody makes wise decisions sometimes. Therefore, everybody is foolish or makes wise decisions one day or another.

13. With the intention of using the translations to detect validity, translate the arguments below. Then derive the Q-conclusion from the Q-premises in each translation.

*a. Some soldiers are heroes. All heroes are worthy of praise. Therefore, some soldiers are worthy of praise.

b. Those who are joyful are wise. Some who are joyful are not rich. Therefore, some who are wise are not rich.

*c. All magicians who are not thieves are registered with the police. All of Mia's brothers are magicians. Some of Mia's brothers are not registered with the police. Therefore, there are thieves.

d. People who hate to waste things are thrifty. Some people hate to waste things. Therefore, some people are thrifty.

*e. No dictators are humane. Some political leaders are humane and popular. Therefore, some political leaders who are not dictators are popular.

14. With the intention of using the translations to detect incompatibility, translate the following. Then derive a contradictory sentence of the form (A & ~A) from the Q-translations in each case. Add valid sentences if warranted.

a. Every even number is in the set. Twelve is not an odd number. Every number is odd or even. Twelve is not in the set.

b. All columnists are men and all reporters are women. But some female reporters are columnists.

PART III

FORMAL LOGICAL SYSTEMS

AN INTRODUCTION
TO FORMAL SYSTEMS

The purpose of a <u>formal system</u> is to capture the essential truths of a specific subject matter. In his *Elements*, the Greek mathematician Euclid (ca. 300 B.C.) gave an axiomatic-deductive treatment of geometry that is well known. It was Aristotle who discovered the formal treatment of logic. Of course, many advances have been made in both geometry and logic since the times of Euclid and Aristotle.

Like other formal systems, logical systems are used to solve problems. However, for beginning students, the study of logical systems has benefits in addition to those of problem solving. Of equal importance is an understanding of how logical words function in inferences and a deeper appreciation of what correct inference involves. Formal logical systems are also of considerable theoretical interest.

The first section of this chapter discusses some general characteristics of logical systems. A formal system is developed in the remaining sections.

9.1 ON THE STRUCTURE OF FORMAL SYSTEMS

This section contains topics that seem most suitably placed at the beginning because of their importance to the construction of a formal system. You may find some of them difficult to grasp on first reading. My advice is to concentrate on the instructions for constructing derivations and return to the other topics for more careful study later.

General Remarks

A system of logic consists of an artificial language, rules governing the steps taken in deriving conclusions from premises, and possibly various <u>axioms</u>. The artificial languages used by logicians are often referred to as <u>formal languages</u>. Which formal language a system uses, which rules of inference it employs, and which axioms (if any) it contains will vary from system to system.

Some differences are insignificant. For example, choosing '·' rather than '&' as the sign for conjunction is of no logical consequence. But other differences in choice of language, axioms, or rules of inference may result in differences with respect to what is derivable. For example, the conclusion of an argument may be derivable from its premises in one system but not in another.

Rules governing steps taken in a <u>derivation</u> are known variously among logicians as rules of deduction, inference, derivation, transformation, and direct consequence. We call them <u>rules of direct consequence</u>. When each sentence in a derivation is either an axiom or follows from preceding items by a rule of direct consequence, the last item is a <u>theorem</u>. Because an axiom can be the last item of such a derivation, axioms also count as theorems.

The derivation below has four items, each of which is an axiom (items 1 and 2) or a direct consequence of preceding items (items 3 and 4) in virtue of a rule of direct consequence.

1	$P \to (P \to P)$	ax cond rep
2	$P \to ((P \to P) \to P)$	ax cond rep
3	$(P \to (P \to P)) \to (P \to P)$	2, dist
4	$P \to P$	1, 3, m p

Notice how each item is numbered on the left and justified on the right. Because each item is either an axiom or a sentence that follows from preceding items by a rule of direct consequence, the last item in the derivation is a theorem in any system that contains those axioms and rules. Detailed explanation of the axiom and rules will come later.

Soundness is a desirable property for deductive systems. A system is <u>sound</u> if and only if it is not possible to derive a false conclusion from true premises. Put another way, a system is not sound if the conclusion of an argument that is not valid is derivable from the premises. Because logicians want to construct formal systems that are sound, they want every rule of direct consequence to be truth-preserving. A rule of direct consequence is truth-preserving if and only if there is no way to derive a false conclusion from true premises using that rule correctly. In other words, a truth-preserving rule can lead from truth to truth, from falsity to truth, or from falsity to falsity, but never from truth to falsity.

Another desirable property for deductive systems is completeness. A system is complete if and only if it is possible to derive the conclusion from the premises of every argument that is valid in terms of the language of the system. For example, a system with C as its formal language is not complete if there is any C-valid argument the conclusion of which is not derivable from the premises. So, if 'Q' is not derivable from '(P & Q)', the system is not complete. By contrast, if '(P & Q)' is derivable from 'Q', the system is not sound.

An undesirable property of systems is inconsistency. A system is inconsistent if both a sentence and its negation are theorems. For example, when both 'Q' and '~Q' are theorems of a system, then the system is inconsistent.

In constructing formal systems, logicians economize on both axioms and rules of direct consequence. Ideally, only as many axioms and rules of direct consequence are included as are needed to insure that the system be both sound and complete. Consequently, in constructing a system, no logician who knows that a theorem is already derivable is likely to adopt it as an axiom. The situation is analogous for rules of direct consequence. If a system is sound and complete without some rule of direct consequence, there is no need to include that rule as an official rule of the system except as a matter of convenience.

When all of the derivable arguments in one system are derivable in another and vice versa, the two systems are the same system from the point of view of logic and are said to be equivalent. We use the phrase 'derivable argument' as short for 'argument the conclusion of which is derivable from the premises'.

One system can be stronger or weaker than another. A system X is stronger than a system Y if there is no argument derivable in Y that is not derivable in X and there are arguments that are derivable in X that are not derivable in Y. For example, if every argument derivable in Y is derivable in X and 'P' is derivable from '~~P' in X but not in Y, then X is stronger that Y. A system is weaker than another if the other is stronger than it.

Axioms and Rules of Direct Consequence

Unlike theorems, axioms are accepted without derivation. Therefore, in constructing a system of logic, by and large only sentences that are believed, and preferably known, to be valid are selected as axioms.

A system containing the **axioms of conditioned repetition** (ax cond rep) has as axioms any and every sentence of the form

$$A \to (B \to A)$$

Items 1 and 2 of the sample derivation on page 260 are axioms of conditioned repetition because each is a sentence of this form. Notice how item 1 results from replacing both '*A*' and '*B*' with '*P*', and item 2 results from replacing '*A*' with '*P*' and '*B*' with '$(P \to P)$'.

Although some rules selected for the construction of a formal system may resemble patterns of correct reasoning regarded as natural, others selected may not. The rule below is an example of a rule that many would regard as having no resemblance to any typical pattern of human reasoning.

Distribution (dist).   In any numbered sequence of sentences having the form below, item i is a direct consequence of item h:

$$
\begin{array}{c|l}
h & A \to (B \to C) \\
i & (A \to B) \to (A \to C) \qquad \text{h, dist}
\end{array}
$$

This rule tells you that given a derivation of this form, item i is justified by writing 'h, dist' to the right; 'dist' is the abbreviated name of the rule of distribution. In the sample derivation on page 260, item 3 is a direct consequence of item 2 in virtue of the rule of distribution, as '2, dist' written to its right indicates.

The next rule reflects its antiquity in its Latin name. In contrast to the rule of distribution, this rule resembles a natural pattern of reasoning.

Modus Ponens (m p).   The consequent of a conditional is a direct consequence of (i) the antecedent of the conditional and (ii) the conditional itself.

Schematically expressed, the rule is as follows:

$$
\begin{array}{c|l}
h & A \to B \\
i & A \\
j & B \qquad\qquad\qquad\qquad \text{h, i, m p}
\end{array}
$$

Notice how 'h, i, m p' is given as the justification for step j, where 'h', 'i', and 'j' stand for numbers (where h < i < j) and 'm p' is the abbreviated name of the rule. In the sample derivation given on page 260, steps 1, 3, and 4 correspond to h, i, and j, respectively. The rule is clearly truth-preserving, as the consequent of a conditional must be true if the conditional and its antecedent are true.

Other seemingly natural rules of direct consequence are the following rules for conjunction.

Conjunction Introduction (conj int).   A conjunction is a direct conse-quence of its left and right conjuncts.

Schematically expressed, the rule is as follows:

$$
\begin{array}{c|ll}
h & A & \\
i & B & \\
j & A \,\&\, B & h, i, \text{conj int}
\end{array}
$$

The rule of conjunction introduction allows you to write a conjunction as an item of a derivation if both its left and right conjuncts (in any order) are preceding items. The rule is clearly truth-preserving, since a conjunction must be true if its conjuncts are.

Conjunction Elimination (conj elim).   Both conjuncts of a conjunction are direct consequences of their conjunction. In other words, a conjunction has as a direct consequence both its right conjunct and its left conjunct.

The following gives a schematic representation of the two parts of the rule.

$$
\begin{array}{c|ll}
h & A \,\&\, B & \\
i & A & h, \text{conj elim}
\end{array}
$$

$$
\begin{array}{c|ll}
h & A \,\&\, B & \\
i & B & h, \text{conj elim}
\end{array}
$$

The rule of conjunction elimination allows you to write either conjunct of a conjunction as an item in a derivation if the conjunction is a preceding item. To be a preceding item, a conjunction need not *immediately* precede a conjunct. There should be no doubt that the rule is truth-preserving as the conjunct of a conjunction (whether left or right) must be true if the conjunc-tion is true.

A derivation with hypotheses differs from one without only in the hypotheses being listed at the beginning and separated from subsequent items by a short horizontal dash. To the right of each hypothesis, 'hyp' is written as a justification. The two derivations that follow each have two hypotheses. They illustrate the fact that in applying the rule of conjunction introduction, either the right or left conjunct may occur first. In the first derivation, the left conjunct appears before the right conjunct.

$$
\begin{array}{c|ll}
1 & P & \text{hyp} \\
2 & Q & \text{hyp} \\
\hline
3 & P \,\&\, Q & 1, 2, \text{conj int}
\end{array}
$$

And in the second derivation, the right conjunct appears before the left.

$$
\begin{array}{ll}
1 \quad & Q & \text{hyp} \\
2 \quad & P & \text{hyp} \\
& \text{-} \\
3 \quad & P\,\&\,Q & \text{1, 2, conj int}
\end{array}
$$

The next derivation illustrates the fact that the rule of conjunction intro-duction requires that the rule be applied to both right and left conjuncts, but that the same item can satisfy the requirement if both conjuncts are the same.

$$
\begin{array}{ll}
1 \quad & P & \text{hyp} \\
& \text{-} \\
2 \quad & P\,\&\,P & \text{1, 1, conj int}
\end{array}
$$

Note that the justification for item 2 is given correctly as '1, 1, conj int'. Two items must be referenced in applying this rule even if the same item is referenced twice.

The following derivations illustrate the range of application of the rule of conjunction elimination.

$$
\begin{array}{ll}
1 \quad & P\,\&\,Q & \text{hyp} \\
& \text{-} \\
2 \quad & P & \text{1, conj elim}
\end{array}
$$

$$
\begin{array}{ll}
1 \quad & P\,\&\,Q & \text{hyp} \\
& \text{-} \\
2 \quad & Q & \text{1, conj elim}
\end{array}
$$

The first derivation leads from a conjunction to its left conjunct; the second derivation, from a conjunction to its right conjunct. Notice how by this rule both left and right conjuncts are derivable from their conjunction.

The next derivation combines the rule of conjunction elimination with that of *modus ponens*.

$$
\begin{array}{ll}
1 \quad & P\,\&\,Q & \text{hyp} \\
2 \quad & P \rightarrow R & \text{hyp} \\
& \text{-} \\
3 \quad & P & \text{1, conj elim} \\
4 \quad & R & \text{2, 3, m p}
\end{array}
$$

Although the previous examples of derivations from hypotheses have had only one or two hypotheses, any finite number of sentences may serve as hypotheses of a derivation. Whether there is one or more, all must be listed at the beginning of the derivation and justified with 'hyp' written to the right.

Derivations and Semantic Properties

Derivations may or may not have hypotheses. The derivation on page 260 has no hypotheses. When a derivation has no hypotheses, every sentence is either an axiom or follows from preceding items by a rule of direct consequence. If a system is sound, all of its axioms are valid and all of its rules of direct consequence are truth-preserving. As a consequence, in a sound system, all items in a derivation from no hypotheses are valid, including the last item which is counted as a theorem. Therefore, if a system is sound, you can establish that a sentence is valid by deriving it as theorem.

If a system has axioms all of which are valid and rules of direct consequence all of which are truth-preserving, no argument derivable in that system can have true premises and a false conclusion. Consequently, in such a system, you can show that an argument is valid by constructing a derivation of the conclusion from the premises. For example, the last derivation on page 264 establishes that the following argument is valid:

$(P \mathbin{\&} Q), (P \rightarrow R) \mathbin{/\therefore} R$

You can also use derivations to show that one sentence implies another. If a sentence is derivable from another, it is implied by the other. For example, we have already derived 'P' from '$(P \mathbin{\&} Q)$'. The derivation shows that '$(P \mathbin{\&} Q)$' implies 'P'. Because two sentences are equivalent if and only if each implies the other, you can verify that any two sentences are equivalent by deriving each from the other. For example, we have already derived '$(P \mathbin{\&} P)$' from 'P'. Derive 'P' from '$(P \mathbin{\&} P)$' and you will have shown that the two sentences are equivalent.

A derivation can also establish that a sentence is contradictory. To show that a sentence is contradictory through a derivation, construct a derivation with the sentence as the sole hypothesis and derive a sentence and its negation as items. If a sentence and its negation are derivable from the hypothesis, then both a truth and a falsehood are derivable from the hypothesis. And as no falsehood is derivable from a truth, the hypothesis cannot be true. Therefore, the hypothesis is contradictory. In an analogous fashion, you can show that a group of sentences is incompatible. Take the sentences as the only hypotheses of a derivation and derive both a sentence and its negation from them.

For example, the following derivation confirms that its hypothesis is contradictory.

1	$(P \,\&\, (P \rightarrow {\sim}Q)) \,\&\, ({\sim}Q \rightarrow {\sim}P)$	hyp
2	$P \,\&\, (P \rightarrow {\sim}Q)$	1, conj elim
3	P	2, conj elim
4	$P \rightarrow {\sim}Q$	2, conj elim
5	${\sim}Q$	3, 4, m p
6	${\sim}Q \rightarrow {\sim}P$	1, conj elim
7	${\sim}P$	5, 6, m p

Note that item 7 is the negation of item 3. The next derivation shows that the hypotheses of the derivation are incompatible.

1	$P \,\&\, {\sim}Q$	hyp
2	$P \rightarrow Q$	hyp
3	P	1, conj elim
4	Q	2, 3, m p
5	${\sim}Q$	1, conj elim

Note that item 5 is the negation of item 4.

Subordinate Derivations

The examples of derivations you have seen so far have only sentences as items. However, in the system we are developing, derivations may also qualify as items of derivations. We call a derivation that is an item of another derivation a <u>subordinate derivation</u> or, for short, a <u>subderivation</u>. Such derivations function as auxiliaries to the derivations to which they are subordinate by assisting in the derivation of their items. A subderivation may be viewed, in effect, as an argument for the sake of the argument.

We refer to a derivation by the sequence of numbers that includes the first and last sentence in the derivation. An example of a subordinate derivation is the derivation 4–7 that is an item of the derivation 1–8 that follows.

1	$P \to S$	hyp
2	$(P \to S) \to (P \to (P \to R))$	hyp
3	$P \to (P \to R)$	1, 2, m p
4	P	hyp (of 4-7)
5	$P \to (P \to R)$	3, reit
6	$P \to R$	4, 5, m p
7	R	4, 6, m p
8	$P \to R$	4-7, cond int

A derivation that is not a subderivation we call the <u>main derivation</u>. Thus, in the example above, the main derivation is the derivation 1-8. This derivation has exactly *five* items bordered on the left by a vertical line extending the length of the column. The first three items are numbered in sequence. The fourth is the whole subordinate derivation referenced '4-7'; and the fifth is the sentence numbered '8'. All five items, that is, 1, 2, 3, 4-7, and 8, are in the same column and lined up under one another. Items 1, 2, and 3 precede the subordinate derivation 4-7 and the subordinate derivation precedes item 8. The second vertical line borders the column of the subordinate derivation 4-7. This derivation has four items, beginning with item 4 and ending with item 7. In the column 4-7, item 4 is the first item and is not preceded by any other. An item <u>precedes</u> another if and only if it is listed anywhere above the other in the very same column.

A subordinate derivation may have as items repetitions of sentences that precede it. The rule allowing this is stated as follows:

Reiteration (reit).   Any sentence that is an item of a derivation can be written as an item of any derivation it precedes.

For example, in the main derivation 1-8 of the sample derivation above, item 3 precedes the subordinate derivation 4-7; therefore, item 3 can be reiterated in 4-7 as item 5. We indicated the reiteration by writing '3, reit' to the right of item 5.

In virtue of the rule of reiteration, every sentence preceding a subordinate derivation can be entered as an item in the subordinate derivation. However, the rule of reiteration does not state that any sentence that is an item of a subderivation can be written as an item in the derivation in which the subderivation is an item. In other words, the rule does allow you to go backward. For example, in the derivation above, item 6 cannot be reiterated as item 8 and item 8 then justified by writing '6, reit' to its right.

The subordinate derivation 4-7 is within the larger derivation 1-8 for the purpose of deriving item 8. Note how '4-7 cond int', appears to the right of item 8. An explanation of the rule that allows you to enter item 8 in a derivation by citing the subderivation 4–7 will be delayed until in the next section.

The summary definition below applies both to main derivations and to subordinate ones in this text.

A derivation is a column of items bordered on the left by a vertical line extending the length of the column. Each item in the column is either (i) a sentence that is a hypothesis, (ii) an axiom, (iii) a direct consequence of preceding items in the *same* column, (iv) a reiteration of a sentence that precedes the column, or (v) a subderivation. To the right of each sentence item is written its justification for appearing in the derivation: (i) 'hyp' as an abbreviation for 'hypothesis' if it is a hypothesis; (ii) what axiom it is if it is an axiom; (iii) reference to the numbers of the preceding items and the rule according to which it is a direct consequence of those items if it is a direct consequence, and (iv) reference to the number of the item that precedes the column and the rule of reiteration if it is a reiteration.

EXERCISES FOR SECTION 9.1

*1. Explain why the following are axioms of conditioned repetition.

   a. $Q \rightarrow (P \rightarrow Q)$

   b. $Q \rightarrow ((P \rightarrow P) \rightarrow Q)$

2. Construct a derivation to show that each of the following is a valid argument.

   *a. $Q, (P \& (Q \rightarrow R)) / \therefore R$

   b. $((P \& Q) \& R) / \therefore P$

   *c. $P, (P \rightarrow Q), (Q \rightarrow R) / \therefore (P \& R)$

*3. Show by a truth table that every axiom of conditioned repetition is valid.

4. Show by a truth table that the rule of *modus ponens* and the rule of distribution are truth-preserving.

5. Look back to the last derivation in this section (p. 267). How many items does the subordinate derivation 4–7 have? How is each sentence item justified? Why is item 3 reiterated in the subordinate derivation? Could *modus ponens* have been applied to items 3 and 4 to derive item 5? If not, why not?

*6. Systems can be complete without being sound. Can you explain why?

Answer to exercise 5. The subordinate derivation 4–7 has *four* items. These items form a vertical column separate from that of the main derivation. Notice that item 4 is a hypothesis of the subordinate derivation and its first item. Item 6 is a direct consequence of items 4 and 5 by the rule of *modus ponens*. You may wonder why we did not apply *modus ponens* to item 3 and 4 and save the trouble of reiterating 3 and then applying the rule of *modus ponens* to items 4 and 5. The reason is quite simple. In a derivation, an item is a direct consequence of other items only if those items precede it in the same column. And items 3 and 4 are not in the same column.

9.2 A NATURAL DEDUCTION SYSTEM

There are rules of direct consequence called introduction rules and others called elimination rules. An <u>introduction rule</u> provides a strategy for deriving a sentence *of* the type after which the rule is named. For example, the rule of conjunction introduction gives you a way to derive a conjunction. In contrast, an <u>elimination rule</u> provides a strategy for deriving a sentence *from* the type after which the rule is named.

For example, the rule of conjunction elimination gives you a way to derive a sentence *from* a conjunction. Because the rule of *modus ponens* gives you a way to derive the consequent of a conditional *from* the conditional and its antecedent, it qualifies as an elimination rule for conditionals in spite of its traditional Latin name. In fact, 'conditional elimination' is that name that some logicians use to refer to the rule we call *modus ponens*.

In this section, we present a rule that allows you to derive a conditional. Not surprisingly, the rule is thought of as an introduction rule. We then discuss derivations with subderivations that themselves have subderivations as items. From the introduction and elimination rules introduced, we begin the construction of a formal system for this text.

Conditional Introduction

The following derivation contains a conditional as its last item. The subderivation preceding the last item is constructed for the purpose of deriving that conditional.

1	$P \rightarrow (R \rightarrow Q)$	hyp
2	R	hyp (of 2–7)
3	$P \rightarrow (R \rightarrow Q)$	1, reit
4	$(P \rightarrow R) \rightarrow (P \rightarrow Q)$	3, dist
5	$R \rightarrow (P \rightarrow R)$	ax cond rep
6	$P \rightarrow R$	2, 5, m p
7	$P \rightarrow Q$	4, 6, m p
8	$R \rightarrow (P \rightarrow Q)$	2–7, cond int

From studying this derivation, one can get an idea of how the new introduction rule works. Note that item 2 is the sole hypothesis of the subderivation 2–7 and that item 7 is the last item of 2–7. Also note that the item immediately below the subderivation is item 8 and to its right is written '2–7, cond int'; '2–7' refers to the subordinate derivation and 'cond int' to the new rule. Also note that item 8 is a conditional with item 2 as its antecedent and item 7 as its consequent.

The new introduction rule is stated precisely below.

Conditional Introduction (cond int). A conditional is a direct consequence of a subordinate derivation if (i) the antecedent of the conditional is the only hypothesis of the subderivation and (ii) the consequent of the conditional is one of the items of the subderivation.

The following schematic expression of the rule shows in a graphic way how the rule leads from a subderivation to a conditional.

h	A	hyp (of h–i)
.	.	
i	B	
j	$A \rightarrow B$	h–i, cond int

[Can you identify which items in derivation 1–8 above correspond to h, i, and j in the schema? Can you make the same identification for those items in the last derivation of the previous section on page 267?]

To see for yourself how to construct the derivation at the beginning of this section, begin as follows by listing the hypothesis as the first item and the sentence you intend to derive as the last.

1	$P \rightarrow (R \rightarrow Q)$	hyp
.	.	
	$R \rightarrow (P \rightarrow Q)$	

Next set up a subordinate derivation with the antecedent of the conditional you want to derive as the only hypothesis and the consequent as its last item.

$$\begin{array}{ll}
1 \quad | \quad P \to (R \to Q) & \text{hyp} \\[4pt]
2 \quad | \quad | \quad R & \text{hyp (of 2-h)} \\[4pt]
. \quad | \quad | \quad . \\[2pt]
h \quad | \quad | \quad P \to Q \\
i \quad | \quad R \to (P \to Q) & \text{2-h, cond int}
\end{array}$$

The idea is that if you can derive the consequent from the antecedent in the subordinate derivation, you can then apply the rule of conditional introduction to the subderivation and get the conditional you desire.

The derivation set up as above reduces your task to completing the subderivation. To complete the subderivation, first reiterate item 1 as below.

$$\begin{array}{ll}
1 \quad | \quad P \to (R \to Q) & \text{hyp} \\[4pt]
2 \quad | \quad | \quad R & \text{hyp (of 2-h)} \\[4pt]
3 \quad | \quad | \quad P \to (R \to Q) & \text{1, reit} \\[2pt]
. \quad | \quad | \quad . \\
h \quad | \quad | \quad P \to Q \\
i \quad | \quad R \to (P \to Q) & \text{2-h, cond int}
\end{array}$$

You can then fill in the missing items and the missing justifications as shown below:

$$\begin{array}{ll}
1 \quad | \quad P \to (R \to Q) & \text{hyp} \\[4pt]
2 \quad | \quad | \quad R & \text{hyp (of 2-7)} \\[4pt]
3 \quad | \quad | \quad P \to (R \to Q) & \text{1, reit} \\
4 \quad | \quad | \quad (P \to R) \to (P \to Q) & \text{3, dist} \\
5 \quad | \quad | \quad R \to (P \to R) & \text{ax cond rep} \\
6 \quad | \quad | \quad P \to R & \text{2, 5, m p} \\
7 \quad | \quad | \quad P \to Q & \text{4, 6, m p} \\
8 \quad | \quad R \to (P \to Q) & \text{2-7, cond int}
\end{array}$$

Notice that once you set up a subordinate derivation with the antecedent of the conditional as the only hypothesis and derive the consequent as an item, you can then enter the conditional as an item in the same column as the subderivation and justify the conditional by referencing the subderivation and citing the rule of conditional introduction.

To understand why the rule of conditional introduction is truth-preserving, it is helpful to think of a subderivation as an argument for the sake of an argument or, more specifically, as a derivation for the sake of the derivation to which it is subordinate. In virtue of the rule of reiteration, you can reiterate any hypothesis of a derivation in a derivation subordinate to it. Therefore, through reiteration, a subderivation can make use of any hypotheses of the derivation to which it is subordinate. In addition, a subderivation often has a hypothesis of its own. Thus what you can derive in a subderivation you could derive in the derivation to which it is subordinate if the hypothesis of the subderivation were added to the hypotheses of that derivation.

So what the rule of conditional introduction says, in effect, is the following: You may enter a conditional as an item in a derivation once you have shown (through a preceding subderivation) that with the addition of the antecedent of the conditional to those hypotheses you could have entered its consequent. This procedure is certain to be truth-preserving. In showing through the subderivation that there is no possibility for the consequent of the conditional to be false while the hypotheses of the derivation and the antecedent of the conditional are true, you also show that there is no possibility for the conditional to be false while the hypotheses of the derivation are true. Remember the only way for a conditional to be false is for its antecedent to be true and its consequent false.

For example, in the derivation at the bottom of page 271, the subderivation 2–7 shows that if item 2 is added to item 1 as a hypothesis of the main derivation, item 7 is derivable in the main derivation. But if item 7 is derivable from items 1 and 2 and the system is sound, then there is no possibility for items 1 and 2 to be true and item 7 false. If there is no possibility for items 1 and 2 to be true and item 7 to be false, then there is no possibility for item 1 to be true and item 8 false.

So far we have only considered examples of subordinate derivations with sentences as items. Subordinate derivations may also have subordinate derivations as items. In fact, any finite number of subordinate derivations may nest one within the other.

A derivation with a subderivation within another subderivation appears at the top of the next page.

1	$P \rightarrow (R \rightarrow Q)$	hyp
2	R	hyp (of 2–8)
3	P	hyp (of 3–7)
4	$P \rightarrow (R \rightarrow Q)$	1, reit
5	R	2, reit
6	$R \rightarrow Q$	3, 4, m p
7	Q	5, 6, m p
8	$P \rightarrow Q$	3–7, cond int
9	$R \rightarrow (P \rightarrow Q)$	2–8, cond int

Observe that the derivation 1–9 has exactly three items (1, 2–8, and 9); the subordinate derivation 2–8 also has exactly three items (2, 3–7, and 8); and the subordinate derivation 3–7 has five (3, 4, 5, 6, and 7). Unlike our previous derivation of the same conclusion from the same hypothesis, this derivation uses neither the rule of distribution nor an axiom of conditioned repetition.

In constructing this derivation, you first set up a subordinate derivation. Let the antecedent of the conditional you wish to derive be the only hypothesis of that subderivation and let the consequent of the conditional be the last item. Then set up a subderivation within the subordinate derivation as follows:

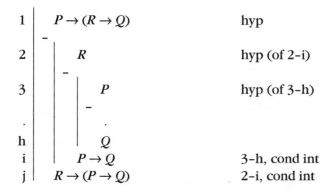

1	$P \rightarrow (R \rightarrow Q)$	hyp
2	R	hyp (of 2–i)
3	P	hyp (of 3–h)
.	.	
h	Q	
i	$P \rightarrow Q$	3–h, cond int
j	$R \rightarrow (P \rightarrow Q)$	2–i, cond int

Because item i will follow by conditional introduction from the innermost subordinate derivation 3–h, your task is now simply to fill in the steps in the innermost subordinate derivation.

Begin by reiterating items 1 and 2 in the innermost subderivation as shown at the top of page 274.

1	$P \to (R \to Q)$	hyp
2	R	hyp (of 2–i)
3	P	hyp (of 3–h)
4	$P \to (R \to Q)$	1, reit
5	R	2, reit
.	.	
h	Q	
i	$P \to Q$	3–h, cond int
j	$R \to (P \to Q)$	2–i, cond int

With items 4 and 5 in place, the derivation now requires the insertion of items between 5 and the last item of the innermost subordinate derivation. You can do this by applying *modus ponens* twice.

With all numerical references inserted, you will have the completed derivation that follows.

1	$P \to (R \to Q)$	hyp
2	R	hyp (of 2–8)
3	P	hyp (of 3–7)
4	$P \to (R \to Q)$	1, reit
5	R	2, reit
6	$(R \to Q)$	3, 4, m p
7	Q	5, 6, m p
8	$P \to Q$	3–7, cond int
9	$R \to (P \to Q)$	2–8, cond int

Compare this derivation with the earlier one (p. 270) that employed the axiom of conditioned repetition instead of a subderivation within a subderivation.

Previously, we said that a derivation is subordinate to the derivation of which it is an item. We also say that a derivation is subordinate to any derivation in which it is an item of an item, and so on. Thus, in the just completed derivation, both 2–8 and 3–7 are subordinate to 1–9. We say that a derivation is <u>directly subordinate</u> only to the derivation in which it is itself an item. So, only 2–8 is directly subordinate to 1–9.

Strictly speaking, an item can only be reiterated from a derivation in a derivation directly subordinate to it. However, as a shortcut, we allow reiterations from a derivation in a derivation that is simply subordinate to it. Thus, in the derivation just completed, we reiterated item 1 directly in the innermost subordinate derivation without first reiterating it in 2–8, which is directly subordinate to 1–9, and then in 3–7, which is directly subordinate to 2–8.

Theorems and Derived Rules

The system that we are developing in this text is a <u>natural deduction system</u>. It has no axioms and its official rules of direct consequence resemble what may be regarded as natural patterns of reasoning. Thus the axioms of conditioned repetition and the rule of distribution are not axioms or among the official rules of direct consequence of this system. Because the system favors introduction and elimination rules, we call it <u>Intelim</u>, following Frederic B. Fitch in his classic *Symbolic Logic* (Ronald Press, 1952). The official rules of this system include the rule of reiteration, *modus ponens* (that is, the elimination rule for conditional), the rule of conditional introduction, and the rules of conjunction introduction and elimination. Still other official rules will be added in subsequent chapters.

In formulating any system, you must state precisely what counts as a theorem in that system. In Intelim, the last item in a derivation without hypotheses is a theorem. It is understood that only rules of Intelim are used in the derivation. The following derivation has no hypotheses and its last item is an Intelim theorem.

1	P	hyp (of 1–4)
2	Q	hyp (of 2–3)
3	P	1, reit
4	$Q \to P$	2–3, cond int
5	$P \to (Q \to P)$	1–4, cond int

Note that the main derivation 1–5 has only two items, the subderivation 1–4 and item 5. Neither of these items is a hypothesis. Therefore, the main derivation has no hypotheses although the two subderivations do.

Intelim has no axioms, not even the axioms of conditioned repetition introduced in section 9.1. This is no problem, however, as all those axioms are derivable as theorems in Intelim. In fact, the derivation above shows how any sentence of the form of

$$P \to (Q \to P)$$

can be derived as a theorem. For example, you can derive

$$(P \mathbin{\&} R) \rightarrow (\sim Q \rightarrow (P \mathbin{\&} R))$$

from no hypotheses by replacing 'P' with '$(P \mathbin{\&} R)$' and 'Q' with '$\sim Q$' throughout the derivation above.

Because the preceding derivation provides a method for proving that any sentence of the form $(A \rightarrow (B \rightarrow A))$ is a theorem, we regard the derivation as a proof of all of those theorems. Whenever you need one in a derivation, you can enter it as an item (as if it were an axiom), citing for its justification the **theorem of conditioned repetition** (th cond rep). Justifying a theorem in this way saves the trouble of deriving it over and over again.

The rule of distribution introduced in section 9.1 is not an official rule of Intelim. But, using it, you will not be able to enter any sentence in a derivation that you could not have entered using only official rules. In general, any such rule can be given the status of a <u>derived rule</u> and you may use it freely in constructing derivations. Having derived rules available is convenient because they often shorten derivations without introducing any result that could not be reached using just the official rules of the system.

The following derivation shows a way to derive any conditional from its own consequent using just official rules.

1	P	hyp
2	$\quad Q$	hyp (of 2–3)
3	$\quad P$	1, reit
4	$Q \rightarrow P$	1–2, cond int

Just replace 'P' with the consequent of the conditional you want to derive and replace 'Q' with the antecedent of the conditional and you will have your derivation. Because we have shown there is a way of deriving any conditional from its consequent using just official rules, we are justified in adopting the following derived rule.

Added Condition (add cond).   A conditional is a direct consequence of its own consequent.

Using the derived rule of added condition, the derivation that proved the theorems of conditioned repetition can be abbreviated as follows:

1	P	hyp (of 1–2)
2	$Q \rightarrow P$	1, add cond
3	$P \rightarrow (Q \rightarrow P)$	1–2, cond int

The notation '1, add cond' to the right of item 2 indicates that this item was obtained from 1 by applying the derived rule of added condition.

The following is a derivation of $(P \to R)$ from the hypotheses $(P \to Q)$ and $(Q \to R)$.

1	$P \to Q$	hyp
2	$Q \to R$	hyp
3	P	hyp (of 3–7)
4	$P \to Q$	1, reit
5	$Q \to R$	2, reit
6	Q	3, 4, m p
7	R	5, 6, m p
8	$P \to R$	3–7, cond int

This derivation justifies the following derived rule.

Transitivity of Conditional (trans cond).   A conditional $(A \to C)$ is a direct consequence of two other conditionals $(A \to B)$ and $(B \to C)$.

This rule is perhaps more easily understood from its schematic expression.

h	$A \to B$	
i	$B \to C$	
j	$A \to C$	h, i, trans cond

In applying the rule, justify the conditional that is the direct consequence by writing to its right the numbers of the other conditionals and the abbreviated name of the rule.

One of the rules of direct consequence used in section 9.1 was the rule of distribution. This rule is not an official rule of Intelim, but it is adopted as a derived rule. The derivation at the top of the next page shows that you cannot enter any sentence in a derivation with the rule of distribution that you could not have entered through a longer derivation using only official rules.

$$
\begin{array}{lll}
1 & P \to (Q \to R) & \text{hyp} \\
2 & \quad P \to Q & \text{hyp (of 2–9)} \\
3 & \qquad P & \text{hyp (of 3–8)} \\
4 & \qquad P \to (Q \to R) & \text{1, reit} \\
5 & \qquad P \to Q & \text{2, reit} \\
6 & \qquad Q & \text{3, 5, m p} \\
7 & \qquad Q \to R & \text{3, 4, m p} \\
8 & \qquad R & \text{6, 7, m p} \\
9 & \quad P \to R & \text{3–8, cond int} \\
10 & (P \to Q) \to (P \to R) & \text{2–9, cond int}
\end{array}
$$

You can now transform derivations previously constructed using axioms of conditioned repetition and the rule of distribution into Intelim derivations. Just let 'dist' stand for the derived rule of distribution and replace 'ax cond rep' with 'th cond rep'.

EXERCISES FOR SECTION 9.2

1. How many items does the initial derivation of $(P \to (Q \to P))$ on page 275 have? What are they (identify by numerical reference)? How many items does the subordinate derivation 1–4 have? What are they? How many items does the innermost subordinate derivation 2–3 have? What are they?

*2. How many items are there in the derivation on page 277 that justifies the derived rule of transitivity of conditional? How many items are there in the subderivation 3–7?

3. Using only official rules, construct a derivation from no hypotheses of

$$(P \to (Q \to R)) \to ((P \to Q) \to (P \to R))$$

4. Using only official rules, construct derivations establishing that the following arguments are derivable in Intelim.

   *a. $(P \to Q) / \therefore (P \to (P \to Q))$
   b. $(P \to (Q \to R)), (P \to Q) / \therefore (P \to R)$
   *c. $Q, ((P \to Q) \to R) / \therefore R$
   d. $(Q \to R) / \therefore ((P \to Q) \to (P \to R))$

*e. $(R \rightarrow Q)$, $(P \rightarrow R)$ /∴ $(P \rightarrow Q)$

 f. Q /∴ $((P \rightarrow (P \rightarrow Q)) \rightarrow Q)$

*g. $(P \rightarrow Q)$ /∴ $(P \rightarrow (R \rightarrow Q))$

 h. $(R \rightarrow (Q \rightarrow P))$ /∴ $(Q \rightarrow (R \rightarrow P))$

5. Using only official rules, prove that $(P \rightarrow P)$ is a theorem of Intelim. Sentences of that form are the theorems of **reflexivity of conditional** (refl cond).

6. Show by a derivation that each of the following is a theorem of Intelim. To shorten derivations, you may use derived rules and theorems already proven.

   *a. $((P \rightarrow R) \mathbin{\&} (R \rightarrow Q)) \rightarrow (P \rightarrow Q)$

    b. $((P \rightarrow P) \rightarrow P) \rightarrow P$

   *c. $((Q \rightarrow Q) \rightarrow P) \rightarrow P$

7. In addition to the official rules of the system, make use of the theorem of reflexivity of conditional (see exercise 5) and the derived rule of transitivity of conditional to show that the following argument is derivable:

$$(R \rightarrow S), ((P \rightarrow P) \rightarrow (Q \rightarrow R)) /∴ (Q \rightarrow S)$$

8. Translate the following arguments into C. For each translation, construct a derivation of the C-conclusion from the C-premises. Then, in those cases where the translations are suitable, decide whether the English arguments are valid. If you consider that a translation is not suitable, give your reasons.

   *a. If the queen is angry, the king will fire the new cook. The queen is angry and the pasta is overcooked. Therefore, the king will fire the new cook.

    b. If Al Pacino is starring in that movie, then his godfather has nothing against it. Al Pacino is starring in that movie. Therefore, Al Pacino is starring in that movie and his godfather has nothing against it.

   *c. Florian will quit whistling only if Orly stops giggling. If Florian quits whistling and Orly stops giggling, the troubadours will start the show. Therefore, if Florian quits whistling, the troubadours will start the show.

    d. If Little Red Riding Hood is smart, then she'll believe the wolf only if he shows her his valid ID. If Little Red Riding Hood is smart, then she'll believe the wolf. Therefore, if Little Red Riding Hood is smart, the wolf will show her his valid ID.

   *e. If the famous detective has already arrived, then both Robert and Ralph are in trouble. Therefore, if the famous detective has already arrived, then Robert is in trouble.

f. If the restless ghost bought itself a gown, then the ghost went shopping. The ghost went shopping only if the gowns were on sale. Therefore, if the restless ghost bought itself a gown, then the gowns were on sale.

*g. If the senator is involved in a major political scandal, he will have to retire; and if he has to retire, he'll have enough time to write fiction. If the senator has enough time to write fiction, he will write the great American novel. Therefore, if the senator is involved in a major political scandal, he will write the great American novel.

h. John will help at the homeless shelter tonight but Mary will help at the homeless shelter tonight only if she can afford a baby-sitter for her son. Therefore, John and Mary will help at the homeless shelter tonight only if she can afford a baby-sitter for her son.

*i. If *Dracula* is on TV tonight, then Dracula will watch it. If Dracula watches *Dracula,* then he will order a pizza; and if he orders a pizza, then *Dracula* is on TV tonight. Therefore, if *Dracula* is on TV tonight, then Dracula will order a pizza.

j. If Michael is Russian and likes caviar, then he will go out and order some in a restaurant. If Michael is Russian, he likes caviar. Michael is Russian. Therefore, Michael will go out and order some caviar in a restaurant.

Answer to exercise 5 on page 279.

$$
\begin{array}{lll}
1 & \quad P & \text{hyp (of 1–1)} \\
 & \quad \text{–} & \\
2 & P \to P & \text{1–1, cond int}
\end{array}
$$

Notice that the subordinate derivation 1–1 has only one item. Though somewhat unusual, there is nothing wrong with this and nothing wrong with item 2 being a direct consequence of 1–1 by conditional introduction. Conditional introduction simply requires (i) that the antecedent of the conditional is the only hypothesis of the subordinate derivation and (ii) that the consequent of that same conditional is one of the items. As item 1 is both the antecedent and the consequent of the conditional, item 1 satisfies both requirements (i) and (ii).

9.3 CONJUNCTIONS, CONDITIONALS, AND BICONDITIONALS

In this section, you will gain more experience using the rules that you already know. In addition, you will learn how defined signs can be used in derivations and see how rules for biconditionals are derived.

Conjunctions, Conditionals, and Defined Signs

The first derivation below is from $(P \rightarrow (Q \rightarrow R)$ to $((P \& Q) \rightarrow R)$.

1	$P \rightarrow (Q \rightarrow R)$	hyp
2	$P \& Q$	hyp (of 2–7)
3	P	2, conj elim
4	Q	2, conj elim
5	$P \rightarrow (Q \rightarrow R)$	1, reit
6	$Q \rightarrow R$	3, 5, m p
7	R	4, 6, m p
8	$(P \& Q) \rightarrow R$	2–7, cond int

The next derivation is in the reverse, that is, from $((P \& Q) \rightarrow R)$ to $(P \rightarrow (Q \rightarrow R))$.

1	$(P \& Q) \rightarrow R$	hyp
2	P	hyp (of 2–8)
3	Q	hyp (of 3–7)
4	P	2, reit
5	$P \& Q$	3, 4, conj int
6	$(P \& Q) \rightarrow R$	1, reit
7	R	5, 6, m p
8	$Q \rightarrow R$	3–7, cond int
9	$P \rightarrow (Q \rightarrow R)$	2–8, cond int

The first of the two derivations shows that $(P \rightarrow (Q \rightarrow R))$ implies $((P \& Q) \rightarrow R)$. The second derivation shows that $((P \& Q) \rightarrow R)$ implies $(P \rightarrow (Q \rightarrow R))$. From these two derivations, it follows that the two sentences are equivalent.

You can also show equivalence through the derivation as theorems of two conditionals with their antecedent and consequent interchanged. The two derivations together show the equivalence of the antecedent and consequent that are interchanged. For example, the next two derivations together show the equivalence of two sentences. [What are those two sentences?]

1		P	hyp (of 1–2)
2		$P \& P$	1, 1, conj int
3	$P \rightarrow (P \& P)$		1–2, cond int

1		$P \& P$	hyp (of 1–2)
2		P	1, conj elim
3	$(P \& P) \rightarrow P$		1–2, cond int

On occasion, you may want to repeat a sentence within the same derivation. Instead of repeating its justification, simply cite the number of the repeated item and write 'rep' for 'repetition'. Be careful not to confuse repetition with reiteration, since repetition involves only the restatement of an item in the same derivation, not in a different though subordinate one. Repetition is often used in connection with a defined sign, such as the triple bar. The triple bar '≡' is defined in section 4.3 as follows:

$$(A \equiv B) =\text{df} ((A \rightarrow B) \& (B \rightarrow A))$$

Defined signs save space and make sentences easier to read. Their use in derivations is indicated by writing 'df', as an abbreviation for 'definition'. The following is an example of the definition of the triple bar used together with repetition.

1	$(P \& Q) \equiv (Q \& P)$	hyp
2	$((P \& Q) \rightarrow (Q \& P)) \& ((Q \& P) \rightarrow (P \& Q))$	1, rep, df

The justification '1, rep, df' written to the right of item 2 means that item 1 is repeated in its unabbreviated form. Another illustration of the use of the definition of the triple bar is the following.

1	$(P \& Q) \rightarrow (Q \& P)$	hyp
2	$(Q \& P) \rightarrow (P \& Q)$	hyp
3	$(P \& Q) \equiv (Q \& P)$	1, 2, conj int, df

The justification '1, 2, conj int, df' written to the right of item 3 means that item 3 is a direct consequence of items 1 and 2 by conjunction introduction and is stated in an abbreviated form. Whether 'df' means an item is being stated in an abbreviated or in an unabbreviated form will be obvious from the context.

We use the definition of the biconditional sign in the following derivation:

1		$P \,\&\, Q$	hyp (of 1–4)
2		P	1, conj elim
3		Q	1, conj elim
4		$Q \,\&\, P$	2, 3, conj int
5		$(P \,\&\, Q) \rightarrow (Q \,\&\, P)$	1–4, cond int
6		$Q \,\&\, P$	hyp (of 6–9)
7		Q	6, conj elim
8		P	6, conj elim
9		$P \,\&\, Q$	7, 8, conj int
10		$(Q \,\&\, P) \rightarrow (P \,\&\, Q)$	6–9, cond int
11		$(P \,\&\, Q) \equiv (Q \,\&\, P)$	5, 10, conj int, df

Observe that the main derivation 1–11, which has no hypotheses, has only five items: the subordinate derivation 1–4, item 5, the subordinate derivation 6–9, and items 10 and 11. Note also that the second subderivation 6–9 is not an item of the first 1–4; therefore, no item of the first subordinate derivation can be reiterated in the second. Because the derivation 1–11 provides a method for deriving as a theorem any sentence of the form

$$(A \,\&\, B) \equiv (B \,\&\, A)$$

such sentences count as theorems, specifically, as the theorems of **commutativity of conjunction** (comm conj).

Any sentence having the form

$$((A \,\&\, B) \,\&\, C) \equiv (A \,\&\, (B \,\&\, C))$$

is a theorem of **associativity of conjunction** (assoc conj). The derivation at the top of the next page shows that any sentence of this form is a theorem.

1	(P & Q) & R		hyp (of 1–7)
2	P & Q		1, conj elim
3	P		2, conj elim
4	Q		2, conj elim
5	R		1, conj elim
6	Q & R		4, 5, conj int
7	P & (Q & R)		3, 6, conj int
8	((P & Q) & R) → (P & (Q & R))		1–7, cond int
9	P & (Q & R)		hyp (of 9–15)
10	P		9, conj elim
11	Q & R		9, conj elim
12	Q		11, conj elim
13	R		11, conj elim
14	P & Q		10, 12, conj int
15	(P & Q) & R		13, 14, conj int
16	(P & (Q & R)) → ((P & Q) & R)		9–15, cond int
17	((P & Q) & R) ≡ (P & (Q & R))		8, 16, conj int, df

Compare the proofs of the theorems of commutativity and associativity above and observe that each exemplifies the following form, where 1–h and j–k are understood as representing correctly formed subordinate derivations.

1	A	hyp (of 1–h)
.	.	
h	B	
i	A → B	1–h, cond int
j	B	hyp (of j–k)
.	.	
k	A	
l	B → A	j–k, cond int
m	A ≡ B	i, l, conj int, df

[As an exercise, study the derivation on page 283 establishing commutativity of conjunction and list the numbers of the two subordinate derivations and the three other items in the derivation that correspond to 1–h, i, j–k, l, and m in the schema just displayed. For example, begin by noting that 1–4 corresponds to 1–h. Do the same for the derivation establishing associativity.]

It is useful to know that whenever a theorem is a biconditional its immediate components are equivalent. To understand this, remember that a biconditional is true if and only if its immediate components have the same truth value. Since there is no possibility that a theorem is false, there is no possibility for a biconditional that is a theorem to have immediate components with different truth values. Therefore, it is not possible for the immediate components of a biconditional that is a theorem to have different truth values. Therefore, any biconditional that is a theorem has immediate components that are equivalent.

Derived Biconditional Rules

There are no official rules in Intelim for the introduction or elimination of biconditionals. Nevertheless, using the definition of the biconditional sign, we can derive such rules. Seeing how these rules are derived is instructive and very interesting. However, you do not need to memorize them as you already have a satisfactory way of dealing with biconditionals.

The derived rule for eliminating a biconditional is as follows:

Biconditional Elimination (bicond elim).   An immediate component of a biconditional is a direct consequence of (i) the biconditional and (ii) its other immediate component.

The derivations below illustrate the range of application of the rule.

$$
\begin{array}{lll}
1 & P & \text{hyp} \\
2 & P \equiv Q & \text{hyp} \\
\\
3 & Q & 1, 2, \text{bicond elim}
\end{array}
$$

$$
\begin{array}{lll}
1 & P & \text{hyp} \\
2 & Q \equiv P & \text{hyp} \\
\\
3 & Q & 1, 2, \text{bicond elim}
\end{array}
$$

Notice that these derivations differ only with respect to one item. [What does the second derivation illustrate that the first does not?]

To justify adoption of the rule of biconditional elimination as a derived rule, we need to verify that we can derive either immediate component of a biconditional from the biconditional and its other immediate component using only official rules. The derivation below demonstrates how the right immediate component of a biconditional can be derived from the biconditional and its left immediate component.

$$
\begin{array}{lll}
1 & P & \text{hyp} \\
2 & P \equiv Q & \text{hyp} \\
& \text{--} & \\
3 & (P \rightarrow Q)\,\&\,(Q \rightarrow P) & 2,\ \text{rep, df} \\
4 & P \rightarrow Q & 3,\ \text{conj elim} \\
5 & Q & 1,\ 4,\ \text{m p}
\end{array}
$$

Note that in this derivation only official rules justify items.

The next derivation shows how to derive the left immediate component of a biconditional from the biconditional and its right immediate component.

$$
\begin{array}{lll}
1 & P & \text{hyp} \\
2 & Q \equiv P & \text{hyp} \\
& \text{--} & \\
3 & (Q \rightarrow P)\,\&\,(P \rightarrow Q) & 2,\ \text{rep, df} \\
4 & P \rightarrow Q & 3,\ \text{conj elim} \\
5 & Q & 1,\ 4,\ \text{m p}
\end{array}
$$

Together these derivations show that whatever is derivable using the derived rule of biconditional elimination could also be derived (with a few more items) using just official rules.

The next derived rule provides a strategy for the introduction of a biconditional. This rule is somewhat more difficult to understand and apply than the elimination rule.

Biconditional Introduction (bicond int).   A biconditional is a direct consequence of two subordinate derivations, (i) one with the left side of the biconditional as its only hypothesis and the right side as an item and (ii) the other with the right side as its only hypothesis and the left side as an item.

With the understanding that 1–h and i–j represent correctly formed subordinate derivations, this rule may also be expressed schematically as shown at the top of the next page.

$$
\begin{array}{lll}
1 & \quad A & \text{hyp (of 1–h)} \\
\cdot & \quad \cdot \\
h & \quad B \\
\\
i & \quad B & \text{hyp (of i–j)} \\
\cdot & \quad \cdot \\
j & \quad A \\
k & A \equiv B & \text{1–h, i–j, bicond int}
\end{array}
$$

Compare the schematic statement of the rule of biconditional introduction above with the schema below, where 1–h and i–j are again understood as representing correctly formed subordinate derivations.

$$
\begin{array}{lll}
1 & \quad A & \text{hyp (of 1–h)} \\
\cdot & \quad \cdot \\
h & \quad B \\
\\
i & \quad B & \text{hyp (of i–j)} \\
\cdot & \quad \cdot \\
j & \quad A \\
k & A \rightarrow B & \text{1–h, cond int} \\
l & B \rightarrow A & \text{i–j, cond int} \\
m & (A \rightarrow B)\,\&\,(B \rightarrow A) & \text{k, l, conj int} \\
n & A \equiv B & \text{m, rep, df}
\end{array}
$$

Notice that this schema differs from the schematic statement of the rule of biconditional introduction in containing three additional items (k, l, and m). Also notice that an official rule justifies each of these additional items and the justification for the last item is 'm, rep, df' instead of '1–h, i–j, bicond int'. From these observations, you should be convinced that any item you derive using the derived rule of biconditional introduction could also be derived with three additional items using only official rules of the system and the definition of the triple bar.

Properties of Biconditional

There are four properties that conjunction, conditional, and biconditional have or fail to have. Knowing which ones each has or does not have will help you gain a firmer grasp of the binary connectives. These properties, all previously mentioned, are reflexivity, transitivity, commutativity, and associativity. Conditional is reflexive and transitive, but is not associative or commutative. Conjunction is associative and commutative, but is not reflexive or transitive. On the other hand, biconditional has all four properties.

The derivation below establishes that biconditional has the property of commutativity.

1		$P \equiv Q$	hyp (of 1–8)
2		Q	hyp (of 2–4)
3		$P \equiv Q$	1, reit
4		P	2, 3, bicond elim
5		P	hyp (of 5–7)
6		$P \equiv Q$	1, reit
7		Q	5, 6, bicond elim
8		$Q \equiv P$	2–4, 5–7, bicond int
9		$Q \equiv P$	hyp (of 9–16)
10		P	hyp (of 10–12)
11		$Q \equiv P$	9, reit
12		Q	10, 11, bicond elim
13		Q	hyp (of 13–15)
14		$Q \equiv P$	9, reit
15		P	13, 14, bicond elim
16		$P \equiv Q$	10–12, 13–15, bicond int
17		$(P \equiv Q) \equiv (Q \equiv P)$	1–8, 9–16, bicond int

Observe that other than the rule of reiteration, only biconditional rules are used in this derivation. In studying this derivation, note that it has only three items: the two subordinate derivations 1–8 and 9–16 and item 17. Of these two subordinate derivations, the second is identical to the first except for having the sentence letters interchanged.

Because the derivation above provides a method for proving that any sentence of the form

$$(A \equiv B) \equiv (B \equiv A)$$

is a theorem, namely, a theorem of **commutativity of biconditional** (comm bicond), we regard the derivation above as a proof of those theorems. That biconditional is associative can be shown by constructing a derivation of

$$((P \equiv Q) \equiv R) \equiv (P \equiv (Q \equiv R))$$

from no hypotheses. Thus we count any sentence of the form of that sentence as a theorem, specifically, a theorem of **associativity of biconditional** (assoc bicond). Proof of this is left to the reader as an exercise.

Besides being commutative and associative, biconditional is also reflexive and transitive. To prove reflexivity requires only the construction of the three-item derivation that follows.

1		P	hyp (of 1–2)
		–	
2		P	1, rep
3	$P \equiv P$		1–2, 1–2, bicond int

This derivation shows, in effect, that every sentence of the form

$$A \equiv A$$

is a theorem, namely, a theorem of **reflexivity of biconditional** (refl bicond).

Biconditional is also transitive, as you can see from the following derivation. This derivation justifies adoption of the derived rule stated on the next page.

$$
\begin{array}{lll}
1 & P \equiv Q & \text{hyp} \\
2 & Q \equiv R & \text{hyp} \\
\\
3 & \quad P & \text{hyp (of 3–7)} \\
\\
4 & \quad\quad P \equiv Q & 1,\ \text{reit} \\
5 & \quad\quad Q & 3,\ 4,\ \text{bicond elim} \\
6 & \quad\quad Q \equiv R & 2,\ \text{reit} \\
7 & \quad\quad R & 5,\ 6,\ \text{bicond elim} \\
\\
8 & \quad R & \text{hyp (of 8–12)} \\
\\
9 & \quad\quad Q \equiv R & 2,\ \text{reit} \\
10 & \quad\quad Q & 8,\ 9,\ \text{bicond elim} \\
11 & \quad\quad P \equiv Q & 1,\ \text{reit} \\
12 & \quad\quad P & 10,\ 11,\ \text{bicond elim} \\
13 & P \equiv R & 3\text{–}7,\ 8\text{–}12,\ \text{bicond int}
\end{array}
$$

Transitivity of Biconditional (trans bicond).   A biconditional $(A \equiv C)$ is a direct consequence of two other biconditionals $(A \equiv B)$ and $(B \equiv C)$.

The following is a schematic expression of the rule.

$$
\begin{array}{lll}
h & A \equiv B & \\
i & B \equiv C & \\
j & A \equiv C & i,\ j,\ \text{trans bicond}
\end{array}
$$

We can also justify the rule of transitivity of biconditional by the following alternative derivation. See how the derivation relies on the definition of the triple bar and does not employ either the derived rule of biconditional introduction or the derived rule of biconditional elimination.

$$
\begin{array}{lll}
1 & P \equiv Q & \text{hyp} \\
2 & Q \equiv R & \text{hyp} \\
\\
3 & P \rightarrow Q & 1,\ \text{rep, df, conj elim} \\
4 & Q \rightarrow P & 1,\ \text{rep, df, conj elim} \\
5 & Q \rightarrow R & 2,\ \text{rep, df, conj elim} \\
6 & R \rightarrow Q & 2,\ \text{rep, df, conj elim} \\
7 & P \rightarrow R & 3,\ 5,\ \text{trans cond} \\
8 & R \rightarrow P & 4,\ 6,\ \text{trans cond} \\
9 & P \equiv R & 7,\ 8,\ \text{conj int, df}
\end{array}
$$

The justification '1, rep, df, conj elim', which is used for both items 3 and 4, means that both items 3 and 4 are direct consequences by the rule of conjunction elimination of the unabbreviated form of item 1.

EXERCISES FOR SECTION 9.3

*1. In the derivation below, we employ the derived rule of transitivity of conditional.

1	$(P \to Q) \& (Q \to R)$	hyp (of 1-4)
2	$P \to Q$	1, conj elim
3	$Q \to R$	1, conj elim
4	$P \to R$	2, 3, trans cond
5	$((P \to Q) \& (Q \to R)) \to (P \to R)$	1-4, cond int

As an exercise, derive the same theorem using only official rules of the system.

2. Making use of only official rules, show that each of the following is a theorem of Intelim.

   a. $((P \& Q) \& R) \to ((Q \& P) \& R)$
   *b. $((P \& Q) \& R) \to (R \& (Q \& P))$
   c. $P \equiv (P \& P)$
   *d. $(((P \& Q) \& R) \to S) \to (P \to (Q \to (R \to S)))$
   e. $(P \to (Q \to (R \to S))) \to (((P \& Q) \& R) \to S)$
   *f. $(P \& (Q \& R)) \to Q$
   g. $((P \to Q) \& (P \to R)) \to (P \to (Q \& R))$
   *h. $((P \to Q) \& (R \to S)) \to ((P \& R) \to (Q \& S))$

3. Making use of only official rules, show that the following arguments are derivable in Intelim.

   a. $P, Q, R /\therefore (P \& (R \& Q))$
   b. $(P \& (R \& Q)) /\therefore R$
   *c. $P, Q /\therefore (P \equiv Q)$

4. Making use of official rules, as well as any theorems or derived rules presented so far, show that the following arguments are derivable in Intelim.

*a. $(P \equiv R)$, $(P \& Q)$ /∴ R

b. $(P \rightarrow R)$, $(R \equiv Q)$ /∴ $(P \rightarrow Q)$

*c. R /∴ $(R \equiv (Q \rightarrow Q))$

5. Construct derivations verifying that the following sentences are theorems of Intelim. In addition to the official rules of the system, you may use both theorems and derived rules.

a. $((P \& R) \equiv (Q \& P)) \rightarrow ((Q \& P) \equiv (P \& R))$

*b. $(P \rightarrow Q) \equiv (P \rightarrow Q)$

ADDITIONAL CONNECTIVE RULES

The purpose of this chapter is to present the official rules of direct consequence for the remaining types of sentences, namely, disjunctions and negations. Besides the official rules, several derived rules are justified and adopted. Additional theorems are also proven.

10.1 RULES ABOUT DISJUNCTION

There are two official rules relating to disjunction, an introduction rule and an elimination rule. With these rules, we are able to demonstrate that disjunction has the properties of commutativity and associativity, establish some theorems relating disjunctions, conjunctions, and conditionals, and add to the list of derived rules.

Disjunction Introduction and Elimination

The rule for introduction of a disjunction gives specific directions for moving to a disjunction, while the rule for elimination gives specific directions for moving away from a disjunction. These rules appear below together with some applications and explanations.

The introduction rule comes first because it is the easier of the two rules to understand and apply.

Disjunction Introduction (disj int).   A disjunction is a direct consequence of either one of its disjuncts.

The rule actually has two parts. Both are covered in the compact statement just given. The first part is the following: a disjunction is a direct consequence of its left disjunct. The second part is the following: a disjunction is a direct consequence of its right disjunct. Since a disjunction is true if at least one of its disjuncts (either left or right) is true, it is not difficult to see that this rule, in both its parts, is truth-preserving.

The derivations below illustrate the first and second parts of the rule.

$$
\begin{array}{ll}
1 \quad\quad P & \text{hyp} \\
\\
2 \quad\quad P \vee Q & \text{1, disj int (first part)}
\end{array}
$$

$$
\begin{array}{ll}
1 \quad\quad Q & \text{hyp} \\
\\
2 \quad\quad P \vee Q & \text{1, disj int (second part)}
\end{array}
$$

Observe that item 2 in the first derivation is the same as item 2 in the second, but item 1 differs. [In which derivation is item 1 the right disjunct? In which derivation is item 1 the left disjunct? Does the statement in chapter 9 of the rule of conjunction elimination include two parts? If so, what are they?]

The second rule about disjunction gives you a strategy for making use of a disjunction.

Disjunction Elimination (disj elim).   A sentence is a direct consequence of a disjunction and two subordinate derivations, one having the left and the other the right disjunct of the disjunction as its only hypothesis, and both having as an item the sentence that is the direct consequence.

With the understanding that 2–h and i–j represent correctly formed subordinate derivations, the following schema may be thought of as embodying this rule.

```
1  │ (A v B)            hyp
   │─
2  │  │  A              hyp (of 2–h)
   │  │─
·  │  │  ·
h  │  │  C
   │  │
i  │  │  B              hyp (of i–j)
   │  │─
·  │  │  ·
j  │  │  C
k  │  C                 1, 2–h, i–j, disj elim
```

The derivation that follows illustrates how to apply the rule.

```
1   │ P v Q             hyp
2   │ P → R             hyp
3   │ Q → R             hyp
    │─
4   │  │  P             hyp (of 4–6)
    │  │─
5   │  │  P → R         2, reit
6   │  │  R             4, 5, m p
    │  │
7   │  │  Q             hyp (of 7–9)
    │  │─
8   │  │  Q → R         3, reit
9   │  │  R             7, 8, m p
10  │  R                1, 4–6, 7–9, disj elim
```

To show how the derivation above relates to English, we have replaced the sentence letters in that derivation with English sentences in the derivation at the top of the next page. [As an exercise, specify which English sentence replaced which sentence letter.]

1	It's the devil v It's the deep blue sea.	hyp
2	It's the devil → I am in trouble.	hyp
3	It's the deep blue sea → I am in trouble.	hyp

4	It's the devil.	hyp
5	It's the devil → I am in trouble.	2, reit
6	I am in trouble.	4, 5, m p

7	It's the deep blue sea.	hyp
8	It's the deep blue sea → I am in trouble.	hyp
9	I am in trouble.	7, 8, m p

10	I am in trouble.	1, 4-6, 7-9, disj elim

An idiomatic rendering of the argument consisting of the hypotheses and last item of the derivation we translated is as follows: "It's the devil or the deep blue sea. If the devil, I am in trouble. If the deep blue sea, I am still in trouble. So, let's face it, I am in trouble."

The introduction and elimination rules for disjunction are both applied in the following derivation.

1	P	hyp
2	$(P \rightarrow Q) \vee (P \rightarrow R)$	hyp

3	$P \rightarrow Q$	hyp (of 3-6)
4	P	1, reit
5	Q	3, 4, m p
6	$R \vee Q$	5, disj int

7	$P \rightarrow R$	hyp (of 7-10)
8	P	1, reit
9	R	7, 8, m p
10	$R \vee Q$	9, disj int

11	$R \vee Q$	2, 3-6, 7-10, disj elim

Notice how 2, 3–6, 7–10, and 11 in this derivation correspond to 1, 2–h, i–j, and k in the schematic expression of the rule of disjunction elimination on page 295. Item 2 is a disjunction, the subderivation 3–6 has the left disjunct of item 2 as its only hypothesis, while the subderivation 7–10 has the right disjunct of item 1 as its only hypothesis. The same sentence occurs as an item in both subderivations and as the last item in the main derivation. See items 6, 10, and 11. The rule of disjunction elimination applied to item 2 (the disjunction) and the two subderivations 3–6 and 7–10 justifies entering the last item in the main derivation.

To see that the rule of disjunction elimination is truth-preserving, study the application above in view of the following considerations. Given the rule of reiteration, you may reiterate in a subordinate derivation any and all of the hypotheses of the derivation to which it is directly subordinate. Thus whatever can be entered as a new item in a subordinate derivation could be entered in the derivation to which it is directly subordinate if that derivation had among its hypotheses the hypothesis of the subordinate derivation. For example, the main derivation 1–11 above has two hypotheses, namely, items 1 and 2. The subderivation 3–6 has only one hypothesis, item 3. Item 1 is reiterated in the subderivation as item 4. Through the rule of reiteration either or both of the hypotheses of the main derivation can be reiterated in the subderivation. Therefore, whatever is derivable in the subderivation 3–6 is derivable from the hypotheses of the main derivation together with the hypothesis of the subordinate derivation. The situation is analogous with the subderivation 7–10. The hypotheses 1 and 2 are available to 7–10 through reiteration. Therefore, whatever is derivable in the subderivation 7–10 is derivable from the hypotheses of the main derivation together with the hypothesis of the subderivation 7–10.

What the rule of disjunction elimination says, in effect, is the following: A sentence may be entered as an item in a derivation if (i) a disjunction is a preceding item and (ii) it has been shown (through subderivations) that the same sentence could be entered in the derivation if either of its disjuncts were added to the hypotheses of the derivation. Notice in the derivation 1–11 above that item 2 is a disjunction, item 3 is the left disjunct of item 2, item 7 is the right disjunct of item 2, and items 6, 10, and 11 are the same sentence. The two subderivations show that item 11 is derivable from items 1 and 2 with the addition of either of the disjuncts of item 2.

As a disjunction is true only if one of its disjuncts is true and the rules of direct consequence previously adopted are truth-preserving, the rule of disjunction elimination is also truth-preserving. If it were not, a false sentence would be derivable by truth-preserving rules from a true disjunction and either of its disjuncts. As one of the disjuncts of a true disjunction must be true, this would mean that a false sentence is derivable from true sentences by truth-preserving rules and that is nonsense.

Properties of Disjunction

We proved the commutativity of conjunction by deriving $(P \mathbin{\&} Q) \equiv (Q \mathbin{\&} P)$ as a theorem and thus showing that any sentence of that form is a theorem. In a similar way, you can show that any sentence of the form

$$(A \mathbin{v} B) \equiv (B \mathbin{v} A)$$

is a theorem of **commutativity of disjunction** (comm disj). To do so, one need only complete the following derivation.

1	$P \mathbin{v} Q$	hyp (of 1–h)
.	.	
h	$Q \mathbin{v} P$	
i	$Q \mathbin{v} P$	hyp (of i–j)
.	.	
j	$P \mathbin{v} Q$	
k	$(P \mathbin{v} Q) \equiv (Q \mathbin{v} P)$	1–h, i–j, bicond int

This is done below through item 6. The rest is left as an exercise.

1	$P \mathbin{v} Q$	hyp
2	P	hyp (of 2–3)
3	$Q \mathbin{v} P$	2, disj int
4	Q	hyp (of 4–5)
5	$Q \mathbin{v} P$	4, disj int
6	$Q \mathbin{v} P$	1, 2–3, 4–5, disj elim
7	$Q \mathbin{v} P$	hyp (of 7–j)
.	.	
j	$P \mathbin{v} Q$	
k	$(P \mathbin{v} Q) \equiv (Q \mathbin{v} P)$	1–6, 7–j, bicond int

Conjunction, biconditional, and disjunction have been shown to have the property of commutativity. They also have the property of associativity. To prove associativity of disjunction, simply construct a derivation of

$$((P \lor Q) \lor R) \equiv (P \lor (Q \lor R))$$

from no hypotheses. The derivation establishes that any sentence of that form is a theorem of **associativity of disjunction** (assoc disj). This can be done by supplying the missing steps in the derivation sketched below.

1	$(P \lor Q) \lor R$	hyp (of 1–h)
.	.	
h	$P \lor (Q \lor R)$	
i	$P \lor (Q \lor R)$	hyp (of i–j)
.	.	
j	$(P \lor Q) \lor R$	
k	$((P \lor Q) \lor R) \equiv (P \lor (Q \lor R))$	1–h, i–j, bicond int

The derivation through item 12 below completes the first subordinate derivation (that of 1–h).

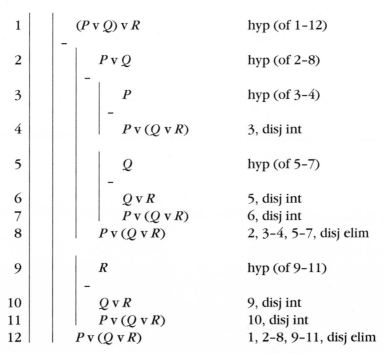

1	$(P \lor Q) \lor R$	hyp (of 1–12)
2	$P \lor Q$	hyp (of 2–8)
3	P	hyp (of 3–4)
4	$P \lor (Q \lor R)$	3, disj int
5	Q	hyp (of 5–7)
6	$Q \lor R$	5, disj int
7	$P \lor (Q \lor R)$	6, disj int
8	$P \lor (Q \lor R)$	2, 3–4, 5–7, disj elim
9	R	hyp (of 9–11)
10	$Q \lor R$	9, disj int
11	$P \lor (Q \lor R)$	10, disj int
12	$P \lor (Q \lor R)$	1, 2–8, 9–11, disj elim

Completing the second subordinate derivation (that of i–j) is left as an exercise.

Distributive Theorems

Among the theorems of Intelim, we have sentences of the form

$$(A \to (B \to C)) \to ((A \to B) \to (A \to C))$$

We also have sentences of the form

$$(A \to (B \to C)) \equiv ((A \to B) \to (A \to C))$$

that are known as the **theorems of distribution** (th dist). Notice how '$A \to$' is "distributed" across the right side of the biconditional. Strengthening of the conditional to a biconditional can easily be justified by a derivation of the left side of the biconditional from the right.

As additional distributive theorems, we also have sentences of the form

$$(A \mathbin{\&} (B \vee C)) \equiv ((A \mathbin{\&} B) \vee (A \mathbin{\&} C))$$

which we call theorems of **distribution of conjunction into disjunction** (dist conj disj). To show that such sentences are theorems, it will suffice to supply what is missing in the following derivation.

1	$P \mathbin{\&} (Q \vee R)$	hyp (of 1–h)
.	–	
h	$(P \mathbin{\&} Q) \vee (P \mathbin{\&} R)$	
i	$(P \mathbin{\&} Q) \vee (P \mathbin{\&} R)$	hyp (of i–j)
.	–	
j	$P \mathbin{\&} (Q \vee R)$	
k	$(P \mathbin{\&} (Q \vee R)) \equiv ((P \mathbin{\&} Q) \vee (P \mathbin{\&} R))$	1–h, i–j, bicond int

The first subordinate derivation (that of 1–h) is completed at the top of the next page.

1	$P \& (Q \vee R)$	hyp (of 1–12)
2	P	1, conj elim
3	$Q \vee R$	1, conj elim
4	Q	hyp (of 4–7)
5	P	2, reit
6	$P \& Q$	4, 5, conj int
7	$(P \& Q) \vee (P \& R)$	6, disj int
8	R	hyp (of 8–11)
9	P	2, reit
10	$P \& R$	8, 9, conj int
11	$(P \& Q) \vee (P \& R)$	10, disj int
12	$(P \& Q) \vee (P \& R)$	3, 4–7, 8–11, disj elim

Completion of the second subordinate derivation required for proving the theorem is left as an exercise for the reader.

There are also theorems of **distribution of disjunction into conjunction** (dist disj conj). These are sentences of the following form:

$$(A \vee (B \& C)) \equiv ((A \vee B) \& (A \vee C))$$

To prove that there are such theorems, you need only complete the following derivation.

1	$P \vee (Q \& R)$	hyp (of 1–h)
.	.	
h	$(P \vee Q) \& (P \vee R)$	
i	$(P \vee Q) \& (P \vee R)$	hyp (of i–j)
.	.	
j	$P \vee (Q \& R)$	
k	$(P \vee (Q \& R)) \equiv ((P \vee Q) \& (P \vee R))$	1–h, i–j, bicond int

Items i–j appear below. For convenience, we number them 1–15.

1		$(P \vee Q) \mathbin{\&} (P \vee R)$	hyp (of 1–15)
2		$P \vee Q$	1, conj elim
3		$P \vee R$	1, conj elim
4		P	hyp (of 4–5)
5		$P \vee (Q \mathbin{\&} R)$	4, disj int
6		Q	hyp (of 6–14)
7		$P \vee R$	3, reit
8		P	hyp (of 8–9)
9		$P \vee (Q \mathbin{\&} R)$	8, disj int
10		R	hyp (of 10–13)
11		Q	6, reit
12		$Q \mathbin{\&} R$	10, 11, conj int
13		$P \vee (Q \mathbin{\&} R)$	12, disj int
14		$P \vee (Q \mathbin{\&} R)$	7, 8–9, 10–13, disj elim
15		$P \vee (Q \mathbin{\&} R)$	2, 4–5, 6–14, disj elim

Completion of 1–h is left for the reader.

Any biconditional that is a theorem is valid. The immediate components of any valid biconditional are equivalent. Thus, by proving that every sentence of the form

$$((A \vee B) \rightarrow C) \equiv ((A \rightarrow C) \mathbin{\&} (B \rightarrow C))$$

is a theorem, you also show that the immediate components of any such sentence are equivalent. The required derivation begins as follows:

1	$(P \lor Q) \to R$	hyp
2	P	hyp (of 2–5)
3	$P \lor Q$	1, disj int
4	$(P \lor Q) \to R$	2, reit
5	R	3, 4, m p
6	$P \to R$	2–5, cond int
7	Q	hyp (of 7–10)
8	$P \lor Q$	7, disj int
9	$(P \lor Q) \to R$	1, reit
10	R	8, 9, m p
11	$Q \to R$	7–10, cond int
12	$(P \to R) \,\&\, (Q \to R)$	6, 11, conj int

Completion is left to the reader as an exercise.

The Rule of Complex Constructive Dilemma

We can adopt the following as a derived rule.

Complex Constructive Dilemma (comp cnst dil).   A disjunction is a direct consequence of three items: (i) a subordinate derivation with the left disjunct as an item and only one hypothesis, (ii) a subordinate derivation with the right disjunct as an item and only one hypothesis, and (iii) a disjunction of the hypotheses of the two subordinate derivations.

With the understanding that 2–h and i–j represent correctly formed subordinate derivations, this rule may be expressed schematically as follows:

$$
\begin{array}{r|l l}
1 & A \lor B & \text{hyp} \\
2 & \quad A & \text{hyp (of 2-h)} \\
. & \quad . & \\
h & \quad C & \\
i & \quad B & \text{hyp (of i-j)} \\
. & \quad . & \\
j & \quad D & \\
k & C \lor D & \text{1, 2-h, i-j, comp cnst dil}
\end{array}
$$

The following is a derivation where the rule of complex constructive dilemma is applied.

$$
\begin{array}{r|l l}
1 & (R \& P) \lor (Q \& S) & \text{hyp} \\
2 & \quad R \& P & \text{hyp (of 2-3)} \\
3 & \quad R & \text{2, conj elim} \\
4 & \quad Q \& S & \text{hyp (of 4-5)} \\
5 & \quad S & \text{4, conj elim} \\
6 & R \lor S & \text{1, 2-3, 4-5, comp cnst dil}
\end{array}
$$

To show that this new derived rule amounts to nothing more than a shortcut, you need to demonstrate that you can achieve the same results with only official rules. You can do this by filling in missing items between j + 1 and k in the following derivation. Each item must, of course, be justified, including the last.

$$
\begin{array}{r|l l}
1 & A \lor B & \text{hyp} \\
2 & \quad A & \text{hyp (of 2-h)}
\end{array}
$$

h	C	
h + 1	$A \rightarrow C$	2–h, cond int
i	B	hyp (of i–j)
j	D	
j + 1	$B \rightarrow D$	i–j, cond int
k	$C \vee D$	

We now fill in the steps between j + 1 and k below, reaching each, including the last, by applying only official rules to preceding items.

1	$A \vee B$	hyp
h + 1	$A \rightarrow C$	2–h, cond int
j + 1	$B \rightarrow D$	i–j, cond int
j + 2	A	hyp (of j + 2 through j + 5)
j + 3	$A \rightarrow C$	h + 1, reit
j + 4	C	j + 2, j + 3, m p
j + 5	$C \vee D$	j + 4, disj int
j + 6	B	hyp (of j + 6 through j + 9)
j + 7	$B \rightarrow D$	j + 1, reit
j + 8	D	j + 6, j + 7, m p
j + 9	$C \vee D$	j + 8, disj int
k	$C \vee D$	1, j + 2 through j + 5, j + 6 through j + 9, disj elim

To shorten the presentation, we omitted the subordinate derivations 2–h and i–j that appeared previously. Notice how we, nevertheless, reference them in justifying items h + 1 and j + 1.

EXERCISES FOR SECTION 10.1

1. For each of the following arguments, construct a derivation with the conclusion as its last item and the premises as the hypotheses. Use only official rules.

   *a. $((P \& Q) v (R \& Q)) / \therefore Q$

   b. $P, ((P v Q) \to R) / \therefore R$

   *c. $(P v Q) / \therefore ((Q v P) v R)$

   d. $((P \& Q) v (S \& T)) / \therefore (P v S)$

   e. $((R \& Q) v R) / \therefore R$

   f. $(P v (Q \& R)) / \therefore ((P v Q) \& (P v R))$

   *g. $((P \& Q) v (P \& R)) / \therefore (P \& (Q v R))$

*2. Each of the following is either a theorem of commutativity of disjunction, associativity of disjunction, distribution of conjunction into disjunction, distribution of disjunction into conjunction, or none of the above. Identify which is which. Are there any that are not theorems?

   a. $(R v ((Q \& P) \& (P \& Q))) \equiv (((R v (Q \& P)) \& (R v (P \& Q)))$

   b. $(((P v R) \& Q) \to (Q v R)) \equiv ((P v R) \to (Q \to (Q v R)))$

   c. $((P v R) v Q) \equiv ((Q v R) v P)$

   d. $(Q \& ((P \to R) v Q)) \equiv ((Q \& (P \to R)) v (Q \& Q))$

   e. $((P \to Q) v (Q \to P)) \equiv ((Q \to P) v (P \to Q))$

3. Establish that each of the following is a theorem. In addition to the official rules, you may also use derived rules and theorems already proven.

   *a. $(P v P) \to P$

   b. $P \to (P v P)$

   *c. $((P v Q) \to P) \to (Q \to P)$

   d. $(P \to (P \& Q)) \to (P \to (Q \& P))$

   *e. $(P v (Q v (P \& R))) \equiv ((P \& R) v (P v Q))$

   f. $(P v P) \equiv P$

   *g. $((P \to Q) \to (P \to R)) \to (P \to (Q \to R))$

4. Use the derived rule of complex constructive dilemma to show that the following arguments are derivable.

   *a. $(P v Q) / \therefore ((P v R) v (Q v S))$

   b. $(((P \& (P \to R)) v (Q \& S)) / \therefore (R v S)$

5. Complete the derivations begun in the text that prove the following theorems:

   *a. commutativity of disjunction

   b. associativity of disjunction

   c. distribution of conjunction into disjunction

   d. distribution of disjunction into conjunction

   e. $((A \vee B) \rightarrow C) \equiv ((A \rightarrow C) \& (B \rightarrow C))$

10.2 RULES ABOUT NEGATION

The official rules for the other connectives have come in pairs, one introduction and one elimination rule for each. In contrast, Intelim has only one official rule for negation. This rule is sufficient for the derivation of any other negation rules one might want.

Indirect Proof

The one and only official negation rule in Intelim is the following:

Indirect Proof (ind pr).   A sentence is a direct consequence of a subordinate derivation with its negation as the only hypothesis and a sentence and its negation as items.

Typical applications of the rule have the form of the schema below, where h–j represents any correctly formed subderivation.

$$
\begin{array}{lll}
\text{h} & \quad {\sim}A & \text{hyp (of h-j)} \\
 & \quad - & \\
\text{i} & \quad B & \\
\text{j} & \quad {\sim}B & \\
\text{k} \quad A & & \text{h-j, ind pr}
\end{array}
$$

    The last step of the next derivation is justified by application of the rule of indirect proof.

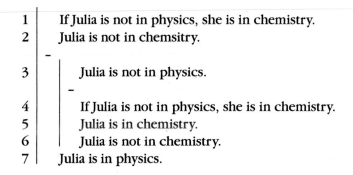

1	~P → Q		hyp
2	~Q		hyp
3		~P	hyp (of 3-6)
4		~P → Q	1, reit
5		Q	3, 4, m p
6		~Q	2, reit
7	P		3-6, ind pr

Notice how items 3, 5, 6, and 7 in this derivation correspond to h, i, j, and k in the schematic expression of the rule of indirect proof. Item 7 is the sentence that is the direct consequence of the subordinate derivation 3-6, item 3 is the negation of item 7, and items 5 and 6 are the sentence and its negation that are derived in the subderivation 3-6. Notice how both of the hypotheses of the main derivation reappear in the subderivation through reiteration.

The following is a translation in English of the sentences in the derivation above.

1	If Julia is not in physics, she is in chemistry.
2	Julia is not in chemsitry.
3	Julia is not in physics.
4	If Julia is not in physics, she is in chemistry.
5	Julia is in chemistry.
6	Julia is not in chemistry.
7	Julia is in physics.

Item 3 is the assumption that Julia is not in physics. With that assumption together with the original hypotheses, you are committed to both items 5 and 6. But items 5 and 6 cannot both be true, as one says that Julia is in chemistry and the other says that she is not. So, it follows that the supposition that she is not in physics is a mistake and that she is in physics if the hypotheses of the main derivation are true.

To understand the rule of indirect proof, you must understand the role of the subordinate derivation. According to the rule of reiteration, you can reiterate in a subderivation any sentence items preceding the subderivation. Therefore, a subderivation has available to it any and all of the hypotheses of the derivation to which it is subordinate. So what the rule of indirect proof says, in effect, is the following: A sentence *A* may be entered as an item in a derivation if it has been shown (through a subderivation) that a sentence *B* as well as its negation *~B* could be entered if *~A* were added to the hypotheses of the derivation.

To see that the rule is truth-preserving, study its application in the derivation above. What the subderivation 3–6 shows is that, if you assume that items 1 and 2 are true and you further assume that item 3 is true, you are committed to the truth of a sentence and its negation. But there is no possibility for both a sentence and its negation to be true. So, there is no way for items 1, 2, and 3 to all be true. If there is no way for all to be true, item 3 must be false if items 1 and 2 are true. Item 3 is the negation of item 7. So, if items 1 and 2 are true, so is item 7.

Double Negation

Although indirect proof is the only official negation rule, we shall give several other negation rules the status of derived rules. These additional rules will make the construction of derivations easier. Moreover, seeing how these rules are derived from the official rules will deepen your understanding of them and of the system as a whole. The following are two of those rules.

Double Negation Introduction (neg$_2$ int).   A double negation is a direct consequence of the sentence it doubly negates.

Double Negation Elimination (neg$_2$ elim).   A sentence is a direct consequence of its double negation.

These rules are represented schematically as follows:

$$
\begin{array}{l|l}
h & A \\
i & \sim\sim A
\end{array} \qquad h, \text{neg}_2 \text{ int}
$$

$$
\begin{array}{l|l}
h & \sim\sim A \\
i & A
\end{array} \qquad h, \text{neg}_2 \text{ elim}
$$

As you can see from the first schema, the rule of double negation introduction allows you to write as an item in any derivation the result of prefixing two tildes to a preceding item. Similarly, the rule of double negation elimination allows you to write as an item in any derivation a sentence if the same sentence prefixed by two tildes is a preceding item.

The following derivation shows that any result one can obtain using the rule of double negation elimination one could obtain in a longer derivation using only official rules.

```
1 |   ~~P              hyp
  |-
2 |   |   ~P           hyp (of 2–3)
  |   |-
3 |   |   ~~P          1, reit
4 |   P                2–3, ind pr
```

Note how item 4 is justified by reference to both the subordinate derivation 2–3, which precedes it, and the rule of indirect proof. In the subordinate derivation, item 2 serves both as the hypothesis and together with item 3 as the sentence and its negation. The following derivation fits the form of the schema precisely, but both derivations are equally correct.

```
1 |   ~~P              hyp
  |-
2 |   |   ~P           hyp (of 2–4)
  |   |-
3 |   |   ~P           2, rep
4 |   |   ~~P          1, reit
5 |   P                2–4, ind pr
```

The following derivation shows that the rule of double negation introduction does not allow you to enter any sentence that you could not have using only official rules.

```
1 |   P                hyp
  |-
2 |   |   ~~~P         hyp (of 2–4)
  |   |-
3 |   |   P            1, reit
4 |   |   ~P           2, neg₂ elim
5 |   ~~P              2–4, ind pr
```

Notice, in this derivation, that the previously derived rule of double negation elimination justifies the derivation of item 4 from item 2. The next derivation uses only official rules.

```
1 │  P                        hyp
  │ ─
2 │ │    ~~~P                 hyp (of 2-6)
  │ │ ─
3 │ │ │    ~~P               hyp (of 3-4)
  │ │ │ ─
4 │ │ │    ~~~P              2, reit
5 │ │    ~P                   3-4, ind pr
6 │ │    P                    1, reit
7 │  ~~P                      2-6, ind pr
```

[What are the official rules used in the derivation?]

Negation Elimination

Another useful negation rule is the following elimination rule. Although by name an "elimination" rule, it is a derived rule, nevertheless.

Negation Elimination (neg elim).   Any sentence is a direct consequence of a sentence and its negation.

The following derivation shows that any transition to any sentence from a sentence and its negation in virtue of the rule of negation elimination could also be made with the official rule of indirect proof and reiteration. This justifies our adoption of the rule of negation elimination as a derived rule.

```
1 │  P                        hyp
2 │  ~P                       hyp
  │ ─
3 │ │    ~Q                   hyp (of 3-5)
  │ │ ─
4 │ │    P                    1, reit
5 │ │    ~P                   2, reit
6 │  Q                        3-5, ind pr
```

Even with this derivation, you may find the derived rule of negation elimination difficult to accept. Nevertheless, it is truth-preserving. Remember, to be truth-preserving a rule cannot allow the derivation of a false sentence from all true ones. The fact that this rule allows you to derive any sentence you like, whether true or false, is not a problem because it allows you that freedom only if you have a sentence and its negation as preceding items. If you have a sentence and its negation as preceding items, there is no danger of deriving a false sentence from all true ones. The reason is simple: a sentence and its negation cannot both be true.

Negation Introduction

Another derived rule is the following:

Negation Introduction (neg int).   A negation is a direct consequence of a subordinate derivation with the sentence it negates as its only hypothesis and a sentence and its negation as items.

Typical applications of the rule have the form of the following schema, where h–j represents a correctly formed subordinate derivation.

$$
\begin{array}{lll}
h & \quad A & \text{hyp (of h–j)} \\
  & \quad \text{–} & \\
i & \quad B & \\
j & \quad \sim B & \\
k & \sim A & \text{h–j, neg int}
\end{array}
$$

Note when items h and k are interchanged and 'neg int' replaced with 'ind pr', the schema is the same as that previously presented for the rule of indirect proof.

   The following derivation illustrates how the rule of negation introduction is applied.

$$
\begin{array}{lll}
1 & \quad P \,\&\, \sim P & \text{hyp (of 1–3)} \\
  & \quad \text{–} & \\
2 & \quad P & \text{1, conj elim} \\
3 & \quad \sim P & \text{1, conj elim} \\
4 & \sim(P \,\&\, \sim P) & \text{1–3, neg int}
\end{array}
$$

Notice how items 1, 2, 3, 1–3, and 4 correspond, respectively, to h, i, j, h–j, and k in the schema above. Now compare the derivation with the one below.

$$
\begin{array}{lll}
1 & \quad \sim\sim(P \,\&\, \sim P) & \text{hyp (of 1–4)} \\
  & \quad \text{–} & \\
2 & \quad P \,\&\, \sim P & \text{1, neg}_2 \text{ elim} \\
3 & \quad P & \text{2, conj elim} \\
4 & \quad \sim P & \text{2, conj elim} \\
5 & \sim(P \,\&\, \sim P) & \text{1–4, ind pr}
\end{array}
$$

Both derivations prove the same Intelim theorem. But, notice that the second derivation uses only official rules with the exception of the derived rule of double negation elimination. We leave it to the reader to construct a third derivation that uses only official rules.

The following schema shows that the rule of negation introduction is acceptable as a derived rule.

1	A	hyp (of 1–i)
h	B	
i	$\sim B$	
j	$\sim\sim A$	hyp (of j–m)
k	A	j, neg$_2$ elim
l	B	{l and m are justified
m	$\sim B$	as in 1–i}.
n	$\sim A$	j–m, ind pr

The subordinate derivation 1–i represents a correctly formed subderivation as in the schematic representation of the rule of negation introduction. Whatever method used in 1–i to obtain items h and i can also be used in the subderivation j–m to obtain items l and m. Thus a transition from the subderivation 1–i to item n can be made using official rules alone. The advantage in having the rule of negation introduction is that it allows you to move to item n from 1–i instead of from j–m.

Although the similarity between the rule of negation introduction and indirect proof is striking, replacing the rule of indirect proof with the rule of negation introduction would result in a weaker system. In other words, some theorems of Intelim would not be provable in the resulting system. Putting both the rule of negation introduction and the rule of negation elimination in the place of the rule of indirect proof would also result in a weaker system. However, if you replace the rule of indirect proof with the rule of double negation elimination together with the rule of negation introduction, you will get a system equivalent to Intelim.

EXERCISES FOR SECTION 10.2

1. Establish that each of the following is a theorem. You can use derived rules and theorems already proven.

   *a. $P \rightarrow (\sim P \rightarrow Q)$

   b. $\sim\sim P \equiv P$

   c. $(P \rightarrow \sim P) \rightarrow \sim P$

2. Show that each of the arguments below is derivable. You can use derived rules and theorems already proven.

   a. $(Q \,\&\, \sim Q) \,/\therefore\, R$

   *b. $(P \vee Q), \sim Q \,/\therefore\, P$

   *c. $(\sim P \vee Q), P \,/\therefore\, Q$

   d. $\sim\sim P, (\sim P \,\&\, Q) \,/\therefore\, R$

   *e. $\sim(P \,\&\, Q), P \,/\therefore\, \sim Q$

   f. $\sim(\sim P \vee Q), \sim P \,/\therefore\, R$

   g. $\sim(P \rightarrow Q), Q \,/\therefore\, R$

   *h. $(P \equiv Q) \,/\therefore\, (\sim P \equiv \sim Q)$

   i. $(P \rightarrow Q), \sim Q \,/\therefore\, \sim P$

3. With the intention of using the translation to detect incompatibility, translate into C each of the following pairs of sentences. Then construct a derivation with the translations as the hypotheses and derive a sentence and its negation as separate items in the main derivation.

   a. Caesar calls me and Brutus writes me letters. But, either Caesar doesn't call me or Brutus doesn't write me letters.

   *b. If our company does not increase its profit by 30 percent, we shall go bankrupt. Yet, our company will not increase its profit by 30 percent and we shall not go bankrupt.

   c. Either Max gets the best house and the best car, or he isn't absolutely happy. Max doesn't get the best house after all and he is absolutely happy.

   *d. Winnie-the-Pooh loves honey; but it is not true that if he has some of it left, he always shares it with Piglet. If Winnie-the-Pooh loves honey and he has some of it left, he always shares it with Piglet.

   e. If George is in a serious mood, then he is very quiet. Yet, it is not the case that George is not quiet only if not in a serious mood.

10.3 OTHER DERIVED RULES ABOUT NEGATION

In this section, we introduce still other derived rules. Unlike the derived rules in section 10.2, however, these rules concern all four of the basic sentence types.

Modus Tollens and Disjunctive Syllogism

Like *modus ponens*, the next rule has a Latin name.

Modus Tollens (m t).   The negation of the antecedent of a conditional is a direct consequence of the same conditional and the negation of its consequent.

This rule is represented schematically as follows:

$$
\begin{array}{c|l}
h & A \to B \\
i & \sim B \\
j & \sim A \qquad\qquad\text{h, i, m t}
\end{array}
$$

The following derivation provides a method by which to transform any derivation using *modus tollens* into a derivation using only official rules. The fact that such a method exists serves as a proof that anything derivable with *modus tollens* is derivable using just official rules. So we can adopt *modus tollens* as a derived rule.

$$
\begin{array}{c|l}
1 & P \to Q \qquad\qquad \text{hyp} \\
2 & \sim Q \qquad\qquad \text{hyp} \\
3 & \quad\; P \qquad\qquad \text{hyp (of 3-6)} \\
4 & \quad\; P \to Q \qquad\; \text{1, reit} \\
5 & \quad\; Q \qquad\qquad \text{3, 4, m p} \\
6 & \quad\; \sim Q \qquad\qquad \text{2, reit} \\
7 & \sim P \qquad\qquad \text{3-6, neg int}
\end{array}
$$

This derivation uses one derived rule, namely, the rule of negation introduction. But we have already justified its adoption, so there is nothing wrong with using it to justify adoption of another derived rule.

The next derived rule is also well known and has the Latin name *modus tollendo ponens*. We use its English name instead in order to avoid confusion with *modus tollens*.

Disjunctive Syllogism (disj syl).   The right disjunct of a disjunction is a direct consequence of the disjunction and a sentence denying the left disjunct. The left disjunct of a disjunction is a direct consequence of the disjunction and a sentence denying the right disjunct. (A sentence is the <u>denial</u> of another if and only if it is either the negation of the other or the other is a negation of it.)

Applications of this rule may have any of the following forms:

h	$A \vee B$		h	$A \vee B$	
i	$\sim A$		i	$\sim B$	
j	B	h, i, disj syl	j	A	h, i, disj syl

h	$\sim A \vee B$		h	$A \vee \sim B$	
i	A		i	B	
j	B	h, i, disj syl	j	A	h, i, disj syl

The next derivation shows that no application of the rule of disjunctive syllogism of the first form would result in the entry of an item that you could not derive through applications of only official rules.

1	$P \vee Q$	hyp
2	$\sim P$	hyp
3	$\quad P$	hyp (of 3–5)
4	$\quad \sim P$	2, reit
5	$\quad Q$	3, 4, neg elim
6	$\quad Q$	hyp (of 6–7)
7	$\quad Q$	6, rep
8	Q	1, 3–5, 6–7, disj elim

Derivations showing that the other three forms are equally acceptable are not difficult and are left as exercises. In constructing these derivations, you can use derived rules that have already been justified. We did this above in deriving item 5 through applying the rule of negation elimination.

Excluded Middle and Contraposition

The following is a derivation of $(P \vee \sim P)$ from no hypotheses.

1	$\sim(P \vee \sim P)$	hyp (of 1–6)
2	$\quad P$	hyp (of 2–4)

3	$P \vee \sim P$	2, disj int
4	$\sim(P \vee \sim P)$	1, reit
5	$\sim P$	2–4, neg int
6	$P \vee \sim P$	5, disj int
7	$P \vee \sim P$	1–6, ind pr

Because the derivation shows how to construct a derivation from no hypotheses for any sentence of the form $(A \vee \sim A)$, we regard it as doing the work for the infinite number of sentences of that form. These are the theorems of **excluded middle** (ex mid), also known summarily as *the principle of excluded middle*.

Unlike Intelim, there are systems of logic that do not have the principle of excluded middle. For example, the systems of Arend Heyting in *Intuitionism* (Amsterdam, 1956) and others developed by Frederic Fitch do not have the principle of excluded middle. These systems have the advantage of being able to accommodate, without the risk of paradox, not only sentences not known to be either true or false but also ones that are neither true nor false, such as 'This sentence itself is false'. These alternative logics, generally known as intuitionistic logic, are a fascinating topic that some reader may want to pursue after mastering the material in this text.

As mentioned previously, you can use theorems as shortcuts in the construction of derivations. This is done by writing a theorem as an item in the derivation and writing its name in the column to the right. You can do this for the theorems of excluded middle and others of the form

$$(A \to B) \equiv (\sim B \to \sim A)$$

known as theorems of **contraposition** (contrapos).

That these are theorems of Intelim can be shown by filling in the missing items in the derivation below.

1	$P \to Q$	hyp (of 1–h)
.		
h	$\sim Q \to \sim P$	
i	$\sim Q \to \sim P$	hyp (of i–j)
.		
j	$P \to Q$	
k	$(P \to Q) \equiv (\sim Q \to \sim P)$	1–h, i–j, bicond int

The missing steps in 1–h are below; those for i–j are left for you to complete.

1	$P \rightarrow Q$	hyp (of 1–8)
2	$\sim Q$	hyp (of 2–7)
3	P	hyp (of 3–6)
4	$P \rightarrow Q$	1, reit
5	Q	3, 4, m p
6	$\sim Q$	2, reit
7	$\sim P$	3–6, neg int
8	$\sim Q \rightarrow \sim P$	2–7, cond int

Negative Conjunctions

Besides those derived rules already given, there are others for the introduction and elimination of negative conjunctions. Negative conjunctions are expressions of the form $\sim(A \ \& \ B)$. The introduction and elimination rules are stated below.

Negative Conjunction Introduction (neg conj int). The negation of a conjunction is a direct consequence of the disjunction of the negations of its conjuncts.

Expressed schematically this rule is as follows:

h	$\sim A \lor \sim B$	
i	$\sim(A \ \& \ B)$	h, neg conj int

Negative Conjunction Elimination (neg conj elim). The disjunction of two negations is a direct consequence of the negation of the conjunction of the negated sentences.

This rule is expressed schematically as follows:

h	$\sim(A \ \& \ B)$	
i	$\sim A \lor \sim B$	h, neg conj elim

The following derivation establishes that the introduction rule is acceptable as a derived rule.

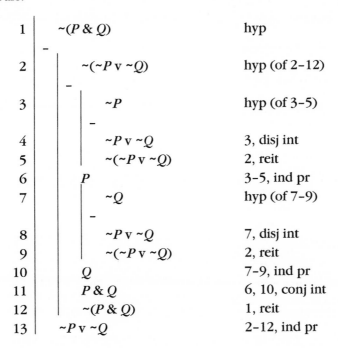

1	~P v ~Q	hyp
2	P & Q	hyp (of 2–6)
3	~P v ~Q	1, reit
4	P	2, conj elim
5	~Q	3, 4, disj syl
6	Q	2, conj elim
7	~(P & Q)	2–6, neg int

The next derivation justifies the adoption of the elimination rule as a derived rule.

1	~(P & Q)	hyp
2	~(~P v ~Q)	hyp (of 2–12)
3	~P	hyp (of 3–5)
4	~P v ~Q	3, disj int
5	~(~P v ~Q)	2, reit
6	P	3–5, ind pr
7	~Q	hyp (of 7–9)
8	~P v ~Q	7, disj int
9	~(~P v ~Q)	2, reit
10	Q	7–9, ind pr
11	P & Q	6, 10, conj int
12	~(P & Q)	1, reit
13	~P v ~Q	2–12, ind pr

Negative Disjunctions

A negative conjunction is any sentence of the form ~(A & B); correspondingly, a negative disjunction is any sentence of the form ~(A v B). Just as there are derived introduction and elimination rules for negative conjunctions, there are also introduction and elimination rules for negative disjunctions.

The introduction rule is below.

Negative Disjunction Introduction (neg disj int).   A negative disjunction is a direct consequence of the conjunction of the negations of its disjuncts.

This rule is expressed schematically as follows:

$$
\begin{array}{l|ll}
h & \sim\!A\ \&\ \sim\!B & \\
i & \sim\!(A \vee B) & h,\ \text{neg disj int}
\end{array}
$$

The following rule is the elimination rule.

Negative Disjunction Elimination (neg disj elim).   A conjunction of two negations is a direct consequence of the negation of the disjunction of the sentences negated.

Expressed schematically the rule is as follows:

$$
\begin{array}{l|ll}
h & \sim\!(A \vee B) & \\
i & \sim\!A\ \&\ \sim\!B & h,\ \text{neg disj elim}
\end{array}
$$

The derivation below shows that the introduction rule does not allow you to derive from hypotheses any sentences that you could not get using official rules.

$$
\begin{array}{ll|ll}
1 & & \sim\!P\ \&\ \sim\!Q & \text{hyp} \\
2 & & \quad P \vee Q & \text{hyp (of 2–6)} \\
3 & & \quad \sim\!P\ \&\ \sim\!Q & 1,\ \text{reit} \\
4 & & \quad \sim\!P & 3,\ \text{conj elim} \\
5 & & \quad Q & 2,\ 4,\ \text{disj syl} \\
6 & & \quad \sim\!Q & 3,\ \text{conj elim} \\
7 & & \sim\!(P \vee Q) & 2–6,\ \text{neg int}
\end{array}
$$

The next derivation justifies adoption of the derived rule for elimination of negative disjunctions.

1	~(P v Q)	hyp
2	P	hyp (of 2–4)
3	P v Q	2, disj int
4	~(P v Q)	1, reit
5	~P	2–4, neg int
6	Q	hyp (of 6–8)
7	P v Q	6, disj int
8	~(P v Q)	1, reit
9	~Q	6–8, neg int
10	~P & ~Q	5, 9, conj int

De Morgan's Theorems

We refer to those sentences exemplifying the forms below jointly as **De Morgan's theorems** (d m).

$$\sim(A \ \& \ B) \equiv (\sim A \ v \ \sim B)$$

$$\sim(\sim A \ \& \ B) \equiv (A \ v \ \sim B)$$

$$\sim(A \ \& \ \sim B) \equiv (\sim A \ v \ B)$$

$$\sim(\sim A \ \& \ \sim B) \equiv (A \ v \ B)$$

$$\sim(A \ v \ B) \equiv (\sim A \ \& \ \sim B)$$

$$\sim(\sim A \ v \ B) \equiv (A \ \& \ \sim B)$$

$$\sim(A \ v \ \sim B) \equiv (\sim A \ \& \ B)$$

$$\sim(\sim A \ v \ \sim B) \equiv (A \ \& \ B)$$

With the introduction and elimination rules for negative conjunction and negative disjunction available, you can easily show that any sentence exemplifying one of the forms above is a theorem.

EXERCISES FOR SECTION 10.3

1. Show through a derivation that each of the sentences a–l at the top of the next page is a theorem. You can use derived rules and theorems from this and previous sections.

a. $((P \vee Q) \mathbin{\&} {\sim}Q) \to P$

*b. ${\sim}({\sim}P \mathbin{\&} Q) \to (P \vee {\sim}Q)$

c. $({\sim}P \vee Q) \to {\sim}(P \mathbin{\&} {\sim}Q)$

d. ${\sim}({\sim}P \mathbin{\&} {\sim}Q) \to (P \vee Q)$

e. $(P \mathbin{\&} {\sim}Q) \to {\sim}({\sim}P \vee Q)$

f. ${\sim}(P \vee {\sim}Q) \to ({\sim}P \mathbin{\&} Q)$

*g. $({\sim}P \vee Q) \to (P \to Q)$

h. $(P \to Q) \to {\sim}(P \mathbin{\&} {\sim}Q)$

i. ${\sim}(P \mathbin{\&} {\sim}Q) \to ({\sim}Q \to {\sim}P)$

*j. $(P \to Q) \to ((P \to {\sim}Q) \to {\sim}P)$

k. $((P \to Q) \mathbin{\&} (P \to {\sim}Q)) \to (P \to R)$

*l. $(P \to {\sim}Q) \to (Q \to {\sim}P)$

*2. Show that the rule of negation elimination could be added as a derived rule in a system with disjunction introduction and disjunctive syllogism as official rules.

3. Show that the following rules of direct consequence can be added to Intelim as derived rules.

> Rule 1. The negation of the right immediate component of a biconditional is a direct consequence of the same biconditional and the negation of the left immediate component.

> Rule 2. The negation of the left immediate component of a biconditional is a direct consequence of the same biconditional and the negation of the right immediate component.

4. Show by a derivation that every sentence of the form $((A \equiv B) \equiv ({\sim}A \equiv {\sim}B))$ is a theorem. Use Rules 1 and 2 in exercise 3.

5. With the intention of using the translations to detect valid arguments, translate the following arguments. Then, derive the C-conclusion from the C-premises of each of your translations.

*a. The clay will not release water if either there is no water in the clay or the particles are too fine. The particles are too fine. Therefore, the clay will not release water.

b. If Alex either dances all night or works all night, he will be exhausted in the morning. Alex will not be exhausted in the morning. Therefore, he will not dance all night and he will not work until daybreak.

*c. The president and the first lady both love animals only if the president has a cocker spaniel and the first lady has a Siamese cat. The first lady does not have a Siamese cat. Therefore, either the president or the first lady does not love animals.

d. The U.S. dollar will increase in value relative to the Japanese yen if the United States does not have a trade deficit with Japan. The United States will not have a trade deficit with Japan if Japan does not have trade barriers unfavorable to the United States. The ability of the United States to sell goods in Japan will not increase if the U.S. dollar increases in value relative to the Japanese yen. Therefore, if Japan does not have trade barriers unfavorable to the United States, the ability of the United States to sell goods in Japan will not increase.

e. If the quality of U.S. goods increases, then the ability of the United States to sell goods to Europe will increase. If the price of U.S. goods declines, then the ability of the United States to sell goods to Europe will increase. The price of U.S. goods will decline unless the quality increases. Therefore, the ability of the United States to sell goods to Europe will increase.

*f. If Tom is sober, then he is interesting and polite. If he is polite and interesting, then Suzy likes him. Therefore, if Tom is sober, Suzy likes him.

*g. Tom is polite only if he is sober. Suzy likes him only if he is polite. Tom is not sober. Therefore, Suzy doesn't like him.

h. Lee is old enough to vote if she is 21 or over. If she's under 21, she'll have to join the Army. So if Lee is not old enough to vote, then she either can't drink legally or will have to join the Army.

6. With the intention of using the translations to detect valid arguments, translate the following arguments. Then, derive the C-conclusion from the C-premises of each of your translations. Add valid and unstated premises if warranted.

*a. I shall eat either salmon or liver. I shall not eat fish. Therefore, I shall eat liver.

b. Pauline was born in the capital of France if she was not born in the capital of Spain. She was not born in Madrid. Therefore, she was born in Paris.

*c. I shall order either a tuna or lobster salad for lunch. If I order a tuna salad, I shall spend $4. If I order a lobster salad, I shall spend $10. I shall not spend more than $6 for lunch. Therefore, I shall order a tuna salad for lunch.

d. If you want to avoid being burglarized, you should have a security system installed or bury all of your valuables. Therefore, you should have a security system installed.

*e. Mr. Cartier will have an allergic reaction if he drinks at least two glasses of wine. Mr. Cartier will drink at least three glasses of wine. Therefore, Mr. Cartier will have an allergic reaction.

f. Buddy will live in the mountains the rest of his life unless he is not indicted for the murder of the lost children. Buddy will be convicted for the murder of the lost children. Therefore, Buddy will live in the mountains the rest of his life.

*g. It was the Fourth of July. Therefore, the mail was not delivered.

h. If the government closes legitimate private companies or ignores problems with public companies, the clock is being turned back on economic reforms. The government is paying no attention to the problems of public companies. Therefore, the economy will decline.

*i. The pro-democracy movement will succeed unless the people are repressed. If the people are repressed, they will fight back until they win. Therefore, the pro-democracy movement will succeed.

j. The president has a cocker spaniel. The first lady has a Siamese cat. If the president has a dog and the first lady has a cat, then they both love animals. Therefore, they both love animals.

10.4 RULES IN REVIEW

Intelim has the rule of reiteration and seven official rules of direct consequence. We have added several derived rules of direct consequence and proven a number of important theorems. In this section, the official and derived rules are restated schematically. Named theorems are also restated.

Official Rules

Rule of Reiteration (reit)

$$
\begin{array}{c|c}
h & A \\
\cdot & \\
\cdot & \vdots \\
i & A \qquad \text{h, reit}
\end{array}
$$

Rule of *Modus Ponens* (m p)

$$
\begin{array}{c|c}
h & (A \rightarrow B) \\
\cdot & \cdot \\
i & A \\
\cdot & \cdot \\
j & B \qquad \text{h, i, m p}
\end{array}
$$

Rule of Conditional Introduction (cond int)

$$
\begin{array}{ll}
h \quad \Big|\;\; \Big|\quad A & \text{hyp (of h–i)} \\[4pt]
\;\;\;\;\;\;\;\; \Big|\quad - \\[4pt]
. \qquad\quad . \\[2pt]
i \qquad\quad B \\[2pt]
. \qquad\;\; . \\[2pt]
j \quad\;\; A \rightarrow B & \text{h–i, cond int}
\end{array}
$$

Rule of Conjunction Introduction (conj int)

$$
\begin{array}{ll}
h \quad\Big|\;\; A \\[2pt]
. \qquad . \\[2pt]
i \qquad B \\[2pt]
. \qquad . \\[2pt]
j \qquad A \,\&\, B & \text{h, i, conj int}
\end{array}
$$

Rule of Conjunction Elimination (conj elim)

$$
\begin{array}{ll}
h \quad\Big|\;\; A \,\&\, B \\[2pt]
. \qquad . \\[2pt]
i \qquad A & \text{h, conj elim}
\end{array}
$$

$$
\begin{array}{ll}
h \quad\Big|\;\; A \,\&\, B \\[2pt]
. \qquad . \\[2pt]
i \qquad B & \text{h, conj elim}
\end{array}
$$

Rule of Disjunction Introduction (disj int)

$$
\begin{array}{ll}
h \quad\Big|\;\; A \\[2pt]
. \qquad . \\[2pt]
i \qquad A \vee B & \text{h, disj int}
\end{array}
$$

$$
\begin{array}{ll}
h \quad\Big|\;\; B \\[2pt]
. \qquad . \\[2pt]
i \qquad A \vee B & \text{h, disj int}
\end{array}
$$

Rule of Disjunction Elimination (disj elim)

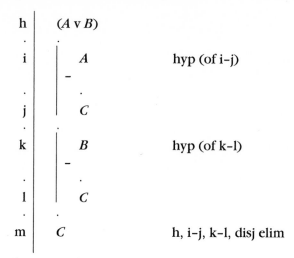

h	(A v B)	
i	A	hyp (of i–j)
j	C	
k	B	hyp (of k–l)
l	C	
m	C	h, i–j, k–l, disj elim

Rule of Indirect Proof (ind pr)

h	~A	hyp (of h–j)
i	B	
j	~B	
k	A	h–j, ind pr

Derived Rules

Derived Rule of Added Condition (add cond)

h	B	
i	A → B	h, add cond

Derived Rule of Transitivity of Conditional (trans cond)

$$
\begin{array}{ll}
\text{h} & A \to B \\
\quad \cdot & \quad \cdot \\
\text{i} & B \to C \\
\quad \cdot & \quad \cdot \\
\text{j} & A \to C \qquad \text{h, i, trans cond}
\end{array}
$$

Derived Rule of Distribution (dist)

$$
\begin{array}{ll}
\text{h} & A \to (B \to C) \\
\quad \cdot & \quad \cdot \\
\text{i} & (A \to B) \to (A \to C) \quad \text{h, dist}
\end{array}
$$

Derived Rule of Biconditional Introduction (bicond int)

$$
\begin{array}{lll}
\text{h} & A & \text{hyp (of h–i)} \\
\quad \cdot & \quad \cdot \\
\text{i} & B \\
\quad \cdot & \quad \cdot \\
\text{j} & B & \text{hyp (of j–k)} \\
\quad \cdot & \quad \cdot \\
\text{k} & A \\
\quad \cdot & \quad \cdot \\
\text{l} & A \equiv B & \text{h–i, j–k, bicond int}
\end{array}
$$

Derived Rule of Biconditional Elimination (bicond elim)

$$
\begin{array}{lll}
\text{h} & A \\
\quad \cdot & \quad \cdot \\
\text{i} & A \equiv B \\
\quad \cdot & \quad \cdot \\
\text{j} & B & \text{h, i, bicond elim}
\end{array}
$$

$$
\begin{array}{lll}
\text{h} & A \\
\quad \cdot & \quad \cdot \\
\text{i} & B \equiv A \\
\quad \cdot & \quad \cdot \\
\text{j} & B & \text{h, i, bicond elim}
\end{array}
$$

Derived Rule of Transitivity of Biconditional (trans bicond)

h | $A \equiv B$

i | $B \equiv C$

j | $A \equiv C$ h, i, trans bicond

Derived Rule of Complex Constructive Dilemma (comp cnst dil)

h | $A \lor B$

i | A hyp (of i–j)

j | C

k | B hyp (of k–l)

l | D

m | $C \lor D$ h, i–j, k–l, comp cnst dil

Derived Rule of Double Negation Introduction (neg$_2$ int)

h | A

i | $\sim\sim A$ h, neg$_2$ int

Derived Rule of Double Negation Elimination (neg$_2$ elim)

h | $\sim\sim A$

i | A h, neg$_2$ elim

Derived Rule of Negation Introduction (neg int)

h	A	hyp (of h–j)
.	.	
i	B	
.	.	
j	$\sim B$	
.	.	
k	$\sim A$	h–j, neg int

Derived Rule of Negation Elimination (neg elim)

h	A	
.	.	
i	$\sim A$	
.	.	
j	B	h, i, neg elim

Derived Rule of *Modus Tollens* (m t)

h	$A \rightarrow B$	
.	.	
i	$\sim B$	
.	.	
j	$\sim A$	h, i, m t

Derived Rule of Disjunctive Syllogism (disj syl)

h	$A \vee B$			h	$A \vee B$	
.	.			.	.	
i	$\sim A$			i	$\sim B$	
.	.			.	.	
j	B	h, i, disj syl		j	A	h, i, disj syl

h	$\sim A \vee B$			h	$A \vee \sim B$	
.	.			.	.	
i	A			i	B	
.	.			.	.	
j	B	h, i, disj syl		j	A	h, i, disj syl

Derived Rule of Negative Conjunction Introduction (neg conj int)

$$
\begin{array}{ll}
\text{h} & \sim\!A \text{ v } \sim\!B \\
\text{.} & \text{.} \\
\text{i} & \sim\!(A \mathrel{\&} B) \qquad \text{h, neg conj int}
\end{array}
$$

Derived Rule of Negative Conjunction Elimination (neg conj elim)

$$
\begin{array}{ll}
\text{h} & \sim\!(A \mathrel{\&} B) \\
\text{.} & \text{.} \\
\text{i} & \sim\!A \text{ v } \sim\!B \qquad \text{h, neg conj elim}
\end{array}
$$

Derived Rule of Negative Disjunction Introduction (neg disj int)

$$
\begin{array}{ll}
\text{h} & \sim\!A \mathrel{\&} \sim\!B \\
\text{.} & \text{.} \\
\text{i} & \sim\!(A \text{ v } B) \qquad \text{h, neg disj int}
\end{array}
$$

Derived Rule of Negative Disjunction Elimination (neg disj elim)

$$
\begin{array}{ll}
\text{h} & \sim\!(A \text{ v } B) \\
\text{.} & \text{.} \\
\text{i} & \sim\!A \mathrel{\&} \sim\!B \qquad \text{h, neg disj elim}
\end{array}
$$

Theorems

Theorem of Conditioned Repetition (cond rep)

$$A \rightarrow (B \rightarrow A)$$

Theorem of Distribution (th dist)

$$(A \rightarrow (B \rightarrow C)) \equiv ((A \rightarrow B) \rightarrow (A \rightarrow C))$$

Theorem of Reflexivity of Conditional (refl cond)

$$A \rightarrow A$$

Theorem of Commutativity of Conjunction (comm conj)

$$(A \mathrel{\&} B) \equiv (B \mathrel{\&} A)$$

Theorem of Associativity of Conjunction (assoc conj)

$$(A \mathrel{\&} (B \mathrel{\&} C)) \equiv ((A \mathrel{\&} B) \mathrel{\&} C)$$

Theorem of Commutativity of Biconditional (comm bicond)

$$(A \equiv B) \equiv (B \equiv A)$$

Theorem of Associativity of Biconditional (assoc bicond)

$$(A \equiv (B \equiv C)) \equiv ((A \equiv B) \equiv C)$$

Theorem of Reflexivity of Biconditional (reflex bicond)

$$A \equiv A$$

Theorem of Commutativity of Disjunction (comm disj)

$$(A \vee B) \equiv (B \vee A)$$

Theorem of Associativity of Disjunction (assoc disj)

$$(A \vee (B \vee C)) \equiv ((A \vee B) \vee C)$$

Theorem of Distribution of Conjunction into Disjunction (dist conj disj)

$$(A \& (B \vee C)) \equiv ((A \& B) \vee (A \& C))$$

Theorem of Distribution of Disjunction into Conjunction (dist disj conj)

$$(A \vee (B \& C)) \equiv ((A \vee B) \& (A \vee C))$$

Theorem of Excluded Middle (ex mid)

$$A \vee {\sim}A$$

Theorem of Contraposition (contrapos)

$$(A \rightarrow B) \equiv ({\sim}B \rightarrow {\sim}A)$$

De Morgan's Theorems (d m)

$$\sim(A \& B) \equiv ({\sim}A \vee {\sim}B)$$

$$\sim({\sim}A \& B) \equiv (A \vee {\sim}B)$$

$$\sim(A \& {\sim}B) \equiv ({\sim}A \vee B)$$

$$\sim({\sim}A \& {\sim}B) \equiv (A \vee B)$$

$$\sim(A \vee B) \equiv ({\sim}A \& {\sim}B)$$

$$\sim({\sim}A \vee B) \equiv (A \& {\sim}B)$$

$$\sim(A \vee {\sim}B) \equiv ({\sim}A \& B)$$

$$\sim({\sim}A \vee {\sim}B) \equiv (A \& B)$$

EXERCISES FOR SECTION 10.4

*1. Both conditional and biconditional are transitive. We demonstrated this by deriving rules of transitivity of conditional and of biconditional. Could corresponding rules for conjunction and disjunction be derived? Explain why or why not.

2. Conjunction, disjunction, and biconditional are associative. This has been shown by proving theorems of associativity for each. Are there theorems of associativity of conditional? If not, why not? (Hint: Only valid sentences are theorems of Intelim. This is a requirement of soundness.)

*3. Conjunction, disjunction, and biconditional are commutative. Is conditional? If not, why not?

4. There are theorems of reflexivity of conditional and biconditional. Would the system be sound if it had as theorems every sentence of the form (A & A) or every sentence of the form (A v A)? Explain why or why not.

5. In the text, the rule of conjunction elimination is characterized as having two parts. What other official rules have more than one part? What are those parts?

*6. As discussed in the text, the rule of conjunction elimination can be thought of as having two parts. Which derived rules can be thought of as rules with two or more parts?

7. With the intention of using the translations to detect valid arguments, translate into C the arguments below. Then, derive the C-conclusion from the C-premises of each of your translations.

   *a. Cindy is either getting married or flying to London, and Clara is either attending the wedding ceremony or flying to Rio de Janeiro. If Cindy is getting married, then Clara is attending the wedding ceremony; and if Cindy is flying to London, then Clara is flying to Rio de Janeiro. Clara is not attending the wedding ceremony. Therefore, Clara is flying to Rio de Janeiro and Cindy is not getting married.

   b. If mercury caused the disorder, then mercury will be banned. If mercury is banned, then the price of mercury will decline. The price of mercury will not decline. Therefore, mercury did not cause the disorder and will not be banned.

   *c. Nancy is either at the movies tonight or unhappy, or she does not want to be at the movies tonight. Nancy does want to be at the movies tonight but she is not there. Therefore, Nancy is unhappy.

   d. If Alex is either a chemist or an engineer, he studied mathematics and physics. If Alex is not a chemist, then he is not a scientist. Alex did not study mathematics. Therefore, Alex is not a scientist.

*e. If you wish upon a star and wait for your fairy godmother to help you, then you will not give up hope. You will give up hope. Therefore, you either do not wish upon a star or you do not wait for your fairy godmother to help you.

8. With the intention of using the translations to detect equivalence, translate into C the pairs of sentences below. Then, derive the C-translation of each from the C-translation of the other.

   *a. (i) Not both Hitler and Nero were communists.
       (ii) Either Hitler or Nero was not a communist.

   b. (i) Either you are rich or you are rich and famous.
      (ii) You are rich.

   *c. (i) It is not the case that Snow White is selfish and has no friends.
       (ii) Either Snow White is not selfish or she has friends.

11

QUANTIFIER RULES

The system of rules we developed in chapters 9 and 10 were intended for the Intelim system, the formal language of which is the language of the logic of connectives. We shall now be developing a system for the language of the logic of quantifiers. This system, which we call Intelim-SQ, makes the assumptions of standard quantification theory. The 'SQ' is short for 'Standard Quantification'.

The Intelim-SQ system includes the rule of reiteration and the official rules already presented for conditional, conjunction, disjunction, and negation, and still others specifically about quantified sentences. Following standard quantification theory, the rules about quantified sentences are truth-preserving only when every singular term designates an individual in the domain. In chapter 12, we develop alternative systems of logic free from the requirement that every singular term designate an individual in the domain.

11.1 RULES ABOUT UNIVERSAL QUANTIFICATION

There are two official rules pertaining to universal sentences, an introduction and an elimination rule. Because the elimination rule is the simpler, we take it up first.

Universal Quantifier Elimination

The elimination rule provides a way to proceed in a derivation from a universal sentence to any one of its instances. The rule is as follows.

Universal Quantifier Elimination (u q elim).   A universal sentence has as a direct consequence any of its instances.

The following is a derivation that makes use of this new rule.

$$
\begin{array}{lll}
1 & (\forall x)(Fx \to Gx) & \text{hyp} \\
2 & (\forall x)Fx & \text{hyp} \\
\\
3 & Fa \to Ga & 1, \text{u q elim} \\
4 & Fa & 2, \text{u q elim} \\
5 & Ga & 3, 4, \text{m p}
\end{array}
$$

Notice that item 3 is an instance of item 1, that item 4 is an instance of item 2, and that 'a' is the instantial term in both cases.

The following is a schematic expression of the rule of universal quantifier elimination. In any derivation of this form, the item corresponding to i is a direct consequence of the item corresponding to h by the rule of universal quantifier elimination.

$$
\begin{array}{lll}
h & (\forall x)A & \\
i & A(a/x) & h, \text{u q elim}
\end{array}
$$

As previously explained, $A(a/x)$ is the result of replacing every free occurrence of x throughout A with a. For example, let A be 'Fy', a be 'b', and x be 'y'. Then $A(a/x)$ is the result of replacing every free occurrence of 'y' throughout 'Fy' with 'b'. The result is 'Fb'. For a detailed discussion of the metalanguage, see section 6.1.

In the simple derivation below, items 1 and 2 correspond, respectively, to h and i in the schema above.

$$
\begin{array}{lll}
1 & (\forall y)Fy & \text{hyp} \\
\\
2 & Fb & 1, \text{u q elim} \\
3 & (\forall y)Fy \to Fb & 1\text{--}2, \text{cond int}
\end{array}
$$

Notice how items 1 and 2 in the derivation relate to items h and i in the schema. To see the relationship, let x be 'y', A be 'Fy', and a be 'b'.

Using the same method as in the derivation above, you can prove that any sentence of the form

$$(\forall x)A \rightarrow A(a/x)$$

is a theorem. Such sentences are known as theorems of **specification** (sp). That the same method works in proving any of the theorems can be seen from studying the metaderivation below.

1		$(\forall x)A$	hyp
		—	
2		$A(a/x)$	1, u q elim
3		$(\forall x)A \rightarrow A(a/x)$	1–2, cond int

A <u>metaderivation</u> is expressed using variables from the metalanguage or, for short, metavariables. It provides a general model for the construction of derivations of that form.

For the system to be sound, every rule of direct consequence must be truth-preserving. In other words, no rule can permit a derivation of a false sentence from true ones. It is not difficult to see that the rule of universal quantifier elimination is truth-preserving. The rule allows you to enter any instance of a preceding universal sentence. Because in standard quantification theory every singular term designates an individual in the domain, an instance is certainly true if the universal sentence is. After all, an instance of a universal sentence only says of an individual in the domain what the universal sentence says is true of every one of them.

Prefixed Derivations

The rule of universal quantifier introduction makes use of a special type of subderivation, a <u>derivation prefixed with a singular term</u> or, for short, a <u>prefixed derivation</u>. In a derivation of this kind, a singular term appears to the left and near the top of the vertical line, bordering the column of items of the derivation. This is the singular term that is the prefix to the derivation. That term cannot appear in any sentence reiterated in the derivation.

An example of a prefixed derivation is the subordinate derivation 3–7 that follows. This derivation is prefixed with the singular term 'a'.

1		$(\forall x)(Fx \rightarrow Gx)$	hyp
2		$(\forall x)Fx$	hyp
3	*a*	$(\forall x)(Fx \rightarrow Gx)$	1, reit
4		$(\forall x)Fx$	2, reit
5		$Fa \rightarrow Ga$	3, u q elim
6		Fa	4, u q elim
7		Ga	5, 6, m p
8		$(\forall x)Gx$	3–7, u q int

Note how the prefixed term is placed to the left and near the top of the vertical line, bordering items 3–7. Also observe that the prefixed term does not appear in any item reiterated in the prefixed subderivation (that is, in items 1 and 2).

As stated, a term prefixed to a derivation is not permitted to occur in any sentence reiterated in the derivation. Therefore, in employing a prefixed derivation, to avoid the error of reiterating a sentence containing the prefixed term, it is advisable to select a "new" singular term for the prefix, that is, one that has not been used previously in the construction of the derivation.

The sequence 3–6 below is an example of a construction that does not qualify as a prefixed derivation because the term that appears near the top of the vertical line, bordering items 3–6, also appears in a sentence (item 5) that is reiterated in 3–6.

1		Gb	hyp
2		$(\forall x)Fx$	hyp
3	*b*	$(\forall x)Fx$	2, reit
4		Fb	3, u q elim
5		Gb	1, reit (Wrong!)
6		$Fb \& Gb$	4, 5, conj int
7		$(\forall x)(Fx \& Gx)$	3–6, u q int

Without the prohibition against reiterating an item containing the prefixed term, the Intelim-SQ system would be unsound. You can see this from the faulty "derivation" above. Let the domain be the natural numbers and assign '$F\_$' to '$\_$ is evenly divisible by 1', '$G\_$' to '$\_$ is evenly divisible by 2', and '*b*' to '14'. Then item 1 translates as '14 is evenly divisible by 2', item 2 translates as 'All natural numbers are evenly divisible by 1', and item 7 translates as 'All natural numbers are evenly divisible by both 1 and 2'. While items 1 and 2 are true, item 7 is false.

Because a singular term prefixed to a subordinate derivation does not appear in any sentence that is reiterated in the subderivation, the prefixed term has a role within the subderivation similar to that of 'John Doe', 'John Q. Public', or '*x*' in informal reasoning. Although treated as if it does, what individual 'John Doe', 'John Q. Public', or '*x*' designates, if indeed there is any, is irrelevant to the reasoning. Similarly, in a prefixed derivation, the prefixed term is assumed to designate an individual in the domain although no particular one. What individual it designates, if in fact any, is irrelevant to the prefixed derivation. Indeed, you may think of the prefixed term as designating an "arbitrary" individual in the sense that the prefixed term can be taken to designate any individual in the domain without disturbing the justification given for any item of the prefixed derivation.

Universal Quantifier Introduction

We now turn to the introduction rule for the universal quantifier. This rule provides a method for deriving a universal sentence.

Universal Quantifier Introduction (u q int).   A universal sentence is a direct consequence of a prefixed subderivation that has no hypotheses but has as an item a generating instance of the universal sentence with the prefixed term as its instantial term.

As defined in section 6.1, an instance of a quantified sentence is a generating instance so long as the instantial term does not occur in the quantified sentence. Thus, although $(a = a)$ and $(a = b)$ are both instances of $(\forall x)(a = x)$, of the two, only $(a = b)$ is a generating instance. [Give examples of other generating instances of $(\forall x)(a = x)$.]

Below is an example of a derivation in which the rule of universal quantifier introduction is used.

1		$(\forall x)(Fx \to Gx)$	hyp
2		$(\forall x)Fx$	hyp
3	a	$(\forall x)(Fx \to Gx)$	1, reit
4		$(\forall x)Fx$	2, reit
5		$Fa \to Ga$	3, u q elim
6		Fa	4, u q elim
7		Ga	5, 6, m p
8		$(\forall x)Gx$	3–7, u q int

Observe that, as required by the rule, the prefixed derivation 3–7 has no hypotheses, item 7 is a generating instance of item 8, the instantial term of 7 is the same as the prefixed term, and item 8 does not contain the prefixed term.

The following is another example of a derivation using both the introduction and elimination rules for universal quantifiers.

1	Gb & $(\forall x)Fx$	hyp
2	Gb	1, conj elim
3	$(\forall x)Fx$	1, conj elim
4	a Fa	3, reit, u q elim
5	Gb	2, reit
6	Gb & Fa	4, 5, conj int
7	$(\forall x)(Gb$ & $Fx)$	4–6, u q int

Notice how 'a' rather than 'b' is picked for the prefixed term. If you replace
'a' with 'b' throughout the prefixed derivation, the result will not be a prefixed
derivation. [Can you explain why?]

Notice how item 1 and item 7 in the preceding derivation become
item 7 and item 1, respectively, of the next derivation. Such derivations are
said to be the <u>converses</u> of one another.

1	$(\forall x)(Gb$ & $Fx)$	hyp
2	a Gb & Fa	1, reit, u q elim
3	Fa	2, conj elim
4	$(\forall x)Fx$	2–3, u q int
5	Gb & Fc	1, u q elim
6	Gb	5, conj elim
7	Gb & $(\forall x)Fx$	4, 6, conj int

You can use these two derivations together with the rule of biconditional
introduction to get the following theorem:

$$(\forall x)(Gb \ \& \ Fx) \equiv (Gb \ \& \ (\forall x)Fx)$$

The rule of universal quantifier introduction could have been stated
through the following schema. According to the rule, in any derivation of
the form below, item j is a direct consequence of the prefixed derivation
h–i.

h	a ·	
·	·	
i	A	
j	$(\forall x)A(x/a)$	h–i, u q int

In any derivation of this form, item i is a generating instance of item j and item j is a direct consequence of the prefixed subderivation h–i. Item i is a generating instance of item j because $A(x/a)$ is the result of replacing every occurrence of a in A with x. Therefore, the instantial term does not occur in $(\forall x)A(x/a)$.

The rule of universal quantifier introduction is truth-preserving. To understand this take note that the rule allows your entering a universal sentence in a derivation only after you have derived a generating instance from no hypotheses in a subderivation prefixed with the instantial term. In a prefixed subderivation, the prefixed term is assumed to designate an individual in the domain but what individual (if any) is irrelevant. So within the prefixed derivation, whatever applies to that "individual" applies equally as well to any individual in the domain.

In a prefixed subderivation with no hypotheses, if the sentences reiterated in that derivation are true, then the sentences in which the prefixed term occurs are also true regardless of what individual in the domain that term designates. If you find that an attribute is true of an "arbitrary" individual, you are justified in concluding that the attribute is true of every individual, and that is just what the rule of universal quantifier introduction, in effect, allows you to do.

Universal Quantifiers and Connectives

The following derivation employs introduction and elimination rules for universal sentences and also for conjunctions.

1		$(\forall x)(Fx \,\&\, Gx)$	hyp
2	a	$(\forall x)(Fx \,\&\, Gx)$	1, reit
3		$Fa \,\&\, Ga$	2, u q elim
4		Fa	3, conj elim
5		$(\forall x)Fx$	2–4, u q int
6	a	$(\forall x)(Fx \,\&\, Gx)$	1, reit
7		$Fa \,\&\, Ga$	6, u q elim
8		Ga	7, conj elim
9		$(\forall x)Gx$	6–8, u q int
10		$(\forall x)Fx \,\&\, (\forall x)Gx$	5, 9, conj int

Notice how none of the reiterates in the prefixed derivations 2–4 and 6–8 contains the prefixed term. The same term is used as a prefix for both subordinate derivations; different terms could also have been used. Usually it is better to pick a "new" term to avoid any possible confusion. Notice that item 4 is a generating instance of item 5 and that item 8 is a generating instance of item 9. You may wonder whether items 2 and 6 are really necessary and whether they might be skipped. Rules of direct consequence can only be applied to preceding items and for one item to precede another both items must be in the same column. So item 1 must be reiterated as item 2 and again as item 6 in order for the rule of universal quantifier elimination to be applied within the subderivations to get items 3 and 7.

Below is another more compact derivation of the same conclusion from the very same hypothesis.

1		$(\forall x)(Fx \mathbin{\&} Gx)$	hyp
2	a	$Fa \mathbin{\&} Ga$	1, reit, u q elim
3		Fa	2, conj elim
4		Ga	2, conj elim
5		$(\forall x)Fx$	2–4, u q int
6		$(\forall x)Gx$	2–4, u q int
7		$(\forall x)Fx \mathbin{\&} (\forall x)Gx$	5, 6, conj int

Items 2 and 3 of the previous derivation are combined in step 2 of this derivation. This is a shortcut. However, the single subordinate derivation is not an abbreviation of the two subderivations in the previous derivation. The rule of universal quantifier introduction does not require an instance to be the last item of a prefixed subderivation; so, the rule is correctly applied to 2–4 to get item 5 and again to get item 6.

You can also derive the hypothesis of the derivation above from its conclusion.

1		$(\forall x)Fx \mathbin{\&} (\forall x)Gx$	hyp
2	a	$(\forall x)Fx \mathbin{\&} (\forall x)Gx$	1, reit
3		$(\forall x)Fx$	2, conj elim
4		$(\forall x)Gx$	2, conj elim
5		Fa	3, u q elim
6		Ga	4, u q elim
7		$Fa \mathbin{\&} Ga$	5, 6, conj int
8		$(\forall x)(Fx \mathbin{\&} Gx)$	2–7, u q int

The following alternative derivation is also correct.

1	$(\forall x)Fx \mathbin{\&} (\forall x)Gx$	hyp
2	$(\forall x)Fx$	1, conj elim
3	$(\forall x)Gx$	1, conj elim

4	a	Fa	2, reit, u q elim
5		Ga	3, reit, u q elim
6		Fa & Ga	4, 5, conj int
7		$(\forall x)(Fx$ & $Gx)$	4-6, u q int

From a derivation in each direction and the rule of biconditional introduction, you can construct a derivation from no hypotheses of

$$(\forall x)(Fx \text{ \& } Gx) \equiv ((\forall x)Fx \text{ \& } (\forall x)Gx)$$

Using the same method, one can also show that any sentence of the following form is a theorem:

$$(\forall x)(A \text{ \& } B) \equiv ((\forall x)A \text{ \& } (\forall x)B)$$

Any sentence having this form is a theorem of **distribution of universal quantification into conjunction** (dist u q conj).

The following is an example of a faulty "derivation."

1		$(\forall x)Fx$ & $(\forall x)Gx$	hyp
2	a	$(\forall x)Fx$ & $(\forall x)Gx$	1, reit
3		Fa	2, u q elim (Wrong!)
4		Ga	2, u q elim (Wrong!)
5		Fa & Ga	3, 4, conj int
6		$(\forall x)(Fx$ & $Gx)$	2-5, u q int

The justification for both items 3 and 4 is incorrect. The rule of universal quantifier elimination can only be applied to a universal sentence and item 2 is a conjunction. The fact that the conjuncts of item 2 are universal should not mislead you. Item 2 is a conjunction and not a universal sentence. If an item is a conjunction, the rule of universal quantifier elimination does not apply under any circumstances.

The following method is also incorrect:

1		$(\forall x)Fx$ & $(\forall x)Gx$	hyp
2		$(\forall x)Fx$	1, conj elim
3		$(\forall x)Gx$	1, conj elim
4		Fa	2, u q elim
5		Ga	3, u q elim
6	a	Fa	4, reit (Wrong!)
7		Ga	5, reit (Wrong!)
8		Fa & Ga	6, 7, conj int
9		$(\forall x)(Fx$ & $Ga)$	6-8, u q int (Wrong!)

Entering item 4 and item 5 as "reiterates" in 6–8 is wrong because the prefixed term occurs in both 4 and 5. Entering item 9 as a "direct consequence" of 6–8 by the rule of universal quantifier introduction is also wrong because item 8 is not a generating instance of 9. Notice how the instantial term appears in item 9.

The following is also not a derivation.

$$
\begin{array}{lll}
1 & \quad Fa & \text{hyp} \\[6pt]
2 & a \;\; Fa & \text{1, reit (Wrong!)} \\
3 & \quad (\forall x)Fx & \text{2–2, u q int}
\end{array}
$$

[Can you explain why it does not qualify as a derivation?] If it was a derivation, you would be able to derive any universal sentence from any one of its instances and the system would be unsound.

Nor is the following a derivation.

$$
\begin{array}{lll}
1 & \quad (\forall x)(x = x) & \text{hyp} \\[6pt]
2 & b \;\; (\forall x)(x = x) & \text{1, reit} \\
3 & \quad\;\; b = b & \text{2, u q elim} \\
4 & \quad (\forall x)(x = b) & \text{2–3, u q int (Wrong!)}
\end{array}
$$

[Can you explain why item 4 is not a direct consequence of the prefixed derivation 2–3?] If you were allowed to derive item 4 from item 1, you would be able to derive a false sentence from one that is true. To see this, let the domain be universal, and '*b*' designate the Pyramid of Cheops. Then item 1 translates as 'Everything is self-identical' while item 4 translates as 'Everything is identical to the Pyramid of Cheops'.

The following derivation uses introduction and elimination rules for universal sentences together with those for disjunctions.

$$
\begin{array}{lll}
1 & \quad Gb \lor (\forall x)Fx & \text{hyp} \\[6pt]
2 & a \;\; Gb \lor (\forall x)Fx & \text{1, reit} \\
3 & \quad\;\; Gb & \text{hyp} \\[6pt]
4 & \quad\;\; Gb \lor Fa & \text{3, disj int} \\[6pt]
5 & \quad\;\; (\forall x)Fx & \text{hyp}
\end{array}
$$

6		*Fa*	5, u q elim
7		*Gb* v *Fa*	6, disj int
8		*Gb* v *Fa*	2, 3-4, 5-7, disj elim
9		(∀*x*)(*Gb* v *Fx*)	2-8, u q int

Notice that this derivation has the form of the metaderivation below.

1		*A* v (∀*x*)*B*	hyp
2	*a*	*A* v (∀*x*)*B*	1, reit
3		*A*	hyp
4		*A* v *B*(*a*/*x*)	3, disj int
5		(∀*x*)*B*	hyp
6		*B*(*a*/*x*)	5, u q elim
7		*A* v *B*(*a*/*x*)	6, disj int
8		*A* v *B*(*a*/*x*)	2, 3-4, 5-7, disj elim
9		(∀*x*)(*A* v *B*)	2-8, u q int

The metaderivation shows that together with an application of the rule of conditional introduction, one can construct a derivation proving as a theorem any sentence of the form

$$(A \text{ v } (\forall x)B) \rightarrow (\forall x)(A \text{ v } B)$$

The following derivation is the converse of the one above.

1		(∀*x*)(*Gb* v *Fx*)	hyp
2		~(*Gb* v (∀*x*)*Fx*)	hyp
3		~*Gb* & ~(∀*x*)*Fx*	2, neg disj elim
4	*a*	(∀*x*)(*Gb* v *Fx*)	1, reit
5		*Gb* v *Fa*	4, u q elim
6		~*Gb*	3, reit, conj elim
7		*Fa*	5, 6, disj syl
8		(∀*x*)*Fx*	4-7, u q int
9		~(∀*x*)*Fx*	3, conj elim
10		*Gb* v (∀*x*)*Fx*	2-9, ind pr

From this derivation, you can construct a metaderivation showing how to prove as a theorem any sentence of the form

$$(\forall x)(A \lor B) \rightarrow (A \lor (\forall x)B)$$

Having proven that any sentence of the form

$$(A \lor (\forall x)B) \rightarrow (\forall x)(A \lor B)$$

is a theorem and that any sentence of the converse form

$$(\forall x)(A \lor B) \rightarrow (A \lor (\forall x)B)$$

is also a theorem, you can easily prove as a theorem any sentence of the form

$$(A \lor (\forall x)B) \equiv (\forall x)(A \lor B)$$

Just use conjunction introduction on the previously proven theorems and the definition of the triple bar.

An example of a derivation using universal quantifier and conditional rules is the following:

1	$(\forall x)(Gb \rightarrow Fx)$		hyp
2	$\quad Gb$		hyp
3	$\quad a \quad Gb$		2, reit
4	$\quad\quad Gb \rightarrow Fa$		1, reit, u q elim
5	$\quad\quad Fa$		3, 4, m p
6	$\quad (\forall x)Fx$		3–5, u q int
7	$Gb \rightarrow (\forall x)Fx$		2–6, cond int

Below is the converse.

1	$Gb \rightarrow (\forall x)Fx$		hyp
2	$a \quad\quad Gb$		hyp
3	$\quad\quad Gb \rightarrow (\forall x)Fx$		1, reit
4	$\quad\quad (\forall x)Fx$		2, 3, m p
5	$\quad\quad Fa$		4, u q elim
6	$\quad Gb \rightarrow Fa$		2–5, cond int
7	$(\forall x)(Gb \rightarrow Fx)$		2–6, u q int

From these two derivations and the rule of biconditional introduction, you can prove as a theorem

$$(Gb \rightarrow (\forall x)Fx) \equiv (\forall x)(Gb \rightarrow Fx)$$

Following the same method, one can construct a derivation of any sentence of the form

$$(A \rightarrow (\forall x)B) \equiv (\forall x)(A \rightarrow B)$$

It is also possible to prove as a theorem any sentence of the form

$$(\forall x)(A \rightarrow B) \rightarrow ((\forall x)A \rightarrow B)$$

Notice that both of the following are expressions of that form.

$$(\forall x)(Fx \rightarrow Ga) \rightarrow ((\forall x)Fx \rightarrow Ga)$$

$$(\forall x)(Fx \rightarrow Gx) \rightarrow ((\forall x)Fx \rightarrow Gx)$$

But only the first is a theorem. The second does not qualify because it is not a sentence.

The following metaderivation indicates how the theorems in question are proven.

1	$(\forall x)(A \rightarrow B)$	hyp
2	$(\forall x)A$	hyp
3	$A(a/x) \rightarrow B$	1, reit, u q elim
4	$A(a/x)$	2, u q elim
5	B	3, 4, m p
6	$(\forall x)A \rightarrow B$	2-5, cond int

Because in B no variable is free, $(A(a/x) \rightarrow B)$ is the same as $(A \rightarrow B)(a/x)$. Recognizing this will help you understand why item 3 can be justified by '1, reit, u q elim'.

As just shown, all sentences of the form $(\forall x)(A \rightarrow B) \rightarrow ((\forall x)A \rightarrow B)$ are theorems. However, those theorems cannot be strengthened to biconditionals if the system is to remain sound. To appreciate this point, consider the following sentence, which is the converse of a theorem listed above.

$$((\forall x)Fx \rightarrow Ga) \rightarrow (\forall x)(Fx \rightarrow Ga)$$

Let the domain consist of human beings and translate '$F\_$' with 'John loves _', '$G\_$' with '_ loves everyone' and 'a' with 'John'. Then the antecedent of the conditional

$$(\forall x)Fx \rightarrow Ga$$

translates

John loves everyone only if John loves everyone.

And the consequent

$$(\forall x)(Fx \rightarrow Ga)$$

translates

> John loves anyone only if John loves everyone.

And the entire conditional translates

> If John loves everyone only if John loves everyone, then John loves anyone only if John loves everyone.

The antecedent of the conditional must be true. So, the conditional is false if the consequent is false, that is, if John loves someone without loving everyone. So, imagine that John loves someone without loving everyone and you have a fairy tale in which the conditional is false. Therefore, if $((\forall x)Fx \rightarrow Ga) \rightarrow (\forall x)(Fx \rightarrow Ga)$ were a theorem, the system would not be sound.

So far we have only considered a prefixed derivation as an item of a regular derivation. Prefixed derivations may also be items of other prefixed derivations. For example, in the derivation below, the prefixed subderivation 2-4 is in the prefixed subderivation 2-5.

1			$(\forall x)(\forall y)Fxy$	hyp
2	b	a	$(\forall x)(\forall y)Fxy$	1, reit
3			$(\forall y)Fay$	2, u q elim
4			Fab	3, u q elim
5			$(\forall x)Fxb$	2-4, u q int
6			$(\forall y)(\forall x)Fxy$	2-5, u q int

Notice that the reiteration of item 1 as item 2 is a shortcut. Not taking the shortcut, you would reiterate item 1 first in the outer subderivation and then in the inner one.

From this derivation, you can easily generate the following metaderivation.

1			$(\forall x)(\forall y)B$	hyp
2	a	b	$(\forall x)(\forall y)B$	1, reit
3			$(\forall y)B(b/x)$	2, u q elim
4			$B(b/x)(a/y)$	3, u q elim
5			$(\forall x)B(a/y)$	2-4, u q int
6			$(\forall y)(\forall x)B$	2-5, u q int

From this, with one application of the rule of conditional introduction, you can prove the following metatheorem:

$$(\forall x)(\forall y)B \rightarrow (\forall y)(\forall x)B$$

which can be strengthened to

$$(\forall x)(\forall y)B \equiv (\forall y)(\forall x)B$$

A <u>metatheorem</u> is expressed using metavariables. Every sentence having the form of a metatheorem is a theorem.

The method used above of removing the universal quantifiers in succession and then returning them in a different order can be used to change the order of any finite number of initially placed universal quantifiers. Thus you can prove any biconditional where the right side differs from the left side only in the order of its initially placed universal quantifiers.

The following is another example of a derivation that has a prefixed derivation, subordinate to another prefixed derivation.

1		$(\forall x)(\forall y)Fxy$	hyp
2	b c	$(\forall x)(\forall y)Fxy$	1, reit
3		$(\forall y)Fby$	2, u q elim
4		Fbc	3, u q elim
5		$(\forall x)Fbx$	2–4, u q int
6		$(\forall y)(\forall x)Fyx$	2–5, u q int

Notice that in this derivation item 6 differs from item 1 in that 'y' has taken the place of 'x' and 'x' the place of 'y' not just in the quantifiers but throughout the expression.

EXERCISES FOR SECTION 11.1

1. Using official and derived rules, show that each of the following is a derivable argument in Intelim-SQ.

   a. $(\forall x)(Fx \rightarrow Gx), (\forall x)(Gx \rightarrow Hx) /\therefore (\forall x)(Fx \rightarrow Hx)$

 *b. $(\forall x)(Fx \text{ v } Gx), (\forall x)\sim Gx /\therefore (\forall x)Fx$

   c. $(\forall x)(Fx \rightarrow Gx) /\therefore (\forall x)(\sim Gx \rightarrow \sim Fx)$

 *d. $(\forall x)(\sim Gx \rightarrow \sim Fx) /\therefore (\forall x)(Fx \rightarrow Gx)$

   e. $(\forall x)(Fx \text{ \& } Gx) /\therefore (\forall x)Fx$

 *f. $(\forall x)(\forall y)(\forall z)Fxyz /\therefore (\forall z)(\forall y)(\forall x)Fxyz$

g. $(\forall x)((Fx \text{ v } Gx) \to Hx), (\forall z)Fz /\therefore (\forall z)Hz$

*h. $((\forall x)(\forall y)Fxy \text{ \& } (\forall z)Gz) /\therefore (\forall z)(\forall y)(\forall x)(Fxy \text{ \& } Gz)$

i. $(\forall x)Fx /\therefore (\forall x)(Gx \text{ v } Fx)$

*j. $(\forall x)((Fx \text{ \& } Gx) \to Hx) /\therefore (\forall x)(Fx \to (Gx \to Hx))$

k. $(\forall x)((Fx \text{ v } Gx) \to Hx) /\therefore ((\forall x)(Fx \to Hx) \text{ \& } (\forall y)(Gy \to Hy))$

*l. $(\forall x)(Fx \to Hx), (\forall y)(Gy \to Hy) /\therefore (\forall z)((Fz \text{ v } Gz) \to Hz)$

m. $(\forall x)(\forall y)Fxy /\therefore (\forall x)Fxx$

2. Using official and derived rules, show that each of the following is a derivable argument in Intelim-SQ.

   a. $(\forall x)Fx /\therefore Fa$

   *b. $(\forall x)(\forall y)Gxy /\therefore Gbc$

   c. $(\forall x)(Fx \to Gx), Fa /\therefore Ga$

   *d. $(\forall x)(Fx \text{ v } Gx), \sim Gc /\therefore Fc$

   e. $(\forall x)(\forall y)(Fxy \text{ v } Fyx), \sim Fab /\therefore Fba$

   *f. $(\forall x)Gx, \sim Ga /\therefore Fa$

   *g. $(\forall x)Fx, (\forall x)Gx /\therefore (Ga \text{ \& } Fa)$

   h. $(\forall x)(Ga \text{ \& } Fx) /\therefore (Ga \text{ \& } Fa)$

3. Using official and derived rules, prove that each of the following is a theorem of Intelim-SQ.

   a. $(\forall y)(Fy \text{ \& } Gc) \equiv ((\forall y)Fy \text{ \& } Gc)$

   *b. $(\forall z)(Fz \text{ v } Ga) \equiv ((\forall z)Fz \text{ v } Ga)$

   c. $(\forall x)Gx \equiv (\forall z)Gz$

   *d. $(\forall y)(Fy \text{ v } (\forall x)Gxy) \to (\forall y)(\forall x)(Fx \text{ v } Gyx)$

4. With the intention of using the translations to detect validity, translate the arguments below. Then derive the Q-conclusion from the Q-premises of each of your translations.

   a. All angels are perfect. But no humans are perfect. Therefore, no humans are angels.

   *b. All who are brave take risks. All who take risks do not give up easily. Therefore, all who give up easily are not brave.

   c. Every one who loves me will cheer for me. Everybody loves me. Therefore, the governor of California will cheer for me.

   *d. Every desperate or confused person will become happy after a while and enlightened after a while. Therefore, anyone who is confused will become happy after a while.

   e. Everybody is foolish sometimes. And everybody makes wise decisions sometimes. Therefore, everybody is foolish or makes wise decisions one day or another.

11.2 RULES ABOUT EXISTENTIAL QUANTIFICATION

Just as there are two official rules pertaining to universal sentences, an introduction and an elimination rule, there are also two such rules for existential sentences. We present the introduction rule first as it is the simpler of the two.

Existential Quantifier Introduction

The introduction rule provides a way to proceed in a derivation to an existential sentence from any one of its instances. The rule is as follows.

Existential Quantifier Introduction (e q int).   An existential sentence is a direct consequence of any one of its instances.

The following is an example of a derivation in which this rule is used.

$$
\begin{array}{ll}
1 \quad | \quad Faa & \text{hyp} \\
\quad\; - & \\
2 \quad | \quad (\exists x)Fxx & 1, \text{e q int}
\end{array}
$$

Study this derivation carefully, being sure to observe that item 1 is an instance of item 2. In the next derivation, item 1 is also an instance of item 2.

$$
\begin{array}{ll}
1 \quad | \quad Faa & \text{hyp} \\
\quad\; - & \\
2 \quad | \quad (\exists x)Fax & 1, \text{e q int}
\end{array}
$$

Similarly, item 1 is again an instance of item 2.

$$
\begin{array}{ll}
1 \quad | \quad Faa & \text{hyp} \\
\quad\; - & \\
2 \quad | \quad (\exists x)Fxa & 1, \text{e q int}
\end{array}
$$

In all three derivations, item 1 is the same sentence. But, in each derivation, item 2 is different. Yet, in all three, because item 1 is an instance of item 2, item 2 is a direct consequence of item 1 by the rule of existential quantifier introduction. Notice that only in the first derivation is the instance a generating instance. In the other two, the instantial term appears in the existential sentence. [As an exercise, let the domain consist of human beings, '$F\_ \_$' translate '_ is acting in the interest of _' and 'a' translate 'Woody Allen'; then translate the sentences in each of the three derivations.]

The rule of existential quantifier introduction may be stated schematically as follows. In any derivation of the form below, item i is a direct consequence of item h.

$$
\begin{array}{c|ll}
\text{h} & A(a/x) & \\
\text{i} & (\exists x)A & \text{h, e q int}
\end{array}
$$

In any derivation of this form, item i is an existential sentence and item h is an instance of item i.

An existential sentence claims that at least one individual in the domain has an attribute, while an instance claims that the attribute applies to the individual its instantial term designates. In standard quantification theory, every singular term designates an individual in the domain. So, in that theory of quantification, the existential sentence is certainly true if an instance is true. Thus, the rule of existential quantifier introduction is truth-preserving in standard logic.

Existential Quantifier Elimination

Like the rule of universal quantifier introduction, the elimination rule for the existential quantifier involves a prefixed derivation. For example, item 5 in the derivation below results from applying the rule of existential quantifier elimination to item 1 and the prefixed derivation 2–4.

$$
\begin{array}{c|cll}
1 & & (\exists x)Fx & \text{hyp} \\
2 & a & Fa & \text{hyp} \\
3 & & Fa \lor Ga & \text{2, disj int} \\
4 & & (\exists x)(Fx \lor Gx) & \text{3, e q int} \\
5 & & (\exists x)(Fx \lor Gx) & \text{1, 2–4, e q elim}
\end{array}
$$

The following is a precise statement of the rule.

Existential Quantifier Elimination (e q elim). A sentence B is a direct consequence of an existential sentence and a prefixed subderivation when (i) the subderivation has a generating instance of the existential sentence as its only hypothesis, (ii) the prefixed term is the instantial term of the generating instance, (iii) B is an item of the prefixed subderivation and (iv) the prefixed term does not occur in B.

Observe that in the derivation above, item 1 is an existential sentence, the subderivation 2-4 is prefixed, item 2 is a generating instance of item 1, the prefixed term is the instantial term of item 2, item 2 is the only hypothesis of 2-4, item 4 is an item of the prefixed subderivation 2-4 but does not contain the prefixed term, and item 4 and item 5 are the same sentence. For these reasons, item 5 is justified correctly by writing '1, 2-4, e q elim'.

The following is not a derivation. Notice that item 2 is not a generating instance of item 1.

1		$(\exists x)Fxa$	hyp
2	a	Faa	hyp
3		$(\exists x)Fxx$	2, e q int
4		$(\exists x)Fxx$	1, 2-3, e q elim (Wrong!)

It is a good thing that 1-4 above is not a derivation. If it were, one could derive a false sentence from a true one. To see this, assign '_ is longer than _' to 'F_ _' and 'the Hudson River' to 'a', and let the domain be rivers. Then item 1 translates as 'There is a river longer than the Hudson River' and item 4 translates as 'There is a river longer than itself'. But the Danube is longer than the Hudson River and no river is longer than itself.

The following is also not a derivation.

1		$(\exists x)Gx$	hyp
2	a	Ga	hyp
3		Ga	2, rep
4		Ga	1, 2-3, e q elim (Wrong!)

The problem here is that the prefixed term occurs in items 3 and 4. If 1-4 were a derivation, you would be able to derive a false sentence from a true one. To understand this, let the domain be unlimited, translate 'G_' with '_ is a river' and 'a' with 'the Gobi desert'. Then item 1 says that there are rivers and item 4 says that the Gobi desert is a river.

With the understanding that the prefixed term a does not occur in B, the rule of existential quantifier elimination may be expressed schematically as shown on the next page.

In any derivation of this form, the sentence k is a direct consequence of h and the prefixed subderivation corresponding to i–j. In such a derivation, the prefixed term a does not occur in either h, j, or k. It does not occur in $(\exists x)A(x/a)$ because $A(x/a)$ is the result of replacing every occurrence of a in A with x. Notice that A is the same sentence as $(A(x/a))(a/x)$, thus A is a generating instance of $(\exists x)A(x/a)$ that has a as its instantial term.

In a prefixed subderivation or in any derivation subordinate to it, it is assumed that there is an individual in the domain that the prefixed term designates but not what individual. The individual is simply not identified by the term. In English, phrases such as 'Mr. X' are used similarly. For example, when one says "Mr. X could solve the mystery of the origin of this diary if he would only come forward," it is assumed that there is an individual in the domain that 'Mr. X' designates but the individual is not identified by 'Mr. X'.

The rule of existential quantifier elimination applies to an existential sentence and a prefixed derivation. The prefixed derivation has as its only hypothesis a generating instance of the existential sentence with the prefixed term as its instantial term and has as an item a sentence B in which the prefixed term does not occur. According to the rule, B is a direct consequence of the existential sentence and the prefixed subderivation.

To understand why the rule is truth-preserving, note that the existential sentence is true if and only if at least one individual in the domain has the attribute that the existential sentence says that at least one does. Also note that the hypothesis of the prefixed derivation is true if and only if some individual in the domain has that same attribute and the prefixed term designates that individual. Remember the hypothesis A is a generating instance of the existential sentence $(\exists x)A(x/a)$.

Now B has been derived in the prefixed derivation on its hypothesis. However, because the prefixed term does not occur in B, the truth of B is not dependent on what individual the prefixed term designates, an individual that is not identified in any case. Therefore, B is true on the condition that the existential sentence is true. Understanding this, you can see that what the rule of existential quantifier elimination says, in effect, is the following: In a derivation with an existential sentence as an item, you can enter a sentence once you have shown through a prefixed derivation that the sentence is true on the condition that the existential sentence is true.

On that condition, the sentence entered is certain to be true if the existential sentence is.

Existential Quantifiers and Connectives

A derivation using existential quantification rules together with disjunction rules is given next.

1	($\exists x$)Fx v ($\exists x$)Gx		hyp
2	($\exists x$)Fx		hyp
3	a	Fa	hyp
4		Fa v Ga	3, disj int
5		($\exists x$)(Fx v Gx)	4, e q int
6	($\exists x$)(Fx v Gx)		2, 3–5, e q elim
7	($\exists x$)Gx		hyp
8	a	Ga	hyp
9		Fa v Ga	8, disj int
10		($\exists x$)(Fx v Gx)	9, e q int
11	($\exists x$)(Fx v Gx)		7, 8–10, e q elim
12	($\exists x$)(Fx v Gx)		1, 2–6, 7–11, disj elim

Notice the similarity between the subderivation 8–10 and the subderivation 3–5. [In what respect do they differ?] Notice how both applications of the rule of existential quantifier elimination lead to existential sentences. This is not uncommon; however, the rule gets its name from the fact that it allows you to reason from existential sentences, not to them.

Now consider the following derivation:

1		$(\exists x)(Fx \lor Gx)$	hyp
2	a	$Fa \lor Ga$	hyp
3		Fa	hyp
4		$(\exists x)Fx$	3, e q int
5		$(\exists x)Fx \lor (\exists x)Gx$	4, disj int
6		Ga	hyp
7		$(\exists x)Gx$	6, e q int
8		$(\exists x)Fx \lor (\exists x)Gx$	7, disj int
9		$(\exists x)Fx \lor (\exists x)Gx$	2, 3-5, 6-8, disj elim
10		$(\exists x)Fx \lor (\exists x)Gx$	1, 2-9, e q elim

From the two derivations above, together with the rule of biconditional introduction, you can prove that

$$(\exists x)(Fx \lor Gx) \equiv ((\exists x)Fx \lor (\exists x)Gx)$$

is a theorem. Using the same method, you can also construct a metaderivation showing that any sentence of the form

$$(\exists x)(A \lor B) \equiv ((\exists x)A \lor (\exists x)B)$$

is a theorem. We call sentences of this form theorems of **distribution of existential quantification into disjunction** (dist e q disj).

By similar methods, you can also obtain as a theorem any sentence having either of the forms below:

$$(\exists x)(A \lor B) \equiv (A \lor (\exists x)B)$$

$$(\exists x)(A \lor B) \equiv ((\exists x)A \lor B)$$

Note that, in any sentence of the form $(A \lor (\exists x)B)$, the left disjunct is a sentence; therefore, the left disjunct contains no free variable. The right disjunct is a sentence with an existential quantifier as its dominant operator. In any sentence $(\exists x)B$, the term variable x occurs free in B.

Although every sentence of the form

$$(\exists x)(A \,\&\, B) \rightarrow ((\exists x)A \,\&\, (\exists x)B)$$

is a theorem, this is not true of the converses of those sentences. So, just as there are *no* theorems of distribution of universal quantification into disjunction, there are *no* theorems of distribution of existential quantification into conjunction. Nevertheless, one can prove that any sentence of either of the following forms is a theorem:

$$(\exists x)(A \ \& \ B) \equiv (A \ \& \ (\exists x)B)$$

$$(\exists x)(A \ \& \ B) \equiv ((\exists x)A \ \& \ B)$$

The following derivation indicates how the right side of a biconditional of the first form can be derived from the left side.

1		$(\exists x)(Gb \ \& \ Fx)$	hyp
2	a	$Gb \ \& \ Fa$	hyp
3		Gb	2, conj elim
4		Fa	2, conj elim
5		$(\exists x)Fx$	4, e q int
6		$Gb \ \& \ (\exists x)Fx$	3, 5, conj int
7		$Gb \ \& \ (\exists x)Fx$	1, 2–6, e q elim

The next derivation provides a method for deriving the left side from the right.

1		$Gb \ \& \ (\exists x)Fx$	hyp
2		Gb	1, conj elim
3		$(\exists x)Fx$	1, conj elim
4	a	Fa	hyp
5		Gb	2, reit
6		$Gb \ \& \ Fa$	4, 5, conj int
7		$(\exists x)(Gb \ \& \ Fx)$	6, e q int
8		$(\exists x)(Gb \ \& \ Fx)$	3, 4–7, e q elim

Notice that these derivations could be converted into metaderivations. Simply replace 'Gb' with 'A', 'Fx' with 'B', and 'Fa' with '$B(a/x)$'.

Within Intelim-SQ, you can prove as a theorem any sentence exemplifying either of the forms below:

$$(\exists x)(A \rightarrow B) \equiv (A \rightarrow (\exists x)B)$$

$$((\exists x)A \rightarrow B) \rightarrow (\exists x)(A \rightarrow B)$$

The following derivation indicates how the right side of a sentence of the first form is derived from the left.

1	$(\exists x)(Gb \rightarrow Fx)$	hyp
2	Gb	hyp
3	$(\exists x)(Gb \rightarrow Fx)$	1, reit
4	a $Gb \rightarrow Fa$	hyp
5	Gb	2, reit
6	Fa	4, 5, m p
7	$(\exists x)Fx$	6, e q int
8	$(\exists x)Fx$	3, 4–7, e q elim
9	$Gb \rightarrow (\exists x)Fx$	2–8, cond int

Notice that this derivation could be converted into a metaderivation simply by replacing 'Gb' with 'A', 'Fx' with 'B', and 'Fa' with '$B(a/x)$'.

A metaderivation showing how any sentence of the second form is a theorem is left to the reader as an exercise. Although such sentences are theorems, not all of their converses are. In other words, not every expression of the form $(\exists x)(A \rightarrow B) \rightarrow ((\exists x)A \rightarrow B)$ is a sentence. The system would not be sound if they were. For example, the following is a sentence of that form.

$$(\exists x)(Fx \rightarrow Gb) \rightarrow ((\exists x)Fx \rightarrow Gb)$$

Let the domain be human beings, '$F\_$' translate 'John loves _', '$G\_$' translate '_ loves everyone', and 'b' translate 'John'. Then the sentence translates 'If there is at least one person whom John loves only if he loves everyone, then John loves someone only if he loves everyone'. The antecedent is true so long as there is someone that John does not love. But the consequent is false if John loves someone but not everyone. Therefore, the sentence is false if John loves Mary but not Carol.

Quantification and Negation

The following are four additional quantifier rules. They are derivable within Intelim-SQ and adopted here as derived rules. Each rule is also stated schematically. You will be asked to provide their justification as derived rules in exercise 5 for section 11.3 (p. 370).

Negative Universal Quantifier Introduction (neg u q int). $\sim(\forall x)A$ is a direct consequence of $(\exists x)\sim A$.

$$
\begin{array}{ll}
h \mid \quad (\exists x)\sim A & \\
i \mid \quad \sim(\forall x)A & \text{h, neg u q int}
\end{array}
$$

Negative Universal Quantifier Elimination (neg u q elim). $(\exists x)\sim A$ is a direct consequence of $\sim(\forall x)A$.

$$
\begin{array}{ll}
h \mid \quad \sim(\forall x)A & \\
i \mid \quad (\exists x)\sim A & \text{h, neg u q elim}
\end{array}
$$

Negative Existential Quantifier Introduction (neg e q int). $\sim(\exists x)A$ is a direct consequence of $(\forall x)\sim A$.

$$
\begin{array}{ll}
h \mid \quad (\forall x)\sim A & \\
i \mid \quad \sim(\exists x)A & \text{h, neg e q int}
\end{array}
$$

Negative Existential Quantifier Elimination (neg e q elim). $(\forall x)\sim A$ is a direct consequence of $\sim(\exists x)A$.

$$
\begin{array}{ll}
h \mid \quad \sim(\exists x)A & \\
i \mid \quad (\forall x)\sim A & \text{h, neg e q elim}
\end{array}
$$

The derivation below makes use of one of these rules.

$$
\begin{array}{lll}
1 & (\forall x)Fx & \text{hyp} \\
2 \quad a & \quad Fa & \text{1, reit, u q elim} \\
3 & \quad \sim\sim Fa & \text{2, neg}_2 \text{ int} \\
4 & (\forall x)\sim\sim Fx & \text{2-3, u q int} \\
5 & \sim(\exists x)\sim Fx & \text{4, neg e q int}
\end{array}
$$

The next derivation is its converse.

$$
\begin{array}{lll}
1 & \sim(\exists x)\sim Fx & \text{hyp} \\
2 & (\forall x)\sim\sim Fx & \text{1, neg e q elim} \\
3 \quad a & \quad \sim\sim Fa & \text{2, reit, u q elim} \\
4 & \quad Fa & \text{3, neg}_2 \text{ elim} \\
5 & (\forall x)Fx & \text{3-4, u q int}
\end{array}
$$

Compare the derivation below to the first of the two at the bottom of the previous page.

1		$(\exists x)Fx$	hyp
2	a	Fa	hyp
3		$\sim\sim Fa$	2, neg_2 int
4		$(\exists x)\sim\sim Fx$	3, e q int
5		$(\exists x)\sim\sim Fx$	1, 2–4, e q elim
6		$\sim(\forall x)\sim Fx$	5, neg u q int

The next derivation is the converse.

1		$\sim(\forall x)\sim Fx$	hyp
2		$(\exists x)\sim\sim Fx$	1, neg u q elim
3	a	$\sim\sim Fa$	hyp
4		Fa	3, neg_2 elim
5		$(\exists x)Fx$	4, e q int
6		$(\exists x)Fx$	2, 3–5, e q elim

Given the derived rules initially listed in this section and the derivations above, we are justified in adopting the following derived rule.

De Morgan's Rule for Quantifiers (d m q).   Any two sentences

$$(\forall x)A \text{ and } \sim(\exists x)\sim A$$

or

$$\sim(\forall x)A \text{ and } (\exists x)\sim A$$

or

$$(\forall x)\sim A \text{ and } \sim(\exists x)A$$

or

$$\sim(\forall x)\sim A \text{ and } (\exists x)A$$

are direct consequences of one another.

This rule encompasses both the rules of negative universal quantifier introduction and elimination (see the second line in the group displayed above) and the rules of negative existential quantifier introduction and elimination (see the third line). The four preceding derivations, in which those rules are applied, indicate how one would construct metaderivations justifying the first and fourth lines of De Morgan's rule for quantifiers.

The following is a derivation using De Morgan's rule for quantifiers.

1		$\sim(\exists x)(Fx\ \&\ Gx)$	hyp
2		$(\exists x)Fx$	hyp
3	a	Fa	hyp
4		$\sim(\exists x)(Fx\ \&\ Gx)$	1, reit
5		$(\forall x)\sim(Fx\ \&\ Gx)$	4, d m q
6		$\sim(Fa\ \&\ Ga)$	5, u q elim
7		$\sim Fa \lor \sim Ga$	6, neg conj elim
8		$\sim Ga$	3, 7, disj syl
9		$(\exists x)\sim Gx$	8, e q int
10		$(\exists x)\sim Gx$	2, 3–9, e q elim

Overlapping Quantifiers

The following derivation illustrates how two initially placed existential quantifiers are interchangeable.

1			$(\exists x)(\exists y)Fxy$	hyp
2	a		$(\exists y)Fay$	hyp
3		b	Fab	hyp
4			$(\exists x)Fxb$	3, e q int
5			$(\exists y)(\exists x)Fxy$	4, e q int
6			$(\exists y)(\exists x)Fxy$	2, 3–5, e q elim
7			$(\exists y)(\exists x)Fxy$	1, 2–6, e q elim

Using the same general method as above, you can also derive the converse and thus, by way of biconditional introduction, establish that

$$(\exists x)(\exists y)Fxy \equiv (\exists y)(\exists x)Fxy$$

is a theorem.

It is not difficult to see how this can also be done for any other sentence of the form

$$(\exists x)(\exists y)A \equiv (\exists y)(\exists x)A$$

In a similar way, you can establish the metatheorem

$$(\exists x)(\exists y)(\exists z)A \equiv (\exists z)(\exists y)(\exists x)A$$

and so on.

You can also obtain as a theorem any conditional of the form

$$(\exists x)(\forall y)A \rightarrow (\forall y)(\exists x)A$$

An example of such a sentence is

$$(\exists x)(\forall y)Fxy \rightarrow (\forall y)(\exists x)Fxy$$

The derivation below shows how this sentence, specifically, and others that have the same form can be proven as theorems.

1			$(\exists x)(\forall y)Fxy$	hyp
2	b		$(\exists x)(\forall y)Fxy$	1, reit
3		a	$(\forall y)Fay$	hyp
4			Fab	3, u q elim
5			$(\exists x)Fxb$	4, e q int
6			$(\exists x)Fxb$	2, 3-5, e q elim
7			$(\forall y)(\exists x)Fxy$	2-6, u q int

If under a translation scheme, '$F\_\_$' translates '_ causes _', then '$(\exists x)(\forall y)Fxy$' (item 1 of the derivation above) translates 'There is an individual x such that, for every individual y, x causes y' or, in idiomatic English, as 'Some one thing causes everything'. On the other hand, '$(\forall y)(\exists x)Fxy$' translates as 'Every individual y is such that there is an individual x such that x causes y' or, in idiomatic English, as 'Each thing has a cause' or 'Everything is caused by something or other'. If some one thing causes everything, it follows that everything has a cause; however, if everything has a cause, it does not follow that some one thing causes everything. Thus it is not surprising that *not* every sentence of the form $(\forall y)(\exists x)A \rightarrow (\exists x)(\forall y)A$ is a theorem.

Although not every sentence of the form $(\forall y)(\exists x)A \rightarrow (\exists x)(\forall y)A$ is a theorem, there are, nevertheless, some that are. For example, the following biconditional is a theorem.

$$(\forall x)(\exists y)(Gx \,\&\, Hy) \equiv (\exists y)(\forall x)(Gx \,\&\, Hy)$$

The right side can be gotten from the left as follows:

1		$(\forall y)(\exists x)(Gx \;\&\; Hy)$		hyp
2		$(\exists x)(Gx \;\&\; Ha)$		1, u q elim
3	b	$Gb \;\&\; Ha$		hyp
4		Gb		3, conj elim
5	c	$(\forall y)(\exists x)(Gx \;\&\; Hy)$		1, reit
6		$(\exists x)(Gx \;\&\; Hc)$		5, u q elim
7	d	$Gd \;\&\; Hc$		hyp
8		Hc		7, conj elim
9		Hc		6, 7–8, e q elim
10		Gb		4, reit
11		$Gb \;\&\; Hc$		9, 10, conj int
12		$(\forall y)(Gb \;\&\; Hy)$		5–11, u q int
13		$(\exists x)(\forall y)(Gx \;\&\; Hy)$		12, e q int
14		$(\exists x)(\forall y)(Gx \;\&\; Hy)$		2, 3–13, e q elim

Now study the following derivation:

1		$(\forall y)(\exists x)(Gx \lor Fy)$		hyp
2	a	$(\forall y)(\exists x)(Gx \lor Fy)$		1, reit
3		$(\exists x)(Gx \lor Fa)$		2, u q elim
4		$(\exists x)(Gx \lor Fa) \equiv ((\exists x)Gx \lor Fa)$		*
5		$(\exists x)Gx \lor Fa$		3, 4, bicond elim
6		$(\forall y)((\exists x)Gx \lor Fy)$		2–5, u q int
7		$(\exists x)Gx \lor (\forall y)Fy$		6, **, bicond elim
8		$(\exists x)Gx$		hyp
9	b	Gb		hyp
10	a	Gb		9, reit
11		$Gb \lor Fa$		10, disj int
12		$(\forall y)(Gb \lor Fy)$		10–11, u q int
13		$(\exists x)(\forall y)(Gx \lor Fy)$		12, e q int
14		$(\exists x)(\forall y)(Gx \lor Fy)$		8, 9–13, e q elim

15		$(\forall y)Fy$	hyp
16	a	$(\forall y)Fy$	15, reit
17		Fa	16, u q elim
18		$Gb \text{ v } Fa$	17, disj int
19		$(\forall y)(Gb \text{ v } Fy)$	16–18, u q int
20		$(\exists x)(\forall y)(Gx \text{ v } Fy)$	19, e q int
21		$(\exists x)(\forall y)(Gx \text{ v } Fy)$	7, 8-14, 15-20, disj elim

$$* \ (\exists x)(A \text{ v } B) = ((\exists x)A \text{ v } B)$$
$$** \ (\forall x)(A \text{ v } B) = (A \text{ v } (\forall x)B)$$

This derivation shows how the right side of the biconditional

$$(\forall x)(\exists y)(Gx \text{ v } Hy) \equiv (\exists y)(\forall x)(Gx \text{ v } Hy)$$

can be gotten from the left. How the left can be gotten from the right is left to the reader as an exercise. Note how item 4 and item 7 are justified by reference to theorems. As the theorems are unnamed, asterisks are used for identification.

EXERCISES FOR SECTION 11.2

1. Using official and derived rules, as well as the theorems proven, show that each of the following is a derivable argument in Intelim-SQ.

   *a. $(\forall x)(Fx \rightarrow Gx), (\exists x)Fx \ / \therefore \ (\exists x)Gx$

   b. $(\forall x)(Fx \rightarrow Gx), \sim(\exists x)Gx \ / \therefore \ \sim(\exists x)Fx$

   *c. $(\forall x)(Fx \text{ v } Gx), (\exists x)\sim Fx \ / \therefore (\exists x)Gx$

   d. $(\forall x)(Fx \rightarrow Gx), (\exists x)\sim Gx \ / \therefore \ (\exists x)\sim Fx$

   *e. $(\exists x)Fxx \ / \therefore \ (\exists x)(\exists y)Fxy$

   f. $(\forall x)(Fx \rightarrow Gx) \ / \therefore \ \sim(\exists x)(Fx \ \& \ \sim Gx)$

   *g. $\sim(\exists x)(Fx \ \& \ \sim Gx) \ / \therefore \ (\forall x)(Fx \rightarrow Gx)$

   h. $(\forall x)(Fx \rightarrow Gx) \ / \therefore \ \sim(\exists x)(Fx \ \& \ Gx)$

   *i. $(\exists x)(Fx \ \& \ Gx) \ / \therefore \ \sim(\forall x)(Fx \rightarrow \sim Gx)$

2. Using only official and derived rules, prove that the following are theorems of Intelim-SQ.

   a. $(\exists x)Gx \equiv (\exists y)Gy$

   *b. $(\exists x)(\exists y)Hxy \equiv (\exists y)(\exists x)Hxy$

   c. $(Hc \text{ v } (\exists y)Gy) \equiv (\exists y)(Hc \text{ v } Gy)$

*d. $(\forall x)(Fx \to Hc) \to ((\exists x)Fx \to Hc)$

e. $((\exists x)Fx \to Hc) \to (\forall x)(Fx \to Hc)$

3. Using official and derived rules, show that each of the following is a derivable argument in Itelim-SQ. For the last argument, you can use the theorem of excluded middle.

   a. $Gb /\therefore (\exists x)Gx$

   *b. $Fac /\therefore (\exists x)(\exists y)Fxy$

   c. $Fbb /\therefore (\exists x)Fxb$

   *d. $Fbb /\therefore (\exists x)(\exists y)Fxy$

   e. $(\exists x)Hx, Hb /\therefore (\exists x)(Hx \ \& \ Hb)$

   *f. $(\exists x)Fax /\therefore (\exists x)(\exists y)Fyx$

   *g. $(Fc \to (\exists x)Gxx) /\therefore (\exists x)(Fc \to Gxx)$

4. With the intention of using the translations to detect validity, translate the arguments below. Then derive the Q-conclusion from the Q-premises of each of your translations. Add valid or unstated premises if warranted.

   a. Some soldiers are heroes. All heroes are worthy of praise. Therefore, some soldiers are worthy of praise.

   *b. Those who are joyful are wise. Some who are joyful are not rich. Therefore, some who are wise are not rich.

   c. All magicians who are not thieves are registered with the police. All Mia's brothers are magicians. Some of Mia's brothers are not registered with the police. Therefore, there are thieves.

   *d. People who hate to waste things are thrifty. Some people hate to waste things. Therefore, some people are thrifty.

   e. No dictators are humane. Some political leaders are humane and popular. Therefore, some political leaders who are not dictators are popular.

   *f. All columnists are men or all reporters are women. Some reporters are women and so are some men. Therefore, all columnists are men.

   g. Everything is identical to everything. Therefore, it is not true that there is more than one thing.

   *h. Everyone likes everyone. So, everyone likes some one or other.

   i. Someone does not like everyone. So, someone does not like someone.

5. With the intention of using the translations to detect incompatibility, translate the following sentences into Q, adding valid sentences if warranted. Then, for each set of sentences, derive from the Q-translation a sentence and its negation.

   a. Every even number is in the set. Twelve is not an odd number. Every number is odd or even. Twelve is not in the set.

       *b. All columnists are men and all reporters are women. but some female reporters are columnists.

       c. All Hans's daughters are beautiful. Only one is married. The one who is married has a daughter. Unfortunately, Hans has no granddaughters.

6. With the intention of using the translations to detect validity, translate the following arguments. Then derive the Q-conclusion from the Q-premises in each translation. Add valid or unstated premises if warranted.

       *a. The interests of the state are the same as the interests of its citizens. The interests of General Motors are the same as the interests of its citizens. Therefore, the interests of the state are the same as the interests of General Motors.

       b. Sebastian gave the *I Ching* to Rachel. Rachel has returned every book that anyone has given her. Therefore, Rachel returned the *I Ching* to Sebastian.

11.3 RULES IN REVIEW

All of the official and derived rules and proven theorems of Intelim belong also to Intelim-SQ. However, only those official and derived rules and proven theorems that belong specifically to Intelim-SQ and not to Intelim are listed next.

Official Rules

Rule of Universal Quantifier Elimination (u q elim)

$$
\begin{array}{ll}
h & (\forall x)A \\
\ \vdots & \quad \cdot \\
i & A(a/x) \qquad\qquad h,\ \text{u q elim}
\end{array}
$$

Rule of Universal Quantifier Introduction (u q int)

$$
\begin{array}{ll}
h \ \big|\ a\ \big| & \cdot \\
\ \vdots \quad\ \big| & \ \ \cdot \\
i \quad\ \ \big| & \ A \\
\ \vdots & \ \cdot \\
j & (\forall x)A(x/a) \qquad\qquad h\text{-}i,\ \text{u q int}
\end{array}
$$

Rule of Existential Quantifier Introduction (e q int)

$$
\begin{array}{l|l}
\text{h} & A(a/x) \\
\cdot & \cdot \\
\text{i} & (\exists x)A \qquad\qquad \text{h, e q int}
\end{array}
$$

Rule of Existential Quantifier Elimination (e q elim)

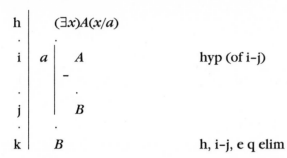

$$
\begin{array}{l}
\text{h} \quad (\exists x)A(x/a) \\
\quad\text{i} \;\; a \quad A \qquad\qquad \text{hyp (of i–j)} \\
\quad\text{j} \qquad B \\
\text{k} \quad B \qquad\qquad\qquad \text{h, i–j, e q elim}
\end{array}
$$

Restriction: The prefixed term cannot occur in *B*.

Derived Rules

Derived Rule of Negative Universal Quantifier Introduction (neg u q int)

$$
\begin{array}{l|l}
\text{h} & (\exists x){\sim}A \\
\cdot & \cdot \\
\text{i} & {\sim}(\forall x)A \qquad\qquad \text{h, neg u q int}
\end{array}
$$

Derived Rule of Negative Universal Quantifier Elimination (neg u q elim)

$$
\begin{array}{l|l}
\text{h} & {\sim}(\forall x)A \\
\cdot & \cdot \\
\text{i} & (\exists x){\sim}A \qquad\qquad \text{h, neg u q elim}
\end{array}
$$

Derived Rule of Negative Existential Quantifier Introduction (neg e q int)

$$
\begin{array}{l|l}
\text{h} & (\forall x){\sim}A \\
\cdot & \cdot \\
\text{i} & {\sim}(\exists x)A \qquad\qquad \text{h, neg e q int}
\end{array}
$$

Derived Rule of Negative Existential Quantifier Elimination (neg e q elim)

$$h \qquad \sim(\exists x)A$$

$$\cdot \qquad \cdot$$

$$i \qquad (\forall x)\sim A \qquad\qquad h, \text{neg e q elim}$$

Derived De Morgan's Rule for Quantifiers (d m q)

Any two sentences

$$(\forall x)A \text{ and } \sim(\exists x)\sim A$$

or

$$\sim(\forall x)A \text{ and } (\exists x)\sim A$$

or

$$(\forall x)\sim A \text{ and } \sim(\exists x)A$$

or

$$\sim(\forall x)\sim A \text{ and } (\exists x)A$$

are direct consequences of one another.

Theorems

For greater generality, metatheorems rather than theorems are listed below when appropriate. No metatheorem listed can be strengthened from a conditional to a biconditional. In other words, when a metatheorem has the form of a conditional, its converse cannot be proven.

Theorem of Specification (sp)

$$(\forall x)A \rightarrow A(a/x)$$

Theorem of Distribution of Universal Quantification into Conjunction (dist u q cond)

$$(\forall x)(A \ \& \ B) \equiv ((\forall x)A \ \& \ (\forall x)B)$$

Theorem of Distribution of Universal Quantification into Conditional (dist u q cond)

$$(\forall x)(A \rightarrow B) \equiv ((\forall x)A \rightarrow (\forall x)B)$$

Theorem of Distribution of Existential Quantification into Disjunction (dist e q disj)

$$(\exists x)(A \ v \ B) \equiv ((\exists x)A \ v \ (\exists x)B)$$

Unnamed Theorems with Universal Quantifiers

$$(\forall x)(A \,\&\, B) \equiv (A \,\&\, (\forall x)B)$$

$$(\forall x)(A \,\&\, B) \equiv ((\forall x)A \,\&\, B)$$

$$((\forall x)A \vee (\forall x)B) \rightarrow (\forall x)(A \vee B)$$

$$(\forall x)(A \vee B) \equiv (A \vee (\forall x)B)$$

$$(\forall x)(A \vee B) \equiv ((\forall x)A \vee B)$$

$$(A \rightarrow (\forall x)B) \equiv (\forall x)(A \rightarrow B)$$

$$(\forall x)(A \rightarrow B) \rightarrow ((\forall x)A \rightarrow B)$$

$$(\forall x)(\forall y)A \equiv (\forall y)(\forall x)A$$

Unnamed Theorems with Existential Quantifiers

$$(\exists x)(A \,\&\, B) \rightarrow ((\exists x)A \,\&\, (\exists x)B))$$

$$(\exists x)(A \,\&\, B) \equiv (A \,\&\, (\exists x)B)$$

$$(\exists x)(A \,\&\, B) \equiv ((\exists x)A \,\&\, B)$$

$$(\exists x)(A \vee B) \equiv (A \vee (\exists x)B)$$

$$(\exists x)(A \vee B) \equiv ((\exists x)A \vee B)$$

$$(\exists x)(A \rightarrow B) \equiv (A \rightarrow (\exists x)B)$$

$$((\exists x)A \rightarrow B) \rightarrow (\exists x)(A \rightarrow B)$$

$$(\exists x)(\exists y)A \equiv (\exists y)(\exists x)A$$

Unnamed Theorems with Existential and Universal Quantifiers

$$(\exists x)(\forall y)A \rightarrow (\forall y)(\exists x)A$$

$$(\forall x)(\exists y)(Gx \vee Hy) \equiv (\exists y)(\forall x)(Gx \vee Hy)$$

$$(\forall x)(\exists y)(Gx \,\&\, Hy) \equiv (\exists y)(\forall x)(Gx \,\&\, Hy)$$

EXERCISES FOR SECTION 11.3

*1. Would you want every sentence of the form

$$(\forall x)(A \vee B) \equiv ((\forall x)A \vee (\forall x)B)$$

to be a theorem of Intelim-SQ? If not, why not?

2. Construct metaderivations showing that any sentence having one of the following forms is a theorem of Intelim-SQ. Use official and derived rules.

*a. $((\forall x)A \mathbin{\&} (\forall x)B) \rightarrow (\forall x)(A \mathbin{\&} B)$

 b. $(\forall x)(A \mathbin{\&} B) \rightarrow ((\forall x)A \mathbin{\&} (\forall x)B)$

*c. $(\forall x)(A \mathbin{v} B) \rightarrow (A \mathbin{v} (\forall x)B)$

 d. $(A \mathbin{v} (\forall x)B) \rightarrow (\forall x)(A \mathbin{v} B)$

*e. $(A \rightarrow (\forall x)B) \rightarrow (\forall x)(A \rightarrow B)$

 f. $(\forall x)(A \rightarrow B) \rightarrow (A \rightarrow (\forall x)B)$

*g. $(A \mathbin{\&} (\forall x)B) \rightarrow (\forall x)(A \mathbin{\&} B)$

 h. $(\forall x)(A \mathbin{\&} B) \rightarrow (A \mathbin{\&} (\forall x)B)$

*i. $(\forall x)(A \rightarrow B) \rightarrow ((\forall x)A \rightarrow B)$

*3. Is it desirable for every sentence of the form

$$(\exists x)(A \mathbin{\&} B) \equiv ((\exists x)A \mathbin{\&} (\exists x)B)$$

to be a theorem of Intelim-SQ? If not, why not? Answer the same question for each of the following forms:

$$(\exists x)(A \rightarrow B) \equiv ((\exists x)A \rightarrow (\exists x)B)$$

$$(\forall x)(A \rightarrow B) \equiv ((\forall x)A \rightarrow (\forall x)B)$$

$$(\forall x)(A \mathbin{v} B) \equiv ((\forall x)A \mathbin{v} (\forall x)B)$$

4. Construct metaderivations showing that any sentence having one of the following forms is a theorem of Intelim-SQ. Use official and derived rules.

 a. $(\exists x)(A \rightarrow B) \rightarrow (A \rightarrow (\exists x)B)$

*b. $(\exists x)(A \rightarrow B) \rightarrow ((\forall x)A \rightarrow B)$

 c. $((\exists x)A \rightarrow B) \equiv (\forall x)(A \rightarrow B)$

*d. $(\exists x)(A \mathbin{v} B) \equiv (A \mathbin{v} (\exists x)B)$

5. Using official and derived rules of Intelim but only the official quantifier rules, justify the adoption of the following derived rules. Once justified, the rule of negative existential quantifier elimination (the rule in 5a) can be used to justify the rule of negative universal quantifier elimination (the rule in 5c).

 a. $(\forall x)\mathord{\sim}A$ is a direct consequence of $\mathord{\sim}(\exists x)A$.

*b. $\mathord{\sim}(\exists x)A$ is a direct consequence of $(\forall x)\mathord{\sim}A$.

*c. $(\exists x)\mathord{\sim}A$ is a direct consequence of $\mathord{\sim}(\forall x)A$.

 d. $\mathord{\sim}(\forall x)A$ is a direct consequence of $(\exists x)\mathord{\sim}A$.

12

IDENTITY AND EXISTENCE

Some properties of relations are important enough to have been given names. In the first section of this chapter, we discuss those properties. In the second section, we present introduction and elimination rules for identity and prove that identity has some of the relational properties previously discussed. In the final section, we develop two formal systems as alternatives to Intelim-SQ. Unlike Intelim-SQ, neither of the alternative systems presupposes that every singular term designates a member of the domain. Consequently, both belong to a class of alternative logics known as free logic. The rules of one of the two systems are truth-preserving in the empty domain, while the rules of the other are truth-preserving only in nonempty domains.

12.1 PROPERTIES OF RELATIONS

There are relations that hold between two individuals. The individuals need not be distinct; in other words, an individual may bear such a relation to itself. For example, the relation of identity is borne by every individual to itself. Relations that hold between two individuals are known as binary relations. These are expressible in Q by using two-place predicate letters, such as F^2, or the identity sign. This section is concerned only with binary relations. So, when relations are mentioned, only binary ones are meant.

One can define a relation F^2 in a domain by listing the class of ordered couples that have F^2 in that domain. A relation can also be defined graphically. Because of the visual appeal of graphs, we begin discussing properties of relations in terms of properties of their graphs. We then state the conditions for relations having those properties in terms of Q.

Graphs of Relations

The graph of a relation in a domain consists of the domain with its individuals so arranged that there is an arrow from one individual to a second (possibly the same) if and only if the first bears the relation to the second. For example, if the relation is F^2 and the domain is $\{a, b\}$, there is an arrow from a to b if and only if Fab and an arrow from a to a if and only if Faa.

To draw a graph of a relation F^2 in a domain, begin by putting an asterisk for each individual in the domain and enclosing the various asterisks within a circle. For example, if the domain is $\{a, b, c, d, e\}$, the following picture represents the domain.

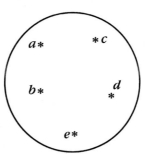

Now for each ordered couple $\langle a, b \rangle$ that has the relation, draw an arrow from a's asterisk to b's asterisk.

For simplicity of expression, we shall use the phrase 'arrow from a to b' as short for 'arrow from a's asterisk to b's asterisk'. When there are arrows going from both a to b and also from b to a, draw one double arrow:

If an ordered couple $\langle c, c \rangle$ has F^2, draw one double arrow from c to itself as illustrated below.

Such a double arrow is called a <u>loop</u>. The resulting diagram, with all arrows and loops, defines the relation.

Now suppose that the extension of F^2 is

$$\{\langle b, a \rangle, \langle a, c \rangle, \langle d, d \rangle, \langle d, e \rangle, \langle c, e \rangle, \langle e, c \rangle, \langle c, d \rangle\}$$

The extension of a relation is the class of those ordered couples that have the relation. Then the graph of F^2 is the following:

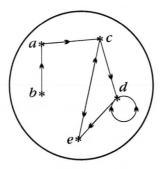

Actually drawing the graph of a relation in a domain is feasible only if the domain is fairly small. Nevertheless, a graph exists for each and every relation regardless of the size of the domain, whether finite or infinite.

We say that there is a <u>broken journey</u> from one individual to a second via a third individual when there is an arrow from the first individual to the third and an arrow from the third to the second. We say that a broken journey has a <u>shortcut</u> when there is also an arrow directly from the first to the second individual.

In the graph above, there is an arrow from b to a and then another from a to c, but there is no arrow from b to c. Thus, in that graph, there is a broken journey from b to c via a, but no shortcut from b to c. Another broken journey without a shortcut is that from d to c via e; the reason is that there is no arrow from d to c. A broken journey with a shortcut is that from c to e via d. [Can you explain why?]

Reflexive and Irreflexive Relations

Every relation in a domain is either reflexive, irreflexive, or nonreflexive in that domain. A relation is <u>reflexive</u> if and only if every individual bears the relation to itself. A relation is <u>irreflexive</u> if and only if no individual bears the relation to itself. And a relation is <u>nonreflexive</u> if and only if it is a relation that is neither reflexive nor irreflexive.

In terms of its graph, a relation is reflexive if and only if there is a loop attached to every individual; irreflexive if and only if there is no loop attached to any individual; and nonreflexive if and only if there are loops attached to some individuals and not to others.

For example, consider the three graphs that follow. Each graph pictures a relation in the domain $\{a, b, c\}$.

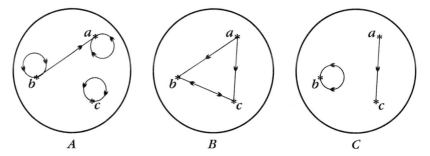

Graph A tells you that the relation is reflexive, as a loop is attached to every individual. Graph B tells you that the relation is irreflexive as no loop is attached to any individual. And graph C tells you that the relation is nonreflexive as a loop is attached to some but not to all individuals.

Reflexive Relations

In terms of Q, a relation F^2 is reflexive in a domain if and only if

$(\forall x)Fxx$

is true in the domain. For example, with '$F\_\_$' translating '$\_$ is the same age as $\_$', '$(\forall x)Fxx$' is equivalent to 'Every individual is the same age as itself', which is true in the domain of people now living. So, the relation of *being the same age as* is reflexive in that domain. Other relations that are reflexive in the domain of people now living are *having the same weight as* and *being as tall as*. [Stop for a moment and think how graphs of these relations would look.]

Now suppose that '$F\_\_$' translates '$\_$ is the mother of $\_$'. In this case, '$(\forall x)Fxx$' is equivalent to 'Every individual is its own mother', which is false in the domain of mammals; therefore, the relation of *being the mother of* fails to be reflexive in that domain. Other examples of relations that fail to be reflexive in a domain are *being greater than* in the domain of numbers and *being smarter than* in the domain of people now living.

If a relation has a property in every domain, we simply say that it is has the property. For example, if you read that a property is reflexive and no mention is made of the domain, what you should understand is that it is reflexive in every domain. The situation is the same for other properties of relations.

Irreflexive Relations

A relation F^2 is irreflexive in a domain if and only if

$$(\forall x)\text{\textasciitilde}Fxx$$

is true in the domain. An example of a relation that is irreflexive is that of *being different from*. Let '$\_$ is different from $\_$' translate '$F\_\_$' and '$(\forall x)\text{\textasciitilde}Fxx$' says that every individual is not different from itself, which is true. Therefore, the relation of *being different from itself* is irreflexive (in every domain). Remember that 'in every domain' is to be understood when no domain is mentioned.

That no irreflexive relation F^2 is reflexive is established through the following derivation.

1	$(\forall x)\text{\textasciitilde}Fxx$	hyp
2	$\text{\textasciitilde}Faa$	1, u q elim
3	$(\exists x)\text{\textasciitilde}Fxx$	2, e q int
4	$\text{\textasciitilde}(\forall x)Fxx$	3, d m q

Although no irreflexive relation is reflexive, it is not true that every relation that is not reflexive is irreflexive. In other words, there are relations that are neither reflexive nor irreflexive.

Nonreflexive Relations

A relation F^2 is nonreflexive in a domain if and only if

$$(\exists x)Fxx \ \& \ (\exists y){\sim}Fyy$$

is true in the domain. In other words, F^2 is nonreflexive just in case it is neither reflexive nor irreflexive. Some familiar relations are nonreflexive. For example, the relation of *being proud of* in the domain of people now living fails to be reflexive but also fails to be irreflexive. Some people now living are proud of themselves, while others are not.

Another relation that is nonreflexive is *being the product of the self-multiplication of* in the domain {0, 1, 2}. Let '$F\_\ \_$' translate '$\_$ is the product of $\_$ being multiplied by itself', '*a*' translate '0', '*b*' translate '1', and '*c*' translate '2'. Then, '*Faa*' and '*Fbb*' are true, but '*Fcc*' is false. [As an exercise, draw a graph of this relation in the domain {0, 1, 2}. Can you think of other nonreflexive relations?]

Symmetrical and Asymmetrical Relations

Every relation in a domain is either symmetrical, asymmetrical, or nonsymmetrical in that domain. A relation is <u>symmetrical</u> if and only if, for any two things, the first bears the relation to the second only if the second bears it to the first. A relation is <u>asymmetrical</u> if and only if, for any two things, the first bears the relation to the second only if the second does not bear it to the first. And a relation is <u>nonsymmetrical</u> if and only if the relation is neither symmetrical nor asymmetrical.

In terms of its graph, a relation is symmetrical if and only if no arrow in the graph is single; asymmetrical if and only if no arrow is double; and nonsymmetrical if and only if some arrows are single and some double.

For example, consider the graphs below.

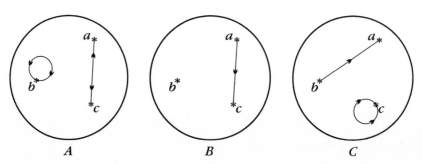

Graph A tells you that the relation is symmetrical, as no arrow is single. Graph B tells you that the relation is asymmetrical, as no arrow is double. And graph

C tells you that the relation is nonsymmetrical, as some arrows are single and some are double.

Symmetrical Relations

In terms of Q, a relation F^2 is symmetrical in a domain if and only if

$$(\forall x)(\forall y)(Fxy \rightarrow Fyx)$$

is true in the domain. For example, the relation of *being a sibling of* is symmetrical. Of any two individuals, if the first is a sibling of the second, the second is a sibling of the first. But the relation of *being a sister of* fails to be symmetrical. A female is a sister of a male without the male's being a sister of the female. [Is the relation of *being a sister of* symmetrical in the domain of females?]

Asymmetrical Relations

A relation F^2 is asymmetrical in a domain if and only if

$$(\forall x)(\forall y)(Fxy \rightarrow \sim Fyx)$$

is true in the domain. An example of a relation that is asymmetrical is the relation of *being the father of*. No son or daughter is the father of his or her own father.

The following derivation demonstrates that any relation which is asymmetrical is also irreflexive.

1	$(\forall x)(\forall y)(Fxy \rightarrow \sim Fyx)$	hyp
2	$\sim(\forall x)\sim Fxx$	hyp
	—	
3	$(\exists x)Fxx$	2, d m q
4	Faa	hyp
	—	
5	$(\forall x)(\forall y)(Fxy \rightarrow \sim Fyx)$	1, reit
6	$Faa \rightarrow \sim Faa$	5, u q elim
7	$\sim Faa$	4, 6, m p
8	$\sim(\exists x)Fxx$	4, 7, neg elim
9	$\sim(\exists x)Fxx$	3, 4–8, e q elim
10	$(\forall x)\sim Fxx$	2–9, ind pr

Although any relation that is asymmetrical is also irreflexive, it is not the case that any relation that is irreflexive is also asymmetrical. The graph of a relation can have no loops and still have some double arrows. Furthermore, the relation of *being the sibling of* is irreflexive and symmetrical.

Nonsymmetrical Relations

A relation F^2 is nonsymmetrical in a domain if and only if

$$(\exists x)(\exists y)(Fxy \ \& \ {\sim}Fyx) \ \& \ (\exists x)(\exists y)(Fxy \ \& \ Fyx)$$

is true in the domain. In other words, a relation is nonsymmetrical in a domain if and only if it is neither symmetrical nor asymmetrical in the domain. For example, the relation of *being the brother of* is nonsymmetrical in the domain of people. Although a male and a female sibling are not each the brother of the other, two male siblings are.

Another example of a relation that is nonsymmetrical in a domain is the relation of *being the sum of a number and itself* in the domain {0, 1, 2}. [As an exercise, draw a graph of this relation. Then, in terms of the graph, explain why the relation is nonsymmetrical. Then, in terms of Q, explain why the relation is nonsymmetrical.]

Transitive and Intransitive Relations

Every relation in a domain is either transitive, intransitive, or nontransitive in that domain. A relation is <u>transitive</u> if and only if, for any three things, the first bears the relation to the second and the second bears the relation to the third only if the first bears the relation to the third. A relation is <u>intransitive</u> if and only if, for any three things, the first bears the relation to the second and the second bears the relation to a third only if the first does not bear the relation to the third. A relation is <u>nontransitive</u> if and only if it is neither transitive nor intransitive.

In terms of a graph, a relation is transitive if and only if whenever there is a broken journey in its graph, there is also a shortcut; intransitive if and only if there are no broken journeys with shortcuts; and nontransitive if and only if there are some broken journeys with shortcuts and some without.

For example, consider the three graphs below.

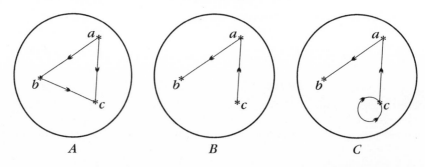

A   B   C

Graph A contains no broken journey without a shortcut; therefore, the relation it graphs is transitive. Graph B contains no broken journey with a shortcut; therefore, the relation it graphs is intransitive. And graph C contains both a broken journey with a shortcut and one without a shortcut; therefore, the relation graphed is nontransitive. The broken journeys in graph C are from c to b via a and from c to c via c. For the first broken journey, there is no shortcut as there is no arrow from c to b. For the second broken journey, there is a shortcut as there is an arrow from c to c.

Transitive Relations

In terms of Q, a relation F^2 is transitive in a domain if and only if

$$(\forall x)(\forall y)(\forall z)((Fxy \mathbin{\&} Fyz) \rightarrow Fxz)$$

is true in the domain. The relation of *being an ancestor of* is an example of a transitive relation. Of three individuals, if the first is an ancestor of the second and the second is an ancestor of the third, then the first is an ancestor of the third. An example of a relation that fails to be transitive is the relation of *sharing a border with* in the domain of nations. Spain shares a border with France and France shares a border with Germany, but Spain does not share a border with Germany.

Intransitive Relations

A relation F^2 is intransitive in a domain if and only if

$$(\forall x)(\forall y)(\forall z)((Fxy \mathbin{\&} Fyz) \rightarrow {\sim}Fxz)$$

is true in the domain. The relation of *being on the same longitude and 5 miles north of* is a relation that is intransitive. Of three individuals, if the first is on the same longitude and 5 miles north of the second and the second is on the same longitude and 5 miles north of the third, then the first is not on the same longitude and 5 miles north of the third. A relation that fails to be intransitive in a domain is the relation of *being a friend of* in the domain of Californians. In this domain, there are friends of friends that are also friends.

Nontransitive Relations

A relation F^2 is nontransitive in a domain if and only if

$$(\exists x)(\exists y)(\exists z)((Fxy \mathbin{\&} Fyz) \mathbin{\&} Fxz) \mathbin{\&} (\exists x)(\exists y)(\exists z)((Fxy \mathbin{\&} Fyz) \mathbin{\&} {\sim}Fxz)$$

is true in the domain. An example of a relation that is nontransitive is the relation of *being 17 kilometers away from* in the domain consisting of villages. One village may be 17 kilometers away from another, which is in turn 17 kilometers away from a third; yet the first village may or may not be 17 kilometers away from the third. Another example of a nontransitive relation is that of *laughing at the jokes of* in the domain of people now living. [Can you explain why? Is the relation of *being a friend of* nontransitive in the domain of people now living?]

Equivalence Relations

If a relation has the properties of reflexivity, symmetry, and also transitivity, it is said to be an <u>equivalence relation</u>. The relation of *being born at the same GMT (Greenwich mean time) as* in the domain of people now living is an equivalence relation. It is a relation such that (i) everything bears the relation to itself (so, it is reflexive); (ii) for any two things, the first bears it to the second only if the second bears it to the first (so, it is symmetrical); and (iii) for any three things, the first bears the relation to the second and the second bears it to the third only if the first bears it to the third (so, it is transitive). Another example of an equivalence relation is that of *equality* in the domain of numbers.

EXERCISES FOR SECTION 12.1

*1. Classify each relation listed below as reflexive, irreflexive, or nonreflexive in the specified domain:

   a. *being a brother of and having the same parents as* in the domain of people
   b. *being a brother of and having the same parents as* in the domain of males
   c. *being a spouse of* in the domain of people
   d. *being proud of* in the domain of people now living
   e. *being as strong as* in the domain of rubber bands
   f. *being taller than* in the domain of office buildings
   g. *being no taller than* in the domain of office buildings
   h. *being more reliable than* in the domain of people now living
   i. *laughing at the jokes of* in the domain of people now living
   j. *having attended one of the schools that ___ attended* in the domain of people

    k. *having the same surname as* in the domain of people
    l. *being the mother of* in the domain of males

2. Classify each relation in exercise 1 as symmetrical, asymmetrical, or nonsymmetrical in the specified domain.

*3. Classify each relation in exercise 1 as transitive, intransitive, or nontransitive in the specified domain.

4. Classify each relation in exercise 1 as equivalent or nonequivalent in the specified domain.

*5. In Intelim-SQ, construct a derivation proving that every intransitive relation is also irreflexive.

6. In Intelim-SQ, construct a derivation proving that every relation that is transitive and irreflexive is also asymmetrical.

7. Using official and derived rules of Intelim-SQ, derive the conclusion of each of the following arguments from its premises.

    *a. $(\forall x)Fxx$ /∴ $\sim(\forall x)\sim Fxx$
    b. $(\forall x)(\forall y)(Fxy \rightarrow Fyx)$, $(\exists x)(\exists y)Fxy$ /∴ $\sim(\forall x)(\forall y)(Fxy \rightarrow \sim Fyx)$
    *c. $(\forall x)(\forall y)(\forall z)((Fxy$ & $Fyz) \rightarrow Fxz)$, $(\exists x)(\exists y)(\exists z)(Fxy$ & $Fyz)$ /∴
        $\sim(\forall x)(\forall y)(\forall z)((Fxy$ & $Fyz) \rightarrow \sim Fxz)$

*8. Is there any domain in which a relation F^2 can be both reflexive and irreflexive?

9. Is there any domain in which a relation F^2 can be both symmetrical and asymmetrical? Is there any domain in which a relation F^2 holds between two individuals (possibly the same) and F^2 is both symmetrical and assymetrical?

*10. Is there any domain in which a relation F^2 is both transitive and intransitive? Is there any domain in which a relation F^2 holds between the first and second and between the second and third of three individuals (possibly the same) and F^2 is both transitive and intransitive?

12.2 IDENTITY

Identity is a relation that each individual bears to itself and to no other. The relation of identity is of such importance in logical analysis that the identity sign is often grouped among the logical symbols. Note that we included the sign '=' among the logical symbols of Q. In Q, identity sentences are of the form ($a = b$) rather than of the form (=ab), but the difference is of no significance. The identity sign has both an introduction and an elimination rule. With their addition to the official rules of Intelim-SQ, the system is complete.

Identity Introduction and Elimination

What is commonly taken to be an axiom may be construed as a rule of direct consequence that requires no preceding item for its application. The introduction rule for identity is a rule of this type.

Identity Introduction (id int).   Any sentence of the form $(a = a)$ is a direct consequence. In other words, any sentence of that form can be entered in a derivation with 'id int' as its sole justification.

An example of a derivation making use of this rule is the following:

$$
\begin{array}{ll}
1 \quad a \mid \quad a = a & \text{id int} \\
2 \quad \quad (\forall x)(x = x) & \text{1-1, u q int}
\end{array}
$$

This derivation from no hypotheses is a proof that any sentence of the form $(\forall x)(x = x)$ is a theorem.

The rule of identity introduction is also applied in the following derivation.

$$
\begin{array}{ll}
1 \quad \quad a = a & \text{id int} \\
2 \quad \quad (\exists x)(x = a) & \text{1, e q int}
\end{array}
$$

This derivation establishes that any sentence of the form $(\exists x)(x = a)$ is a theorem of Intelim-SQ. Some logicians do not consider this a logical truth and, therefore, regard it as undesirable as a theorem of any system of logic. With the assumption of standard quantification theory that every singular term designates an individual in the domain, it is valid. This issue is discussed further in the next section.

The elimination rule for identity will remind you of the rule for replacing equals for equals in mathematics.

Identity Elimination (id elim).   Any sentence that results from replacing in a sentence the right side of an identity with its left side everywhere the right side occurs is a direct consequence of the identity and the original sentence.

The rule is expressed schematically as follows:

$$
\begin{array}{ll}
h & A \\
i & a = b \\
j & A(a/b) \qquad\qquad \text{h, i, id elim}
\end{array}
$$

where j is understood to be a direct consequence of h and i in any sequence of items having the form h, i, j.

The derivation below illustrates how the elimination rule works.

$$
\begin{array}{lll}
1 & b = c & \text{hyp} \\
2 & Fc & \text{hyp} \\
3 & b = c & \text{1, reit} \\
4 & Fb & \text{2, 3, id elim} \\
5 & Fc \rightarrow Fb & \text{2–4, cond int} \\
6 & b = c \rightarrow (Fc \rightarrow Fb) & \text{1–5, cond int}
\end{array}
$$

Notice how items 2, 3, and 4 correspond to items h, i, and j in the schematic representation above.

The derivation above is included in the following derivation which adds two applications of the rule of universal quantifier introduction.

$$
\begin{array}{lll}
1 & b \quad c \quad b = c & \text{hyp} \\
2 & Fc & \text{hyp} \\
3 & b = c & \text{1, reit} \\
4 & Fb & \text{2, 3, id elim} \\
5 & Fc \rightarrow Fb & \text{2–4, cond int} \\
6 & b = c \rightarrow (Fc \rightarrow Fb) & \text{1–5, cond int} \\
7 & (\forall y)(b = y \rightarrow (Fy \rightarrow Fb)) & \text{1–6, u q int} \\
8 & (\forall x)(\forall y)(x = y \rightarrow (Fy \rightarrow Fx)) & \text{1–7, u q int}
\end{array}
$$

Notice how items 1–6 correspond to items 1–6 in the previous derivation.

From this derivation together with the derived rule for identity elimination soon to be presented in "Other Identity Rules" (see p. 385), you should be able to see how to derive as a theorem

$$(\forall x)(\forall y)(x = y \rightarrow (Fy \equiv Fx))$$

This theorem can be construed as saying that two individuals are identical only if they have the same attributes. From this derivation, which is left to the reader, a metaderivation can be easily constructed showing that any sentence of the form

$$(\forall x)(\forall y)(x = y \rightarrow (A(y/a) \equiv A(x/a)))$$

is a theorem.

Equivalence of Identity

Identity is an equivalence relation because it has the properties of reflexivity, symmetry, and transitivity. That identity has these properties is proven by deriving the following as theorems.

Reflexivity of Identity (refl id)

$$(\forall x)(x = x)$$

Symmetry of Identity (sym id)

$$(\forall x)(\forall y)(x = y \rightarrow y = x)$$

Transitivity of Identity (trans id)

$$(\forall x)(\forall y)(\forall z)((x = y \ \& \ y = z) \rightarrow x = z)$$

We have already proved the theorems of reflexivity of identity. The following derivation serves as a proof of the theorems of symmetry.

1	a	c		$a = c$	hyp
2				$c \neq a$	hyp
3				$a = c$	1, reit
4				$a \neq a$	2, 3, id elim
5				$a = a$	id int
6				$c = a$	2–5, ind pr
7				$a = c \rightarrow c = a$	1–6, cond int
8				$(\forall y)(a = y \rightarrow y = a)$	1–7, u q int
9				$(\forall x)(\forall y)(x = y \rightarrow y = x)$	1–8, u q int

The next derivation is a proof of the theorems of transitivity.

$$
\begin{array}{ll}
1 \quad | \; a \; | \; b \; | \; c \; | \qquad\quad a = b \;\&\; b = c & \text{hyp} \\[4pt]
2 \qquad\qquad\qquad\qquad\quad a \neq c & \text{hyp} \\[4pt]
3 \qquad\qquad\qquad\qquad\qquad a = b & \text{1, reit, conj elim} \\
4 \qquad\qquad\qquad\qquad\qquad b = c & \text{1, reit, conj elim} \\
5 \qquad\qquad\qquad\qquad\qquad a = c & \text{3, 4, id elim} \\
6 \qquad\qquad\qquad\qquad\; a = c & \text{2-5, ind pr} \\
7 \qquad\qquad\qquad (a = b \;\&\; b = c) \to a = c & \text{1-6, cond int} \\
8 \qquad\quad (\forall z)((a = b \;\&\; b = z) \to a = z) & \text{1-7, u q int} \\
9 \qquad (\forall y)(\forall z)((a = y \;\&\; y = z) \to a = z) & \text{1-8, u q int} \\
10 \quad (\forall x)(\forall y)(\forall z)((x = y \;\&\; y = z) \to x = z) & \text{1-9, u q int}
\end{array}
$$

Other Identity Rules

It is interesting to compare the following metaderivation with the official rule of identity elimination on pages 382–383.

$$
\begin{array}{ll}
1 \quad | \; A & \text{hyp} \\
2 \quad | \; a = b & \text{hyp} \\[6pt]
3 \qquad | \; \sim A(b/a) & \text{hyp} \\[6pt]
4 \qquad | \; a = b & \text{2, reit} \\
5 \qquad | \; A & \text{1, reit} \\
6 \qquad | \; A(a/b) & \text{4, 5, id elim} \\
7 \qquad | \; \sim A(a/b) & \text{3, 4, id elim} \\
8 \quad | \; A(b/a) & \text{3-7, ind pr}
\end{array}
$$

Note that this derivation sanctions replacement of the left side of an identity with its right side throughout. The official rule only sanctions replacement of the right side with the left throughout. In other words, this derivation justifies a derived rule stating that a sentence $A(b/a)$ that results from replacing in the sentence A every occurrence of the left side of the identity $(a = b)$ with the right side is a direct consequence of A and $(a = b)$.

Stated schematically, the rule is as follows:

$$
\begin{array}{ll}
\text{h} \quad | \; A & \\
\text{i} \quad | \; a = b & \\
\text{j} \quad | \; A(b/a) & \text{h, i, id elim (derived version)}
\end{array}
$$

where j is understood to be a direct consequence of h and i in any sequence of items of the form h, i, and j. As a convenience, we shall adopt this rule as a derived rule and employ it together with the official rule of identity elimination, using the same name for both the official and derived versions.

To convince yourself that the original rule of identity elimination is truth-preserving, note that (i) if an identity is true, then the right and left sides designate the same individual; and (ii) if one sentence results from replacing in another the right side of a true identity with the left, then the two sentences express the same proposition. From (i) and (ii) it follows that the sentence which results from such a replacement is true if the identity and the original sentence are true. The derived rule of identity elimination differs from the original rule only in having 'right' and 'left' interchanged. That the derived rule is truth-preserving should be equally as obvious.

It is also possible to derive a more general rule that states that a sentence that results from replacing one or more occurrences of one side of an identity with its other side is a direct consequence of the identity and the original sentence. The following is a derivation showing that you can replace one or more occurrences of the left side of an identity with the right side.

1	$A(a/b)$	hyp
2	$a = b$	hyp
3	$\sim A$	hyp
4	$a = b$	2, reit
5	$\sim A(a/b)$	3, 4, id elim
6	$A(a/b)$	1, reit
7	A	3–6, neg elim

A derivation showing that one can replace one or more occurrences of the right side of an identity with the left side is left to the reader.

The two derivations sanction our adoption of the following derived rule.

General Identity Elimination (gen id elim).   A sentence that results from replacing in the original sentence one or more occurrences of one side of an identity with its other side is a direct consequence of the identity and the original sentence.

EXERCISES FOR SECTION 12.2

1. Using official and derived rules of Intelim-SQ, derive the conclusion of each of the following arguments from its premises.

   a. $(a = b), Fb /\therefore Fa$

   *b. $(Gc \mathbin{\&} {\sim}Gb), (\forall x)(\forall y)((Gx \mathbin{\&} x \neq y) \rightarrow Fxy) /\therefore Fcb$

   c. $(a = a) /\therefore (\exists x)(x = a)$

   *d. $(\forall y)(y = a), {\sim}Fa /\therefore {\sim}(\exists x)Fx$

   e. $(\forall y)(y = a), (b \neq a) /\therefore {\sim}(\exists x)(b = x)$

   *f. $(\forall y)(y = a), (b \neq a) /\therefore (a \neq a)$

   *g. $(\exists x)(Fx \mathbin{\&} (\forall y)(Fy \rightarrow y = x) \mathbin{\&} x = a), Hc, (a = c) /\therefore (\exists x)(Fx \mathbin{\&} (\forall y)(Fy \rightarrow y = x) \mathbin{\&} Hx)$

   h. $(\forall x)(Fx \rightarrow x = a), Fb /\therefore (b = a)$

2. Using official and derived rules of Intelim-SQ, derive the following from no hypotheses.

   *a. ${\sim}(\exists x){\sim}(x = x)$

   b. $(\forall x)(\exists y)(x = y)$

   *c. $(\forall x)(\exists y)((Fx \mathbin{\&} {\sim}Fy) \rightarrow x \neq y)$

   d. $(\forall x)(Gx \rightarrow (\forall y)(y = x \rightarrow Gy))$

   *e. $(\forall x)(\forall y)((Fx \mathbin{\&} {\sim}Fy) \rightarrow x \neq y)$

   f. $(\forall x)(\forall y)(x = y \rightarrow (Fy \equiv Fx))$

   *g. $(\forall x)(\forall y)(x \neq y \rightarrow y \neq x)$

3. In the theorems of symmetry of identity, replace '=' with '≠'. Are the results also theorems? Justify your answer.

*4. In the theorems of transitivity of identity, replace '=' with '≠'. Are the results also theorems? Justify your answer.

*5. Derive

$$(\forall x)(\forall y)(x = y \rightarrow (Fy \equiv Fx))$$

as a theorem. Then establish

$$(\forall x)(\forall y)(x = y \rightarrow (A(y/a) \equiv A(x/a)))$$

as a metatheorem.

6. Translate into English the arguments in exercise 1. Use your own translation scheme and domain.

*7. Translate into English the sentences in exercise 2.

8. With the intention of showing that the argument is valid, translate into Q each of the arguments below. Then derive the Q-conclusion from the Q-premises in Intelim-SQ.

*a. James and Jimmy are not the same individual. James is my brother and so is Jimmy. Therefore, I have at least two brothers.

b. Betty and Elizabeth are the same individual. Therefore either Betty is an astrophysicist or Elizabeth is not.

c. Nancy likes any Fiji islander who likes her. Platt likes Nancy but Nancy does not like Platt. Therefore, Platt is not a Fiji islander.

*d. Peter is smarter than every philosophy major. Peter is not smarter than Susan. There is a philosophy major who is not smarter than Peter. Therefore, Susan is not the philosophy major who is not smarter than Peter.

e. There are two Nobel Prize winners at the wedding reception; I will photograph one and Harold will photograph another. There are no more than two Nobel Prize winners at the wedding reception. Therefore, every Nobel Prize winner at the wedding reception will be photographed by either Harold or myself. ($F\_$: _ is a Nobel Prize winner at the wedding reception, $G\_$: I photograph _, $H\_$: Harold photographs _).

12.3 EXISTENCE ASSUMPTIONS AND FREE LOGIC

Standard quantification theory assumes that every singular term designates an individual in the domain and, consequently, that the domain is nonempty. Intelim-SQ is in this sense a standard logical system. Both of the following are valid in standard quantification theory and both are theorems of Intelim-SQ.

(1) $(\exists x)(x = x)$

(2) $(\exists x)(x = a)$

The first says that something exists and the second says that a exists. Under the assumption that every singular term designates an individual in the domain, one would want both of these as theorems, as well as the following:

(3) $(\forall x)Fx \rightarrow Fa$

(4) $Fa \rightarrow (\exists x)Fx$

Theorem (3) says that a has the attribute F if everything in the domain does and (4) says that something in the domain has the attribute F if a does.

Unlike standard theory, <u>free quantification theory</u> does not assume that every singular term designates an individual in the domain. In this section, we begin by explaining some of the motivations for the development of free logic and then construct two such systems. The first system, called Intelim-FQ, results from weakening two of the rules of direct consequence of Intelim-SQ: the rule of universal quantifier elimination and the rule of existential quantifier introduction. Just as we use 'SQ' to indicate that Intelim-SQ is a standard logic, we use 'FQ' to indicate that Intelim-FQ is a free logic. In Intelim-FQ, (1) through (4) are not theorems.

The second system of free logic we call <u>Intelim-FQE</u>. The 'FQE' indicates that Intelim-FQE is a free logic with an existence assumption. This system results from adding to Intelim-FQ a rule which is truth-preserving only if the domain is nonempty. Because of this rule, (1) is a theorem of Intelim-FQE, although (2) through (4) are not. For short, we refer to the three systems as SQ, FQ, and FQE, respectively.

Advantages of Free Logic

In standard logic, some arguments that have the following form are not valid.

(5) $(\forall x)(A \to B) \mathbin{/} \therefore (\exists x)(A \mathbin{\&} B)$

For example, the argument below has this form, yet there is a translation with respect to some domain on which the premise is true and the conclusion false.

(6) $(\forall x)((Fx \mathbin{\&} Gx) \to Gx) \mathbin{/} \therefore (\exists x)((Fx \mathbin{\&} Gx) \mathbin{\&} Gx)$

To convince yourself of this, let '$F\_$' translate '$\_$ is a square' and '$G\_$' translate '$\_$ is round'. Then, (6) translates

(6′) All round squares are round. Therefore, there is at least one round square that is round.

The premise is true, but the conclusion is false.

The following is a special case of (5).

(7) $(\forall x)(x = a \to B) \mathbin{/} \therefore (\exists x)(x = a \mathbin{\&} B)$

Every argument of this form is valid in standard logic. However, some of these arguments are not valid in free logic. For example,

(8) $(\forall x)(x = a \to Gx) \mathbin{/} \therefore (\exists x)(x = a \mathbin{\&} Gx)$

is not valid in free logic. To see this, restrict the domain to actual, nonmythical entities, let '*a*' translate 'Pegasus', and '*G_*' translate '_ has wings'. Then (8) will translate into English as follows.

> **(8′)** Anything that is identical to Pegasus has wings. Therefore, Pegasus exists and has wings.

The premise is true and the conclusion is false.

There are various motivations for the development of free logic. One is to have a formal language that will translate singular terms that designate no individual in the domain. For example, when 'Pegasus' does not designate an individual in the domain, (8′) cannot be translated as (8) in standard logic. This is important for arguments, such as (8′), that contain a singular term that one knows does not designate an individual in the domain. It is also important when one is uncertain about whether or not a singular term designates an individual in the domain.

For example, consider the argument below with the domain limited to actresses.

> **(9)** Ruby Keller took the part of Peggy Sawyer. So, Ruby Keller took someone's part.

Is 'Peggy Sawyer' the name of an actress? Or is 'Peggy Sawyer' the name of a fictional character? If 'Peggy Sawyer' is the name of a fictional character that Ruby Keller played the part of, the premise of (9) is true but the conclusion is false.

In standard logic, (9′) below has no translation with respect to a domain on which the premise is true and the conclusion is false.

> **(9′)** *Fa* /∴ (∃*x*)*Fx*

Therefore, in standard logic, you cannot translate (9) as (9′) without committing yourself to the proposition that (9) is valid. The advantage of free logic is that you can translate (9) as (9′) without that commitment. [To translate (9) as (9′), what would you use as your translation scheme?]

Some other reasons for favoring free logic are less practical than philosophical. The proposition (∃*x*)(*x* = *x*), that is, that something exists, is indisputably true. But is it a truth of logic? In SQ and other standard systems, every sentence of the form (∃*x*)(*x* = *x*) is a theorem. For those who prefer that the soundness of a system not depend on the assumption that something exists, there is FQ, the first system of free logic developed below. In FQ, no sentence of the form (∃*x*)(*x* = *x*) is a theorem.

Universal Quantifiers in Free Logic

For its justification, the rule of universal quantifier introduction does not depend upon the assumption that every singular term designates an individual in the domain. Consequently, the rule is the same in both SQ and FQ. The situation is different for the standard rule of universal quantifier elimination. That rule is not truth-preserving in FQ.

According to the rule of universal quantifier elimination, a universal sentence has as a direct consequence any one of its instances. When each and every instantial term designates an individual in the domain, the rule is truth-preserving. But, in free logic, where an instantial term need not designate an individual in the domain, such a rule can lead from true premises to a false conclusion.

For example, you can get the conclusion of the following argument from its premise by one application of the standard rule of universal quantifier elimination.

$(\forall x)Fx \ /\therefore \ Fa$

But, the argument is not valid in free logic. Let the domain be companies listed on the New York Stock Exchange and translate 'F_' with '_ is a for profit organization' and 'a' with 'the Museum of Fine Arts, Boston'. Then the argument translates as

All are for-profit organizations. Therefore, the Museum of Fine Arts, Boston, is a for-profit organization.

Given the domain, the premise is true, but the conclusion is false.

In a system of free logic, we need an elimination rule for universal quantifiers that is truth-preserving when not every singular term designates an individual in the domain. The following is such a rule.

Free Universal Quantifier Elimination (free u q elim). In a prefixed derivation and in any of its subordinate derivations, a universal sentence has as a direct consequence the instance that has the prefixed term as its instantial term.

Thus, in any derivation (or part of a derivation) of the form below, item i is a direct consequence of item h by the rule of free universal quantifier elimination.

$$
\begin{array}{c|c|l}
h & a & (\forall x)A \\
\cdot & & \cdot \\
i & & A(a/x) \qquad\qquad \text{h, free u q elim}
\end{array}
$$

The rule allows you to enter in a prefixed derivation and in any of its subordinate derivations an instance of a preceding universal sentence when the prefixed term is the instantial term. In a prefixed derivation and in any derivation subordinate to it, the prefixed term is assumed to designate an individual in the domain. So, given a preceding universal sentence, there can be no danger in entering the instance that has the prefixed term as its instantial term. Certainly, with the assumption that the instantial term designates an individual in the domain, the universal sentence is true only if that instance is also true.

Many of the derivations and metaderivations in chapter 11 can be converted using the rule of universal quantifier elimination into ones in FQ simply by replacing the justification 'u q elim' with 'free u q elim'. But some cannot be. For example, consider the following metaderivation for SQ, which proves the theorems of specification.

$$
\begin{array}{lll}
1 & (\forall x)A & \text{hyp} \\
\\
2 & A(a/x) & 1, \text{u q elim} \\
3 & (\forall x)A \to A(a/x) & 1\text{-}2, \text{cond int}
\end{array}
$$

Replace 'u q elim' with 'free u q elim' and you get

$$
\begin{array}{lll}
1 & (\forall x)A & \text{hyp} \\
\\
2 & A(a/x) & 1, \text{free u q elim (Wrong!)} \\
3 & (\forall x)A \to A(a/x) & 1\text{-}2, \text{cond int}
\end{array}
$$

Step 2 is not justified by the free rule. The reason is that the instantial term is not prefixed to the subderivation 1–2. The rule of free universal quantifier elimination requires the prefix.

You may think that the following qualifies as a derivation. But it does not.

$$
\begin{array}{llll}
1 & a & (\forall x)A & \text{hyp} \\
\\
2 & & A(a/x) & 1, \text{free u q elim} \\
3 & & (\forall x)A \to A(a/x) & 1\text{-}2, \text{cond int (Wrong!)}
\end{array}
$$

The rule of conditional introduction only applies to regular subordinate derivations and never to prefixed derivations. Rules of direct consequence apply to prefixed derivations only when prefixed derivations are specified and not otherwise.

There are no erroneous steps in the next metaderivation, where *a* is assumed not to occur in *A*.

$$
\begin{array}{llll}
1 & a & (\forall x)A & \text{hyp} \\
\\
2 & & A(a/x) & 1, \text{free u q elim} \\
3 & & (\forall x)A \to A(a/x) & 1\text{-}2, \text{cond int} \\
4 & & (\forall y)((\forall x)A \to A(y/x)) & 1\text{-}3, \text{u q int}
\end{array}
$$

The following is an example of a derivation of that form. Studying this derivation will help you understand the metaderivation.

1	a	$(\forall x)Fx$	hyp
2		Fa	1, free u q elim
3		$(\forall x)Fx \rightarrow Fa$	1–2, cond int
4		$(\forall y)((\forall x)Fx \rightarrow Fy)$	1–3, u q int

Notice that free universal quantifier elimination can be applied to item 1 to get item 2, because the derivation 1–2 is subordinate to a derivation prefixed with the instantial term. The rule of conditional introduction can be applied to the subderivation 1–2, as that derivation is a regular subderivation. Finally, the rule of universal quantifier introduction can be applied to the prefixed subderivation 1–3 to get item 4, as the subderivation has no hypothesis and item 3 is a generating instance of item 4 with the prefixed term as its instantial term. The subderivation 1–3 shows that item 3 is true if the prefixed term designates any individual in the domain. What is true of any individual is certainly true of every individual.

The derivation below is another example of a derivation in SQ that cannot be converted into a derivation in FQ simply by replacing 'u q elim' with 'free u q elim'.

1	$(\forall x)(Fx \rightarrow Gx)$	hyp
2	$(\forall x)Fx$	hyp
3	$Fa \rightarrow Ga$	1, free u q elim (Wrong!)
4	Fa	2, free u q elim (Wrong!)
5	Ga	3, 4, m p

However, you can get a derivation in FQ if you prefix the instantial term to the derivation as follows:

1	a	$(\forall x)(Fx \rightarrow Gx)$	hyp
2		$(\forall x)Fx$	hyp
3		$Fa \rightarrow Ga$	1, free u q elim
4		Fa	2, free u q elim
5		Ga	3, 4, m p

Notice that because the derivation is prefixed with the instantial term, items 3 and 4 are direct consequences of items 1 and 2, respectively, by the rule of free universal quantifier elimination.

The following is an example of a derivation in FQ that results from simply replacing 'u q elim' with 'free u q elim' in a derivation in SQ that appears in chapter 11.

1		$(\forall x)Fx$	hyp
2		$(\forall x)(Fx \rightarrow Gx)$	hyp
3	a	$(\forall x)Fx$	1, reit
4		$(\forall x)(Fx \rightarrow Gx)$	2, reit
5		Fa	3, free u q elim
6		$Fa \rightarrow Ga$	4, free u q elim
7		Ga	5, 6, m p
8		$(\forall x)Gx$	3–7, u q int

Such an exchange of rules works in just those cases where the conditions for application of the rule of free universal quantifier elimination are satisfied.

The theorems of distribution of universal quantification into conjunction and into conditional are theorems of both SQ and FQ, as are sentences of the following form.

$$(A \text{ v } (\forall x)B) \equiv (\forall x)(A \text{ v } B)$$

The metaderivation below shows how to derive the second half of the biconditional, that is, the left from the right side. In derivations of this form x does not occur in A and the prefixed term a does not occur either in A or in B.

1			$(\forall x)(A \text{ v } B)$	hyp
2			$\sim(A \text{ v } (\forall x)B)$	hyp
3			$\sim A \text{ \& } \sim(\forall x)B$	2, neg disj elim
4			$\sim A$	3, conj elim
5		a	$A \text{ v } B(a/x)$	1, reit, free u q elim
6			$\sim A$	4, reit
7			$B(a/x)$	5, 6, disj syl
8			$(\forall x)B$	5–7, u q int
9			$A \text{ v } (\forall x)B$	8, disj int
10			$A \text{ v } (\forall x)B$	2–9, ind pr

Notice how step 5 is justified.

Every sentence exemplifying one of the forms below is a theorem of FQ as well as SQ.

$$(A \ \& \ (\forall x)B) \ \rightarrow \ (\forall x)(A \ \& \ B)$$

$$(\forall x)(\forall y)B \ \equiv \ (\forall y)(\forall x)B$$

In contrast, although every sentence of one of the following forms is a theorem of SQ, not all are theorems of FQ.

$$(\forall x)(A \ \& \ B) \ \equiv \ (A \ \& \ (\forall x)B)$$

$$(\forall x)(A \ \rightarrow \ B) \ \rightarrow \ ((\forall x)A \ \rightarrow \ B)$$

That not all are theorems of FQ is to be expected. After all, FQ allows for the possibility that the domain is empty. In the empty domain, there is nothing and thus nothing that fails to have the attribute that a universal sentence says that they all do. So, in the empty domain, all universal sentences are true. Consequently, with the domain empty and '*Fa*' false, the left side of the following biconditional is true but the right side is false.

$$(\forall x)(Fa \ \& \ Gx) \ \equiv \ (Fa \ \& \ (\forall x)Gx)$$

Therefore, the biconditional is false.

Existential Quantifiers in Free Logic

Like the standard rule of universal quantifier introduction, the standard rule of existential quantifier elimination is truth-preserving without the assumption that every singular term designates an individual in the domain. Therefore, it may be adopted as a rule of FQ without modification. This is not the case, however, with the standard rule of existential quantifier introduction.

According to the standard rule of existential quantifier introduction, an existential sentence is a direct consequence of any of its instances. This rule is truth-preserving in standard quantification theory because that theory assumes that every singular term designates an individual in the domain. But, without that assumption, the rule is not truth-preserving. And free logic does not make that assumption.

For example, the following argument is derivable in SQ using the standard rule of existential quantifier introduction and is valid in standard logic.

$$(a = a) \ / \therefore \ (\exists x)(x = a)$$

But, in free logic, there is a translation of this argument that has a true premise and a false conclusion. If you let '*a*' translate 'Peter Pan' and the domain consist of nonfictional entities, the argument translates as the following:

Peter Pan is identical to Peter Pan. Therefore, Peter Pan exists.

Consequently, we must weaken the standard rule of existential quantifier introduction to get a rule for FQ that is truth-preserving.

The following rule is truth-preserving regardless of whether every singular term designates an individual in the domain.

Free Existential Quantifier Introduction (free e q int).   In a prefixed derivation and in any derivation subordinate to it, an existential sentence is a direct consequence of the instance that has the prefixed term as its instantial term.

Thus, in any derivation or part of a derivation of the form below, item i is a direct consequence of item h by the rule of free existential quantifier introduction.

$$
\begin{array}{c|c|l}
\text{h} & a & A(a/x) \\
\cdot & & \cdot \\
\text{i} & & (\exists x)A \qquad\qquad\qquad \text{h, free e q int}
\end{array}
$$

Notice that, in order for a derivation to qualify as a prefixed derivation of the form above, step h must (i) be an instance of the existential sentence and (ii) have as its instantial term the same singular term that prefixes the derivation.

The free rule allows you to enter an existential sentence in a prefixed derivation and in any of its subordinate derivations when there is a preceding instance with the prefixed term as its instantial term. In such derivations, the prefixed term is assumed to designate an individual in the domain. What individual (if there are any in the domain) is irrelevant to the assumption. So, given a preceding instance with the prefixed term as its instantial term, there can be no problem in entering the existential sentence. Certainly, with the assumption that the instantial term designates an individual in the domain, the instance is true only if the existential sentence is also true.

Many of the derivations and metaderivations in chapter 11 that use the rule of existential quantifier introduction can be converted into derivations in FQ by replacing 'e q int' with 'free e q int'. The following is the derivation that results from replacing 'e q int' with 'free e q int' in a derivation that appears on page 352 in chapter 11.

$$
\begin{array}{c|c|l}
1 & & (\exists x)Fx & \text{hyp} \\
2 & a & Fa & \text{hyp} \\
3 & & Fa \lor Ga & \text{2, disj int} \\
4 & & (\exists x)(Fx \lor Gx) & \text{3, free e q int} \\
5 & & (\exists x)(Fx \lor Gx) & \text{1, 2-4, e q elim}
\end{array}
$$

Study the prefixed subderivation 2–4 carefully and be sure to observe that 3 is an instance of 4 and its instantial term is the same as the prefixed term. Replacing 'e q int' with 'free e q int' works in those derivations prefixed with the instantial term.

Derivations proving that any sentence of one of the following forms is a theorem of SQ can all be converted into derivations in FQ by just replacing 'e q int' with 'free e q int'. Thus these sentences are all theorems of FQ:

$$(\exists x)(A \lor B) \equiv ((\exists x)A \lor (\exists x)B)$$

$$(\exists x)(A \lor B) \rightarrow (A \lor (\exists x)B)$$

$$(\exists x)(A \lor B) \rightarrow ((\exists x)A \lor B)$$

$$(\exists x)(A \& B) \equiv (A \& (\exists x)B)$$

$$(\exists x)(A \& B) \equiv ((\exists x)A \& B)$$

$$(\exists x)(A \rightarrow B) \rightarrow (A \rightarrow (\exists x)B)$$

$$(\exists x)(\exists y)A \equiv (\exists y)(\exists x)A$$

$$(\exists x)(\forall y)A \rightarrow (\forall y)(\exists x)A$$

$$(\exists x)(\forall y)(Gx \lor Hy) \rightarrow (\forall y)(\exists x)(Gx \lor Hy)$$

$$(\exists x)(\forall y)(Gx \& Hy) \rightarrow (\forall y)(\exists x)(Gx \& Hy)$$

In section 11.2, we said that any sentence of one of the following forms is a theorem in SQ.

$$((\exists x)A \rightarrow B) \rightarrow (\exists x)(A \rightarrow B)$$

$$(\forall y)(\exists x)(Gx \lor Hy) \rightarrow (\exists x)(\forall y)(Gx \lor Hy)$$

$$(\forall y)(\exists x)(Gx \& Hy) \rightarrow (\exists x)(\forall y)(Gx \& Hy)$$

However, it is not true that any sentence having one of these forms is a theorem of FQ. This is desirable, as none of these sentences is true in the empty domain. [Can you explain why?]

In SQ, the following metaderivation establishes that any sentence of the form $(A(a/x) \rightarrow (\exists x)A)$ is a theorem, specifically, a theorem of **particularization** (part).

1	$A(a/x)$	hyp
2	$(\exists x)A$	1, e q int
3	$A(a/x) \rightarrow (\exists x)A$	1–2, cond int

In SQ, step 2 is justified by the standard rule of existential quantifier introduction. The rule of free existential quantifier introduction cannot be used to justify step 2. The free rule can be applied *only* to an instance of an existential sentence in a derivation prefixed with its instantial term, and 1–2 is not a prefixed derivation.

The following are the closest approximations of the theorems of particularization and specification that are derivable in FQ.

$$((\forall x)A \ \& \ (\exists x)(x = a)) \rightarrow A(a/x)$$

$$(A(a/x) \ \& \ (\exists x)(x = a)) \rightarrow (\exists x)A$$

The following metaderivations establish that any sentence of either form is a theorem of FQ. In a derivation of either form *b* does not occur in *A*.

1		$(\forall x)A$	hyp
2		$(\exists x)(x = a)$	hyp
3	*b*	$b = a$	hyp
4		$(\forall x)A$	1, reit
5		$A(b/x)$	4, free u q elim
6		$A(a/x)$	3, 5, id elim
7		$A(a/x)$	2, 3–6, e q elim

1		$A(a/x)$	hyp
2		$(\exists x)(x = a)$	hyp
3	*b*	$b = a$	hyp
4		$A(a/x)$	1, reit
5		$A(b/x)$	3, 4, id elim
6		$(\exists x)A$	5, free e q int
7		$(\exists x)A$	2, 3–6, e q elim

Existence Assumption

A system of logic is free if it does not assume that every singular term designates an individual in the domain. FQ does not make that assumption and is, therefore, free. Because FQ does not even assume that the domain is nonempty, FQ is said to be <u>universally free</u>. The second system of free logic that we present in this text does not assume that every singular term designates an individual in the domain, but it does assume that the domain is nonempty. This is the system FQE.

FQE results from adding to FQ the following rule which is truth-preserving only if the domain is nonempty.

Existence Assumption (ex a). A sentence that is an item of a prefixed derivation with no hypotheses is a direct consequence of the derivation so long as the prefixed term does not occur in the sentence. In other words, a sentence is a direct consequence of a prefixed derivation with no hypotheses in which the sentence is an item so long as the prefixed term does not occur in the sentence.

With the understanding that a does not occur in B, this rule may be expressed schematically as follows:

$$
\begin{array}{ll|l|l}
h & a & \cdot & \\
  &   & \cdot & \\
  &   & \cdot & \\
i &   & B & \\
j &   & B & \qquad\qquad\qquad \text{h–i, ex a}
\end{array}
$$

That this rule is truth-preserving only if the domain is nonempty is evident from the derivation below of $(\exists x)(x = x)$ as a theorem in FQE.

$$
\begin{array}{lll}
1 & a \quad a = a & \text{id int} \\
2 & \quad\ (\exists x)(x = x) & \text{1, free e q int} \\
3 & (\exists x)(x = x) & \text{1–2, ex a}
\end{array}
$$

Item 3 is derived from 1–2 by the rule of existence assumption. Notice that the prefixed term does not occur in item 3. The assumption within the prefixed derivation that the prefixed term designates an individual in the domain is not carried into the main derivation. However, the assumption that the domain is nonempty is carried into the main derivation. Also note that 3 is the last item of a derivation with no hypotheses; therefore, any sentence of the form $(\exists x)(x = x)$ is a theorem of FQE.

The following is a derivation of the rule of existence assumption in FQ given that $(\exists x)(x = x)$. It is assumed that a does not occur in B.

$$
\begin{array}{ll|l}
h & & (\exists x)(x = x) \\
i & a & \cdot \\
\cdot & & \cdot \\
j & & B \\
k & & B \qquad\qquad \text{h, i–j, e q elim}
\end{array}
$$

You may be puzzled by our justifying step k by application of the rule of existential quantifier elimination to h and i–j without a suitable instance of h appearing as an hypothesis of i–j. Close scrutiny of the rule of existential quantifier elimination will show, however, that the rule only requires that i-j have such an instance "as its only hypothesis" (if it has any). The rule may be applied without i-j having any hypothesis.

Of the three systems including rules of quantifier introduction and elimination we have discussed, SQ is the strongest. As FQE results from adding the rule of existence assumption to the rules of FQ, FQE is, not surprisingly, stronger than FQ. Derivable in FQE but not in FQ are the following:

$$(\forall x)(A \text{ \& } B) \rightarrow (A \text{ \& } (\forall x)B)$$

$$(\forall x)(A \text{ \& } B) \rightarrow ((\forall x)A \text{ \& } B)$$

$$(\forall x)(A \rightarrow B) \rightarrow ((\forall x)A \rightarrow B)$$

$$((\exists x)A \rightarrow B) \rightarrow (\exists x)(A \rightarrow B)$$

$$(\forall y)(\exists x)(Gx \text{ v } Hy) \rightarrow (\exists x)(\forall y)(Gx \text{ v } Hy)$$

$$(\forall y)(\exists x)(Gx \text{ \& } Hy) \rightarrow (\exists x)(\forall y)(Gx \text{ \& } Hy)$$

Here is a derivation in FQE that uses the rule of existence assumption.

1		$(\forall x)(Gb \text{ \& } Fx)$	hyp
	–		
2	a	$Gb \text{ \& } Fa$	1, reit, free u q elim
3		Gb	2, conj elim
4		Fa	2, conj elim
5		$(\forall x)Fx$	2–4, u q int
6		Gb	2–4, ex a
7		$Gb \text{ \& } (\forall x)Fx$	5, 6, conj int

Notice how step 6 is justified by the rule of existence assumption. In FQ, 'Gb' is not a direct consequence of 2–4. You can use the same method to construct a metaderivation showing that every sentence of the form

$$(\forall x)(A \text{ \& } B) \rightarrow (A \text{ \& } (\forall x)B)$$

is a theorem of FQE. This derivation is left as an exercise for the reader.

The metaderivation below establishes that every sentence of the form

$$((\exists x)A \rightarrow B) \rightarrow (\exists x)(A \rightarrow B)$$

is a theorem of FQE. In a derivation of this form, a does not occur in A or in B.

1			$(\exists x)A \rightarrow B$	hyp
		–		
2		a	$A(a/x)$	hyp
			–	

3				$(\exists x)A$	2, free e q int
4				$(\exists x)A \to B$	1, reit
5				B	3, 4, m p
6			$A(a/x) \to B$		2–5, cond int
7			$(\exists x)(A \to B)$		6, free e q int
8		$(\exists x)(A \to B)$			2–7, ex a
9	$((\exists x)A \to B) \to (\exists x)(A \to B)$				2–8, cond int

The theorems of SQ are valid under the assumption that every singular term designates an individual in the domain. On the other hand, the theorems of FQE are valid under the more modest assumption that the domain is nonempty. Neither assumption is thought to be a "logical" assumption, that is, an assumption required by the interpretation or meaning of the logical constants. Therefore, it would appear that some of the theorems of SQ and even FQE are not "logical" truths. In contrast, the theorems of FQ are true regardless of what is assumed about the size of the domain or about which singular terms designate. Therefore, unlike SQ and FQE, there is no disagreement over the logical validity of the theorems of FQ.

EXERCISES FOR SECTION 12.3

1. Using only official rules of FQ, derive the conclusion from the premises in the following arguments.

    *a. $(\forall x)Gx, (\exists x)(x = a) / \therefore Ga$

    b. $Ga, (\exists x)(x = a) / \therefore (\exists x)Gx$

2. In exercise 1 of section 11.1 (p. 349), you are asked to construct derivations showing that arguments a–m are derivable in SQ. In which of these arguments is the conclusion derivable from the premises in FQ? Are there any for which there are derivations in FQE but not in FQ?

*3. Answer the same questions for exercise 2 in section 11.1.

4. Answer the same questions for exercise 3 of section 11.1.

*5. Answer the same questions for exercise 2 of section 11.3.

6. Answer the same questions for exercise 1 of section 11.2.

*7. Answer the same questions for exercise 3 of section 11.2.

*8. Answer the same questions for exercise 4 of section 11.3.

9. Using official and derived rules of FQ, show that each of the following is a theorem of FQ.

   a. $((\forall y)Fy \,\&\, Gc) \rightarrow (\forall y)(Fy \,\&\, Gc)$

   b. $(\forall z)(Fz \,v\, Ga) \equiv ((\forall z)Fz \,v\, Ga)$

   c. $(\forall x)Gx \equiv (\forall z)Gz$

   d. $(\forall y)(Fy \,v\, (\forall x)Gxy) \rightarrow (\forall y)(\forall x)(Fx \,v\, Gyx)$

10. Using official and derived rules of FQ, prove that the following are metatheorems of FQ.

   *a. $((\forall x)A \,\&\, (\forall x)B) \rightarrow (\forall x)(A \,\&\, B)$

   b. $(\forall x)(A \,\&\, B) \rightarrow ((\forall x)A \,\&\, (\forall x)B)$

   *c. $(\forall x)(A \,v\, B) \rightarrow (A \,v\, (\forall x)B)$

   d. $(A \,v\, (\forall x)B) \rightarrow (\forall x)(A \,v\, B)$

   *e. $(A \rightarrow (\forall x)B) \rightarrow (\forall x)(A \rightarrow B)$

   f. $(\forall x)(A \rightarrow B) \rightarrow (A \rightarrow (\forall x)B)$

   *g. $(A \,\&\, (\forall x)B) \rightarrow (\forall x)(A \,\&\, B)$

11. Using official and derived rules of FQE, prove that the following are metatheorems of FQE.

   a. $(\forall x)(A \,\&\, B) \rightarrow (A \,\&\, (\forall x)B)$

   *b. $(\forall x)(A \rightarrow B) \rightarrow ((\forall x)A \rightarrow B)$

   c. $((\exists x)A \rightarrow B) \rightarrow (\exists x)(A \rightarrow B)$

12. Using official and derived rules of FQE, prove that the following are theorems of FQE.

   a. $(\forall y)(Fy \,\&\, Gc) \rightarrow ((\forall y)Fy \,\&\, Gc)$

   *b. $(\forall y)(\exists x)(Gx \,\&\, Hy) \rightarrow (\exists x)(\forall y)(Gx \,\&\, Hy)$

13. Using official and derived rules, prove the following are theorems of FQE. In your proof of the last theorem, you can use the previous two.

   *a. $(\exists x)(Gx \,v\, Fa) \rightarrow ((\exists x)Gx \,v\, Fa)$

   b. $(\forall y)((\exists x)Gx \,v\, Fy) \rightarrow ((\exists x)Gx \,v\, (\forall y)Fy)$

   *c. $(\forall y)(\exists x)(Gx \,v\, Hy) \rightarrow (\exists x)(\forall y)(Gx \,v\, Hy)$

14. Show that the rule of free universal quantifier elimination could be adopted as a derived rule in SQ.

15. With the intention of deciding whether the argument is valid, translate into Q each of the arguments in exercise 8 of section 12.2 (p. 388). For each of the translations decide whether the Q-conclusion can be derived from the Q-premises in FQ. For those that can, construct derivations in FQ.

12.4 RULES IN REVIEW

In this section, we restate the rules for identity and theorems of identity that belong to all three systems, SQ, FQ, and FQE. The system FQ includes all of the rules of SQ with the exception of the rule of universal quantifier elimination and the rule of existential quantifier introduction. The versions of those rules for free logic are restated together with theorems of FQ. The system FQE results from adding one rule to FQ. That rule is also restated with some theorems of FQE that are not theorems of FQ. To distinguish FQE from SQ, we also restate certain theorems of SQ that are not theorems of FQE.

Identity Rules and Theorems

The systems SQ, FQ, and FQE all include the official introduction and elimination rules for identity and the derived rules and theorems below.

Official Rules

Rule of Identity Introduction (id int)

$$h \qquad a = a \qquad\qquad \text{id int}$$

Rule of Identity Elimination (id elim)

$$
\begin{array}{ll}
h & A \\
i & a = b \\
j & A(a/b) \qquad\qquad \text{h, i, id elim}
\end{array}
$$

Derived Rules

Derived Rule of Identity Elimination (id elim)

$$
\begin{array}{ll}
h & A \\
i & a = b \\
j & A(b/a) \qquad\qquad \text{h, i, id elim (derived version)}
\end{array}
$$

Derived Rule of General Identity Elimination (gen id elim)

A sentence that results from replacing in the original sentence one or more occurrences of one side of an identity with its other side is a direct consequence of the identity and the original sentence.

Theorems

Theorems are stated through metatheorems. Any sentence having the form of a metatheorem is a theorem.

Theorem of Reflexivity of Identity (refl id)

$$(\forall x)(x = x)$$

Theorem of Symmetry of Identity (sym id)

$$(\forall x)(\forall y)(x = y \rightarrow y = x)$$

Theorem of Transitivity of Identity (trans id)

$$(\forall x)(\forall y)(\forall z)((x = y \ \& \ y = z) \rightarrow x = z)$$

Unnamed Theorem

$$(\forall x)(\forall y)(x = y \rightarrow (A(y/a) \equiv A(x/a)))$$

FQ Rules and Theorems

FQ includes all the official rules of SQ with the exception of the rule of universal quantifier elimination and the rule of existential quantifier introduction. Instead of those rules, FQ has the rule of free universal quantifier elimination and the rule of free existential quantifier introduction. These two rules are restated below. Although not all rules derivable in SQ are derivable in FQ, those that have been derived for SQ in the text are also derived rules for FQ.

Official Rules

Rule of Free Universal Quantifier Elimination (free u q elim)

$$
\begin{array}{cc|ll}
h & a & (\forall x)A & \\
\ \cdot & & \ \cdot & \\
i & & A(a/x) & \text{h, free u q elim}
\end{array}
$$

Rule of Free Existential Quantifier Introduction (free e q int)

$$
\begin{array}{ccll}
\text{h} & a & A(a/x) & \\
\cdot & & \cdot & \\
\text{i} & & (\exists x)A & \text{h, free e q int}
\end{array}
$$

Derived Rules

In addition to the rules and derived rules for identity, the system FQ includes the derived rules of Intelim and the rules derived for SQ in the text, namely, the introduction and elimination rules for negative universal quantifier and negative existential quantifier and De Morgan's rule for quantifiers.

Theorems

Theorems are stated through metatheorems. Any sentence having the form of a metatheorem is a theorem.

Theorems with Universal Quantifiers

$$((\forall x)A \,\&\, (\forall x)B) \equiv (\forall x)(A \,\&\, B)$$

$$((\forall x)A \rightarrow (\forall x)B) \equiv (\forall x)(A \rightarrow B)$$

$$(A \,\&\, (\forall x)B) \rightarrow (\forall x)(A \,\&\, B)$$

$$((\forall x)A \,\&\, B) \rightarrow (\forall x)(A \,\&\, B)$$

$$(A \rightarrow (\forall x)B) \equiv (\forall x)(A \rightarrow B)$$

$$((\forall x)A \,v\, (\forall x)B) \rightarrow (\forall x)(A \,v\, B)$$

$$(A \,v\, (\forall x)B) \equiv (\forall x)(A \,v\, B)$$

$$((\forall x)A \,v\, B) \equiv (\forall x)(A \,v\, B)$$

$$(\forall y)((\forall x)A \rightarrow A(y/x))$$

$$(\forall x)(\forall y)B \equiv (\forall y)(\forall x)B$$

Theorems with Existential Quantifiers

$$(\exists x)(A \,v\, B) \equiv ((\exists x)A \,v\, (\exists x)B)$$

$$(\exists x)(A \,\&\, B) \rightarrow ((\exists x)A \,\&\, (\exists x)B)$$

$$(\exists x)(A \,\&\, B) \equiv (A \,\&\, (\exists x)B)$$

$$(\exists x)(A \,\&\, B) \equiv ((\exists x)A \,\&\, B)$$

$$(\exists x)(A \rightarrow B) \rightarrow (A \rightarrow (\exists x)B)$$

$$(\exists x)(A \text{ v } B) \rightarrow (A \text{ v } (\exists x)B)$$

$$(\exists x)(A \text{ v } B) \rightarrow ((\exists x)A \text{ v } B)$$

$$(\exists x)(\exists y)A \equiv (\exists y)(\exists x)A$$

Theorems with Existential and Universal Quantifiers

$$((\exists x)A \rightarrow B) \equiv (\forall x)(A \rightarrow B)$$

$$(\exists x)(\forall y)A \rightarrow (\forall x)(\exists y)A$$

Theorems with Quantifiers and Identity

$$((\forall x)A \text{ \& } (\exists x)(x = a)) \rightarrow A(a/x)$$

$$(A(a/x) \text{ \& } (\exists x)(x = a)) \rightarrow (\exists x)A$$

FQE Rules and Theorems

The system FQE results from adding one official rule to FQ, the rule of existence assumption. Consequently, all theorems and derived rules of FQ are theorems and derived rules of FQE. But the rule of existence assumption is not derivable in FQ and neither the rule of universal quantifiers elimination nor the rule of existential quantifier introduction is derivable in FQE. Thus, there are theorems of FQE that are not theorems of FQ and theorems of SQ that are not theorems of FQE. So the system FQE is stronger than FQ but weaker than SQ.

Official and Derived Rules

In addition to the official and derived rules of FQ, the system FQE has the rule of existence assumption below.

Rule of Existence Assumption (ex a)

$$
\begin{array}{ll}
\text{h} & a \quad \cdot \\
\cdot & \quad \cdot \\
\text{i} & \quad B \\
\cdot & \quad \cdot \\
\text{j} \quad B & \qquad\qquad \text{h–i, ex a}
\end{array}
$$

Restriction: There is no occurrence of a in B.

LIST OF SYMBOLS

∴	symbol immediately preceding the conclusion of an argument; it is to be read 'therefore'.
$\hat{x}(...)$	designates an attribute or its extension. An attributive expression fills the dots.
$(\exists x)$	existential quantifier; it is to be read 'there is at least one individual x such that'.
$(\forall x)$	universal quantifier; it is to be read 'every individual x is such that'.
{...}	designates a class, set, or domain, when a general term fills the dots or when singular terms fill the dots and are separated by commas.
~	tilde (the negation sign); to be read 'it is not the case that'.
&	ampersand (the conjunction sign); to be read 'and'.
v	*vel* (the disjunction sign); to be read 'or'.
→	arrow (the conditional sign); to be read 'if . . . then'.
|	Sheffer's stroke (the alternative denial sign); to be read 'either it is not the case that . . . or it is not the case that'.
↓	dagger (the joint denial sign); to be read 'neither . . . nor'.
≡	triple bar (the biconditional sign); to be read 'if and only if'.

$\veebar$	*aut* (the exclusive disjunction sign); to be read 'either . . . or . . . but not both'.
=df	used for the purpose of introducing defined connectives; it is to be read 'is equal by definition'.
=	identity sign.
$A(a/x)$	designates the quasi-sentence that results from replacing every free occurrence of x in A with a, where x is a term variable, A is a quasi-sentence, and a is a singular term.
$A(t_1/t_2)$	designates the quasi-sentence that results from replacing every occurrence of a singular term or free occurrence of a term variable t_2 in a quasi-sentence A with a singular term or term variable t_1 that does not become bound in the resulting expression.
$\langle\ ,\ \rangle$	designates an ordered couple, when the comma separates two singular terms instead of spaces.
$\langle \ldots \rangle$	designates an ordered n-tuple, when n singular terms (where $n > 1$) fill the dots and are separated by commas.
$\neq$	nonidentity sign.
$:\,:$	appears in the statement of two-way rules to indicate that inference is allowed both ways.

GLOSSARY

CHAPTER 1

Proposition Something one can believe, know, and reason from and to. 3

Premises Propositions one starts reasoning with. 3

Conclusion In reasoning, the terminal proposition one reaches and affirms on the basis of premises. 3

Fact (truth) True proposition. 4

Error of fact (untruth) False proposition. 4

Declarative sentence A sentence customarily used to express a true or false proposition. 4

Verbalization (of a proposition) Linguistic expression of a proposition. 4

Argument (premise-conclusion argument) Sequence of propositions one of which is the conclusion and the others of which are premises. 5

Inductive reasoning Reasoning in which the reasoner considers the truth of the premises to make the conclusion only probable and not certain. 6

Deductive reasoning Reasoning in which the reasoner considers the truth of the premises to require the truth of the conclusion. 7

Valid argument Argument in which the truth of the premises requires the truth of the conclusion. 7

Error of deductive reasoning Reasoning from the premises to the conclusion of an invalid argument. 8

Sound argument A valid argument that has all true premises and a true conclusion; an argument that is free from errors of fact and errors of deductive reasoning. 8

Implication A relation that holds between the premises and conclusion of a valid argument. 9

Inference An act of moving from premises to a conclusion. If it turns out that the premises imply the conclusion, then the inference is correct. 9

Syntax of a language   The structure or grammar of a language considered independently of what specific meaning its expressions may have. In an artificial language, the syntax is defined according to structure without reference to any meaning the expressions might have. 12

Semantics of a language   The meaning of words and phrases of the language and conditions under which sentences of the language are true or false. 12

Truth value   Value that a sentence has according to the truth or falsehood of the proposition it expresses. A sentence has the truth value *true* if the proposition is true; it has the truth value *false* if the proposition is false. 12

Valid sentence   A sentence that does not have the semantic possibility of being false. 13

Semantic possibility   Possibility with respect to the truth values of sentences that is conditioned only by the constraints of the language itself. 13

Contradictory (self-contradictory) sentence   A sentence that does not have the semantic possibility of being true. 13

Logical content   The meaning that a sentence or argument has apart from the specific meaning of its nonlogical expressions. 13

Logical expressions   Nondescriptive expressions; they may occur in any book on any subject. Examples: 'and', 'or', 'if . . .then'. 15

Nonlogical expressions   Descriptive expressions that are used to refer to things or to say something about them and that do not contain logical expressions. 15

Incompatible sentences   Sentences for which the semantic possibility of being true together does not exist. 15

Equivalent sentences   Sentences for which the semantic possibility of having different truth values does not exist; these sentences are either true together or false together. 15

Fairy-tale method   Method for detecting invalidity in an argument by describing a possible situation where the premises of the argument are true but the conclusion is false. 20

Counterargument (counterexample) method   Method for detecting invalidity in an argument by constructing a new argument that is similar to the original argument in having the logical content of the original argument but dissimilar in having true premises and a false conclusion. The counterargument shows that the original argument is not valid in virtue of its logical content. 21

Plural substantive general term   An expression that takes a plural verb, can serve as a subject in a sentence, and is true of any one of a class of things. Referred to as a 'general term' for short. 22

CHAPTER 2

Logical connectives   Logical expressions that are used to form sentences from other sentences. 30

Negation   Sentence formed from a simpler sentence that is true if and only if the simpler sentence is false. The connective 'it is not the case that' is often used to form negations. 30

Conjunction   Sentence formed from two simpler sentences that is true if and only if the two simpler sentences are both true. The connectives 'and' and 'but' are often used to form conjunctions. 30

Telescoped version of a sentence A sentence formed from a longer sentence by using a connective to join two (or more) subjects of the longer sentence with a common predicate or to join two (or more) predicates of the longer sentence with a common subject. 31

Conjuncts Two sentences of which a conjunction is composed. 31

Disjunction Sentence formed from two simpler sentences that is true if and only if at least one of the two simpler sentences is true. The connective 'or' is often used to form disjunctions. 31

Disjuncts Two sentences of which a disjunction is composed. 32

Conditional Sentence formed from two simpler sentences using the connectives 'if' and 'only if'. 32

Antecedent One of the two sentences connected to form a conditional; the antecedent follows 'if' when a conditional is formed using 'if'. 32

Consequent One of the two sentences connected to form a conditional; the consequent follows 'only if' when a conditional is formed using 'only if'. 32

Material conditional Conditional that is false if and only if its antecedent is true and its consequent is false. 33

Truth conditions of a sentence Conditions under which the sentence is or would be true. 33

A-type sentence A sentence of the form 'All F are G', where 'F' and 'G' are placeholders for general terms. 35

E-type sentence A sentence of the form 'No F are G', where 'F' and 'G' are placeholders for general terms. 36

I-type sentence A sentence of the form 'Some F are G', where 'F' and 'G' are placeholders for general terms. 36

O-type sentence A sentence of the form 'Some F are not G', where 'F' and 'G' are placeholders for general terms. 36

Logical form A structural representation of logical content; a sentence exemplifies a logical form if and only if the form displays logical content that is contained in the proposition the sentence expresses. 37

Sentence placeholders Letters that stand for sentences and are replaceable only with sentences. These letters are 'A', 'B', 'C', 'D', and 'E'. 37

General term placeholders The letters 'F', 'G', 'H', 'I', and 'J', which stand for and are replaceable only with general terms. 38

Idiomatic variant of a linguistic expression A linguistic expression that is interchangeable with another linguistic expression without a change in meaning. 38

Principal logical form of a sentence A sentence exemplifies (or has) a form if and only if the sentence or an idiomatic variant results from making replacements in the form, the same replacement for the same placeholder throughout. A form is the principal logical form if and only if (i) the replacements for different placeholders are different and (ii) none of the replacements contains a logical expression explicitly or implicitly. 39

Basic forms Certain typical sentence forms for negations, conjunctions, disjunctions, and conditionals, along with the sentence forms for A-type, E-type, I-type, and O-type sentences. 40

Complex forms Sentence forms constructed from basic forms by replacing one or more sentence placeholders with basic form. 41

Logically valid argument An argument that is valid in virtue of its logical content. 43

Disjunctive syllogism   Valid argument with two premises in which one premise is a disjunction, the other premise is the negation of one disjunct of that disjunction, and the other disjunct is the conclusion of the argument. 44

Modus ponens   Valid argument with two premises in which one premise is a conditional, the other premise is the antecedent of that conditional, and its consequent is the conclusion of the argument. 44

Chain argument   Valid argument composed of three A-type sentences so related that (i) the subject and predicate terms of the conclusion are, respectively, the subject term of the first premise and the predicate term of the second and (ii) the predicate term of the first premise is the subject term of the second. 44

Fallacy of affirming the consequent   Invalid argument with two premises in which one premise is a conditional, the other premise is the consequent of that conditional, and its antecedent is the conclusion of the argument. 45

CHAPTER 3

Individual   Thing or entity. 55

Designatory sentence   Sentence that designates an individual and says that a certain attribute is true of the individual. 56

Attribute   Property that an individual may or may not have. 56

Existential sentence   Sentence that says that a certain attribute is true of at least one from a group of individuals. 56

Universal sentence   Sentence that says that a certain attribute is true of every one from a group of individuals. 56

Singular term   Linguistic expression used to designate an individual. 57

Concrete individuals   Individuals (such as physical objects and historical events) that have spatial and temporal locations. 57

Abstract individuals   Individuals (such as numbers and relations) that have no spatial or temporal locations. 57

Applies   An attribute applies to an individual when the attribute is true of that individual or, in other words, the individual has the attribute. 58

Assignment of an attribute (by a sentence)   A sentence assigns an attribute to an individual when the sentence says that the attribute is true of the individual. 58

Attributive expression   Expression that is formed from a designatory sentence by (i) selecting one or more singular terms that occur in that sentence and designate one and the same individual and (ii) replacing each of those singular terms with 'x'. 58

Extension of an attribute   Class of individuals that have the attribute. 59

Empty (null) class   Class that has no members. 59

Abstract   Expression which results from replacing 'Fx' in '$\hat{x}(Fx)$' with an attributive expression, regardless of how often 'x' occurs in that expression. 59

Complement of an attribute   Attribute that applies to just those individuals (if any) that the attribute of which it is a complement does not apply to. 60

Union of two attributes   Attribute that applies to just those individuals (if any) that have either attribute. 61

Intersection of two attributes   Attribute that applies to just those individuals (if any) that have each of the two attributes. 61

Domain (or universe) of discourse   Class of individuals talked about. 64

Designatory use of 'it' 'It' used in place of a singular term to designate an individual and assign a certain attribute to that individual. 65

Existential use of 'it' 'It' used in an existential sentence to say that a certain attribute applies to at least one individual in the domain. 65

Universal use of 'it' 'It' used in an universal sentence to say that a certain attribute is true of every individual in the domain. 65

Existential quantifier The phrase 'there is at least one individual x such that'; this is abbreviated '$(\exists x)$'. 66

Universal quantifier The phrase 'every individual x is such that'; abbreviated '$(\forall x)$'. 67

Overlapping attributes Two attributes for which there exists at least one individual possessing both attributes. 72

Disjoint attributes Two attributes that do not overlap. 73

Extension of an attribute outside another An attribute F extends outside an attribute G if and only if some individual that has the attribute F does not have the attribute G. 73

Inclusion of an attribute in another An attribute F is included in an attribute G if and only if every individual that has attribute F also has attribute G. 73

CHAPTER 4

Language C Language of the logic of connectives. 88

C-sentence Expression that qualifies as a sentence in language C. 88

Sentence letters Letters 'P', 'Q', 'R', 'P_1', 'Q_1', 'R_1'. . . . Nonlogical symbols of language C that express propositions. 88

Translation scheme Collection of one or more assignments of English sentences to sentence letters of language C in which the assigned sentence is the translation of the sentence letter and the sentence letter is the translation of the assigned sentence. 88

Sentence connective Expression that takes one or more sentences to form another sentence. 88

Tilde Negation sign '~'. 88

Ampersand Conjunction sign '&'. 88

Vel Disjunction sign 'v'. 88

Arrow Material conditional sign '$\rightarrow$'. 88

Form of a sentence A sentence has *a* form if and only if the sentence results from replacing placeholders in that form with sentences. A form is *the* form of a sentence if and only if that form differs from the sentence only in having placeholders where the sentence has sentence letters. 91

Dominant connective (of a sentence) An occurrence of a connective in a sentence such that within that sentence, there is no shorter sentence in which the occurrence appears. The connective is then said to *dominate* the sentence. 92

Negation A sentence with a tilde as its dominant connective. 92

Conjunction A sentence with an ampersand as its dominant connective. 92

Disjunction A sentence with a *vel* as its dominant connective. 92

Conditional A sentence with an arrow as its dominant connective. 92

Component of a sentence The sentence itself and every shorter sentence appearing in it. 92

Immediate components (of a sentence) Components that the dominant connective of the sentence takes to form the sentence. 93

Conjuncts The immediate components of a conjunction. 93

Disjuncts The immediate components of a disjunction. 94

Antecedent The left immediate component of a conditional. 94

Consequent The right immediate component of a conditional. 94

Atomic component (of a sentence) Component which is a sentence letter. 94

Scope (of a connective) The sentence that a connective dominates. 94

Truth-functional connective Dominant connective of a sentence the truth value of which is determined solely by (i) the meaning of the connective and (ii) the truth values of the immediate components of the sentence, regardless of what those truth values might be. 98

Valuation rules Rules that state the truth conditions of sentences dominated by a tilde, ampersand, *vel*, or arrow. 99

Truth table Codification of a valuation rule in the form of a table that can be used in a mechanical fashion to determine truth values of sentences. 99

Complex forms Forms with more than one connective. 103

Basic forms Forms with one connective. They are $\sim\!A$, $(A \;\&\; B)$, $(A \lor B)$, and $(A \to B)$. 103

Alternative denial A sentence with a Sheffer's stroke as its dominant connective. 106

Joint denial A sentence with a dagger as its dominant connective. 107

Biconditional A sentence with a triple bar as its dominant connective. 108

Exclusive disjunction A sentence with an *aut* as its dominant connective. 109

Defined connective Sentence connective that does not belong to the language proper but is introduced as a convenient device to abbreviate sentences containing official connectives. 109

Official connective Sentence connective that belongs to the language and is not introduced by a definition. 109

Sheffer's stroke The alternative denial sign ' $|$ '. 109

Dagger The joint denial sign ' $\downarrow$ '. 109

Triple bar The biconditional sign ' $\equiv$ '. 109

Aut The exclusive disjunction sign ' $\veebar$ '. 109

C-valid sentence Sentence that is true upon every row of its truth table. 113

C-contradictory sentence Sentence that is false upon every row of its truth table. 113

C-equivalent sentences Sentences for which, in a joint truth table, there is no row upon which the sentences differ from one another in truth value. 115

C-valid argument Argument for which, in a joint truth table, every row upon which all the premises are true is one upon which the conclusion is also true. 117

C-incompatible sentences Sentences for which, in a joint truth table, there is no row upon which all the sentences in question are true. 119

CHAPTER 5

Weaker sentence A sentence that is implied by a given other sentence but does not imply it. 127

Stronger sentence Of any two sentences, the first is stronger than the second if and only if the second is weaker than the first. 128

Subjunctive conditional Conditional that makes a claim about what would be the case if something else were the case. 134

Counterfactual Subjunctive conditional with an antecedent that claims something contrary to what was, is, or will be the case. 134

Enthymeme An argument that has one or more unstated premises or an unstated conclusion. 145

CHAPTER 6

Language Q Language of the logic quantifiers. 153

Terms Singular terms and term variables. 155

Singular terms $a, b, c, a_1, b_1, c_1, \ldots$, etc. These are used to translate English singular terms. 155

Term variables $x, y, z, x_1, y_1, z_1, \ldots$, etc. 156

Predicate letters Symbols in Q used to translate English phrases, such as '_ runs' and '_ likes _'. 156

One-place predicate letters $F\_, G\_, H\_, F_1\_, G_1\_, H_1\_, \ldots$, etc. 156

n-place predicate letters (where $n > 1$) $F^2\_ \_, G^2\_ \_, H^2\_ \_, \ldots, F^n\_ \cdots \_,$ $G^n\_ \cdots \_, H^n\_ \cdots \_, \ldots$. If $n = 2$, the superscript is '2' and the predicate letter is two-place; if $n = 3$, the superscript is '3' and the predicate letter is three-place; and so on. 156

Quasi-sentence Expression in the language Q that is a sentence if it contains no free occurrence of a term variable, no vacuous quantifiers, and no overlapping quantifiers in the same variable. 156

Atom An n-place predicate letter with n singular terms in its n blank places. 157

Quantifier Expression that is formed by placing one of the quantifier symbols, $\exists$ or $\forall$, before a term variable and enclosing the result in parentheses. 157

Existential quantifier A quantifier that contains the symbol $\exists$. 157

Universal quantifier A quantifier that contains the symbol $\forall$. 157

Quantifier in the variable A quantifier is a quantifier in the variable that occurs in it. For example, $(\forall x)$ is a quantifier in the variable x. 157

Q-sentence Expression that qualifies as a sentence in the language Q. Q-sentences are a subclass of the quasi-sentences. 159

Logical operators Sentence connectives and quantifiers. 159

Dominant operator An occurrence of an operator in a quasi-sentence such that within that quasi-sentence, there is no shorter quasi-sentence in which the occurrence appears. The occurrence is then said to *dominate* the sentence. 159

Scope (of an occurrence of an operator) Quasi-sentence that an occurrence of an operator dominates. 159

Overlapping quantifiers Quantifiers one of which occurs within the scope of another. 160

Overlapping quantifiers in the same variable Overlapping quantifiers each of which contains an occurrence of the same variable. 160

Bound occurrence of a term variable An occurrence of a term variable is bound if it is within the scope of a quantifier in that variable. 160

Free occurrence of a term variable   An occurrence of a term variable which is not bound. 160

Vacuous quantifier   Quantifier in a variable that occurs in the quantifier and nowhere else in the scope of the quantifier. 161

Existentially quantified sentence (existential sentence)   A sentence with an existential quantifier as its dominant operator. 161

Universally quantified sentence (universal sentence)   A sentence with a universal quantifier as its dominant operator. 162

Instance (of a quantified sentence)   An expression formed from a quantified sentence by dropping the dominant operator, which is either an existential or universal quantifier, and replacing every occurrence of the variable that becomes free with the same singular term throughout. 162

Instantial term   For a given instance of a quantified sentence, the singular term that replaces the variable that becomes free after dropping the dominant operator. 162

Generating instance   An instance of a quantified sentence that has as its instantial term a singular term that does not appear in the quantified sentence. 169

Identity sentences   Sentences formed from placing the identity sign between two singular terms and enclosing the result in parentheses. 173

Natural translation   Translation that uses words and phrases from a natural language to specify the individuals that singular terms designate, the attributes or relations that predicate letters express, and the propositions that sentence letters express. 173

Ordered couple   Pair of individuals that are in order, one first and the other second. An ordered couple of individuals is designated by placing the names of the two individuals in their proper order in angular parentheses. 174

Ordered n-tuple n-individuals that are in order, one first, another second, and so on. An ordered n-tuple of individuals is designated by placing the names of the individuals in their proper order in angular parentheses. 174

Extensional translation   Translation that assigns to a one-place predicate letter a class of individuals, to an n-place predicate letter a class of n-tuples, and to a sentence letter a truth value. 178

Abstract translation   Translation that uses singular terms themselves to specify the individuals in a domain and the extensional method to translate predicate letters and sentence letters. 179

Standard quantification theory (standard logic)   Quantification theory that makes the following existential assumptions: (i) the domain is nonempty; (ii) every singular term designates exactly one individual in the domain. The theory does not assume that every individual in the domain is designated by at least one singular term. 180

Q-valid sentence   A sentence such that there is no translation with respect to any domain on which the sentence is false. 184

Q-contradictory sentence   A sentence such that there is no translation with respect to any domain on which the sentence is true. 184

Q-valid argument   An argument for which there is no translation with respect to any domain on which all the premises are true and the conclusion is false. 185

Q-equivalent sentences   Sentences for which there is no translation with respect to any domain on which those sentences have different truth values. 185

Q-incompatible sentences   Sentences for which there is no translation with respect to any domain on which all of them are true. 185

Model domain A domain that is specified by placing a finite number of singular terms in braces. The members of the domain are not otherwise identified. All that is known about the domain is its minimum and maximum size. 186

One-member domain A model domain that contains only one individual. 186

Two-member domain A model domain that contains at least one and no more than two individuals. 186

Expansion (of a sentence relative to an n-member domain) A sentence that contains no quantifiers and is equivalent to the original sentence relative to the domain in question. 186

Decision procedure Mechanical method that gives a definite answer to a certain question in a finite number of steps. 189

Monadic predicate logic What remains of the Q-language after the identity sign and *n*-place predicate letters are removed. 189

CHAPTER 7

Universal claim Claim made by a sentence that states that every individual has a certain attribute. 197

Existential claim Claim made by a sentence that states that there is at least one individual which has a certain attribute. 197

Definite description An English expression of the form 'the so-and-so'. 201

CHAPTER 8

Derivation (deduction or proof) Sequence of sentences, some of which are hypotheses and the others of which are each sanctioned by application of a rule of inference. 220

Rules of inference Rules that allow one to take steps from the hypotheses to the conclusion of a derivation. 220

Conclusion (of a derivation) Last sentence of a derivation. 220

One-way rule Inference rule that applies to entire steps only and works in one direction only. 221

Two-way rule Inference rule that applies to components of steps as well as to entire steps and works in both directions. 221

One-premise rule Rule of inference that applies to one and only one preceding step in a derivation. 225

Two-premise rule Rule of inference that applies to two and only two preceding steps in a derivation. 225

Truth-preserving (rule of inference) Rule for which it is not possible for the step or steps to which you apply the rule to be true and the result of the application to be false. 231

Direct method Method of demonstrating an argument's validity by deriving the conclusion from the premises. 232

Indirect method Method of demonstrating an argument's validity by deriving a sentence of the form $(A \mathbin{\&} {\sim}A)$ from the premises together with the negation of the conclusion. 232

Conditional proof method Method of demonstrating the validity of an argument that concludes with a conditional by deriving the consequent of the conditional from the premises together with the antecedent of the conditional. 232

***Reductio ad absurdum* method** Method of showing the validity of a sentence by deriving a sentence of the form (A & ~A) from the negation of the sentence in question. 234

Instantiation rule Rule of inference that allows you to move from a universal or existential sentence to one of its instances. 239

Generalization rule Rule of inference that allows you to move to a universal or existential sentence from one of its instances. 239

CHAPTER 9

Formal system System consisting of an artificial language, rules governing the steps taken in deriving conclusions from premises, and possibly various axioms. Such systems are designed to capture the essential truths of a specific subject matter. 259

Axiom Statement accepted without proof. 260

Formal language Language of a formal system. 260

Derivation A column of items bordered on the left by a vertical line extending the length of the column. Each item on the column is either (i) a sentence that is a hypothesis, (ii) an axiom, (iii) a direct consequence of preceding items in the *same* column, (iv) a reiteration of a sentence that precedes the column, or (v) a subderivation. To the right of each sentence item is written its justification for appearing in the derivation: (i) 'hyp' as an abbreviation for 'hypothesis' if it is a hypothesis; (ii) what axiom it is if it is an axiom; (iii) reference to the numbers of the preceding items and the rule according to which it is a direct consequence of those items if it is a direct consequence, and (iv) reference to the number of the item that precedes the column and the rule of reiteration if it is a reiteration. 260

Rule of direct consequence Rule governing steps taken in a derivation. 260

Theorem The last item in a derivation with no hypotheses. 260

Sound system A system that does not allow derivation of a false conclusion from true premises. 260

Truth-preserving rule A rule of direct consequence by which there is no way to derive a false conclusion from true premises if the rule is used correctly. 261

Complete system Systems in which, if an argument is valid, then it is also derivable (that is, its conclusion is derivable from its premises). 261

Inconsistent system A system that contains both a sentence and its negation among the theorems of the system. 261

Official rules (of a system) Rules of direct consequence on the basis of which the system is constructed and which are introduced explicitly for that purpose. 261

Equivalent systems Systems for which all of the derivable arguments in one system are derivable in the other and vice versa. 261

Stronger system For a given system Y, a system X such that there is no argument derivable in Y that is not derivable in X, but there are arguments that are derivable in X that are not derivable in Y. 261

Weaker system For a given system Y, a system X such that Y is stronger than X. 261

Subordinate derivation (subderivation) A derivation that is an item of another derivation. Such a derivation is said to be subordinate to the derivation in which it is an item and also to the derivation in which it is an item of an item, and so on. 266

Main derivation A derivation that is not a subderivation. 267

Preceding item (in a derivation) An item precedes another if and only if it is listed anywhere above the other in the very same column. 267

Introduction rule A rule of direct consequence that provides a strategy for deriving a sentence *of* the type after which the rule is named. 269

Elimination rule A rule of direct consequence that provides a strategy for deriving a sentence *from* the type after which the rule is named. 269

Directly subordinate derivation A derivation is directly subordinate to and only to the derivation in which it is itself an item. 274

Natural deduction system A system that has no axioms and whose official rules of direct consequence resemble natural patterns of reasoning. 275

Intelim The system developed in this text consisting of the C-language, the rule of reiteration, the introduction and elimination rules for conjunction, disjunction, and conditional, and the rule of indirect proof. 275

Derived rule A rule that does not belong to the set of official rules of the system but provides a shortcut method for arriving at a result when to reach that same result would require application of a combination of official rules. 276

CHAPTER 10

Denial A sentence is the denial of another if and only if it is either the negation of the other or the other is a negation of it. 315

Intuitionistic logic Logic that does not hold that every sentence of the form $(A \vee {\sim}A)$ is valid and does not have every sentence of that form as theorem. In intuitionistic logic, not every sentence is assumed to be either true or false. 317

CHAPTER 11

Intelim-SQ System that has as its formal language Q and has, in addition to the rules of direct consequence of Intelim, introduction and elimination rules for both quantifiers. The system is a standard quantificational logic; 'SQ' is short for 'Standard Quantification'. 335

Metaderivation A metaderivaton is expressed using metavariables. It provides a general model for the construction of derivations of that form. 337

Prefixed derivation (a derivation prefixed with a singular term) A derivation in which the singular term appears to the left and near the top of the vertical line, bordering the column of items of the derivation. A term prefixed to a derivation is not permitted to occur in any sentence reiterated in the derivation. 337

Converse (of a derivation) A derivation with exactly one hypothesis is a converse of another with exactly one hypothesis if the hypothesis of the first derivation is the last item of the second and the last item of the first derivation is the hypothesis of the second. The converse of a conditional is a conditional with the antecedent and consequent of the original conditional interchanged. 340

Metatheorem A metatheorem is expressed using metavariables. Every sentence having the form of a metatheorem is a theorem. 349

CHAPTER 12

Free logic Logic that does not presuppose that every singular term designates a member of the domain. 371

Binary relation Relation that holds or fails to hold between two individuals. 371–372

Graph of a relation A graph of a relation in a domain consists of the domain with its individuals so arranged that there is an arrow from one individual to a second (possibly the same) if and only if the first bears the relation to the second. 372

Loop A double arrow from an individual to itself. A loop represents a relation's holding between an individual and itself. 373

Broken journey There is a broken journey from one individual to a second via a third individual when there is an arrow from the first individual to the third and an arrow from the third to the second. 373

Shortcut A broken journey from one individual to a second via a third has a shortcut when there is also an arrow directly from the first to the second individual. 374

Reflexive relation A relation such that every individual bears the relation to itself. 374

Irreflexive relation A relation such that no individual bears the relation to itself. 374

Nonreflexive relation A relation that is neither reflexive nor irreflexive. 374

Symmetrical relation A relation such that, for any two things, the first bears the relation to the second only if the second does bears it to the first. 376

Asymmetrical relation A relation such that, for any two things, the first bears the relation to the second only if the second does not bear it to the first. 376

Nonsymmetrical relation A relation that is neither symmetrical nor asymmetrical. 376

Transitive relation A relation such that, for any three things, the first bears the relation to the second and the second bears the relation to the third only if the first bears the relation to the third. 378

Intransitive relation A relation such that, for any three things, the first bears the relation to the second and the second bears the relation to the third only if the first does not bear the relation to the third. 378

Nontransitive relation A relation that is neither transitive nor intransitive. 378

Equivalence relation A relation that is reflexive, symmetrical, and transitive. 380

Free quantification theory Quantification theory that does not assume that every singular term designates an individual in the domain. 389

Intelim-FQ Free-logic system that results from weakening two of the rules of direct consequence of Intelim-SQ, namely, the rule of universal quantifier elimination and the rule of existential quantifier introduction. 389

Intelim-FQE Free-logic system that results from adding to Intelim-FQ a rule that is truth-preserving only if the domain is nonempty. That rule is the rule of existence assumption. 389

Universally free system of logic A free-logic system that does not assume that the domain is nonempty. 398

SOLUTIONS TO SELECTED EXERCISES

CHAPTER 1

SECTION 1.1

2. No. A verbalized proposition is a proposition expressed by a sentence.

4. No. To be an argument, a collection of propositions must meet the following requirement: one of the propositions must be a conclusion and the rest premises.

5. In a given situation two individuals might use the same propositions, but verbalize them in different languages. Thus a problem may be solved the same way even though the solution is verbalized in different languages.

7. Expressions to indicate premises: since, in reference to, based upon, assuming, from, considering.

   Expressions to indicate conclusion: thus, obviously, then, that is why, it implies that.

10. Given only the premises and the conclusion, one cannot always determine what kind of support the reasoner considers the premises give the conclusion. If the conclusion follows necessarily from the premises, one can be sure that the reasoning is deductive; if the conclusion is only probable given the premises, the reasoning is obviously inductive.

12. The answer would more likely be "yes" if the reasoning were deductive. In reasoning deductively, one considers one's conclusion certain, not just probable, given that the premises are true.

14. This definition is too narrow: it limits logic to the study of deductive reasoning but ignores the fact that logic is also concerned with inductive reasoning. Besides that, "truth" and "validity" cannot be treated as synonyms: propositions and sentences are true or false while arguments are valid or invalid. Logic is concerned with the validity of arguments, not with the truth or falsity of propositions. However, the strong point of this definition is that logic is identified with the study of reasoning.

16. An implication is a relationship between propositions. Although an individual may verbalize a proposition, it is the proposition which implies other propositions.

18. An individual can commit an error of fact (use false premises or arrive at a false conclusion from false premises) while reasoning from the premises to the conclusion of a valid argument. An individual can also commit an error of reasoning (that is, use an argument that is not valid) while reasoning from true premises to a true conclusion.

19. In Argument A, the first premise states that Timothy has a certain attribute, namely, the one of being a poet; the second premise ascribes another attribute, the one of being poor, to all poets. So under the circumstances described by the premises, there is no way for Timothy to be a poet without being poor.

    Argument B has only one premise, which states that there exists one person loved by everyone. Given the truth of the premise, the conclusion is obvious: everyone loves at least someone. For the conclusion to be false, there would have to be at least one individual who loves no one, but in this case the premise of the argument would have to be false.

    Arguments C and D are not valid because the conclusion of each could be false even if the premises are true. The second premise of Argument

C says only that some poets happen to be poor and, of course, there is no guarantee that Timothy is one of those poor creatures.

With respect to Argument D, everyone could love at least someone without everyone's loving the same person. Therefore, reasoning deductively from the premises to the conclusions of Argument D would be incorrect.

SECTION 1.2

1. Yes, it is semantically possible for both sentences to be true. But February 19, 1999, may fall on a Monday and not be the day George Washington's birthday is observed; in other words, the first sentence may be true while the second is false. The current convention of the birthday being observed on the third Monday of February may not be in use in 1999. And if the first sentence is false, then February 19, 1999, does not fall on a Monday. Therefore, the second sentence must be false when the first is false. Finally, in cases in which February 19, 1999, does not fall on a Monday, both sentences are false.

2. Sentences a, d, and e are valid; b, c, and f are not.

5. Yes. If a sentence is not contradictory, then it is semantically possible for it to be true; so, there can be a situation in which a valid sentence and a noncontradictory one are both true. For example,

    (1) Charlie is either a student or not a student

    is a valid sentence.

    (2) Charlie loves ice cream

    is a noncontradictory sentence.

    If Charlie loves ice cream, then we have a situation where both sentences are true, since (1) is true anyway.

7. No. It is not possible for a self-contradictory sentence to be true. Therefore, it cannot be true together with any other sentence.

8. Yes, self-contradictory sentences are equivalent but incompatible. They are equivalent because every such sentence must be false, so they can never have different truth values. They are incompatible because they can never be true together. for example, the two sentences that follow are equivalent but not compatible:

    (1) Today is and is not Monday.

    (2) This square is round.

10. a. false   e. true   i. true
     b. true   f. true   j. true
     c. false   g. false
     d. true   h. false

13. The first premise of each argument uses 'if . . . then'. Where 'Shanghai has a larger population than Paris' occurs in one, 'Bugs Bunny has floppy ears' occurs in the other. Similarly, where 'Shanghai has a larger population than London' occurs in one, 'Bugs Bunny is an elephant' occurs in the other.

15. Assume that all chimpanzees eat bananas, but none eat oranges (in this case the first premise is true but the conclusion is false), and that giraffes eat both bananas and oranges (making the second premise true).

SECTION 1.3

1. d. No. The logical expressions and their placement is not the same.

    f. No. The premises of argument ii are all false.

2. a. Suppose that all physics majors do eat collard greens as well as okra, and there are some chemistry majors who eat collard greens but cannot stand okra.

    c. Suppose that 'I' in this case refers to a Martian who is mortal.

    e. Suppose that the premises are both true and that in addition, some football players are history majors and friends of Sarah.

3. a.   (1) All U.S. presidents are human beings.
         (2) All U.S. presidents are Americans.
       ∴ (3) All human beings are Americans.

    b.   (1) Shakespeare's Hamlet is a commoner or unhappy.
       ∴ (2) Shakespeare's Hamlet is a commoner.

    c.   (1) If William Faulkner is a movie star, then he is famous.
         (2) William Faulkner is famous.
       ∴ (3) William Faulkner is a movie star.

    d.   (1) All deer are animals.
         (2) Some animals are lions.
       ∴ (3) Some lions are deer.

e. (1) No cats are gamblers.
    (2) No animals are gamblers.
∴ (3) No cats are animals.

4. b. invalid

    d. invalid

    f. invalid

    h. valid

    j. valid (but not simply because of its logical content)

CHAPTER 2

SECTION 2.1

2. a and b are completed in the text as examples.

    d. (i) A and B A: All grapefruit are edible.
                                    B: Some grapefruit do not have seeds.

        (ii) All F are G and some F are not H F: Grapefruit
                                                           G: Edible things
                                                           H: Seeded things

    f. (i) If A then B

        A: Caesar and Brutus win and Cleopatra comes in second.
        B: Marcus Antonius will have a banana split if there are bananas
             in the Forum.

      • (ii) If (A and B) then C

        A: Caesar and Brutus win.
        B: Cleopatra comes in second.
        C: Marcus Antonius will have a banana split if there are bananas
             in the Forum.

        (iii) If ((A and B) and C) then (D if E)

        A: Caesar wins.
        B: Brutus wins.
        C: Cleopatra comes in second.
        D: Marcus Antonius will have a banana split.
        E: There are bananas in the Forum.

(iv) If ((*A* and *B*) and *C*) then (*D* if some *F* are *G*)

    A: Caesar wins.
    B: Brutus wins.
    C: Cleopatra comes in second.
    D: Marcus Antonius will have a banana split.
    F: bananas
    G: things in the Forum

4. b. *A* and *B*

    A: Johann Strauss is Austrian.
    B: Johann Strauss is a composer.

  c. Either *A* or *B*

    A: Marcus Antonius will speak to Cleopatra.
    B: Julius Caesar will speak to Cleopatra.

  e. Some *F* are not *G*

    F: men
    G: tennis players

  g. No *F* are *G*

    F: camels
    G: things with humps

  i. *A* if not *B*

    A: Jack will pass.
    B: Jack will fail.

  j. *A* but some *F* are not *G*

    A: This apple is red.
    F: apples
    G: red things

5. Antecedent of 2c: The United States is not at war.
    Consequent of 2c: The United States will prosper.

    Antecedent of 2e: Caesar and Brutus win.
    Consequent of 2e: Cleopatra will not win.

    Antecedent of 2f: Caesar and Brutus win and Cleopatra comes in second.
    Consequent of 2f: Marcus Antonius will have a banana split if there are bananas in the Forum.

    Antecedent of 4i: Jack does not fail.
    Consequent of 4i: Jack will pass.

8. A-Type: 4f
    I-Type: 2b
    E-Type: 4g
    O-Type: 4e

9. a. Conditional with same antecedent and consequent.

    c. Negation of a disjunction.

    d. Disjunction with a negation as its left disjunct.

    h. Conditional with an O-type sentence as an antecedent and an I-type sentence as a consequent. The I-type and O-type sentences have the same general terms in the same order.

    i. Conjunction of an A-type and an E-type sentence in that order; the second general term in the A-type is the same as the first general term in the E-type sentence.

10. a. If I like to write, then I like to read.

    b. Julius Caesar did not write *Hamlet*.

    c. It is not the case that either Jim got the job or Cindy got the job.

    d. I will not give up this chance or I will lose my money.

    e. It is not the case that George Washington lived in the twentieth century and wrote science fiction.

    f. Not all animals are meat eaters.

    g. Some actors are movie stars and some are not.

    h. If some magicians are not comedians, then some magicians are comedians.

    i. All chemists are scientists, but no scientists are alchemists.

12. Valid: Today is not tomorrow and tomorrow is not today.

    Contradictory: Yesterday in London it was raining cats and dogs and there was no precipitation.

    Neither valid nor contradictory: Tom Sawyer was thirsty and hungry.

SECTION 2.2

1. b. Translation scheme for first form:
        A: Harvey is annoyed.
        B: Jack is annoyed.
        C: Jack is not annoyed.

Translation scheme for second form:
A: Harvey is annoyed.
B: Jack is annoyed.

d. Translation scheme for first form:
A: All piano players are European.
B: No piano players are Chinese.

Translation scheme for second form:
F: piano players
G: Europeans
H: Chinese

2. Principal logical form of argument in 1a:
  (1) *A* or *B*
∴ (2) *A*

Principal logical form of argument in 1b:
  (1) *A* if *B*
  (2) Not *B*
∴ (3) Not *A*

Principal logical form of argument in 1c:
  (1) No *F* are *G*
  (2) Some *G* are *H* and some *G* are not *H*
∴ (3) No *F* are *H*

Principal logical form of argument in 1d:
  (1) If all *F* are *G* then no *F* are *H*
  (2) All *F* are *G*
∴ (3) No *F* are *H*

4. a. (1) All *F* are *G*   *F*: my sisters-in-law
     (2) All *F* are *H*   *G*: New Englanders
   ∴ (3) All *G* are *H*   *H*: descendants of Paul Revere

   c. (1) If *A* then *B*   *A*: I am a dolphin.
      (2) *A*   *B*: I am a cetacean.
    ∴ (3) *B*

   e. (1) *A* only if *B*   *A*: Harry will come.
      (2) *A* or *C*   *B*: John will come.
      (3) Not *B*   *C*: Peter will come.
    ∴ (4) *C*

   g. (1) If not *A* then *B*   *A*: Harvey is old enough to vote.
      (2) *C* if and only if not *B*   *B*: Harvey is under 21.
    ∴ (3) *C* only if *A*   *C*: Harvey can drink legally.

i.   (1)   Some *F* are not *G*   *F*: apple
     ∴ (2)   Some *G* are not *F*   *G*: yellow things

k.   (1)   All *F* are *G*   *F*: canines
     ∴ (2)   All *G* are *F*   *G*: pets

m.   (1)   Some *F* are not *G*   *F*: apples
     ∴ (2)   Not all *F* are *G*   *G*: red things

o.   (1)   Some *F* are *G*   *F*: apples
     ∴ (2)   It is not the case that no *F* are *G*   *G*: red things

5.   The only arguments in exercise 4 that are invalid are: 4a, 4b, 4f, 4i, 4k. The remainder are valid. A fairy tale or counterargument for each of the invalid arguments appears below.

Counterargument for 4a:
     (1) All men are animals.
     (2) All men are mammals.
   ∴ (3) All animals are mammals.

Counterargument for 4b:
     (1) All oranges are fruits or all oranges are vegetables.
   ∴ (2) All oranges are vegetables.

Fairy tale for 4f:
     Imagine that to vote you must be 21 or over but to drink you must be 20 or over and Harvey is 20. In this case, the premises are true and the conclusion is false.

Counterargument for 4i:
     (1) Some females are not mothers.
   ∴ (2) Some mothers are not females.

Counterargument for 4k:
     (1) All humans are animals.
   ∴ (2) All animals are humans.

7.   Forms b, c, and f exemplify form a.

9.   Valid: b, c, e, f, h, j, k, l, m, n, p, r, s, u, z.
     Invalid: a, d, g, i, o, q, t, v, w, x, y.

For each invalid form, a replacement scheme is given below. You can construct an English argument with true premises and a false conclusion by making replacements as indicated by the scheme.

Replacement scheme for a:
A: Bo Jackson is president of the United States.
B: Bo Jackson is an American.

Replacement scheme for d:
F: humans
G: reptiles
H: mammals

Replacement scheme for g:
A: Mars is inhabitable by humans.
B: The earth is inhabitable by humans.

Replacement scheme for i:
A: It is raining.
B: It is cloudy.

Replacement scheme for o:
F: humans
G: animals

Replacement scheme for q:
F: humans
G: animals
H: mammals

Replacement scheme for t:
F: humans
G: mammals

Replacement scheme for v:
A: Canada is in South America.
B: 2 + 2 = 5

Replacement scheme for w:
F: mammals
G: human

Replacement scheme for x:
A: Bill Clinton is a father.
B: Bill Clinton is a grandfather.

Replacement scheme for y:
F: humans
G: animals
H: reptiles

CHAPTER 3

SECTION 3.1

1. b. Singular terms: President Lincoln (a physical object), the assassination of President Lincoln (an event), 1865 (a time period).

    d. Singular terms: seven, three, four, seven minus three (numbers).

    e. Singular term: maternity (a relation).

    f. Singular terms: to err, to forgive (actions).

2. a. The Eiffel Tower is shorter than the World Trade Center.

    c. I forgot the answer on the exam.

    e. Class has been scheduled for tomorrow.

    g. Beauty is in the eyes of the beholder.

    h. John is sitting next to Joan, and Joan is sitting next to Harry.

3. a. the union of the attribute of *being a rational number* with the attribute of *being an irrational number*

    c. the union of the attribute of *being a sister* with the attribute of *being a brother*

    e. the union of the attribute of *being an animal* with the attribute of *being a vegetable* and the attribute of *being a mineral*

4. a. $\hat{x}(x$ is a rational number or x is an irrational number)

    b. $\hat{x}(x$ is a mother or x is a father)

    c. $\hat{x}(x$ is a sister or x is a brother)

    d. $\hat{x}(x$ is Great Britain or x is Ireland or x is one of the Channel Islands)

    e. $\hat{x}(x$ is an animal or x is a vegetable or x is a mineral)

    f. $\hat{x}(x$ is a biology major or x a chemistry major or . . .)

5. a. the intersection of the attribute of *being a man* with the attribute of *being unmarried*

    c. the intersection of the attribute of *belonging to the seventeenth century* with the attribute of *being a philosopher*

    e. the intersection of the attribute of *being a triangle* with the attribute of *having two sides of equal length*

7. a. Nietzsche is a philosopher.

   c. Nietzsche is a human.

   e. Nietzsche is a philosopher or a composer.

   g. Nietzsche is a philosopher and not a logician.

   i. If Nietzsche is a philosopher, then Nietzsche is not a logician.

SECTION 3.2

1. a. nonuniversal, nonempty   f. nonuniversal, nonempty

   b. nonuniversal, nonempty   g. nonuniversal, nonempty

   c. universal, nonempty   h. nonuniversal, nonempty

   d. nonuniversal, empty   i. nonuniversal, nonempty

   e. universal, nonempty

3. The intersection of an attribute and its complement is always empty because the complement applies to just those things that the attribute does not apply to. The intersection of an attribute and its complement includes only those individuals to which both apply. For example, $\hat{x}(x$ is red and $\hat{x}$ is not red) is the intersection of the attribute $\hat{x}(x$ is red) with its complement; the intersection is empty. The union of an attribute and its complement is empty if the domain itself is empty; otherwise, the union is always nonempty.

4. a. Overlaps with a (the attribute of *being a poodle*): a, b, e, f, i, j
      Included by a: a

   c. Overlaps with c: c, e, f, g, h, j
      Included by c: c

   e. Overlaps with e: a, b, c, e, f, g, h, i, j
      Included by e: a, b, c

   g. Overlaps with g: b, c, d, e, f, g, h, i, j, k, l
      Included by g: c, d, h, k, l

   i. Overlaps with i: a, b, d, e, f, g, h, i, j, k, l
      Included by i: a, b, d, i, k, l

   k. Overlaps with k: d, f, g, h, i, j, k, l
      Included by k: d, l

5. a. Disjoint from a (the attribute of *being a poodle*): c, d, g, h, k, l
      Extends outside but is not disjoint from a: b, e, f, i, j

   b. Disjoint from b (the attribute of *being a dog*): c, d, h, k, l
      Extends outside but is not disjoint from b: e, f, g, i, j

    c. Disjoint from c (the attribute of *being a cat*): a, b, d, i, k, l
       Extends outside but is not disjoint from c: e, f, g, h, j

    d. Disjoint from d (the attribute of *being a grasshopper*): a, b, c, e, j, l
       Extends outside but is not disjoint from d: f, g, h, i, k

6. a. Domain: animals
      (1) All are either vegetarians or carnivores.
      (2) Some are vegetarians.
    ∴ (3) Some are carnivores.

   c. Domain: dogs
      (1) Gentle ones are desirable.
      (2) Pit bull terriers are not gentle.
    ∴ (3) Pit bull terriers are not desirable.

7. Paraphrase of 6a with unlimited domain:
      (1) $(\forall x)$(if x is an animal, then x is a vegetarian or a carnivore)
      (2) $(\exists x)$(x is an animal and x is a vegetarian)
    ∴ (3) $(\exists x)$(x is an animal and x is a carnivore)

Paraphrase of 6b with unlimited domain:
      (1) $(\forall x)$(if x is a hat and x is new, then x is red)
      (2) $(\forall x)$(if x is a hat and x is red, then x is not for children)
    ∴ (3) $(\forall x)$(if x is a hat and x is for children, then x is not new)

Paraphrase of 6c with unlimited domain:
      (1) $(\forall x)$(if x is a dog and x is gentle, then x is desirable)
      (2) $(\forall x)$(if x is a pit bull terrier, then x is not gentle)
    ∴ (3) $(\forall x)$(if x is a pit bull terrier, then x is not desirable)

Paraphrase of 6d with unlimited domain:
      (1) $(\forall x)$(if x is a student and x is prepared for class, then x will pass)
      (2) $(\exists x)$(x is a philosophy major and x will not pass)
    ∴ (3) $(\exists x)$(x is a philosophy major and x is not prepared for class)

10. Sentence (1) is true because it says that all apples are red. The domain as specified includes everything in the world with the exception of apples that are not red; therefore, every apple in the domain is red. Sentence (2) is false because it says that everything is a red apple. The domain as specified includes everything in the world with the exception of apples that are not red; therefore, not everything in that domain is a red apple. For example, I am in that domain and I am not a red apple. However, both sentences would be true if the domain contained only red apples.

SECTION 3.3

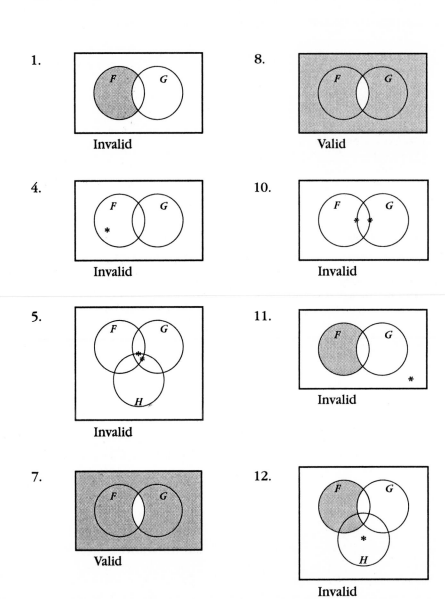

1. Invalid

8. Valid

4. Invalid

10. Invalid

5. Invalid

11. Invalid

7. Valid

12. Invalid

CHAPTER 4

SECTION 4.1

1. a. Natural languages are, primarily, spoken. Formal languages are, primarily, written. Natural languages develop over a long period of time to express feelings or thoughts or to describe the external world. Formal languages are constructed for specific purposes of analysis and problem-solving. Natural languages are vague, ambiguous, and changeable. Formal languages are precise, unambiguous, and fixed.

    c. 'to fly high' (one example)

2. b. Circle arrow.   k. Circle tilde.

    d. Circle arrow.   m. Circle ampersand.

    f. Circle arrow.   o. Circle ampersand.

    g. Circle arrow.   q. Circle vel.

    i. Circle arrow.   s. Circle ampersand.

4. 2b, 2d, 2f, 2g, 2i, 2j, 2r, and 2t are conditionals. Their antecedents and consequents are listed below.

    (2b) antecedent: P; consequent: Q

    (2d) antecedent: $\sim Q$; consequent: $\sim P$

    (2f) antecedent: $\sim P$; consequent: Q

    (2g) antecedent: $\sim Q$; consequent: P

    (2i) antecedent: P; consequent: $\sim Q$

    (2j) antecedent: Q; consequent: $\sim P$

    (2r) antecedent: $(P \vee Q)$; consequent: R

    (2t) antecedent: $((P \rightarrow Q) \,\&\, (Q \rightarrow R))$; consequent: $(P \rightarrow R)$

6. Components of 2p: $((P \vee Q) \,\&\, \sim(P \,\&\, Q))$, $(P \vee Q)$, $\sim(P \,\&\, Q)$, $(P \,\&\, Q)$, P, Q

    Components of 2q: $((P \,\&\, \sim Q) \vee (Q \,\&\, \sim P))$, $(P \,\&\, \sim Q)$, $(Q \,\&\, \sim P)$, P, $\sim Q$, Q

    The components that 2p and 2q have in common are the two atomic components, P and Q.

7. b. 2m, 2o, 2p, 2s

    d. 2b, 2d, 2f, 2g, 2i, 2j, 2r, 2t

f. 2c, 2k

h. none

j. 2t

8. 7a is the form of no sentences in exercise 2.

7b is the form of no sentences in exercise 2.

7c is the form of 2e.

7d is the form of 2b.

7e is the form of 2m.

7f is the form of 2k.

7g is the form of 2n.

7h is the form of no sentences in exercise 2.

7i is the form of 2o.

7j is the form of no sentences in exercise 2.

10. In 2c, the scope of the ampersand is $(P \& \sim Q)$.

In 2k, the scope of the ampersand is $(P \& Q)$.

In 2n, the scope of the first ampersand is $(P \& Q)$; the scope of the second is $(\sim P \& \sim Q)$.

In 2p, the scope of the first ampersand is $((P \lor Q) \& \sim(P \& Q))$; the scope of the second is $(P \& Q)$.

In 2q, the scope of the first ampersand is $(P \& \sim Q)$; the scope of the second is $(Q \& \sim P)$.

In 2t, the scope of the ampersand is $((P \to Q) \& (Q \to R))$.

12. b. P P: Some gourmets eat camels humps.

d. $(P \& Q)$ P: All grapefruit are edible.
                             Q: Some grapefruit do not have seeds.

f. $((P \& Q) \& R) \to (S \to T)$ P: Caesar wins.
                             Q: Brutus wins.
                             R: Cleopatra comes in second.
                             S: There are bananas in the Forum.
                             T: Marcus Antonius will have a banana split.

h. $P \& Q$ P: Johann Strauss is an Austrian.
                             Q: Johann Strauss is a composer.

j. $\sim P$ P: I did bury Paul.

l. P P: All philosophers drink wine.

13. b.   (1) $P \rightarrow Q$ P: Jack is annoyed.
          (2) $\sim P$ Q: Harvey is annoyed.
          (3) $\sim Q$

     d.   (1) $P \rightarrow Q$ P: All piano players are European.
          (2) P Q: No piano players are Chinese.
          $\therefore$ (3) Q

     f.   (1) $P \rightarrow Q$ P: I am a dolphin.
          (2) P Q: I am a cetacean.
          $\therefore$ (3) Q

     h.   (1) $\sim P \rightarrow Q$ P: Harvey is old enough to vote.
          (2) $\sim Q \rightarrow R$ Q: Harvey is under 21.
          $\therefore$ (3) $R \rightarrow P$ R: Harvey can drink legally.

14. $(P \rightarrow Q)$ does not have the form $(A \rightarrow A)$ because the antecedent and consequent of $(P \rightarrow Q)$ are not the same; consequently, there is no way of replacing the placeholder in $(A \rightarrow A)$ to get $(P \rightarrow Q)$.

     $(A \rightarrow B)$ is only a form of $(P \rightarrow P)$ and not the form. The antecedent and consequent of $(P \rightarrow P)$ are the same.

     $(A \rightarrow A)$ is the form of $(P \rightarrow P)$ because the two differ only in one have the placeholder A where the other has the sentence letter P.

SECTION 4.2

1. No. Something can be the case with or without its being required by law. For example, you could drive no faster than 55 miles per hour on Interstate 95 with or without it being required by law.

3. Yes. The truth value of the sentence is determined solely by the meaning of 'neither . . . nor' and the truth values of 'John will come' and 'Mary will come', regardless of what those truth values might be.

5. a. F   e. F
    c. T   g. F

6. a. T   e. T
    b. T   f. T
    c. T   g. F
    d. T   h. F

SECTION 4.3

1. a. false   f. true   k. true   p. true
   b. false   g. true   l. false   q. true
   c. false   h. true   m. false   r. false
   d. false   i. true   n. false   s. false
   e. true   j. true   o. false   t. true

3. Sentences l, m, n, o, and p are false; the rest are true.

5. a.

A	B	$\sim A$	$\sim A \vee B$
T	T	F	T
T	F	F	F
F	T	T	T
F	F	T	T

c.

A	B	$\sim A$	$\sim B$	$A \mathrel{\&} \sim B$	$B \mathrel{\&} \sim A$	$(A \mathrel{\&} \sim B) \vee (B \mathrel{\&} \sim A)$
T	T	F	F	F	F	F
T	F	F	T	T	F	T
F	T	T	F	F	T	T
F	F	T	T	F	F	F

e.

A	B	$\sim B$	$\sim B \to A$
T	T	F	T
T	F	T	T
F	T	F	T
F	F	T	F

g.

A	B	$B \to A$	$A \to (B \to A)$
T	T	T	T
T	F	T	T
F	T	F	T
F	F	T	T

i.

A	B	C	A v B	(A v B) → C
T	T	T	T	T
T	T	F	T	F
T	F	T	T	T
T	F	F	T	F
F	T	T	T	T
F	T	F	T	F
F	F	T	F	T
F	F	F	F	T

6. a is of form (iii).

c is of form (i).

e is of form (v).

g is of form (ii).

8. a. ~(P & Q) & ~R

P: Shakespeare is an American.
Q: Byron is an American.
R: *Macbeth* was written in New York.

It is not the case that both Shakespeare and Byron are Americans, and *Macbeth* was not written in New York.

b. (P & ~(Q & S)) v ((Q & S) & ~P)

P: Jeff makes a lot of money.
Q: Cindy is employed.
S: Greg is employed.

Jeff makes a lot of money and not both Cindy and Greg are employed; or both Cindy and Greg are employed but Jeff does not make a lot of money.

c. ~Q v ~R

Q: Caesar had ice cream for dessert.
R: Cleopatra was hungry.

Caesar did not have ice cream for dessert or Cleopatra wasn't hungry.

d. ~(Q v ~R)

Q: The government will raise taxes.
R: The country will prosper.

It is not the case that the government will raise taxes or the country will not prosper.

e. $(\sim P \rightarrow \sim Q) \ \& \ (\sim Q \rightarrow \sim P)$

   P: The princess is well.
   Q: The princess goes for a walk.

If the princess is not well, then she will not go for a walk; and if she does not go for a walk, then she is not well.

f. $((P \ \& \ R) \ \& \ (Q \ \& \ R)) \ v \ (\sim(P \ \& \ R) \ \& \ \sim(Q \ \& \ R))$

   P: The banker ordered a drink.
   Q: The farmer ordered a drink.
   R: The baker ordered a drink.

The banker and the baker ordered drinks and the farmer and the baker ordered drinks, or not both the banker and baker ordered drinks and not both the farmer and baker did.

g. $\sim(\sim Q \ \& \ \sim P)$

   P: Jack Nicholson won an Oscar.
   Q: Al Pacino won an Oscar.

It is not the case that both Al Pacino and Jack Nicholson did not win an Oscar.

h. $(Q \ v \ P) \ \& \ \sim(Q \ \& \ P)$

   P: Sam plays golf.
   Q: Sam plays chess.

Sam plays chess or golf, but not both.

9. b. $(Q \downarrow \sim R)$: $\sim Q \ \& \ \sim\sim R$

   d. $\sim(Q \ \underline{\vee} \ P)$: $\sim((Q \ v \ P) \ \& \ \sim(Q \ \& \ P))$

SECTION 4.4

1. b. Neither C-valid nor C-contradictory

   d. C-contradictory

   f. C-valid

   h. Neither C-valid nor C-contradictory

   j. C-contradictory

3. Sentences a, d, and h are C-equivalent to one another; b and e are C-equivalent to each other; and c, f, i, and j are mutually C-equivalent as well. Sentence g is equivalent to none of the other sentences.

4. b.   Not C-valid

P	Q	R	(P & R) → Q	Q	P & R
T	T	T	T	T	T
T	T	F	T	T	F

d.   Not C-valid

P	Q	~(P & Q)	Q	P
T	T	F	T	T
T	F	T	F	T
F	T	T	T	F
F	F	T	F	F

f.   C-valid

P	Q	P v Q	~P	Q
T	T	T	F	T
T	F	T	F	F
F	T	T	T	T
F	F	F	T	F

5. a. Q, $(Q \rightarrow \sim R)$ /∴ $\sim R$ is of form (i): A, $(A \rightarrow B)$ /∴ B

c. $(Q \rightarrow \sim R)$, $\sim\sim R$ /∴ $\sim Q$ is of form (iii): $(A \rightarrow B)$, $\sim B$ /∴ $\sim A$

e. $(Q$ v $\sim R)$, $\sim\sim R$ /∴ Q is of form (v): $(A$ v $B)$, $\sim B$ /∴ A

g. $(Q$ & $\sim R)$ /∴ Q is of form (vii): $(A$ & $B)$ /∴ A

i. Q /∴ $(\sim R \rightarrow Q)$ is of form (ix): A /∴ $(B \rightarrow A)$

k. Q, $\sim R$ /∴ $(Q$ & $\sim R)$ is of form (xi): A, B /∴ $(A$ & $B)$

l. $(Q \rightarrow \sim R)$, $(\sim R \rightarrow P)$ /∴ $(Q \rightarrow P)$ is of form (ii): $(A \rightarrow B)$, $(B \rightarrow C)$ /∴ $(A \rightarrow C)$

n. $(Q$ & $Q)$ /∴ Q is of form (vii): $(A$ & $B)$ /∴ A

p. $(\sim Q \rightarrow R)$, $(\sim P \rightarrow R)$, $(\sim P$ v $\sim Q)$ /∴ R is of form (x): $(A \rightarrow C)$, $(B \rightarrow C)$, $(A$ v $B)$ /∴ C

r. $((P$ v $Q) \rightarrow R)$, $(R \rightarrow R)$ /∴ $(((P$ v $Q)$ v $R) \rightarrow R)$ is of form (iv): $(A \rightarrow B)$, $(C \rightarrow B)$ /∴ $((A$ v $C) \rightarrow B)$

t. $(Q \rightarrow R)$, $(\sim(P$ v $R) \rightarrow R)$ /∴ $((Q$ v $\sim(P$ v $R)) \rightarrow R)$ is of form (iv): $(A \rightarrow B)$, $(C \rightarrow B)$ /∴ $((A$ v $C) \rightarrow B)$

6. a.

A	B	A	(B → ~A)
T	T	T	F
T	F	T	T
F	T	F	T
F	F	F	T

C-compatible

c.

A	B	C	~(A v ~B)	(A → (~B & C))
T	T	T	F	F
T	T	F	F	F
T	F	T	F	T
T	F	F	F	F
F	T	T	T	T
F	T	F	T	T
F	F	T	F	T
F	F	F	F	T

C-compatible

e.

A	B	(A ≡ ~B)	~A	~B
T	T	F	F	F
T	F	T	F	T
F	T	T	T	F
F	F	F	T	T

C-incompatible

7. a. Yes.

c. Yes.

e. A conditional *is* C-valid if its consequent is C-valid; however, there are conditionals that are not C-valid even though their antecedents are.

g. No.

i. Yes.

CHAPTER 5

SECTION 5.1

1. a. The first is neither weaker, nor stronger, nor equivalent to the second.

   c. The first is stronger than the second.

   e. The first is weaker than the second.

   g. The first is neither weaker, nor stronger, nor equivalent to the second.

   j. The first is equivalent to the second.

   l. The first is stronger than the second.

   n. The first is equivalent to the second.

   p. The first is stronger than the second.

   r. The first is neither stronger, nor weaker, nor equivalent to the second.

2. a. $((P \lor Q) \lor R)$ or $(P \lor (Q \lor R))$

   c. $P \& {\sim}R$

   e. $({\sim}P \& {\sim}S)$ or $({\sim}S \to {\sim}P)$

   g. ${\sim}(R \lor Q)$ or $({\sim}R \& {\sim}Q)$

   i. $(P \& {\sim}R) \lor (R \& {\sim}P)$

3. With 'P' translating 'John will win' and 'T' translating 'John is tired', '$(P \to {\sim}T)$' is true if John is not tired regardless of whether he wins or not. The English sentence is true only if John wins. Translating the sentence as '$(P \to {\sim}T)$' results in a translation that is weaker than the English sentence. Translating the sentence as '$(P \& {\sim}T)$' also results in a translation that is weaker than the English, but one that is stronger than '$(P \to {\sim}T)$'. More specifically, unlike the English, neither '$(P \& {\sim}T)$' nor '$(P \to {\sim}T)$' claim that John's winning is causal connected to his not being tired, but '$(P \& {\sim}T)$' reveals more content than '$(P \to {\sim}Q)$'. Note that '$(P \& {\sim}T)$' is true only if John wins and is not tired. Therefore, as a translation of the English, '$(P \& {\sim}T)$' is preferable to '$(P \& {\sim}T)$'.

SECTION 5.2

1. a. *P & Q*   *P*: Hans hit the ball.
                                     Q: Hans ran for the first base.

    The English sentences uses the connective 'and then', which expresses temporal order. The translation does not express any temporal order.

    c. *((P & Q) v R)*   *P*: Jack is jovial.
                                         Q: Jack is charming.
                                         R: Jack's stepmother is present.

    A causal connection is indicated in the English sentence but not in the translation.

    e. *P & Q*   *P*: Mr. Stevens paused from his task of
                                             repairing a scythe.
                                     Q: A small bird alighted beside Mr. Stevens.

    The simultaneity indicated by the English sentence is not transmitted in the translation.

    f. *P → Q*   *P*: Charles will become the King of England.
                                     Q: Charles will remain married to Di.

    The English indicates a causal relationship but the translation does not.

2. b. The sentence 'All teenagers are unemployed' says that each and every teenager is unemployed. On the other hand, 'Not all teenagers are employed' says that not every teenager is employed but does not exclude the possibility that some are employed.

3. a. *R → P*   Weaker translation

    c. *~R*   Equivalent translation

    d. *Q → ~R*   Weaker translation

    g. *P → (R & Q)*   Weaker translation

    i. *~(R & Q)*   Equivalent translation

    k. *Q & R*   Equivalent translation

    m. *(Q v R)* or *(~R → Q)*   Weaker translation

    n. *~(Q → P)*   Stronger translation

    q. *(R v S) & ~(R & S)*   Equivalent translation

    r. *(Q → ~R) & (~R → Q)* or *(Q ≡ ~R)*   Equivalent translation

4. a. *P* v *T*

    c. *(Q ≡ R)* or *((Q → R) & (R → Q))*

    e. *(~(P & R) & ~(P & Q)) & ~(R & Q)*

    f. *((P v R) v Q) & ((~(P & R) & ~(P & Q)) & ~(R & Q))* or
        ((P & (~Q & ~R)) v (R & (~Q & ~P))) v (Q & (~P & ~R))

5.

A *B*	*A* only if *B*	*A* unless *B*
T T	?	?
T F	F	?
F T	?	?
F F	?	F

6. b. (v) *P* v *Q*   Equivalent translation
        P: Everyone is invited.
        Q: No one is invited.

    d. (ii) *P → Q*   Weaker translation
        P: You invite her.
        Q: She will be pleased.

    f. (viii) *~(P v Q)*   Equivalent translation
        P: The Alpha team will score.
        Q: The Beta team will score.

    h. (vi) *~(P & Q)*   Stronger translation
        P: The boat sank.
        Q: The boat was attacked by whales.

    j. (viii) *~(P v Q)*   Equivalent translation
        P: Photography is permitted during the procession.
        Q: Photography is permitted in the church.

    l. (ix) *P* v *~P*   Equivalent translation
        P: Someone is invited.

    n. (ii) *P → Q*   Weaker translation
        P: Life is too short.
        Q: No day is too long.

7. a. Jack is jovial and charming if his stepmother is not present.

    d. You will not be elected if you do not campaign.

8. a. Tom and Barbara will marry unless Barbara does not have a job.

    c. Barbara and Tom are working unless they are not getting married.

    e. Harry will not win unless John does not.

g. She will be pleased unless you do not invite her.

h. She will not be pleased unless you invite her.

9. Sentences a, c, and d are equivalent to one another. Sentence b is equivalent to e. No sentence is stronger than any other.

SECTION 5.3

1. a. *P*: Spain is a land of castles.
   Q: Spain is a land of cathedrals.
   (P v Q) v ~(P v Q)

   Translation is C-valid; therefore, English sentence is valid.

   c. *P*: Joe is an astronaut.
   ~(P v ~P)

   Translation is C-contradictory; therefore, English sentence is contradictory.

2. Translation scheme:
   P: Church is a painter.
   Q: Bierstadt is a painter.

   a. (i) *~(P v Q)*   (ii) *~(P & Q)*
   (i) and (ii) are not C-equivalent. The translation scheme contributes nothing to equivalence; therefore, the English sentences are not equivalent.

   c. (i) *(P & Q)*   (ii) *~~(P & Q)*
   (i) and (ii) are C-equivalent; therefore, the sentences they translate are equivalent.

3. a. *P*: The clay will release water.
   Q: There is water in the clay.
   R: The particles are too fine.
   ((~Q v R) → ~P), R /∴ ~P

   Translation is C-valid; therefore, the English argument is valid.

   c. *P*: The child is blowing bubbles through a straw into a glass of milk.
   Q: The child will be spanked.
   R: The child stops blowing bubbles through a straw into a glass of milk.
   S: The child will be sent to her room.
   P, (~R → Q), ~R /∴ (Q & S)

Translation is not C-valid. The translation scheme contributes nothing to validity; therefore, the English argument is not valid.

e. Use translation scheme from c.

$P, (Q \rightarrow \sim R), \sim R /\therefore Q$

Translation is not C-valid. The translation scheme contributes nothing to validity; therefore, the English argument is not valid.

f. P: You forget your opera glasses.
Q: I will supply you with a long thin tube.
R: You will be able to look at the exotic landscape in small sections.
$(P \rightarrow Q), (Q \rightarrow R) /\therefore (P \rightarrow R)$

Translation is C-valid; therefore, if the C-conclusion is equivalent to the English conclusion, the English argument is valid.

i. P: Alex dances all night.
Q: Alex works all night.
R: Alex will be exhausted in the morning.
$((P \vee Q) \rightarrow R), \sim R /\therefore \sim P \& \sim Q$

Translation is C-valid; therefore, the English argument is valid.

k. P: The president has a cocker spaniel.
Q: The first lady has a Siamese cat.
R: The president loves animals.
S: The first lady loves animals.
T: The president belongs to the Animal Rights Society.
U: The first lady belongs to the Animal Rights Society.
$P, Q, ((P \& Q) \rightarrow (R \& S)), ((T \& U) \rightarrow (R \& S)) /\therefore ((R \& S) \&$
$(T \& U))$

Translation is not C-valid. The translation scheme contributes nothing to validity; therefore, the English argument is not valid.

m. P: The United States has a trade deficit with Japan.
Q: The Japanese yen will increase in value relative to the U.S. dollar.
R: The U.S. dollar will increase in value relative to the Japanese yen.
S: The ability of the United States to sell goods in Japan will increase.
T: Japan has trade barriers unfavorable to the United States.
$(P \rightarrow Q), (Q \rightarrow (S \vee T)) /\therefore (\sim S \rightarrow (T \vee \sim P))$

Translation is C-valid; therefore, if the C-conclusion is equivalent to the English conclusion, the English argument is valid.

o. Use translation scheme from m.

$(\sim P \to R)$, $(\sim T \to \sim P)$, $(R \to \sim S)$ /∴ $(\sim T \to \sim S)$

Translation is C-valid; therefore, if the C-conclusion is equivalent to the English conclusion, the English argument is valid.

q. *P*: The ability of the United States to sell goods to Europe will increase.

Q: The quality of U.S. goods increases.

R: The price of U.S. goods declines.

$(Q \to P)$, $(R \to P)$, $(R \vee Q)$ /∴ P

Translation is C-valid; therefore, the English argument is valid.

s. *P*: Tom is sober.

Q: Tom is interesting.

R: Tom is polite.

S: Suzy likes Tom.

$(P \to (Q \mathbin{\&} R))$, $((R \mathbin{\&} Q) \to S)$ /∴ $(P \to S)$

Translation is C-valid; therefore, if the C-conclusion is equivalent to the English conclusion, the English argument is valid.

u. *P*: Lee is old enough to vote.

Q: Lee is 21.

R: Lee is over 21.

S: Lee can drink legally.

T: Lee will have to join the Army.

$((Q \vee R) \to P)$, $((\sim(Q \vee R) \to \sim S) \mathbin{\&} (R \to T))$ /∴ $(P \to (\sim S \vee T))$

Translation is not C-valid. The translation scheme contributes nothing to validity; therefore, the English argument is not valid.

w. *P*: Bill heard Nancy.

Q: Bill was eavesdropping.

R: Bill was in the pay of the FBI.

$(P \to Q)$, $(R \to Q)$ /∴ $(\sim R \to \sim P)$

Translation is not C-valid. The translation scheme contributes nothing to validity; therefore, the English argument is not valid.

y. *P*: The number of hens stays about the same.

Q: People start buying more eggs.

R: Omelettes will cost more.

S: Chicken farmers will make a fortune.

$((P \mathbin{\&} Q) \to R)$, $(R \to S)$, $(P \mathbin{\&} Q)$ /∴ S

Translation is C-valid; therefore, the English argument is valid.

4. a. *P*: The mayor will follow tradition.
   Q: The mayor will visit his "lucky" subway stop.
   $(P \rightarrow Q)$, $(\sim P \ \& \ Q)$

   The translations are C-compatible. The translation scheme contributes nothing to incompatibility; therefore, the English sentences are compatible.

   c. *P*: Dinkins will win.
   Q: Dinkins has the support of the labor unions.
   R: Giuliani will win.
   $(P \ v \sim Q)$, $(R \rightarrow \sim P)$, $(\sim P \ \& \ Q)$

   The translations are C-incompatible; therefore, the English sentences are incompatible.

   d. *P*: Representatives of the Sons of the Revolution were at the Hale ceremony.
   Q: Representatives of the Yale Club were at the Hale ceremony.
   R: Giuliani did attend the Hale ceremony.
   S: Giuliani gets the votes from the Yale Club.
   T: Giuliani will win the election.
   $((P \ \& \ Q) \ \& \sim R)$, $(\sim S \rightarrow \sim T)$, $(\sim R \rightarrow \sim S)$, T

   The translations are C-incompatible; therefore, the English sentences are incompatible.

5. a. *P*: I will eat salmon.
   Q: I will eat liver.
   R: I will eat fish.
   $(P \ v \ Q)$, $\sim R$, $(P \rightarrow R)$ /∴ Q C-valid
   '$(P \rightarrow R)$' is added as a valid premise.

   The translation with the added valid premise is C-valid; therefore, the English argument is valid.

   c. *P*: I will order tuna salad for lunch.
   Q: I will order lobster salad for lunch.
   R: I will spend $4.
   S: I will spend $10.
   T: I will spend more than $6 for lunch.
   $(P \ v \ Q)$, $(P \rightarrow R)$, $(Q \rightarrow S)$, $\sim T$, $(S \rightarrow T)$ /∴ P   C-valid
   '$(S \rightarrow T)$' is added as an unstated premise.

   The translation with the unstated premise is C-valid; therefore, the English argument with that unstated premise is valid.

e. *P*: Mr. Cartier will have an allergic reaction.
   Q: Mr. Cartier drinks at least two glasses of wine.
   R: Mr. Cartier drinks at least three glasses of wine.
   $(Q \rightarrow P)$, *R*, $(R \rightarrow Q)$ /∴ *P*   C-valid
   '$(R \rightarrow Q)$' is added as an unstated premise.

   The translation with the unstated premise is C-valid; therefore, the English argument with that unstated premise is valid.

g. *P*: Buddy will live in the mountains the rest of his life.
   Q: Buddy is indicted for the murder of the lost children.
   R: Buddy will be convicted for the murder of the lost children.
   $(P \lor \sim Q)$, *R*, $(R \rightarrow Q)$ /∴ *P*   C-valid
   '$(R \rightarrow Q)$' is added as an unstated premise.

   The translation with the unstated premise is C-valid; therefore, the English argument with that unstated premise is valid.

i. *P*: The government closes legitimate private companies.
   Q: The government ignores problems with public companies.
   R: The clock is being turned back on economic reforms.
   S: The economy will decline.
   $((P \lor Q) \rightarrow R)$, *Q*, $(R \rightarrow S)$ /∴ *S*   C-valid
   '$(R \rightarrow S)$' is added as an unstated premise.

   The translation with the unstated premise is C-valid; therefore, the English argument with that unstated premise is valid.

k. *P*: The president has a cocker spaniel.
   Q: The first lady has a Siamese cat.
   R: The president has a dog.
   S: The first lady has a cat.
   T: The president and the first lady love animals.
   P, *Q*, $((R \& S) \rightarrow T)$, $((P \rightarrow R) \& (Q \rightarrow S))$ /∴ *T*   C-valid
   '$((P \rightarrow R) \& (Q \rightarrow S))$' is added as a valid premise.

   The translation with the valid premise is C-valid; therefore, the English argument is valid.

CHAPTER 6

SECTION 6.1

1. a. quasi-sentence but not sentence

    b. neither sentence nor quasi-sentence

    c. quasi-sentence but not sentence

    d. sentence

e. neither

f. neither

g. neither

h. sentence

i. sentence

j. sentence

k. sentence

l. sentence

m. sentence

n. sentence

o. sentence

p. quasi-sentence but not sentence

3. d. $(\exists z)(Fz \ \& \ Ga)$ [existential quantifier]

h. $(\exists z)F^2zz$ [existential quantifier]

i. $(\exists y)Gy$ [existential quantifier]; $(\forall x)Fx$ [universal quantifier]

j. $(\exists x)(Gx \ \& \ (\exists y)F^2xy)$ and $(\exists y)F^2xy$ [existential quantifiers]

k. $(\exists y)(\forall x)F^2xy$ [existential quantifier]; $(\forall x)F^2xy$ [universal quantifier]

l. $(\exists x)Fx$ [existential quantifier]; $(\forall y)Gy$ [universal quantifier]

m. $(\exists y)(Fy \rightarrow Gx)$ [existential quantifier]; $(\forall x)(\exists y)(Fy \rightarrow Gx)$ [universal quantifier]

n. $(\exists x)(\exists y)F^2xy$ and $(\exists y)F^2xy$ [existential quantifiers]

5. a. $Ga \ \text{v} \ Ha$ [the instantial term is a]

$Gb \ \text{v} \ Hb$ [the instantial term is b]

c. $(Fa \ \& \ Ga) \rightarrow Ha$ [instantial term a]

$(Fb \ \& \ Gb) \rightarrow Hb$ [instantial term b]

e. $Fa \ \& \ (\exists x)(Fx \ \& \ G^2xa)$ [instantial term a]

$Fb \ \& \ (\exists x)(Fx \ \& \ G^2xb)$ [instantial term b]

g. $(\forall y)(a = y)$ [instantial term a]

$(\forall y)(b = y)$ [instantial term b]

6. b. Platt lives on an island and Platt is a sailor. (More idiomatically: Platt is an island dweller who sails.)

d. Someone lives on an island.

f. At least one human being lives on an island and at least one human being lives on an island. (More idiomatically: Someone is an island dweller.)

h. Someone does not live on an island.

i. It's not true that some island dwellers sail. (Alternatively: No island dweller is a sailor.)

k. There are people who sail but are not island dwellers.

m. Some are island dwellers and some are not.

o. It is not the case that both Platt and Nancy are island dwellers.

q. If Platt lives on an island, then Platt is a sailor.

s. If Platt lives on an island, then he is not a sailor.

u. If Platt lives on an island and is a sailor, then he eats fish.

w. All island dwellers are sailors.

y. Anyone who lives on an island and sails does not eat fish. (Alternatively: No island dweller who sails eats fish.)

z. Anyone who lives on an island or sails eats fish. (Alternatively: All island dwellers and sailors eat fish.)

7. b. If Platt likes Nancy, then Nancy likes Platt.

d. Platt likes Nancy or Platt does not like Nancy.

f. Everyone is liked by both Nancy and Platt.

h. Everyone is liked by either Nancy or Platt.

j. Anyone whom Platt likes likes Platt.

l. Platt likes everyone or Nancy likes everyone.

n. Platt likes all sailors.

p. If everyone likes Platt, then everyone likes Nancy.

r. If someone likes Platt, then everyone likes Nancy.

t. There is an island dweller whom Nancy does not like.

v. It is not the case that all island dwellers are liked by Nancy.

x. If you live on an island or eat fish then you are not a sailor. (Alternatively: No island dwellers or fish eaters are sailors.)

z. If everyone likes him- or herself, then Nancy likes herself.

8. b. Ga

d. $(\forall x)(Fx \rightarrow (Hx \ \& \ Gx))$ or $(\forall x)(Fx \rightarrow Hx) \ \& \ (\forall x)(Fx \rightarrow Gx))$

f. $(\forall x)(Fx \rightarrow (Hx \ \& \ Gx))$

h. $\sim(Hb \ v \ Ha)$ or $(\sim Hb \ \& \ \sim Ha)$

j. $\sim(\exists x)(Gx \ \& \ Hx)$

l. $(\exists x)(Gx \ \& \ Hx) \rightarrow Ha$ or $(\forall x)((Gx \ \& \ Hx) \rightarrow Ha)$

n. $(\forall x)((Gx \ \& \ Fx) \rightarrow Hx)$

p. $(\forall x)(Fx \rightarrow Gx)$

r. $(\forall x)(Gx \rightarrow Hx) \ \& \ (\forall x)(Hx \rightarrow Gx)$ or $(\forall x)(Gx \equiv Hx)$

t. $(\exists x)(Hx \ \& \ \sim Gx)$

v. ~($\forall x$)($Hx \rightarrow$ (Gx v Fx))

w. ($\exists x$)($\exists y$)((Gx & Fy) & (~Hx & ~Hy))

y. (Gb & ~Hb) & ($\forall x$)((Gx & ~Hx) $\rightarrow$ ($x = b$))

z. ($\forall x$)($\forall y$)((Fx & Gy) $\rightarrow$ Ixy)

SECTION 6.2

1. '($\exists y$)Gz' is not an existential sentence because it contains both a vacu-
    ous quantifier and a free variable.

3. a. One is even or two is odd.

    b. One is greater than two or two is less than one.

    c. If three is greater than two, then three is greater than one.

    d. One is greater than two if and only if two is less than one.

    e. It is not the case that two is equal to three.

    f. Two is the sum of two and one.

    g. If three is the sum of two and two, then two is the sum of one
        and one.

    h. If three is the sum of one and two, then three is equal to two.

    i. One is greater than one and two is greater than two.

    j. If one is the sum of one and two, then one is greater than two.

4. a. false   e. true   i. true   m. false   q. true

    b. true   f. true   j. true   n. false   r. true

    c. false   g. true   k. true   o. true   s. true

    d. false   h. false   l. false   p. false

7. b. True. There is at least one x such that x is even and x is not odd.
        At least one number in the set is even but not odd.

    d. True. Two is even and there is at least one x such that x is less
        than two. Two is even and one number in the set is less than two.

    g. True. Every x is such that for every y if x is even and y is odd,
        then it is not the case that x is equal to y. No odd number in the
        set is identical to any that are even.

    i. True. Every x is such that for every y, if it is not the case that x
        is equal to y, then x is less than y or x is not less than y. Given
        any two numbers in the set that are not identical, one is less than
        or not less than the other.

j. True. Every x such that for every y and for every z, if x is greater than y and y is greater than z, then x is greater than z. Given any three numbers from the set, if the first is greater than the second and the second is greater than the third, then the first is greater than the third.

8. a. false   e. true   h. true

    b. false   f. true   i. true

    c. false   g. false   j. false

    d. false

9. b. $\{3, 4\}$ h. $\{2, 3, 4\}$

    d. empty   j. $\{1\}$

    f. $\{\langle 1, 3\rangle, \langle 3, 1\rangle, \langle 2, 2\rangle\}$ k. $\{4\}$

10. a. true   d. true   f. true

    b. false   e. true   g. true

    c. false

SECTION 6.3

1. a. $F\_:\_$ is odd, a: 1
    Domain: {natural numbers}
    If 1 is odd, then every natural number is odd.

    c. $G\_:\_$ is a vegetable, $H\_:\_$ is a mineral
    Whatever is either a vegetable or a mineral is a mineral.

    e. $F\_:\_$ is an orange, $G\_:\_$ is a grapefruit
    If there are grapefruits and there are oranges, then there are grapefruits that are oranges.

    f. $F\_:\_$ was elected president of the United States in 1988
    $G\_:\_$ was married to Barbara Bush in 1988
    Domain: {people}
    Someone was elected president of the United States in 1988 and someone was married to Barbara Bush in 1988 and they are not the same person.

2. b. $G\_$: $\{a\}$, Domain: $\{a, b\}$

    d. $F\_$: $\{a, b\}$, $G\_$: $\{a, b\}$, Domain: $\{a, b\}$

3. b. *G_*: _ lives in Russia, *b*: Mikhail Gorbachev
    Domain: {people}

    If someone lives in Russia, then Mikhail Gorbachev lives in Russia.

    d. *F_*: _ is living, *G_*: _ is dead

    Something is living and is not dead.

    f. *F_*: _ is a mammal, *G_*: _ is a bird

    Something is a mammal and something is a bird and they are not
    the same thing.

4. a. *F_*: {*a*}, Domain: {*a*}

    c. *F_*: {*a*, *b*}, *G_*: {*a*}, Domain: {*a*, *b*}

    e. *F_*: {*a*, *b*}, *G_*: {*a*, *b*}, Domain: {*a*, *b*}

    f. *F_*: {*a*}, *G_*: {*b*}, Domain: {*a*, *b*}

5. a. *F_*: _ is a tulip, *G_*: _ is a flower, *H_*: _ blooms in the spring

    All tulips are flowers. All tulips bloom in the spring. Therefore, all
    flowers bloom in the spring.

    c. *a*: President Clinton, *b*: Lassie, *F_*: _ is a man, *G_*: _ is a human
    being

    President Clinton is a man. Lassie is not a human being. Therefore,
    something is a man yet is not a human being.

    e. *F_*: _ is a mammal, *G_*: _ is an animal, *H_*: _ is a reptile

    Everything that is a mammal is an animal. Something is an animal
    and a reptile. Therefore, something is a mammal and a reptile.

    g. *F_*: _ is mortal, *G_*: _ is immortal
    Domain: {mammals}

    Each individual is either mortal or immortal. Therefore, each indi-
    vidual is immortal.

6. b. *F_*: empty class, *G_*: {*a*}, Domain: {*a*}

    d. *F_*: {*a*}, *G_*: {*a*, *b*}, Domain: {*a*, *b*}

    f. *F_*: {*a*}, *G_*: empty class, Domain: {*a*}

    h. *G_*: {⟨*a*, *a*⟩, ⟨*b*, *b*⟩}, Domain: {*a*, *b*}

7. b. *F_*: _ is male, *G_*: _ is female
    Domain: {human beings}

    Everyone is both male and female. Everyone is male or female.

8. a. *F_*: {*a*}, *G_*: {*b*}
    Domain: {*a*, *b*}

    The first sentence is true and the second is false.

    c. *F_*: {⟨*a*, *b*⟩, ⟨*b*, *a*⟩}, Domain: {*a*, *b*}

    The first sentence is false and the second is true.

9. b. ((*Fa* & *Fb*) & *Fc*) → ((*Ga* v *Gb*) v *Gc*)

    e. ((*a* = *a*) & (*a* = *b*) & (*a* = *c*)) & ((*b* = *a*) & (*b* = *b*) & (*b* = *c*))
        & ((*c* = *a*) & (*c* = *b*) & (*c* = *c*))

    g. ((*a* = *a*) & (*a* = *b*) & (*a* = *c*)) v ((*b* = *a*) & (*b* = *b*) & (*b* = *c*))
        v ((*c* = *a*) & (*c* = *b*) & (*c* = *c*))

10. b. ((*Ga* v *Gb*) → *Gb*)   {*a*, *b*}

Ga	*Gb*	*Ga* v *Gb*	(*Ga* v *Gb*) → *Gb*
T	T	T	T
T	F	T	F

The first row of truth values provides a translation with respect to
the domain {*a*, *b*} on which the original sentence ((∃*x*)*Gx* → *Gb*)
is true. The second row of truth values provides a translation on
which it is false. Therefore, the original sentence is neither Q-valid
nor Q-contradictory.

d. (*Fa* & ~*Ga*)   {*a*}

Fa	*Ga*	*Fa* & ~*Ga*
T	F	T
T	T	F

The first row of truth values provides a translation with respect to
the domain {*a*} on which the original sentence (∃*x*)(*Fx* & ~*Gx*) is
true. The second row of truth values provides a translation on
which it is false. Therefore, the original sentence is neither Q-valid
nor Q-contradictory.

11. a. (*Fa* → *Ga*), (*Fa* → *Ha*) /∴ (*Ga* → *Ha*)   {*a*}

Fa	*Ga*	*Ha*	*Fa* → *Ga*	*Fa* → *Ha*	*Ga* → *Ha*
F	T	F	T	T	F

The row of truth values provides a translation with respect to the
domain {*a*} on which the original argument has true premises and
a false conclusion. Therefore, the original argument is not Q-valid.

c. *Fa, ~Gb* /∴ *((Fa & ~Ga) v (Fb & ~Gb))*   {*a, b*}

Fa	*Ga*	*Fb*	*Gb*		*Fa*	*~Gb*		*(Fa & ~Ga) v (Fb & ~Gb)*
T	T	F	F		T	T		F

The row of truth values provides a translation with respect to the domain {*a, b*} on which the original argument has true premises and a false conclusion. Therefore, the original argument is not Q-valid.

e. *(Fa → Ga), (Ga & Ha)* /∴ *(Fa & Ha)*   {*a*}

Fa	*Ga*	*Ha*		*Fa → Ga*		*Ga & Ha*		*Fa & Ha*
F	T	T		T		T		F

The row of truth values provides a translation with respect to the domain {*a*} on which the original argument has true premises and a false conclusion. Therefore, the original argument is not Q-valid.

g. *(Fa v Ga)* /∴ *Ga*   {*a*}

Same table as in f.

The row of truth values provides a translation with respect to the domain {*a*} on which the original argument has true premises and a false conclusion. Therefore, the original argument is not Q-valid.

12. a. *(Fa v Ga), (Fa & Ga)*   {*a*}

Fa	*Ga*		*Fa v Ga*		*Fa & Ga*
T	F		T		F

The row of truth values provides a translation with respect to the domain {*a*} on which the original sentences have different truth values. Therefore, the original sentences are not Q-equivalent.

c. *((Faa & Fab) v (Fba & Fbb)), ((Faa v Fab) & (Fba v Fbb))*   {*a*}

Faa	*Fab*	*Fba*	*Fbb*		*(Faa & . . . & Fbb)*		*(Faa v . . . v Fbb)*
T	T	F	F		T		F

The row of truth values provides a translation with respect to the domain {*a*} on which the original sentences have different truth values. Therefore, the original sentences are not Q-equivalent.

13. a. There is only one predicate letter in $(\exists x)(Fx$ v $~Fx)$; therefore, if its expansion for the model domain {*a, b*} is Q-valid, then $(\exists x)(Fx$ v $~Fx)$ is valid. The expansion $((Fa$ v $~Fa)$ v $(Fb$ v $~Fb))$ is Q-valid by the truth table test.

    c. There is only one predicate letter in $(\forall x)(Fx \rightarrow (\exists x)Fx)$; therefore if its expansion for the model domain $\{a, b\}$ is Q-valid, then it is Q-valid. The expansion $((Fa \ \& \ Fb) \rightarrow (Fa \ v \ Fb))$ is Q-valid by the truth table test.

    d. There is only one predicate letter in $(\forall x)Fx \rightarrow Fa$; therefore, if its expansion for the model domain $\{a, b\}$ is Q-valid, then it is Q-valid. The expansion $(Fa \ \& \ Fb) \rightarrow Fa$ is Q-valid by the truth table test.

14. a. Expand sentences for domain $\{a, b, c, d\}$.
      (i) $(Fa \ \& \ {\sim}Ga) \ v \ (Fb \ \& \ {\sim}Gb) \ v \ (Fc \ \& \ {\sim}Gc) \ v \ (Fd \ \& \ {\sim}Gd)$
      (ii) ${\sim}((Fa \rightarrow Ga) \ \& \ (Fb \rightarrow Gb) \ \& \ (Fc \rightarrow Gc) \ \& \ (Fd \rightarrow Gd))$.
      Show Q-equivalence by applying the truth table test.

    c. Expand sentences for domain $\{a, b, c, d\}$.
      (i) ${\sim}((Fa \ \& \ {\sim}Ga) \ v \ (Fb \ \& \ {\sim}Gb) \ v \ (Fc \ \& \ {\sim}Gc) \ v \ (Fd \ \& \ {\sim}Gd))$
      (ii) $((Fa \rightarrow Ga) \ \& \ (Fb \rightarrow Gb) \ \& \ (Fc \rightarrow Gc) \ \& \ (Fd \rightarrow Gd))$
      Show Q-equivalence by applying the truth table test.

    e. Expand sentences for domain $\{a, b, c, d\}$.
      (i) ${\sim}((Fa \ \& \ Ga) \ v \ (Fb \ \& \ Gb) \ v \ (Fc \ \& \ Gc) \ v \ (Fd \ \& \ Gd))$
      (ii) $((Fa \rightarrow {\sim}Ga) \ \& \ (Fb \rightarrow {\sim}Gb) \ \& \ (Fc \rightarrow {\sim}Gc) \ \& \ (Fd \rightarrow {\sim}Gd))$
      Show Q-equivalence by applying the truth table test.

15. a. Expand argument for domain $\{a, b\}$.
      Fa & Fb $/\therefore$ *Fa*
      A truth table will show that the argument is Q-valid.

    c. Expand argument for domain $\{a, b, c, d\}$.
      (Fa & Ga) v *(Fb & Gb)* v *(Fc & Gc)* v *(Fd & Gd)* $/\therefore$ *(Ga* v *Gb* v *Gc* v *Gd)*.
      A truth table will show that the argument is Q-valid.

    e. Expand argument for domain $\{a, b\}$.
      (~Fa v *~Fb)* $/\therefore$ *~(Fa & Fb)*
      A truth table will show that the argument is Q-valid.

g. Expand argument for domain {*a*, *b*, *c*, *d*, *e*, *f*, *g*, *h*}.

((*Fa* → *Ga*) & (*Fb* → *Gb*) & (*Fc* → *Gc*) & (*Fd* → *Gd*) & (*Fe* → *Ge*) & (*Ff* → *Gf*) & (*Fg* → *Gg*) & (*Fh* → *Gh*)), (*Ga* → *Ha*) & (*Gb* → *Hb*) & (*Gc* → *Hc*) & (*Gd* → *Hd*)) & (*Ge* → *He*) & (*Gf* → *Hf*) & (*Gg* → *Hg*) & (*Gh* → *Hh*)) /∴ ((*Fa* → *Ha*) & (*Fb* → *Hb*) & (*Fc* → *Hc*) & (*Fd* → *Hd*) & (*Fe* → *He*) & (*Ff* → *Hf*) & (*Fg* → *Hg*) & (*Fh* → *Hh*))

A truth table will show that the argument is Q-valid.

i. Expand argument for domain {*a*, *b*, *c*, *d*, *e*, *f*, *g*, *h*}.

((*Fa* → *Ga*) & (*Fb* → *Gb*) & (*Fc* → *Gc*) & (*Fd* → *Gd*) & (*Fe* → *Ge*) & (*Ff* → *Gf*) & (*Fg* → *Gg*) & (*Fh* → *Gh*)), ((*Ha* & ~*Ga*) v (*Hb* & ~*Gb*) v (*Hc* & ~*Gc*) v (*Hd* & ~*Gd*)) v ((*He* & ~*Ge*) v (*Hf* & ~*Gf*) v (*Hg* & ~*Gg*) v (*Hh* & ~*Gh*)) /∴ ((*Ha* & ~*Fa*) v (*Hb* & ~*Fb*) v (*Hc* & ~*Fc*) v (*Hd* & ~*Fd*) v (*He* & ~*Fe*) v (*Hf* & ~*Ff*) v (*Hg* & ~*Fg*) v (*Hh* & ~*Fh*))

A truth table will show that the argument is Q-valid.

16. a. *F_*: _ is mortal, *a*: Ronald Reagan
    Domain: {human beings}

    Every human being is mortal. Therefore, Ronald Reagan is mortal.

c. *F_*: _ is a mother, *G_*: _ is female
    Domain: {human beings}

    Some human being is both a mother and female. Therefore, some human is a female.

e. *F_*: _ is happy
    Domain: {human beings}

    Somebody is not happy. Therefore, not everyone is happy.

g. *F_*: _ is Cinderella's sister, *G_*: _ is wicked,
    *H_*: _ deserves punishment

    All of Cinderella's sisters are wicked. All wicked people deserve punishment. Therefore, all of Cinderella's sisters deserve punishment.

i. *F_*: _ is a violinist, *G_*: _ is a musician, *H_*: _ is a philosopher

    All violinists are musicians. Some philosophers are not musicians. Therefore, some philosophers are not violinists.

CHAPTER 7

SECTION 7.1

1. a. F_ _ _: _ is sitting between _ and _
        a: Pansy, *b*: Lily, *c*: Rose
        Fabc

        G_ _: Pansy is sitting between _ and _
        a: Lily, *b*: Rose
        Gab

    c. F_: _ is sitting between Lily and Rose
        ~(∃*x*)*Gx*

        G_ _ _: _ is sitting between _ and _
        a: Lily, *b*: Rose
        ~(∃*x*)*Gxab* or (∀*x*) ~*Gxab*

    e. F_ _: _ plus 3 is 7 only if 7 minus 3 is _
        (∀*x*)*Fxx*

        F_ _ _: _ plus _ is _ , G_ _ _: _ minus _ is _
        a: 3, *b*: 7
        (∀*x*)(*Fxab* → *Gbax*)

2. b. *Fa* → *Ga*

    d. (∃*x*)(*Fx* & ~*Hx*) & *Hb*

    f. ~(∃*x*)((*Hx* & *Fx*) & *Gx*) or (∀*x*)((*Hx* & *Fx*) → ~*Gx*)

    g. (∃*x*)((*Fx* & *Hx*) & ~*Gx*)

    i. (∀*x*)((*Hx* v *Fx*) → *Gx*)

    k. *Gb* [weaker than English]

    m. (∃*x*)(*Hx* & ~*Gx*) & (∃*x*) (*Fx* & ~*Gx*)

    o. (∀*x*)(*Iax* → ~*Ibx*)

    q. (∃*x*)(*Hx* & *Ibx*)

    s. (∀*x*)((*Hx* & *Ixb*) → *Ixa*)

3. '(∀*x*)((*Fx* & *Gx*) → *Hx*)' says that any doctor who is a lawyer is a professional. The English sentence says that any doctor or lawyer is a professional. Therefore, '(∀*x*)((*Fx* & *Gx*) → *Hx*)' is not an equivalent translation of the English. An equivalent translation is '(∀*x*)((*Fx* v *Gx*) → *Hx*)'.

4. a. $(\forall x)(\exists y)(Hx \rightarrow Ixy)$

    c. $(\forall x)(Ibx \rightarrow (x = b))$

    e. $(\forall x)((Hx \ \& \ Iax) \rightarrow (x \neq b))$

    g. $\sim(\exists x)(Hx \ \& \ Ixb) \rightarrow \sim Ibb$ or $(\forall x)(Hx \rightarrow \sim Ixb) \rightarrow \sim Ibb$

    i. $(\forall x)(Gx \rightarrow ((x = a) \ \mathrm{v} \ (x = b)))$ or $\sim(\exists x)(Gx \ \& \ ((x \neq a) \ \& \ (x \neq b)))$

SECTION 7.2

1. b. $(\exists x)(Fx \ \& \ Gx) \rightarrow Ga$ or $(\forall x)((Fx \ \& \ Gx) \rightarrow Ga)$

    c. $(\forall x)(Fx \rightarrow Gx) \rightarrow Ga$

    e. $\sim(\exists x)(Hx \ \& \ Gx)$ or $(\forall x)(Hx \rightarrow \sim Gx)$

    f. $\sim(\exists x)(\sim Hx \ \& \ Gx)$ or $(\forall x)(Gx \rightarrow Hx)$

    h. $(\forall x)((Gx \rightarrow (Hx \ \& \ Ix))$

    j. $\sim(\exists x)((Ix \ \& \ Gx) \ \& \ \sim Hx)$ or $(\forall x)((Ix \ \& \ Gx) \rightarrow Hx)$

    l. $(\forall x)(Gx \rightarrow Hx)$

    n. $\sim(\exists x)((Fx \ \& \ Gx) \ \& \ \sim Hx)$ or $(\forall x)((Fx \ \& \ Gx) \rightarrow Hx)$

    p. $(\forall x)((Ix \ \& \ Gx) \rightarrow Hx)$

    q. $(\forall x)(Hx \rightarrow (Ix \ \& \ Gx))$

    r. $(\forall x)((Ix \ \& \ Hx) \rightarrow Gx)$

2. a. $F\_$: _ is a man, $G\_$: _ lives in Manhattan, $H\_ \ \_$: _ is richer than _, a: Mr. Trump

    $(Fa \ \& \ Ga) \ \& \ (\forall x)((Fx \ \& \ Gx) \rightarrow \sim Hxa)$

    b. $F\_$: _ is a woman, $G\_$: _ lives in Manhattan, $H\_ \ \_$: _ is richer than _, c: Mrs. Astor

    $(\exists x)((Fx \ \& \ Gx) \ \& \ Hxc)$

    d. $G\_$: _ laughs at, $F\_$: _ is a person, b: Bozo

    $Gbb \ \& \ (\forall x)(Gxb \rightarrow (x = b))$

    f. $F\_ \ \_$: _ loves _, a: John, b: Mary

    $Fab \ \& \ (\forall x)(Fax \rightarrow (x = b))$

3. $F\_$: _ is a brother of Abby, $G\_$: _ is a sister of Abby

    a. $(\exists x)(\exists y)(Fx \ \& \ Fy \ \& \ (x \neq y))$

    d. $(\exists x)(\exists y)((Fx \ \mathrm{v} \ Gx) \ \& \ (Fy \ \mathrm{v} \ Gy) \ \& \ (x \neq y) \ \& \ (\forall z)((Fz \ \mathrm{v} \ Gz) \rightarrow ((z = x) \ \mathrm{v} \ (z = y))))$

    e. $(\forall x)(\forall y)(\forall z) ((Gx \ \& \ Gy \ \& \ Gz) \rightarrow ((x = y) \ \mathrm{v} \ (y = z) \ \mathrm{v} \ (x = z)))$

4. $F\_\ \_$: _ likes _

    a. $(\forall x)(\forall y)Fxy$

    c. $(\forall x)(\forall y)((x \neq y) \rightarrow Fxy)$

    e. $(\exists x)(\exists y)(Fxy)$

    g. $(\exists x)(\forall y)Fxy$

    i. $(\exists x){\sim}(\forall y)Fxy$ or $(\exists x)(\exists y){\sim}Fxy$

6. $F\_$: _ is a friend of mine, $G\_$: _ is fair-minded

    a. $(\forall x)(Fx \rightarrow Gx)$

    c. ${\sim}(\exists x)(Fx \ \& \ {\sim}Gx)$ or $(\forall x)(Fx \rightarrow Gx)$

    e. $(\forall x)(Gx \rightarrow Fx)$

    g. $(\forall x)(Fx \rightarrow Gx)$

7.   b. $(\forall x)(x \neq x)$ or ${\sim}(\exists x)(x = x)$

      Contradictory. There is no translation of $(\forall x)(x \neq x)$ with respect to any domain on which it is true. The expansion for $\{a\}$ is $(a \neq a)$, the expansion for $\{a, b\}$ is $((a \neq a) \ \& \ (b \neq b))$, and so on.

    d. $(\exists x)(x = x)$

      Valid. There is no translation of $(\exists x)(x = x)$ with respect to any domain on which it is false. The expansion for $\{a\}$ is $(a = a)$, the expansion in $\{a, b\}$ is $((a = a) \ \text{v} \ (b = b))$, and so on.

    f. $(\exists x)(\exists y)(x \neq y)$

      Neither valid nor contradictory. There is a translation of $(\exists x)(\exists y)(x \neq y)$ with respect to a domain on which it is false and a translation on which it is true. The expansion for $\{a, b\}$ is $((a \neq a) \ \text{v} \ (a \neq b)) \ \text{v} \ ((b \neq a) \ \text{v} \ (b \neq b))$. The expansion is false when a and b are the same individual but true when a and b are not the same individual.

    h. $F\_$: _ is red, $G\_$: _ is black

      $(\exists x)Fx \rightarrow {\sim}(\exists x)(Fx \ \text{v} \ Gx)$

      There is a translation of $((\exists x)Fx \rightarrow {\sim}(\exists x)(Fx \ \text{v} \ Gx))$ with respect to a domain on which it is false and a translation on which it is true. The expansion for $\{a\}$ is $((Fa \rightarrow {\sim}(Fa \ \text{v} \ Ga))$; and the expansion is true if Fa is false, but false if Fa is true. Thus $((\exists x)Fx \rightarrow {\sim}(\exists x)(Fx \ \text{v} \ Gx))$ is neither valid not contradictory. But, with the arrow translating the English 'if . . . then', $((\exists x)Fx \rightarrow {\sim}(\exists x)(Fx \ \text{v} \ Gx))$ may be weaker than the English sentence it translates. The English sentence does seem to be contradictory.

j. *F_*: _ is a woman, *G_*: _ is a man, *H_*: _ attends
(∃x)(Fx & Hx) → ~(∃x)(Gx & Hx)

There is a translation of ((∃x)(Fx & Hx) → ~(∃x)(Gx & Hx)) with respect to a domain on which it is false and a translation on which it is true. The expansion for {*a, b*} is ((Fa & Ha) v (Fb & Hb)) → ~((Ga & Ha) v (Gb & Hb)). If *Fa* and *Fb* are both false, the expansion is true. However, if *Fa* and *Ha* are both true and *Ga* and *Gb* are true, the expansion is false. If the Q-translation is equivalent to the English sentence, the English sentence is neither valid nor contradictory.

l. *F_*: _ is a dinosaur
(∀x)Fx → (∃x)~Fx

There is a translation of ((∀x)Fx → (∃x)~Fx) with respect to a domain on which it is false and a translation on which it is true. The expansion for {*a*} is (Fa → ~Fa). The expansion is false if *Fa* is true, but the expansion is true if *Fa* is false. The English sentence seems contradictory; however, with 'if . . . then' understood as having the same meaning as the arrow, the English sentence is neither valid nor contradictory.

n. *F_*: _ is coming, *a*: John
Domain: {human beings}
(∃x)Fx & ~Fa

Neither valid nor contradictory. There is a translation of ((∃x)Fx & ~Fa) with respect to a domain on which it is false and a translation on which it is true. The expansion for {*a*} is (Fa & ~Fa) and that is false. The expansion for {a, b} is ((Fa v Fb) & ~Fa). The expansion is true if *Fa* is false and *Fb* is true. However, the expansion is false if both *Fa* and *Fb* are false.

p. *F_ _*: _ caused _
(∃x)(∀y)Fxy & ~(∀x)(∃y)Fyx

Contradictory. There is no translation of (∃x)(∀y)Fxy & ~(∀x)(∃y)Fyx with respect to any domain on which it is true.

8. a. *F_*: _ is an even number, *G_*: _ is an odd number,
*H_*: _ is in the set, *J_*: _ is a number, *a*: 12

(∀x)(Fx → Hx), ~Ga, (∀x)(Jx → (Fx v Gx)), ~Ha
Valid sentence: *Ja*

  c. $F\_$: _ is a man, $G\_$: _ is a woman, $H\_$: _ is a columnist, $J\_$: _ is a reporter

   $(\forall x)(Hx \to Fx)$ & $(\forall x)(Jx \to Gx)$, $(\exists x)(Gx$ & Jx & $Hx)$
   Valid sentence: $(\forall x)(Fx \equiv \sim Gx)$

  e. $C\_$: _ comes, $S\_$: _ will be surprised, j: Jack, i: I
   Domain: {human beings}

   $(Cj \to \sim Si)$, $(Si \to ((\exists x)Cx$ v $(\forall x)\sim Cx))$

9. b. $(\forall x)(x = x)$ /∴ $(\forall x)(\forall y)(x = y)$

  c. $N\_$: _ is a Nobel Prize winner, $W\_$: _ is at the wedding reception, $P\_\_$: _ will photograph _, i: I, h: Harold

   $(\exists x)(\exists y)((((Nx$ & $Wx)$ & $(Ny$ & $Wy))$ & $(x \ne y))$ & $(\forall z)((Nz$ & $Wz)$ $\to ((x = z)$ v $(y = z))))$, $(\exists x)(\exists y)((Nx$ & Wx & $Pix)$ & $(Ny$ & Wy & $Phy)$ /∴ $(\forall x)((Nx$ & $Wx) \to (Pix$ v $Phx))$

  d. $I\_\_\_$: _ gave _ to _, $R\_\_\_$: _ returned _ to _, $B\_$: _ is a book, $P\_$:_ is a person, s: Sebastian, r: Rachel, i: I Ching

   $Isir$, $(\forall x)(\forall y)((Bx$ & Py & $Iyxr) \to Rrxy)$, Bi, Ps /∴ $Rris$
   Unstated premises: Bi, Ps

  e. $S\_\_$: _ spoke to _
   Domain: {individuals at the party}

   $(\exists x)(\forall y)$ Syx /∴ $(\forall x)(\exists y)Sxy$

CHAPTER 8

SECTION 8.1

1. The rule of simplification has two parts. One part allows you to write the right conjunct of a conjunction as a step in a derivation if the conjunction is a preceding step. The other part allows you to write the left conjunct of a conjunction as a step in a derivation if the conjunction is a preceding step. Each scheme expresses one and only one part of the rule. So, one scheme would not be sufficient.

3. | i | A v B | | i | A v $\sim B$ | |
    |---|---|---|---|---|---|
    | j | $\sim B$ | | j | B | |
    | k | A | i, j, DS | k | A | i, j, DS |

5.   1 If Pat is employed as a CIA agent, then Pat will not be bored.
     2 If Pat is employed as a financial analyst, then Pat will not be bored.
     3 Pat is employed as either a financial analyst or a CIA agent.
     4 If Pat is employed as either a financial analyst or a CIA agent, then Pat will not be bored.
     5 Pat will not be bored.
     6 Pat is employed as either a financial analyst or a CIA agent and Pat will not be bored.

6. b. 1 $P \& (Q \& \sim R)$ Hyp
        2 $Q \& \sim R$ 1, Simp
        3 $\sim R$ 2, Simp

    d. 1 Q Hyp
        2 $\sim(P \& Q)$ Hyp
        3 $\sim R$ Hyp
        4 $Q \& \sim(P \& Q)$ 1, 2, Conj

    f. 1 $Q \to \sim R$ Hyp
        2 $\sim P \to \sim R$ Hyp
        3 $(\sim P \vee Q) \to \sim R$ 1, 2, CD

    h. 1 $(Q \to R) \& (\sim P \to S)$ Hyp
        2 $\sim R \vee \sim S$ Hyp
        3 $\sim Q \vee \sim\sim P$ 1, 2, DD

    j. 1 $R \to S$ Hyp
        2 $\sim S$ Hyp
        3 $\sim R$ 1, 2, MT

10. a. 1 $(P \vee \sim R) \vee (Q \& R)$ Hyp
        2 $P \vee (\sim R \vee (Q \& R))$ 1, Assoc

    c. 1 $Q \& (P \vee R)$ Hyp
        2 $Q \& (R \vee P)$ 1, Com

    e. 1 $(P \& Q) \to R$ Hyp
        2 $\sim(P \& Q) \vee R$ 1, Con Exch

    g. 1 $P \to (Q \& R)$ Hyp
        2 $\sim(P \& \sim(Q \& R))$ 1, Con Exch

    i. 1 $P \& (Q \vee Q)$ Hyp
        2 $P \& Q$ 1, Taut

k. 1 $P \& (\sim Q \lor R)$ Hyp
    2 $(P \& \sim Q) \lor (P \& R)$ 1, Dist

11. b. 1 $(P \& Q) \lor (P \& \sim Q)$ Hyp
         2 $P \to Q$ Hyp
         3 $\sim(P \& \sim Q)$ 2, Con Exch
         4 $P \& Q$ 1, 3, DS

     d. 1 $P \to (Q \lor R)$ Hyp
         2 $\sim Q$ Hyp
         3 $\sim R$ Hyp
         4 $\sim Q \& \sim R$ 2, 3, Conj
         5 $\sim(Q \lor R)$ 4, DeM
         6 $\sim P$ 1, 5, MT

     f. 1 $P \to (Q \to R)$ Hyp
         2 $P \& Q$ Hyp
         3 P 2, Simp
         4 $Q \to R$ 1, 3, MP
         5 Q 2, Simp
         6 R 4, 5, MP

13. De Morgan's Law cannot be applied to step 1 to get step 2 in the given sequence because step 1 does not have the form of either the right or the left member in either of the two pairs that follow.

   $\sim(A \lor B) :: (\sim A \& \sim B)$

   $\sim(A \& B) :: (\sim A \lor \sim B)$

14. a. 1 $\sim(P \& \sim Q)$ Hyp
         2 $\sim P \lor \sim\sim Q$ 1, DeM

     d. 1 $\sim P \& Q$ Hyp
         2 $\sim P \& \sim\sim Q$ 1, DN
         3 $\sim(P \lor \sim Q)$ 2, DeM

     g. 1 $P \& Q$ Hyp
         2 $P \to R$ Hyp
         3 P 1, Simp
         4 R 2, 3, MP
         5 $R \lor S$ 4, Add

     j. 1 $(P \& Q) \to R$ Hyp
         2 $\sim R$ Hyp
         3 $\sim(P \& Q)$ 1, 2, MT

	4	~P v ~Q	3, DeM
	5	P → ~Q	4, Con Exch
m.	1	P → Q	Hyp
	2	Q → R	Hyp
	3	~R	Hyp
	4	~Q	2, 3, MT
	5	~P	1, 4, MT

15. No. A conditional can be true even though its consequent is false; therefore, such a rule would not be truth-preserving.

19. The first derivation shows that ($\sim Q \to \sim P$) is derivable from $\sim(\sim Q$ & P); the second shows that $\sim(\sim Q$ & P) is derivable from ($\sim Q \to \sim P$). When one sentence is derivable from another, it is implied by the other. If two sentences imply one another, they are equivalent.

21.	a.	1	P	Hyp
		2	P v ~Q	1, Add
		3	~Q v P	2, Com
		4	Q → P	3, Con Exch
	c.	1	P	Hyp
		2	P v Q	1, Add
	e.	1	P → (Q v R)	Hyp
		2	~P v (Q v R)	1, Con Exch
		3	(~P v ~P) v (Q v R)	2, Taut
		4	~P v (~P v (Q v R))	3, Assoc
		5	~P v ((~P v Q) v R)	4, Assoc
		6	~P v (R v (~P v Q))	5, Com
		7	(~P v R) v (~P v Q)	6, Assoc
		8	(P → R) v (~P v Q)	7, Con Exch
		9	(P → R) v (P → Q)	8, Con Exch
		10	(P → Q) v (P → R)	9, Com
22.	b.	1	P v Q	Hyp
		2	~P & ~Q	Hyp
		3	~P	2, Simp
		4	Q	1, 3, DS
		5	~Q	2, Simp
		6	Q & ~Q	5, 6, Conj

SECTION 8.2

1. | 1 | $(\forall x)Fx \ \& \ (\forall y)Gy$ | Hyp |
    |---|---|---|
    | 2 | $(\forall x)Fx$ | 1, Simp |
    | 3 | $(\forall y)Gy$ | 1, Simp |
    | 4 | Fa | 2, UI |
    | 5 | Gb | 3, UI |
    | 6 | $Fa \ \& \ Gb$ | 4, 5, Conj |

    1 All first ladies are kindhearted and all first ladies are self-sacrificing.
    2 All first ladies are kindhearted.
    3 All first ladies are self-sacrificing.
    4 Martha Washington is kindhearted.
    5 Dolly Madison is self-sacrificing.
    6 Martha Washington is kindhearted and Dolly Madison is self-sacrificing.

3. | 1 | Gb | |
    |---|---|---|
    | 2 | Fb | |
    | 3 | $Gb \ \& \ Fb$ | |
    | 4 | $(\exists x)(Gx \ \& \ Fx)$ | |

5. $(a = b)$ is an instance of $(\exists x)(a = x)$; the instantial term is b. $(a = b)$ is also an instance of $(\exists x)(x = b)$ but, in this case, the instantial term is a.

7. a. | 1 | $(\forall x)Fx$ | Hyp |
    |---|---|---|
    | 2 | Fa | 1, UI |
    | 3 | $Fa \ v \ Ga$ | 2, Add |
    | 4 | $(\forall x)(Fx \ v \ Gx)$ | 3, UG |

    c. | 1 | $(\forall x)Fx$ | Hyp |
    |---|---|---|
    | 2 | $(\forall x)Gx$ | Hyp |
    | 3 | Fa | 1, UI |
    | 4 | Ga | 2, UI |
    | 5 | $Fa \ \& \ Ga$ | 3, 4, Conj |
    | 6 | $(\forall y)(Fy \ \& \ Gy)$ | 5, UG |

    e. | 1 | $(\forall x)(Gx \rightarrow Fx)$ | Hyp |
    |---|---|---|
    | 2 | $(\exists x)Gx$ | Hyp |
    | 3 | Ga | 2, EI |
    | 4 | $Ga \rightarrow Fa$ | 1, UI |
    | 5 | Fa | 3, 4, MP |
    | 6 | $(\exists x)Fx$ | 5, EG |

g. 1 $(\forall x)(Gx \rightarrow Fx)$ Hyp
    2   $(\forall x)Gx$ Hyp
    3   $Ga \rightarrow Fa$ 1, UI
    4   Ga 2, UI
    5   Fa 3, 4, MP
    6   $(\forall x)Fx$ 5, UG

i. 1 $(\forall x)(Fx \rightarrow Gx)$ Hyp
    2   $(\exists x)(Fx \& Hx)$ Hyp
    3   $Fa \& Ha$ 2, EI
    4   $Fa \rightarrow Ga$ 1, UI
    5   Fa 3, Simp
    6   Ga 4, 5, MP
    7   Ha 3, Simp
    8   $Ga \& Ha$ 6, 7, Conj
    9   $(\exists x)(Gx \& Hx)$ 8, EG

k. 1 $(\exists x)(Fx \& {\sim}Gx)$ Hyp
    2   $(\forall x)(Fx \rightarrow (Hx \vee Gx))$ Hyp
    3   $Fa \& {\sim}Ga$ 1, EI
    4   $Fa \rightarrow (Ha \vee Ga)$ 2, UI
    5   Fa 3, Simp
    6   $Ha \vee Ga$ 4, 5, MP
    7   ${\sim}Ga$ 3, Simp
    8   Ha 6, 7, DS
    9   $(\exists x)Hx$ 8, EG

m. 1 $(\forall x)(Fx \rightarrow Gx)$ Hyp
    2   $(\forall x)(Hx \rightarrow Ix)$ Hyp
    3   $(\forall x)({\sim}Gx \vee {\sim}Ix)$ Hyp
    4   $Fa \rightarrow Ga$ 1, UI
    5   $Ha \rightarrow Ia$ 2, UI
    6   ${\sim}Ga \vee {\sim}Ia$ 3, UI
    7   $(Fa \rightarrow Ga) \& (Ha \rightarrow Ia)$ 4, 5, Conj
    8   ${\sim}Fa \vee {\sim}Ha$ 6, 7, DD
    9   $(\forall x)({\sim}Fx \vee {\sim}Hx)$ 8, UG

9. a. 1 ${\sim}(\exists x)(Fx \& Gx)$ Hyp
        2   $(\forall x){\sim}(Fx \& Gx)$ 1, QN
        3   ${\sim}(Fa \& Ga)$ 2, UI
        4   ${\sim}Fa \vee {\sim}Ga$ 3, DeM
        5   $Fa \rightarrow {\sim}Ga$ 4, Con Exch
        6   $(\forall x)(Fx \rightarrow {\sim}Gx)$ 5, UG

c. 1 $(\exists x)(Fx \& Gx)$ Hyp
    2   $Fa \& Ga$ 1, EI
    3   $Ga \& Fa$ 2, Com
    4   $(\exists x)(Gx \& Fx)$ 3, EG

e. 1 $(\forall x)(Fx \rightarrow \sim Gx)$ Hyp
    2   $(\forall x)(Hx \rightarrow Gx)$ Hyp
    3   $Fa \rightarrow \sim Ga$ 1, UI
    4   $Ha \rightarrow Ga$ 2, UI
    5   $\sim\sim Ga \rightarrow \sim Fa$ 3, Contra
    6   $Ga \rightarrow \sim Fa$ 5, DN
    7   $Ha \rightarrow \sim Fa$ 4, 6, HS
    8   $(\forall x)(Hx \rightarrow \sim Fx)$ 7, UG

g. 1 $(\forall y)(Fy \vee Gy)$ Hyp
    2   $(\forall y)(\sim Gy \vee Hy)$ Hyp
    3   $Fa \vee Ga$ 1, UI
    4   $\sim Ga \vee Ha$ 2, UI
    5   $\sim\sim Fa \vee Ga$ 3, DN
    6   $\sim Fa \rightarrow Ga$ 5, Con Exch
    7   $Ga \rightarrow Ha$ 4, Con Exch
    8   $\sim Fa \rightarrow Ha$ 6, 7, HS
    9   $\sim\sim Fa \vee Ha$ 8, Con Exch
   10   $Fa \vee Ha$ 9, DN
   11   $(\forall z)(Fz \vee Hz)$ 10, UG

h. 1 $(\forall y)((Fy \vee Gy) \rightarrow Hy)$ Hyp
    2   $(\forall x)((Hx \rightarrow (Ix \& Jx))$ Hyp
    3   $(Fa \vee Ga) \rightarrow Ha$ 1, UI
    4   $Ha \rightarrow (Ia \& Ja)$ 2, UI
    5   $(Fa \vee Ga) \rightarrow (Ia \& Ja)$ 3, 4, HS
    6   $\sim(Fa \vee Ga) \vee (Ia \& Ja)$ 5, Con Exch
    7   $(\sim Fa \& \sim Ga) \vee (Ia \& Ja)$ 6, DeM
    8   $((\sim Fa \& \sim Ga) \vee Ia) \& ((\sim Fa \& {}$ 7, Dist
        $\sim Ga) \vee Ja)$
    9   $(\sim Fa \& \sim Ga) \vee Ia$ 8, Simp
   10   $Ia \vee (\sim Fa \& \sim Ga)$ 9, Com
   11   $(Ia \vee \sim Fa) \& (Ia \vee \sim Ga)$ 10, Dist
   12   $Ia \vee \sim Fa$ 11, Simp
   13   $\sim Fa \vee Ia$ 12, Com
   14   $Fa \rightarrow Ia$ 13, Con Exch
   15   $(\forall z)(Fz \rightarrow Iz)$ 14, UG

j. 1 $(\forall x)(Fx \rightarrow (Gx \lor Hx))$ Hyp
    2   $\sim(\exists x)(Fx \;\&\; Hx)$ Hyp
    3   $(\forall x)\sim(Fx \;\&\; Hx)$ 2, QN
    4   $\sim(Fa \;\&\; Ha)$ 3, UI
    5   $\sim Fa \lor \sim Ha$ 4, DeM
    6   $Fa \rightarrow \sim Ha$ 5, Con Exch
    7   $\sim\sim Ha \rightarrow \sim Fa$ 6, Contra
    8   $Ha \rightarrow \sim Fa$ 7, DN
    9   $Fa \rightarrow (Ga \lor Ha)$ 1, UI
    10 $Fa \rightarrow (\sim\sim Ga \lor Ha)$ 9, DN
    11 $Fa \rightarrow (\sim Ga \rightarrow Ha)$ 10, Con Exch
    12 $(Fa \;\&\; \sim Ga) \rightarrow Ha$ 11, Exp
    13 $(Fa \;\&\; \sim Ga) \rightarrow \sim Fa$ 8, 12, HS
    14 $\sim(Fa \;\&\; \sim Ga) \lor \sim Fa$ 13, Con Exch
    15 $(\sim Fa \lor \sim\sim Ga) \lor \sim Fa$ 14, DeM
    16 $\sim Fa \lor (\sim Fa \lor \sim\sim Ga)$ 15, Com
    17 $(\sim Fa \lor \sim Fa) \lor \sim\sim Ga$ 16, Assoc
    18 $\sim Fa \lor \sim\sim Ga$ 17, Taut
    19 $Fa \rightarrow \sim\sim Ga$ 18, Con Exch
    20 $Fa \rightarrow Ga$ 19, DN
    21 $(\forall x)(Fx \rightarrow Gx)$ 20, UG

10. a. 1 $\sim(\forall x)(Fx \rightarrow \sim Gx)$ Hyp
        2   $(\exists x)\sim(Fx \rightarrow \sim Gx)$ 1, QN
        3   $(\exists x)\sim\sim(Fx \;\&\; \sim\sim Gx)$ 2, Con Exch
        4   $(\exists x)(Fx \;\&\; \sim\sim Gx)$ 3, DN
        5   $(\exists x)(Fx \;\&\; Gx)$ 4, DN

    b. 1 $(\exists x)(Fx \;\&\; Gx)$ Hyp
        2   $\sim(\forall x)\sim(Fx \;\&\; Gx)$ 1, QN
        3   $\sim(\forall x)(\sim Fx \lor \sim Gx)$ 2, DeM
        4   $\sim(\forall x)(Fx \rightarrow \sim Gx)$ 3, Con Exch

The two derivations together show that $(\exists x)(Fx \;\&\; Gx)$ and $\sim(\forall x)(Fx \rightarrow \sim Gx)$ are equivalent.

11. b.   1 $(\forall x)(Fx \to \sim Gx)$ Premise
          2   $(\exists x)Fx \to (\forall x)(Gx \vee Hx)$ Premise
          3   $\sim(\sim(\exists x)Hx \to (\forall x)\sim Fx)$ Negation of Conclusion
          4   $\sim\sim(\sim(\exists x)Hx \,\&\, \sim(\forall x)\sim Fx)$ 3, Con Exch
          5   $\sim(\exists x)Hx \,\&\, \sim(\forall x)\sim Fx$ 4, DN
          6   $\sim(\exists x)Hx$ 5, Simp
          7   $(\forall x)\sim Hx$ 6, QN
          8   $\sim(\forall x)\sim Fx$ 5, Simp
          9   $(\exists x)Fx$ 8, QN
         10   $(\forall x)(Gx \vee Hx)$ 2, 9, MP
         11   Fa 9, EI
         12   $Fa \to \sim Ga$ 1, UI
         13   $\sim Ga$ 11, 12, MP
         14   $Ga \vee Ha$ 10, UI
         15   Ha 13, 14, DS
         16   $\sim Ha$ 7, UI
         17   $Ha \,\&\, \sim Ha$ 15, 16, Conj

12. a. $(\forall x)(Fx \to Gx),\ (\forall x)(Hx \to \sim Gx) \ /\therefore\ (\forall x)(Hx \to \sim Fx)$

          1   $(\forall x)(Fx \to Gx)$ Hyp
          2   $(\forall x)(Hx \to \sim Gx)$ Hyp
          3   $Fa \to Ga$ 1, UI
          4   $Ha \to \sim Ga$ 2, UI
          5   $\sim Ga \to \sim Fa$ 3, Contra
          6   $Ha \to \sim Fa$ 4, 5, HS
          7   $(\forall x)(Hx \to \sim Fx)$ 6, UG

     c. $(\forall x)(Fx \to Gx),\ (\forall x)Fx \ /\therefore\ Ga$

          1   $(\forall x)(Fx \to Gx)$ Hyp
          2   $(\forall x)Fx$ Hyp
          3   $Fa \to Ga$ 1, UI
          4   Fa 2, UI
          5   Ga 3, 4, MP

     e. $(\forall y)Fy,\ (\forall x)Gx \ /\therefore\ (\forall x)(Fx \vee Gx)$

          1   $(\forall y)Fy$ Hyp
          2   $(\forall x)Gx$ Hyp
          3   Fa 1, UI
          4   $Fa \vee Ga$ 3, Add
          5   $(\forall x)(Fx \vee Gx)$ 3, UG

13. a. $(\exists x)(Fx \& Gx)$, $(\forall x)(Gx \to Hx)$ /∴ $(\exists x)(Fx \& Hx)$

1	$(\exists x)(Fx \& Gx)$	Hyp
2	$(\forall x)(Gx \to Hx)$	Hyp
3	$Fa \& Ga$	1, EI
4	$Ga \to Ha$	2, UI
5	Ga	3, Simp
6	Ha	4, 5, MP
7	Fa	3, Simp
8	$Fa \& Ha$	6, 7, Conj
9	$(\exists x)(Fx \& Hx)$	8, EG

c. $(\forall x)((Fx \& \sim Gx) \to Hx)$, $(\forall x)(Ix \to Fx)$, $(\exists x)(Ix \& \sim Hx)$ /∴ $(\exists x)Gx$

1	$(\forall x)((Fx \& \sim Gx) \to Hx)$	Hyp
2	$(\forall x)(Ix \to Fx)$	Hyp
3	$(\exists x)(Ix \& \sim Hx)$	Hyp
4	$Ia \& \sim Ha$	3, EI
5	$Ia \to Fa$	2, UI
6	Ia	4, Simp
7	Fa	5, 6, MP
8	$\sim Ha$	4, Simp
9	$(Fa \& \sim Ga) \to Ha$	1, UI
10	$\sim(Fa \& \sim Ga)$	8, 9, MT
11	$\sim Fa \lor \sim \sim Ga$	10, DeM
12	$\sim \sim Ga$	7, 11, DS
13	Ga	12, DN
14	$(\exists x)Gx$	13, EG

e. $(\forall x)(Fx \to \sim Gx)$, $(\exists x)((Hx \& Gx) \& Jx)$ /∴ $(\exists x)((Hx \& \sim Fx) \& Jx)$

1	$(\forall x)(Fx \to \sim Gx)$	Hyp
2	$(\exists x)((Hx \& Gx) \& Jx)$	Hyp
3	$(Ha \& Ga) \& Ja$	2, EI
4	$Ha \& Ga$	3, Simp
5	Ga	4, Simp
6	$Fa \to \sim Ga$	1, UI
7	$\sim Fa$	5, 6, MT
8	Ha	4, Simp
9	$Ha \& \sim Fa$	7, 8, Conj
10	Ja	3, Simp
11	$(Ha \& \sim Fa) \& Ja$	9, 10, Conj
12	$(\exists x)((Hx \& \sim Fx) \& Jx)$	11, EG

CHAPTER 9

SECTION 9.1

1.   a. Any sentence of the form $(A \rightarrow (B \rightarrow A))$ is an axiom of conditioned repetition; $(Q \rightarrow (P \rightarrow Q))$ results from replacing 'A' with 'Q' and 'B' with 'P'.

     b. $Q \rightarrow ((P \rightarrow P) \rightarrow Q)$ is also of the form $(A \rightarrow (B \rightarrow A)$; it results from replacing 'A' with 'Q' and 'B' with '$(P \rightarrow P)$'.

2.   a.

1	Q	hyp
2	$P \& (Q \rightarrow R)$	hyp
–		
3	$Q \rightarrow R$	2, conj elim
4	R	1, 3, m p

     c.

1	P	hyp
2	$P \rightarrow Q$	hyp
3	$Q \rightarrow R$	hyp
–		
4	Q	1, 2, m p
5	R	3, 4, m p
6	$P \& R$	1, 5, conj int

3.   Axiom of Conditioned Repetition

A	B	A	$(B \rightarrow A)$	$(A \rightarrow (B \rightarrow A))$
T	T	T	T	T
T	F	T	T	T
F	T	F	F	T
F	F	F	T	T

6.   The fact that a system is complete guarantees that it is possible to derive the conclusion from the premises of every argument which is valid in terms of the semantics of the system. A system is sound if and only if it is not possible to derive an argument that is not valid. If every argument (valid or not valid) is derivable in a system, then the system is complete. But no such system is sound because the derivable arguments include those that are not valid.

SECTION 9.2

2. The derivation of $(P \rightarrow R)$ from the hypotheses $(P \rightarrow Q)$ and $(Q \rightarrow R)$ has four items: 1, 2, 3–7, 8. The subordinate derivation 3–7 has five items: 3, 4, 5, 6, and 7.

4. a.

1	$P \rightarrow Q$	hyp
2	P	hyp of 2–3
3	$P \rightarrow Q$	1, reit
4	$P \rightarrow (P \rightarrow Q)$	2–3, cond int

c.

1	$(P \rightarrow Q) \rightarrow R$	hyp
2	Q	hyp
3	P	hyp of 3–4
4	Q	2, reit
5	$P \rightarrow Q$	3–4, cond int
6	R	1, 5, m p

e.

1	$R \rightarrow Q$	hyp
2	$P \rightarrow R$	hyp
3	P	hyp of 3–7
4	$P \rightarrow R$	2, reit
5	R	3, 4, m p
6	$R \rightarrow Q$	1, reit
7	Q	5, 6, m p
8	$P \rightarrow Q$	3–7, cond int

g. 1 | $P \to Q$ | hyp
2 | P | hyp of 2-7
3 | R | hyp of 3-6
4 | $P \to Q$ | 1, reit
5 | P | 2, reit
6 | Q | 4, 5, m p
7 | $R \to Q$ | 3-6, cond int
8 | $P \to (R \to Q)$ | 2-7, cond int

6. a. 1 | $(P \to R) \& (R \to Q)$ | hyp of 1-4
2 | $P \to R$ | 1, conj elim
3 | $R \to Q$ | 1, conj elim
4 | $P \to Q$ | 2, 3, trans cond
5 | $((P \to R) \& (R \to Q)) \to (P \to Q)$ | 1-4, cond int

c. 1 | $(Q \to Q) \to P$ | hyp of 1-3
2 | $Q \to Q$ | refl cond
3 | P | 1, 2, m p
4 | $((Q \to Q) \to P) \to P$ | 1-3, cond int

8. a. *P*: The queen is angry.
Q: The king will fire the new cook.
R: The pasta is overcooked.

$(P \to Q)$, $(P \& R)$ /∴ Q

1 | $P \to Q$ | hyp
2 | $P \& R$ | hyp
3 | P | 2, conj elim
4 | Q | 1, 3, m p

c. *P*: Florian will quit whistling.
   Q: Orly stops giggling.
   R: The troubadours will start the show.

   $(P \rightarrow Q)$, $((P \,\&\, Q) \rightarrow R)$ /∴ $(P \rightarrow R)$

1	$P \rightarrow Q$	hyp
2	$(P \,\&\, Q) \rightarrow R$	hyp
3	P	hyp of 3–8
4	$P \rightarrow Q$	1, reit
5	Q	3, 4, m p
6	$P \,\&\, Q$	3, 5, conj int
7	$(P \,\&\, Q) \rightarrow R$	2, reit
8	R	6, 7, m p
9	$P \rightarrow R$	3–8, cond int

e. *P*: The famous detective has already arrived.
   Q: Robert is in trouble.
   R: Ralph is in trouble.

   $(P \rightarrow (Q \,\&\, R))$ /∴ $(P \rightarrow Q)$

1	$P \rightarrow (Q \,\&\, R)$	hyp
2	P	hyp of 2–5
3	$P \rightarrow (Q \,\&\, R)$	1, reit
4	$Q \,\&\, R$	2, 3, m p
5	Q	3, conj elim
6	$P \rightarrow Q$	2–5, cond int

g. *P*: The senator is involved in a major political scandal.
   Q: The senator will have to retire.
   R: The senator will have enough time to write fiction.
   S: The senator will write the great American novel.

   $((P \rightarrow Q) \,\&\, (Q \rightarrow R))$, $(R \rightarrow S)$ /∴ $(P \rightarrow S)$

1	$(P \rightarrow Q) \,\&\, (Q \rightarrow R)$	hyp
2	$R \rightarrow S$	hyp

3		P	hyp of 3-10
4		$(P \to Q)\,\&\,(Q \to R)$	1, reit
5		$P \to Q$	4, conj elim
6		$Q \to R$	4, conj elim
7		Q	3, 5, m p
8		R	6, 7, m p
9		$R \to S$	2, reit
10		S	8, 9, m p
11	$P \to S$		3-10, cond int

i. *P*: *Dracula* is on TV tonight.
  Q: Dracula will watch *Dracula*.
  R: Dracula will order a pizza.

$(P \to Q)$, $((Q \to R)\,\&\,(R \to P))$ / $\therefore$ $(P \to R)$

1	$P \to Q$	hyp
2	$(Q \to R)\,\&\,(R \to P)$	hyp
3	P	hyp of 3-8
4	$P \to Q$	1, reit
5	Q	3, 4, m p
6	$(Q \to R)\,\&\,(R \to P)$	2, reit
7	$Q \to R$	6, conj elim
8	R	5, 7, m p
9	$P \to R$	3-8 cond int

SECTION 9.3

1.

1	$(P \to Q)\,\&\,(Q \to R)$	hyp of 1-8
2	P	hyp of 2-7
3	$(P \to Q)\,\&\,(Q \to R)$	1, reit
4	$P \to Q$	3, conj elim
5	Q	2, 4, m p
6	$Q \to R$	3, conj elim
7	R	5, 6, m p
8	$P \to R$	2-7, cond int
9	$((P \to Q)\,\&\,(Q \to R)) \to (P \to R)$	1-8, cond int

2. b.

	1	$(P \& Q) \& R$	hyp of 1-7
	2	$P \& Q$	1, conj elim
	3	P	2, conj elim
	4	Q	2, conj elim
	5	R	1, conj elim
	6	$Q \& P$	3, 4, conj int
	7	$R \& (Q \& P)$	5, 6, conj int
	8	$((P \& Q) \& R) \rightarrow (R \& (Q \& P))$	1-7, cond int

d.

	1	$((P \& Q) \& R) \rightarrow S$	hyp of 1-13
	2	P	hyp of 2-12
	3	Q	hyp of 3-11
	4	R	hyp of 4-10
	5	Q	3, reit
	6	P	2, reit
	7	$P \& Q$	5, 6, conj int
	8	$(P \& Q) \& R$	4, 7, conj int
	9	$((P \& Q) \& R) \rightarrow S$	1, reit
	10	S	8, 9, m p
	11	$R \rightarrow S$	4-10, cond int
	12	$Q \rightarrow (R \rightarrow S)$	3-11, cond int
	13	$P \rightarrow (Q \rightarrow (R \rightarrow S))$	2-12, cond int
	14	$(((P \& Q) \& R) \rightarrow S) \rightarrow (P \rightarrow (Q \rightarrow (R \rightarrow S)))$	1-13 cond int

f.

	1	$P \& (Q \& R)$	hyp of 1-3
	2	$Q \& R$	1, conj elim
	3	Q	2, conj elim
	4	$(P \& (Q \& R)) \rightarrow Q$	1-3, cond int

h. 1 | $(P \to Q)\ \&\ (R \to S)$ | hyp of 1-12

   2 | $P \to Q$ | 1, conj elim
   3 | $R \to S$ | 1, conj elim
   4 | $P\ \&\ R$ | hyp of 4-11

   5 | P | 4, conj elim
   6 | R | 4, conj elim
   7 | $P \to Q$ | 2, reit
   8 | $R \to S$ | 3, reit
   9 | Q | 5, 7, m p
  10 | S | 6, 8, m p
  11 | $Q\ \&\ S$ | 9, 10, conj int
  12 | $(P\ \&\ R) \to (Q\ \&\ S)$ | 4-11, cond int
  13 | $((P \to Q)\ \&\ (R \to S)) \to$ | 1-12, cond int
     | $((P\ \&\ R) \to (Q\ \&\ S))$ |

3. c. 1 | P | hyp
    2 | Q | hyp

    3 | P | hyp of 3-4

    4 | Q | 2, reit
    5 | $P \to Q$ | 3-4, cond int
    6 | Q | hyp of 6-7

    7 | P | 1, reit
    8 | $Q \to P$ | 6-7, cond int
    9 | $P \equiv Q$ | 5, 8, conj int, df

4. a. 1 | $P \equiv R$ | hyp
    2 | $P\ \&\ Q$ | hyp

    3 | P | 2, conj elim
    4 | $(P \to R)\ \&\ (R \to P)$ | 1, rep, df
    5 | $P \to R$ | 4, conj elim
    6 | R | 3, 5, m p

c. 1 | R hyp

    2 | | R hyp of 2–3

    3 | | $Q \rightarrow Q$ refl cond
    4 | $R \rightarrow (Q \rightarrow Q)$ 2–3, cond int
    5 | | $Q \rightarrow Q$ hyp of 5–6

    6 | | R 1, reit
    7 | $(Q \rightarrow Q) \rightarrow R$ 5–6, cond int
    8 | $R \equiv (Q \rightarrow Q)$ 4, 7, conj int, df

5. b.   1 | $(P \rightarrow Q) \equiv (P \rightarrow Q)$ refl bicond

CHAPTER 10

SECTION 10.1

1. a.   1 | $(P \& Q) \vee (R \& Q)$ hyp

        2 | | $P \& Q$ hyp of 2–3

        3 | | Q 2, conj elim

        4 | | $R \& Q$ hyp of 4–5

        5 | | Q 4, conj elim
        6 | Q 1, 2–3, 4–5, disj elim

    c.   1 | $P \vee Q$ hyp

        2 | | P hyp of 2–4

        3 | | $Q \vee P$ 2, disj int
        4 | | $(Q \vee P) \vee R$ 3, disj int

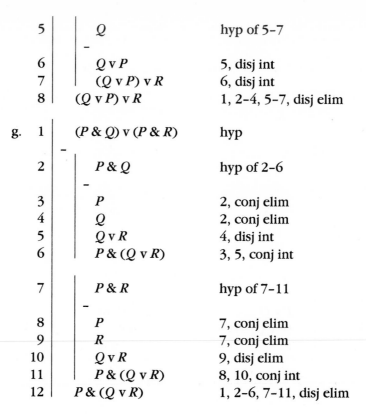

5		Q	hyp of 5–7
6		$Q \vee P$	5, disj int
7		$(Q \vee P) \vee R$	6, disj int
8	$(Q \vee P) \vee R$		1, 2–4, 5–7, disj elim

g. 1	$(P \& Q) \vee (P \& R)$		hyp
2		$P \& Q$	hyp of 2–6
3		P	2, conj elim
4		Q	2, conj elim
5		$Q \vee R$	4, disj int
6		$P \& (Q \vee R)$	3, 5, conj int
7		$P \& R$	hyp of 7–11
8		P	7, conj elim
9		R	7, conj elim
10		$Q \vee R$	9, disj elim
11		$P \& (Q \vee R)$	8, 10, conj int
12	$P \& (Q \vee R)$		1, 2–6, 7–11, disj elim

2. a. $(R \vee ((Q \& P) \& (P \& Q))) \equiv ((R \vee (Q \& P)) \& (R \vee (P \& Q)))$ is a theorem of distribution of disjunction into conjunction, as it has the form $(A \vee (B \& C)) \equiv ((A \vee B) \& (A \vee C))$.

   b. $(((P \vee R) \& Q) \rightarrow (Q \vee R)) \equiv ((P \vee R) \rightarrow (Q \rightarrow (Q \vee R)))$ is a theorem but none of the above.

   c. $((P \vee R) \vee Q) \equiv ((Q \vee R) \vee P)$ is a theorem but none of the above.

   d. $(Q \& ((P \rightarrow R) \vee Q)) \equiv ((Q \& (P \rightarrow R)) \vee (Q \& Q))$ is a theorem of distribution of conjunction into disjunction, as it has the form $(A \& (B \vee C)) \equiv ((A \& B) \vee (A \& C))$.

   e. $((P \rightarrow Q) \vee (Q \rightarrow P)) \equiv ((Q \rightarrow P) \vee (P \rightarrow Q))$ is a theorem of commutativity of disjunction, as it has the form $(A \vee B) \equiv (B \vee A)$.

3. a.
1	$P \lor P$	hyp of 1–6
2	P	hyp of 2–3
3	P	2, rep
4	P	hyp of 4–5
5	P	4, rep
6	P	1, 2–3, 4–5, disj elim
7	$(P \lor P) \to P$	1–6, cond int

c.
1	$(P \lor Q) \to P$	hyp of 1–6
2	Q	hyp of 2–5
3	$P \lor Q$	2, disj int
4	$(P \lor Q) \to P$	1, reit
5	P	3, 4, m p
6	$Q \to P$	2–5, cond int
7	$((P \lor Q) \to P) \to (Q \to P)$	1–6, cond int

e.
1	$P \lor (Q \lor (P \,\&\, R))$	hyp of 1–5
2	$((P \lor Q) \lor (P \,\&\, R)) \equiv (P \lor (Q \lor (P \,\&\, R)))$	assoc disj
3	$(P \lor Q) \lor (P \,\&\, R)$	1, 2, bicond elim
4	$((P \lor Q) \lor (P \,\&\, R)) \equiv ((P \,\&\, R) \lor (P \lor Q))$	comm disj
5	$(P \,\&\, R) \lor (P \lor Q)$	3, 4, bicond elim
6	$(P \,\&\, R) \lor (P \lor Q)$	hyp of 6–10
7	$((P \,\&\, R) \lor (P \lor Q)) \equiv ((P \lor Q) \lor (P \,\&\, R))$	comm disj
8	$(P \lor Q) \lor (P \,\&\, R)$	6, 7, bicond elim
9	$((P \lor Q) \lor (P \,\&\, R)) \equiv (P \lor (Q \lor (P \,\&\, R)))$	assoc disj
10	$P \lor (Q \lor (P \,\&\, R))$	8, 9, bicond elim
11	$(P \lor (Q \lor (P \,\&\, R))) \equiv ((P \,\&\, R) \lor (P \lor Q))$	1–5, 6–10, bicond int

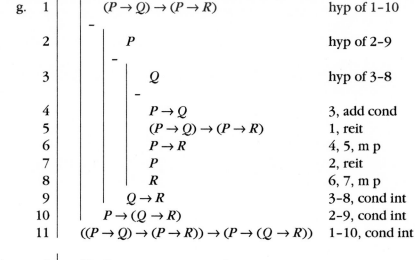

g. 1 $(P \rightarrow Q) \rightarrow (P \rightarrow R)$ hyp of 1–10

    2   P hyp of 2–9

    3   Q hyp of 3–8

    4             $P \rightarrow Q$ 3, add cond
    5             $(P \rightarrow Q) \rightarrow (P \rightarrow R)$ 1, reit
    6             $P \rightarrow R$ 4, 5, m p
    7   P 2, reit
    8   R 6, 7, m p
    9         $Q \rightarrow R$ 3–8, cond int
    10    $P \rightarrow (Q \rightarrow R)$ 2–9, cond int
    11    $((P \rightarrow Q) \rightarrow (P \rightarrow R)) \rightarrow (P \rightarrow (Q \rightarrow R))$ 1–10, cond int

4. a. 1 $P \vee Q$ hyp

       2   P hyp of 2–3

       3        $P \vee R$ 2, disj int
       4   Q hyp of 4–5

       5        $Q \vee S$ 4, disj int
       6    $(P \vee R) \vee (Q \vee S)$ 1, 2–3, 4–5, comp cnst dil

5. a. The following completes the derivation begun in the text proving
        the theorems of commutativity of disjunction.

        7     $Q \vee P$ hyp of 7–12

        8   Q hyp of 8–9

        9         $P \vee Q$ 8, disj int

        10   P hyp of 10–11

        11        $P \vee Q$ 10, disj int
        12    $P \vee Q$ 7, 8–9, 10–11, disj elim
        13    $(P \vee Q) \equiv (Q \vee P)$ 1–6, 7–12, bicond int

SECTION 10.2

1. a.

1	P	hyp of 1-5
2	$\sim P$	hyp of 2-4
3	P	1, reit
4	Q	2, 3, neg elim
5	$\sim P \to Q$	2-4, cond int
6	$P \to (\sim P \to Q)$	1-5, cond int

2. b.

1	$P \vee Q$	hyp
2	$\sim Q$	hyp
3	Q	hyp of 3-5
4	$\sim Q$	2, reit
5	P	3, 4, neg elim
6	P	hyp of 6-6
7	P	1, 3-5, 6-6, disj elim

c.

1	$\sim P \vee Q$	hyp
2	P	hyp
3	$\sim P$	hyp of 3-5
4	P	2, reit
5	Q	3, 4, neg elim
6	Q	hyp of 6-6
7	Q	1, 3-5, 6-6, disj elim

e. 1 | ~(P & Q)   hyp
    2 | P   hyp

    3 | | Q   hyp of 3–6

    4 | | P   2, reit
    5 | | P & Q   3, 4, conj int
    6 | | ~(P & Q)   1, reit
    7 | ~Q   3–6, neg int

h. 1 | P ≡ Q   hyp

    2 | | ~Q   hyp of 2–7

    3 | | | P   hyp of 3–6

    4 | | | P ≡ Q   1, reit
    5 | | | Q   3, 4, bicond elim
    6 | | | ~Q   2, reit
    7 | | ~P   3–6, neg int

    8 | | ~P   hyp of 8–13

    9 | | | Q   hyp of 9–12

    10 | | | P ≡ Q   1, reit
    11 | | | P   9, 10, bicond elim
    12 | | | ~P   8, reit
    13 | | ~Q   9–12, neg int
    14 | ~P ≡ ~Q   2–7, 8–13, bicond int

3. b. (~P → Q), (~P & ~Q)

    1 | ~P → Q   hyp
    2 | ~P & ~Q   hyp

    3 | ~P   2, conj elim
    4 | Q   1, 3, m p
    5 | ~Q   2, conj elim

The sentence and its negation are items 4 and 5.

d. $(P \& \sim(Q \to R)), ((P \& Q) \to R)$

1	$P \& \sim(Q \to R)$	hyp
2	$(P \& Q) \to R$	hyp
3	Q	hyp of 3-8
4	$P \& \sim(Q \to R)$	1, reit
5	P	4, conj elim
6	$P \& Q$	3, 5, conj int
7	$(P \& Q) \to R$	2, reit
8	R	6, 7, m p
9	$Q \to R$	3-8, cond int
10	$\sim(Q \to R)$	1, conj elim

The sentence and its negation are items 9 and 10.

SECTION 10.3

1. b.

1	$\sim(\sim P \& Q)$	hyp of 1-7
2	$\sim\sim P \vee \sim Q$	1, neg conj elim
3	$\sim\sim P$	hyp of 3-4
4	P	3, neg_2 elim
5	$\sim Q$	hyp of 5-6
6	$\sim Q$	5, rep
7	$P \vee \sim Q$	2, 3-4, 5-6, comp cnst dil
8	$\sim(\sim P \& Q) \to (P \vee \sim Q)$	1-7, cond int

g.

1	$\sim P \vee Q$	hyp of 1-5
2	P	hyp of 2-4
3	$\sim P \vee Q$	1, reit
4	Q	2, 3, disj syl
5	$P \to Q$	2-4, cond int
6	$(\sim P \vee Q) \to (P \to Q)$	1-5, cond int

j. 1 | | | $P \rightarrow Q$ | hyp of 1–9
2 | | | $P \rightarrow \sim Q$ | hyp of 2–8
3 | | | P | hyp of 3–7
4 | | | $P \rightarrow Q$ | 1, reit
5 | | | Q | 3, 4, m p
6 | | | $P \rightarrow \sim Q$ | 2, reit
7 | | | $\sim Q$ | 3, 6, m p
8 | | | $\sim P$ | 3–7, neg int
9 | | | $(P \rightarrow \sim Q) \rightarrow \sim P$ | 2–8, cond int
10 | | | $(P \rightarrow Q) \rightarrow ((P \rightarrow \sim Q) \rightarrow \sim P)$ | 1–9, cond int

l. 1 | | | $P \rightarrow \sim Q$ | hyp of 1–6
2 | | | Q | hyp of 2–5
3 | | | $\sim\sim Q$ | 2, neg$_2$ int
4 | | | $P \rightarrow \sim Q$ | 1, reit
5 | | | $\sim P$ | 3, 4, m t
6 | | | $Q \rightarrow \sim P$ | 2–5, cond int
7 | | | $(P \rightarrow \sim Q) \rightarrow (Q \rightarrow \sim P)$ | 1–6, cond int

2. The metaderivation below shows that the rule of negation elimination does not allow derivation of any sentence that could not be derived using the rules of disjunction introduction and disjunctive syllogism.

1 | A | hyp
2 | $\sim A$ | hyp
3 | $\sim A \vee B$ | 2, disj int
4 | B | 1, 3, disj syl

5. a. P: The clay will release water.
     Q: There is water in the clay.
     R: The particles are too fine.

1 | $(\sim Q \vee R) \rightarrow \sim P$ | hyp
2 | R | hyp
3 | $\sim Q \vee R$ | 2, disj int
4 | $\sim P$ | 1, 3, m p

[Note: the translation for 5a is fully expressed in the hypotheses and the conclusion of the derivation at the bottom of the preceding page.]

c. *P*: The president has a cocker spaniel.
   Q: The first lady has a Siamese cat.
   R: The president loves animals.
   S: The first lady loves animals.

1	$(R \,\&\, S) \to (P \,\&\, Q)$	hyp
2	$\sim Q$	hyp
3	$\sim P \lor \sim Q$	2, disj int
4	$\sim (P \,\&\, Q)$	3, neg conj int
5	$\sim (R \,\&\, S)$	1, 4, m t
6	$\sim R \lor \sim S$	5, neg conj elim

f. *P*: Tom is sober.
   Q: Tom is interesting.
   R: Tom is polite.
   S: Suzy likes Tom.

1	$P \to (Q \,\&\, R)$	hyp
2	$(R \,\&\, Q) \to S$	hyp
3	$\quad P$	hyp of 3–10
4	$\quad\quad P \to (Q \,\&\, R)$	1, reit
5	$\quad\quad Q \,\&\, R$	3, 4, m p
6	$\quad\quad Q$	5, conj elim
7	$\quad\quad R$	5, conj elim
8	$\quad\quad R \,\&\, Q$	6, 7, conj int
9	$\quad\quad (R \,\&\, Q) \to S$	2, reit
10	$\quad\quad S$	8, 9, m p
11	$P \to S$	3–10, cond int

g. Same translation scheme as f.

1	$R \to P$	hyp
2	$S \to R$	hyp
3	$\sim P$	hyp
4	$\sim R$	1, 3, m t
5	$\sim S$	2, 4, m t

6. a. *P*: I will eat salmon.
      Q: I will eat liver.
      R: I will eat fish.

1	$P \vee Q$	hyp
2	$\sim R$	hyp
3	$P \rightarrow R$	valid premise
	—	
4	$\sim P$	2, 3, m t
5	Q	1, 4, disj syl

c. *P*: I will order tuna salad for lunch.
     Q: I will order lobster salad for lunch.
     R: I will spend $4.
     S: I will spend $10.
     T: I will spend more than $6 for lunch.

1	$P \vee Q$	hyp
2	$P \rightarrow R$	hyp
3	$Q \rightarrow S$	hyp
4	$\sim T$	hyp
5	$S \rightarrow T$	unstated premise
	—	
6	$\sim S$	4, 5, m t
7	$\sim Q$	3, 6, m t
8	P	1, 7, disj syl

e. *P*: Mr. Cartier will have an allergic reaction.
     Q: Mr. Cartier drinks at least two glasses of wine.
     R: Mr. Cartier drinks at least three glasses of wine.

1	$Q \rightarrow P$	hyp
2	R	hyp
3	$R \rightarrow Q$	unstated premise
	—	
4	Q	2, 3, m p
5	P	1, 4, m p

g. *P*: It was the Fourth of July.
   Q: The mail was not delivered.

1	*P*	hyp
2	*P* → *Q*	unstated premise
3	*Q*	1, 2, m p

i. *P*: The pro-democracy movement will succeed.
   Q: The people are repressed.
   R: The people will fight back until they win.

1	*P* v *Q*	hyp
2	*Q* → *R*	hyp
3	*R* → *P*	unstated premise
4	*P*	hyp of 4–5
5	*P*	4, rep
6	*Q*	hyp of 6–10
7	*Q* → *R*	2, reit
8	*R* → *P*	3, reit
9	*R*	6, 7, m p
10	*P*	8, 9, m p
11	*P*	1, 4–5, 6–10, disj elim

SECTION 10.4

1. The rule of transitivity of conjunction is expressed schematically as
   follows:

h	*A* & *B*	
i	*B* & *C*	
j	*A* & *C*	h, i, trans conj

The metaderivation below shows that the rule of transitivity of conjunction could be adopted as a derived rule.

1	$A \& B$	hyp
2	$B \& C$	hyp
	–	
3	A	1, conj elim
4	C	2, conj elim
5	$A \& C$	3, 4, conj int

No corresponding rule of transitivity of disjunction is derivable. If it were, the system would be unsound and it is not. Because the system is sound, only truth-preserving rules are derivable. That such a rule is not truth-preserving is shown by the following truth-table row:

A	B	C	$A \lor B$	$B \lor C$	$A \lor C$
F	T	F	T	T	F

3. Conditionals are not commutative because not every sentence of the form $((A \rightarrow B) \equiv (B \rightarrow A))$ is valid.

6. The derived rule of biconditional elimination has two parts. One part says that the right immediate component of a biconditional is a direct consequence of the biconditional and its left immediate component. The other part says that the left immediate component of a biconditional is a direct consequence of the biconditional and its right immediate component.

The derived rule of disjunctive syllogism has four parts. Part one says that B is a direct consequence of $(A \lor B)$ and $\sim A$. Part two says that A is a direct consequence of $(A \lor B)$ and $\sim B$. Part three says that B is a direct consequence of $(\sim A \lor B)$ and A. Part four says that A is a direct consequence of $(A \lor \sim B)$ and B.

7. a. P: Cindy is getting married.
   Q: Cindy is flying to London.
   R: Clara is attending the wedding ceremony.
   S: Clara is flying to Rio de Janeiro.

   $((P \lor Q) \& (R \lor S)), ((P \rightarrow R) \& (Q \rightarrow S)), \sim R \ /\therefore \ (S \& \sim P)$

1	$(P \lor Q) \& (R \lor S)$	hyp
2	$(P \rightarrow R) \& (Q \rightarrow S)$	hyp
3	$\sim R$	hyp
	–	

4	$R \vee S$	1, conj elim
5	S	3, 4, disj syl
6	$P \rightarrow R$	2, conj elim
7	$\sim P$	3, 6, m t
8	$S \,\&\, \sim P$	5, 7, conj int

c. *P*: Nancy is at the movies tonight.
    Q: Nancy is unhappy.
    R: Nancy wants to be at the movies tonight.
    $((P \vee Q) \vee \sim R)$, $(R \,\&\, \sim P)$ /∴ *Q*

1	$(P \vee Q) \vee \sim R$	hyp
2	$R \,\&\, \sim P$	hyp
3	R	2, conj elim
4	$P \vee Q$	1, 3, disj syl
5	$\sim P$	2, conj elim
6	Q	4, 5, disj syl

e. *P*: You wish upon a star.
    Q: You wait for your fairy godmother to help you.
    R: You give up hope.
    $((P \,\&\, Q) \rightarrow \sim R)$, R /∴ $(\sim P \vee \sim Q)$

1	$(P \,\&\, Q) \rightarrow \sim R$	hyp
2	R	hyp
3	$\sim\sim R$	2, neg$_2$ int
4	$\sim(P \,\&\, Q)$	1, 3, m t
5	$\sim P \vee \sim Q$	4, neg conj elim

8. a. (i) $\sim(P \,\&\, Q)$
        (ii) $\sim P \vee \sim Q$

1	$\sim(P \,\&\, Q)$	hyp of 1–2
2	$\sim P \vee \sim Q$	1, neg conj elim
3	$\sim P \vee \sim Q$	hyp of 3–4
4	$\sim(P \,\&\, Q)$	3, neg conj int
5	$\sim(P \,\&\, Q) \equiv (\sim P \vee \sim Q)$	1–2, 3–4, bicond int

c. (i) ~(P & ~Q)

(ii) ~P v Q

1		~(P & ~Q)	hyp of 1–7
2		~P v ~~Q	1, neg conj elim
3		~P	hyp of 3–4
4		~P	3, rep
5		~~Q	hyp of 5–6
6		Q	5, neg₂ elim
7		~P v Q	2, 3–4, 5–6, comp cnst dil
8		~P v Q	hyp of 8–15
9		~~(P & ~Q)	hyp of 9–14
10		P & ~Q	9, neg₂ elim
11		~P v Q	8, reit
12		P	10, conj elim
13		Q	11, 12, disj syl
14		~Q	10, conj elim
15		~(P & ~Q)	9–14, ind pr
16		~(P & ~Q) ≡ (~P v Q)	1–7, 8–15, bicond int

CHAPTER 11

SECTION 11.1

1. b.

1		$(\forall x)(Fx \text{ v } Gx)$	hyp
2		$(\forall x)\text{~}Gx$	hyp
3	a	$(\forall x)(Fx \text{ v } Gx)$	1, reit
4		$(\forall x)\text{~}Gx$	2, reit
5		Fa v Ga	3, u q elim
6		~Ga	4, u q elim
7		Fa	5, 6, disj syl
8		$(\forall x)Fx$	3–7, u q int

d.

1		$(\forall x)(\sim Gx \rightarrow \sim Fx)$		hyp
2	a	$(\forall x)(\sim Gx \rightarrow \sim Fx)$		1, reit
3		$\sim Ga \rightarrow \sim Fa$		2, u q elim
4		Fa		hyp of 4–9
5		$\sim Ga$		hyp of 5–8
6		$\sim Ga \rightarrow \sim Fa$		3, reit
7		$\sim Fa$		5, 6, m p
8		Fa		4, reit
9		Ga		5–8, ind pr
10		$Fa \rightarrow Ga$		4–9, cond int
11		$(\forall x)(Fx \rightarrow Gx)$		2–10, u q int

f.

1				$(\forall x)(\forall y)(\forall z)Fxyz$	hyp
2	c	b	a	$(\forall x)(\forall y)(\forall z)Fxyz$	1, reit
3				$(\forall y)(\forall z)Fayz$	2, u q elim
4				$(\forall z)Fabz$	3, u q elim
5				$Fabc$	4, u q elim
6				$(\forall x)Fxbc$	2–5, u q int
7				$(\forall y)(\forall x)Fxyc$	2–6, u q int
8				$(\forall z)(\forall y)(\forall x)Fxyz$	2–7, u q int

h.

1				$(\forall x)(\forall y)Fxy \,\&\, (\forall z)Gz$	hyp
2	a	b	c	$(\forall x)(\forall y)Fxy \,\&\, (\forall z)Gz$	1, reit
3				$(\forall z)Gz$	2, conj elim
4				Ga	3, u q elim
5				$(\forall x)(\forall y)Fxy$	2, conj elim
6				$(\forall x)Fxb$	5, u q elim
7				Fcb	6, u q elim
8				$Fcb \,\&\, Ga$	4, 7, conj int
9				$(\forall x)(Fxb \,\&\, Ga)$	2–8, u q int
10				$(\forall y)(\forall x)(Fxy \,\&\, Ga)$	2–9, u q int
11				$(\forall z)(\forall y)(\forall x)(Fxy \,\&\, Gz)$	2–10, u q int

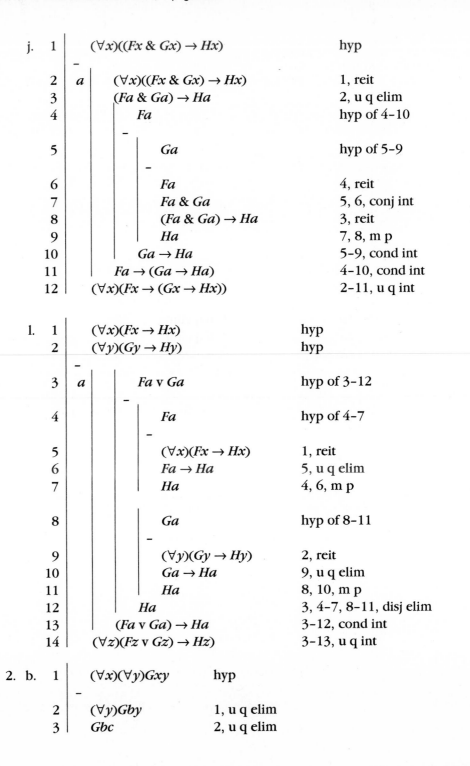

j. 1 | $(\forall x)((Fx \;\&\; Gx) \rightarrow Hx)$ | hyp

2 a | $(\forall x)((Fx \;\&\; Gx) \rightarrow Hx)$ | 1, reit
3 | $(Fa \;\&\; Ga) \rightarrow Ha$ | 2, u q elim
4 | Fa | hyp of 4–10

5 | Ga | hyp of 5–9

6 | Fa | 4, reit
7 | $Fa \;\&\; Ga$ | 5, 6, conj int
8 | $(Fa \;\&\; Ga) \rightarrow Ha$ | 3, reit
9 | Ha | 7, 8, m p
10 | $Ga \rightarrow Ha$ | 5–9, cond int
11 | $Fa \rightarrow (Ga \rightarrow Ha)$ | 4–10, cond int
12 | $(\forall x)(Fx \rightarrow (Gx \rightarrow Hx))$ | 2–11, u q int

l. 1 | $(\forall x)(Fx \rightarrow Hx)$ | hyp
2 | $(\forall y)(Gy \rightarrow Hy)$ | hyp

3 a | $Fa \;v\; Ga$ | hyp of 3–12

4 | Fa | hyp of 4–7

5 | $(\forall x)(Fx \rightarrow Hx)$ | 1, reit
6 | $Fa \rightarrow Ha$ | 5, u q elim
7 | Ha | 4, 6, m p

8 | Ga | hyp of 8–11

9 | $(\forall y)(Gy \rightarrow Hy)$ | 2, reit
10 | $Ga \rightarrow Ha$ | 9, u q elim
11 | Ha | 8, 10, m p
12 | Ha | 3, 4–7, 8–11, disj elim
13 | $(Fa \;v\; Ga) \rightarrow Ha$ | 3–12, cond int
14 | $(\forall z)(Fz \;v\; Gz) \rightarrow Hz)$ | 3–13, u q int

2. b. 1 | $(\forall x)(\forall y)Gxy$ | hyp

2 | $(\forall y)Gby$ | 1, u q elim
3 | Gbc | 2, u q elim

d. 1 | $(\forall x)(Fx \lor Gx)$ | hyp
    2 | $\sim Gc$ | hyp
    |—
    3 | $Fc \lor Gc$ | 1, u q elim
    4 | Fc | 2, 3, disj syl

f. 1 | $(\forall x)Gx$ | hyp
    2 | $\sim Ga$ | hyp
    |—
    3 | Ga | 1, u q elim
    4 | Fa | 2, 3, neg elim

g. 1 | $(\forall x)Fx$ | hyp
    2 | $(\forall x)Gx$ | hyp
    |—
    3 | Fa | 1, u q elim
    4 | Ga | 2, u q elim
    5 | $Ga \ \& \ Fa$ | 3, 4, conj int

3. b. 1 | $(\forall z)(Fz \lor Ga)$ | hyp of 1–10
    |—
    2 | $\sim((\forall z)Fz \lor Ga)$ | hyp of 2–9
    |—
    3 | $\sim(\forall z)Fz \ \& \ \sim Ga$ | 2, d m
    4 | b | $(\forall z)(Fz \lor Ga)$ | 1, reit
    5 | $Fb \lor Ga$ | 4, u q elim
    6 | $\sim Ga$ | 3, reit, conj elim
    7 | Fb | 5, 6, disj syl
    8 | $(\forall z)Fz$ | 4–7, u q int
    9 | $\sim(\forall z)Fz$ | 3, conj elim
    10 | $(\forall z)Fz \lor Ga$ | 2–9, ind pr

    11 | $(\forall z)Fz \lor Ga$ | hyp of 11–19
    |—
    12 | b | $(\forall z)Fz \lor Ga$ | 11, reit
    13 | $(\forall z)Fz$ | hyp of 13–15
    |—
    14 | Fb | 13, u q elim
    15 | $Fb \lor Ga$ | 14, disj int

16				Ga	hyp of 16–17

16	Ga	hyp of 16–17
17	$Fb \lor Ga$	16, disj int
18	$Fb \lor Ga$	12, 13–15, 16–17, disj elim
19	$(\forall z)(Fz \lor Ga)$	12–18, u q int
20	$(\forall z)(Fz \lor Ga) \equiv ((\forall z)Fz \lor Ga)$	1–10, 11–19, bicond int

d.

1	$(\forall y)(Fy \lor (\forall x)Gxy)$	hyp of 1–9
2	b	a	$Fa \lor (\forall x)Gxa$	1, reit, u q elim
3	Fa	hyp of 3–4
4	Fa	3, rep
5	$(\forall x)Gxa$	hyp of 5–6
6	Gba	5, u q elim
7	$Fa \lor Gba$	2, 3–4, 5–6, comp cnst dil
8	$(\forall x)(Fx \lor Gbx)$	2–7, u q int
9	$(\forall y)(\forall x)(Fx \lor Gyx)$	2–8, u q int
10	$(\forall y)(Fy \lor (\forall x)Gxy) \rightarrow$ $(\forall y)(\forall x)(Fx \lor Gyx)$	1–9, cond int

4.　b. $(\forall x)(Fx \rightarrow Gx)$, $(\forall x)(Gx \rightarrow {\sim}Hx)$ /∴ $(\forall x)(Hx \rightarrow {\sim}Fx)$
　　　$F\_$: _ is brave, $G\_$: _ takes risks, $H\_$: _ gives up easily

1	$(\forall x)(Fx \rightarrow Gx)$	hyp
2	$(\forall x)(Gx \rightarrow {\sim}Hx)$	hyp
3	a	$Fa \rightarrow Ga$	1, reit, u q elim
4	$Ga \rightarrow {\sim}Ha$	2, reit, u q elim
5	$Fa \rightarrow {\sim}Ha$	3, 4, trans cond
6	Ha	hyp of 6–9
7	$Fa \rightarrow {\sim}Ha$	5, reit
8	${\sim}{\sim}Ha$	6, neg$_2$ int
9	${\sim}Fa$	7, 8, m t
10	$Ha \rightarrow {\sim}Fa$	6–9, cond int
11	$(\forall x)(Hx \rightarrow {\sim}Fx)$	3–10, u q int

d. $(\forall x)((Fx \lor Gx) \to (Hx \& Ix)) \; / \therefore \; (\forall x)(Gx \to Hx)$
$F\_:$ _ is desperate, $G\_:$ _ is confused, $H\_:$ _ will become happy after a while, $I\_:$ _ will become enlightened after a while
Domain: {people}

1		$(\forall x)((Fx \lor Gx) \to (Hx \& Ix))$		hyp
2	a	Ga		hyp of 2-7
3		$(\forall x)((Fx \lor Gx) \to (Hx \& Ix))$		1, reit
4		$(Fa \lor Ga) \to (Ha \& Ia)$		3, u q elim
5		$Fa \lor Ga$		2, disj int
6		$Ha \& Ia$		4, 5, m p
7		Ha		6, conj elim
8		$Ga \to Ha$		2-7, cond int
9		$(\forall x)(Gx \to Hx)$		2-8, u q int

SECTION 11.2

1. a.

1		$(\forall x)(Fx \to Gx)$	hyp
2		$(\exists x)Fx$	hyp
3	a	Fa	hyp of 3-6
4		$Fa \to Ga$	1, reit, u q elim
5		Ga	3, 4, m p
6		$(\exists x)Gx$	5, e q int
7		$(\exists x)Gx$	2, 3-6, e q elim

c.

1		$(\forall x)(Fx \lor Gx)$	hyp
2		$(\exists x)\sim Fx$	hyp
3	a	$\sim Fa$	hyp of 3-6
4		$Fa \lor Ga$	1, reit, u q elim
5		Ga	3, 4, disj syl
6		$(\exists x)Gx$	5, e q int
7		$(\exists x)Gx$	2, 3-6, e q elim

e. 1 | $(\exists x)Fxx$ | hyp
    2 | a | Faa | hyp 2–4
    3 | $(\exists y)Fay$ | 2, e q int
    4 | $(\exists x)(\exists y)Fxy$ | 3, e q int
    5 | $(\exists x)(\exists y)Fxy$ | 1, 2–4, e q elim

g. 1 | $\sim(\exists x)(Fx\ \&\ \sim Gx)$ | hyp
    2 | $(\forall x)\sim(Fx\ \&\ \sim Gx)$ | 1, neg e q elim
    3 | a | Fa | hyp of 3–9
    4 | $\sim(Fa\ \&\ \sim Ga)$ | 2, reit, u q elim
    5 | $\sim Fa\ \lor\ \sim\sim Ga$ | 4, d m
    6 | $\sim\sim Fa$ | 3, neg_2 int
    7 | $\sim\sim Ga$ | 5, 6, disj syl
    8 | Ga | 7, neg_2 elim
    9 | $Fa \to Ga$ | 3–8, cond int
    10 | $(\forall x)(Fx \to Gx)$ | 3–9, u q int

i. 1 | $(\exists x)(Fx\ \&\ Gx)$ | hyp
    2 | a | $Fa\ \&\ Ga$ | hyp of 2–8
    3 | $Fa \to \sim Ga$ | hyp of 3–6
    4 | Fa | 2, reit, conj elim
    5 | $\sim Ga$ | 3, 4, m p
    6 | Ga | 2, reit, conj elim
    7 | $\sim(Fa \to \sim Ga)$ | 3–6, neg int
    8 | $(\exists x)\sim(Fx \to \sim Gx)$ | 7, e q int
    9 | $(\exists x)\sim(Fx \to \sim Gx)$ | 1, 2–8, e q elim
    10 | $\sim(\forall x)(Fx \to \sim Gx)$ | 9, neg u q int

2. b. 1 | $(\exists x)(\exists y)Hxy$ | hyp
       2 | a | $(\exists y)Hay$ | hyp of 2–6

3			*b*	*Hab*	hyp of 3-5
4				(∃*x*)*Hxb*	3, e q int
5				(∃*y*)(∃*x*)*Hxy*	4, e q int
6			(∃*y*)(∃*x*)*Hxy*		2, 3-5, e q elim
7		(∃*y*)(∃*x*)*Hxy*			1, 2-6, e q elim
8		(∃*y*)(∃*x*)*Hxy*			hyp of 8-14
9		*a*	(∃*x*)*Hxa*		hyp of 9-13
10			*b*	*Hba*	hyp of 10-12
11				(∃*y*)*Hby*	10, e q int
12				(∃*x*)(∃*y*)*Hxy*	11, e q int
13			(∃*x*)(∃*y*)*Hxy*		9, 10-12, e q elim
14		(∃*x*)(∃*y*)*Hxy*			8, 9-13, e q elim
15	(∃*x*)(∃*y*)*Hxy* ≡ (∃*y*)(∃*x*)*Hxy*				1-7, 8-14, bicond int

d.

1		(∀*x*)(*Fx* → *Hc*)			hyp of 1-7
2			(∃*x*)*Fx*		hyp of 2-6
3			*a*	*Fa*	hyp of 3-5
4				*Fa* → *Hc*	1, reit, u q elim
5				*Hc*	3, 4, m p
6			*Hc*		2, 3-5, e q elim
7		(∃*x*)*Fx* → *Hc*			2-6, cond int
8	(∀*x*)(*Fx* → *Hc*) → ((∃*x*)*Fx* → *Hc*)				1-7, cond int

3. b.

1	*Fac*	hyp
2	(∃*y*)*Fay*	1, e q int
3	(∃*x*)(∃*y*)*Fxy*	2, e q int

d.

1	*Fbb*	hyp
2	(∃*y*)*Fby*	1, e q int
3	(∃*x*)(∃*y*)*Fxy*	2, e q int

f. 1 | $(\exists x)Fax$ | hyp

2   b | Fab | hyp of 2–4

3 | $(\exists y)Fyb$ | 2, e q int
4 | $(\exists x)(\exists y)Fyx$ | 3, e q int
5 | $(\exists x)(\exists y)Fyx$ | 1, 2–4, e q elim

g. 1 | $Fc \to (\exists x)Gxx$ | hyp of 1–18

2 | $Fc \lor \sim Fc$ | ex mid
3 | Fc | hyp of 3–11

4 | $Fc \to (\exists x)Gxx$ | 1, reit
5 | $(\exists x)Gxx$ | 3, 4, m p
6   a | Gaa | hyp of 6–10

7 | Fc | hyp of 7–8

8 | Gaa | 6, reit
9 | $Fa \to Gaa$ | 7–8, cond int
10 | $(\exists x)(Fx \to Gxx)$ | 9, e q int
11 | $(\exists x)(Fx \to Gxx)$ | 5, 6–10, e q elim

12 | $\sim Fc$ | hyp of 12–17

13 | Fc | hyp of 13–15

14 | $\sim Fc$ | 12, reit
15 | Gaa | 13, 14, neg elim
16 | $Fc \to Gaa$ | 13–15, cond int
17 | $(\exists x)(Fc \to Gxx)$ | 16, e q int
18 | $(\exists x)(Fc \to Gxx)$ | 2, 3–11, 12–17, disj elim
19 | $(Fc \to (\exists x)Gxx) \to (\exists x)(Fc \to Gxx)$ 1–18, cond int

4. b. $(\forall x)(Fx \rightarrow Gx)$, $(\exists x)(Fx \;\&\; \sim Hx)$ /$\therefore$ $(\exists x)(Gx \;\&\; \sim Hx)$

   $F\_:$ _ is joyful, $G\_:$ _ is wise, $H\_:$ _ is rich

1		$(\forall x)(Fx \rightarrow Gx)$	hyp
2		$(\exists x)(Fx \;\&\; \sim Hx)$	hyp
3	a	$Fa \;\&\; \sim Ha$	hyp of 3-9
4		$Fa \rightarrow Ga$	1, reit, u q elim
5		Fa	3, conj elim
6		Ga	4, 5, m p
7		$\sim Ha$	3, conj elim
8		$Ga \;\&\; \sim Ha$	6, 7, conj int
9		$(\exists x)(Gx \;\&\; \sim Ha)$	8, e q int
10		$(\exists x)(Gx \;\&\; \sim Hx)$	2, 3-9, e q elim

   d. $(\forall x)(Fx \rightarrow Gx)$, $(\exists x)Fx$ /$\therefore$ $(\exists x)Gx$

   $F\_:$ _ hates to waste things, $G\_:$ _ is thrifty
   Domain: {people}

1		$(\forall x)(Fx \rightarrow Gx)$	hyp
2		$(\exists x)Fx$	hyp
3	a	Fa	hyp of 3-6
4		$Fa \rightarrow Ga$	1, reit, u q elim
5		Ga	3, 4, m p
6		$(\exists x)Gx$	5, e q int
7		$(\exists x)Gx$	2, 3-6, e q elim

   f. $((\forall x)(Fx \rightarrow Gx) \;\text{v}\; (\forall x)(Hx \rightarrow Ix))$, $((\exists x)(Hx \;\&\; Ix) \;\&\; (\exists y)(Hy \;\&\; Gy))$, $(\forall x)(Gx \equiv \sim Ix)$ /$\therefore$ $(\forall x)(Fx \rightarrow Gx)$

   $F\_:$ _ is a columnist, $G\_:$ _ is a man, $H\_:$ _ is a reporter,
   $I\_:$ _ is a woman
   Valid premise: $(\forall x)(Gx \equiv \sim Ix)$

1	$(\forall x)(Fx \rightarrow Gx)$ v $(\forall x)(Hx \rightarrow Ix)$	hyp
2	$(\exists x)(Hx \& Ix) \& (\exists y)(Hy \& Gy)$	hyp
3	$(\forall x)(Gx \equiv \sim Ix)$	hyp
4	$\quad (\forall x)(Hx \rightarrow Ix)$	hyp of 4–14
5	$\quad (\exists y)(Hy \& Gy)$	2, reit, conj elim
6	$a \quad Ha \& Ga$	hyp of 6–13
7	$\quad\quad Ha$	6, conj elim
8	$\quad\quad Ha \rightarrow Ia$	4, reit, u q elim
9	$\quad\quad Ia$	7, 8, m p
10	$\quad\quad Ga \equiv \sim Ia$	3, reit, u q elim
11	$\quad\quad Ga$	6, conj elim
12	$\quad\quad \sim Ia$	10, 11, bicond elim
13	$\quad\quad \sim(\forall x)(Hx \rightarrow Ix)$	9, 12, neg elim
14	$\quad \sim(\forall x)(Hx \rightarrow Ix)$	5, 6–13, e q elim
15	$\sim(\forall x)(Hx \rightarrow Ix)$	4–14, neg int
16	$(\forall x)(Fx \rightarrow Gx)$	1, 15, disj syl

h. $(\forall x)(\forall y)Fxy$ /∴ $(\forall x)(\exists y)Fxy$

$F\_ \_: \_$ likes $\_$ Domain: {people}

1	$(\forall x)(\forall y)Fxy$	hyp
2	$b \quad (\forall y)Fby$	1, reit, u q elim
3	$\quad Fba$	2, u q elim
4	$\quad (\exists y)Fby$	3, e q int
5	$(\forall x)(\exists y)Fxy$	2–4, u q int

5. b. $F\_: \_$ is a man, $G\_: \_$ is a woman, $H\_: \_$ is a columnist, $J\_: \_$ is a reporter

$((\forall x)(Hx \rightarrow Fx) \& (\forall x)(Jx \rightarrow Gx))$, $(\exists x)(Gx \& Jx \& Hx)$
Valid sentence: $(\forall x)(Fx \equiv \sim Gx)$

1	$(\forall x)(Hx \rightarrow Fx) \&$ $(\forall x)(Jx \rightarrow Gx)$	hyp
2	$(\exists x)(Gx \& Jx \& Hx)$	hyp
3	$(\forall x)(Fx \equiv \sim Gx)$	hyp
4	$a \quad (Ga \& Ja) \& Ha$	hyp of 4–13

5	$Ga \mathbin{\&} Ja$	4, conj elim
6	Ga	5, conj elim
7	$(\forall x)(Hx \rightarrow Fx)$	1, reit, conj elim
8	$Ha \rightarrow Fa$	7, u q elim
9	Ha	4, conj elim
10	Fa	8, 9, m p
11	$Fa \equiv {\sim}Ga$	3, reit, u q elim
12	${\sim}Ga$	10, 11, bicond elim
13	${\sim}(\forall x)(Fx \equiv {\sim}Gx)$	6, 12, neg elim
14	${\sim}(\forall x)(Fx \equiv {\sim}Gx)$	2, 4–13, e q elim

Item 14 is the negation of 3.

6. a. $S\_$: _ is an interest of the state, $C\_$: _ is an interest of the citizens, $G\_$: _ is an interest of General Motors

   $(\forall x)(Cx \equiv Sx)$, $(\forall x)(Cx \equiv Gx)$ /$\therefore$ $(\forall x)(Gx \equiv Sx)$

1		$(\forall x)(Cx \equiv Sx)$	hyp
2		$(\forall x)(Cx \equiv Gx)$	hyp
3	a	$Ca \equiv Sa$	1, reit, u q elim
4		$Ca \equiv Ga$	2, reit, u q elim
5		$(Ga \equiv Ca) \equiv (Ca \equiv Ga)$	comm bicond
6		$Ga \equiv Ca$	4, 5, bicond elim
7		$Ga \equiv Sa$	3, 6, trans bicond
8		$(\forall x)(Gx \equiv Sx)$	3–7, u q int

SECTION 11.3

1. No. Intelim-SQ would not be sound if every sentence of the form

   $(\forall x)(A \mathbin{\text{v}} B) \rightarrow ((\forall x)A \mathbin{\text{v}} (\forall x)B)$

   were a theorem. For example,

   $(\forall x)(Fx \mathbin{\text{v}} Gx) \rightarrow ((\forall x)Fx \mathbin{\text{v}} (\forall x)Gx)$

   is such a sentence and it is false if $F\_$: $\{a\}$, $G\_$: $\{b\}$, and the domain is $\{a, b\}$. No theorem of a sound system can be false.

2. a.

1		$(\forall x)A \mathbin{\&} (\forall x)B$	hyp of 1–8
2	a	$(\forall x)A \mathbin{\&} (\forall x)B$	1, reit
3		$(\forall x)A$	2, conj elim
4		$(\forall x)B$	2, conj elim
5		$A(a/x)$	3, u q elim
6		$B(a/x)$	4, u q elim
7		$A(a/x) \mathbin{\&} B(a/x)$	5, 6, conj int
8		$(\forall x)(A \mathbin{\&} B)$	2–7, u q int
9		$((\forall x)A \mathbin{\&} (\forall x)B) \rightarrow (\forall x)(A \mathbin{\&} B)$	1–8, cond int

In no derivation of this form does a occur in A or in B.

c.

1		$(\forall x)(A \vee B)$	hyp of 1–10
2		$\sim(A \vee (\forall x)B)$	hyp 2–9
3		$\sim A \mathbin{\&} \sim(\forall x)B$	2, d m
4	a	$(\forall x)(A \vee B)$	1, reit
5		$A \vee B(a/x)$	4, u q elim
6		$\sim A$	3, reit, conj elim
7		$B(a/x)$	5, 6, disj syl
8		$(\forall x)B$	4–7, u q int
9		$\sim(\forall x)B$	3, conj elim
10		$A \vee (\forall x)B$	2–9, ind pr
11		$(\forall x)(A \vee B) \rightarrow (A \vee (\forall x)B)$	1–10, cond int

In any derivation of this form, a does not occur in A or in B and x does not occur in A.

e.

1		$A \rightarrow (\forall x)B$	hyp of 1–7
2	a	A	hyp of 2–5
3		$A \rightarrow (\forall x)B$	1, reit
4		$(\forall x)B$	2, 3, m p
5		$B(a/x)$	4, u q elim
6		$A \rightarrow B(a/x)$	2–5, cond int
7		$(\forall x)(A \rightarrow B)$	2–6, u q int
8		$(A \rightarrow (\forall x)B) \rightarrow (\forall x)(A \rightarrow B)$	1–7, cond int

In no derivation of this form does a occur in A or in B

g. 1 | $A \& (\forall x)B$ | hyp of 1-7

2 a | $A \& (\forall x)B$ | 1, reit
3 | A | 2, conj elim
4 | $(\forall x)B$ | 3, conj elim
5 | $B(a/x)$ | 4, u q elim
6 | $A \& B(a/x)$ | 3, 5, conj int
7 | $(\forall x)(A \& B)$ | 2-6, u q int
8 | $(A \& (\forall x)B) \to (\forall x)(A \& B)$ | 1-7, cond int

In any derivation of this form, a occurs neither in A nor in B.

i. 1 | $(\forall x)(A \to B)$ | hyp of 1-6

2 | $(\forall x)A$ | hyp of 2-5

3 | $A(a/x) \to B$ | 1, reit, u q elim
4 | $A(a/x)$ | 2, u q elim
5 | B | 3, 4, m p
6 | $(\forall x)A \to B$ | 2-5, cond int
7 | $(\forall x)(A \to B) \to ((\forall x)A \to B)$ | 1-6, cond int

In any derivation of this form, x does not occur in B.

3. No, because not all sentences of the form

$$((\exists x)A \& (\exists x)B) \to (\exists x)(A \& B)$$

are Q-valid, even though their converses are. The same is true of the second form because not every sentence of the form

$$(\exists x)(A \to B) \to ((\exists x)A \to (\exists x)B)$$

is Q-valid. For example, take

$$(\exists x)(Fx \to Gx) \to ((\exists x)Fx \to (\exists x)Gx)$$

and let $F\_$: $\{a\}$, $G\_$: empty set, and the domain be $\{a, b\}$. Then the antecedent is true but the consequent is false. The same is also true of the fourth form because not every sentence of the form

$$(\forall x)(A \text{ v } B) \to ((\forall x)A \text{ v } (\forall x)B)$$

is Q-valid. However, every sentence of the third form is Q-valid, so all those sentence are desirable as theorems.

4. b.

1	$(\exists x)(A \rightarrow B)$		hyp of 1–8
2	$(\forall x)A$		hyp of 2–7
3	$(\exists x)(A \rightarrow B)$		1, reit
4	a	$A(a/x) \rightarrow B$	hyp of 4–6
5	$A(a/x)$		2, reit
6	B		4, 5, m p
7	B		3, 4–6, e q elim
8	$(\forall x)A \rightarrow B$		2–7, cond int
9	$(\exists x)(A \rightarrow B) \rightarrow ((\forall x)A \rightarrow B)$		1–8, cond int

In any derivation of this form, a does not occur in A or in B and x does not occur in B.

d.

1	$(\exists x)(A \vee B)$		hyp of 1–9
2	a	$A \vee B(a/x)$	hyp of 2–8
3	A		hyp of 3–4
4	$A \vee (\exists x)B$		3, disj int
5	$B(a/x)$		hyp of 5–7
6	$(\exists x)B$		5, e q int
7	$A \vee (\exists x)B$		6, disj int
8	$A \vee (\exists x)B$		2, 3–4, 5–7, disj elim
9	$A \vee (\exists x)B$		1, 2–8, e q elim
10	$A \vee (\exists x)B$		hyp of 10–19
11	A		hyp of 11–13
12	$A \vee B(b/x)$		11, disj int
13	$(\exists x)(A \vee B)$		12, e q int
14	$(\exists x)B$		hyp of 14–18

15	c	$B(c/x)$	hyp of 15–17
16		$A \vee B(c/x)$	15, disj int
17		$(\exists x)(A \vee B)$	16, e q int
18		$(\exists x)(A \vee B)$	14, 15–17, e q elim
19		$(\exists x)(A \vee B)$	10, 11–13, 14–18, disj elim
20		$(\exists x)(A \vee B) \equiv (A \vee (\exists x)B)$	1–9, 10–19, bicond int

In any derivation of this form, neither a nor c appears in A or in B and x does not occur in A.

5. b.

1		$(\forall x)\sim A$	hyp
2		$(\exists x)A$	hyp of 2–6
3	a	$A(a/x)$	hyp of 3–5
4		$\sim A(a/x)$	1, reit, u q elim
5		$\sim(\exists x)A$	3, 4, neg elim
6		$\sim(\exists x)A$	2, 3–5, e q elim
7		$\sim(\exists x)A$	2–6, neg int

In a derivation of this form, a cannot occur in A.

c.

1		$\sim(\forall x)A$	hyp
2		$\sim(\exists x)\sim A$	hyp of 2–7
3		$(\forall x)\sim\sim A$	2, rule 5a
4	a	$\sim\sim A(a/x)$	3, reit, u q elim
5		$A(a/x)$	4, neg_2 elim
6		$(\forall x)A$	4–5, u q int
7		$\sim(\forall x)A$	1, reit
8		$(\exists x)\sim A$	2–7, ind pr

In a derivation of this form, a cannot occur in A.

CHAPTER 12

SECTION 12.1

1. a. irreflexive   e. reflexive   i. nonreflexive
    b. irreflexive   f. irreflexive   j. reflexive
    c. irreflexive   g. reflexive   k. reflexive
    d. nonreflexive   h. irreflexive   l. irreflexive

3. a. transitive   g. transitive
    b. transitive   h. transitive
    c. transitive   i. nontransitive
    d. nontransitive   j. nontransitive
    e. transitive   k. transitive
    f. transitive   l. transitive and intransitive

5.

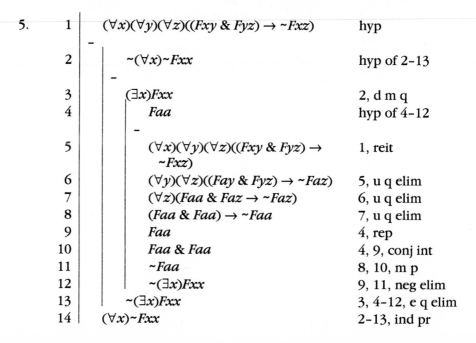

1	$(\forall x)(\forall y)(\forall z)((Fxy \mathbin{\&} Fyz) \to {\sim}Fxz)$	hyp
2	${\sim}(\forall x){\sim}Fxx$	hyp of 2–13
3	$(\exists x)Fxx$	2, d m q
4	Faa	hyp of 4–12
5	$(\forall x)(\forall y)(\forall z)((Fxy \mathbin{\&} Fyz) \to {\sim}Fxz)$	1, reit
6	$(\forall y)(\forall z)((Fay \mathbin{\&} Fyz) \to {\sim}Faz)$	5, u q elim
7	$(\forall z)(Faa \mathbin{\&} Faz \to {\sim}Faz)$	6, u q elim
8	$(Faa \mathbin{\&} Faa) \to {\sim}Faa$	7, u q elim
9	Faa	4, rep
10	$Faa \mathbin{\&} Faa$	4, 9, conj int
11	${\sim}Faa$	8, 10, m p
12	${\sim}(\exists x)Fxx$	9, 11, neg elim
13	${\sim}(\exists x)Fxx$	3, 4–12, e q elim
14	$(\forall x){\sim}Fxx$	2–13, ind pr

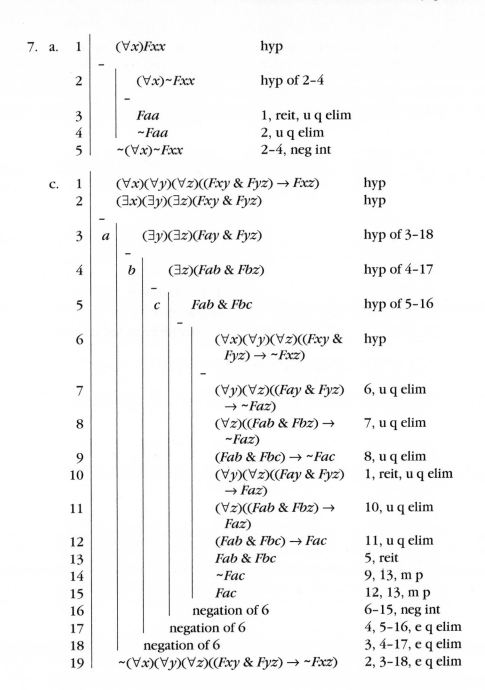

7. a.

1	$(\forall x)Fxx$	hyp
2	$(\forall x)\sim Fxx$	hyp of 2–4
3	Faa	1, reit, u q elim
4	$\sim Faa$	2, u q elim
5	$\sim(\forall x)\sim Fxx$	2–4, neg int

c.

1	$(\forall x)(\forall y)(\forall z)((Fxy \,\&\, Fyz) \to Fxz)$	hyp
2	$(\exists x)(\exists y)(\exists z)(Fxy \,\&\, Fyz)$	hyp
3	a $(\exists y)(\exists z)(Fay \,\&\, Fyz)$	hyp of 3–18
4	b $(\exists z)(Fab \,\&\, Fbz)$	hyp of 4–17
5	c $Fab \,\&\, Fbc$	hyp of 5–16
6	$(\forall x)(\forall y)(\forall z)((Fxy \,\&\, Fyz) \to \sim Fxz)$	hyp
7	$(\forall y)(\forall z)((Fay \,\&\, Fyz) \to \sim Faz)$	6, u q elim
8	$(\forall z)((Fab \,\&\, Fbz) \to \sim Faz)$	7, u q elim
9	$(Fab \,\&\, Fbc) \to \sim Fac$	8, u q elim
10	$(\forall y)(\forall z)((Fay \,\&\, Fyz) \to Faz)$	1, reit, u q elim
11	$(\forall z)((Fab \,\&\, Fbz) \to Faz)$	10, u q elim
12	$(Fab \,\&\, Fbc) \to Fac$	11, u q elim
13	$Fab \,\&\, Fbc$	5, reit
14	$\sim Fac$	9, 13, m p
15	Fac	12, 13, m p
16	negation of 6	6–15, neg int
17	negation of 6	4, 5–16, e q elim
18	negation of 6	3, 4–17, e q elim
19	$\sim(\forall x)(\forall y)(\forall z)((Fxy \,\&\, Fyz) \to \sim Fxz)$	2, 3–18, e q elim

8. There is no domain in which a relation F^2 is both reflexive and irre-flexive. This is proven by the derivation of the conclusion of 7a from its premise.

10. A relation F^2 is both transitive and intransitive in a domain if F^2 does not hold between the first and the second and the second and the third of any three of the individuals. For example, the relation of *being taller than* is both transitive and intransitive in the domain of individuals all of the same height. The derivation of the conclusion of 7c from its premises shows that in a domain where a relation F^2 holds between the first and the second and between the second and the third of three individuals, F^2 cannot be both transitive and intransitive.

SECTION 12.2

1. b.

1		$Gc \& {\sim}Gb$	hyp
2		$(\forall x)(\forall y)((Gx \& x \neq y) \rightarrow Fxy)$	hyp
3		$c = b$	hyp of 3–7
4		$Gc \& {\sim}Gb$	1, reit
5		Gc	4, conj elim
6		${\sim}Gb$	4, conj elim
7		${\sim}Gc$	3, 6, id elim
8		$c \neq b$	3–7, neg int
9		Gc	1, conj elim
10		$Gc \& c \neq b$	8, 9, conj int
11		$(\forall y)((Gc \& c \neq y) \rightarrow Fcy)$	2, u q elim
12		$(Gc \& c \neq b) \rightarrow Fcb$	11, u q elim
13		Fcb	10, 12, m p

d.

1		$(\forall y)(y = a)$	hyp
2		${\sim}Fa$	hyp
3	b	$b = a$	1, reit, u q elim
4		${\sim}Fa$	2, reit
5		${\sim}Fb$	3, 4, id elim
6		$(\forall x){\sim}Fx$	3–5, u q int
7		${\sim}(\exists x)Fx$	6, d m q

f.

1		$(\forall y)(y = a)$	hyp
2		$b \neq a$	hyp
3		$b = a$	1, u q elim
4		$a \neq a$	2, 3, id elim

g. 1 | $(\exists x)((Fx \,\&\, (\forall y)(Fy \to y = x)) \,\&\, x = a)$ | hyp
   2 | Hc | hyp
   3 | $a = c$ | hyp

   4 | Ha | 2, 3, id elim
   5 | b $(Fb \,\&\, (\forall y)(Fy \to y = b)) \,\&\, b = a$ | hyp of 5–11

   6 | $Fb \,\&\, (\forall y)(Fy \to y = b)$ | 5, conj elim
   7 | $b = a$ | 5, conj elim
   8 | Ha | 4, reit
   9 | Hb | 7, 8, id elim
   10 | $(Fb \,\&\, (\forall y)(Fy \to y = b)) \,\&\, Hb$ | 6, 9, conj int
   11 | $(\exists x)((Fx \,\&\, (\forall y)(Fy \to y = x)) \,\&\, Hx)$ | 10, e q int
   12 | $(\exists x)((Fx \,\&\, (\forall y)(Fy \to y = x)) \,\&\, Hx)$ | 1, 5–11, e q elim

2. a. 1 | a $a = a$ | id int
   2 | $(\forall x)(x = x)$ | 1–1, u q int
   3 | $\sim(\exists x)\sim(x = x)$ | 2, d m q

c. 1 | a $Fa \,\&\, \sim Fb$ | hyp of 1–7

   2 | $a = b$ | hyp of 2–6

   3 | $Fa \,\&\, \sim Fb$ | 1, reit
   4 | Fa | 3, conj elim
   5 | Fb | 2, 4, id elim
   6 | $\sim Fb$ | 3, conj elim
   7 | $a \neq b$ | 2–6, neg int
   8 | $(Fa \,\&\, \sim Fb) \to a \neq b$ | 1–7, cond int
   9 | $(\exists y)((Fa \,\&\, \sim Fy) \to a \neq y)$ | 8, e q int
   10 | $(\forall x)(\exists y)((Fx \,\&\, \sim Fy) \to x \neq y)$ | 1–9, u q int

e. 1 | a b $Fa \,\&\, \sim Fb$ | hyp of 1–8

   2 | Fa | 1, conj elim
   3 | $\sim Fb$ | 1, conj elim
   4 | $a = b$ | hyp of 4–7

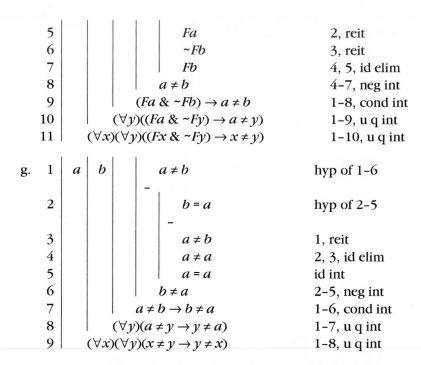

5		*Fa*	2, reit
6		~*Fb*	3, reit
7		*Fb*	4, 5, id elim
8		*a* ≠ *b*	4–7, neg int
9		(*Fa* & ~*Fb*) → *a* ≠ *b*	1–8, cond int
10		(∀*y*)((*Fa* & ~*Fy*) → *a* ≠ *y*)	1–9, u q int
11		(∀*x*)(∀*y*)((*Fx* & ~*Fy*) → *x* ≠ *y*)	1–10, u q int

g.

	1	*a*	*b*	*a* ≠ *b*	hyp of 1–6
	2			*b* = *a*	hyp of 2–5
	3			*a* ≠ *b*	1, reit
	4			*a* ≠ *a*	2, 3, id elim
	5			*a* = *a*	id int
	6			*b* ≠ *a*	2–5, neg int
	7			*a* ≠ *b* → *b* ≠ *a*	1–6, cond int
	8			(∀*y*)(*a* ≠ *y* → *y* ≠ *a*)	1–7, u q int
	9			(∀*x*)(∀*y*)(*x* ≠ *y* → *y* ≠ *x*)	1–8, u q int

4. No. '(∀*x*)(∀*y*)(∀*z*)((*x* ≠ *y* & *y* ≠ *z*) → *x* ≠ *z*)' is not a theorem. The fact that the first individual is not identical to the second and the second is not identical to the third does not guarantee that the first is not identical to the third. After all, the third individual could be the same individual as the first. For example, assume that the domain consists of Scott and his younger sister Mary, who is also called "Misty." Even though Mary is not identical with Scott and Scott is not identical with Misty, Mary is identical with Misty.

5. The derivation of '(∀*x*)(∀*y*)(*x* = *y* → (*Fy* ≡ *Fx*))' is the same as that for 2f. The following is a derivation of the metatheorem.

1	*a*	*b*	*a* = *b*	hyp of 1–2
2			*A* ≡ *A*	reflex bicond
3			*A*(*b*/*a*) ≡ *A*	1, 2, gen id elim
4			*a* = *b* → (*A*(*b*/*a*) ≡ *A*)	1–3, cond int
5			(∀*y*)(*a* = *y* → (*A*(*y*/*a*) ≡ *A*))	1–4, u q int
6			(∀*x*)(∀*y*)(*x* = *y* → (*A*(*y*/*a*) ≡ *A*(*x*/*a*)))	1–5, u q int

In any derivation of this form, *A*(*y*/*a*) must be the same as (*A*(*b*/*a*))(*y*/*b*). Therefore, in no derivation of this form does *b* occur in *A*.

7. a. It is not true that there is something that is not self-identical.

b. Everything is identical to something.

c. Nothing black is identical to something that is not black.

d. Anything identical to anything that is green is also green.

e. If one individual is a father and one is not, then the two are not the same individual.

f. If two individuals (possibly the same) are the same individual, then the second was born on the Fourth of July if and only if the first was.

g. If one individual is not identical to a second, then the second is not identical to the first.

8. a. $(b \neq a)$, $(Fa \ \& \ Fb)$ /$\therefore$ $(\exists y)(\exists x)((Fx \ \& \ Fy) \ \& \ y \neq x)$

1	$b \neq a$	hyp
2	$Fa \ \& \ Fb$	hyp
3	$(Fa \ \& \ Fb) \ \& \ b \neq a$	1, 2, conj int
4	$(\exists x)((Fx \ \& \ Fb) \ \& \ b \neq x)$	3, e q int
5	$(\exists y)(\exists x)((Fx \ \& \ Fy) \ \& \ y \neq x)$	4, e q int

d. $(\forall x)(Fx \rightarrow Gax)$, $\sim Gab$, $(\exists x)(Fx \ \& \ \sim Gxa)$ /$\therefore$ $(\exists x)((Fx \ \& \ \sim Gxa) \ \& \ x \neq b)$

1		$(\forall x)(Fx \rightarrow Gax)$	hyp
2		$\sim Gab$	hyp
3		$(\exists x)(Fx \ \& \ \sim Gxa)$	hyp
4	c	$Fc \ \& \ \sim Gca$	hyp of 4–14
5		$\quad c = b$	hyp of 5–11
6		$\quad Fc \ \& \ \sim Gca$	4, reit
7		$\quad Fc$	6, conj elim
8		$\quad Fc \rightarrow Gac$	1, u q elim
9		$\quad Gac$	7, 8, m p
10		$\quad Gab$	5, 9, id elim
11		$\quad \sim Gab$	2, reit
12		$c \neq b$	5–11, neg int
13		$(Fc \ \& \ \sim Gca) \ \& \ c \neq b$	4, 12, conj int
14		$(\exists x)((Fx \ \& \ \sim Gxa) \ \& \ x \neq b)$	13, e q int
15		$(\exists x)((Fx \ \& \ \sim Gxa) \ \& \ x \neq b)$	3, 4–14, e q elim

SECTION 12.3

1. a.

1		$(\forall x)Gx$	hyp
2		$(\exists x)(x = a)$	hyp
3	b	$b = a$	hyp of 3-6
4		$(\forall x)Gx$	1, reit
5		Gb	4, free u q elim
6		Ga	3, 5, id elim
7		Ga	2, 3-6, e q elim

3. Derivable in FQ: none

Derivable in FQE but not in FQ: none

5. Derivable in FQ: a, b, c, d, e, f, g

Derivable in FQE but not in FQ: h, i

7. Derivable in FQ: e

Derivable in FQE but not in FQ: g

8. Derivable in FQ: a, b, c, e, f, g, h

Derivable in FQE but not in FQ: d

10. Replace 'u q elim' with 'free u q elim' in the metaderivations of 2a, 2c, 2e, and 2g in section 11.3 and you will have proven that 10a, 10c, 10e, and 10g, respectively, are metatheorems of FQ.

11. b.

1		$(\forall x)(A \rightarrow B)$	hyp of 1-7
2		$(\forall x)A$	hyp of 2-6
3	a	$A(a/x) \rightarrow B$	1, reit, free u q elim
4		$A(a/x)$	2, reit, free u q elim
5		B	3-4, m p
6		B	3-5, ex a
7		$(\forall x)A \rightarrow B$	2-6, cond int
8		$(\forall x)(A \rightarrow B) \rightarrow ((\forall x)A \rightarrow B)$	1-7, cond int

In no derivation of this form can a occur either in A or in B.

12. b.

1			$(\forall y)(\exists x)(Gx \mathbin{\&} Hy)$		hyp
2	a		$(\exists x)(Gx \mathbin{\&} Ha)$		1, reit, free u q elim
3		b	$Gb \mathbin{\&} Ha$		hyp of 3–13
4			Gb		3, conj elim
5		c	$(\forall y)(\exists x)(Gx \mathbin{\&} Hy)$		1, reit
6			$(\exists x)(Gx \mathbin{\&} Hc)$		5, free u q elim
7		d	$Gd \mathbin{\&} Hc$		hyp of 7–8
8			Hc		7, conj elim
9			Hc		6, 7–8, e q elim
10			Gb		4, reit
11			$Gb \mathbin{\&} Hc$		9, 10, conj int
12			$(\forall y)(Gb \mathbin{\&} Hy)$		5–11, u q int
13			$(\exists x)(\forall y)(Gx \mathbin{\&} Hy)$		12, free e q int
14			$(\exists x)(\forall y)(Gx \mathbin{\&} Hy)$		2, 3–13, e q elim
15			$(\exists x)(\forall y)(Gx \mathbin{\&} Hy)$		2–14, ex a

13. a.

1			$(\exists x)(Gx \mathbin{v} Fa)$		hyp
2	b		$Gb \mathbin{v} Fa$		hyp of 2–8
3			Gb		hyp of 3–5
4			$(\exists x)Gx$		3, free e q int
5			$(\exists x)Gx \mathbin{v} Fa$		4, disj int
6			Fa		hyp of 6–7
7			$(\exists x)Gx \mathbin{v} Fa$		6, disj int
8			$(\exists x)Gx \mathbin{v} Fa$		2, 3–5, 6–7, disj elim
9			$(\exists x)Gx \mathbin{v} Fa$		1, 2–8, e q elim
10			$(\exists x)(Gx \mathbin{v} Fa) \rightarrow ((\exists x)Gx \mathbin{v} Fa)$		1–9, cond int

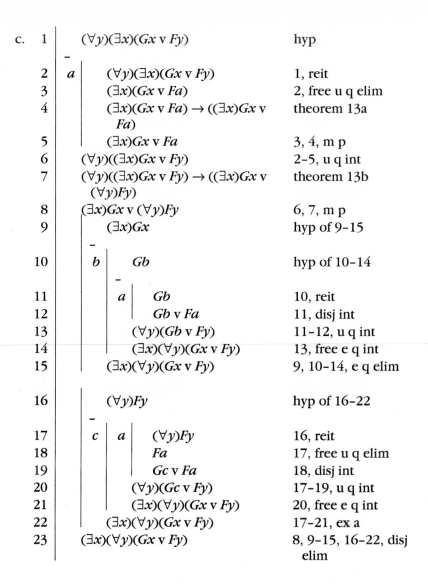

c.	1			$(\forall y)(\exists x)(Gx \lor Fy)$	hyp
	2	a		$(\forall y)(\exists x)(Gx \lor Fy)$	1, reit
	3			$(\exists x)(Gx \lor Fa)$	2, free u q elim
	4			$(\exists x)(Gx \lor Fa) \to ((\exists x)Gx \lor Fa)$	theorem 13a
	5			$(\exists x)Gx \lor Fa$	3, 4, m p
	6			$(\forall y)((\exists x)Gx \lor Fy)$	2–5, u q int
	7			$(\forall y)((\exists x)Gx \lor Fy) \to ((\exists x)Gx \lor (\forall y)Fy)$	theorem 13b
	8			$(\exists x)Gx \lor (\forall y)Fy$	6, 7, m p
	9			$(\exists x)Gx$	hyp of 9–15
	10	b		Gb	hyp of 10–14
	11		a	Gb	10, reit
	12			$Gb \lor Fa$	11, disj int
	13			$(\forall y)(Gb \lor Fy)$	11–12, u q int
	14			$(\exists x)(\forall y)(Gx \lor Fy)$	13, free e q int
	15			$(\exists x)(\forall y)(Gx \lor Fy)$	9, 10–14, e q elim
	16			$(\forall y)Fy$	hyp of 16–22
	17	c	a	$(\forall y)Fy$	16, reit
	18			Fa	17, free u q elim
	19			$Gc \lor Fa$	18, disj int
	20			$(\forall y)(Gc \lor Fy)$	17–19, u q int
	21			$(\exists x)(\forall y)(Gx \lor Fy)$	20, free e q int
	22			$(\exists x)(\forall y)(Gx \lor Fy)$	17–21, ex a
	23			$(\exists x)(\forall y)(Gx \lor Fy)$	8, 9–15, 16–22, disj elim

INDEX

STAFF

Editors Jacqueline T. Cannon and Joshua Safran

Production Manager Brenda S. Filley

Designer Harry Rinehart

Typesetting Supervisor Libra Ann Cusack

Typesetter Juliana Arbo

Graphic Coordinator Shawn Callahan

RULES OF INTELIM

Reiteration (reit)

A

   A

Modus Ponens (m p)

$A \rightarrow B$

A

B

Conditional Introduction (cond int)

   A

-

   .

   B

$A \rightarrow B$

Conjunction Introduction (conj int)

A

B

$A \,\&\, B$

Conjunction Elimination (conj elim)

$A \,\&\, B$

A

$A \,\&\, B$

B

Disjunction Introduction (disj int)

A

$A \text{ v } B$

B

$A \text{ v } B$

Disjunction Elimination (disj elim)

$A \text{ v } B$

   A

-

   .

   C

   B

-

   .

   C

C

Indirect Proof (ind pr)

   $\sim\!A$

-

   .

   B

   $\sim\!B$

A

RULES OF INTELIM-SQ

Universal Quantifier Elimination (u q elim)

$(\forall x)A$

$A(a/x)$

Universal Quantifier Introduction (u q int)

a .

   A

$(\forall x)A(x/a)$